Vinny Cahill and Donal Lafferty

Learning to Program the Object-oriented Way with C#

Springer

Vinny Cahill, BA, MSc, PhD, FTCD
Trinity College Dublin, Ireland

Donal Lafferty, BSc, PEng
Trinity College Dublin, Ireland

British Library Cataloguing in Publication Data
Cahill, V. (Vinny)
    Learning to program the object-oriented way with C#
    1.C# (Computer program language)   2.Object-oriented programming (Computer Science)
    I.Title   II.Lafferty, Donal
    0.05.1'33
    ISBN 1852336021

Library of Congress Cataloging-in-Publication Data
Cahill, V. (Vinny)
    Learning to program the object-oriented way with C# / Vinny Cahill and
    Donal Lafferty.
        p.   cm.
    Includes bibliographical references and index.
    ISBN 1-85233-602-1 (alk. paper)
    1. C# (Computer program language).   2. Object-oriented programming (Computer Science)
    I. Lafferty, Donal, 1973-   II. Title.
    QA76.73.C178 2002
    005.13'3--dc21   2002021738

ISBN 1-85233-602-1 Springer-Verlag London Berlin Heidelberg
a member of BertelsmannSpringer Science+Business Media GmbH
http://www.springer.co.uk

Typesetting: Digital by Design Ltd, Cheltenham
Printed and bound at the Athenæum Press Ltd, Gateshead, Tyne & Wear
34/3830-543210 Printed on acid-free paper SPIN 10868272

Foreword

In my professional career, I've attended quite a few design meetings. When discussing the details of how a system will work, it's fairly common for somebody to say, "that's just an implementation detail". This means that a specific detail isn't important to the design of the system, and can safely be determined when the design is implemented. Ignoring implementation details focuses attention on the important aspects of the design.

That distinction is important in books on programming as well. Concepts, modelling and programming techniques are the important parts of programming, and their expression in a specific language is an implementation detail. Many books spend lots of time on the syntax of the language while not spending enough time on the important high-level subjects, or they discuss them at the same time.

The thing that I like the most about *Learning to Program the Object-oriented Way with C#* is that it does a great job at explaining a subject in the abstract, and then implements those concepts in C# sample code. This separation of the conceptual from the implementation highlights the importance of the concepts. Not only does that make it easier to learn object-oriented programming, but the conceptual matter is relevant for any object-oriented language.

I heartily recommend this book for those who are interested in learning object-oriented programming.

Eric Gunnerson
Program Manager, Visual C# Team
Author, *A Programmer's Introduction to C#*

Preface

Can you swim? Yes? Great! No? Well, you really should learn! In any case, we hope you'll appreciate that learning to swim is something that you have to do for yourself. No one can teach you to swim. Swimming is a skill that you acquire through practice. While you might well take swimming lessons under the supervision of a swimming instructor, you basically have to learn it for yourself. Your instructor is there to help you along, suggest practices and corrections to your technique, and, of course, to make sure you don't drown in the process!

Believe it or not, learning to program is much like learning to swim. Programming is also a skill that you learn through constant practice. No instructor, and certainly no textbook, can teach you to program. Our intension in this book is to guide you through the process of learning to program. We expect that you will be using this book as part of a first course in programming. We don't expect you to have programmed before. We do expect that you will practice your programming skills by doing the exercises and programming tasks that we suggest in the book, hopefully under the supervision of your course instructor.

Writing programs is not easy! In particular, writing programs that perform correctly in a variety of different situations is not easy. It requires that you develop a way of thinking about problems and developing solutions to those problems that is probably quite different from anything you have done before. Developing these skills is the essence of learning to program. Once you've acquired these skills, they will be equally applicable to the design of programs for video games, airline reservation systems, or sending electronic mail. They will be equally applicable no matter what type of computer (or computers) your program is to run on or what computer programming language it is written in! Thus, our emphasis in this book is on developing the problem solving skills necessary to write correct computer programs given some problem to be solved.

Recognizing that programming is difficult, computer scientists have developed a number of different approaches to the design of programs. Different approaches, or methodologies, exist. Some are more applicable to certain types of problem than others. One of the most widely used, and maybe even the most widely applicable, approaches to program design that is used in the computer industry today is known as the object-oriented approach. This is the approach that we advocate in this book. Using the object-oriented approach to programming gives you a common framework for tackling different problems that will hopefully help you to write correct programs. Unfortunately, using the object-oriented (or indeed any other) approach to program design cannot guarantee that you will get a correct program at the end. It serves only as a guide to the design of the program. Writing a correct program depends ultimately on your own skill and application.

When you write a computer program to solve a particular problem, there are three goals that should be borne in mind. In order of importance they are correctness, clarity, and efficiency.

Correctness is of paramount importance! You programs should work correctly in all reasonable circumstances. That is, they should solve the problem at hand and handle all reasonable eventualities that might arise while the program is running! This is a strong requirement. While you might only need 40% to pass your programming course, nobody wants a program that only gets the answer right 40% of the time, or handles 40% of the possible cases! What makes programming difficult is that you have to consider all the possibilities and make sure your solutions are applicable in all cases!

Clarity demands that not only do your programs work correctly but that they obviously work correctly! Someone else should be able to take your programs and understand how and why they work. It is common in the computer industry for one program to be worked on by several people over time. Thus, it is imperative that someone else can take a program that you have written and easily, without wasted effort, understand it. Unfortunately, it is all too easy to write programs that others will not understand. In fact, it is often the case that even the author of a program is not be able to understand their own program when they come to read it sometime later!

Efficiency requires that your programs take no longer than necessary to solve the problem at hand. In fact, in most circumstances efficiency is not an issue and any correct program will suffice. In some circumstances, for example when dealing with very complex problems or problems whose solutions are time-critical, it is necessary to put considerable effort into making sure your programs operate efficiently. Making a program work efficiently is called "program tuning". Such program tuning is best left until you have a working program. In keeping with this advice, we largely ignore the efficiency of the programs we develop in this book and concentrate instead on our main goal – correctness.

The skills that you develop as you learn to program are, as we said before, independent of the use of any particular language. However, we need to have a programming language in which to actually write our programs. Of course, we would like to choose one that supports the object-oriented approach to designing programs, that is, an object-oriented programming language. Moreover, we would like to choose one that is widely used and that you can continue to use to write serious applications in the future. As it happens, the C# language fits the bill exactly!

C# is a new object-oriented language that can be used to write applications that can be distributed over the worldwide computer network known as the Internet. Applications that might be distributed to hundreds and thousands of computers across the world have to be correct! Thus, the designers of C# paid special attention to making it easy to write correct programs in C#. This together with the object-oriented approach of C# makes it an ideal language for the new programmer.

Why did we write this book? Well, mainly because we could not find another textbook that introduced the object-oriented approach to programming using C#. There are other introductory books on object-oriented programming. If you had used one of those, you would have missed out on C#. There are other books on C#. However, because C# is so new, they are mainly aimed at existing programmers who want to find out about C# quickly. They are not designed to help you develop your programming skills, which is our primary aim in writing this book.

As we have hinted already, we advocate a practical approach to learning to program. Each chapter of this book introduces some new programming techniques (as supported by C#). In general, we try to motivate why each technique is required and, by means of numerous examples, how it is used in C#. We hope that these examples will be sufficient to allow you to understand the why and the how of each technique and allow you to try to use the various techniques in your own programs. At the end of the day, you will really only learn to program by actually trying to write some programs!

So anyway, what about those swimming lessons?

Acknowledgements

As experience has now taught us, writing a textbook such as this is no trivial undertaking and could not possibly have been completed successfully without help and support from many good friends.

The authors would particularly like to acknowledge the contributions of Stefan Weber, Brendan Bruen, and Anthony Harrington at Trinity College Dublin. Between them they co-authored, tested, and debugged many of the programs in this book – in some cases long into the night when we had long since gone home!

Greg O'Shea of Microsoft Research provided the early encouragement and support that turned a vague idea for a textbook on C# into a realistic plan. Eric Gunnerson of Microsoft reviewed many parts of the text and we are particularly grateful to have had the benefit of his expertise. Berverley Ford recognized the book as a valuable contribution, and pushed for approval to publish, while Rebecca Mowat handled the logistics of getting the work to press.

Vinny would like to thank 'Trish for all her support during the writing of the book and he promises to spend some weekends away from the office now that it is done!

Donal would like to thank Irenee, for her confidence, assistance, and considerable patience during the project, his parents, for pushing him to finish, and Kate for distracting them when the book was late.

Finally, the authors would like to thank the very many students that have passed through our introductory programming courses at Trinity over many years. We couldn't have written this book without their experience and we hope that it will prove beneficial to many future students of programming at Trinity and elsewhere.

Contents

Objects and Classes 1

This chapter:

- introduces the object-oriented approach to computer programming
- describes how object-oriented programs are made up of collections of interacting objects
- describes how objects are defined by the class to which they belong
- describes how to define a new class of objects in C#...
- ... and how to write a C# program that uses this class

In today's world, computers, and the programs that control them, are to be found in just about every aspect of our daily lives. Computers are to be found in our homes, offices, schools, colleges, and factories. Computers are to be found on our desks, embedded in our washing machines, and buried in complex systems such as aeroplanes and cars.

Despite the endless variety of different types of computer, and the very different uses to which they are put, it might surprise you to hear that the capabilities of most computers are very similar. Computers are simply machines capable of storing and processing large amounts of information very quickly. The operations that most computers are capable of performing on the information that they process are very simple; they are typically limited to performing simple arithmetic and logical operations on the information that they store. What makes computers so useful is the speed at which they can perform these simple operations (typically hundreds of millions of operations per second), the huge amount of information that they are capable of storing (the equivalent of millions of pages of text at any time), and the flexibility with which different sequences of operations can be arranged to carry out complex tasks.

What really distinguishes different computers are the *programs* that control them. A program is nothing more than a sequence of instructions to the computer describing how to carry out some task. Different programs typically control different computers. For example, the program that controls your washing machine is likely to be very different from the program that controls the computer system used in your local bank!

Computer programs such as those that are used in banks, hospitals, factories, and aircraft control are incredibly complex. Writing such programs may involve thousands of hours of programming effort and be the work of hundreds of programmers. Why? Well, these programs have to take account of the hundreds of different situations and possibilities with which they might be asked to deal while they are in use and handle all of them correctly. Given that a program might be in use continually for years or even decades, writing such a program is no mean feat! Not only that, programs also have to be written in a way that allows them to be modified incrementally in order to take account of new requirements as they arise.

On top of all that, and given the huge effort that may be involved in writing a program, programs are often written so that some parts of the program can be reused in future programs – avoiding the need for the programmers to have to redo the same work over again. For example, it might be possible to reuse part of a program written for a bank in a new program for an insurance company.

Fortunately, the computer industry has developed techniques to allow computer programs to be written that meet all of these requirements. One such technique is the technique that we will study in this book. It's called *object-oriented programming*. Today object-oriented programming is the technique of choice for writing complex computer programs and is used in writing just about every type of program.

Introducing Object-oriented Programming

At the heart of object-oriented programming is the old saying:

divide and conquer

In other words, the best way to master the complexity of writing a large computer program is to carve it up into manageable chunks and tackle each chunk more or less separately. The divide and conquer strategy allows us to turn a large problem into a series of smaller, hopefully more easily solved, subproblems. If we can successfully identify different chunks of a program that can be tackled separately (which is a bit tricky!) we are well on our way to handling all of the problems that we mentioned previously.

For example, we can assign different chunks of the program to different programmers giving us a convenient way of dividing up the effort of writing the program among the many programmers involved. Each programmer can tackle one or more chunks of the program without having to worry about what everybody else is doing. Since programmers only have to worry about their own part of the program, they have a better chance of making sure that their part works correctly and handles all of the functions that it is supposed to carry out properly in different situations. If a change to the program is required, hopefully that change can be limited to one or at most a few chunks. In other words, we hopefully won't have to change every part of the program. Moreover, if we choose our chunks carefully, some chunks might be reusable in future programs. For example, if we write a chunk of program that deals with calculating the tax to be paid by the employees of a bank, we might be able to reuse that same chunk of program in another program that deals with the employees of a different type of business.

All very well you say, but how do we choose the chunks and what has this got to do with object-oriented programming? As it turns out, the divide and conquer strategy has been used in writing computer programs for many years – long before object-oriented programming. One of the main contributions of object-oriented programming is to suggest a way of dividing up programs into meaningful chunks. Object-oriented programming says let's look at the sort of entities (or *objects*) with which the program deals and let's write the part of the program that handles each type of entity separately. For example, in a banking program objects might represent customers, their bank accounts, individual cheques, bank statements, the bank's employees, and its branches. In a program that implements a video game, the objects might represent the characters in the game, the players' scores, or the joystick used to control the movement of the characters. When we come to write a program using the object-oriented approach, we first need to identify the sort of entities with which the program deals and then we describe the characteristics and behaviour of each of these types of entity as a (chunk of) computer program!

Introducing Objects and Classes

The fundamental idea in object-oriented programming is that running programs are made up of collections of interacting *objects*. As we explained, an object is a component of a program that represents some entity of interest to the program. For example, in a banking program objects might represent customers, their accounts, and the cheques they write. Objects of the same *type* represent the same kind of entity. As you can see, even in a single program, there are likely to be many different types of objects. Moreover, there are likely to be many different objects of the same type representing different entities. For example, in our banking program there are likely to be different objects representing my account and your account and presumably everybody elses' accounts. In a different program, we will very likely have different types of objects. For example, in a program concerned with air traffic control, we may well have objects representing individual planes, airports, and radar screens. In a program that is concerned with the management of a college, we might find objects representing students, teachers, and courses.

OK, so an object *represents* some entity with which a program is concerned, but what *is* an object? It's probably easiest to think of an object as being a collection of information, stored in the computer, that describes the entity in question. Thus, an object that represents a student is a collection of information that might include the student's name, the student's college identification number, the student's address, the courses that the student is taking, and so on. An object that represents a different student will contain a different name, a different identification number, a different address (assuming that the two students aren't sharing a house!), and, very likely, a different set of courses.

Attributes

Every object has a set of *attributes* that fully describe the entity represented by the object. As Figure 1.1 shows, the attributes of an object that represents a person might include things like age, eye colour, hair colour, height, gender, name, occupation, spouse, and shoe size.

As Figure 1.2 shows, every one of these attributes has a *value*. Taken together the values of all of the attributes tell us everything that we want to know about the entity represented by the object. This collection of information is usually referred to as the *state* of the object.

Objects of the same type (i.e., those that represent the same kind of entity) all have the same attributes. Thus, as shown in Figure 1.3, all the objects that represent people have exactly the same set of attributes: age, eye colour, hair colour, height, gender, name, occupation, spouse, and shoe size!

Of course, different objects (i.e., objects that represent different entities) will probably have different values for some or all of their attributes. For example, Figure 1.4 shows two objects representing people. Both have the same set of attributes. However, they have different values for those attributes: one has black hair and blue eyes, while the other has brown hair and green eyes; one is male and one is female; both are 45!

It's worth re-emphasizing that the attributes that an object has depend on the *kind* of entity that it represents, while the values of those attributes depend on the *particular* entity that it represents. For example, objects that represent cars are likely to have a completely different set of attributes from those that represent people. For example, as shown in Figure 1.5, an

Figure 1.1   Objects have attributes.

object representing a car might have attributes such as manufacturer, engine size, number of doors, registration number, colour, model number, and current speed. Objects representing different cars will have different values for these attributes.

In general, the values of an object's attributes can change over time. For example, Figure 1.6 shows what happens if our good friend Sean gets a promotion on his 46th birthday! Notice that the values of both the age and occupation attributes have changed.

Of course, the values don't change spontaneously. It might be more correct to say that the values of an object's attributes *can be changed* over time, typically by the program of which the object is a part. We'll see how this works soon. For now, it's enough to realize that while the set of attributes that an object has is fixed, the values of the attributes aren't and can be changed during the course of a program.

Attributes have one other important characteristic. As well as having a value, every attribute has a *type*. The type of an attribute tells us what sort of value is expected to be stored in that

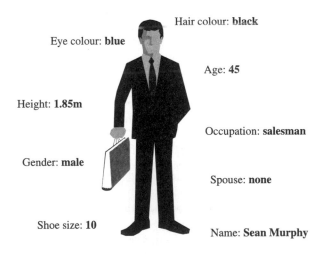

Figure 1.2   Attributes have values.

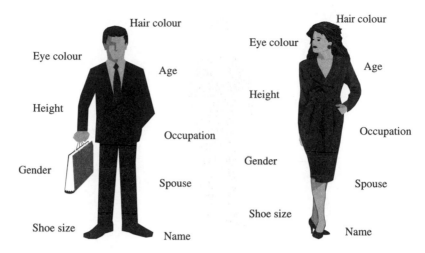

Figure 1.3   Objects of the same type have the same attributes.

Figure 1.4   Different objects have different values for their attributes.

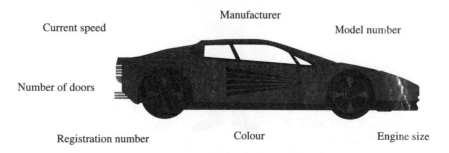

Figure 1.5   Objects of different types have different attributes.

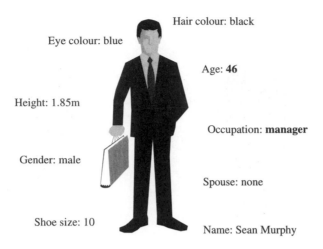

Figure 1.6   The values of an object's attributes can be changed over time.

attribute. For example, we don't expect the age attribute of a person to contain the name "Sean Murphy", rather we expect it to contain a number such as 45. Thus, the type of the age attribute is "integer number". On the other hand, the type of the name attribute is "string of text". Figure 1.7 shows the types of the other attributes of objects that represent people.

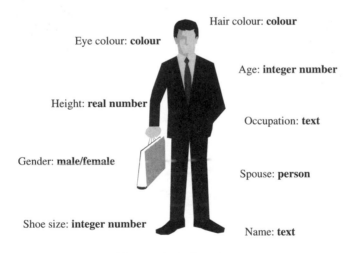

Figure 1.7   Attributes have types.

Object References

As explained above, a typical program contains lots and lots of objects, perhaps even millions! However, every object is unique. To emphasize this fact every object is given its own unique name that distinguishes it from every other object. These object names aren't names that we would recognize, like "Joe" or "Fred", but then they aren't meant to be used by humans. Instead, object names are typically large numbers like 85950351 or 54763881 as shown in Figure 1.8 (actually I'm only guessing what they might look like because I've never actually

Figure 1.8   Every object has a unique name.

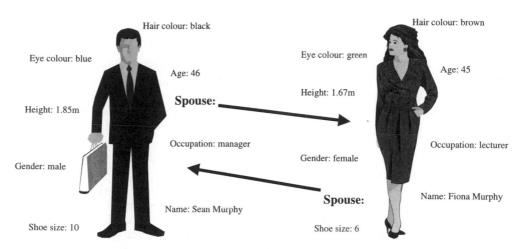

Figure 1.9   The value of an attribute might be a reference to another object.

seen one and you probably won't either!). Object names are intended to be used by programs and objects to refer to other objects. For this reason, object names are usually called *object references*.

As an example of the use of object references, Figure 1.9 shows what happens if Sean and Fiona get married. Now the spouse attribute in the object representing Sean refers to the object representing Fiona and vice versa. The value of the spouse attribute is actually a reference to (i.e., the unique name of) another object and is represented as an arrow in the figure.

Recall that every attribute has a type. Notice that the type of the spouse attribute of a person is type person! This makes sense because we expect a person's spouse to be another person and not, for example, a colour, a string of text, or an integer number. The values of type person are person objects and hence the attribute contains a reference to another person object.

Object references are very important because they allow objects to refer to other objects via their attributes. This means that we can store information about the relationships between objects in the objects themselves. Car objects might, for example, have an attribute that refers

Grow

Dye hair

Change job

Marry

Die

Figure 1.10 Objects have methods.

to their owner – a person object. Likewise, person objects might have an attribute that refers to their car!

Methods

So far, we have seen that every object contains information that describes some entity. Actually, there is a little more to an object than that. As well as containing information describing some entity, every object provides a collection of small programs that can be used to manipulate that information, for example, to change the value of an attribute or calculate a value that depends on the current value of some attributes. These small programs are called *methods*. The methods of an object describe the things that the object can do, i.e., they describe its *behaviour*. You might like to think of methods as commands to which the object is capable of responding when ordered!

Thus, as shown in Figure 1.10 an object that represents a person might respond to methods to dye its hair, change its job, or get married. Typically, when a method is carried out it will change the values of some of the attributes of the object to which it is applied. Thus, the dye hair method will most likely change the current value of the hair-colour attribute. Likewise, the change job method will probably change the value of the occupation attribute of the object.

The set of methods to which an object responds depends on the kind of entity that the object represents. Thus, all the objects that represent people will respond to the same set of methods, e.g., dye hair, change job. Other types of objects will respond to other sets of methods. Objects that represent cars might respond to methods such as accelerate, brake, and refuel as Figure 1.11 shows.

Refuel

Accelerate

Brake

Change gear

Figure 1.11 Objects of different types respond to different sets of methods.

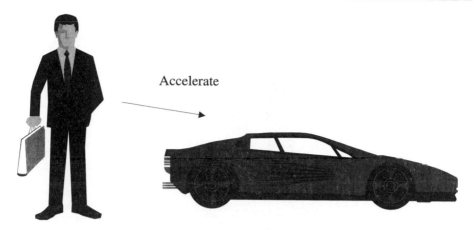

Figure 1.12 Objects interact by invoking each other's methods.

The orders to carry out these methods come from the program or from other methods. The order to an object to carry out a method is called an *invocation* and we say that *methods are invoked on an object*. A typical program begins by invoking a method on some object, which results in that method invoking further methods on other objects that it knows about and so on. Thus, objects interact by invoking each other's methods as shown in Figure 1.12. In fact, method invocation is essentially the way in which we get things done in an object-oriented program!

Classes

As we've seen, a program typically contains different sets of objects representing different types of entities. All the objects that represent one type of entity have the same set of attributes and respond to the same set of methods. Of course, when writing a program, we don't define every object individually, rather we define the different types of objects that the program will use by describing their common characteristics: the set of attributes that they have and the set of methods to which they respond. A description of a set of objects that represents the same kind of entity is called a *class*. Every class describes a particular type of object. For example, we might have different classes that describe objects representing people, or cars, or bank accounts, or aeroplanes. Every object is described by some class. We say that every object is an *instance* of some class. Thus, an object that represents a person will be an instance of class "Person". An object that represents a car will be an instance of a different class, presumably class "Car".

A class lists the attributes and methods that all the instances of that class have in common. Actually it does more than that. It describes the type of each attribute and also describes how each method works, i.e., it describes the sequence of operations that is carried out when the method is invoked on an instance of the class. For example, Figure 1.13 shows an outline of a class whose instances represent people. We'll see a real class definition later in the chapter.

You can think of a class as a template from which lots of different objects of the same type can be created. All of the objects will have the same set of attributes and respond to the same set of methods, although each will represent a different entity and probably store different values in each of its attributes.

```
class Person {
    Colour eyeColour
    Colour hairColour
    integer age
    integer shoeSize
    real height
    Person spouse
    Text name
    Text occupation
    Gender gender

    Marry ...
    Grow ...
    ChangeJob ...
    DyeHair ...
    Die ...
}
```

Figure 1.13 A class definition.

Writing a C# Class

In the previous sections we looked at the major ideas in object-oriented programming: objects and classes, attributes, types and values, object references, and, of course, methods. In this section we will look at putting all this theory into practice by actually writing a (small) program.

The program will be written in a programming language called C#, which is, of course, the language that we will be using throughout this book. C# is just one of the many different object-oriented programming languages that exist. Most of these languages are quite similar but vary in the notation that they use and some of the features that they provide. If you can master one object-oriented programming language, hopefully you won't have too much difficulty in learning to use another. In fact, most of the concepts and techniques that we will study in this book are independent of the use of any particular language, although the exact details of how to use them are typically language-specific. In any case, learning another object-oriented language, once you know one, is much easier than, for example, learning to speak French or another natural language when your native language is English!

As an example, to start us off, let's write a program to calculate the area and perimeter of a rectangle given its dimensions, i.e., its length and width.

Where do we start? In the spirit of object-oriented programming, the first question that we need to ask is what types of entity will our program deal with? Put another way, what types of objects will the program use? Or, in yet other words, what classes will we need to define?

Hopefully, you will see immediately that this program deals with rectangles and not much else! Hence, we will need to define a single class describing objects that represent rectangles. We can then use that class in our program.

Defining Class `Rectangle`

We saw earlier that a class definition lists the attributes and methods to be provided by instances of that class. Every object-oriented programming language has its own rules for

```
class <class name>
{

        <list of instance variables>

        <list of methods>

}
```

Figure 1.14   The syntax of a C# class declaration.

how such class definitions are written. Such rules correspond to the grammatical rules of a natural language and are usually called the *syntax rules* of the language. The syntax rules of the language not only dictate how class definitions are written but also how attributes are defined, how methods are defined, and so on. The syntax rules of C# specify that class definitions (called *class declarations* in C#'s terminology) basically take the form shown in Figure 1.14.

We will use figures like Figure 1.14 to illustrate many of the syntax rules of C# throughout the remainder of the book. In these figures, text that appears **in this font** is text that must appear exactly as shown in the figure in the final class declaration. By the way, when we say that this text must appear exactly as shown, we really mean exactly! C# is very unforgiving and will refuse to accept anything that doesn't conform exactly to the syntax rules. Text that appears between angled brackets <like this> represents placeholder text that we can fill in with our own text (subject to various rules) in the final class declaration.

As you can see, a C# class declaration always begins with the keyword `class` (notice that we also use `this font` whenever we refer to text that appears in a program). This keyword is followed by the name of the class. We get to choose the name of the class ourselves. Essentially, we can use any single word for the name. Of course, it should be a word that describes what the instances of the class represent! The name of the class is followed by an opening brace ({). This opening brace is followed by two lists: a list of the attributes that each of the instances of the class will have and a list of the methods that the instances will respond to. The contents of these lists will obviously differ from class to class and there are further syntax rules that govern how they are written. A single closing brace (}) completes the class declaration.

Let's decide to call our class `Rectangle` since that's what instances of the class are supposed to represent! Notice that we like to give classes names that begin with capital letters. Having made this decision we can begin to fill in our template as shown in Figure 1.15.

```
class Rectangle
{

    <list of instance variables>

    <list of methods>

}
```

Figure 1.15   The Rectangle class (step 1 – choosing the class name).

Defining the Attributes of a `Rectangle`

Having decided what classes we need to use in our program and having chosen names for each, the next major step in designing an object-oriented program is deciding what attributes each class should provide. Put another way, we need to decide what information, or what state, the instances of each class should contain.

Actually, the decision as to what attributes to include depends on the program we are writing. For example, if we are designing a class to represent people, we might choose different attributes depending on whether that class is going to be used in a banking program or a hospital program. For example, a bank probably doesn't want to store information about its customers' doctors, while a hospital probably would. It's up to us as the programmers to make an informed choice of attributes depending on the program that we are writing.

You can probably imagine lots of different attributes of a rectangle: its length, its width, its position, its colour and so on. However, since our program is only concerned with calculating the area and perimeter of a rectangle, the only attributes of interest are the length and width, so these are the only attributes that we will include in our class.

```
private <type> <instance variable name>;
```

Figure 1.16   The syntax of a C# instance variable declaration.

As Figure 1.16 shows, the declaration of an attribute usually begins with the keyword `private`. After that, we have to give the type of the attribute and its name in that order. We get to choose both the type (i.e., what sort of values the attribute will store) and the name of the attribute ourselves. The declaration is always finished off with a single semicolon (`;`). By the way, attributes are usually called *fields, member variables* or *instance variables* in C#: *instance* because they belong to the instances of a class and *variables* because their values can be changed. The terms "field" and "instance variable" are used interchangeably throughout the remainder of this book.

We will call the two instance variables to be provided by our `Rectangle` class `length` and `width` respectively. Both of these instance variables will contain numbers. For now, we will limit ourselves to whole numbers. Luckily, C# provides a type to represent whole numbers. The name of this type is `int`, which is short for "integer". Thus, both of our instance variables will be of type `int`. We can now complete the list of instance variables in our class declaration as shown in Figure 1.17. Notice that the placeholder for the list of attributes has been replaced with the declarations of the two instance variables.

```
class Rectangle
{
    private int length;
    private int width;

    <list of methods>

}
```

Figure 1.17   The Rectangle class (step 2 – declaring the instance variables).

Defining the Methods of a `Rectangle`

So far, so good. We are declaring a class whose instances will represent rectangles and we've decided what instance variables each instance of the class will have. The next step, in common with the design of any other class, is to decide what methods the class should provide. Put another way, what do we want to be able to ask instances of the class to do for us?

Again, what methods we provide depends on the program in which we want to use the class. In our case, we would like to be able to ask an instance of `Rectangle` to calculate its area or perimeter and give us the result. The straightforward way to do this is by providing two methods: one to calculate the area and another to calculate the perimeter.

As Figure 1.18 shows, a method declaration usually begins with the keyword `public`. Following that we have to specify the type of value calculated (or *returned* in C#'s terminology) by the method. Different methods will typically return different types of value, so we get to choose the appropriate type ourselves. Next, we have to specify the name of the method. Again, we get to choose the name of the method ourselves. This name can be any single word and should describe what the method does or what it calculates. After that, we can give a list of the input values required by the method enclosed in brackets. A method can always use the values stored in the instance variables of the object on which it is invoked. However, it may need to use some other values in order to do its work. The input values, usually called *parameters*, provide a way of specifying these values. The parameters are optional. We don't have to specify any if the method doesn't need them. However, the brackets are not optional and have to be included.

The body of the method is enclosed in braces and usually consists of two parts. A list of *local variable* declarations and a list of the commands that the method carries out to perform its work where each command is followed by a single semicolon (`;`). Such commands are called *statements* in C#'s terminology. Local variables are not unlike instance variables in that they are used to store information. However, unlike instance variables, local variables are used to store information that is needed temporarily by a method while it is executing. We won't need to use any local variables in our `Rectangle` class but we will use some later in our program.

Let's think about the methods to calculate the area and perimeter of a rectangle. First off, let's give them names: `CalculateArea` and `CalculatePerimeter` seem appropriate. OK, so "CalculateArea" isn't a single word in English but, as long as it contains no spaces, C# treats it as a single word!

What should `CalculateArea` do? Essentially it multiplies the length of the current rectangle by its width to determine the area and then returns the resulting value. Since both the

```
public <type> <method name>(<parameters>)
{

  <list of local variables>

  <statement 1>;
  <statement 2>;
  <statement 3>;
  ...
  <Statement n>;
}
```

Figure 1.18   The syntax of a C# method declaration.

```
public int CalculateArea()
{
   return this.length * this.width;
}
```

Figure 1.19   The declaration of the CalculateArea method.

length and width of the rectangle are `int` values and since the result of multiplying one `int` by another is also an `int`, the type returned by `CalculateArea` will also be `int`. Moreover, since calculating the area of a rectangle only requires us to know its length and width, as given by the instance variables, `CalculateArea` doesn't need any parameters. Hence, the parameter part of the method declaration will be empty. To actually calculate the area of the current rectangle, we simply multiply its length by its width using the multiplication operator (`*`) and return the value to the invoker of the method using C#'s `return` statement. The full definition of the method is shown in Figure 1.19. Notice that when we want to refer to the instance variables of the object on which the method was invoked, we say "`this.length`" rather than just "`length`" to re-emphasize that we are talking about the length of *this* rectangle – the one that the method was invoked on.

The `CalculatePerimeter` method is, as shown in Figure 1.20, very similar. This method calculates and returns an `int` value by adding twice the length of this rectangle to twice its width.

Figure 1.21 shows the declaration of class `Rectangle` resulting from replacing the placeholder for the list of methods with the declarations of the methods.

```
public int CalculatePerimeter()
{
   return (2 * this.length) + (2 * this.width);
}
```

Figure 1.20   The declaration of the CalculatePerimeter method.

```
class Rectangle
{
   private int length;
   private int width;

   public int CalculateArea()
   {
      return this.length * this.width;
   }

   public int CalculatePerimeter()
   {
      return (2 * this.length) + (2 * this.width);
   }
}
```

Figure 1.21   The Rectangle class (step 3 – declaring the methods).

Initializing a New Instance of Class `Rectangle`

You may think that the declaration of class `Rectangle` is now finished. After all, we have declared the instance variables to be contained in instances of class `Rectangle` and declared methods that allow instances of class `Rectangle` to calculate their area and perimeter using the values of their instance variables. One question remains however, how do the instance variables ever get values? Given class `Rectangle` as it is defined in Figure 1.21, a program can create an instance of the class and ask that instance for its area and perimeter. However, that's not much use because there is no way to tell the object what its dimensions are! We need a way to initialize the values of the instance variables in a new object. The way to do this in C# is by providing another, special, method called a *constructor*, which is used only to initialize the instance variables of a new object.

Figure 1.22 shows the syntax of a constructor declaration. It's actually very similar to a method declaration. There are two main differences. Firstly, the name of the constructor can't be chosen arbitrarily – it has to be the same as the name of the class to which it belongs, i.e., a constructor for class `Rectangle` has to be called `Rectangle`. Secondly, a constructor is not used to calculate a value, it is used to give the instance variables of a new object their first values. Hence, a constructor never returns a value and therefore we don't have to say what type of value it returns!

Since the job of a constructor is to give initial values to the instance variables of a new object, it has to get those values from somewhere. Typically, these values are supplied as parameters to the constructor. While any method may have parameters, a constructor almost always does. Our `Rectangle` constructor will have two parameters, one to specify the length of the new rectangle and another to specify its width. When we define a parameter, as shown in Figure 1.23, we specify the type of the parameter and give it a name. As usual, the name can be any single word.

The declaration of our constructor is shown in Figure 1.24. Our constructor has to store the value of each of the parameters into the corresponding instance variable. Thus, there are two steps to carry out: store the value of the parameter giving the length into the length instance variable in the current object and then store the value of parameter giving the width into the

```
public <class name>(<parameters>)
{

  <list of local variables>

  <statement 1>;
  <statement 2>;
  <statement 3>;
  ...
  <statement n>;
}
```

Figure 1.22   The syntax of a C# constructor declaration.

```
<type> <parameter name>
```

Figure 1.23   The syntax of a C# parameter declaration.

```
public Rectangle (int length, int width)
{
  this.length = length;
  this.width = width;
}
```

Figure 1.24   The declaration of the Rectangle constructor.

width instance variable in the current object. The body of the constructor uses the assignment statement represented by the symbol = (a single equals sign) to store the value of each of the parameters into the corresponding instance variable. In C#'s terminology we say that the constructor *assigns* the value of parameter length to instance variable this.length. In other words, whatever value is specified as the length of the new rectangle when the constructor is called is stored in the instance variable length. The assignment statement is very important because it provides the means of changing the value stored in an instance variable. As we'll see, we're not limited to using assignment only in constructors; we can use assignment statements in any method.

```
/* A class whose instances represent rectangles */
class Rectangle
{
  /* declare the instance variables */
  private int length;  // used to store the length of the rectangle
  private int width;   // used to store the width of the rectangle

  /* declare a constructor to initialise */
  /* new instances of class Rectangle */
  public Rectangle(int length, int width)
  {
    this.length = length;      // store the value of l into length
    this.width = width;        // store the value of w into width
  }

  /* declare the other methods */
  /* a method to calculate the area of a rectangle */
  public int CalculateArea()
  {
    return this.length * this.width;
  }

  /* a method to calculate the perimeter of a rectangle */
  public int CalculatePerimeter()
  {
    return (2 * this.length) + (2 * this.width);
  }
}
```

Program 1.1   A class whose instances represent rectangles.

Now that we have a constructor, our class declaration is complete. The full declaration is shown in Program 1.1. Class `Rectangle` describes a set of objects that represent rectangles. Every instance of this class has two instance variables: `length` and `width`. Both of these instance variables are of type `int`, i.e., they can store a single whole number. When we create a new instance of this class (we haven't seen how to do this yet!), we can use the constructor for the class to give values to the instance variables of the new object. After that, we can invoke the `CalculateArea` and `CalculatePerimeter` methods on the object as often as we want to have it calculate and report its area or perimeter respectively.

A Comment about Comments

You may have noticed that Program 1.1 includes some additional text apart from the declaration of the class. This text is intended to explain what the class represents and how it works. Text that is included in a class declaration to explain how it works is referred to as being a *comment*. C# ignores comments – they don't affect the meaning of the class declaration in any way. Their only purpose is to help anyone who reads the class declaration to understand it. As such, comments are often very helpful and you should get into the habit of adding comments to all your class declarations as a matter of course.

There are essentially two ways of including a comment. First of all, any text included between the symbol /* (a backslash immediately followed by an asterisk without any space in between) and the symbol */ (an asterisk immediately followed by a backslash) is a comment. For example:

```
/* This is a comment */
```

Such a comment can extend over several lines.

```
/* This is a longer comment that extends
over a couple of lines before finishing here */
```

As a rule when we want to include several lines of comments, we usually use a separate comment for each line:

```
/* This is a longer comment that has been made into */
/* two separate comments on different lines */
```

This technique avoids any confusion about where the end of the comment is located (which may be difficult to find in a long program).

Remember that C# ignores everything between /* and */ so don't forget to include the closing */ or C# will ignore the rest of your class declaration! It's a common and confusing error to forget to finish a comment properly. It sometimes happens accidentally because you forget to type either the * or the /, or because you mistype them.

The second type of comment is intended only for single line comments. Any text between the symbol // (two backslashes without any space between them) and the end of the current line is a comment.

```
// This is a single line comment
```

This form of comment is commonly used to annotate part of the class declaration written on the same line. For example, you might see something like:

```
int length; // the length of the rectangle
```

Take a look at Program 1.1 to see the style in which comments are used. You should get into the habit of using a similar style in your programs.

Writing a Program that Uses Class `Rectangle`

OK, so we have a class to represent rectangles. How do we use it to find the area and perimeter of a particular rectangle of specified dimensions? Well, the answer is that we write a C# program that creates an instance of class `Rectangle` with the appropriate dimensions and we ask that object to tell us its area and perimeter!

Figure 1.25 shows the syntax of a C# program. Actually it's just a class declaration that includes a special method called `Main` defined as shown in Figure 1.25. When we ask C# to run a program it always begins by executing the statements contained in the `Main` method of the program. Thus, the statements that we include in the `Main` method determine what the program does.

The `Main` method of our program will be somewhat more complicated than the methods in the `Rectangle` class. So, before going any further, we need to think about exactly what the steps to be carried out by this method are. The first step is obviously to create the rectangle object with the correct dimensions. Then we can ask the object to calculate its area and then its perimeter. After that we should print out the area on the computer screen and, finally, print out the length of the perimeter. Figure 1.26 lists the steps involved.

Notice that once we create our rectangle object we will have to store it somewhere so that we can use it later. We saw previously that a method can declare its own local variables to store information that it uses while it is executing. The `Main` method is no exception. While we didn't use any local variables in any of the methods of class `Rectangle`, we will need to use a local variable in our `Main` method to store our rectangle object. Likewise, we will have to store the area and perimeter of the rectangle between the time that we calculate them and the time that we print them out. Again, we can use local variables for this.

As Figure 1.27 shows, the syntax of a local variable declaration is similar to the syntax of an instance variable declaration except that it isn't preceded by the keyword `private` (and, of course, it occurs within a method rather than just within a class). The `Rectangle` object will be stored in a variable called `shape`, which is of type `Rectangle` – a type corresponding to the class that we just defined. In fact, every class defines a corresponding type that can be used as the type of any variable that stores an instance of that class. The area and perimeter will be stored in variables of type `int` since they're just numbers.

```
class <class name>
{

  public static void Main()
  {

    <list of local variables>

    <statement 1>;
    <statement 2>;
    <statement 3>;
    ...
    <statement n>;
  }

}
```

Figure 1.25   The syntax of a C# application declaration.

1. Create a new rectangle object with specified dimensions

2. Ask rectangle for its area

3. Ask rectangle for its perimeter

4. Print the area on the computer screen

5. Print the perimeter on the computer screen

Figure 1.26   The steps of the Main method.

The first statement in our `Main` method creates a new instance of `Rectangle` by using the C# new command (or *operator* as it is properly called) and specifying the name of the class of object to be created – in this case `Rectangle`. The new operator creates an object of the appropriate type and automatically calls its constructor to initialize the instance variables of the new object. Our `Rectangle` constructor needed two parameters; we provide the values for these parameters in the brackets following the name of the class. So, this program will create an instance of `Rectangle` with length 15 and width 30. The result of new is a new object that is immediately stored into the local variable `shape` as a result of the assignment. We can subsequently use this variable to refer to our new `Rectangle` object.

Next, `Main` invokes the `CalculateArea` method on the object stored in `shape` using the . (a single full stop) operator. This causes the `CalculateArea` method to execute and return the area of the object. The area is immediately stored in the variable `area` by means of another assignment. `Main` then invokes the `CalculatePerimeter` method on the object stored in `shape` and stores the result in the variable `perimeter`.

Having succeeded in calculating the area and perimeter of our rectangle, we now want to print out the results on the screen. To do so, we first need to create an instance of class `Terminal` using new in much the same way that we previously created an instance of `Rectangle`. `Terminal` is the name of a pre-defined class that we can use in any program that needs to print information on our computer screen (or indeed to read information entered by the user of the program). `Terminal` is a good example of reusing existing classes in new programs! In C#, reusable classes are collected together in so-called *assemblies* where each assembly typically contains a set of related classes, e.g., classes that describe similar kinds of objects. The `Terminal` class is contained in an assembly called `tcdIO`. To use the `Terminal` class in our program we have to declare that we want to use the `tcdIO` assembly as shown in Program 1.2.

Unlike the `Rectangle` constructor, the `Terminal` constructor needs no parameters. The newly created object is stored in yet another local variable called `terminal`.

To print out a message on the screen, `Main` uses the `WriteLine` method from class `Terminal`. `WriteLine`, as the name suggests, prints out a line of text that we give as a

```
<type> <local variable name>;
```

Figure 1.27   The syntax of a local variable declaration.

```
/* A program to calculate the area and perimeter of a rectangle */

using tcdIO;

class RectangleProgram
{
  public static void Main ()
  {
    Terminal terminal; // used to store object representing the terminal
    Rectangle shape;   // used to store object representing the rectangle
    int area;          // used to store area of rectangle
    int perimeter;     // used to store perimeter of rectangle

    /* create an object representing a 15 by 30 rectangle */
    shape = new Rectangle(15, 30);

    /* ask the rectangle object for its area */
    area = shape.CalculateArea();

    /* ask the rectangle object for its perimeter */
    perimeter = shape.CalculatePerimeter();

    /* create an object representing the terminal */
    terminal = new Terminal();

    /* Write the area of the rectangle on the screen */
    terminal.WriteLine("The area of the rectangle is: " + area);

    /* Write the perimeter of the rectangle on the screen */
    terminal.WriteLine("The perimeter of the rectangle is: " + perimeter);
  }
}
```

Program 1.2   A program to calculate the area and perimeter of a rectangle.

parameter on the computer screen. The WriteLine method therefore needs a single input – the string of text to be printed out. In our case we want to print out a message including the area of the rectangle. We make this message by joining the string of text "The area of the rectangle:" with the string representing the value of the area using the + operator. In this case the + operator means string addition (or *concatenation* as it is properly called) rather than integer addition. Of course, you may have noticed that the area is a number and not a string of text. However, C# is able to deduce from the context that we really want a textual representation of the area and convert the number stored in the variable area to the corresponding sequence of characters. We repeat exactly the same sequence of statements to print out the perimeter. The full program is shown in Program 1.2 and the result of running it is shown in Figure 1.28.

By the way, although we've said that the shape and terminal variables are used to store objects, what they actually contain are references to the corresponding objects. For now we'll ignore the distinction, latter you'll see that this is a crucial difference.

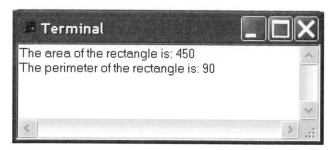

Figure 1.28   The execution of Program 1.2.

All of this may seem like an awful lot of effort just to print out the area and perimeter of a rectangle. However, this program illustrates all of the main features of object-oriented programming and how they are expressed in C#. We've already seen how to declare a new class that includes instance variables and methods, how to write a constructor to initialize a new object, how to create a new instance of that class and have it initialized, how to invoke the methods of an object, and how to reuse existing classes. In fact, there isn't an awful lot more to object-oriented programming, so we've already covered a lot of what this book is about!

Summary

- programs are made up of collections of interacting objects
- an *object* is a component of a program that represents some entity of interest
- objects of the same *type* represent the same kind of entity
- all objects of the same type have the same set of *attributes*
- ... and can carry out the same set of *methods*
- a *class* is a description of a particular type of object
- every object is an *instance* of some class
- objects can refer to each other by means of their *references*
- objects *interact* by invoking each other's methods
- in C#, a class is defined in a *class declaration*
- a class declaration includes *instance variable (or field) declarations* and *method declarations*
- a method can include *local variable declarations* and *statements*
- a C# *program* is defined by a special method called `Main`
- the new operator is used to create a new object
- a *constructor* is used to initialize a new object

Exercises

(1) List five classes of object that might be found in each of the following programs:
- a supermarket stock control program,
- an air traffic control program,
- a hospital management program.

(2) List (some of) the attributes of instances of each of the classes that you identified in Exercise 1. In each case describe what the type of the attribute is (i.e., what kind of value does it store?)

(3) List (some of) the methods that might be provided by each of the classes that you identified in Exercise 1.

(4) Modify Program 1.2 so that it prints out a message describing the purpose of the program on the screen before printing out the area and perimeter of the rectangle.

(5) Modify Program 1.2 so that it creates two different rectangles with different dimensions and prints out the areas and perimeters of each rectangle in turn.

(6) Modify your program from Exercise 5, so that is first prints the areas of both rectangles and then prints the perimeters of the two rectangles.

(7) Write a program that creates ten different rectangles and prints out the area and perimeter of each. Your program shouldn't use any more local variables than Program 1.2.

(8) Write a class whose instances represent squares and provides methods to calculate the area and perimeter of a square. Use your class in a program that prints out the area and perimeter of some square.

(9) Write a C# program that creates a rectangle and a square and then prints out the area of each.

(10) Write a class whose instances represent cubes and which provides methods to calculate the area of one side of the cube, to return the volume of the cube, and any other methods that you think appropriate.

(11) Write a C# program that first creates two different cubes and then prints out the areas of their sides and their volumes.

Computers, Programming Languages, and C# 2

This chapter:

- describes the main components of a typical computer system
- describes how a computer stores data and instructions and how instructions are executed
- introduces *machine language, assembly language,* and *high-level programming languages*
- describes the role of *compilers* and *interpreters* in translating high-level languages into instructions that can be directly executed by a computer
- motivates the use of C# as a programming language
- describes in detail how C# programs are translated into instructions that can be executed by a computer
- introduces the Visual Studio.Net development environment and how it is used to execute a C# program

In Chapter 1 we introduced a computer as a machine that is capable of storing and processing large amounts of information very quickly. We saw that the operations that computers perform on the information that they process are usually very simple (limited to simple arithmetic and logical operations) but can be performed at very high speeds. We also saw that it is possible to write a program in the C# programming language and run that program on most computers. Chapter 1 left one very important question unanswered – how is a C# program translated into instructions that the underlying computer can understand so that it can be executed?

In this chapter we will look in more detail at the components of a typical computer and how they work. Hopefully, this will allow you to understand in detail what's involved in getting a program written in C# to actually execute on some computer!

The Components of a Typical Computer

Figure 2.1 illustrates the components of a typical desktop computer system. The computer in question might be a typical PC, an Apple Macintosh, or a workstation used for computer-aided design or scientific computing. In fact, I have examples of all three of these types of computer sitting in my office! The most striking thing about them is that, although they all have different capabilities, they all have more or less the same basic components:

- a monitor on which information is displayed
- a keyboard and mouse used to input information

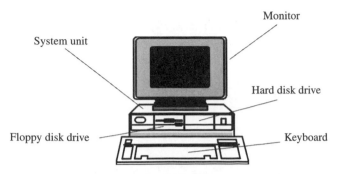

Figure 2.1 The components of a desktop computer system.

- a cabinet – usually referred to as *the system unit* – containing the computer's central processing unit (CPU), or *processor*, and its *primary memory*, as well as additional *secondary storage* devices such as hard disk drives, CD-ROM drives, and floppy disk drives.

In some cases, extra storage devices such as additional hard disk drives or CD-ROM drives may be provided outside of the system unit to which they are then attached in much the same way as the monitor or keyboard. Other devices that may be attached to a typical desktop computer might include joysticks, modems (a modem is a device used to interconnect computers via the telephone system), or printers. Taken together the entire collection of components that makes up the computer system is often referred to as being the computer's *hardware* (as distinct from its *software*, which consists of the collection of programs provided with the computer system).

While the input and output devices (including the storage devices) attached to a computer are its most visible components, the heart of any computer system is its processor and the associated electronic components including the computer's primary memory and so-called *peripheral interfaces*. These components are usually to be found on a printed circuit board (PCB) housed inside the system unit and often referred to as the computer's *motherboard*. These components are implemented as small electronic devices, usually referred to as *integrated circuits* or *chips*. Figure 2.2 illustrates the components to be found on a typical motherboard.

While a computer system that is embedded in a machine such as a video recorder or motor car will probably not have a monitor or keyboard, and may not even have any secondary storage devices, it will certainly have a PCB containing a processor, some memory, and one or more peripheral interfaces. In this case, the peripheral interfaces are required to allow the computer to interact with sensors or valves that control parts of the machine in which the computer is embedded.

The Processor

The processor is the component of a computer system that actually executes instructions. Every computer system has a processor. In fact, some computer systems may have more than one processor, although this is still relatively rare. Typically, the processor contains no memory (other that a small set of memory cells called *processor registers* that are used as a kind of scratch pad while executing instructions). Hence, when running a program, the processor repeatedly fetches its instructions from the memory, decodes them, and carries out the specified operation as illustrated in Figure 2.3. This process is usually referred to as

to/from peripheral device
(e.g., hard disk, floppy disk, CD-ROM)

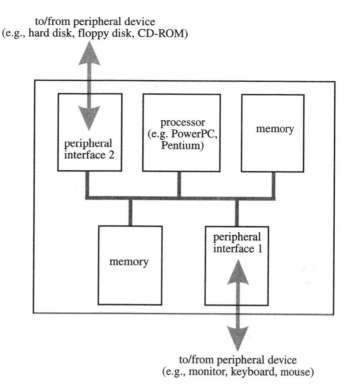

Figure 2.2 The motherboard of a typical computer system.

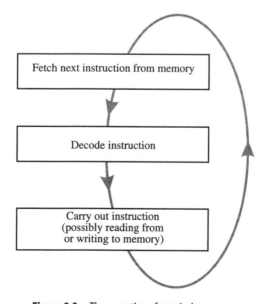

Figure 2.3 The operation of a typical processor.

the *fetch–decode–execute cycle*. Carrying out an instruction might involve fetching further information from memory or storing information into memory depending on the specific instruction in question.

There are a variety of different types of processor available. You may have heard of processors such as Intel's Pentium processor or Motorola's PowerPC processor. However, there are literally hundreds of others. Types of processor differ in a variety of ways. From our perspective, the most important thing to note it that different types of processors understand and are capable of carrying out different sets of instructions. Thus, the Pentium processor understands a different *instruction set* from the PowerPC processor. Any program written using the instructions understood by the Pentium processor can (probably) be executed on any computer whose processor is a Pentium, but not on a computer whose processor is a PowerPC. Likewise, a program written using the instructions understood by the PowerPC processor can't be executed on a computer whose processor is a Pentium. As a result, different versions of a program are usually required if that program is to run on computers with different types of processors. Clearly, such duplication of effort is undesirable. We'll see later how this problem can be alleviated.

Bits, Bytes, and Words

In computer science, a single binary digit is normally referred to as one *bit*. A bit has only two possible values – 0 and 1.

A *byte* is a collection of eight bits. Since each of the eight bits has two possible values, a single byte has 2^8 or 256 possible values (i.e., 00000000, 00000001, 00000010, 00000011, ..., 11111111). A byte might be used to represent a number in the range 0 to 255, a number in the range -128 to 127, or, possibly, a single character.

A *word* is a collection of 16 bits and has 2^{16} or 65536 possible values. Similarly, a *longword* is a collection of 32 bits and has a large number of possible values!

More interestingly, a *kilobyte* (KB) is 2^{10} or 1024 bytes. If a byte can store a single character, 1 KB can store approximately one page of text.

A *megabyte* (MB) is 2^{20} bytes (or if you prefer 2^{10} KB) and can store a lot of information. Finally, a *gigabyte* (GB) is 2^{30} bytes.

Primary Memory

Primary memory is where instructions and data are stored while the computer is running. As Figure 2.4 shows, the primary memory of a computer is organized as a collection of directly addressable *memory locations* where each memory location is capable of storing 16, 32, or 64 bits depending on the type of processor being used. Every available memory location has its own distinct *address* that can be used by a program running on the processor to refer to that location when its contents are required or are about to be changed. Typically, addresses also consist of 32 or 64 bits meaning that a very large number (2^{32} or 2^{64}) of distinct memory locations can theoretically be provided. In practice, typical desktop computers now include 256 MB or more of memory.

All information stored in memory must, of course, be encoded as a collection of binary numbers. However, the contents of a single memory location, although encoded as a binary number, might actually represent a single instruction, the address of another memory location, a positive or negative number, a single character, or some other type of data.

For the most part, the contents of primary memory are *volatile*. In other words, when power is turned off (whether deliberately using the computer system's on/off button or accidentally

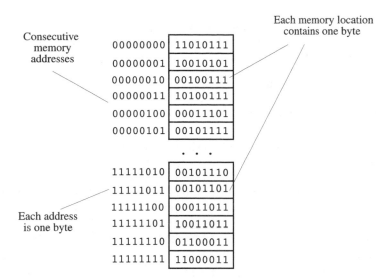

Figure 2.4　Primary memory is organized as a collection of addressable locations.

due, for example, to a power cut) the contents of primary memory are usually lost. In contrast, secondary storage devices such as hard disks and CD-ROMs provide long-term *persistent* storage for programs and data. Information (whether instructions or other types of data) that must be saved even when the computer is turned off is therefore usually stored on secondary storage. However, this information must be brought into the computer's primary memory in order to be used because, as we explained above, the processor obtains all of its instructions and data directly from primary memory. In any case, storing and retrieving data to or from primary memory is usually much faster than storing and retrieving data to or from secondary storage. Hence, it makes good sense to store instructions and data in primary memory while they are in use.

Peripheral Interfaces

As well as the processor and primary memory, the motherboard usually includes a collection of peripheral interfaces. Secondary storage devices and other types of input and output devices (including sensors and valves in the case of an embedded computer system) are often referred to as being *peripherals*. Peripheral interfaces are the electronic components that provide the connection between these peripheral devices and the processor and its primary memory. In some sense, they provide a gateway to and from the outside world. For example, the processor will make use of the peripheral interfaces to fetch data from secondary storage or from the computer's keyboard into primary memory and to output data from primary memory to secondary storage or the monitor. Different types of peripheral interfaces are used to form the gateway to different types of peripheral device.

The System Bus

The system bus is the medium through which the processor is connected to the other components on the motherboard – the primary memory and peripheral interfaces. You can think of the bus as a set of (tiny) electrical leads that interconnect the various components.

Any information that has to be transferred between the processor, primary memory, and the peripheral interfaces is transferred over the bus. Typically, the bus can only transfer about the equivalent of the contents of one memory location at a time – 16 to 64 bits.

Programming Languages

This book is about computer programming. Given some computer, we are concerned with describing the sequence of instructions that the computer should carry out in order to accomplish some task. This sequence of instructions, *a computer program*, must be described using a programming language. In fact, just as there are many different natural languages in existence, there are also many different programming languages. They differ in the types of computer for which they are suitable, the types of program for which they are intended, the approach to programming that they support, and the details of their syntax. In this section, we explore the characteristics of the three fundamental types of programming languages that are available: machine languages, assembly languages, and high-level programming languages.

Machine Language

We've already seen that a typically computer, or more correctly its processor, is capable of executing only the instructions defined by its instruction set. The instruction sets of most processors include only about 100–200 very simple instructions. For example, typical instructions would include those to:

- fetch a word from a specified memory location into a specified processor register,
- store a word from a specified register into a specified memory location,
- add the word in a specified register to that in a specified memory location, or
- subtract the word in a specified register from that in a specified memory location.

Individual instructions are referred to as *machine instructions*. Machine instructions are very *low level* in the sense that they typically refer to specific processor registers and memory locations and other hardware-specific details of the computer system. While it is possible to write a program directly using machine instructions, doing so is a painstaking and error-prone task, not least because it demands that the programmer keep track of the current use of every processor register and relevant memory location! Nevertheless, *all* programs whether written in a language like C# or directly using machine instructions must eventually be transformed into a corresponding set of machine instructions before they can be executed.

When stored in the memory of a computer, individual machine instructions are represented using binary code numbers. This binary representation of machine instructions is referred to as *machine code* or *machine language*. The code numbers used to represent each instruction are defined by the type of processor being used. Thus, every type of processor understands its own distinct machine language. For example, Program 2.1 shows a machine language program to add two numbers written using Pentium machine language. Each instruction includes not only the code number for that particular instruction but also additional data required by the instruction such as the address of any memory location that it effects or the number of any processor register that it uses. Given the right tools, we could load this machine language program into the memory of a suitable computer (i.e., one that has a Pentium processor) and execute it.

```
1101 1000 0010 0100 1010 0101 0010 1000 0001 0101 0101
1110 0100 1010 1000 1010 1011 1011 1011 1111 0001 1010
0001 0001 0111 0101 1101 1010 1001 0100 1010 1111 1101
1101 0101 1110 0101 0101 1001 0100 1001 1101 1011 1101
0001 0100 1000 1001 1101 0110 1010 1100 1111 0010 1010
1000 1010 1110 1011 0010 0101 0110 1001 0010 1010 1010
1101 0101 1110 0101 0101 1001 0100 1001 1101 1011 1101
```

Program 2.1 A machine language program.

Assembly Language

Writing programs using machine code is difficult not only because of the fact that we have to deal with individual machine instructions but also because we have to work in binary! In particular, we have to know the binary code number for each instruction and be careful not to enter it incorrectly! A slightly better alternative to using machine language is to use what is called *assembly language*. In assembly language, each machine instruction is represented by a simple mnemonic – usually a word that describes the meaning of the corresponding instruction. For example, rather than writing the binary number 11110101 to represent the instruction to add the word in a specified processor register to that in a specified memory location, we might instead write an assembly language instruction such as addw, for "add word". Program 2.2 shows the assembly language version of Program 2.1. Hopefully, it's a little easier to understand! Notice that, as well as using mnemonics to represent instructions, assembly language programs use mnemonics to represent processor registers too. In addition, they usually use hexadecimal, rather than binary, numbers to represent memory addresses and other numeric values.

It's important to understand that there is a one-to-one mapping between assembly language instructions and machine language instructions. In other words, for each machine instruction there is exactly one corresponding assembly language instruction and vice versa. Thus, both Programs 2.1 and 2.2 describe exactly the same sequence of instructions. The only difference is that the instructions are represented in a different form. The complexity of writing the program is the same except that when writing the assembly language version it wasn't necessary to work in binary. Notice that this means that the assembly language to be used with each different type of processor is different since each type of processor has a different instruction set. Thus, a program written in either machine language or assembly language can only be executed on one type of processor.

Writing programs in assembly language is clearly preferable to writing in machine language and, as a result, almost nobody ever uses machine language when writing a program. However,

```
mov     esi,edx
xor     cl,cl
shld    edx,eax,1
shld    esi,eax,2
adc     cl,0
xor     edx,esi
xchg    eax,edx
xor     dl,cl
```

Program 2.2 An assembly language program.

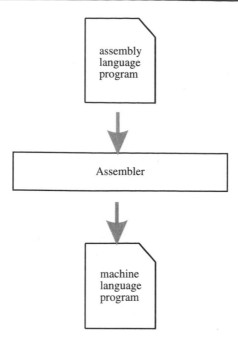

Figure 2.5 An assembler translates assembly language into machine language.

the use of assembly language introduces another problem because, as we know, computers don't actually understand assembly language! Before a program written in assembly language can be executed, the text of the program must be translated into the corresponding machine language before it can then be loaded into some computer's memory and executed. This translation is carried out by a program called an *assembler*. An assembler is simply a program that translates assembly language into the corresponding machine language as illustrated in Figure 2.5. Most computers come with an assembler already installed. Typically, the assembler takes a file containing the text of an assembly language program as its input and produces a file containing the corresponding machine language program as its output. The resulting program can then be loaded into the computer and executed just as if it had originally been written in machine language.

Note that, in general, the entire assembly language program has to be translated into machine language before the resulting machine language program can be executed. However, once the translation is complete, the machine language program can be stored away safely and executed as often as required.

High-level Programming Languages

As you've probably guessed, most programs aren't written in machine language, or even assembly language, but in what are usually termed *high-level programming languages*. These languages are *high level* in the sense that they provide statements that are closer to commands expressed in a natural language such as English than to individual machine instructions. Moreover, statements written in such a language don't refer to individual processor registers or memory locations but to more meaningful concepts such as "my salary" or "the area of the rectangle".

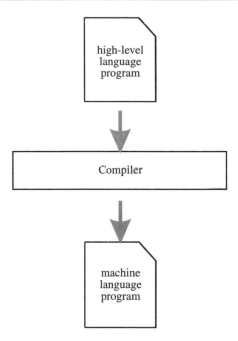

Figure 2.6   A compiler translates a high-level language into machine language.

Apart from being easier to use, high-level languages have another major advantage. The use of a high-level language is independent of the use of any particular type of processor in the computer. For example, the *same* program written in a high-level language such as C# can be executed on computers with Pentium processors or PowerPC processors or, indeed, many other types of processors. Before any program written in a high-level language can be executed it must first be translated into machine language. When we come to do the translation we can choose what sort of machine language we want to translate the program into. Thus, we can translate the same program into Pentium machine language or PowerPC machine language or some other machine language! In fact, having written the program once, we can potentially translate it into a number of different types of machine language for use on different computers!

A program that translates programs written in a high-level language into machine language is known as a *compiler* as illustrated in Figure 2.6. Different compilers are required to translate programs written in different languages. For example, to translate programs written in the Pascal programming language into machine language, a Pascal compiler is required. Likewise, to translate C++ programs into machine language, a C++ compiler is required. Typically, a different version of the compiler is required for each type of machine language into which programs are to be translated. Thus, different versions of the Pascal compiler would be required to translate Pascal programs into Pentium machine language and PowerPC machine language.

A compiler usually takes a file containing the text of the program to be translated as its input and produces a file containing the corresponding machine language program as its output. In general, the entire high-level language program must be translated before the resulting machine language program can be executed. However, the translation only needs to be done once and then the translated program can be executed as often as required thereafter. Of course, the translation has to be done once for each type of machine on which the program is to be executed using the appropriate version of the compiler for that type of machine.

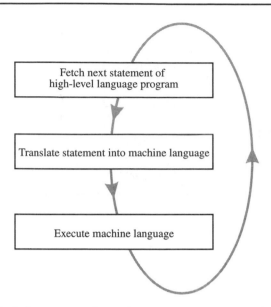

Figure 2.7 An interpreter translates and executes a program statement-by-statement.

An *interpreter* is another type of program that does essentially the same job as a compiler but operates statement by statement as illustrated in Figure 2.7. Thus, an interpreter takes a single statement of the program, translates it and then immediately executes it before moving on to the next statement. Moreover, while a compiler typically produces a file containing the translated program as its output, which is subsequently executed, interpreters normally do not provide a translated version of the program that can be executed separately. Thus, each time a program is to be executed it must go through the same interpretation. In fact, if there are statements in the program that are executed multiple times, each statement may be translated every time that it is about to execute!

Clearly, when we use an interpreter, the overall speed at which the program runs is reduced because each statement has to be translated before being executed. However, the advantage is that we don't have to go through a separate translation phase before starting to run our program.

It's worth pointing out that we usually don't get a choice as to whether to use a compiler or an interpreter to do the translation. Some languages are compiled while others are interpreted!

Comparison of Machine, Assembly, and High-level Programming Languages

Machine language and assembly language are more or less indistinguishable from the point of view of their usability for writing programs. However, compared with the use of a high-level programming language, machine/assembly language has two main disadvantages:

- programs are machine dependent,
- programming is tedious and error prone.

A given machine/assembly language program will run only on computers with the type of processor for which the program was written. Thus, to execute such a program on another type of computer usually requires that the entire program be rewritten. On the other hand, machine/assembly language does have some advantages:

- it is possible to write programs that access specific features of the computer's hardware, such as its peripheral interfaces, which may not be possible from a high-level language,
- it is sometimes possible to write more efficient programs (i.e., programs that execute using fewer instructions) than is possible using a high-level language since the compiler may not minimize the number of instructions used in the same way that a human programmer can.

So, while it is sometimes necessary or desirable to program in assembly language, by far the vast majority of programs are written in a suitable high-level language.

Operating Systems and Portability

A bare computer, i.e., one without any software, would be very difficult to use. At the very least we would need some way of loading programs into primary memory and executing them.

To solve this problem, most computers come equipped with an *operating system* – a program or set of programs provided to assist the user of the computer in creating, managing, and running their own programs. You may have already met operating systems such as Windows XP, Windows 2000, or Linux. As well as allowing their users to run programs, a typical operating system will provide facilities to allow multiple users to use a single machine simultaneously without them necessarily being aware of each other. Moreover, an operating system will almost certainly include the software necessary to allow the various peripherals attached to the computer system to be used. Typically, each type of peripheral needs specialized software tailored to the characteristics of the particular device. Rather than having every programmer write this software for themselves, it's usually provided as part of the operating system so that any other program that executes on the computer can use it.

The role of the operating system can be seen as hiding the idiosyncrasies of the computer's hardware, e.g., the size of its primary memory or the details of how to use the peripherals attached to the computer, from users of the computer and their programs. An operating system provides a standard way for programs to interact with the underlying hardware without every program having to know all the details of how the hardware works. Thus, an operating system might provide facilities to allow programs to read or write data to or from a hard disk that work independently of what kind of disk is attached to the computer. The details of what facilities are provided and how programs use them differ from operating system to operating system.

Computers of different types can use the same operating system. Likewise, computers of the same type might use different operating systems. Thus, we might have one computer with a Pentium processor that uses the Windows 2000 operating system and another that uses the Linux operating system. At same time we could have a computer with a PowerPC processor that uses Linux.

Normally, programs are written to run using a particular operating system. Thus, we might have one version of a program that is intended for use on computers that use the Windows 2000 operating system and another that is intended to run on computers that use the Linux operating system. Most of the program will be the same independent of which operating system is used (since it performs the same task in either case). However, the parts of the program that interact with the operating system, e.g., those parts that use the devices attached to the computer, may need to be changed for different versions of the program.

The task of modifying a program that was written to execute on one type of computer using one operating system to execute on another type of computer possibly using a different operating system is referred to as *porting* the program. Thus, we might "port" the Windows 2000 version of our program to Linux, meaning that we are modifying it to use the facilities provided by Linux in place of those provided by Windows 2000. The ease with which a program can be ported to a different system is referred to as the *portability* of the program. A *portable* program is one that is easily modified to work on different types of computers and operating systems.

C#

So far in this chapter we have taken a look at how programs written in high-level languages are typically translated into corresponding machine language programs that can be executed on a computer of a certain type. In this section, we look in some detail at how C# programs are translated into a form that can be executed on a computer. As you'll see, C# uses a two-stage compilation to allow C# programs to be translated only *once* into a form that can be used on *any* machine that supports C#.

One of the uses of C# is to write programs that can be distributed over the world-wide computer network known as the Internet. The Internet is a collection of hundreds of thousands of interconnected computers that routinely share information with each other. Typically, information is exported by one computer, usually referred to as a *server*, and imported by other *client* computers that need to use it. One of the goals of the C# design was to allow a program exported by one computer on the Internet to be imported and executed by many other computers. Since pretty much any kind of computer can be attached to the Internet, there is no way of knowing in advance what types of computers might import a program that was been exported in this way or of knowing what operating system they might be using. Hence, the question arises as to what format the program should be made available in. There are two obvious possibilities:

- export the high-level language version of the program. In this case, whenever the program was imported by a computer it would have to be compiled into the corresponding machine language program. Moreover, this strategy would only work if the same program could be run on computers that used different operating systems. For example, there are significant differences in how services are accessed in WindowsXP as opposed to Linux. In addition, it would result in a significant delay before an imported program could be run (i.e., while the compilation takes place) and clearly involves considerable duplication of effort (since the program has to be compiled on every computer that imports it).
- export one or more different machine language versions of the program suitable for use on different types of computer using different operating systems. While this solution avoids most of the problems associated with the first approach, it introduces some new problems. Firstly, we would have to port the program and compile it for every different type of computer before exporting it. Moreover, we would have to make all these different versions available. For example, Windows NT4.0 runs on Alpha and Intel processors. Since these machines have considerably different machine languages, two completely separate versions of the same operating system are required. In our case, anyone who wants to import our program would be faced with the problem of working out which is the appropriate version for his or her machine!

To overcome these potential problems, the designers of C# packaged all platform dependencies into a software framework. They began by defining the ideal processor on which to run C# programs. This processor doesn't correspond to any existing processor (at least not quite yet!). The Common Language Runtime (CLR), as it is called, is defined by

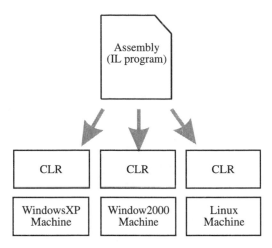

Figure 2.8   The Common Language Runtime (CLR).

its instruction set – in this case the set of instructions that it should be able to execute. The instructions defined by the CLR are known as *intermediate language* (IL) and, at least in principle, correspond to the machine instructions of a real processor.

Given the definition of the CLR, the next step was to implement it as a program in such a way that it can potentially be ported to lots of different types of computers that use different operating systems. Now, given an implementation of the CLR, any computer can execute programs consisting of sequences of IL. Moreover, exactly the same IL program, or assembly as they are called, can execute on any machine on which the CLR executes as shown in Figure 2.8.

Given a C# program, the C# compiler is used not to translate that program into machine language but to translate it into IL. IL is then converted to machine language by the CLR, as shown in Figure 2.9.

By taking responsibility for platform dependencies, the CLR allows assemblies to execute on multiple machines and operating systems. The architecture of the CLR allows it to factor out hardware and operating system dependencies. The CLR contains an IL compiler that is responsible for converting the IL representation of an assembly into machine language corresponding to the platform on which the assembly will be executed. In order to avoid assemblies being dependent on a particular operating system, the designers of the CLR provided a set of assemblies, just like the tcdIO assembly that we used in Chapter 1, that contain classes providing all the facilities usually provided by the operating system. Rather than using the facilities provided by the local operating system, C# programs are expected to make use of these assemblies. These assemblies can then be implemented and made available on each type of computer on which C# programs are to run. As long as a C# program only uses these packages and not the facilities provided by the operating system, it will be independent of what operating system is being used! Taken together this set of assemblies is referred to as the Base Classes.

Thus, given a C# program, we can translate it once into IL form using the C# Compiler and then export the resulting assembly to anyone who wants to import it. In order to execute the assembly, importers will need to have a CLR installed on their own computers. Once they have, they can execute any C# assembly.

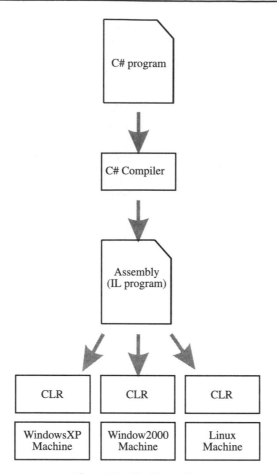

Figure 2.9 The C# compiler.

Developing Programs with VisualStudio.NET

Now that we have seen the context in which we are developing our programs, it is time to take a quick tour of the VisualStudio.NET environment for some hands on experience with program development. This section provides a tutorial for using the Visual Studio to create a simple program to write "Hello world!" in a window on the computer monitor using classes in the `tcdIO` assembly. If you have access to VisualStudio.NET, you would be advised to work through the example.

Creating a VisualStudio.NET Project

The first step in developing any application in VisualStudio is to create an appropriate project. A VisualStudio project groups files that will be compiled into a single end product be it a stand alone program or an assembly that will be included in other programs. To create a Project, start by selecting the File | New | Project menu item, as pictured in Figure 2.10. This will open the New Project window.

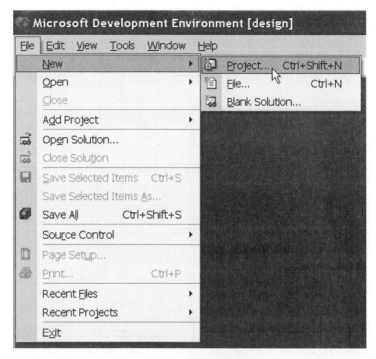

Figure 2.10   Create the project.

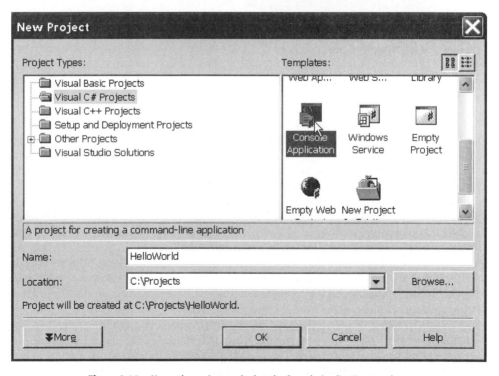

Figure 2.11   Name the project, and select the Console Application template.

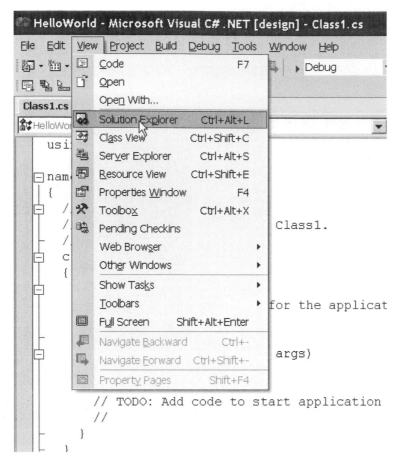

Figure 2.12   Open Solution Explorer window.

The New Project window, shown in Figure 2.11, allows us to select a template, name the project, and select its location. For this demonstration, it does not matter where we put the project folder. If you are following along on your own computer, you should name the project "HelloWorld" to keep your project consistent with the figures. Templates are available for creating different kinds of components. Some are programs that execute on their own, while others are files that contain classes that other programs will use. Throughout this book, we will use the Console Application template and rely on the tcdIO classes to display text to the screen and read the keyboard for input. Later, when we look at GUI development, we will make use of the Windows Application template.

After entering the project information and pressing the "OK" button, the project should now be visible in the Solution Explorer window. To guarantee that the window is on the screen, select the Solution Explorer item from the View menu, as shown in Figure 2.12.

The Solution Explorer, shown in Figure 2.13, displays the projects in the solution. A solution can be thought of as a basket for collecting projects. Each project is contained by a solution. So we if create a new project, it will be added to the solution that is currently open or a new solution will be created to contain the project. As mentioned, projects correspond to a collection of files that are compiled into a single unit. Under each project is a list of the files and References in the project. Our project's name is "HelloWorld". The Application Console template results in three files being added to our project. Two files, `App.ico` and an `AssemblyInfo.cs`, are of little interest. The other, `Class1.cs` file, will contain a `Main` method. When the project is compiled, or built, an executable file will be produced.

Making Changes to a Class

The `Main` method in the `Class1.cs` file is the starting point of execution when the application is run. Thus, we will have to add code to this method to get the message "Hello world!" to display when the application is run, so we will open this file for editing. To do so, select the file name and right click. In the menu that appears, select the "Open" option, as shown in Figure 2.13.

To allow the `Main` method to reference classes in the `tcdIO` assembly, the file needs a `using` statement that refers to the assembly. Later in the text we will explain the meaning of this keyword. For now, put the text `using tcdIO;` on a separate line above the `using System;` statement, as shown in Figure 2.14.

To display "Hello world!" we need to add code to create a `Terminal` class object, and to display the text "Hello world!" in the `Terminal` object's window. To do so, the following code must be added to the body of the `Main` method.

```
Terminal terminal;
terminal = new Terminal();
terminal.WriteLine("Hello world!");
```

The code added to `Class1.cs` is highlighted in Figure 2.15

Figure 2.13 Opening the `Class1.cs` file for editing.

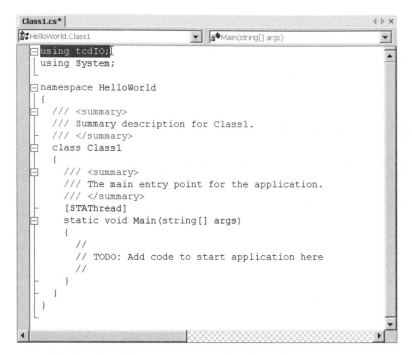

Figure 2.14 Add `using tcdIO;` above the `using System;`.

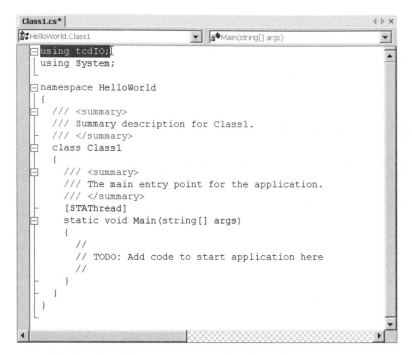

Figure 2.15 Add code to create a `Terminal` object, and to display the text "Hello world!".

Using Other Assemblies

The inclusion of a `using` statement does not automatically tell the project where to find the assembly. This information is held in the project's References. Unfortunately, the `tcdIO` assembly is not among the References in the HelloWorld project, which are shown in Figure 2.16.

To open the Add Reference dialog, select the References text, and activate the right click menu. From the options that appear, click on the "Add Reference" option, as shown in Figure 2.17.

The `tcdIO` assembly is stored in a file called `tcdIO.dll`. This file will be stored in a folder on the computer. To select the file for inclusion in the References, open the file browser by selecting the "Browse" button, as shown in Figure 2.18.

Use the browser to navigate to the folder containing `tcdIO.dll`. In this example, the file is in the same folder as the HelloWorld project folder; however, the location will vary from computer to computer. When in the folder containing `tcdIO.dll`, select the file and press the "Open" button, as shown in Figure 2.19.

Figure 2.16　References in the HelloWorld Project.

Figure 2.17　Open the Add Reference dialog.

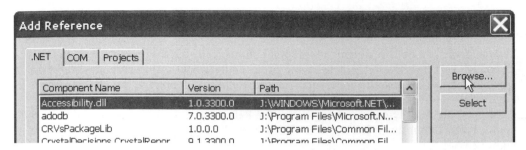

Figure 2.18 Open file browser to locate the tcdIO.dll file.

The `tcdIO` file will now appear in the "Selected Components:" box at the bottom of the Add Reference Dialog, shown in Figure 2.20. However, the `tcdIO` library is in turn dependent on the `System.Windows.Forms` assembly, and the HelloWorld project does not have a reference for this assembly either. Unlike `tcdIO`, the `System.Windows.Forms` assembly is registered as a .NET assembly. Thus, the corresponding file can be selected by scrolling down to the bottom of the list of files in the .NET tab, clicking on the assembly's name, and pressing the select button, as shown in Figure 2.20.

Now that the "Selected Components" box lists both the `tcdIO` and `System.Windows.Forms` assembly, we can close the Add Reference dialog by pressing the "OK" button, as shown in Figure 2.21.

The Solution Explorer window will be updated, and the References list for the HelloWorld project should contain two new entries. We have highlighted them in Figure 2.22 to distinguish them from the existing entries.

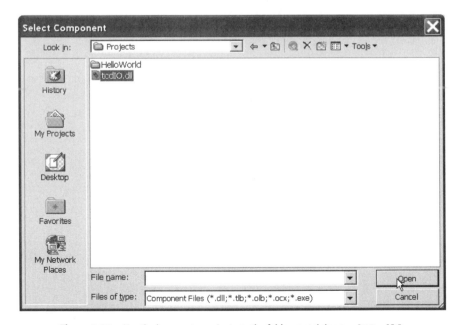

Figure 2.19 Use the browser to navigate to the folder containing `tcdIO.dll`.

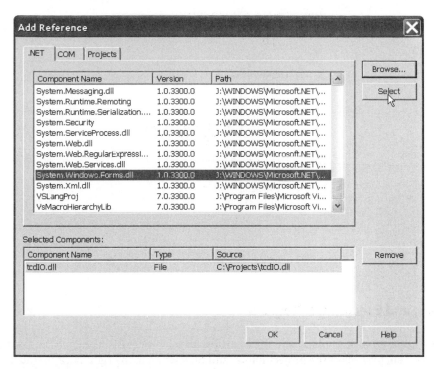

Figure 2.20   Select the `System.Windows.Forms.dll` file and press the Select button.

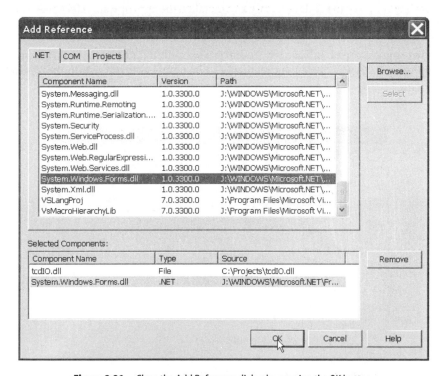

Figure 2.21   Close the Add Reference dialog by pressing the OK button.

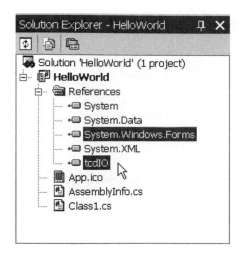

Figure 2.22   Updated References list for HelloWorld project.

Building and Executing a Program

With the updated code in place, and the appropriate references installed, we can compile the code. To do so, first select the project name, and then activate the right click menu. Selecting the Rebuild option, pictured in Figure 2.23, will cause VisualStudio to compile the source code of the project and create an executable program.

Since we have entered the code correctly and installed the appropriate references, the project will compile correctly. After the build completes, the Output window should appear as shown in Figure 2.24.

With the program correctly built, we can start its execution. The Debug | Start menu option, shown in Figure 2.25, will cause the executable to be launched from within the VisualStudio environment.

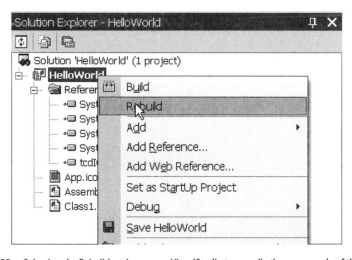

Figure 2.23   Selecting the Rebuild option causes VisualStudio to compile the source code of the project.

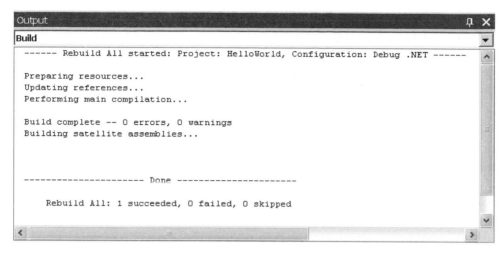

Figure 2.24   After the build completes, the Output window should appear as shown.

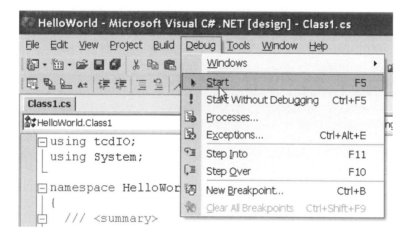

Figure 2.25   Start program execution with the Debug | Start menu option.

The result of executing the program is that the window displayed in Figure 2.26 will appear. Now that we have some background with VisualStudio.NET, it will be possible to complete the end of chapter programming exercises in the later chapters.

Figure 2.26   Execution of HelloWorld project.

Summary

- the *processor* is the component of a computer system that actually executes instructions
- different types of processors understand and are capable of carrying out different *instruction sets*
- *primary memory* is where instructions and data are stored while the computer is running
- the contents of primary memory are *volatile*
- *secondary storage* devices provide long-term *persistent* storage for programs and data
- the binary representation of *machine instructions* is referred to as *machine language*
- in *assembly language*, each machine instruction is represented by a simple mnemonic
- an *assembler* is a program that translates assembly language into the corresponding machine language
- C# classes are compiled into assemblies that contain IL. These assemblies are executed by the CLR.
- VisualStudio.NET provides an environment for developing C# applications.

Variables, Types, and Assignment 3

This chapter:

- motivates the use of *variables* as a means of storing information
- describes how variables are declared, initialized, and modified
- describes how *types* are used to describe the values that may be stored in a variable
- describes how classes are used to introduce new types
- introduces the types that C# provides to represent numbers
- describes how *assignment* is used to change the value of a variable
- describes how *expressions* are written in C#
- describes how the instance variables of an object are initialized
- describes how *constants* are used to associate meaningful names with values

In Chapter 1 we saw that an object typically contains a collection of *attributes* or *instance variables* that are used to store the *state* of the object, i.e., to store the information that describes the entity represented by the object. We also saw that methods, such as the `Main` method of a C# program, typically have their own *local variables* to store additional information used by the method as it executes.

Thus, variables, whether instance variables or local variables, serve as *containers* for information. In particular, variables provide the means for programs to store the information on which they are working. Since most programs are concerned with processing stored information, understanding the use of variables is fundamental to being able to write useful programs. This chapter looks in detail at the use of variables in C# programs.

Storing Information – Variables

It is probably best to think of a variable as simply a container for a value. For example, a variable that is used to store the colour of somebody's eyes would contain a colour value such as "green" or "blue". Likewise, a variable that is used to store the radius of a circle would contain a numeric value such as 15.57 or 8.9. Finally, a variable that stores my current salary would also contain a (hopefully large) numeric value such as 17895.76. Different variables will typically contain different values. Thus, the variable that stores my salary would probably contain a different value from the one that stores my boss's salary. Moreover, the same variable will very often contain different values at different times. The variable that stores my current salary will contain different values as I get promoted and (hopefully) earn more. Thus, a

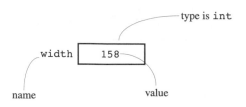

Figure 3.1 Variables in C#.

defining characteristic of a variable is that the value stored in it can be changed over time – it is *variable*!

Variables in C#

In C#, every variable has a *name*, a *type*, and a (current) *value* as depicted in Figure 3.1. The name of a variable allows that variable to be referred to by the program to which it belongs. The programmer, subject to certain rules that are described later, can choose the name of a variable. The name should be chosen to describe the value that is stored in the variable. For example, a variable might be called eyeColour, radius, or mySalary. Clearly, you would not expect a variable called eyeColour to contain a number nor would you expect a variable called mySalary to contain a colour. Thus, the choice of variable name is very important in helping people to understand what is going on in a program.

The type of a variable describes the kind of values that can be stored in that variable. We'll say a lot more about types later in this chapter. For now, the important thing to realize is that a type characterizes a set of possible values. For example, the type Colour might consist of the set of values {"blue", "green", "red", "white", "black"}. When we then say that a variable named eyeColour has type Colour, we mean that the variable can only store one of the values of type Colour. Thus, it might store the value "red" or the value "green" but it cannot store the value "yellow" (because "yellow" is not one of the values included in type Colour). Moreover, it cannot store a numeric value such as 54.7 or any other value that is not one of the values provided by type Colour.

It is important to realize that *every* variable has a type that describes the kind of values that it is allowed to store. The type of a variable cannot be changed. Thus, every variable is constrained to store only one type of value. When we introduce a new variable in a program, we have to say explicitly what its type is, i.e., we have to say what kind of values it is intended to store. After that, C# will prevent us from storing the wrong kind of value in that variable. Not all programming languages enforce this rule. For this reason, C# is said to be a *strongly-typed* language. Strong typing is very helpful in detecting programming errors. It prevents programs from carrying out meaningless actions, such as trying to store a number in a variable that is intended to store a colour, that are indicative of programming mistakes.

Naming Variables

In C#'s terminology names are called *identifiers*. Thus variables have identifiers rather than names. In fact, it's not only variables that have identifiers but every entity defined by a program that might need to be referred to by another part of the program (or even another program). Thus, classes, types, and methods all have identifiers and the same rules apply to choosing the identifiers of each.

abstract	as	base	bool	break
byte	case	catch	char	checked
class	const	continue	decimal	default
delegate	do	double	else	enum
event	explicit	extern	false	finally
fixed	float	for	foreach	goto
if	implicit	in	int	interface
internal	is	lock	long	namespace
new	null	object	operator	out
override	params	private	protected	public
readonly	ref	return	sbyte	sealed
short	sizeof	stackalloc	static	string
struct	switch	this	throw	true
try	typeof	uint	ulong	unchecked
unsafe	ushort	using	virtual	void
volatile	while			

Figure 3.2   C#'s keywords.

Formally, an identifier can be any sequence of characters (i.e., letters, the decimal digits and some punctuation marks) as long as it begins with a letter or an underscore ("_"). Letters include both uppercase ("A"..."Z") and lowercase ("a"..."z") letters. Thus, the following are valid C# identifiers:

```
MyAge     person1   aLongIdentifier   time2Go
_label    my_name   noOfDollars
```

while the following are not valid identifiers:

a+b – we can't use the plus sign as part of an identifier,

2Down – an identifier must begin with a letter,

Help! – we can't use the exclamation mark as part of an identifier,

My Salary – this is actually two separate identifiers (spaces are not allowed).

One thing to watch out for is that uppercase and lowercase letters are considered to be different, i.e., case is significant. Thus, myAge and myage are different identifiers.

A further complication is that C# uses a number of keywords to introduce various parts of a program (among other things). These keywords cannot be used as identifiers. This full list is given in Figure 3.2.

C# won't let us use an identifier that doesn't comply with these rules, although it will allow us to use any identifier that does. However, just because an identifier complies with the rules doesn't make it a good identifier. A good identifier is one that helps people who read our programs to understand what the program is doing. You should put some effort into trying to choose good identifiers. Here's some advice:

- try to choose identifiers that convey the role of the entity being named,
- in the case of a class, choose an identifier that names the type of entities represented by the instances of the class, e.g. Car, House, or Invoice,
- in the case of a variable, choose an identifier that describes what the variable stores, e.g., I hope it's fairly obvious what's going to be stored in each of the following variables: mySalary, birthday, phoneNumber,
- in the case of a method, choose an identifier that describes what the method does or what value it returns, e.g. IncreaseSalary, TurnLeft, ComputeInterest,

- never use a variable whose name has only a single letter – identifiers such as x or p are rarely meaningful,
- try to avoid using punctuation characters in identifiers, e.g., use myName rather than my_name,
- avoid using identifiers that differ only in their capitalization or that are in any way similar to any of C#'s keywords, e.g. don't use area and Area in the same program,
- don't be afraid to use multi-word identifiers, e.g. phoneNumber conveys a lot more information than number.

Apart from the rules above, there are a few conventions used by C# programmers when choosing identifiers. These are only conventions and are not enforced by C#. If you ignore them, you run the risk of making yourself very unpopular with other programmers. The identifier of a class should begin with a capital letter. The identifier of a variable should normally begin with a lowercase letter and of a method with an uppercase letter. If an identifier consists of multiple words, the second and subsequent words should begin with capital letters, e.g., turnLeft is much more readable than turnleft.

Describing Information – Types

The C# language provides a number of predefined types that describe common sets of values, such as whole numbers or single characters, and facilities that allow us to define our own new types.

C# provides 13 so-called *simple types* whose values represent fundamental entities such as numbers and single characters. In addition, every class defines a new type. The values of such a *class type* are the instances of the class. Thus, the possible values of type Person, where Person is the name of a class, are all the objects that are instances of class Person. For reasons that we will explain below, such class types are called *reference types* in C#.

Simple Types

Figure 3.3 lists the 13 simple types provided by C# and describes their values. Notice that most of the simple types describe numbers. Type char describes single characters. Type bool has only two values true and false.

We can declare variables of any of these types. To declare a variable, we write the identifier of its type followed by the identifier of the variable. Thus, to declare a single variable of type int named age we write:

```
int age;
```

which introduces a new container for integer numbers that can be referred to by the identifier age. To declare three distinct integer variables, called one, two, and three, we can write:

```
int one, two, three;
```

i.e., we give the name of the type just once and follow it with a list of the identifiers of the variables that we want to declare separated by commas.

Program 3.1 is a simple program that declares an int variable called number and stores a sequence of different values into that variable. After each change to the value of the variable, its current value is written to the screen as shown in Figure 3.4. Notice the use of assignment

Type	Represents	Example
sbyte	Integer numbers	...-3,-2,-1,0,1,2,3...
short	Integer numbers	...-3,-2,-1,0,1,2,3...
int	Integer numbers	...-3,-2,-1,0,1,2,3...
long	Integer numbers	...-3,-2,-1,0,1,2,3...
byte	Natural numbers	0,1,2,3,4,5,6...
ushort	Natural numbers	0,1,2,3,4,5,6...
uint	Natural numbers	0,1,2,3,4,5,6...
ulong	Natural numbers	0,1,2,3,4,5,6...
float	Real numbers	...-57.321...0.0...4543.23
double	Real numbers	...-57.321...0.0...4543.23
decimal	Real numbers	...-57.321...0.0...4543.23
char	Single characters	...'a','Z','!'...
bool	Truth values	true, false

Figure 3.3   C#'s simple types.

```
/* A program to illustrate changing */
/* the value of an integer variable */

using tcdIO;

class ChangeInteger
{
   public static void Main()
   {
      Terminal terminal;
      int number; // declare an integer variable called number

      /* create an object to represent the terminal */
      terminal = new Terminal();

      number = 7865; // store 7865 in number
      terminal.WriteLine("The value of number is " + number + ".");

      number = -5678; // now store -5678 in number
      terminal.WriteLine("The value of number is now " + number + ".");

      number = 27;  // finally store 27 in number
      terminal.WriteLine("The value of number is now " + number + ".");
   }
}
```

Program 3.1   A program to illustrate changing the value of an integer variable.

to store different values into the variable. As this example shows, we can change the value of a variable as often as we want during a program.

As declared, the variable number in Program 3.1 can only ever contain a value of type int. It could never, for example, contain a real number or a character. Thus, it might contain the value 18 but never the value 18.43. To declare a variable capable of storing a real number we can use type float. For example, to declare a variable of type float named salary we write:

```
float salary;
```

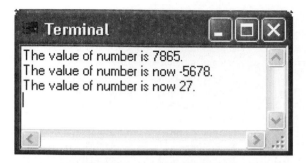

Figure 3.4   The execution of Program 3.1.

This introduces a new container for real numbers that can be referred to by the identifier salary.

As declared here, salary can only ever contain a value of type float. Thus, perhaps surprisingly, it might contain the value 18.43 but never the value 18 (although 18.00 would be OK!).

Program 3.2 declares three float variables and stores values into all three before eventually writing these values out to the screen as shown in Figure 3.5. Notice that the letter "F" always follows a value of type float when written in a C# program.

Finally, to declare a variable of type char named gender we write:

```
char gender;
```

This declaration introduces a new container for single characters that can be referred to by

```
/* A program to illustrate the use */
/* of floating point variables */

using tcdIO;

class UseFloats
{
    public static void Main()
    {
        Terminal terminal;
        float number1, number2, number3; // declare three variables

        /* create an object to represent the terminal */
        terminal = new Terminal();

        /* store values into each of the floating point variables */
        number1 = -7289.45F;
        number2 = 234.67F;
        number3 = 34.567F;

        /* now Write out the stored values */
        terminal.WriteLine("The value of number1 is " + number1 + ".");
        terminal.WriteLine("The value of number2 is " + number2 + ".");
        terminal.WriteLine("The value of number3 is " + number3 + ".");
    }
}
```

Program 3.2   A program to illustrate the use of floating-point variables.

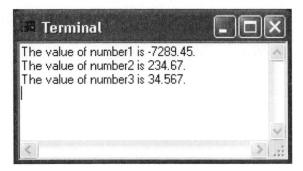

Figure 3.5　The execution of Program 3.2.

the identifier `gender`. As declared, `gender` can only ever contain a single character such as "A" or "!".

As an example of strong typing in action, look at Program 3.3. This program tries to store the `float` value contained in the variable `number` into the `char` variable `letter`. Figure 3.6 shows the result of trying to compile this program. As you can see, the C# compiler refuses to compile the program and complains about not being able to "convert type 'float' to 'char'". As this example illustrates, attempts to violate strong typing are usually caught at compile time!

```
/* A program to illustrate type safety in action */

using tcdIO;

class TypeSafety
{
    public static void Main()
    {
        Terminal terminal;
        float number; // declare a floating point variable
        char letter;  // declare a character variable

        /* create an object to represent the terminal */
        terminal = new Terminal();

        /* store values into each of the variables */
        number = -345.7F;
        letter = 'V';

        /* now Write out the stored values */
        terminal.WriteLine("The number is " + number + ".");
        terminal.WriteLine("The letter is " + letter + ".");

        /* finally, store the value of number in letter and Write it out */
        letter = number;
        terminal.WriteLine("The letter is now " + letter + ".");
    }
}
```

Program 3.3　A program to illustrate type safety in action.

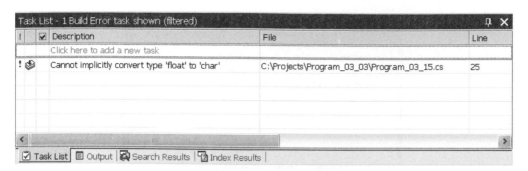

Figure 3.6 The compilation of Program 3.3.

Reference Types

As we saw in Chapter 1, every class defines a corresponding type that can be used as the type of any variable that is intended to store an object of that type. In fact, in C# a variable that is declared to be of such a class type does not contain an instance of the specified class. Instead, it contains a reference to an instance of the class. This is the reason why class types are called reference types in C#.

For example, C# provides a pre-defined class called `string` whose instances represent sequences of characters. Thus, an instance of `string` can contain the sequence of characters "Hello there!" or the sequence of characters "Albert Einstein". Strings are used heavily in programs that need to read and write messages from and to their users, as well as in programs that perform any kind of text processing. Now, say that we want to declare a variable called `userName` that will be used to store the name of our program's user. As usual we write the identifier of the type followed by the identifier of the variable:

```
string userName;
```

We might expect this declaration to give us a container capable of holding the object containing the sequence of characters making up the user's name. What it actually gives us, as Figure 3.7 shows, is a container capable of holding a reference to that object. The actual object is stored somewhere else. Note that, as in Figure 3.7, we usually draw variables as rectangles and objects as circles. We use arrows to depict object references.

A variable of type `string` can only contain (a reference to) a `string` object but it might contain references to different instances of `string` at different times.

The difference between containing an object and containing a reference to an object might not appear all that important. However, there is one possibility that arises from this that is fundamentally important. It is simply this: two or more different variables can contain references to the same object. We will return to discuss the implications of this fact later. For now it is sufficient to emphasize that this means we have to be very careful to distinguish

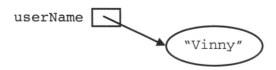

Figure 3.7 A `string` variable.

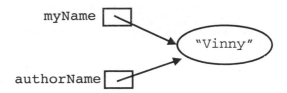

Figure 3.8   `string` variables referring to the same object.

between the value of an object and the value of any variable that refers to that object, since the two are distinct as shown in Figure 3.8.

For example, Program 3.4 declares two `string` variables, `myName` and `authorName`, and uses assignment to store references to the same object in both. This allows either variable to be used to print out the value of the `string` object, as shown in Figure 3.9.

```
/* A program to illustrate the */
/* use of object references */

using tcdIO;

class ObjectReferences
{
   public static void Main()
   {
      Terminal terminal;
      string myName, authorName; // declare two string variables

      /* create an object to represent the terminal */
      terminal = new Terminal();

      /* create an object to represent my name */
      myName = "Vinny";

      /* make authorName refer to the same object as myName */
      /* by storing the value of myName in authorName */
      authorName = myName;

      /* now write out the name */
      terminal.WriteLine("Hello there " + myName + " !");

      /* finally, use authorName to write out the name again */
      terminal.WriteLine("Hello again " + authorName + " !");
   }
}
```

Program 3.4   A program to illustrate the use of object references.

As another example Program 3.5 creates an instance of our class `Rectangle` from Chapter 1 and stores references to it in two different variables. Notice that the area of the rectangle is calculated by invoking the `CalculateArea` method on the object using the variable `shape` while the perimeter of the rectangle is calculated by invoking the `CalculatePerimeter`

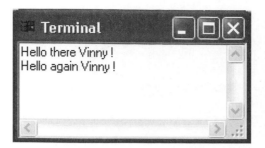

Figure 3.9   The execution of Program 3.4.

method on the *same* object using the variable `rectangle`. Figure 3.10 shows the resulting output.

Note that while a variable of type `Rectangle` can contain a reference to an instance of class `Rectangle`, such a variable could never contain a reference to an instance of class `string`. Although the variables `authorName` and `rectangle` in the examples above both contain object references, they contain references to different types of objects. Just as we can't store a character in a variable intended to store a number, we can't store a reference to an instance of `Rectangle` in a variable intended to store a reference to an instance of `string`.

```
/* A program to illustrate the use of different */
/* variables to refer to the same object */

using tcdIO;

class DifferentVariables
{
    public static void Main()
    {
        Terminal terminal;
        Rectangle shape, rectangle; // declare two Rectangle variables
        int area, perimeter;

        /* create an object to represent the terminal */
        terminal = new Terminal();

        /* create an object to represent a 10 X 15 rectangle */
        shape = new Rectangle(10, 15);
        /* make rectangle refer to the same object as shape */
        rectangle = shape;

        /* calculate the area of the rectangle using shape */
        area = shape.CalculateArea();
        terminal.WriteLine("The area of the rectangle is " + area + ".");

        /* calculate the perimeter of the rectangle using rectangle */
        perimeter = rectangle.CalculatePerimeter();
        terminal.WriteLine("The perimeter of the rectangle is "
                                        + perimeter + ".");
    }
}
```

Program 3.5   A program to illustrate the use of different variables to refer to the same object.

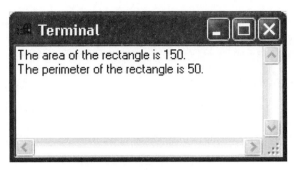

Figure 3.10 The execution of Program 3.5.

Working with Whole Numbers – Type `int`

Now that we have looked at the concept of type in general, let's take a look at one particular type, the type `int`, in detail.

Type `int` represents positive and negative whole numbers such as −2 756, −23, 0, or 36 789. In C#, 4 bytes of memory are used to store a value of type `int`. Thus, the possible values of type `int` range from −2 147 483 648 to 2 147 483 647! While this might seem like a fabulously large range of values, it is important to realize that, as large as it is, it is still a finite set of values. Thus, while there are mathematically an infinite number of positive and negative whole numbers, type `int` only represents a subset of them. This gives rise to the possibility that when we perform an operation, such as addition or subtraction, with `int` values, the result might be too big or too small to be represented by type `int`, a condition known as *integer overflow* or *integer underflow* respectively.

Describing Integer Values

In a program, we can write values of type `int` using conventional decimal notation (without commas). Thus:

```
0 −123 23000 1000000 −7456 3990276
```

are all valid `int` values. A value written directly into a program is called a *literal*. Thus, `23000` is an *integer literal*.

We can also write values of type `int` using hexadecimal (base 16). The hexadecimal notation uses the letters A to F (in uppercase or lowercase) to represent the hexadecimal digits with values 10–15. A hexadecimal number is always preceded by the symbol `0x` (zero followed by an uppercase or lowercase x). Thus, the following are valid hexadecimal literals (with their decimal equivalents in brackets):

```
0xFFFFFF85(-123) 0x59D8(23000) 0x0(0)
0xF4240(1000000) 0xFFFFE2E0(-7456) 0x3CE304(3990276)
```

Storing Integers

As we've seen already we can declare a variable of type `int` in the usual way. For example,

```
int mySalary;
```

declares a single variable called my Salary that is capable of storing a single int value. The variable my Salary occupies 4 bytes of memory and can contain only allowable values of type int. The declaration

```
int cost, price, quantity;
```

declares three separate int variables called cost, price, and quantity respectively.

We can use assignment to store an int value into an int variable. The value to be stored can be specified as a literal or by giving the name of another variable. Thus, the statement:

```
cost = 540;
```

stores the value 540 in the variable cost. The statement:

```
price = cost;
```

stores the current value of the variable cost into the variable price.

Calculating Integers

As Figure 3.11 shows, C# provides five operators for performing arithmetic on values of type int. These operators implement the standard mathematical operations of addition, subtraction, multiplication, division, and modulus (remainder). All of these operators take two values of type int and produce a value of type int as their result. Because they take two values as operands, they are described as being *binary operators*. Note that the result of these operators is always a value of type int. Thus, division of one integer by another returns the quotient, i.e., the whole number part of the result. The remainder operator can be used to get the remainder from the division. Thus, 15/2 is 7 and not 7.5 (which is not a value of type int) and 15%2 is 1 (the remainder on dividing 15 by 2). The operands of any of these operators can be literals or the values of variables.

Operator	Use	Meaning	Examples
+	op1 + op2	add values of op1 and op2	newSalary = oldSalary + rise; count = count +1;
−	op1 - op2	subtract op2 from op1	newSalary = oldSalary -100;
*	op1 * op2	multiply op1 by op2	area = length * breath; minutes = hours * 60;
/	op1 / op2	divide op1 by op2	length = area / breath;
%	op1 % op2	remainder on dividing op1 by op2	pounds = pence / 100 pence = pence % 100;

Figure 3.11 Operators on type int.

We can also write arithmetic expressions that involve multiple operators. For example, we might calculate our salary as follows:

```
pay = salary + bonus - tax;
```

or our monthly salary as:

```
monthlyPay = (salary + bonus - tax) / 12;
```

Notice the use of the brackets in the last example. If we had written the expression without brackets as in:

```
monthlyPay = salary + bonus - tax / 12;
```

then the division operation would have been done first dividing tax by 12 before taking the result from the sum of salary and bonus. The reason is that / has a higher precedence than + and hence / is always carried out before +. The brackets force the addition to be carried out before the division.

In general, *, /, and % have equal precedence that is higher than + and – which also have equal precedence. Operators with equal precedence are evaluated in left to right order. Thus, in the expression above, salary is first added to bonus and then tax is subtracted from the result. Such operators are said to be left associative.

Reading and Writing Integers

We've already seen that an `int` can be printed out using the `WriteLine` method from class `Terminal`. Class `Terminal` also provides a method for reading an `int` from the user. This method is called `ReadInt`. To use `ReadInt`, we supply a `string` value as its single parameter and it returns the next `int` read from the user as its result. The `string` that we supply is used as a prompt to the user. So, `ReadInt` displays the prompt string on the screen and then waits for the user to type in an `int`. The `int` is then returned as the result of the call to the `ReadInt` method. If the user types something that doesn't represent a valid C# `int` value, `ReadInt` will prompt the user again, using the same prompt, until the user eventually enters an acceptable value. Program 3.6 uses `ReadInt` twice to read in two integers from the user and then uses `WriteLine` to print out their sum.

The Rectangle Program Revisited

Armed with our knowledge of type `int`, let's change the rectangle program from Chapter 1 to allow its user to specify the dimensions of the rectangle. We will need to read the length and width of the rectangle from the user using `ReadInt`. We will store the dimensions in two variables, which will then be used to provide the input values to the `Rectangle` constructor. As before, the area and perimeter of the rectangle are calculated by invoking the corresponding methods on the object and the values returned are printed out. Notice that the values of the two parameters to the `Rectangle` constructor are now obtained from the variables `len` and `wide` rather than being written directly into the program. Clearly, this makes the program a lot more flexible since it allows this same program to be used to calculate the area and perimeter of a different rectangle each time that it is executed. Figure 3.12 shows the output generated by the program.

```
/* A program to illustrate */
/* reading integers from the user */

using tcdIO;

class ReadIntegers
{
    public static void Main()
    {
        Terminal terminal;
        int number1, number2, total; // declare some int variables

        /* create an object to represent the terminal */
        terminal = new Terminal();

        /* Read in the values of number1 and number 2 */
        number1 = terminal.ReadInt("Enter first number: ");
        number2 = terminal.ReadInt("Enter second number: ");

        /* add the numbers and store the result in total */
        total = number1 + number2;

        /* Write out the result */
        terminal.WriteLine("The sum of " + number1 + " plus "
                            + number2 + " is " + total + ".");
    }
}
```

Program 3.6 A program to illustrate reading integers from the user.

```
/* A program to illustrate the use of type int */
/* Calculates the area and perimeter of a rectangle */
/* whose dimensions are specified by the user */

using tcdIO;

class RectangleProgram
{
    public static void Main()
    {
        Terminal terminal;
        Rectangle shape;
        int area, perimeter;
        int len, wide;

        /* create an object to represent the terminal */
        terminal = new Terminal();

        /* ask user for length of rectangle */
        len = terminal.ReadInt("Enter length of rectangle: ");

        /* ask user for width of rectangle */
        wide = terminal.ReadInt("Enter width of rectangle: ");

        /* create a new Rectangle with given dimensions */
        shape = new Rectangle(len, wide);
```

```
        /* ask the rectangle object for its area */
        area = shape.CalculateArea();
        /* Write out the area */
        terminal.WriteLine("The area of the rectangle is: " + area + ".");

        /* ask the rectangle obejct for its perimeter */
        perimeter = shape.CalculatePerimeter();
        /* Write out the perimeter */
        terminal.WriteLine("The perimeter of the rectangle is: "
                                        + perimeter + ".");
    }
}
```

Program 3.7   A program to illustrate the use of type `int`.

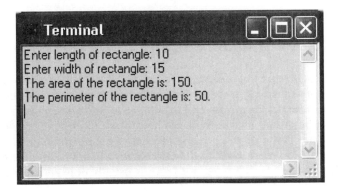

Figure 3.12   The execution of Program 3.7.

Other Integer Types

C# actually provides four simple types that represent integers (i.e., positive and negative whole numbers). Apart from type `int`, the other integer types are called `sbyte`, `short`, and `long`. These four types differ only in the amount of memory that C# uses to store values of the type and therefore in the range of values that each type supports. Not surprisingly, values of type `sbyte` occupy 1 byte in memory. Thus, the possible values of type `sbyte` range from −128 to 127. Values of type `short` occupy 2 bytes. The range of possible values of type `short` is therefore −32 768 to 32 767. The name `short` derives from the fact that a value of type `short` is a short integer. Finally, values of type `long` occupy 8 bytes in memory and can range from −9 223 372 036 854 775 808 to 9 223 372 036 854 775 807! Of course, the name `long` derives from the fact that a value of type `long` is a long integer!

Apart from the fact that each of the integer types has a different range of values, essentially all of the same rules apply to each of these types as to type `int`. Thus, we can write literals of any of these types, declare variables of any of these types, and use values of these types in integer expressions using exactly the same operators as for type `int`.

Faced with a choice of four integer types, you may wonder which to use in a given situation. The main difference between the types is obviously the range of values that they can represent, so try to pick the type that most closely matches the range of values that you expect to use. We recommend using type `int` as the default choice when the likely range is not well defined.

Natural Number Types

In addition to the four simple types that represent integer values, C# also provides four types representing natural numbers, i.e., positive whole numbers. There is one such type corresponding to each of the integer types. Thus, a variable of type `uint` occupies 4 bytes of memory and can store values in the range 0 to 4 294 967 295! Likewise there are types `ulong`, `ushort` and `byte` corresponding to the integer types `long`, `short`, and `sbyte`.

In C# terminology these types are referred to as unsigned types. Hence, `uint` stands for "unsigned int", `ulong` stands for "unsigned long", and so on. Confusingly, `byte` is an unsigned type while `sbyte`, for "signed byte" is its signed equivalent!

Where would we use such types? Well, it is very common to have to deal with whole number values that can't be negative. For example, we might (and probably should) have used `uint` in our `Rectangle` class, since the length and width of a rectangle can never be negative.

Working with Real Numbers – Type `float`

Floating-point numbers represent real numbers, i.e., positive and negative numbers that have a decimal part. As we've seen, C# provides the simple type `float` to represent real numbers. Just as the range of values of the integer types is limited by the amount of space used to store a value of the type, both the range and the accuracy of a floating-point value is limited. In the case of C#, a value of type `float` occupies 4 bytes of memory and can store a number in the range $\pm 1.5 \times 10^{-45}$ to $\pm 3.4 \times 10^{38}$ with an accuracy of seven significant decimal digits. Since the accuracy of `float`s is limited, a `float` is usually only an *approximation* for the real number to be represented.

Describing Floating-point Values

Values of type `float` are written using conventional decimal notation. If the number contains an exponent (i.e., a power of ten by which the value is to be multiplied), the value of the exponent is written after the letter "E". In addition, the letter "F" always follows a value of type `float`. Thus, the following are all examples of literals of type `float`:

```
-123F  30.6F  0.0F  -1.0E8F  -7.4E-5  -399.02E+7F
```

Notice that the exponent may be positive or negative.

Storing Floating-point Values

As we saw previously, we can declare variables of type `float` in the same way that we declare variables of other types. For example,

```
float temperature;
```

declares a single variable called `temperature` that is capable of storing a single `float`.

```
float radius, pi;
```

declares two separate `float` variables called `radius` and `pi` respectively.

Operator	Use	Meaning	Examples
+	op1 + op2	add values of op1 and op2	`newSalary = oldSalary + rise;` `distance = distance + 10.2F;`
-	op1 - op2	subtract op2 from op1	`time = hours - 0.6F;`
*	op1 * op2	multiply op1 by op2	`area = radius * PI;` `area = radius * 3.14F;`
/	op1 / op2	divide op1 by op2	`length = area / breath;`

Figure 3.13   Operators on type `float`.

As before, we can use assignment to store a `float` value into a `float` variable. The value to be stored can be specified as a literal, by giving the name of a variable that contains the value, or by giving an expression that will be evaluated to obtain the value. Thus, the statement

```
temperature = 17.5F;
```

stores the value `17.5F` into the variable `temperature`. The statement

```
distance = numKilometres;
```

stores the current value of the variable `numKilometres` into the variable `distance`.

Calculating Floating-point Values

As Figure 3.13 shows, C# provides four binary operators for performing arithmetic on floating-point numbers. These operators implement the standard mathematical operations of addition, subtraction, multiplication, and real division. All of these operators take two values of type `float` and produce a result of type `float`. The operands can be literals or the values of variables. Notice that the division operator implements real division. Thus, `5F/2F` is `2.5F`.

The precedence of the operators is the same as the corresponding integer operators. For example,

```
distanceToTravel = miles * kmPerMile - kmTravelled;
```

multiplies the value of `miles` by the value of `kmPerMile` and subtracts `kmTravelled` before storing the result in `distanceToTravel`.

Reading and Writing Floating-point Values

A `float` can be printed out using the `WriteLine` method from class `Terminal` in much the same way as an `int` can. In addition, class `Terminal` provides a method – `ReadFloat` – to read a `float` from the user. Like, `ReadInt`, `ReadFloat` displays the specified prompt on the screen, waits for the user to type in a valid `float` and then returns the value read to its caller. Program 3.8, uses `ReadFloat` twice to read in two `floats` from the user and then uses `WriteLine` to print out their sum.

```
/* A program to illustrate reading */
/* floating-point numbers from the user */

using tcdIO;

class ReadFloats
{
    public static void Main()
    {
        Terminal terminal;
        float number1, number2, total; // declare some float variables

        /* create an object to represent the terminal */
        terminal = new Terminal();

        /* Read in the values of number1 and number 2 */
        number1 = terminal.ReadFloat("Enter first number: ");
        number2 = terminal.ReadFloat("Enter second number: ");

        /* add the numbers and store the result in total */
        total = number1 + number2;

        /* Write out the result */
        terminal.WriteLine("The sum of " + number1 + " plus "
                        + number2 + " is " + total + ".");
    }
}
```

Program 3.8   A program to illustrate reading floating-point numbers from the user.

Type double

As well as type float, C# provides another type that represents floating-point numbers – the type double. In C#, a value of type double occupies 8 bytes of memory and can represent a number in the range $\pm 5.0E-324$ to $\pm 1.7E+308$ with an accuracy of 15 significant decimal digits. Apart from supporting a larger range of values and greater accuracy, double can be used in much the same way as float. Literals of type double can, but need not, be followed by "D" rather than "F". Thus, 1234.7 and 1234.7D represent values of type double, while 1234.7F represents a value of type float.

Calculating the Area and Circumference of a Circle

As an example of the use of floating-point numbers, let's write a program to calculate the area and circumference of a circle. Since our program deals with circles, it seems natural to introduce a class Circle whose instances will represent individual circles. Our program will create an instance of class Circle and then ask that object for its area and circumference by means of methods CalculateArea and CalculateCircumference provided by Circle.

While a circle might have many attributes, the most important for our purposes is its radius. Thus, our class will provide a single instance variable radius to store the radius of the current Circle. Since there's no reason why the radius of a circle should be limited to being a whole number, radius will be of type double. The Circle class will provide a constructor to initialize new instances of the class. In this case, each call to the constructor requires a single

```
/* A class whose instances represent circles */
class Circle
{
   private double radius;

   /* initialize new circle object */
   public Circle(double radius)
   {
      this.radius = radius;
   }

   /* calculate area of circle */
   public double CalculateArea()
   {
      return this.radius * this.radius * 3.1416;
   }

   /* calculate circumference of circle */
   public double CalculateCircumference()
   {
      return 2.0 * 3.1416 * this.radius;
   }
}
```

Program 3.9 Class `Circle`.

parameter that gives the radius of the new circle. In our constructor, this value is also referred to by the identifier `radius` and is used to initialize the `radius` attribute of the new object.

Neither `CalculateCircumference` nor `CalculateArea` require any parameters. Since the radius of the circle is a real number and since the formulae for calculating the area and circumference of a circle use the value of π ($\sim$3.1416), the value returned in each case is a `double`. `CalculateCircumference` uses the formula $2\pi r$ to calculate the circumference, while `CalculateArea` uses the formula πr^2 to calculate the area as shown in Program 3.9.

Program 3.10 shows a program that uses the `Circle` class to report the area and circumference of a circle whose radius is supplied by the user. Figure 3.14 shows the output generated by the program.

Working with Real Numbers – Type `decimal`

As we saw in the previous section, floating-point numbers of type `float` or `double` can be used to represent real numbers. As we also saw, both the range and the accuracy of floating-point values are limited. In mathematics, there are, of course, an infinite number of values between any two real values. Obviously, we can't hope to represent all of these values, so the floating-point types provide approximations for many real numbers. In fact, even an apparently straightforward number such as 0.1 can only be represented approximately with a floating-point type! For many programs, these approximations are sufficient. For other programs, a much higher degree of accuracy is required. To accommodate such programs, C# provides another type, `decimal`, to represent real numbers with high precision.

In C#, a value of type `decimal` occupies 12 bytes of memory and can represent a number in the range $\pm 1.0\mathrm{E}{-}28$ to $\pm 7.9\mathrm{E}{-}28$ with an accuracy of 28 significant decimal digits. Notice

```
/* A program to illustrate the use of type double */
/* Calculates the area and circumference of a circle */
/* whose radius is supplied by the user */

using tcdIO;

class CircleProgram
{
    public static void Main()
    {
        Terminal terminal;
        Circle shape; // the circle object
        double input; // used to store radius
        double area, circumference;

        /* create an object to represent the terminal */
        terminal = new Terminal();

        /* ask user for radius */
        input = terminal.ReadDouble("Enter radius of circle: ");

        /* create a new circle with the given radius */
        shape = new Circle(input);

        /* ask the Circle object for its area */
        area = shape.CalculateArea();
        /* Write out the area to the screen */
        terminal.WriteLine("The area of the circle is: " + area + ".");

        /* ask the Circle object for its circumference */
        circumference = shape.CalculateCircumference();
        /* write out the perimeter to the screen */
        terminal.WriteLine("The circumference of the circle is: "
                                        + circumference + ".");
    }
}
```

Program 3.10   A program to illustrate the use of type double.

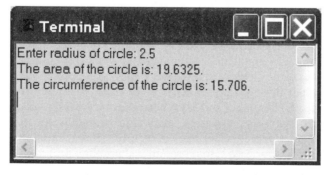

Figure 3.14   The execution of Program 3.10.

that while the range of values that type decimal can represent is much smaller than for float or double, the precision, 28 significant digits, is much higher. Most importantly, type decimal represents the real numbers in the range that it covers *exactly*.

Describing Decimal Values

Values of type decimal are written using conventional decimal notation. If the number contains an exponent, the value of the exponent is written after the letter "E". However, the letter "M" always follows a value of type decimal. Thus, the following are all examples of literals of type decimal:

```
-123.78M  302.6M  0.0M  -1.0E-8M  -7.4E-5M  -399.02E+7M
```

As before, the exponent may be positive or negative.

Storing and Calculating Decimal Values

We can declare variables of type decimal in the usual ways and can use assignment to store a value into such a variable. Moreover, we can use the usual four binary operators ($+$, $-$, $*$, and $/$) to perform addition, subtraction, multiplication and division of decimal values. For example,

```
decimal temperature;
```

declares a variable capable of storing a single decimal at a time.

```
decimal area, radius, pi;
```

declares three decimal variables called area, radius, and pi respectively. Given these declarations, we can then do

```
temperature = 17.5M;
```

to store the value 17.5M into the variable temperature. The statement:

```
area = pi * radius * radius;
```

calculates the area of a circle and stores the result into the variable area.

Reading and Writing Decimal Values

A decimal can be also printed out using the WriteLine method from class Terminal, which also provides a method – ReadDecimal – to read a decimal from the user. Like, ReadInt and ReadFloat, ReadDecimal displays the specified prompt on the screen, waits for the user to type in a valid decimal and then returns the value read to its caller.

Conversions Between Numeric Types

As we've explained things so far, all the (binary) operators on numeric types take two values of the same type and return a result of that type. Clearly, there are times when it makes sense to be able to multiply an int by a float, for example, or to subtract a float from a double.

C# allows this by allowing the type of a value to be converted to another (meaningful) type for the duration of such an operation. For example, say we want to calculate my monthly salary by dividing my annual salary by 12. Given,

```
double yearlySalary, monthlySalary;
```

we could say:

```
monthlySalary = yearlySalary / 12;
```

Since `yearlySalary` is of type `double` and 12 of type `int`, we don't have an operator capable of performing this calculation unless we either convert the value of `yearlySalary` to type `int` or convert 12 to type `double`. If we were to convert `yearlySalary` to type `int` we would risk losing part of its value. For example, if `yearlySalary` had a fractional part, we would not be able to represent that part in an `int`. Likewise, and remembering that the range of numbers that can be represented by a `double` is much larger than can be represented by an `int`, if I were lucky enough to earn more than the maximum integer value (some hope!), that could not be represented in an `int` either. Thus, it makes more sense to convert the integer value 12 to `double` and perform real division to calculate my monthly salary. That's exactly what C# does. Notice that any integer value can always be represented as a `double` without the risk of losing part of the value so this conversion should always give the correct answer. In other words the set of possible values of type `double` is a superset of the possible values of type `int`.

In general C# will automatically perform any conversion that is safe in the sense that the type to which to convert contains a superset of the values of the type of the value being converted. This means that:

- values of any integer type or type `float` can be converted to type `double`
- values of any integer type can be converted to type `float`
- values of type `sbyte`, `short` or `int` can be converted to type `long` (and likewise `sbyte` and `short` to `int` or `sbyte` to `short`), and
- values of type `byte`, `ushort` or `uint` can be converted to type `ulong` (and likewise `byte` and `ushort` to `uint` or `byte` to `ushort`).

For example, if we try to add an `int` to a `long`, the `int` will be converted to `long` because the value of an `int` is always guaranteed to be representable as a `long`. However, the value of a `long` may not be representable as an `int`! For the same reason, if we try to store a value of type `long` into a variable of type `double`, C# will actually allow it by converting the `long` value to a `double` before storing it. For example, in Program 3.11 we store the value of `aLongNumber` into `aDoubleNumber` and then print out the values of both variables. Notice the difference between the two values displayed on the screen as shown in Figure 3.15.

Program 3.12 calculates the monthly salary for an employee by dividing the yearly salary by 12. Since `yearlySalary` is a `double`, `numMonths` is treated as a `double` for the purposes of the division and real division is used. The result is a floating-point value that is stored in `monthlySalary` before being printed to the screen as shown in Figure 3.16.

Sometimes, we may actually want to store, for example, a `double` into an `int` variable – even though this will almost certainly result in some information being lost. At the very least, the fractional part of the floating-point number will be truncated. Since this is clearly very dangerous, C# won't allow it unless we explicitly say that it should be done. To do so, we have

```
/* A program to illustrate conversion */
/* of type long to type double */

using tcdIO;

class LongToDouble
{
    public static void Main()
    {
        Terminal terminal;
        long aLongNumber;
        double aDoubleNumber;

        /* create an object to represent the terminal */
        terminal = new Terminal();

        /* Read in number */
        aLongNumber = terminal.ReadLong("Enter your number: ");;

        /* store number into floating point variable */
        aDoubleNumber = aLongNumber;

        /* Write out the results */
        terminal.WriteLine("aLongNumber is: " + aLongNumber + ".");
        terminal.WriteLine("aDoubleNumber is: " + aDoubleNumber + ".");
    }
}
```

Program 3.11   A program to illustrate conversion of type long to type double.

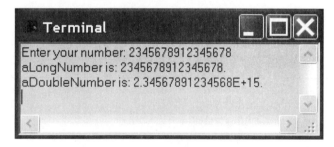

Figure 3.15   The execution of Program 3.11.

to use a *type cast* by preceding the value to be stored with the name of the type to which we want to convert it (enclosed in parenthesis). For example, given:

```
int months;
double salary;
```

consider the following:

```
salary = months; // allowed to store an int in a double
months = salary; // not allowed to store a double in an int
months = (int)salary; // unless we do an explicit conversion
```

One interesting case arises when dealing with type decimal. Since decimal has both a smaller range and a higher precision that either of the floating-point types, conversions

```
/* A program to illustrate the use of different */
/* numeric types in one expression */
/* Calculates the monthly salary of an employee */

using tcdIO;

class SalaryProgram
{
    public static void Main()
    {
        Terminal terminal;
        double yearlySalary, monthlySalary;
        int numMonths;

        /* create an object to represent the terminal */
        terminal = new Terminal();

        /* initialize number of months */
        numMonths = 12;

        /* Read in yearly salary */
        yearlySalary = terminal.ReadDouble("Enter yearly salary: ");;

        /* calculate monthly salary */
        monthlySalary = yearlySalary / numMonths;

        /* Write out the result */
        terminal.WriteLine("Your monthly salary is: " + monthlySalary + ".");
    }
}
```

Program 3.12   A program to illustrate the use of different numeric types in one expression.

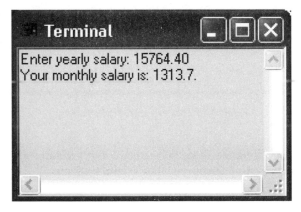

Figure 3.16   The execution of Program 3.12.

between decimal and either float or double, in either direction, require casts. For example, given:

```
double bonus;
decimal yearlySalary, basicSalary;
```

we cannot write:

```
yearlySalary = basicSalary + bonus;
```

but can say

```
yearlySalary = basicSalary + (decimal)bonus;
```

Having said all that, you should note that casts are inherently dangerous since they allow C#'s string typing to be overridden. Over use of casts is a sure sign of bad programming. Avoid them!

Changing the Value of a Variable – Assignment

We have already seen examples of assignment in several of the programs that we have written. Assignment is extremely important because it is the *only* means of changing the value of a variable, i.e., of storing information into a variable. Thus, whenever we want to change the current value of a variable we use an assignment statement. No matter what the type of the variable is, what value we want to store in the variable, or how we calculated that value, we always use assignment to store the value into a variable.

Every assignment statement has the syntax shown in Figure 3.17. The left-hand side of the assignment is *always* the name of a variable, while the right-hand side of the assignment is *always* an expression. An expression is anything that can be evaluated to give a single value. It might be a literal, in which case its value is the value represented by the literal. It might be a variable name, in which case its value is the *current* value of the variable. It might be a method call, in which case its value is the value returned by the method. Finally, it might be some combination of the above combined using appropriate operators. Thus, the following are all valid assignments that use different kinds of expressions:

```
width = 12;
length = width;
rectangleArea = length * width;
width = rectangle.CalculateArea() / length;
```

Of course, the value of the expression must be the same type as the variable to which it is to be assigned. When an assignment statement is executed in the course of a program, the expression is first evaluated and then its value is stored into the specified variable as Figure 3.18 illustrates.

Assignment is Destructive

It is important to realize that assignment is *destructive* in the sense that it overwrites the value that was previously stored in the variable. In other words, when we do an assignment, the old value of the variable is lost. So, before we carry out an assignment to a variable we need to be very sure that we won't need the value that's stored in that variable again!

```
<variable name>   =   <expression>;
```

Figure 3.17   The syntax of C#'s assignment statement.

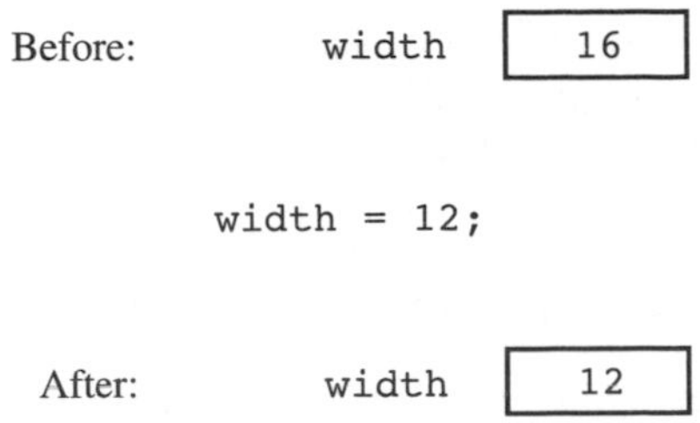

Before: width   [16]

width = 12;

After: width   [12]

Figure 3.18   The effect of an assignment.

Let's look at an example. Program 3.13 apparently swaps the values of the two variables width and breadth by storing the value of width into breadth and vice versa using two assignment statements. As Figure 3.19 shows, the output form the program is not what we might have expected. Let's trace through the execution of the program step by step and see why not.

Assume that we enter the values 16 and 34 for width and breadth as in Figure 3.19. Thus, the initial contents of the two variables are as shown in Figure 3.20.

When the first assignment is executed, the value of breadth is stored into width. As Figure 3.21 shows, the value of width is overwritten and both variables now have the same value.

```
/* A program to illustrate that assignment */
/* is destructive Tries to swap the values of two variables */
/* but gets it wrong! */

using tcdIO;

class SwapIntegers1
{
    public static void Main()
    {
        Terminal terminal;
        int width, breadth;

        /* create an object to represent the terminal */
        terminal = new Terminal();

        /* Read in two values */
        width = terminal.ReadInt("Enter the value of width: ");
        breadth = terminal.ReadInt("Enter the value of breadth: ");

        /* swap them */
        width = breadth;
        breadth = width;

        /* Write out the results */
        terminal.WriteLine("The value of width is : " + width + ".");
        terminal.WriteLine("The value of breadth is : " + breadth + ".");
    }
}
```

Program 3.13   A program to illustrate that assignment is destructive.

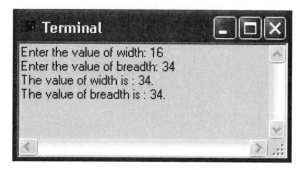

Figure 3.19   The execution of Program 3.13.

width $\boxed{\quad 16 \quad}$ breadth $\boxed{\quad 34 \quad}$

Figure 3.20   Program 3.13: the initial situation.

width $\boxed{\quad 34 \quad}$ breadth $\boxed{\quad 34 \quad}$

Figure 3.21   Program 3.13: the value of width is lost.

width $\boxed{\quad 34 \quad}$ breadth $\boxed{\quad 34 \quad}$

Figure 3.22   Program 3.13: the final situation.

The second assignment copies the value of width into breadth. Since both variables already had the same value, this assignment has no real effect as can be seen in Figure 3.22.

The flaw in our program is that it overwrites the value of width before we have a chance to store it into breadth. The solution is to save the value of width until we need it. To save this value we need to introduce a third variable – saved – to hold the saved value. The resulting program is shown in Program 3.14 and its output in Figure 3.23. Figure 3.24 illustrates how the variables change during the course of the program. Notice that when the value of width is overwritten, its value has already been saved in saved and is not lost.

Evaluating Expressions with Assignment

As mentioned already, when an assignment statement is executed, the expression is evaluated first and then the result of the expression is stored in the variable. It's important to realize that the evaluation of the expression is finished before the variable is altered, for one very important reason: the expression might use the current value of the variable! If so, the expression implicitly uses the value of the variable prior to the assignment being carried out. Here's a simple example,

```
counter = counter + 1;
```

If counter has the value 16 before the assignment statement is executed, then the expression counter+1 yields the value 17. Only then is the value 17 stored into counter.

```
/* A program to swap the values of two variables */
using tcdIO;

class SwapIntegers2
{
   public static void Main()
   {
      Terminal terminal;
      int width, breadth;
      int saved;

      /* create an object to represent the terminal */
      terminal = new Terminal();

      /* Read in two values */
      width = terminal.ReadInt("Enter the value of width: ");
      breadth = terminal.ReadInt("Enter the value of breadth: ");

      /* swap them */
      saved = width;    // save the value of width
      width = breadth;  // overwrite width
      breadth = saved;  // store saved value of width into breadth

      /* Write out the results */
      terminal.WriteLine("The value of width is : " + width + ".");
      terminal.WriteLine("The value of breadth is : " + breadth + ".");
   }
}
```

Program 3.14   A program to swap the values of two variables.

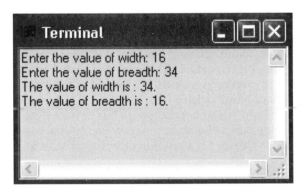

Figure 3.23   The execution of Program 3.14.

Another detail to watch out for arises from the fact that = is an operator in C#. That means that an assignment is itself an expression and consequently has a value! The value of an assignment is the value that is eventually stored into the variable concerned. Thus, the value of the assignment,

```
mySalary = 24000;
```

is 24 000.

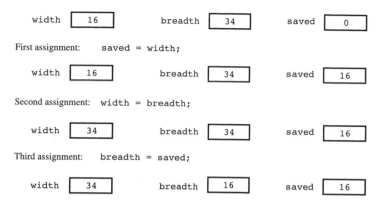

Figure 3.24   The variables of Program 3.14.

The fact that an assignment is an expression means that we can use an assignment anywhere that a value is required. The assignment will give us a value and store that value in the specified variable too!

One interesting use of assignment as an expression is when an assignment makes up the expression part of another assignment statement, as is:

```
yourSalary = mySalary = 24000;
```

To understand this statement, you need to know that the assignment operator is right associative. Thus, we could have rewritten this assignment as:

```
yourSalary = (mySalary = 24000);
```

The first assignment carried out is:

```
mySalary = 24000
```

This stores 24 000 in the variable mySalary and yields the value 24 000 as its result. So, the value 24 000 is also stored in yourSalary.

Assigning Object References

Just as we can assign values of simple types to variables of those types, we can, of course, assign (references to) objects to variables of the appropriate type. For example, Figure 3.25

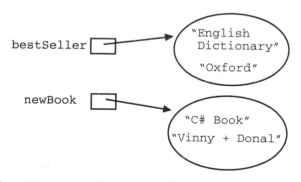

Figure 3.25   Two variables referring to different instances of class Book.

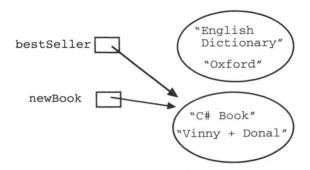

Figure 3.26   Two variables referring to a single instance of class Book.

shows a situation where we have two variables of type Book referring to two different objects representing two different books. Given this situation, the assignment:

```
bestSeller = newBook;
```

has the effect of copying the reference contained in the variable newBook to the variable bestSeller. The resulting situation is shown in Figure 3.26.

The interesting thing about Figure 3.26 is that we have two different variables referring to the same object. This is a very common situation in object-oriented programming. In fact, it is usual to have many different variables referring to the same object. Assignment gives us the means of copying references arbitrarily between variables. As noted previously, it is important to distinguish between variables and objects: an object is a distinct instance of some class; a variable is a container for a reference to an object. The same variable can refer to different objects at different times as a result of assignments to that variable. Many different variables can refer to the same object at the same or different times. Recall that when two or more variables refer to the same object, we can use any of them to interact with the object. The effects of access via one variable or another are visible through any of the variables.

Getting Rid of Useless Objects – Garbage Collection

Using assignment to change the value of a variable that contains a reference to an object gives rise to another possibility. Because, assignment is destructive and overwrites the value of the variable assigned, we might actually overwrite the only (remaining) reference to some object, making the object inaccessible to our program. For example, in Figure 3.26 notice that as a result of the assignment to the variable bestSeller, there is now no variable that contains a reference to the object representing the dictionary. Thus, there is now *no way* to refer to the dictionary since our only reference to the object has been *overwritten*. If we can't refer to the object, we can't access it! For example, there is now no way to retrieve the name of its author.

While this situation might, at first glance, appear erroneous, in fact, objects are commonly created to be used for a short period of time. When no longer required, any remaining references to the objects are overwritten in the knowledge that they will not be needed again. Such inaccessible objects are referred to as being *garbage*. Garbage objects, although inaccessible, still exist and occupy space in the computer's memory. The space occupied by these objects is not available for use by new objects. Since this is clearly wasteful, we should delete those objects and, in doing so, free up the space that they are using. Some languages require that programs explicitly delete objects that they are not going to use again. However, leaving it to the program to delete objects is error-prone: a program might forget to delete some object (and thereby waste the corresponding memory space) or it might accidentally delete an object that is still required. Moreover, in order to be able to delete an object, the program must have a reference to the object. Hence, programs must be careful not to overwrite the last reference to an object before deleting the object. This leaves open the possibility that the last reference might be accidentally overwritten before the object is deleted, thereby preventing the program from reclaiming the space that it occupies.

To overcome these problems, and make our lives a lot easier, C# does not require that programs explicitly delete objects. Instead, C# will automatically *delete* an object when it detects that there are no more references to the object (and hence no way to use it). The process of finding and deleting inaccessible objects is known as *garbage collection*. Garbage collection is usually invisible to programs: as long as an object is referenced by any variable, it will never be garbage collected. Only when there are no variables referring to an object and, hence no way for a program to use the object, will it be garbage collected.

All About Nothing – `null`

As we've seen, variables of reference types such as `string` or `Book` usually contain references to objects of the corresponding type. Sometimes, such a variable does not contain a reference to any object, perhaps because we haven't yet stored any value into the variable or have discarded its value. Such a variable contains the special value called `null`. You can think of `null` as a value that denotes the absence of an object.

`null` is unusual in that it is a value of *all* reference types. That means that the value `null` can be stored into a variable of any reference type, such as `string`, `Rectangle`, or `Book`, to signify the fact that the variable does not currently refer to an object. For example, we can say:

```
bestSeller = null; // no Book
userName = null;   // no string
shape = null;      // no Rectangle
```

Storing the value `null` into a variable overwrites its previous value. As a result the reference that was previously stored there is destroyed. This may, of course, result in the corresponding object becoming garbage and eventually being deleted (if the variable held the last remaining reference to that object).

Another question that arises is what happens when we store the value `null` into a variable and then try to use that variable to invoke a method. For example, what happens if we write:

```
bestSeller = null;
name = bestSeller.GetAuthor();
```

Clearly, since `bestSeller` doesn't refer to any `Book`, we can't retrieve the author. Trying to use a `null`-valued variable in this manner results in an error. We'll talk much more about this possibility later in the book!

Calculating New Values – Expressions

We have already seen lots of examples of expressions, usually on the right-hand side of some assignment statement. Formally speaking, an *expression* is any properly constructed sequence

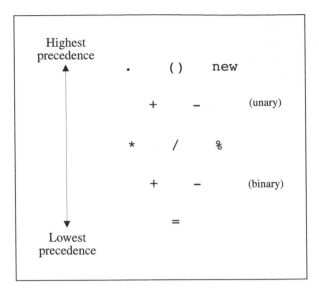

Highest
precedence

.   ( )   new

+   –   (unary)

*   /   %

+   –   (binary)

=

Lowest
precedence

Figure 3.27   The relative precedence of C#'s operators.

of values, variables, operators, and method invocations that *yields some value*. In other words, the most important feature of an expression is that it can be evaluated to give us a value. Put another way, any C# construct that has a value is an expression. As such, an expression can be a *simple expression* as in the following examples:

```
15                     // a literal is an expression whose value
                       // is the specified value
length                 // a variable is an expression whose value
                       // is the current value of the variable
myCircle.GetArea()     // a method call is an expression whose
                       // value is the return value of the method
```

or a *compound expression*, i.e., a series of simple expressions combined with appropriate operators:

```
myCircle.GetArea() * 5.7
"Hello" + "Vinny"
(salary + bonus - tax) / 12
PI * radius * radius
new Lecturer("Cahill");
lba2Lecturer = newBook;
```

As we have already seen, the order in which the operators are evaluated is important and is determined by the relative precedence of the operators involved and whether they are left associative or right associative. Figure 3.27 summarizes the relative precedence of all the operators that we have met so far and their associativity.

As well as the arithmetic operators, Figure 3.27 includes the method selector (i.e., the . operator) and method call operators (i.e., the ( ) operator). Note that these operators have equal precedence and are left associative. Hence, we can chain together method calls on objects returned as the result of previous method calls as in the following example:

```
name = myBook.GetAuthor().GetName();
```

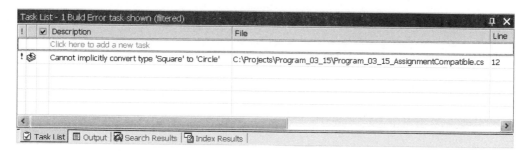

Figure 3.28 The compilation of Program 3.15.

Here `myBook.GetAuthor()` is evaluated first and returns a reference to a `Person` object on which we immediately invoke the `GetName` method to obtain the `string` representing the author's name.

Notice too that in C#, new is an operator whose value is always a reference to a new object. Finally, and as we mentioned before, assignment is an operator.

It is important to understand that every expression has a type. The type of an expression is essentially the type of the value returned by that expression. Thus, the types of each of the following expressions are as given in the comments following the expression:

```
15                                      // int
length                                  // int
myCircle.GetArea()                      // double
"Vinny"                                 // string
myCircle.GetArea()* 5.7                 // double
"Hello" + "Vinny"                       // string
(salary + bonus - tax) / 12            // int
PI * radius * radius                    // double
new Book("C\# Book", "Vinny + Donal"); // Book
bestSeller = newBook;                   // Book
```

The type of an expression is used to decide if a particular assignment statement is legal. In particular, C# enforces the rule that the type of an expression must be the same as the type of the variable to which its value is being assigned. In other words, it enforces the rule that "you can't put a square peg in a round hole"!

Because the type of an expression can be determined from the types of its component parts, C# can usually detect such attempts when a program is being compiled rather that when the program is running. For example, Figure 3.28 shows what happens when you try to compile Program 3.15. Notice that the program contains the assignment statement:

```
myCircle = new Square(15);
```

Since `myCircle` has type `Circle` and the expression `new Square(15)` has type `Square`, they are not assignment compatible and an error is detected.

Class `string`

We have already seen that any sequence of characters enclosed in double quotes is a string and we have used strings frequently when writing messages to the screen.

```
/* A program to illustrate assignment compatibility */
using tcdIO;

class AssignmentCompatibility
{
   public static void Main()
   {
      Circle myCircle;      // a placeholder for a circle
      Square mySquare;      // a placeholder for a square

      /* create a new Square */
      myCircle = new Square(15);
   }
}
```

Program 3.15 A program to illustrate assignment compatibility.

In fact, strings are instances of a predefined C# class string. Thus, individual strings are, in fact, represented by objects. A sequence of characters in double quotes is a literal of type string denoting the value of some string object.

Because string is a fully-fledged class, we can declare variables of type string as usual and give them values using assignment. For example, we can say

```
string name, address;
name = "Vinny";
address = "Trinity College Dublin.";
```

since C# implicitly creates an instance of string corresponding to every string literal used in a program. Note that there is no need to use the new operator to create an instance of string.

To read a string from the terminal we use the ReadString method from class Terminal. Like ReadInt and ReadDouble, ReadString takes a single string as input and uses it as a prompt to the user. ReadString reads any text that the user types before pressing <ENTER> and then returns a reference to an instance of string containing this text. For example, to read the user's name, we might write:

```
name = terminal.ReadString("Enter name: ");
terminal.println("Hello " + name);
```

As we've seen, the + operator allows us to concatenate strings:

```
name = "Vinny" + "Cahill";
   // gives "VinnyCahill"
authors = name + "Donal Lafferty";
   // gives "VinnyCahillDonal Lafferty"
myCourseCodes = "1ba2" + ", 4ba8" + ", nds103";
   // gives "1ba2, 4ba8, nds103"
```

The + operator applied to two strings creates a new instance of `string` containing the concatenation of the original strings. Note that there is no way to modify (edit) a C# string once its been created, although you can use an instance of `string` to make a new `string` using +. A variable that refers to an instance of `string` can, of course, be made refer to a different instance:

```
bookTitle = "C\#";
bookTitle = bookTitle + "Programming";
```

Initializing New Objects – Constructors

We have seen already that a *constructor* is used to initialize the instance variables of a new object. Typically, a constructor takes a number of parameters that are used to provide the initial values of the instance variables. Of course, the constructor can take as many inputs as required and can determine the initial values of the instances variables in any way that is appropriate. In other words, there doesn't have to be a one-to-one correspondence between inputs to the constructor and instance variables of the class.

Program 3.16 shows a class `StudentMark` whose instances are used to keep track of the marks awarded to a student in some course. The class declares three instance variables giving the name and identification number of the student and the number of marks scored by the student so far. The constructor, however, takes only two parameters corresponding to the

```
/* A class whose instances contain the marks */
/* obtained by a student in some course */
class StudentMark
{
   private string name;
   private int idNumber;
   private int totalMark;

   /* initialize new object */
   public StudentMark(string name, int idNumber)
   {
      this.name = n;        // set name of student
      this.idNumber = i;    // set id. number of student
      this.totalMark = 0;   // always start with no marks
   }

   /* record a mark for an exercise */
   public void AddMark(int mark)
   {
      this.totalMark = this.totalMark + mark;
   }

   /* return marks achieved so far */
   public int GetMark()
   {
      return this.totalMark;
   }
}
```

Program 3.16   Class `StudentMark`.

```
/* A class whose instances contain the marks */
/* obtained by a student in a course (revised) */
class StudentMark2
{
    private string name;
    private int idNumber;
    private int totalMark = 0;   // always start with no marks

    /* initialize new object */
    public StudentMark2(string name, int idNumber)
    {
        this.name = n;          // set name of student
        this.idNumber = i;      // set id. number of student
    }

    /* record a mark for an exercise */
    public void AddMark(int mark)
    {
        this.totalMark = this.totalMark + mark;
    }

    /* return marks achieved so far */
    public int GetMark()
    {
        return this.totalMark;
    }
}
```

Program 3.17   Class StudentMark (revised).

name and identification number of the student. Thus, every new object is initialized with the name and identification number supplied as parameters to its constructor, while the mark field in every new instance of the class in always set to zero initially.

While most classes do provide constructors to initialize new instances of the class, it is not compulsory for a constructor to be provided. If the programmer doesn't define a constructor for a class, C# automatically provides a *default constructor* that is used to initialize all new instances of the class. The default constructor takes *no* inputs and sets all the instance variables to *default values*. In particular, instance variables of numeric types are set to zero while variables of reference types are set to the value null.

In the common case where an instance variable is always initialized to the same value in *all* new instances of a class, C# allows the initialization of the instance variable to be combined with its declaration. Variable initialization takes the form of an assignment to the variable where the expression part of the assignment gives the initial value of the variable. Program 3.17 uses this facility to initialize the totalMark attribute in new instances of class StudentMark.

Not only is totalMark initialized in exactly the same way for every instance of the class, but also the initialization cannot depend on the parameters to the constructor. Thus, instance variables that should be initialized in a different way in different instances of the class or those whose initialization depends in some way on the values supplied by the creator of the new object should be initialized in a constructor.

We can also initialize a local variable where it is declared in exactly the same way that we can initialize an instance variable. In the absence of any explicit initialization, local variables of numeric types are set to zero while variables of reference types are set to the value null.

Giving Names to Values – Constants

You may have noticed that many of the classes and programs, which we have written, included numeric and even `string` values in the program. For example, our `Circle` class (Program 3.9) made use of the value of π (~3.1416) in several places. Since the value of π is well known and since it never changes, we can write that value into our program as a literal. In the same way, if we were writing a program to calculate the income tax due on a salary, we might need to use the value of the tax rate (e.g., 27%) in this way. Thus we might write,

```
taxDue = salary * 0.27;
```

Just as was the case with the value of π in the `Circle` program, it's likely that this value will appear in several places in the program.

There are two problems with this approach. Firstly, while `3.1416` may be instantly recognizable as the value of π, it may not be so obvious to somebody reading a long program what the value `0.27` (or any other such value) represents. Secondly, while the value of π never changes, the value of the tax rate might change occasionally. This would require us to modify the program. That's acceptable. However, if the value occurs in many places in the program we will have to find and modify all of them. If we miss one the program will be incorrect.

To tackle these problems, C# allows us to associate an identifier with a literal and use that identifier in place of the corresponding literal throughout the program. Such a named value is called a *constant*. By choosing meaningful identifiers for such values, we can improve the clarity of our programs. Moreover, because the actual value only appears once in the declaration of the constant, if we ever need to modify the program to change the value, we're sure that it only has to be changed in one place.

To define the constant `TAXRATE` with the value `0.27`, we write:

```
private const double TAXRATE = 0.27;
```

which looks very much like the definition of an instance variable except for the inclusion of the keyword `const` which indicates that the value of `TAXRATE` can never be changed (unless we rewrite the program). Notice that, by convention, constants are defined in a class before any of its instance variables and are given identifiers consisting entirely of capital letters. Now we can write:

```
taxDue = salary * TAXRATE;
```

where `TAXRATE` stands for the value `0.27`. Hopefully you'll agree that the meaning of this statement is now much clearer! As another example, Program 3.18 is a modified version of class `Circle` that uses a constant (`PI`) for the value of π.

We recommend that you use named constants whenever your need to write a specific value into a program. You'll see lots of example of constants in our programs, later in the book.

Case Study: The Traveling Salesperson

As an example of the use of the various features of C# that we have looked at in this chapter let's consider the following problem. A traveling salesperson travels between five cities. Supposing that the latitude and longitude of each city are supplied as input, write a C# program that reports the total distance traveled by the salesperson and the direct distance between the first and last cities on the route.

```
/* A class whose instances represent circles (revised) */
class Circle
{
   private const double PI = 3.1416;
   private double radius;

   /* initialize new circle object */
   public Circle(double radius)
   {
      this.radius = radius;
   }

   /* calculate area of circle */
   public double CalculateArea()
   {
      return this.radius * this.radius * PI;
   }

   /* calculate circumference of circle */
   public double CalculateCircumference()
   {
      return 2.0 * PI * this.radius;
   }
}
```

Program 3.18   Class `Circle` (revised).

Choosing the Classes – Class `City`

As always when beginning to design a new program, we start by considering what types of entity
the program deals with and, hence, what classes we will need. In this case, there seem to be two
types of entity of interest: traveling salespeople and cities. While our program represents the
traveling salesperson, each of the cities will be represented by objects (instances of class `City`,
in fact). From the description of the problem, it is clear that a city has its latitude and longitude
as attributes. Thus, the class `City` will provide two instance variables of type `double` to store
the coordinates of the corresponding city. These instance variables are declared as follows:

```
private double latitude, longitude;
```

A city surely has lots of other attributes, its name, its population, its altitude, and so forth. For
our purposes, we do not need to use any of this information and hence we will not include
any of these attributes in our class.

Our class will, as usual, have a constructor to initialize the instance variables of each new city.
Since the values of the instance variables vary on a per-city basis, these values are supplied as
parameters to the constructor as each new city is created. Our class will also provide methods
to allow the latitude and longitude of a city to be retrieved.

Our program is concerned with calculating the distances between cities. When we want to
find the distance from one city to another it seems natural to ask one of the cities concerned.
Hence, our class `City` will provide a method to calculate the distance between the current
city and another specified city. The method `GetDistance` will take (a reference to) another

$$Distance = \sqrt{(x_2 - x_1)^2 + (y_2 - y_1)^2}$$

Figure 3.29   Formula for distance between two points.

city as its parameter and return the distance between the two cities as its result. Its heading is therefore:

```
public double GetDistance(City next);
```

In order to write the method `GetDistance`, we will treat the cities as points in a two-dimensional space – this isn't strictly correct since the earth isn't flat but its close enough for our purposes! Remembering our coordinate geometry, we can calculate the distance between two points with coordinates (x_1, y_1) and (x_2, y_2) using the formula in Figure 3.29.

In the case of `GetDistance`, (x_1, y_1) corresponds to the latitude and longitude of the current city as given by its `latitude` and `longitude` instance variables. (x_2, y_2) corresponds to the coordinates of the next city. These can be obtained by invoking the `GetLatitude` and `GetLongitude` methods on the object that represents this city as given by the `next` parameter to the `GetDistance` method, i.e., `next.GetLatitude()`, `next.GetLongitude()`.

To take the square root we need to use a standard method `Math.Sqrt` provided in a C# assembly called `System`. The `System` assembly provides a lot of useful classes and methods. We'll use more later! For now it's enough to say that `Math.Sqrt` is defined as follows:

```
double Math.Sqrt(double number)
```

i.e., it takes a `double` value (whose square root is required) as its single parameter and returns a `double` value (the square root) as its result. Thus, the code to calculate and return the distance between the cities is as follows:

```
tmpX = next.GetLatitude() - this.latitude;
tmpY = next.GetLongitude() - this.longitude;
return Math.Sqrt((tmpX*tmpX) + (tmpY*tmpY));
```

The full code for class `City` is given in Program 3.19.

The Traveling Salesperson Program

Our traveling salesperson program will obviously need to create five instances of class `City` to represent the cities visited by the salesperson. For each city the program reads the coordinates of the city from the user and then creates a new object to represent that city. Rather than creating all the objects representing the cities at once, instances of city need only be created at they are required. In particular, at any time the program must keep track of *the current city* and *the next city* to which the salesperson will travel. Two local variables are used to store references to the corresponding objects:

```
City currentCity, nextCity;
```

```
/* A class whose instances represent cities */
/* with latitude and longitude*/

using System;

class City
{
   private double longitude, latitude; // only attributes of interest
                                       // are latitude and longitude

   /* initialize a new City */
   public City(double longitude, double latitude)
   {
      this.longitude = longitude;
      this.latitude = latitude;
   }

   /* return longitude coordinate */
   public double GetLongitude()
   {
      return this.longitude;
   }

   /* return latitude coordinate */
   public double GetLatitude()
   {
      return this.latitude;
   }

   /* get distance to some other city */
   public double GetDistance(City next)
   {
      double tmpX, tmpY;        // local variables for this method

      tmpX = next.GetLongitude() - this.longitude; // (x2 - x1)
      tmpY = next.GetLatitude - this.latitude;      // (y2 - y1)
      return Math.Sqrt((tmpX*tmpX) + (tmpY*tmpY));
   }
}
```

Program 3.19   Class `City`.

As the salesperson travels, the `GetDistance` method is used to calculate the distance from the current city to the next city and this distance added to a running total for the distance traveled so far:

```
distance = distance + currentCity.GetDistance(nextCity);
```

As we move, what was the next city becomes the current city:

```
currentCity = nextCity;
```

Notice that this overwrites our reference to the object representing the current city, potentially making the corresponding object garbage! However, we need to keep a reference to the first city so that we can calculate the direct distance between the first and the last cities at the end of the program. Thus, we introduce an additional local variable to store this object.

```
City firstCity;
```

and initialize it at the beginning of the program when `currentCity` still refers to the object representing the first city on the path.

```
firstCity = currentCity;
```

At the end of the program, we ask the first city for its distance to the last city:

```
distance = firstCity.GetDistance(currentCity);
```

where by this time `currentCity` refers to the object representing the last city on the path. The full code for the traveling salesperson program is given in Program 3.20.

```
/* A program to calculate distance */
/* travelled by salesperson */

using tcdIO;

class Salesperson
{
    public static void Main()
    {
        Terminal terminal;
        City currentCity; // reference to city we're in
        City nextCity;    // reference to city we're going to
        City firstCity;   // reference to 1st city
        double longitude, latitude;    // used to get input
        double distance;  // running total

        /* create an object to represent the terminal */
        terminal = new Terminal();

        /* ask user for position of 1st city */
        terminal.WriteLine("Enter position of first city:");
        longitude = terminal.ReadDouble("Longitude:");
        latitude = terminal.ReadDouble("Latitude:");
        /* create object to represent 1st city */
        currentCity = new City(longitude, latitude);
        firstCity = currentCity;    // remember 1st city for later

        /* ask user for position of next city */
        terminal.WriteLine("Enter position of second city:");
        longitude = terminal.ReadDouble("Longitude:");
        latitude = terminal.ReadDouble("Latitude:");
        /* create object to represent 2nd city */
        nextCity = new City(longitude, latitude);
```

```
        /* get distance between 1st and 2nd cities */
        distance = currentCity.GetDistance(nextCity);
        currentCity = nextCity;        // move to 2nd city

        /* ask user for position of next city */
        terminal.WriteLine("Enter position of third city:");
        longitude = terminal.ReadDouble("Longitude:");
        latitude = terminal.ReadDouble("Latitude:");
        /* create object to represent 3rd city */
        nextCity = new City(longitude, latitude);

        /* update distance with distance between 2nd and 3rd cities */
        distance = distance + currentCity.GetDistance(nextCity);
        currentCity = nextCity;        // move to 3rd city

        /* ask user for position of next city */
        terminal.WriteLine("Enter position of fourth city:");
        longitude = terminal.ReadDouble("Longitude:");
        latitude = terminal.ReadDouble("Latitude:");
        /* create object to represent 4th city */
        nextCity = new City(longitude, latitude);

        /* update distance with distance between 3rd and 4th cities */
        distance = distance + currentCity.GetDistance(nextCity);
        currentCity = nextCity;        // move to 4th city

        /* ask user for position of next city */
        terminal.WriteLine("Enter position of fifth city:");
        longitude = terminal.ReadDouble("Longitude:");
        latitude = terminal.ReadDouble("Latitude:");
        /* create object to represent 5th city */
        nextCity = new City(longitude, latitude);

        /* update distance with distance between 4th and 5th cities */
        distance = distance + currentCity.GetDistance(nextCity);
        currentCity = nextCity;        // move to 5th city

        /* Write out result */
        terminal.WriteLine("Distance travelled is: " + distance + ".");

        /* calculate direct distance between 1st and 5th cities */
        distance = firstCity.GetDistance(currentCity);
        terminal.WriteLine("Direct distance is: " + distance + ".");
    }
}
```

Program 3.20 The traveling salesperson program.

Say that the coordinates of the five cities are as follows:

(0, 0) (4, 3) (8, 6) (12, 9) (16, 12)

These coordinates represent points on a straight line with a distance of five between each pair of points. The total distance to be traveled and the straight-line distance between the first and last cities are both 20. Figure 3.30 shows the execution of the program for this sequence of

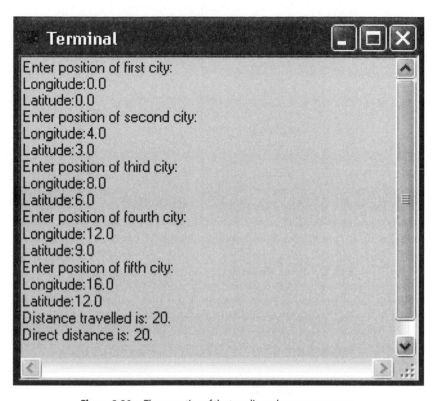

Figure 3.30   The execution of the traveling salesperson program.

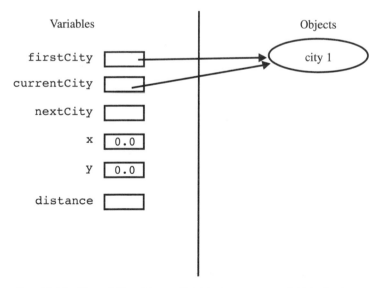

Figure 3.31   The variables of the traveling salesperson program (initial values).

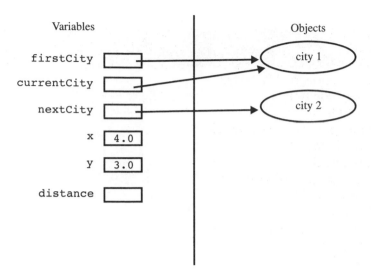

Figure 3.32 The variables of the traveling salesperson program (step 1).

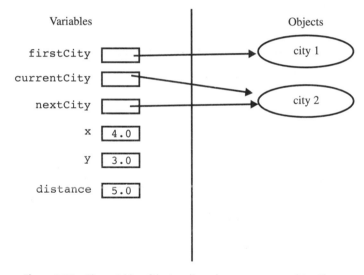

Figure 3.33 The variables of the traveling salesperson program (step 2).

inputs while Figures 3.31–3.39 illustrate what happens to the variables of the program as it executes.

This is by far the largest program we have looked at up to now. It uses most of the features of C# that we have examined. It's worth spending the time to make sure you fully understand how the program works before proceeding further. As you can see, things are starting to get a little more complicated now!

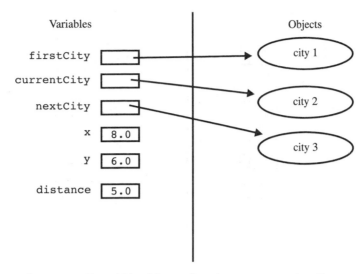

Figure 3.34 The variables of the traveling salesperson program (step 3).

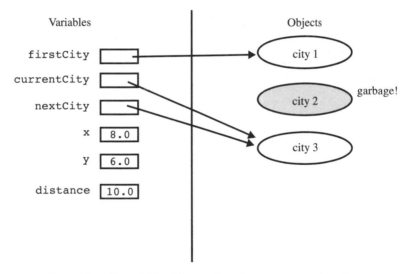

Figure 3.35 The variables of the traveling salesperson program (step 4).

Summary

- a *variable* is a container for a *value*
- every variable has a *name*, a *type*, and a (current) *value*
- the *type* of a variable describes the set of values that can be stored in that variable
- C# is a *strongly-typed* language
- *simple types* describe simple values like numbers and letters
- every class defines a corresponding type whose values are the instances of the class
- class types are called *reference types* in C#

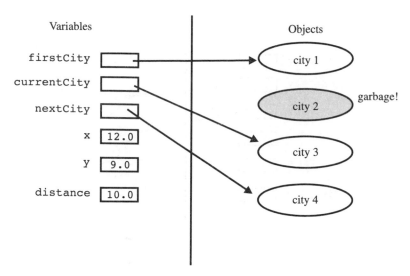

Figure 3.36 The variables of the traveling salesperson program (step 5).

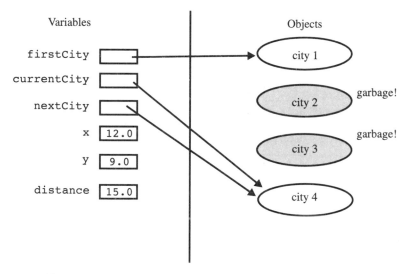

Figure 3.37 The variables of the traveling salesperson program (step 6).

- a variable of a reference type stores a reference to an object of that type
- two or more different variables can contain references to the same object
- integer types represent positive and negative whole numbers
- floating-point types represent real numbers (approximately)
- an *assignment* is used to change the current value of a variable
- think of an assignment as storing the value of an expression into a specified variable
- during an assignment, the previous value of the variable is *lost*
- we can assign object references between variables
- every *expression* yields a value of some type

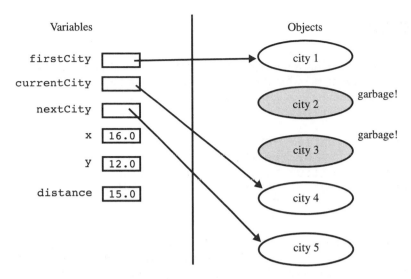

Figure 3.38   The variables of the traveling salesperson program (step 7).

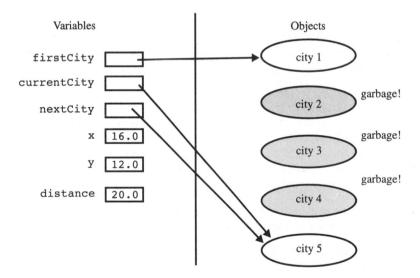

Figure 3.39   The variables of the traveling salesperson program (final values).

- the type of an expression must be the *same* as the type of the variable to which its value is being assigned
- a *string* is any sequence of characters enclosed in double quotes
- *constants* are used to associate meaningful identifiers with values

Exercises

(1) Say whether each of the following tokens is a C# keyword, a valid identifier, or a literal. In the case of a literal, say what the type of the literal is. In the case of an integer literal say what base the number is in and its value in decimal.

```
myName      while    ELSE           5.0E3      0x56A1
02547L      numOf    2345.78F       timeToGo   timetogo
1110        01110    8945.89e-10D   class      an_identifier
2tired      "c"      "Vinny"        2,345      0xFFFF
```

(2) Our `Rectangle` class from Chapter 1 has instance variables of type `int`. However, there is no good reason why the dimensions of a rectangle should be whole numbers. Rewrite class `Rectangle` to have attributes of type `double`. Now rewrite Program 3.7, the program to calculate the area and perimeter of a rectangle, to use your new class.

(3) Using your `Rectangle` class from Exercise 2 above, write a C# program that creates three different rectangles with dimensions specified by the user and then prints out the area of each.

(4) Declare a C# class whose instances represent books. Such a class might include instance variables giving the title of the book, its authors, the publisher, and the date of publication, and provide methods including those to obtain the title, authors, publisher and date of publication from a book. Use your class in a program that creates a number of books whose details are provided by the user and then prints out the titles of each.

(5) Using the types `int`, `double`, and `string`, as well as any types that you define yourself, give a declaration for class `Person` whose instances represent people. Include at least ten attributes and any methods that seem appropriate. Use your class in a program that creates two instances of `Person` (representing a male and a female) and makes each the spouse of the other. Your program should then invoke each object to find out its spouse and, having done so, should print out the name of the spouse.

Suggestion: you might want to consider defining additional classes such as one whose instances represent the person's home or business address.

Hint: the question should give you clues as to some of the attributes and methods that you should provide.

(6) Write a C# program that will read the start time of some event (in hours and minutes) and its duration (also in hours and minutes), and then print out the time at which the event will finish. For example, an event starting at 11:45 hrs and lasting 2 hours, 37 minutes finishes at 14:22 hrs.

Hint: think about what classes are required and make sure you consider all the possibilities that might arise when adding a duration to a time.

(7) Program 3.14 swaps the value of two variables using a third variable to temporarily remember the value of one of the variables to be swapped. Write a fragment of code that swaps the values of two `int` variables without using a third variable.

(8) A complex number consists of a real part and an imaginary part where the imaginary part is the coefficient of i (iota, the square root of -1). Write a class whose instances represent complex numbers, and which provides methods to add, subtract, and multiply (but, for now, not divide) complex numbers. Use your class in a program that allows its users to perform each of these operations on two complex numbers that they enter.

Making Decisions – Selection in C# 4

This chapter:

- motivates the need for programs to be able to make decisions and take different courses of action each time they run
- describes the type `bool` and the operators that are available to manipulate `bool` values
- describes how to compare the values of simple types, object references, and objects
- describes the `if` statement – a C# statement that provides one means for programs to choose between alternative courses of action
- describes the `switch` statement – a C# statement that provides another means for programs to choose between many different courses of action

So far, every program that we have written has consisted of a single sequence of statements. When such a program is run, each statement in the sequence is executed in turn. Likewise, every method that we have written has consisted of a single sequence of statements. When such a method is invoked, its statements are executed one after another in turn. Notice that, in all the programs and methods that we have written up to now, exactly the *same* sequence of statements is executed every time that the program or method runs!

It should be obvious that programs and methods like these are very inflexible since they have no opportunity to take different courses of action, i.e., to execute different sequences of statements, in different circumstances. The ability to respond to prevailing circumstances by carrying out different actions is clearly essential.

As an example, consider the problem of getting from your home to the nearest airport. You might decide that you will always go by bus. Most of the time this is likely to be an efficient and, indeed, cheap, strategy. However, what if there is a bus strike? Clearly, in this circumstance, you need to take an alternative course of action such as going by taxi. The resulting algorithm for getting to the airport might be stated as follows:

> if there is a bus strike today
> then take a taxi to the airport;
> otherwise take a bus to the airport.

This algorithm illustrates the basic approach to writing programs that incorporate the necessary flexibility to take different courses of action in different circumstances. Essentially, we have identified two different courses of action – "take a taxi to the airport" and "take a bus to the airport" – and a condition for choosing which course of action to take – "there is a bus strike today". The condition is either true (when there is a bus strike) or false. When you want to go to the airport on a given day, you first evaluate the condition and, based on its value, choose whether to take a taxi or a bus. On different days the condition is likely to have different values. In either case, you're covered and will not be left waiting at the bus stop while your plane takes off! Notice that the two courses of action are alternatives to each other and are mutually exclusive. On any given journey to the airport, you will either take a taxi or a bus but not both.

C# provides means for specifying alternative courses of action that a program or method can take and for specifying conditions for deciding between these alternatives. In programming terms, each possible course of action corresponds to a different sequence of statements. A mechanism for choosing between alternative courses of action is known as a *selection* mechanism because it allows us to select an appropriate sequence of statements to execute. C# provides two different selection mechanisms, the `if` statement and the `switch` statement, which we describe in detail later in this chapter. However, before we can look further at selection in C#, we need to look at how conditions are described in a C# program.

Describing Conditions – Type `bool`

`bool` is the name of a C# type rather like `int` or `double`. While `int` is used to represent whole numbers and `double` to represent floating-point numbers, type `bool` represents the value of a condition. As we have just seen, a condition is a statement that can be either true or false depending on prevailing circumstances. For example, the statement "it's sunny" is a condition. Sometimes it's true and sometimes, unfortunately, it's false.

While type `int` has many values, all of which are numbers such as -234243 and 67, type `bool` has only two values called, unsurprisingly, `true` and `false`. These two values are, of course, sufficient to represent the value of any condition.

Formally, `bool`, `true`, and `false` are C# keywords. While `bool` is the identifier of a simple type, `true` and `false` are literals representing the only values of that type.

In a program, we can use type `bool` in essentially all the same ways that we can use other simple types. Thus, we can have:

- variables of type `bool` – such a variable either stores the value `true` or the value `false`,
- expressions that yield values of type `bool`,
- methods that take inputs of type `bool`, and
- methods that return values of type `bool`.

We will see examples of each of these in the following sections.

`bool` **Variables and Assignment**

A `bool` variable can be used to store the value of some condition. Put another way, `bool` variables are used to remember simple facts. For example, the current value of the condition "it's raining outside" could be represented by a single `bool` variable – let's call it `rainingOut`. `rainingOut` is declared as follows:

```
bool rainingOut;
```

To record the fact that it's currently raining (i.e., that the condition is true) we write:

```
rainingOut = true; // it's raining!
```

i.e., we assign the value `true` to the variable `rainingOut`. Note that we can use assignment to store a (`bool`) value in a `bool` variable in the same way that we previously used assignment to store, for example, an (int) value in an int variable. To record the fact that it's dry out (i.e., that the condition is false) we write:

```
rainingOut = false; // it's not raining!
```

If we were writing a program to help determine who is allowed in to a night-club (as we will later), we might want to remember the value of the condition "customer is allowed into club". Again, we use a single bool variable:

```
bool allowedIn;
```

To record the fact that the customer is not allowed in, we write:

```
allowedIn = false; // customer is under age
```

Of course, we can assign the result of any expression that gives a value of type bool to a bool variable. We'll see lots of examples below.

The bool **Operators**

Just as we can manipulate integers by means of operators that perform addition, subtraction, and other mathematical operations, we can also manipulate bool values by means of a number of operators. These operators allow us to express complex conditions as bool expressions whose values depend on the values of simpler expressions, including the values of one or more bool variables.

The most important bool operators are called *and*, *or*, and *not*. These operators are sometimes called the *conditional operators* or the *s*. Thus, you may see the *and* operator referred to as the *conditional-and* or *logical-and* operator.

The *and* operator is a binary operator. It takes two bool values as its operands and gives a single bool value as its result in much the same way that the integer + operator takes two int values as its operands and gives a single int as its result.

The *and* operator is represented by the symbol && (two ampersands without any space between them) and its operation is defined by the truth table shown in Figure 4.1. A truth table for a bool operator lists all the possible combinations of the values of its operands and the result returned for that combination of the operands. Notice that there are only four possible combinations of the operands. && gives true only if both operands are true. If either operand is false, && gives false.

As an example of the use of &&, consider the following three conditions: "I can buy petrol", "I have money", and "the garage is open". The three conditions are related in that "I can only buy petrol if I have money *and* the garage is open". In other words, the first condition is true

a	b	a && b
false	false	false
false	true	false
true	false	false
true	true	true

Figure 4.1   The truth table for the && operator.

a	b	a || b
false	false	false
false	true	true
true	false	true
true	true	true

Figure 4.2 The truth table for the \|\| operator.

only if both of the other conditions are true. The value of the first condition can be obtained from the value of the other two conditions. If the three conditions are represented by `bool` variables as follows:

```
bool buyPetrol, haveMoney, garageOpen;
```

then we can calculate the value of `buyPetrol` using `&&` as follows:

```
buyPetrol = haveMoney && garageOpen;
```

Notice that if both `haveMoney` and `garageOpen` are `true`, `buyPetrol` will be `true`. If either `buyPetrol` or `garageOpen` is `false`, `buyPetrol` will be `false`.

The *or* operator is also a binary operator that takes two `bool` values as its operands and gives a single `bool` value as its result. The *or* operator is represented by the symbol `||` (two vertical bars without any space between them). The operation of the `||` operator is defined by the truth table shown in Figure 4.2. Notice that `||` gives `true` if either of its operands is `true`. If both operands are `false`, `||` gives `false`.

As an example of the use of `||`, consider the following conditions: "I should wear my coat", "it's cold outside", and "it's raining outside". Again, these conditions are related in that "I should wear my coat if it's cold outside *or* it's raining outside". The first is true if either of the others if true. Hence, the value of the first condition can be calculated from the values of the others using the `||` operator. Let's represent the conditions as `bool` variables:

```
bool coatOn, coldOut, rainingOut;
```

We can say:

```
coatOn = coldOut || rainingOut;
```

Notice that if either `coldOut` or `rainingOut` is `true`, `coatOn` will be `true`. If both are `false`, `coatOn` will be `false`.

The final `bool` operator that we will introduce here is the *not* operator. The *not* operator is a unary operator that takes a single `bool` value as its only operand and gives a `bool` value as its result. The *not* operator is represented by the symbol `!` (a single exclamation mark) that is placed immediately before its operand. `!` gives `true` when its operand is `false` and `false` when its operand is `true`. Thus, if `windyOut` is a `bool` variable, `!windyOut` is `true` when `windyOut` is `false` and vice versa. `!` is said to *invert* or *complement* its single operand. Thus, `!windyOut` is said to be the *inverse* or the *complement* of `windyOut`. The truth table for `!` is shown in Figure 4.3.

As an example of the use of `!`, consider the following conditions: "I can fly my kite", "it's windy outside", "it's raining outside". Again, these conditions are related in that "I can only

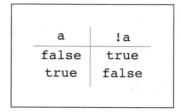

Figure 4.3   The truth table for the ! operator.

fly my kite if it's windy outside and it's not raining". So, the first condition is true if the second condition is true and the third condition is false. If we represent the three conditions as `bool` variables:

```
bool flyKite, windyOut, rainingOut;
```

then we can say that:

```
flyKite = windyOut && (!rainingOut);
```

`flyKite` will be `true` when `windyOut` is `true` and `!rainingOut` is `true`. Notice the use of the brackets to ensure that `!` is evaluated before `&&`. This is actually unnecessary because, as we will see below, `!` has a higher precedence than `&&`. However, we feel that the use of the brackets makes the expression a little clearer.

Having introduced some new operators, we need to describe the relative precedence of these operators to each other and to the operators that we have met already. Figure 4.4 shows the relative precedence of all the operators that we have met so far.

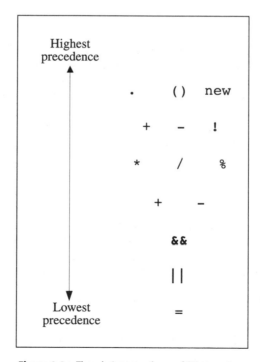

Figure 4.4   The relative precedence of C#'s operators.

Note that of the three `bool` operators ! has the highest precedence followed by `&&` and then `||`. Both `&&` and `||` are left associative, i.e., they are evaluated in left to right order.

Comparing Numeric Values

It is very common for people to want to compare numbers to see if they are equal or to check if one is greater than another. For example, I might want to check whether or not my salary is greater than that of one of my colleagues. The same is true of many programs – it's quite common for a program to need to compare two numeric values. In C#, we can, for example, compare two `ints` to see if they are equal, or compare two `doubles` to see if one is greater than the other.

==	equals
!=	not equals
>	greater than
<	less than
>=	greater than or equals
<=	less than or equals

Figure 4.5   The numeric relational operators.

C# provides a set of six binary operators for comparing numeric values. These six operators are listed in Figure 4.5. Collectively, they are referred to as *relational operators* because they are used to test relations between numbers. Each takes two numeric values as its operands and returns a `bool` value indicating whether or not the specified relation between the numbers holds. Note that the two operands must be of the same numeric type (other than `byte`, `sbyte`, `ushort`, or `short`) although conversions may be used to compare values of different types. Moreover, since the comparison is really a condition, the result is always of type `bool`.

For example, given the following variable definitions:

```
bool answer;
int counter = 5;
double salary = 27000.0, bonus = 2000.0;
```

we can perform the following comparisons. Note that in each case the result of the comparison is either `true` or `false` and is stored in the `bool` variable `answer` by means of an assignment. The difference between the assignment operator (a single equals sign) and the equals operator (two equals signs without any space between them) is also worth noting.

```
answer = counter == 5; // true
```

In this first example we check to see if the current value of `counter` is 5 using the equals operator and store the result in `answer`. As we note in the comment, the result is `true`.

```
answer = bonus > salary; // false - pity!
```

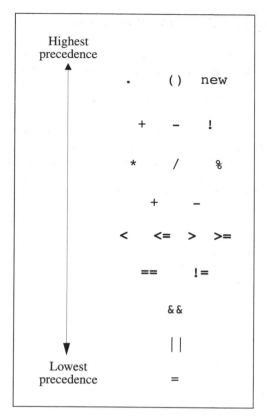

Figure 4.6   The relative precedence of C#'s operators.

In the second example we check to see if the current value of bonus is greater than the current value of salary using the greater than operator. Unfortunately, it isn't. Thus, the result is false.

```
answer = salary >= 27000.0; // true
```

In the third example we check to see if the current value of salary is greater than or equal to 27000.0. Happily, it is. Thus, the result is true.

```
answer = bonus != 2000.0; // false
```

In the fourth example we check to see that the current value of bonus is not equal to 2000.0. Since bonus is equal to 2000.0, the result is false.

```
answer = (counter > 0) && (counter <= 10);
// true -- counter is in range 1-10
```

In the final example, we are checking that the value of counter is in the range 1-10. This requires that we check that counter is both greater than 0 and less than or equal to 10. In this case we have to perform two separate comparisons (each of which yields a bool result) and combine the results using the && operator. The use of the brackets is unnecessary here since, as Figure 4.6 shows, && has a lower precedence than any of the relational operators.

Choosing Between Alternative Courses of Action – `if`

As we described at the beginning of this chapter, programs often need to be able to *make decisions* based on prevailing circumstances and *select* one of a number of possible alternative courses of action. For example, consider Program 4.1 that creates a circle whose radius is specified by the user of the program and then calculates the area and circumference of the circle.

Of course, the radius of a circle should be positive. However, this program allows the user to enter a negative radius since it accepts any value of type `double` as input. Implicitly, we are relying on the user to provide a valid (positive) value for the radius. Relying on users to provide valid input is not a good idea. Instead, we should detect any cases where invalid input is provided and, rather than trying to create an instance of `Circle`, complain to the user.

```
/* A program to illustrate the need for selection */
/* Calculates the area and circumference of a circle */
/* whose radius is supplied by the user */

using tcdIO;

class CircleProgram
{
  public static void Main ()
  {
    Terminal terminal;
    Circle shape; // the circle object
    double input; // used to store radius
    double area, circumference;

    /* create an object to represent the terminal */
    terminal = new Terminal();

    /* ask user for radius */
    input = terminal.ReadDouble("Enter radius of circle: ");

    /* create a new circle with the given radius */
    shape = new Circle(input);

    /* ask the Circle object for its area */
    area = shape.CalculateArea();
    /* Write out the area to the screen */
    terminal.WriteLine("The area of the circle is: " + area + ".");

    /* ask the Circle object for its circumference */
    circumference = shape.CalculateCircumference();
    /* Write out the perimeter to the screen */
    terminal.WriteLine("The circumference of the circle is: "
                                        + circumference + ".");
  }
}
```

Program 4.1   A program to illustrate the need for selection.

```
if (<boolean expression>)
{
   <statement sequence 1>
}
else
{
   <statement sequence 2>
}
```

Figure 4.7   The syntax of the C# if statement.

As in the case of the airport example at the beginning of the chapter, we now have two possible courses of action from which to choose ("create a circle and calculate its area and circumference" or "complain to the user") and a condition for choosing between them ("the specified radius is positive"). Our algorithm might be restated as follows:

ask the user for the radius;

if the specified radius is positive

then create a circle; calculate the area of the circle; calculate the circumference of the circle;

otherwise complain to the user that the radius entered was negative.

Each time the program is run, the user will enter a value for the radius. Sometimes (hopefully, most of the time) the value will be positive. Sometimes it will be negative. In either case, the program will do something sensible by selecting the appropriate sequence of statements to execute. For any given execution of the program, only one of the two mutually exclusive courses of action is taken.

To write this program in C#, we need to use an if statement. As Figure 4.7 illustrates, an if statement consists of three parts, a condition represented by a bool expression (and written within brackets) and two statement sequences (usually written between braces). The condition is used to select one of the statement sequences to execute. In particular, the first statement sequence is executed when the condition is true, while the second statement sequence is executed when the condition is false. Fundamentally, only *one* of the statement sequences is ever carried out when an if statement is executed. Thus, the two statement sequences constitute *alternative* courses of action and the condition provides a means of choosing between them.

When an if statement is executed, the condition is always evaluated first yielding a value of true or false. Based on this value, one of the two alternative statement sequences is then chosen and executed. Thus, the flow of control through an if statement is as shown in Figure 4.8.

Returning to our program, we can use an if statement to select the appropriate course of action to take each time that the program is executed depending on what value the user enters for the radius. The condition that determines which course of action to take is whether or not the input is valid, i.e., whether or not the radius supplied by the user is greater than zero (zero is not an acceptable value for the radius either). The corresponding bool expression is:

```
radius > 0
```

which gives true when the value of the variable radius is greater than zero. Thus, the outline of our program becomes:

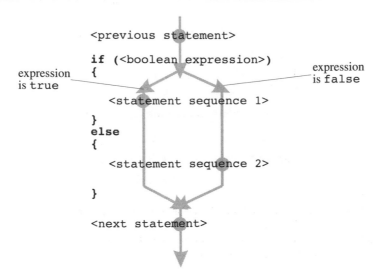

Figure 4.8 The flow of control through a C# if statement.

```
// ask the user for the radius
if (radius > 0)
{
   // create circle, calculate area, calculate circumference
}
else
{
   // complain to user that radius entered was negative
    or zero
}
```

The full program is shown in Program 4.2. The first statement sequence, which is executed only when radius > 0 is true, creates an instance of Circle and calculates its area and circumference as in Program 4.1. The second statement sequence simply prints a message on the screen.

```
/* A program to illustrate the use of the if statement */
/* Calculates the area and circumference of a circle */
/* whose radius is supplied by the user */

using tcdIO;

class CircleProgram
{
   public static void Main ()
   {
      Terminal terminal;
      Circle shape; // the circle object
      double input; // used to store radius
      double area, circumference;
```

```
/* create an object to represent the terminal */
terminal = new Terminal();

/* ask user for radius */
input = terminal.ReadDouble("Enter radius of circle: ");

/* check that the radius is positive and non-zero */
if (input > 0)
{
    /* radius is positive and non-zero */
    /* create a new circle with the given radius */
    shape = new Circle(input);

    /* ask the Circle object for its area */
    area = shape.CalculateArea();
    /* Write out the area to the screen */
    terminal.WriteLine("The area of the circle is: " + area + ".");

    /* ask the Circle object for its circumference */
    circumference = shape.CalculateCircumference();
    /* Write out the perimeter to the screen */
    terminal.WriteLine("The circumference of the circle is: " +
                                        circumference + ".");
}
else
{
    /* radius is negative or zero */
    /* complain to the user */
    terminal.WriteLine("You entered an invalid value for the radius.");
}
}
}
```

Program 4.2   A program to illustrate the use of the `if` statement.

Figures 4.9 and 4.10 show the result of running the program when the user provides valid input and invalid input respectively. Notice that different courses of action are executed in each case, resulting in different output being produced by the same program.

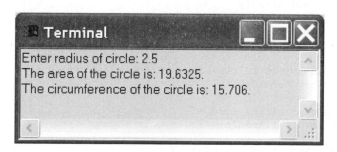

Figure 4.9   The execution of Program 4.2 when the user's input is valid.

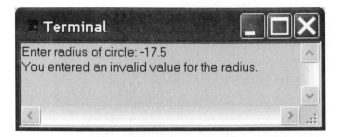

Figure 4.10 The execution of Program 4.2 when the user's input is invalid.

More Complicated `if` Statements

In Program 4.2, the condition that controlled the execution of the `if` statement was a very simple one – it just performed a test on the value of a single variable. In general, the condition can be arbitrarily complex. It can, in fact, be any `bool` expression involving any appropriate combination of `bool` values and operators such as `&&`, `||`, and `!`.

For example, Program 4.3 is a program to help its users decide whether or not they need to wear a coat when going out. The program uses the rule that the user should wear a coat if it's cold or raining outside. It asks the user to say whether or not it is cold and then whether or not it is raining and stores the answers as `int` values (where 1 means yes and any other value means no). Based on the answers to these questions, the program uses an `if` statement to decide whether to tell the user to wear a coat or not. The condition used to decide whether or not to wear a coat is as follows:

```
(coldOut == YES) || (rainingOut == YES)
```

where YES is a constant with the value 1. If it is cold out *or* it is raining out the condition will be `true` and the message `"You better wear a coat today!"` will be displayed.

```
/* A program to illustrate the use of a complex */
/* condition in an if statement Advises the user whether or */
/* not to wear a coat when going out. */

using tcdIO;

class WearCoat
{
 private const int YES = 1;

 public static void Main ()
 {
    Terminal terminal;
    int coldOut, rainingOut; // used to store weather conidtions

    /* create an object to represent the terminal */
    terminal = new Terminal();

    /* ask the user if its cold */
    coldOut = terminal.ReadInt("Is it cold today? ");

    /* ask the user if its raining */
    rainingOut = terminal.ReadInt("Is it raining today? ");
```

```
    /* check if its cold or raining */
    if ((coldOut == YES) || (rainingOut == YES))
    {
      /* yes - advise the user to wear a coat */
      terminal.WriteLine("You better wear a coat today!");
    }
    else
    {
      /* no - advise the user not to wear a coat */
      terminal.WriteLine("There's no need to wear a coat today!");
    }
  }
}
```

Program 4.3   A program to illustrate the use of a complex condition in an `if` statement.

Figure 4.11 shows the result of running the program when the user answers that it's not cold and not raining. Figure 4.12 shows the result of running the program when the user answers that it's cold but not raining.

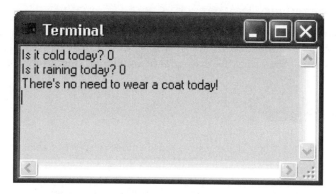

Figure 4.11   The execution of Program 4.3 on a fine day.

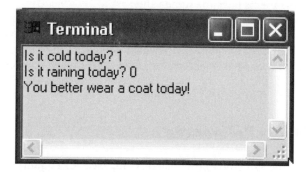

Figure 4.12   The execution of Program 4.3 on a cold day.

Comparing `bool` Values

We saw earlier that we can test values of most numeric types to see if they are equal or to compare their relative magnitudes. We can also compare values of type `bool` for equality and inequality. However, it makes no sense to compare the relative magnitude of two `bool` values. Thus, the only operators available to compare `bool`s are `==` and `!=`. In particular, note that we can't use `>`, `<`, `>=`, or `<=` with `bool` values.

Given the following variable definitions:

```
bool answer, gameOver = false;
int period = 2;
```

we can perform the following comparisons. In each case the result of the comparison is either `true` or `false` and is stored in the `bool` variable `answer` by means of an assignment.

```
answer = gameOver == true; // false
```

In this first example, we compare the current value of `gameOver` with the value `true`. Since they are not equal, the answer is `false`.

```
answer = gameOver == false; // true
```

In the second example, we compare the current value of `gameOver` with the value `false`. Since the values are equal, the answer is `true`.

```
answer = gameOver != (period < 4); // true
```

In the final example, we compare the current value of `gameOver` with the value of the condition `period < 4`. Since `period < 4` is `true`, the values are not equal. However, since we are testing that the values are not equal (using the `!=` operator), the answer is `true`.

Comparing Objects

So far, we have seen that it is possible to compare values of most of the simple types that we have met. As we will see in this section and the next, it is also possible to compare objects and object references.

In fact, we can also use `==` and `!=` to compare two objects to see whether or not they contain the same value. For example, we might want to see if two different instances of `string` actually contain the same sequence of letters. To do so we simply use `==` to compare the objects as shown in Program 4.4. As the output from the program (shown in Figure 4.13) shows, the answer is that the two objects have the same value.

In general, `==` and `!=` compare the entire contents of the two objects concerned in order to decide whether or not they are equal. If both objects have exactly the same values for all of their attributes then they are considered to be equal, otherwise they are not. As usual, `==` and `!=` can only be used to compare objects of the same type. Clearly, objects of different types could never be equal.

Comparing Object References

Object references (of the same type) can also be compared for equality and inequality using the `==` and `!=` operators. Two object references are equal only when they both refer to the

```
/* a program to compare the contents of two strings */
using tcdIO;

class CompareStringValues
{
  public static void Main()
  {
    Terminal terminal;
    string professor, lecturer;

    /* create an object to represent the terminal */
    terminal = new Terminal();

    /* create two strings with the same value */
    professor = "Prof. Smith";
    lecturer = string.Copy("Prof. Smith");

    /* check if the strings have the same value */
    if (professor == lecturer)
    {
      terminal.WriteLine("Professor and lecturer have the same value.");
    }
    else
    {
      terminal.WriteLine("Professor and lecturer have different values.");
    }
  }
}
```

Program 4.4   A program to illustrate comparison of string values.

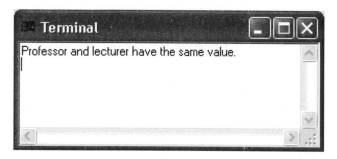

Figure 4.13   The execution of Program 4.4.

same object (or when they are both null). Two object references are not equal if they refer
to different objects.

For example, Program 4.5 describes a simple class whose instances represent cities, where
each city has a name, a latitude, and a longitude. Program 4.6 creates two different instances
of the class City representing Dublin and London. The variable City1 refers to the object
representing Dublin, while City2 refers to the object representing London. We use an if
statement to compare the two references and report whether or not they are equal. Notice
that to indicate that we want to compare the references rather than the values of the objects,
we have to precede the identifier of each variable with (object). In this case, since the two

```
/* A class whose instances represent cities */

class City
{
  private string name;
  private double latitude, longitude;

  /* initialize a new instance of City */
  public City(string newName, double newLatitude, double newLongitude)
  {
    this.name = newName;
    this.latitude = newLatitude;
    this.longitude = newLongitude;
  }

  /* return name of city */
  public string GetName()
  {
    return this.name;
  }

  /* return latitude */
  public double GetLatitude()
  {
    return this.latitude;
  }

  /* return longitude */
  public double GetLongitude()
  {
    return this.longitude;
  }
}
```

Program 4.5   Class City.

```
/* A program to illustrate comparison */
/* of object references */

using tcdIO;

class CompareReferences
{
  public static void Main ()
  {
    Terminal terminal;
    City city1, city2; // two references to instances of City

    /* create an object to represent the terminal */
    terminal = new Terminal();

    /* create an object to represent Dublin */
    city1 = new City("Dublin", 64.5, 4.5);

    /* create an object to represent London */
    city2 = new City("London", 61.5, 1.5);
```

```
    /* check if city1 and city2 refer to the same object */
    if ((object)city1 == (object)city2)
    {
      /* yes - tell the user */
      terminal.WriteLine("city1 and city2 refer to the same object!");
    }
    else
    {
      /* no - tell the user */
      terminal.WriteLine("city1 and city2 refer to different objects!");
    }
  }
}
```

Program 4.6   A program to illustrate comparison of object references.

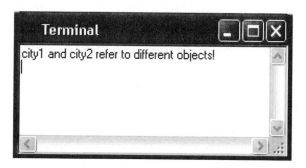

Figure 4.14   The execution of Program 4.6.

references refer to different objects, the program will always print the message "city1 and
city2 refer to different objects!" as shown in Figure 4.14.

  Figure 4.15 illustrates the variables and objects that exist just before the if statement in
Program 4.6 is executed. There are two different variables and each refers to a different object.
Now let's modify the program slightly by adding an assignment statement in which we assign
the value of city1 to city2 as shown in Program 4.7. Figure 4.16 illustrates the variables
and objects that now exist just before the if statement is executed. Here, both variables refer
to the same object – the instance of City representing Dublin. When we compare the two
references, we will always find that they are equal as shown in Figure 4.17.

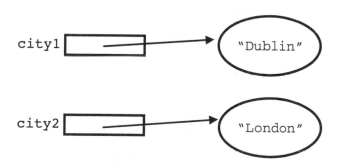

Figure 4.15   The variables and objects used by Program 4.6.

```
/* A program to illustrate comparison of object references (revised) */

using tcdIO;

class CompareReferences2
{
  public static void Main ()
  {
    Terminal terminal;
    City city1, city2; // two references to instances of City

    /* create an object to represent the terminal */
    terminal = new Terminal();

    /* create an object to represent Dublin */
    city1 = new City("Dublin", 64.5, 4.5);

    /* create an object to represent London */
    city2 = new City("London", 61.5, 1.5);

    /* copy reference to object representing Dublin to city2 */
    city2 = city1;

    /* check if city1 and city2 refer to the same object */
    if ((object)city1 == (object)city2)
    {
      /* yes - tell the user */
      terminal.WriteLine("city1 and city2 refer to the same object!");
    }
    else
    {
      /* no - tell the user */
      terminal.WriteLine("city1 and city2 refer to different objects!");
    }
  }
}
```

Program 4.7　A program to illustrate comparison of object references (revised).

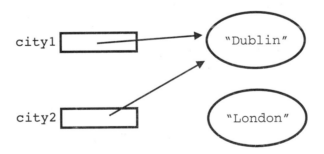

Figure 4.16　The variables and objects used by Program 4.7.

As another example, Program 4.8 compares two different instances of class `string` (which happen to contain the same value) as shown in Figure 4.18.

When the program executes, we find that `professor` and `lecturer` are not equal. This shouldn't be a surprise. As Figure 4.18 shows, `professor` and `lecturer` refer to different objects (albeit objects that have the same value). When we compare references we are not

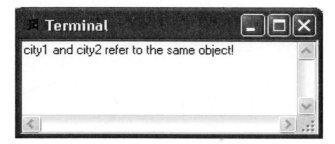

Figure 4.17   The execution of Program 4.7.

```
/* A program to illustrate comparison */
/* of references to strings */

using tcdIO;

class CompareStringReferences
{
    public static void Main()
    {
        Terminal terminal;
        string professor, lecturer;

        /* create an object to represent the terminal */
        terminal = new Terminal();

        /* create two Strings with copy of the same value */
        professor = "Prof. Smith";
        lecturer = string.Copy("Prof. Smith");


        /* check if the references are equal */
        if ((object)professor == (object)lecturer)
        {
            /* true if both references refer to the same object */
            terminal.WriteLine("Professor and lecturer" +
                                    "refer to the same object.");
        }
        else
        {
            terminal.WriteLine("Professor and lecturer refer to" +
                                    "different objects.");
        }
    }
}
```

Program 4.8   A program to illustrate comparison of references to strings.

asking if the referenced objects have the *same value*, rather we are asking if the referenced objects are the *same object*. Again, the distinction between an object's identity and its value is crucial. It is, of course, quite possible that different objects may have the same value!

By the way, did you notice that Program 4.8 uses a method to copy a `string` when making the second `string` object:

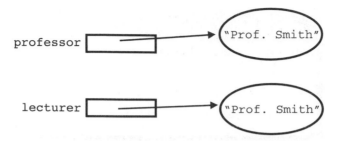

Figure 4.18 The variables and objects used by Program 4.8.

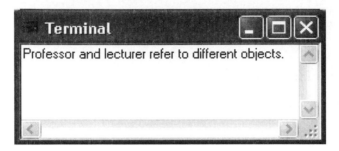

Figure 4.19 The execution of Program 4.8.

```
professor = "Prof. Smith";
lecturer = string.Copy("Prof. Smith");
```

If it didn't, for example, if we had written

```
professor = "Prof. Smith";
lecturer = "Prof. Smith";
```

then both variables would have referred to the same object! In fact, C# uses only a single instance of class `string` to represent all `string` literals that have the same contents even if that literal occurs several times in the program.

Nested `if` Statements

As we have seen, an `if` statement specifies two alternative sequences of statements to be executed depending on the value of some condition. Both of these statement sequences can contain any statements we want. In particular, either might include one or more further `if` statements. Thus, an `if` statement might contain one or more further `if` statements within it. These `if` statements are called *nested* `if` statements and are said to be *nested within* the outer enclosing `if` statement.

As an example of the use of nested `if` statements, consider writing a program to assist your friendly local "bouncer" in deciding who to allow into his night-club. Faced with a potential customer our program has to make a decision as to whether or not that person should be allowed into the club according to the following rules:

- nobody under 25 is allowed in
- scruffy people are not normally allowed in, but
- scruffy people are allowed in if they agree to put on a tie.

We will rely on the bouncer to provide the information about the age and scruffiness of the customer, and their willingness to put on a tie, and the program will report whether or not the potential customer is allowed in.

We might implement the first rule as a simple if statement where the condition is that the customer's age, to be input by the bouncer, is greater than 25:

```
int age;
age = terminal.ReadInt("Enter customer's age:");
if (age >= 25)
{
  terminal.WriteLine("Allowed in!");
}
else
{
terminal.WriteLine("Customer is too young!");
}
```

Note, however, that being old enough is not sufficient. There is another condition to be satisfied before the customer can be allowed in: the customer has to be neatly dressed. In other words, in the case where the customer is old enough to enter, we need to check that they are also neat enough. Checking this condition can be implemented with another if statement. This if statement replaces the call to print the "Allowed in!" message.

```
int age;
string answer;
age = terminal.ReadInt("Enter customer's age:");
if (age >= 25)
{
  answer = terminal.ReadString("Is customer neatly dressed?");
  if (answer == "yes")
  {
    terminal.WriteLine("Allowed in!");
  }
  else
  {
    terminal.WriteLine("Customer is too scruffy!");
  }
} else {
    terminal.WriteLine("Customer is too young!");
}
```

The second rule is implemented by a nested if statement contained within the first part of the enclosing if statement. The program asks the bouncer if the customer is neatly dressed. If the answer is yes then the customer will be allowed in.

We still have one rule to incorporate in our program. In the case where the customer is deemed to be too scruffy to get in, we should give him or her(!) a chance to put on a tie. The program asks the bouncer if the customer is willing to wear a tie. If so, they are allowed in, otherwise they are refused. We use yet another (nested) if statement to implement the check:

```
int age;
string answer;
age = terminal.ReadInt("Enter customer's age:");
if (age >= 25)
{
  answer = terminal.ReadString("Is customer neatly dressed?");
  if (answer == "yes")
  {
    terminal.WriteLine("Allowed in!");
  }
  else
  {
  answer = terminal.ReadString("Will customer put on a tie?");
  if (answer == "yes")
  {
    terminal.WriteLine("Allowed in!");
  }
  else
  {
    terminal.WriteLine("Customer is too scruffy!");
  }
  }
}
else
{
  terminal.WriteLine("Customer is too young!");
}
```

This final if statement is nested within the else part of the previous nested if statement. If fact, we can nest if statements anywhere within the statements of another if statement.

The full program is shown in Program 4.9. The execution of the program is illustrated in Figure 4.20 (where the customer is refused entry due to their age) and Figure 4.21 (where a scruffy customer is allowed in after agreeing to put on a tie).

```
/* A program to illustrate the use of */
/* nested if statements */

using tcdIO;

class Nightclub
{
  const int AGELIMIT = 25;  // no kiddies allowed
  const string GOODANSWER = "yes";

  public static void Main ()
  {
    Terminal terminal;
    int age;
    string answer;
```

```
   /* create an object to represent the terminal */
   terminal = new Terminal();

   /* check customers age */
   age = terminal.ReadInt("Enter customer's age: ");
   if (age >= AGELIMIT)
   {
     // so far so good - check customers dress
     answer = terminal.ReadString("Is customer neatly dressed? ");
     if (answer == GOODANSWER)
     {
       terminal.WriteLine("Allowed in!");
     }
     else
     {
       // give scruffy people a chance - check for tie
       answer = terminal.ReadString("Will customer put on a tie? ");
       if (answer == GOODANSWER)
       {
          terminal.WriteLine("Allowed in!");
       }
       else
       {
          terminal.WriteLine("Customer is too scruffy!");
       }
     }
   }
   else
   {
     terminal.WriteLine("Customer is too young!");
   }
 }
}
```

Program 4.9   A program to illustrate the use of nested if statements.

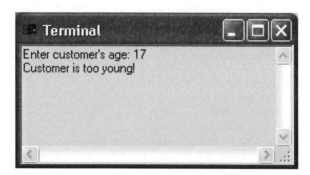

Figure 4.20   The execution of Program 4.9 when the customer is too young.

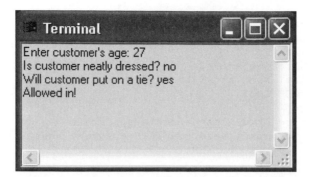

Figure 4.21   The execution of Program 4.9 when the customer is allowed in.

Note that in the special case where the statement sequences making up each of the alternative courses of action in an if statement consist of only a single statement, the braces that normally surround the statement sequence can be omitted. Thus, Program 4.9 can be rewritten as shown in Program 4.10. Notice that a single if statement, including all the statements that make up its statement sequences, counts as just a single statement.

```
/* A program to illustrate the use of */
/* nested if statements (revised) */

using tcdIO;

class Nightclub
{
  const int AGELIMIT = 25;  // no kiddies allowed
  const string GOODANSWER = "yes";

  public static void Main ()
  {
    Terminal terminal;
    int age;
    string answer;

    /* create an object to represent the terminal */
    terminal = new Terminal();

    /* check customers age */
    age = terminal.ReadInt("Enter customer's age: ");
    if (age >= AGELIMIT)
    {
      // so far so good - check customers dress
      answer = terminal.ReadString("Is customer neatly dressed? ");
      if (answer == GOODANSWER)
       terminal.WriteLine("Allowed in!");
      else
      {
```

```
      // give scruffy people a chance - check for tie
      answer = terminal.ReadString("Will customer put on a tie? ");
      if (answer == GOODANSWER)
        terminal.WriteLine("Allowed in!");
      else
        terminal.WriteLine("Customer is too scruffy!");
    }
  }
  else
    terminal.WriteLine("Customer is too young!");
  }
}
```

Program 4.10   A program to illustrate the use of nested i f statements (revised).

Using if to Select One of Many Alternative Courses of Action

We have seen that we can use C#'s if statement to choose one of two different courses of action depending on the value of a bool condition. Sometimes, however, we want to choose from a larger number of possible courses of action. For example, there may be three or four different possibilities from which we want to choose just one. In such cases we can make use of multiple if statements to decide on the course of action to be taken.

As an example of using multiple if statements to select one of many alternative courses of action, consider a program to calculate the bonus due to an employee according to the following rules (see Program 4.11 and Figure 4.22):

- if the employee's salary is less than $10 000, the bonus is 1%,
- if the employee's salary is between $10 000 and $20 000 the bonus is 2%,
- if the employee's salary is between $20 000 and $30 000 the bonus is 3%,
- if the employee's salary is greater than $30 000 the bonus is 5%.

The program will make use of a sequence of nested if statements. The first tests if the salary is less than $10 000. If so, a bonus of 1% is calculated in the if part. The else part consists of a nested if statement that handles the remaining cases. This nested if statement tests if the salary is between $10 000 and $20 000. If so, the if part calculates the bonus of 2% while the corresponding else part handles the remaining cases. A final nested if statement is used to distinguish the last two cases. Notice that we need three nested if statements to choose one out of the four possible courses of action.

```
double salary, bonus;
if (salary < 10000.0)
  bonus = salary * 0.01;
else if ((salary >= 10000.0) && (salary < 20000.0))
  bonus = salary * 0.02;
else if ((salary >= 20000.0) && (salary < 30000.0))
  bonus = salary * 0.03;
else // salary > 30K
  bonus = salary * 0.05;
```

You should also notice the style in which the if statements are written to emphasize that they represent four mutually exclusive courses of action. The code below shows the same example modified to print out the bonus that the employee is to receive as it is calculated.

```
/* A program to illustrate the use of multi-way selection */

using tcdIO;

class Bonus
{
  const double ONEPERCENT = 0.01;
  const double TWOPERCENT = 0.02;
  const double THREEPERCENT = 0.03;
  const double FIVEPERCENT = 0.05;

  public static void Main ()
  {
    Terminal terminal;
    double salary, bonus;

    /* create an object to represent the terminal */
    terminal = new Terminal();

    /* ask user to enter salary */
    salary = terminal.ReadDouble("How much do you earn? ");

    /* now calulcate bonus due according to sliding scale */
    if (salary < 10000.0)
      bonus = salary * ONEPERCENT;
    else if ((salary >= 10000.0) && (salary < 20000.0))
      bonus = salary * TWOPERCENT;
    else if ((salary >= 20000.0) && (salary < 30000.0))
      bonus = salary * THREEPERCENT;
    else // salary > 30K
      bonus = salary * FIVEPERCENT;

    /* report bonus due */
    terminal.WriteLine("You are due a bonus of: $" + bonus + ".");
  }
}
```

Program 4.11 A program to illustrate the use of multi-way selection.

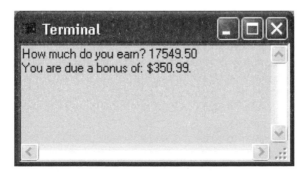

Figure 4.22 The execution of Program 4.11.

It serves only to illustrate what a nested `if` statement that has multiple statements in each course of action looks like. Notice the use of braces.

```
double salary, bonus;
if (salary < 10000.0)
{
  terminal.println("1%");
  bonus = salary * 0.01;
}
else if ((salary >= 10000.0) && (salary < 20000.0))
{
  terminal.println("2%");
  bonus = salary * 0.02;
}
else if ((salary >= 20000.0) && (salary < 30000.0))
{
  terminal.println("3%");
  bonus = salary * 0.03;
}
else
{
  terminal.println("5%");
  bonus = salary * 0.05;
}
```

Defensive Programming

Now that we are armed with the `if` statement, we can write programs that are capable of reacting to different circumstances each time they are run. In particular, we can write programs that are prepared to deal with any undesirable or illegal situations that might arise, for example, because users input incorrect values in certain situations. Programs can then be written to detect such possible errors and handle them appropriately when they occur. By writing programs in this manner, we ensure that our programs always do something sensible and always produce meaningful results! This style of programming is often referred to as *defensive programming*.

As an example, consider Program 4.12, which simply adds the two positive `int`s entered by the user and prints the result. This program will work most of the time as shown in Figure 4.23. However, if the user enters two large positive numbers, the program will produce unpredictable results due to integer overflow as shown in Figure 4.24.

In particular, execution of the statement:

```
result = value1 + value2;
```

will cause an overflow if:

```
value1 + value2 > int.MaxValue
```

where `int.MaxValue` is a constant defining the largest possible value of type `int`.

To guard against this possibility, we can use an `if` statement to make sure that the addition can be carried out safely. For example, we could try:

```
/* A program to illustrate the need for defensive programming*/

using tcdIO;

class IntAdder
{
  public static void Main ()
  {
    Terminal terminal;
    int value1, value2, result;

    /* create an object to represent the terminal */
    terminal = new Terminal();

    /* ask user to enter the numbers to be added */
    value1 = terminal.ReadInt("Enter first number: ");
    value2 = terminal.ReadInt("Enter second number: ");

    /* now do the addition */
    result = value1 + value2;

    /* Write out the answer */
    terminal.WriteLine("The answer is: " + result + ".");
  }
}
```

Program 4.12   A program to illustrate the need for defensive programming.

```
    if (value1 + value2 <= int.MaxValue)
      result = value1 + value2;
    else
      // handle error
```

Unfortunately, this might still result in an overflow error when we compute value1 + value2 as part of the comparison! In fact, we need to check that:

```
    value1 + value2 <= int.MaxValue
```

without actually computing value1 + value2! More specifically, we need to rearrange

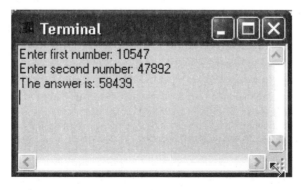

Figure 4.23   The execution of Program 4.12 for small values.

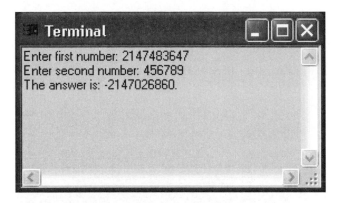

Figure 4.24   The execution of Program 4.12 for large values.

the comparison so that it does not require the addition to be performed. One possibility is as follows:

```
value1 <= int.MaxValue - value2
```

The resulting if statement becomes:

```
if (value1 <= int.MaxValue - value2)
  result = value1 + value2;
else
  // handle error
```

Program 4.13 shows the full program, while Figures 4.25 and 4.26 show its output.

```
/* A program to illustrate defensive programming */

using tcdIO;

class IntAdder
{
  public static void Main ()
  {
    Terminal terminal;
    int value1, value2, result;

    /* create an object to represent the terminal */
    terminal = new Terminal();

    /* ask user to enter the numbers to be added */
    value1 = terminal.ReadInt("Enter first number: ");
    value2 = terminal.ReadInt("Enter second number: ");

    /* check if addition is possible without overflow */
    if (value1 <= int.MaxValue - value2)
    {
      /* yes - do the addition and Write out the result */
      result = value1 + value2;
      terminal.WriteLine("The answer is: " + result + ".");
```

```
    }
    else
    {
      /* no - report that addition is not possible */
      terminal.WriteLine("These integers are too large to add.");
    }
  }
}
```

Program 4.13 A program to illustrate defensive programming.

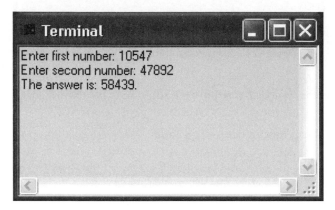

Figure 4.25 The execution of Program 4.13 for small values.

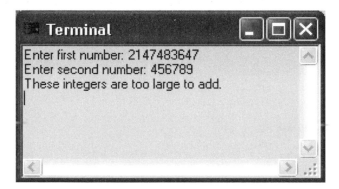

Figure 4.26 The execution of Program 4.13 for large values.

Using an `if` Statement Without `else`

As well as allowing us to chose between two alternative courses of action, the `if` statement can be used to handle special cases that arise occasionally. For example, say we want to calculate the number of days in a year. Most years have 365 days. However, in a leap year, we need to add an extra day. Handling the leap year constitutes a special case for which a special course of action must be taken. To write a program that determines the number of days in a given year, we can use an `if` statement to test for a leap year and add on the extra day. In this case no action is required if the year is not a leap year. Thus, no `else` part is required.

```
int numDays;
bool leapYear;
....
numDays = 365; // default
if (leapYear)
   numDays = numDays + 1;
terminal.println("This year has " + numDays + " days.");
```

In this program, we assign the default value of 365 days to numDays. Only in the special case of a leap year, do we add 1 to numDays. If the condition specified in the `if` statement is `true`, the corresponding statement sequence is executed and the program continues with the next statement. If the condition is `false`, the `if` part is not executed and execution simply continues with the statement following the `if` statement.

More About && and ||

As we have described them so far `&&` gives `true` only when both of its arguments are `true`, while `||` gives `true` when at least one of its arguments is `true`. However, you should note that it may not be necessary to evaluate both of the arguments of `&&` or `||` in order to determine what the result will be. For example, if the first argument of `&&` evaluates to `false`, then the result of the `&&` operator must be `false`, irrespective of the value of the second argument. Likewise, if the first argument of `||` evaluates to `true`, then the result of the `||` operator must be `true`, irrespective of the value of the second argument.

C# takes advantage of this to avoid evaluating the arguments of `&&` and `||` when possible. Thus, if the first argument of `&&` evaluates to `false`, the second argument is not evaluated and the result is `false`. Likewise, if the first argument of `||` evaluates to `true`, the second argument is not evaluated and the result is `true`. Thus, `&&` and `||` are said to be evaluated in *short-circuit* form.

In some sense, we can consider each of these operators to be implemented using an `if` statement. For example, the expression:

```
answer = boolVariable1 && boolVariable2;
```

can be considered to be equivalent to:

```
if (!boolVariable1) // i.e. if boolVariable1 is false
   answer = false;   // assign false to answer immediately
else
   answer = boolVariable2;
     // assign the value of boolVariable2 to answer
```

Likewise,

```
answer = boolVariable1 || boolVariable2;
```

```
/* A program to illustrate short circuit evaluation of && */

using tcdIO;

class CheckFactor
{
  public static void Main ()
  {
    Terminal terminal;
    int number, factor;

    /* create an object to represent the terminal */
    terminal = new Terminal();

    /* ask user to enter the numbers  */
    number = terminal.ReadInt("Enter number: ");
    factor = terminal.ReadInt("Enter factor: ");

    if ((factor != 0) && (number % factor == 0))
      terminal.WriteLine(number + " is divisible by " + factor + ".");
    else
      terminal.WriteLine(number + " is not divisible by " +
                                              factor + ".");
  }
}
```

Program 4.14   A program to illustrate short circuit evaluation of &&.

can be considered to be equivalent to:

```
if (boolVariable1) // i.e. if boolVariable1 is true
  answer = true;   // assign true to answer immediately
else
  answer = boolVariable2;
    // assign the value of boolVariable2 to answer
```

As an example of the use of short-circuit evaluation, consider Program 4.14 which reads two ints from the user and reports whether or not the first is exactly divisible by the second. To check if one integer is exactly divisible by another, we take the remainder on dividing the first by the second and see if it is zero. If so, the numbers divide exactly. However, because

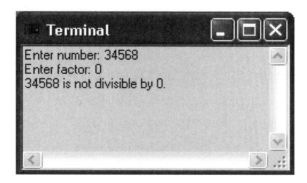

Figure 4.27   The execution of Program 4.14 when the divisor is zero.

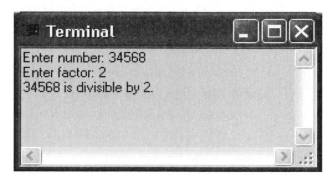

Figure 4.28   The execution of Program 4.14 when the divisor is non-zero.

the user of the program enters the divisor, we first need to check that it is not zero. We could use nested `if` statements to perform the two checks. However, we can combine the two tests using `&&` as shown in the program listing. Because of the short circuit evaluation of `&&`, we are guaranteed that the `%` operation in the second part of the condition will not be attempted if the test for zero in the first part of the condition fails.

The C# `switch` Statement

The `if` statement is designed primarily to allow a program to choose one of two alternative courses of action to execute. We saw earlier that a program can use multiple `if` statements to choose one of many alternative courses of action based on the current values of some set of conditions. Notice that using multiple `if` statements in this way may require that several conditions be evaluated before the one that selects the required course of action is found.

In fact, C# provides an alternative selection statement designed specifically to be used when a choice of one (or indeed more) of many possible courses of action to be executed is to be made. This statement is called the `switch` statement. While the decision as to which branch of an `if` statement is to be executed can only be based on the value of a `bool` expression, the decision as to which branch of a `switch` statement is to be executed is based on the value of a numeric, character, or `string` expression. Essentially, every branch of a `switch` statement is associated with a possible value of the expression. When a `switch` statement is executed, the expression is evaluated and the branch (if any) associated with the resulting value is executed.

Thus, as Figure 4.29 illustrates, a `switch` statement consists of an expression (in brackets) and a list of the possible courses of action to be taken (in braces). The expression may be of any predefined type such as `byte`, `short`, `int`, `char`, or `string`. Each possible course of action consists of one or more labels (each followed by a colon) and a statement sequence. A label specifies a possible value of the expression that will result in the corresponding course of action being selected and its statement sequence executed. The keyword `case` is used to introduce a label.

The `switch` statement imposes one very significant restriction on how the value of a label is specified – the value of a label must be specified as a constant expression. A constant expression is one that can be evaluated fully at compile time. Typically, a constant expression is composed of some combination of literals and constants combined with appropriate operators. This restriction means that there may be times when it is more appropriate to

```
switch (<expression>) {

  case <constant expression1>:

    <statement sequence 1>

  case <constant expression2>:

    <statement sequence 2>

  ....

  case <constant expressionN>:

    <statement sequenceN>
}
```

Figure 4.29 The syntax of the C# `switch` statement.

use multiple `if` statements rather than a single `switch` statement to choose one of many alternatives.

When a `switch` statement is executed, its expression is evaluated. If the value of one of the labels *matches* the value of the expression then the corresponding statement sequence is executed. To avoid any ambiguity, no two labels may have the same value. Perhaps surprisingly, once a statement sequence is executed, the programmer must decide the next statement to execute. Typically, we include a C# `break` statement as the last statement in each statement sequence in order to cause the execution of the enclosing `switch` statement to terminate as illustrated in Figure 4.30.

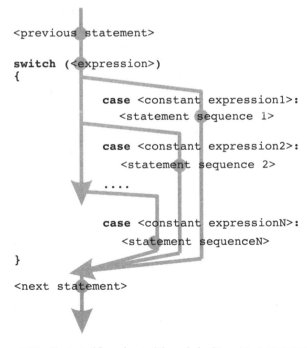

Figure 4.30 The typical flow of control through the C# `switch` statement.

As an example of the use of the `switch` statement let's consider writing a program to calculate the postage to be paid to send a parcel to one of the fifteen countries in the European Union. Typically, the cost of the postage will be different depending on the country to which the parcel is being sent. Our program will make use of a class `Parcel` whose instances represent individual parcels (as shown in Program 4.15). Every parcel has as attributes an address (to which it is to be delivered) and a weight. Addresses are represented by instances of class `Address` and each address includes the name of the appropriate street and town as well as a code identifying the country to which it belongs. The codes for each of the countries are defined as constants in class `Address` as shown in Program 4.16.

The most important method in class `Parcel` is the one to calculate the cost of the postage due on the parcel. In our example, the postage depends only on the country to which the

```
/* A class whose instances represent parcels */

class Parcel
{
  private Address address;
  private double weight;
  private bool delivered = false;

  /* initialize a new instace of Parcel */
  public Parcel(Address addr, double wght)
  {
    this.address = addr;
    this.weight = wght;
  }

  /* report whether or not the parcel has been delivered */
  public bool IsDelivered()
  {
    return this.delivered;
  }

  /* record the delivery of the parcel */
  public void Deliver()
  {
    this.delivered = true;
  }

  /* determine the cost of sending the package */
  public double CalculatePostage()
  {
    double cost = 0.0;

    switch (address.GetCountry())
    {
     case Address.IRELAND:
        cost = 5.0;
        break;
     case Address.UK:
        cost = 10.0;
        break;
     case Address.FRANCE:
        cost = 15.0;
        break;
```

```
        case Address.GERMANY:
            cost = 15.0;
            break;
        case Address.AUSTRIA:
            cost = 15.0;
            break;
        case Address.SPAIN:
            cost = 20.0;
            break;
        case Address.PORTUGAL:
            cost = 20.0;
            break;
        case Address.ITALY:
            cost = 20.0;
            break;
        case Address.GREECE:
            cost = 20.0;
            break;
        case Address.DENMARK:
            cost = 25.0;
            break;
        case Address.SWEDEN:
            cost = 25.0;
            break;
        case Address.FINLAND:
            cost = 25.0;
            break;
        case Address.BELGIUM:
            cost = 12.0;
            break;
        case Address.HOLLAND:
            cost = 12.0;
            break;
        case Address.LUXEMBURG:
            cost = 12.0;
            break;
    }
    return cost;
  }
}
```

Program 4.15 Class `Parcel`.

package is to be delivered. `CalculatePostage` uses a `switch` statement to choose between the 15 different possibilities based on the value of the country code in the parcel's address. Notice that every possible country code is associated with exactly one statement sequence and every statement sequence ends with a `break` statement. Thus, every time that the method is run, exactly one of the specified sequences is executed to give a value to `cost`.

Program 4.17 shows a program to calculate the postage due on a parcel whose address and weight are entered by the user. Notice the use of an `if` statement to ensure that the country code entered by the user corresponds to one of the countries of the European Union! The execution of the program is illustrated in Figure 4.31.

It may of course happen that there are values of the expression for which there is no associated statement sequence. In that case, the execution of the `switch` statement terminates immediately after the evaluation of the expression. On the other hand, there may be times

```
/* A class whose instances represent addresses */

class Address
{
  /* define some contry codes */
  public const int IRELAND = 0;
  public const int UK = 1;
  public const int FRANCE = 2;
  public const int GERMANY = 3;
  public const int AUSTRIA = 4;
  public const int SPAIN = 5;
  public const int PORTUGAL = 6;
  public const int ITALY = 7;
  public const int GREECE = 8;
  public const int DENMARK = 9;
  public const int SWEDEN = 10;
  public const int FINLAND = 11;
  public const int BELGIUM = 12;
  public const int HOLLAND = 13;
  public const int LUXEMBURG = 14;

  private string street;
  private string town;
  private int country;

  /* initialize a new instance of Address */
  public Address(string s, string t, int c)
  {
    this.street = s;
    this.town = t;
    this.country = c;
  }

  /* return the street name */
  public string GetStreet()
  {
    return this.street;
  }

  /* return the town name */
  public string GetTown()
  {
    return this.town;
  }

  /* return the country code */
  public int GetCountry()
  {
    return this.country;
  }
}
```

Program 4.16   Class Address.

```
/* A program to illustrate the use of the C# switch statement */
/* Calculates the postage due on a parcel */

using tcdIO;

class Postage
{
  public static void Main ()
  {
    Terminal terminal;
    Address address;
    Parcel parcel;
    double weight;
    string street, town;
    int country;

    /* create an object to represent the terminal */
    terminal = new Terminal();

    /* get details of parcel from user*/
    terminal.WriteLine("Please enter the details of your parcel.");
    weight = terminal.ReadDouble("Enter weight of parcel: ");
    terminal.WriteLine("Enter destination address: ");
    street = terminal.ReadString("Street: ");
    town = terminal.ReadString("Town: ");
    country = terminal.ReadInt("Country code: ");

    /* check that the counrty code is valid before proceeding */
    if ((country >= Address.IRELAND) && (country <= Address.LUXEMBURG))
    {
      /* create objects to represent address and parcel */
      address = new Address(street, town, country);
      parcel = new Parcel(address, weight);
      /* report the cost of sending the parcel */
      terminal.WriteLine("The cost of sending this parcel is $"
                                  + parcel.CalculatePostage() + ".");
    }
    else
      terminal.WriteLine("Sorry, can't be done!");
  }
}
```

Program 4.17 A program to illustrate the use of the C# switch statement.

when several different values of the switch expression should result in the same statement sequence being executed. To handle these cases, C# allows multiple labels to be associated with each statement sequence. If the expression evaluates to any of the corresponding values then that statement sequence is executed, as illustrated in Figure 4.32.

Program 4.18 shows a modified version of class Parcel that takes advantage of these rules. Notice that we have initialized cost to 5.00 – the cost of sending a parcel to Ireland – and left out the case for Ireland from the switch statement. Thus, whenever, the code for Ireland is entered, no case in the switch statement will be selected and the value of cost will remain 5.00. Notice too that we have combined those cases that result in the same value being assigned to cost simply by using multiple labels for the corresponding statement sequence. Figures 4.33 and 4.34 show the execution of the program for parcels to Ireland and Spain respectively.

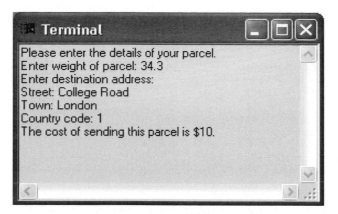

Figure 4.31   The execution of Program 4.17.

Sometimes there are cases where only a small subset of the values of the expression require different actions to be taken, while most of the values require the same default action to be taken. To handle such cases, the switch statement allows us to include a catch-all statement sequence that is executed whenever the value of the expression does not match any of the specified labels. Such a catch-all action, is introduced by the keyword default in place of the case label and must come at the end of the switch statement after all the other cases. For example, Program 4.19 shows another modification to class Parcel to allow the cost of sending a parcel to any other country in the world to be calculated using a flat rate of $50. As

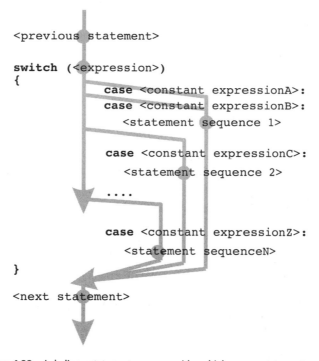

Figure 4.32   Labeling a statement sequence with multiple case statements.

```csharp
/* A class whose instances represent parcels */

class Parcel
{
  private Address address;
  private double weight;
  private bool delivered = false;

  /* initialize a new instace of Parcel */
  public Parcel(Address addr, double wght)
  {
    this.address = addr;
    this.weight = wght;
  }

  /* report whether or not the parcel has been delivered */
  public bool IsDelivered()
  {
    return  this.delivered;
  }

  /* record the delivery of the parcel */
  public void Deliver()
  {
    this.delivered = true;
  }

  /* determine the cost of sending the package */
  public double CalculatePostage()
  {
    double cost = 5.0;    // default to Ireland

    switch (address.GetCountry())
    {
     case Address.UK:
         cost = 10.0;
         break;
     case Address.FRANCE:    // France, Germany
     case Address.GERMANY:   // and Austria cost the same
     case Address.AUSTRIA:
         cost = 15.0;
         break;
     case Address.SPAIN:     // Likewise for Spain,
     case Address.PORTUGAL:  // Italy, Portugal and Greece
     case Address.ITALY:
     case Address.GREECE:
         cost = 20.0;
         break;
     case Address.DENMARK:   // Scandanavian countries
     case Address.SWEDEN:    // also cost the same
     case Address.FINLAND:
         cost = 25.0;
         break;
     case Address.BELGIUM:   // as do Benelux countries
     case Address.HOLLAND:
     case Address.LUXEMBURG:

         cost = 12.0;
         break;
```

```
  }
    return cost;
  }
}
```

Program 4.18   Class `Parcel` (revised).

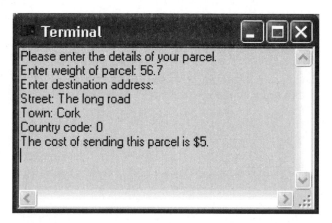

Figure 4.33   The execution of Program 4.18 when the parcel is to be delivered to Ireland.

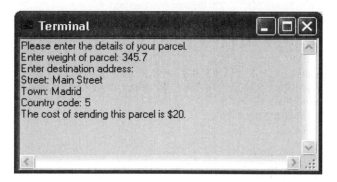

Figure 4.34   The execution of Program 4.18 when the parcel is to be delivered to Spain.

```
/* A class whose instances represent parcels (revised)*/

class Parcel
{
  private Address address;
  private double weight;
  private bool delivered = false;

  /* initialize a new instance of Parcel */
  public Parcel(Address addr, double wght)
  {
    this.address = addr;
    this.weight = wght;
  }
```

```csharp
/* report whether or not the parcel has been delivered */
public bool IsDelivered()
{
  return  this.delivered;
}

/* record the delivery of the parcel */
public void Deliver()
{
  this.delivered = true;
}

/* determine the cost of sending the package */
public double CalculatePostage()
{
  double cost = 0.0;
  switch (address.GetCountry())
  {
   case Address.IRELAND:
       cost = 5.0;
       break;
   case Address.UK:
       cost = 10.0;
       break;

   case Address.FRANCE:     // France, Germany
   case Address.GERMANY:    // and Austria cost the same
   case Address.AUSTRIA:
       cost = 15.0;
       break;
   case Address.SPAIN:      // Likewise for Spain,
   case Address.PORTUGAL:   // Italy, Portugal and Greece
   case Address.ITALY:
   case Address.GREECE:
       cost = 20.0;
       break;
   case Address.DENMARK:    // Scandanavian countries
   case Address.SWEDEN:     // also cost the same
   case Address.FINLAND:
       cost = 25.0;
       break;
   case Address.BELGIUM:    // as do Benelux countries
   case Address.HOLLAND:
   case Address.LUXEMBURG:
       cost = 12.0;
       break;
   default:                 // anywhere else in the world
       cost = 50.00;
       break;
  }
  return cost;
}
}
```

Program 4.19   Class `Parcel` (revised).

```
/* A program to illustrate the use of the C# switch statement (revised) */
/* Calculates the postage due on a parcel */

using tcdIO;

class Postage
{
  public static void Main ()
  {
    Terminal terminal;
    Address address;
    Parcel parcel;
    double weight;
    string street, town;
    int country;

    /* create an object to represent the terminal */
    terminal = new Terminal();

    /* get details of parcel from user*/
    terminal.WriteLine("Please enter the details of your parcel.");
    weight = terminal.ReadDouble("Enter weight of parcel: ");
    terminal.WriteLine("Enter destination address: ");
    street = terminal.ReadString("Street: ");
    town = terminal.ReadString("Town: ");
    country = terminal.ReadInt("Country code: ");

    /* check that the counrty code is valid before proceeding */
    if ((country >= Address.IRELAND))
    {
      /* create objects to represent address and parcel */
      address = new Address(street, town, country);
      parcel = new Parcel(address, weight);
      /* report the cost of sending the parcel */
      terminal.WriteLine("The cost of sending this parcel is $"
                              + parcel.CalculatePostage() + ".");
    }
    else
      terminal.WriteLine("Sorry, can't be done!");
  }
}
```

Program 4.20   A program to illustrate the use of the C# switch statement (revised).

Program 4.20 shows, the program has also been modified to allow the user to enter country codes other than those for the European Union countries by changing the condition on the if statement. The effect is to treat any positive number that has not been defined as a country code for one of the European Union countries as a country code for some other country. The execution of the program is shown in Figures 4.35 and 4.36 respectively.

Case Study: Solving Quadratic Equations

As a complete example of the use of the if statement consider writing a program to solve a quadratic equation. A quadratic equation is an equation of the form:

$$ax^2 + bx + c = 0$$

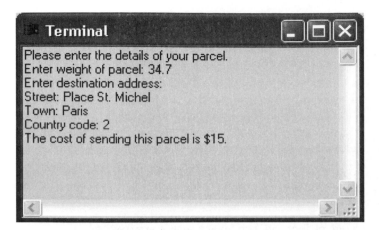

Figure 4.35   The execution of Program 4.20 for an European Union country.

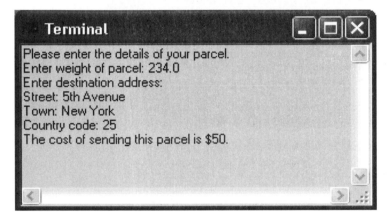

Figure 4.36   The execution of Program 4.20 for a non-European Union country.

where a, b, and c are real numbers. Such an equation usually describes a curve that crosses the x-axis in two places. For example, a graph of the equation:

$$-0.1x^2 + 1.5x - 5 = 0$$

is shown in Figure 4.37. Notice that this curve crosses the x-axis at x =5 and x =10.

The two values of x at which the curve crosses the x-axis are known as the *roots* of the equation. Given, the values of a, b, and c our program should calculate these values of x.

Fortunately, there is a well-known formula for calculating the roots of a quadratic equation. In particular, the two roots are given by the two values of:

$$\frac{-b \pm \sqrt{b^2 - 4ac}}{2a}.$$

Unfortunately, the equation does not work for all possible values of a, b, and c. Depending on the values of a, b, and c, the equation may degenerate to a non-quadratic equation (when a is 0) that may or may not have a single root; it may have only one root (when b^2 is equal to

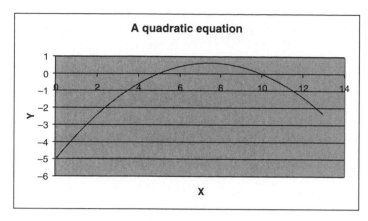

Figure 4.37   A quadratic equation.

$4ac$); or it may have two complex roots (when b^2 is less than $4ac$). The full set of possibilities is as follows:

- for $a = 0$ and $b = 0$, there is no solution,
- for $a = 0$ and $b <> 0$, there is one root,
- for $b^2 = 4ac$, there is one root,
- for $b^2 > 4ac$, there are two real roots,
- for $b^2 < 4ac$, there are two complex roots.

To write the program, we will not introduce any new classes. The Main method of the program will simply read the values of a, b, and c from the user and calculate the root(s) if possible. To do so we will use nested if statements to determine the appropriate action to take, as follows:

```
// read a, b, c from user
if (a == 0)
{
  if (b == 0)
    // no solution possible -- write error message
  else
    // calculate single root
}
else if (b*b == 4*a*c)
{
  // calculate single root
}
else if (b*b > 4*a*c)
{
  // calculate first real root
  // calculate second real root
}
else
{
  // calculate first imaginary root
  // calculate second imaginary root
}
```

The full program is shown in Program 4.21 and its execution in Figure 4.39.

```
/* A program to solve the quadratic equation */
/* ax^2 + bx + c = 0 */

using tcdIO;   // allow us to Read from terminal
using System;

class Quadratic
{
    public static void Main ()
    {
        Terminal terminal;
        double  a, b, c, underSqrt, tmp1, tmp2;

        /* create an object to represent the terminal */
        terminal = new Terminal();

        /* get a-c from user */
        a = terminal.ReadDouble("Enter a: ");
        b = terminal.ReadDouble("Enter b: ");
        c = terminal.ReadDouble("Enter c: ");

        /* solve equation and Write results */
        underSqrt = (b * b) - (4 * a * c);
        if (a == 0)
            if (b == 0)
                terminal.WriteLine("Sorry - no solution!");
            else
                terminal.WriteLine("Single root is: " + -c/b + ".");
        else if (underSqrt == 0)
            // b*b == 4*a*c
            terminal.WriteLine("Single root is: " + -b/(2 * a) + ".");
        else if (underSqrt > 0)
        {
            // b*b > 4*a*c
            // calculate real roots
            tmp1 = (-b + Math.Sqrt(underSqrt))/(2 * a);
            terminal.WriteLine("First root is: " + tmp1 + ".");
            tmp1 = (-b - Math.Sqrt(underSqrt))/(2 * a);
            terminal.WriteLine("Second root is: " + tmp1 + ".");
        }
        else
        {
            // b*b < 4*a*c
            // calculate imaginary roots
            tmp1 = -b/(2 * a);
            tmp2 = Math.Sqrt(-underSqrt)/(2 * a);
            terminal.WriteLine("First root is: " + tmp1
                                        + " + " + tmp2 + "i.");
            terminal.WriteLine("Second root is: " + tmp1
                                        + " - " + tmp2 + "i.");
        }
    }
}
```

Program 4.21   A program to solve the quadratic equation $ax^2 + bx + c = 0$.

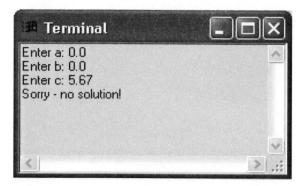

Figure 4.38   The execution of Program 4.21 when there are no roots.

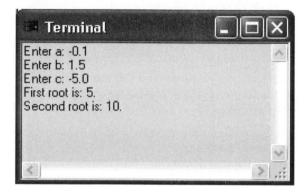

Figure 4.39   The execution of Program 4.21 when there are two real roots.

Summary

- type `bool` represents the value of a condition and has only two possible values: `true` and `false`
- we can have variables of type `bool`, expressions that yield values of type `bool`, methods that take inputs of type `bool`, and methods that return values of type `bool`
- the most important `bool` operators are `&&`, `||`, and `!`
- values of most of the simple numeric types can be compared using the `==`, `!=`, `<`, `>`, `<=`, and `>=` operators
- the `if` statement allows a program to choose between two alternative courses of action to be executed
- we can compare values of type `bool` for equality and inequality
- we can compare objects (i.e., their values) and object references for equality and inequality
- two objects are equal if they contain exactly the same values in each of their instance variables
- two object references are equal is they both refer to the same object (or are both `null`)
- an `if` statement may be nested within another `if` statement
- the `else` part of an `if` statement is optional

- the `switch` statement allows a program to choose one (or more) of many alternative courses of action to execute

Exercises

(1) Given the following declarations:

```
bool yes = true, no = false, maybe = true;
```

say what the value of each of the following conditions is:

```
yes && (no || maybe)
no || (!yes && maybe)
yes || no || maybe
no || yes && maybe
(!no && yes) || (!no && maybe)
```

(2) Write `bool` expressions to represent each of the following italicized expressions:

I can go to a club if *I have enough money and I'm dressed neatly and I'm not drunk*
I should stop if *I've found the house I'm looking for or I'm at the end of the road*
I should continue while *I haven't found the house and there are more houses*

(3) Write a C# program that reads six numbers (a, b, c, d, e, f) from the user and uses them to solve the simultaneous equations:

```
ax + by = c
dx + ey = f
```

for x and y, using the well-known formula for solving simultaneous equations. Make sure that your program takes account of the fact that there may not necessarily be a solution.

(4) Write a class whose instances represent circles and which includes the current position of a circle (i.e., its *x* and *y* coordinates) among its attributes. Provide methods to move a circle to a new position and to determine if two circles overlap.
Use your `Circle` class in a program that reads the dimensions and positions of two circles from the user and reports whether or not the circles overlap.

(5) Write a class `Date` that includes a method to report whether or not the current date falls within a leap year. Use your class in a program that reads a date and reports whether or not it falls within a leap year.

Note: a leap year occurs every four years, but only every fourth whole century (i.e., 100, 200, 300 etc. are NOT leap years but 400, 800, 1200 etc. are).

(6) Rewrite the nightclub program so that it uses only a single `if` statement.

Hint: your program will probably need to obtain all the information describing potential customers before making the decision as to whether or not to admit them.

(7) Write a C# program that can be used by a cinema ticket seller to decide whether or not to admit someone to a film.
A film may be rated G, P, R, or X. Anyone can go to a G or P rated film. Anyone over 21 can go to any film. Those under 21 can go to an R rated film only if accompanied by someone over 21 and can never go to an X rated film.

(8) A computer-dating agency maintains records describing each of its clients. Potential couples must have similar physical, occupational, and social characteristics. In particular, the agency applies the following rules to selecting couples:

- each couple should consist of one male and one female,
- if the male is under 26, then the female should be no more than 1 year older,
- the male should not be shorter nor more than 25 cm taller than the female,
- if both are employed, they should work the same shift pattern (day or night),
- if either smokes, they should both smoke,
- their places of residence should be in the same postal district.

Write a class whose instances represent clients of the computer-dating agency and that includes a method to determine if two clients would make a compatible couple. Use your class in a program that reads in descriptions of two clients and reports whether or not they would make a couple.

(9) Our program for calculating the postage due on a parcel is a little unrealistic since the cost of sending a parcel usually depends not only on its destination but also on its weight. Assuming that the cost of sending a parcel is as before with the addition of a supplement depending on the weight of the parcel which is calculated as follows:

- 0–100 grams: no extra charge,
- 100 grams–1 kg: $10 extra,
- 1 kg–5 kg: $25 extra,
- 5 kg–10 kg: $60 extra,
- greater than 10 kg: $100 extra.

Rewrite Program 4.20 and especially class `Parcel` accordingly.

(10) We've seen lots of programs that allow users to calculate the areas or perimeters of different types of shapes. Typically each of these programs dealt with only one type of shape. Write a program which allows the user to select the type of shape in which they are interested and then reads the dimensions of the chosen shape before reporting its area and circumference. The program should deal with squares, circles, rectangles, and triangles at least!

Doing Things Repeatedly – Iteration in C# 5

This chapter:

- motivates the need for a program to be able to execute the same sequence of statements a variable number of times
- describes the while statement – a C# statement that provides one means for a program to carry out the same sequence of statements a number of times
- describes the do statement – a C# statement that provides another means for a program to carry out the same sequence of statements a number of times

Consider writing a program to print out the numbers from 1 to 5. By now, you should find writing this program pretty easy! We might describe the steps to be carried out by the program as follows:

print out the number 1;

print out the number 2;

print out the number 3;

print out the number 4;

print out the number 5;

Easy! Our program basically consists of the same statement repeated five times (although printing out a different value each time). In the same way, we could easily write a program to print out the numbers from 1 to 10, or a program to print out the numbers from 1 to 100, or, even, a program to print out the numbers from 1 to 1000. Apart from the fact that the program would be very long, and writing it very tedious, the idea is reasonably straightforward – we simply write the required number of print statements into our program and they get executed one after another every time that the program is run.

Now suppose that we want to write a program to print out the numbers from 1 up to some value specified by the user. How should we go about it? We can't use our previous strategy because we don't know how many numbers have to be printed at the time that we are writing the program. In fact, we won't know how many numbers to print until the program is actually running. Moreover, the user can specify a different number each time that the program runs so the program may need to execute a different number of print statements each time!

The solution to our problem lies in the observation that what we want to do is essentially to execute *the same statement* but *a different number of times*. So, in our program we would like to be able to write the statement (or statements) to be repeated just once along with a description of how many times those statements should be executed. For example, we might describe the program for printing out the numbers from 1 up to the value specified by the user as follows:

get the final number from the user;
while we haven't printed the final number
print out the next number;

So, we write the statement to be executed ("print out the next number") just once and also specify a condition that describes how long we should keep executing that statement ("while we haven't printed the final number"). We don't specify exactly how many times to execute the print statement and, in fact, we don't know how many times it will be executed until the program actually runs.

Luckily, C# provides means for specifying sequences of statements that should be executed multiple times including specifying how often they should be repeated. Executing the same sequence of statements repeatedly is called *iteration* and C# provides a number of different ways of specifying iteration. In this chapter, we will look at two different ways: the `while` statement and the `do` statement.

Repeating a Sequence of Statements – The `while` Statement

A `while` statement allows us to execute some sequence of statements a number of times. As such, it consists of two main parts: a single sequence of statements to be executed and a condition that controls how often that sequence is to be repeated. As an example, let's consider writing the program to print out the numbers from 1 to 5 using a `while` statement.

The first thing that we have to do is to identify the statements that we want executed repeatedly. In this case, that's the statement corresponding to printing out a number. OK, but what number? We don't want to print out the same number all the time; we want to print a different number. Thus, the number that we print will have to be given by the value of a variable – let's call it `currentNumber`. The statement to be repeated will print out the *current* value of this variable each time it's executed. Once we've printed out the value of the variable, we need to increment its value so that the next time the value of the variable is printed, it will contain the new number to be printed. So, it turns out that there are actually two statements to be repeated:

print out the value of `currentNumber`;
increment `currentNumber`;

Now we have to specify the condition that controls how often we want these statements to be executed. The condition is specified as a `bool` expression. When this condition is `true`, the statements will be repeatedly executed. Once the condition becomes `false`, the statements will not be executed again. In our case, assuming that we start with `currentNumber` having the value 1, we want to keep printing out the value of `currentNumber` until we have printed the value 5, or, put another way, until the value of `currentNumber` is greater than 5. Thus, the condition under which the statements should continue to be executed is:

while `currentNumber` is less than or equal to 5

Program 5.1 shows how to write this program in C# by using a `while` statement to pull all the pieces together, while Figure 5.1 shows the program in action.

As Figure 5.2 shows a `while` statement is introduced by the keyword `while` and consists of a condition represented by a `bool` expression (and written within brackets) and a

```
/* A program to illustrate */
/* the use of the while statement */

using tcdIO;

class OneToFive
{
    public static void Main ()
    {
        Terminal terminal;
        int currentNumber = 1; // start at 1

        /* create an object to represent the terminal */
        terminal = new Terminal();
        terminal.WriteLine("The list is:");
        while (currentNumber <= 5)
        {
            /* print out the value of currentNumber */
            terminal.WriteInt(currentNumber);
            /* increment currentNumber */
            currentNumber = currentNumber + 1;
        }
        /* print a message to say that the program is finished */
        terminal.WriteLine("Finished!");
    }
}
```

Program 5.1   A program to illustrate the use of the while statement.

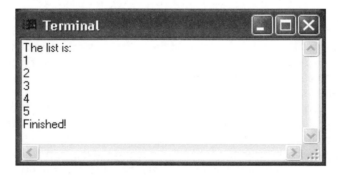

Figure 5.1   The execution of Program 5.1.

```
while (<bool expression>)
{
  <statement sequence>
}
```

Figure 5.2   The syntax of the C# while statement.

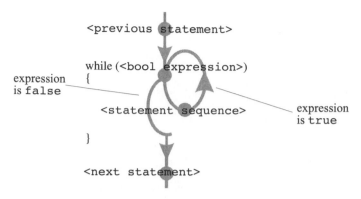

Figure 5.3   The flow of control through a C# while statement.

single statement sequence (usually written between braces). The condition is known as the *terminating condition* since it controls when the execution of the while statement terminates. The statement sequence is usually called the *body* of the while statement.

When a while statement is executed, the terminating condition is always evaluated first yielding a value of true or false. If the value is true, then the body of the while statement is executed exactly once, control is returned to the beginning of the while statement and the terminating condition is evaluated as before. If the value of the condition is false, the body is not executed and the execution of the while statement terminates. Figure 5.3 shows the flow of control through a while statement. Notice that when the body of the while statement is executed, control "loops" back to the beginning and starts over again. For this reason, while statements (and indeed other iteration statements) are often called *loops*. A single execution of the body of a loop is often called *an iteration of the loop*.

Note that the first thing that happens when a while loop is executed is always the evaluation of the terminating condition. Likewise, the last thing that happens is always the evaluation of the terminating condition! The terminating condition is re-evaluated only after the body has been executed fully. Thus, if the execution of the body causes the terminating condition to become false, the remainder of the body will still be executed as usual before the condition is re-evaluated. When the execution of the while loop completes the terminating condition is always false.

As a further example of the use of the while statement, let's modify Program 5.1 to print out the numbers from 1 up to some number specified by the user. As usual when writing a while loop, we have to identify both the sequence of statements to be repeated and the terminating condition to be used to control the execution of the loop.

Not surprisingly, the body of this loop is exactly the same as in the previous example – it simply prints out the value of currentNumber and then calculates the next number to be printed. However, the terminating condition is different. This time we want to keep printing out numbers until we get to the value specified by the user. If we assume that this value is stored in the variable usersNumber, then we want to continue while:

```
currentNumber <= usersNumber
```

Program 5.2 shows the full program.

Now let's look at what happens when we run the program and supply different values for the input. Figure 5.4 shows what happens when the user enters the value 0. In this case, no numbers are printed! The reason is that when the terminating condition for the while loop is evaluated for the first time, the condition currentNumber (which is 1) <= usersNumber

```
/* A program to illustrate the use of
 * the while statement (revised) */

using tcdIO;

class UserChoice
{
    public static void Main ()
    {
        Terminal terminal;
        int currentNumber = 1; // start at 1
        int usersChoice;

        /* create an object to represent the terminal */
        terminal = new Terminal();

        /* get the user's number */
        usersChoice = terminal.ReadInt(
            "Enter the highest number to print: ");

        /* now print out the list */
        terminal.WriteLine("The list is:");
        while (currentNumber <= usersChoice)
        {
            /* print out the value of currentNumber */
            terminal.WriteInt(currentNumber);
            /* increment currentNumber */
            currentNumber = currentNumber + 1;
        }

        /* print a message that the program is finished */
        terminal.WriteLine("Finished!");
    }
}
```

Program 5.2   A program to illustrate the use of the `while` statement (revised).

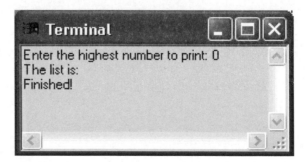

Figure 5.4   The execution of Program 5.2 when the user enters 0.

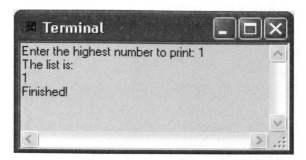

Figure 5.5   The execution of Program 5.2 when user enters 1.

(which is 0) is already `false`. Since the terminating condition is `false`, the body of the loop is not executed and the `while` loop terminates. It's important to realize that the body of a `while` loop need not be executed at all if the terminating condition is already `false` when the loop is executed.

Figure 5.5 shows what happens when the user enters the value 1. In this case, when the terminating condition is first evaluated, it is `true` (`currentNumber` (which is 1) `<=` `usersNumber` (which is also 1) is `true`). Thus, the body of the loop is executed once resulting in the value 1 being printed and `currentNumber` being incremented to 2. The terminating condition is now re-evaluated and found to be `false` (`currentNumber` is now greater than `usersNumber`). Thus, the execution of the loop terminates.

Finally, Figure 5.6 shows what happens when the user enters 5. As you might expect the body of the loop is now executed five times. After each execution of the body, the terminating condition is re-evaluated; after the fifth iteration, the condition becomes `false` and the `while` loop terminates.

Taken together, these three scenarios show that the same sequence of statements can be executed a different number of times depending on prevailing circumstances – exactly what we wanted to achieve!

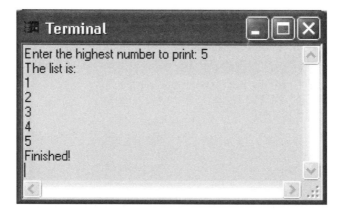

Figure 5.6   The execution of Program 5.2 when the user enters the value 5.

Calculating $n!$

The factorial of a non-zero positive number n (i.e., $n!$) is given by the formula:

$$n! = n * n - 1 * n - 2 * \cdots * 2 * 1 \quad \text{for } n \geq 0$$

Thus, to calculate $n!$ we multiply n by each of the positive numbers that are lower than it. To write a program to calculate $n!$ for some value of n specified by the user of the program, we need to use a loop to perform the appropriate number of multiplications. We *need* to use a loop because we don't know in advance how many multiplications will have to be performed. Thus, a possible strategy is to use a `while` loop that performs one multiplication on each iteration of the loop.

As usual, to use a while loop we need to decide on two things:

- what sequence of statements is to be repeated,
- for how long is that sequence of statements to be repeated.

In this case, we will need to keep a running total for the factorial and multiply it by successively lower values of n. Thus, on each iteration of the loop, we have two things to do:

- multiply the factorial by the current value of n, and
- get the next lower value of n.

Starting at the value supplied by the user, we want to execute the body of the loop once for each value of n down to 1. Thus, the terminating condition is:

- continue while current value of n is greater than 1.

Program 5.3 shows the resulting program. Notice the use of an `if` statement to make sure that the value entered by the user is greater than 1 to start with.

Figure 5.7 shows the result of executing the program when the user enters 5. In this case, the body of the loop is executed four times for the values 5, 4, 3, and 2.

Reading Input from the User

We've seen lots of examples of programs that read input from the user and need to check that the values supplied are acceptable for their intended use. Until now we have usually used an

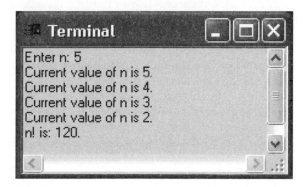

Figure 5.7   The execution of Program 5.3 when the user enters the value 5.

```
/* A program to calculate n! */

using tcdIO;

class Factorial
{
   public static void Main ()
   {
      Terminal terminal;
      int n;
      int factorialN = 1; // running total; initialize to 1

      /* create an object to represent the terminal */
      terminal = new Terminal();

      /* get value of n from user */
      n = terminal.ReadInt("Enter n: ");
      /* check that value is acceptable */
      if (n > 1)
      {
         /* calculate n! */
         while (n > 1)
         {
            terminal.WriteLine("Current value of n is " + n + ".");
            /* multiply factorial by current n */
            factorialN = factorialN * n;
            /* get next lower n */
            n = n - 1;
         }
         /* print out the result */
         terminal.WriteLine("n! is: " + factorialN + ".");
      }
      else
      {
         /* illegal value for n */
         terminal.WriteLine("Unable to calculate factorial
                                      of " + n + ".");
      }
   }
}
```

Program 5.3   A program to calculate *n*!.

if statement to check if the values are acceptable and print a message if not. The problem
with this approach is that when the user enters unacceptable values, the program finishes
without giving them a chance to re-enter acceptable values. To accomplish this we can use a
while statement to repeatedly ask for input until we get values that are acceptable. Notice
that a while loop is necessary since we can't predict in advance how many attempts the user
will need before they enter acceptable values.

For example, let's return to our program to calculate the area and perimeter of a rectangle
with dimensions specified by the user. We need to ensure that the dimensions supplied by the
user are valid (i.e., positive and non-zero). Essentially, we will use a while loop to repeatedly
ask the user for the dimensions until valid dimensions are entered. As ever, we need to decide
on two things:

- what sequence of statements is to be repeated,
- for how long is that sequence of statements to be repeated.

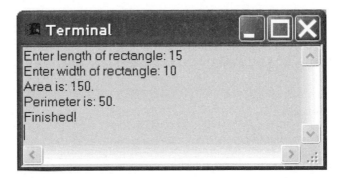

Figure 5.8   The execution of Program 5.4 when the user enters valid dimensions.

In this case, the step to be repeated is asking for valid dimensions, i.e.,

- reading in the length of the rectangle, and
- reading in the width of the rectangle.

We want to repeat this sequence of statements while the dimensions are invalid. Thus, the terminating condition is:

- while either the length is <= 0 or the width is <= 0.

We can express this condition as a `bool` expression by making use of the || operator, as follows:

```
(length <= 0) || (width <= 0)
```

Remember that we can use any `bool` expression (using any appropriate combination of operators) as the terminating condition of a `while` loop.

Program 5.4 shows the resulting program. Notice that we read in the length and width of the rectangle before executing the `while` loop. This means that when we come to evaluate the terminating condition of the loop for the first time, `length` and `width` already have values. Moreover, the body of the loop is only executed if invalid values have already been entered and can therefore print an appropriate message. Figure 5.8 shows the result of executing the program when the user enters valid dimensions and Figure 5.9 the execution of the program when the user enters an invalid length.

The code to read in the dimensions of the rectangle actually serves as a useful template for reading input from the user and checking its validity. Figure 5.10 illustrates a fragment of code that can be adapted to any such program.

Getting the Terminating Condition Right

When Program 5.4 is run, the number of times that the body of the loop is executed depends entirely on the input supplied by the user during each iteration of the loop. As long as the user continues to supply invalid input, the body of the loop will be executed again. Theoretically, the body of the loop might be executed an infinite number of times! This illustrates one of the main dangers of using loops – the possibility that the execution of the loop will never end. In our previous examples we were guaranteed that the loop would always terminate after a number of iterations. In Program 5.2, the loop terminates when `currentNumber` is greater than `usersNumber` and we are sure that `currentNumber` will eventually reach

```
/* A program to calculate the area */
/* and perimeter of a rectangle */

using tcdIO;

class RectangleProgram
{
   public static void Main ()
   {
      Terminal terminal;
      Rectangle shape;
      int length, width;
      int area, perimeter;

      /* create an object to represent the terminal */
      terminal = new Terminal();

      /* ask user for width and length */
      length = terminal.ReadInt("Enter length of rectangle: ");
      width = terminal.ReadInt("Enter width of rectangle: ");

      /* check that width and length are valid */
      while ((length <= 0) || (width <= 0))
      {
         /* width or length is invalid - try again */
         terminal.WriteLine("The dimensions entered are invalid.");
         length = terminal.ReadInt("Please enter positive length: ");
         width = terminal.ReadInt("Please enter positive width: ");
      }
      /* now we have valid dimensions */

      /* create a new Rectangle with given dimensions */
      shape = new Rectangle(length, width);

      /* ask the rectangle object for its area */
      area = shape.CalculateArea();
      /* Write out the area to the screen */
      terminal.WriteLine("Area is: " + area + ".");

      /* ask the rectangle obejct for its perimeter */
      perimeter = shape.CalculatePerimeter();
      /* Write out the perimeter to the screen */
      terminal.WriteLine("Perimeter is: " + perimeter + ".");

      /* print a message to say that the program is finished */
      terminal.WriteLine("Finished!");
   }
}
```

Program 5.4   A program to calculate the area and perimeter of a rectangle.

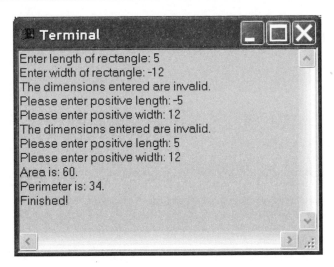

Figure 5.9   The execution of Program 5.4 when the user enters invalid dimensions.

```
<read new input from the user>
while (<the input is not valid>)
{
  <print out an error message>
  <read the input from the user>
}
/* loop ends only when input is valid */
```

Figure 5.10   A template for reading input from the user and checking its validity.

usersNumber because we increment currentNumber each time that the body of the loop executes. In Program 5.3 the loop terminates when n reaches 1 and we are sure that n will eventually reach 1 because we know that n is greater than 1 initially and we subtract 1 from n each time that the body of the loop is executed.

All of these examples have the common characteristic that the execution of the body of the loop eventually causes the terminating condition to become false and the execution of the loop to stop. When we write a loop, we should always check that the execution of its body will eventually cause the terminating condition to become false and the loop to stop; otherwise we risk the loop continuing infinitely – a so-called *infinite loop*.

Combining Iteration and Selection

We've seen that the body of a while loop contains a sequence of statements that is to be executed repeatedly. So far, the bodies of all of our while loops have been made up of simple statements such as assignment statements and method invocations to print out

```
/* A program to find the largest number in */
/* a list of positive integers entered by the user */

using tcdIO;

class Largest
{
   public static void Main ()
   {
      Terminal terminal;
      int number;
      int maxSoFar = 0; // initially smaller than any number

      /* create an object to represent the terminal */
      terminal = new Terminal();

      /* Read the first number */
      number = terminal.ReadInt("Enter number: ");
      /* now process list of numbers */
      while (number >= 0)
      {
         /* check if number is largest so far */
         if (number > maxSoFar)
         {
            /* if so, remember it */
            maxSoFar = number;
         }
         /* Read the next number */
         number = terminal.ReadInt("Enter number: ");
      }
      /* print out the largest number */
      terminal.WriteLine("The largest number was: " + maxSoFar + ".");
   }
}
```

Program 5.5   A program to illustrate the use of an `if` statement within a `while` loop.

messages on the screen. However, you should realize that the body of a `while` loop can contain
any other statements that you want to include, for example, further `while` statements, `if`
statements and `switch` statements as well as assignment statements and method invocations.
Likewise, any branch of an `if` statement or `switch` statement can contain one or more `while`
statements.

As a simple example of combining iteration and selection, let's write a program to determine
the largest number in a list of numbers to be entered by the user. Let's assume that the list
consists of an arbitrary number of positive integers. Thus, a negative number can be used to
signify the end of the list. For example, the list might be:

```
57, 2345, 0, 485745, 94243, 647893, 27653, -34
```

Since we don't know in advance how many numbers are to be entered, we will use a `while`
to loop to repeatedly read in numbers. In addition, since we don't want to store up all the
numbers until the last one has been entered, we will need to process each number as we read
it. Thus, we need to keep track of the largest number entered so far and, whenever we read a

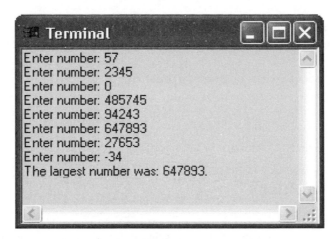

Figure 5.11   The execution of Program 5.5.

new number, check if that number is larger than the previous largest. To perform this check we will need to use an if statement to compare each new number with the largest so far. The if statement will be within the body of our loop!

As usual when writing a while loop, we need to decide on two things:

- what sequence of statements is to be repeated,
- for how long is that sequence of statements to be repeated.

In this case, the statements to be repeated are:

- read in a new number,
- if it is larger than the largest so far,
- remember that it is the largest so far,

and we want to continue executing the loop:

- while the number is positive.

Program 5.5 shows the resulting program. We read in the first number before executing the while loop. This means that when we come to evaluate the terminating condition of the loop for the first time, currentNumber already has a value. Moreover, if the first number in the list is negative, the body of the loop will not be executed at all. Because the first number is read before the loop, the order in which the statements in the body of the loop are executed is slightly different from what is described above. Since we already have a new number when we start to execute the body, we first check if it is the largest so far and only after that do we read the next number in preparation for re-evaluating the terminating condition. Figure 5.11 shows the result of executing the program when the user enters the list of numbers above.

Incidentally, Program 5.5 also serves as a template for any program that needs to process a list of items entered by the user where the end of the list is identified by a special item – known as a *sentinel*. Figure 5.12 illustrates a fragment of code that can be adapted to any such program. Notice that in Program 5.5, the items to be processed are positive integers and the sentinel is any negative integer.

```
<read the next element from the user>
while (<the element is not equal to the sentinel>)
{
    <process the current element>
    <read an element of the list from the user>
}
```

Figure 5.12   A template for processing a list of items entered by the user.

Generating Functions

A generating function allows us to generate one term of a sequence of terms from one or more of the previous terms. For example, the famous Fibonacci Sequence consists of the sequence of terms:

$$1, 1, 2, 3, 5, 8, 13, 21, \ldots$$

Each term after the first two is the sum of the previous two terms. If we number the terms T_0 to T_n, where T_0 is the first term then we can say that:

$$T_0 = 1, \quad T_1 = 1, \quad T_n = T_{n-2} + T_{n-1} \quad \text{for } n > 1.$$

Now let's consider writing a program to print out a specified number of terms of the Fibonacci Sequence. Of course, we will use a loop to calculate each new term from the previous two terms. We will need three variables Tn, Tn1, and Tn2 corresponding to T_n, T_{n-1}, and T_{n-2}. Each time through the loop we update Tn as follows:

```
Tn = Tn2 + Tn1;
```

A possible program to generate the Fibonacci Sequence is shown in Program 5.6 and the resulting output in Figure 5.13.

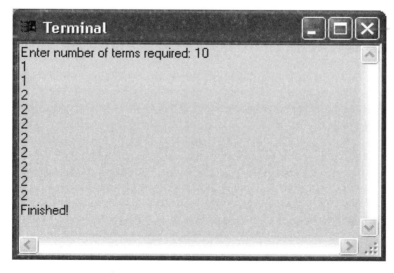

Figure 5.13   The execution of Program 5.6.

```
/* A program to generate the Fibonacci Sequence */
/* Stops when a specified number of terms have been generated */

using tcdIO;

class Fibonacci
{
    public static void Main ()
    {
        Terminal terminal;
        int Tn, Tn1, Tn2;      // Tn, Tn-1, Tn-2
        int termsToDo, count; // count number of terms done

        /* create an object to represent the terminal */
        terminal = new Terminal();

        termsToDo = terminal.ReadInt("Enter number of terms required: ");
        /* make sure that the user wants more than 2 terms */
        while (termsToDo < 2)
        {
            terminal.WriteLine("At least two terms must be generated.");
            termsToDo = terminal.ReadInt("Enter number of terms required: ");
        }
        /* generate the first two terms */
        Tn2 = 1; terminal.WriteInt(Tn2);  // T0
        Tn1 = 1; terminal.WriteInt(Tn1);  // T1
        count = 2;  // two terms done
        /* generate as many more terms as needed */
        while (count < termsToDo)
        {
            Tn = Tn2 + Tn1;          // generate new term
            terminal.WriteInt(Tn); // print out new term
            count = count + 1;
        }
        /* print a message to say that the program is finished */
        terminal.WriteLine("Finished!");
    }
}
```

Program 5.6   A program to generate the Fibonacci Sequence.

Oooops! Not what we might have expected! We've clearly done something wrong. The problem is that when we computed a new value for Tn, we neglected to update the values of Tn-1 and Tn-2 to reflect the fact that another term has been generated. We need to modify the body of the loop as follows:

```
Tn = Tn2 + Tn1; // generate new term
Tn2 = Tn1;      // what was Tn-1 is now Tn-2
Tn1 = Tn;       // what was Tn is now Tn-1
```

The finished program is shown in Program 5.7 and its output in Figure 5.14.

Notice that our Fibonacci program stops once a specified number of terms has been generated. This is, of course, not the only condition under which the program could be terminated. For example, we might want to keep generating terms until one that exceeds a certain value, perhaps entered by the user, is generated. For example, if the target value is stored in a variable called upperBound, then we could keep generating new terms while Tn

```
/* A program to generate the Fibonacci Sequence (revised) */
/* Stops when a specified number of terms have been generated */

using tcdIO;

class Fibonacci
{
    public static void Main ()
    {
        Terminal terminal;
        int Tn, Tn1, Tn2;      // Tn, Tn-1, Tn-2
        int termsToDo, count; // count number of terms done

        /* create an object to represent the terminal */
        terminal = new Terminal();

        termsToDo = terminal.ReadInt("Enter number of terms required: ");
        /* make sure that the user wants more than 2 terms */
        while (termsToDo < 2)
        {
            terminal.WriteLine("At least two terms must be generated.");
            termsToDo = terminal.ReadInt("Enter number of terms required: ");
        }

        /* generate the first two terms */
        Tn2 = 1; terminal.WriteInt(Tn2); // T0
        Tn1 = 1; terminal.WriteInt(Tn1); // T1
        count = 2;   // two terms done

        /* generate as many more terms as needed */
        while (count < termsToDo)
        {
            Tn = Tn2 + Tn1;         // generate new term
            terminal.WriteInt(Tn); // print out new term
            Tn2 = Tn1;              // update Tn-2
            Tn1 = Tn;               // and Tn-1
            count = count + 1;
        }

        /* print a message to say that the program is finished */
        terminal.WriteLine("Finished!");
    }
}
```

Program 5.7   A program to generate the Fibonacci Sequence (revised).

was less than upperBound as shown in Program 5.8. The result of executing the program is shown in Figure 5.15.

Calculating e^x

As a further example of the use of generating functions let's look at a program to calculate $e^x \cdot e^x$ is given by the formula:

$$e^x = 1 + x + x^2/2! + x^3/3! + \cdots + x_n/n!$$

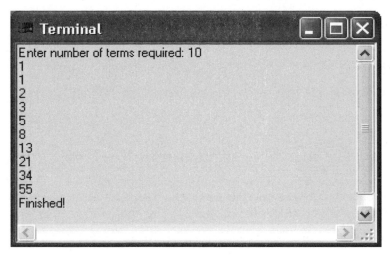

Figure 5.14   The execution of Program 5.7.

Each of the terms of this formula can be calculated from the previous term. In other words, each term is given by a generating function. If we number the terms T_0 to T_n, where T_0 is the first term then we can say that:

$$T_0 = 1, \quad T_1 = x, \quad T_2 = x^2/2!, \quad T_3 = x^3/3!$$

and in general:

$$T_n = x_n/n! \quad \text{for } n > 1.$$

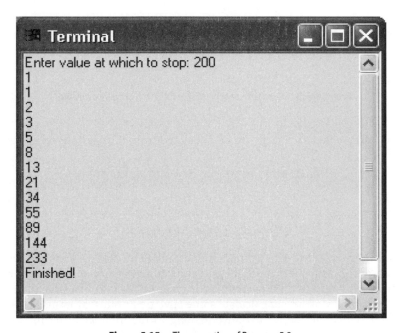

Figure 5.15   The execution of Program 5.8.

```
/* A program to generate the Fibonacci Sequence (revised) */
/* Stops when a term whose value is greater than the value specified */
/* by the user has been generated */

using tcdIO;

class Fibonacci
{
    public static void Main ()
    {
        Terminal terminal;
        int Tn, Tn1, Tn2;       // Tn, Tn-1, Tn-2
        int upperBound;

        /* create an object to represent the terminal */
        terminal = new Terminal();

        upperBound = terminal.ReadInt("Enter value at which to stop: ");

        /* generate the first two terms */
        Tn2 = 1; terminal.WriteInt(Tn2); // T0
        Tn1 = 1; terminal.WriteInt(Tn1); // T1
        Tn = 0;                          // not yet calculated

        /* generate new terms until the current term */
        /* exceeds the specifed upper bound */
        while (Tn < upperBound)
        {
            Tn = Tn2 + Tn1;           // generate new term
            terminal.WriteInt(Tn); // print out new term
            Tn2 = Tn1;                // update Tn-2
            Tn1 = Tn;                 // and Tn-1
        }

        /* print a message to say that the program is finished */
        terminal.WriteLine("Finished!");
    }
}
```

Program 5.8   A program to generate the Fibonacci Sequence (revised).

Moreover, we can see that each term can be calculated from the previous term as follows:

$$T_1 = T_0 \cdot x \quad T_2 = T_1 \cdot x/2 \quad T_3 = T_2 \cdot x/3.$$

So, in general:

$$T_n = T_{n-1} \cdot x/n \quad \text{for } n > 1.$$

We can use these rules to write a program to calculate e^x. Not surprisingly, we will use a loop to calculate successive terms of the generating function and add them to the running total. We can employ various different terminating conditions to control the number of terms generated. The simplest is just to calculate some specific number of terms specified by the program's user. Thus, the loop is executed as long as the number of terms that has been generated is less than the number specified by the user.

```
/* A program to calculate eX */

using tcdIO;

class eX
{
    public static void Main ()
    {
        Terminal terminal;
        double eX, x, Tn;
        int n, termsToDo;

        /* create an object to represent the terminal */
        terminal = new Terminal();

        /* Read x and number of terms to generate */
        x = terminal.ReadDouble("Enter x: ");
        termsToDo = terminal.ReadInt("Enter number of terms to generate: ");
        while (termsToDo < 1)
        {
            terminal.WriteLine("At least one term must be generated.");
            termsToDo = terminal.ReadInt("Enter number of terms to generate: ");
        }
        /* calculate eX */
        n = 0; Tn = 1; eX = Tn;   // T0
        while (n < termsToDo-1)
        {
            /* generate another term */
            n = n + 1;
            Tn = (x/n) * Tn;
            /* add to eX */
            eX = eX + Tn;
        }
        /* print out result */
        terminal.WriteLine("Result is: " + eX + ".");
    }
}
```

Program 5.9   A program to calculate e^x.

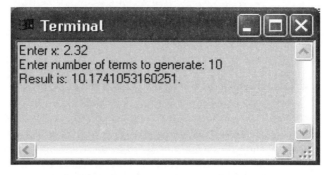

Figure 5.16   The execution of Program 5.9.

```
/* Program 6.10: a program to calculate eX (revised) */

using tcdIO;
using System;

class eX
{
    public static void Main ()
    {
        Terminal terminal;
        double eX, x, Tn;
        int n;

        /* create an object to represent the terminal */
        terminal = new Terminal();

        /* Read x */
        x = terminal.ReadDouble("Enter x: ");

        /* calculate eX */
        n = 0; Tn = 1; eX = Tn;   // T0
        while (Math.Abs(Tn) >= 0.0001)
        {
            /* generate another term */
            n = n + 1;
            Tn = (x/n) * Tn;
            /* add to eX */
            eX = eX + Tn;
        }
        /* print out result */
        terminal.WriteLine("Result is: " + eX + ".");
    }
}
```

Program 5.10   A program to calculate e^x (revised).

The resulting program is shown in Program 5.9 and its execution in Figure 5.16. Program 5.10 shows a revised version of the program that keeps generating new terms as long as each new term makes a significant contribution to the accuracy of e^x. In this case, the program generates new terms as long as the magnitude of each new term is greater than 0.0001.

Notice that, since terms can be negative as well as positive, we need to be able to take the absolute value of each term. To do this, we use the method

```
double Math.Abs(double number);
```

Repeating a Sequence of Statements One or More Times – do

C# provides a number of other iteration statements apart from the while loop. In this section, we will look at another one of C#'s iteration statements – the do statement. In fact, the do statement is very similar to the while statement with two important differences. Firstly, a while statement allows us to execute a sequence of statements zero or more times (i.e., it is possible that the body of a while loop will not be executed if the terminating condition is already false when execution of the loop begins). On the other hand, the statements

```
do {

    <statement sequence>

} while (<bool expression>)
```

Figure 5.17   The syntax of the C# do statement.

contained in a do loop are always executed at least once. This is actually a consequence of the second important difference between while loops and do loops. In a while loop the terminating condition is always evaluated *before* the body of the loop is executed; in a do loop the terminating condition is only evaluated *after* the body of the loop has been executed.

As Figure 5.17 shows, a do statement is introduced by the keyword do and consists of a single statement sequence (usually written between braces) and a terminating condition represented by a bool expression (introduced by the keyword while and written within brackets as usual). Notice that the terminating condition is written *after* the statement sequence making up the body of the loop to emphasize the fact that it is evaluated only after each iteration of the loop.

When a do statement is executed, the body of the loop is always executed first. Once the body has been executed, the terminating condition is then evaluated to give a value of true or false. If the value is true, control is returned to the beginning of the do statement, the body of the do statement is executed again, and then the terminating condition re-evaluated. If the value of the terminating condition is false, the execution of the do statement terminates immediately. Figure 5.18 shows the flow of control through a do statement.

Note that the first thing that happens when a do statement is executed is always the execution of the body. The last thing that happens is always the evaluation of the terminating condition! Notice that the terminating condition is evaluated only after the body has been executed fully. Thus, if the execution of the body causes the terminating condition to become false, the remainder of the body will still be executed as usual before the condition is evaluated. When the execution of the do loop completes, the terminating condition is always false.

The do statement is slightly less general purpose than the while statement because of the fact that it can only be used where the body of the loop definitely has to be executed at least once. As a result, use of do statements is relatively rare compared with the use of the other iteration statements provided by C#. Since the while statement can do everything that the

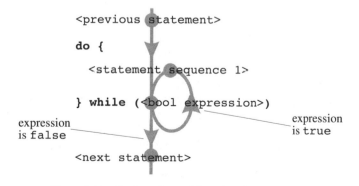

Figure 5.18   The flow of control through a C# do statement.

```
/* A program to illustrate the use of the do statement */

using tcdIO;

class RectangleProgram
{
    public static void Main ()
    {
        Terminal terminal;
        Rectangle shape;
        int length, width;
        int area, perimeter;

        /* create an object to represent the terminal */
        terminal = new Terminal();

        do
        {
            /* ask user for width and length */
            length = terminal.ReadInt("Please enter length of rectangle: ");
            width = terminal.ReadInt("Please enter width of rectangle: ");
            /* now check that length and width are valid */
        } while ((length <= 0) || (width <= 0));
        /* now we have valid dimensions */

        /* create a new Rectangle with given dimensions */
        shape = new Rectangle(length, width);

        /* ask the rectangle object for its area */
        area = shape.CalculateArea();
        /* Write out the area to the screen */
        terminal.WriteLine("Area is: " + area + ".");

        /* ask the rectangle obejct for its perimeter */
        perimeter = shape.CalculatePerimeter();
        /* Write out the perimeter to the screen */
        terminal.WriteLine("Perimeter is: " + perimeter + ".");

        /* print a message to say that the program is finished */
        terminal.WriteLine("Finished!");
    }
}
```

Program 5.11   A program to illustrate the use of the do statement.

do statement can, we prefer to use while in most cases and only use do where we really want to emphasize that the body of the loop is going to be executed at least once.

Once case where we might consider using do is when reading input from the user. We saw in Program 5.4 that we can use a loop to ensure that the user provides valid input when requested before allowing the rest of the program to proceed. In Program 5.4 we used a while loop. Moreover, notice that we read the user's initial input before executing the loop and read further input, if necessary, in the body of the loop. Since, the body of the loop reads input from the user and since input has to be read at least one, this is clearly a case where a do loop could be used as Program 5.11 illustrates.

In Program 5.11, the body of the loop is executed once to request the user's initial input. If the input in valid, as in Figure 5.19, the terminating condition is false and the loop

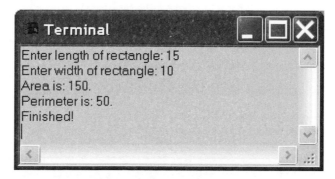

Figure 5.19   The execution of Program 5.11 when the user enters valid dimensions.

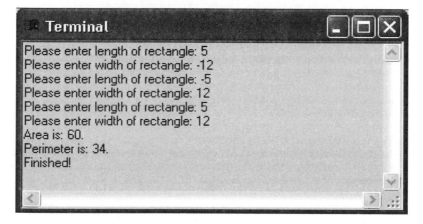

Figure 5.20   The execution of Program 5.11 when the user enters invalid dimensions.

terminates. If, however, the input is invalid, as in Figure 5.20, the terminating condition is `true` and the body of the loop is executed again to request new input.

Case Study: The Traveling Salesperson Revisited

To complete our discussion of iteration in C#, let's look at using iteration in one of the larger programs that we have written previously – the traveling salesperson program from Chapter 3. Recall that the problem was to write a C# program that reports the total distance traveled by a salesperson in traveling between a number (actually five) of cities as well as the direct distance between the first and last cities on the route. Our previous solution is shown in Program 5.12.

There are two points that are worth noting about this program. Firstly, the program only handles a path consisting of a fixed number of cities. In Chapter 3, we were limited to handling a fixed number of cities because our program depended on including the code to calculate the distance from one city to the next for each pair of cities. Thus, the same code is repeated four times in the course of the program. This brings us to the second point to note. The original program was rather long due to all the duplicated code that we were forced to include.

```
/* A program to calculate the distance travelled by salesperson */

using tcdIO;

class Salesperson
{
    public static void Main ()
    {
        Terminal terminal;
        City currentCity; // reference to city we're in
        City nextCity;    // reference to city we're going to
        City firstCity;   // reference to 1st city
        double x, y;       // used to get input
        double distance;   // running total

        /* create an object to represent the terminal */
        terminal = new Terminal();

        /* ask user for coordinates of 1st city */
        terminal.WriteLine("Enter coordinates of first city:");
        x = terminal.ReadDouble("X:"); y = terminal.ReadDouble("Y:");
        /* create object to represent 1st city */
        currentCity = new City(x, y);
        firstCity = currentCity;      // remember 1st city for later

        /* ask user for coordinates of next city */
        terminal.WriteLine("Enter coordinates of second city:");
        x = terminal.ReadDouble("X:"); y = terminal.ReadDouble("Y:");
        /* create object to represent 2nd city */
        nextCity = new City(x, y);

        /* get distance between 1st and 2nd cities */
        distance = currentCity.GetDistance(nextCity);
        currentCity = nextCity;      // move to 2nd city

        /* ask user for coordinates of next city */
        terminal.WriteLine("Enter coordinates of third city:");
        x = terminal.ReadDouble("X:"); y = terminal.ReadDouble("Y:");
        /* create object to represent 3rd city */
        nextCity = new City(x, y);

        /* update distance with distance between 2nd and 3rd cities */
        distance = distance + currentCity.GetDistance(nextCity);
        currentCity = nextCity;      // move to 3rd city

        /* ask user for coordinates of next city */
        terminal.WriteLine("Enter coordinates of fourth city:");
        x = terminal.ReadDouble("X:"); y = terminal.ReadDouble("Y:");
        /* create object to represent 4th city */
        nextCity = new City(x, y);

        /* update distance with distance between 3rd and 4th cities */
        distance = distance + currentCity.GetDistance(nextCity);
        currentCity = nextCity;      // move to 4th city
```

```
        /* ask user for coordinates of next city */
        terminal.WriteLine("Enter coordinates of fifth city:");
        x = terminal.ReadDouble("X:"); y = terminal.ReadDouble("Y:");
        /* create object to represent 5th city */
        nextCity = new City(x, y);

        /* update distance with distance between 4th and 5th cities */
        distance = distance + currentCity.GetDistance(nextCity);
        currentCity = nextCity;        // move to 5th city

        /* Write out result */
        terminal.WriteLine("Distance travelled is: " + distance + ".");

        /* calculate direct distance between 1st and 5th cities */
        distance = firstCity.GetDistance(currentCity);
        terminal.WriteLine("Direct distance is: " + distance + ".");
    }
}
```

Program 5.12   The traveling salesperson program.

Now that we are armed with iteration, we can rewrite the program to allow a path consisting of a variable number of cities to be followed, and in doing so, shorten the program considerably! In rewriting the program to use a loop, we first need to identify what sequence of statements is to be repeated and then determine the appropriate terminating condition.

To answer the first question, let's look at the original program. Notice that every city (except the first) is processed in the same way:

```
    /* ask user for coordinates of next city */
    terminal.WriteLine("Enter coordinates of next city:");
    x = terminal.ReadDouble("X: ");
    y = terminal.ReadDouble("Y: ");
    /* create object to represent next city */
    nextCity = new City(x, y);
    /* get distance between current and next cities */
    distance = currentCity.GetDistance(nextCity);
    /* move to next city */
    currentCity = nextCity;
```

Since every city other than the first is processed in this way, we can simply include this code in the body of a loop that is executed once for each city on the route. Interestingly, the loop creates a new object on each iteration, calculates the distance from the current city to the city represented by the new object, and then discards the object representing the current city by overwriting the reference to it that was stored in currentCity.

Each iteration of the loop essentially handles one city, hence if we ask the user to specify how many cities are to be visited, we can use a simple counter to control the termination of the loop. We want to keep executing the loop while the number of cities that has been visited is less than the number specified by the user.

The full program is shown in Program 5.13. Notice that it is both significantly more flexible and shorter than its counterpart in Program 5.12. The output from the program is shown in Figure 5.21.

```
/* A program to calculate distance */
/* travelled by salesperson (revised) */

using tcdIO;

class Salesperson
{
    public static void Main ()
    {
        Terminal terminal;
        City currentCity;       // reference to city we're in
        City nextCity;          // reference to city we're going to
        City firstCity;         // reference to 1st city
        double x, y;            // used to get input
        double distance = 0;    // running total
        int citiesVisited, citiesToVisit;   // used to count cities

        /* create an object to represent the terminal */
        terminal = new Terminal();

        /* ask user for number of cities to visit */
        citiesToVisit = terminal.ReadInt("How many cities are on the
                                                        route? ");

        if(citiesToVisit > 0)
        {
            citiesVisited = 1;
            /* ask user for coordinates of first city */
            terminal.WriteLine("Enter coordinates of city: " +
                                        citiesVisited + ".");
            x = terminal.ReadDouble("X: "); y = terminal.ReadDouble("Y: ");
            /* create object to represent first city */
            currentCity = new City(x, y);
            firstCity = currentCity;        // remember first city for later

            while (citiesVisited < citiesToVisit)
            {
                /* process next city */
                citiesVisited = citiesVisited + 1;

                /* ask user for coordinates of next city */
                terminal.WriteLine("Enter coordinates of city: " +
                                            citiesVisited + ".");
                x = terminal.ReadDouble("X: ");
                y = terminal.ReadDouble("Y: ");
                /* create object to represent next city */
                nextCity = new City(x, y);

                /* get distance between current and next cities */
                distance = distance + currentCity.GetDistance(nextCity);
                /* move to next city */
                currentCity = nextCity;
            }

            /* Write out result */
            terminal.WriteLine("Distance travelled is: " + distance + ".");
```

```
            /* now calculate straight-line distance between */
            /* first and last cities */
            distance = firstCity.GetDistance(currentCity);
            terminal.WriteLine("Direct distance is: " + distance + ".");
        }
        else
        {
            /* number of cities entered is negative or zero */
            terminal.WriteLine("You entered an invalid value for the
                                            number of cities.");
        }

    }
}
```

Program 5.13   The traveling salesperson program (revised).

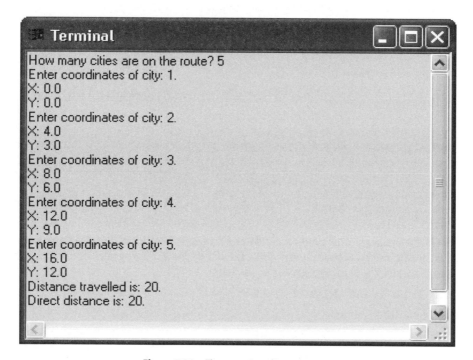

Figure 5.21   The execution of Program 5.13.

Summary

- *iteration* provides the means for a program to execute some sequence of statements repeatedly
- the number of times that the sequence of statements is to be executed need not be known until the program is running and can be different every time that the program is run
- an iteration statement describes both a sequence of statements to be executed repeatedly and the number of times that it is to be repeated
- iteration statements are usually called *loops*

- C# provides a number of different iteration statements including the `while` statement and the `do` statement
- the *body* of a `while` statement is executed repeatedly for as long as its *terminating condition* remains `true`
- a `while` statement terminates once its terminating condition becomes `false`
- the body of a `do` statement is executed repeatedly for as long as its terminating condition remains `true`
- a `do` statement terminates once its terminating condition becomes `false`
- the body of a `do` statement is always executed at least once

Exercises

(1) Consider the following fragment of a C# program:

```
/* x > 0 and y > 0 */
a = x;
b = y;
while (a != b)
{
  if (a > b)
    a = a - b;
  else
    b = b - a;
}
terminal.WriteLine(a);
```

If x is 69 and y is 15, what does the program print out? In general what does the program compute?

(2) Write a C# program that reads a list of positive numbers from the user and prints out the list to the screen replacing any 1s in the list by 2s. The program should stop when a negative number is read. For example, the list:

```
2 3 11 1 5 6 10 1 2 1 -9
```

should be printed out as:

```
2 3 11 2 5 6 10 2 2 2 -9
```

(3) Now modify your program from Exercise 2 so that it replaces a 1 followed immediately by a 2 to instead be a 3 followed by a 4:

```
2 3 11 1 5 6 10 1 2 1 -9
```

should be written out as:

```
2 3 11 1 5 6 10 3 4 1 -9
```

(4) The Taylor series for $\sin(x)$ is:

$$\sin(x) = x - x^3/3! + x^5/5! - x^7/7! + \cdots.$$

Write a C# program that calculates $\sin(x)$ to four decimal places of accuracy.

(5) Write an program that reports whether or not a given positive number obtained from its user is prime, i.e. has no factors other than itself and 1.

Modify your program to reads a list of positive integers from the keyboard and reports whether or not they are prime.

(6) Write a C# program that reads a year and the day of the week on which the 1st of January falls in that year and is capable of outputting the calendar for any month of the year when requested.

Hint: you may(!) want to use the Date class that you wrote as one of the exercises in Chapter 4 although you might need to add a method to increment the current date to the class (if you didn't have the foresight to provide such a method originally!).

(7) A list of pairs of integers is called *admissible* if, for each pair (X, Y), Y is 2 * X and also, for any two consecutive pairs, pair (X, Y) and pair (U, V), U is 3 * Y. For example, the following list is admissible:

```
(3, 6)  (18, 36)  (108, 216)  (648, 1296)
```

Write a C# program that prints out an admissible list of 50 pairs of integers starting with a pair of integers entered by the user.

Hint: use a class whose instances represent each pair of integers and which provides a method to return the pair of integers that would follow the current pair in an admissible list.

(8) A number's divisors are the numbers that divide it evenly. For example, the divisors of 12 are 1, 2, 3, 4, 6, and 12. A number is said to be *perfect* if the sum of its divisors (less the number itself) is equal to the number itself. For example, 6 is perfect because its divisors are 1, 2, 3 and 6, and 1 + 2 + 3 = 6.
Write a C# program that determines which integers between 2 and 1000 are perfect.

(9) Friday 13th is often thought to be an unlucky date. Since "forewarned is forearmed", it would be nice to have a program that, when given a date (e.g., Wednesday the 23rd of July 1997), will determine which, if any, months of the given year have the 13th falling on a Friday. So write it!

Hint: dates again!

More About Methods 6

This chapter:

- describes in detail how a method can refer to the object on which it was invoked
- describes how methods that don't return any value can be written
- describes how parameters are usually passed to methods in C#
- describes the use of *class variables and methods*
- describes how C#'s *scope rules* allow the same identifier to be used to name different things at different points in a program
- describes how different versions of a method can be provided by the same class using *method overloading*
- describes how *destructors* are used to inform an object that it is about to be deleted

A class typically provides a collection of methods to which the instances of that class respond when requested. Methods essentially implement commands that the instances of the class are capable of carrying out. As such, methods are said to describe the *behaviour* exhibited by the instances of the class. As we've seen, methods typically return a result that depends in some way on the values of some of the instance variables of the object on which they are invoked. Of course, a method may also change the values of some of these instance variables.

Methods provide the only way of actually getting any work done in an object-oriented program. Every C# program begins with the execution of its `Main` method. `Main` typically creates some objects and then invokes methods on those objects. These methods may, in turn, invoke further methods and so on. Thus, the execution of the entire program consists of a series of method invocations. Understanding methods is therefore essential to understanding how object-oriented programs work. This chapter looks in detail at methods and their use in C# programs.

Referring to the Current Object

Program 6.1 shows a new version of our old friend, class `Circle`. The circles represented by this version of `Circle` have both a position (described by the x and y coordinates of the centre of the circle) and a radius. Moreover, this version of the class provides a method, `Overlaps`, to check if two circles overlap. Two circles overlap if the distance between their centres is less than the sum of their radii.

177

```
/* A class whose instances represent cirlces with position */

using System;

class Circle
{
    private const double PI = 3.1416;
    private double x, y; // position
    private double radius;

    /* initialize new circle object */
    public Circle(double x, double y, double radius)
    {
        this.x = x;
        this.y = y;
        this.radius = radius;
    }

    /* return x coordinate of circle */
    public double GetX()
    {
        return this.x;
    }

    /* return y coordinate of circle */
    public double GetY()
    {
        return this.y;
    }

    /* return radius of circle */
    public double GetRadius()
    {
        return this.radius;
    }

    /* calculate area of circle */
    public double CalculateArea()
    {
        return PI * this.radius * this.radius;
    }

    /* calculate circumference of circle */
    public double CalculateCircumference()
    {
        return 2.0 * PI * this.radius;
    }

    /* check if specified circle overlaps with current circle */
    public bool Overlaps(Circle other)
    {
        double distance, tmpX, tmpY;

        /* get distance between centres of circles */
        tmpX = other.GetX() - this.x;
        tmpY = other.GetY() - this.y;
```

```
        distance = Math.Sqrt((tmpX * tmpX) + (tmpY * tmpY));
        /* determine if circles overlap */
        return distance <= (other.GetRadius() + this.radius);
    }
}
```

Program 6.1   Class `Circle`.

Now, suppose that we have a variable of type `Circle` that refers to an instance of this class. For example,

```
Circle outerCircle = new Circle(0.0, 0.0, 15.4);
```

We might invoke a method, such as its `CalculateArea` method, on this object as follows:

```
area = outerCircle.CalculateArea();
```

Notice that the method is invoked on a particular object – the one referred to by the variable `outerCircle`. When the invocation is carried out, control is transferred to the statements in the `CalculateArea` method of class `Circle` *in the context of* the object referred to by `outerCircle`. The statements in the body of the method use the instance variables of this object to calculate the result. We might later invoke the same method on a different object:

```
Circle innerCircle = new Circle(1.0, 1.0, 76.2);
area = innerCircle.CalculateArea();
```

Now, the same statements are executed (as specified by the declaration of `CalculateArea` in class `Circle`) but in the context of a different object. This time the statements in the body of the method will access the instance variables of this new object in calculating the result.

While this might all seem obvious, the important thing to realize is that *a method executes in the context of some object* – the particular object on which it was invoked. While the method is executing that object is *the current object* for the program. A method can always access the instance variables of the current object but not necessarily those of other objects.

Using `this` to Refer to the Current Object

Since the same method can be invoked on different objects at different times, it is sometimes necessary for a method to be able to find out exactly which object it has been invoked on. In other words, in may be necessary for a method to be able to *refer* to the current object. For this reason C# provides a keyword, `this`, whose value is always a reference to the current object and which can be used by any method that has been invoked on an object. Whenever, a method is invoked on an object, the value of `this` is updated to refer to that object so that while the method is executing `this` always refers to the current object.

If a method invokes a method on a different object, that object becomes the current object while this new method is executing. Moreover, the value of `this` is updated to refer to that object for the duration of the method invocation. When the invocation is complete, control returns to the original method and the value of `this` is updated to refer to the object on which that method was invoked once again.

As an example of the use of `this`, let's consider the `Overlaps` method of class `Circle`. As in Program 6.1, `Overlaps` should take a parameter of type `Circle` referring to the object with which the current object (i.e., the instance of `Circle` on which `Overlaps` is being invoked) is to be compared and, as ever, return a result of type bool, i.e., its heading is:

```
public bool Overlaps(Circle other);
```

When do two circles overlap? As we noted before, two circles overlap if the distance between their centres is less than the sum of their radii. However, we should also realize that a circle always overlaps with itself. In other words, if other happens to refer to the current object, then we don't need to go to the trouble of comparing the coordinates and radii. How do we know if other refers to the current object? We need to compare other with a reference to the current object. Fortunately, the value of this is exactly that – a reference to the current object! Thus, a better version of Overlaps is:

```
public bool Overlaps(Circle other)
{
  double distance, tmpX, tmpY;
  if ((object)this == (object)other)
  {
    /* other refers to the current object and an object */
    /* always overlaps with itself so return true */
    return true;
  }
  else
  {
    /* other refers to a different object */
    /* get distance between centres of circles */
    tmpX = other.GetX() - this.x;
    tmpY = other.GetY() - this.y;
    distance = Math.Sqrt((tmpX * tmpX) + (tmpY * tmpY));
    /* determine if circles overlap */
    return distance <= (other.GetRadius() + this.radius);
  }
}
```

Whenever Overlaps is executed, this always refers to the object on which it was invoked and that object may or may not be the same object that is referred to by other depending on how the method was called.

In passing, notice that Overlaps also invokes some methods on the object referred to by other. While these methods are executing, that object becomes the current object for the program and the value of this becomes a reference to that object.

Program 6.2 shows the revised version of class Circle including the Overlaps method.

We can use this in almost all the same ways that we can use any variable that contains (a reference to) an object. However, there are two things that we have to bear in mind when using this. Firstly, we can't change the value of this ourselves, for example, by using this as the variable on the left-hand side of an assignment. Since C# automatically updates this as the current object changes, we never need to either! Secondly, the type of this changes with the current object. The type of this is always a reference type. Which reference type it is depends on the type of the current object. When used in a method of class Circle, this is of type Circle. In general, the type of this is always the type corresponding to the class in which it is being used.

```csharp
/* A class whose instance represent cirlces with position (revised) */

using System;

class Circle
{
    private const double PI = 3.1416;
    private double x, y; // position
    private double radius;

    /* initialize new circle object */
    public Circle(double x, double y, double radius)
    {
        this.x = x;
        this.y = y;
        this.radius = radius;
    }

    /* return x coordinate of circle */
    public double GetX()
    {
        return this.x;
    }

    /* return y coordinate of circle */
    public double GetY()
    {
        return this.y;
    }

    /* return radius of circle */
    public double GetRadius()
    {
        return this.radius;
    }

    /* calculate area of circle */
    public double CalculateArea()
    {
        return PI * this.radius * this.radius;
    }

    /* calculate circumference of circle */
    public double CalculateCircumference()
    {
        return 2.0 * PI * this.radius;
    }

    /* check if specified circle overlaps with current circle */
    public bool Overlaps(Circle other)
    {
        double distance, tmpX, tmpY;
        if ((object)this == (object)other)
        {
            /* other refers to the current circle and a circle */
            /* always overlaps with itself so return true */
            return true;
        }
```

```
      else
      {
         /* other refers to a different circle *
         /* get distance between centres of circles */
         tmpX = other.GetX() - this.x;
         tmpY = other.GetY() - this.y;
         distance = Math.Sqrt((tmpX * tmpX) + (tmpY * tmpY));
         /* determine if circles overlap */
         return distance <= (other.GetRadius() + this.radius);
      }
   }
}
```

Program 6.2   Class `Circle` (revised).

Methods Without Values – `void`

So far, apart from constructors, all the methods that we have written have returned some value to their caller. For example, the value returned might have been the area of a rectangle, an indication as to whether or not two circles overlap, or the distance between two cities. In addition, we've seen that methods can, and often do, change the values of the instance variables of the object on which they are invoked.

It is also possible to write a method that, like a constructor, does not return any value. In contrast to methods that return values, such a method is called for the *effect* that it has rather than to obtain some result. The effect will usually be to change the values of some of the instance variables of the object on which it was invoked.

A method, other than a constructor, that is not intended to return a value must be declared to have the return type `void`. `void` is a C# keyword that represents the absence of a type. The only place that `void` is used is in the declaration of a method that returns no value.

As an example, let's add a method to class `Circle` to move a circle to a new position. The `MoveTo` method should take the new *x* and *y* coordinates of the circle as its parameters. Its only effect will be to change the values of the x and y instance variables of the object on which it is invoked to the values specified by its parameters. As such, there is no need for it to return any result. Hence, the declaration of `MoveTo` is as follows:

```
public void MoveTo(double x, double y)
{
   this.x = x;
   this.y = y;
}
```

Notice that the keyword `void` is used in place of the return type of the method to specify that the method returns no result. Moreover, since `MoveTo` returns no result, there is no `return` statement in the body of the method. When `MoveTo` is invoked, the statements in its body are executed one after another in turn. When the execution of the last statement in the method is complete, the invocation returns immediately just as is the case for a constructor.

In a similar way we could write separate methods to change the x and y instance variables of a circle object individually or indeed to change its radius.

```
public void SetX(double x)
{
   this.x = x;
}
public void SetY(double y)
{
   this.y = y;
}
public void SetRadius(double radius)
{
   this.radius = radius;
}
```

The MoveTo, SetX, SetY and SetRadius methods are used for their effect. After an invocation of one of these methods is complete that state of the object on which it was invoked will have been changed. Methods that are called for their effect rather than their value are very common. Another good example is the WriteLine method from class Terminal, which we have already used frequently. Notice that WriteLine does not return any value. It is used for the effect that it has. In the case of WriteLine, the effect is to change what appears on the terminal screen.

In passing, note that our Circle class now includes a set of methods to allow us to query the value of its instances variables (GetX, GetY, and GetRadius) and another set to allow us to change the values of its instance variables (SetX, SetY, and SetRadius). It is in fact quite common for a class to provide such methods. The former are often referred to as *accessor* methods and the latter as *modifier* methods.

Functions and Procedures

Methods like MoveTo and WriteLine can really be thought of as commands to the objects concerned. Invoking MoveTo on a circle is really saying to the circle "move to this new position". Invoking WriteLine is ordering the terminal to "write this string". In C# terms, an invocation of such a method is a *statement*. On the other hand, an invocation of a method that returns a value is treated as an *expression* (because it has a value) and can be part of a larger expression. Thus, we can say:

```
myCircle.MoveTo(0.0, 0.0);
area = myCircle.CalculateArea();
totalArea = myCircle.CalculateArea() + yourCircle.CalculateArea();
terminal.Writeln("Area is " + myCircle.CalculateArea());
```

but not:

```
yourCircle = myCircle.MoveTo(x1, y1);
```

The latter simply makes no sense because MoveTo returns no value and hence there is nothing to store in the variable yourCircle.

Thus, an invocation of a method that returns a result is an expression that can be used as part of a larger expression. An invocation of a method that returns no result is a statement and must be used alone as a command to an object.

Methods that return values are usually called *functions*. Methods that return no result are sometimes called *procedures*. While a function is invoked for its value, a procedure it invoked for its effect. Since a function can also modify the instance variables of the object on which it is invoked, a function may also have an effect. Since functions are really intended to return values, such effects are usually referred to as *side effects*. Thus, the side effect of some function may be to change the state of the object on which it was invoked.

For example, let's add another method to class `Circle` to report whether or not the current circle was at the specified location and, if not, to move the circle to that location. Thus, `IsAt` will take a pair of coordinates as its parameters and return a `bool` result to say whether or not the circle was already located at that position. `IsAt` will also have the additional side effect of moving the circle to that position if it was not already located there.

```csharp
public bool IsAt(double x, double y)
{
   if ((this.x == x) && (this.y == y))
   {
      /* circle is already at the specified position */
      return true;
   }
   else
   {
      /* circle is not at the specified */
      /* position so move it */
      this.x = x;
      this.y = y;
      return false;
   }
}
```

Notice that `IsAt` reports whether or not the circle was located at the specified coordinates when the method was invoked but, in any case, after `IsAt` is complete the circle will always be located at those coordinates. Since `IsAt` is a function we can use it as part of an expression:

```csharp
bool movedObject = !myCircle.IsAt(0.0, 0.0);
if (myCircle.IsAT(x, y))...
```

Moreover, since `IsAt` also has an effect, we can choose to ignore its result and use it as a command to move the object to the specified location. Thus, we can say:

```csharp
myCircle.IsAt(6.0, 7.0); // move circle only if necessary
```

We can always invoke a function as a statement. However, it makes no sense to do so unless the function has side effects. For example, we could write:

```csharp
myCircle.GetArea();
```

as a statement. However, this statement is completely superfluous since it has no effect other than calculating a value and that value is not used anywhere!

Passing Parameters to Methods

Let's take a closer look at the heading of the MoveTo method of our Circle class:

```
public void MoveTo(double x, double y);
```

Properly speaking the parameters x and y are called the *formal parameters or formal arguments* of MoveTo. As we know, formal parameters are used to *supply* additional information that a method needs in order to carry out its task. In the case of MoveTo, x and y are used to provide the method with the coordinates of the position to which the circle is to be moved. In general, the formal parameters of a method can be thought of as placeholders for values to be supplied to the method when it is invoked. They also provide names by which the method can refer to these values.

A method can have any number of formal parameters (including none!). Every formal parameter has a name and a type and the name can be any valid C# identifier. Of course, all the formal parameters of a method must have different names. The type of a formal parameter can be any valid C# type including a simple type (like int, double, or bool) or a reference type (like Circle or Person).

The formal parameters of a method can be used exactly as if they are local variables that are declared within the method. MoveTo uses x and y to initialize this.x and this.y. It could have used them in any way that any other local variable can be used. For example, let's write a new version of the Overlaps method, which, instead of taking another instance of Circle as a parameter, takes the coordinates and radius of some circle as its parameters, i.e.,

```
public bool Overlaps(double x, double y, double radius);
```

Our previous version of Overlaps used three local variables, distance, tmpX and tmpY in calculating the distance between the two circles. However, the new version of Overlaps uses the formal parameters x and y in place of the local variables tmpX and tmpY:

```
public bool Overlaps(double x, double y, double radius)
{
    double distance;
    x = x - this.x;
    y = y - this.y;
    distance = Math.Sqrt((x * x) + (y * y));
    return distance <= (radius + this.radius);
}
```

Notice that during the method x is changed to hold the difference between the *x* coordinates of the two circles, which is subsequently used in calculating the distance between the circles. y is likewise used to hold the difference between the *y* coordinates of the circles. x and y are used in the same way as the local variables tmpX and tmpY were used previously. The values stored in x and y are even changed during the course of the method!

In general, the only difference between a local variable, like distance, and a formal parameter, like x or y, is that the initial values of the formal parameters are provided by the invoker of the method. Thus, when this method starts executing, x and y already have the values supplied as inputs to the method when it was invoked while distance is only given a value within the method.

Actual Parameters and Call-by-value

When we invoke a method, we must supply a *value* for each of the formal parameters. The values that we supply are called the *actual parameters* or *actual arguments*. For example, to call MoveTo we might write:

```
// move circle1 to position (27.5, 14.5)
circle1.MoveTo(27.5, 14.5);
```

Here, 27.5 and 14.5 are the *actual parameters* of this *invocation* of MoveTo. Obviously, the actual parameters may be different every time that the method is invoked. Indeed, that's the whole point of using parameters, to supply information to the method that may be different every time that the method is called!

When we invoke a method, we supply one actual parameter for each formal parameter specified in the declaration of the method. Moreover, the type of the actual parameter must be the same as the type of the corresponding formal parameter. The declaration of MoveTo specifies two formal parameters of type double, hence whenever we invoke MoveTo we have to supply two values of type double as its actual parameters.

An actual parameter can be any *expression* that gives a *value* of the required type. Thus, the following are all valid ways of invoking MoveTo:

```
circle1.MoveTo(27.5, 14.5); // actual parameters are literals
circle1.MoveTo(newX, newY); // actual parameters are variables
circle1.MoveTo((endX-startX)/2.0,(endY-startY)/2.0);
        // actual parameters are arbitrary expressions
circle1.MoveTo(0.0, (lowY+highY)*factor);
        // actual parameters are some combination of the above
```

When an invocation is carried out, the actual parameters are evaluated first and then the required method invoked with the values of the actual parameters being used to initialize the corresponding formal parameters. In some sense, the values of the actual parameters are *copied* to the corresponding formal parameters. This method of passing parameters to a method is known as *call-by-value* since methods are called with the values of their actual parameters.

Figure 6.1 shows in more detail the sequence of events that occurs when MoveTo is invoked.

As another example, Figure 6.2 shows in detail what happens when Overlaps is invoked as follows:

```
centreX = 12.0; centreY = 37.0; newRadius = 3.0;
if (circle1.Overlaps(centreX, centreY, newRadius))
{
...
```

You might ask what values do centreX, centreY, and newRadius have after the invocation of Overlaps is complete. Of course, they have exactly the same values as they had before! We didn't do anything to change them and *using call-by-value* there is no way for a method to change the values of its actual parameters. Even though the formal parameters x and y are changed during the course of the method, that has no effect on the corresponding actual parameters centreX and centreY. The actual parameters are only used to give initial values to the formal parameters. Thereafter, there is no connection between the actual and formal parameters and, therefore, no possibility of a method ever changing the values of its actual parameters when using call-by-value.

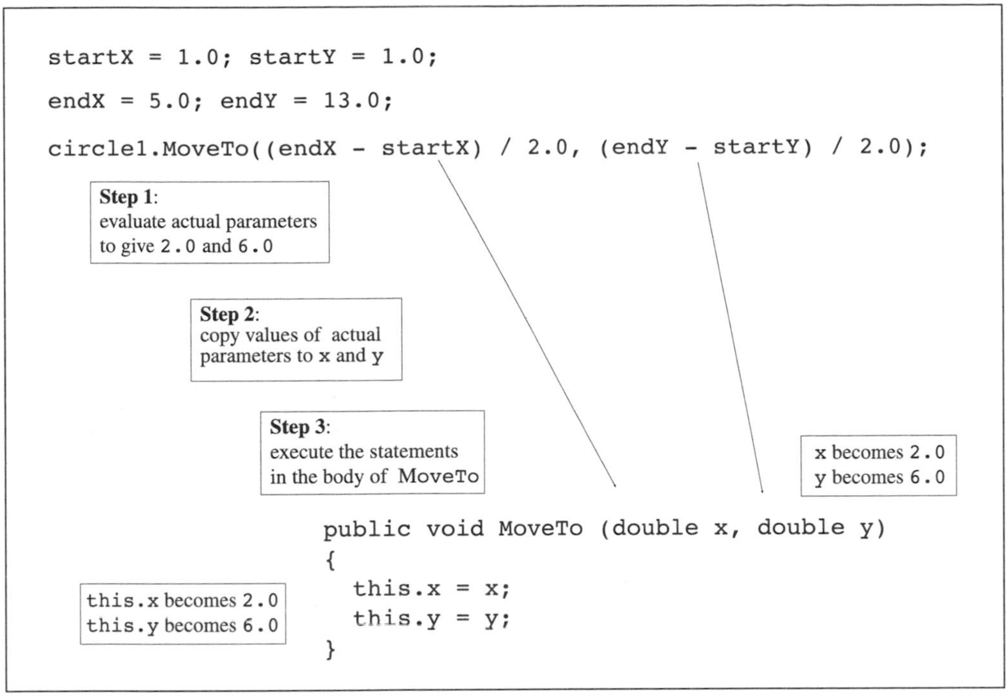

```
startX = 1.0; startY = 1.0;

endX = 5.0; endY = 13.0;

circle1.MoveTo((endX - startX) / 2.0, (endY - startY) / 2.0);
```

Step 1:
evaluate actual parameters
to give `2.0` and `6.0`

Step 2:
copy values of actual
parameters to x and y

Step 3:
execute the statements
in the body of `MoveTo`

`x` becomes `2.0`
`y` becomes `6.0`

```
public void MoveTo (double x, double y)
{
    this.x = x;
    this.y = y;
}
```

`this.x` becomes `2.0`
`this.y` becomes `6.0`

Figure 6.1   Call-by-value in action.

Passing Object References as Parameters

As we've seen already, the type of a formal parameter can be a reference type. For example, our original version of the Overlaps method of class Circle has a single formal parameter of type Circle called other:

```
public bool Overlaps(Circle other);
```

When we invoke Overlaps, we must supply (a reference to) an instance of class Circle as its actual parameter. For example, we might write:

```
newCircle = new Circle(0.0, 0.0, 5.0);
if (circle1.Overlaps(newCircle)) ...
```

In this case, the value of newCircle becomes the initial value of other when Overlaps is invoked. The interesting thing to notice here is that now, as Figure 6.3 shows, both newCircle and other refer to the same object!

Of course, a method can use an object reference that has been passed to it as a parameter to invoke methods on that object. For example, Overlaps invokes the GetX, GetY, and GetRadius methods on the object referred to by its formal parameter other.

As a further example, let's add a method to class Circle to position a specified circle at the same coordinates as the current circle, i.e., to centre the two circles at the same point. Our new method, let's call it Centre, will take a single formal parameter of type Circle to specify the other circle.

```
public void Centre(Circle other);
```

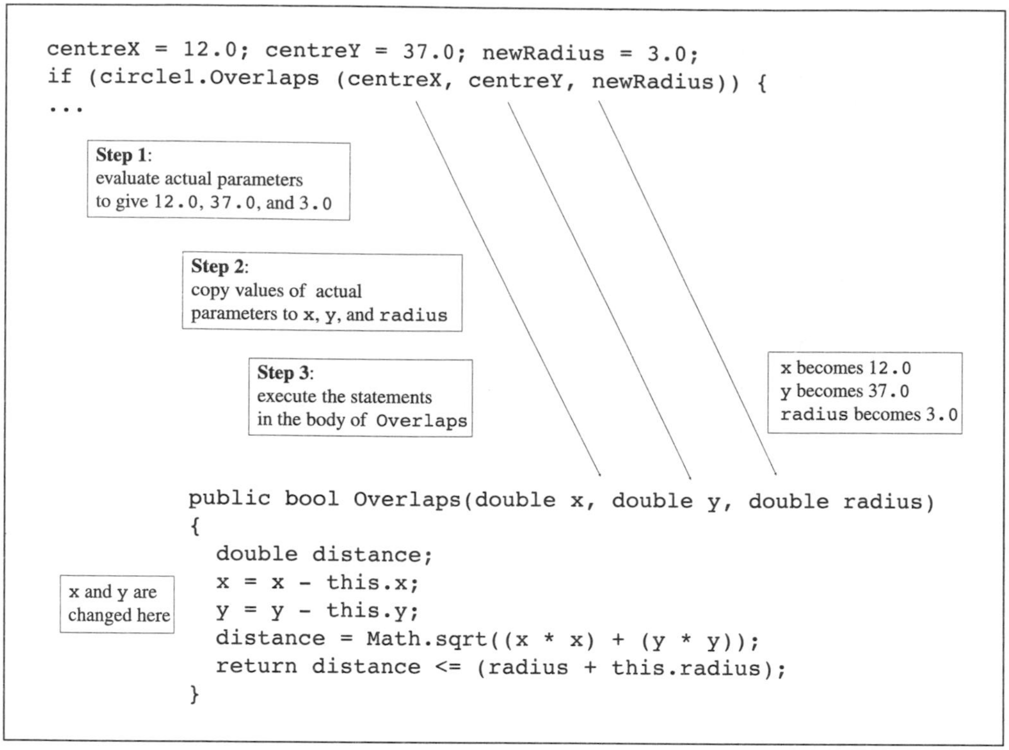

```
centreX = 12.0; centreY = 37.0; newRadius = 3.0;
if (circle1.Overlaps (centreX, centreY, newRadius)) {
...
```

Step 1:
evaluate actual parameters
to give 12.0, 37.0, and 3.0

Step 2:
copy values of actual
parameters to x, y, and radius

Step 3:
execute the statements
in the body of Overlaps

x becomes 12.0
y becomes 37.0
radius becomes 3.0

```
public bool Overlaps(double x, double y, double radius)
{
    double distance;
    x = x - this.x;
    y = y - this.y;
    distance = Math.sqrt((x * x) + (y * y));
    return distance <= (radius + this.radius);
}
```

x and y are
changed here

Figure 6.2   Call-by-value is one way.

Notice that Centre returns no value – it is intended to be used only for its effect.

To centre the specified circle at the same point as the current circle, we simply invoke the MoveTo method on the other circle to move it to the point given by the *x* and *y* coordinates of the current circle.

```
public void Centre(Circle other) {
    if ((object)this != (object)other) // no need to move
    {
        other.MoveTo(this.x, this.y);
    }
}
```

Invoking this method may cause the x and y instance variables of the circle referred to by other to change! Put another way, a method can change an object to which it is passed a reference as a parameter. Thus, the effect of a method may not be to change the state of the current object but to change the state of one or more other objects! Figure 6.4 shows the effect of invoking Centre on an instance of Circle.

Notice that, although the state of the object referred to by the actual parameter circle2 has changed, the actual parameter itself *is not changed*. circle2 still refers to the same object (although the state of that object has been changed). Put another way, object references are also passed by value.

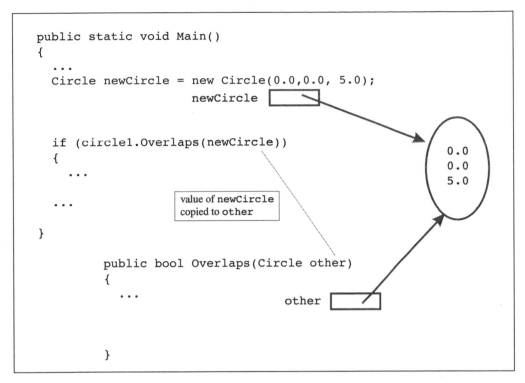

Figure 6.3   Passing an object reference by value.

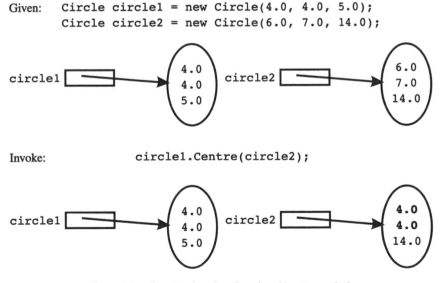

Figure 6.4   Changing the value of another object in a method.

Swapping the Values of Actual Parameters

As a final example, let's consider writing a class, let's call it `IntSwapper`, that provides a method to swap the values of two `int` variables. For example, we should be able to write:

```
int var1 = 12, var2 = 14;
swapper = new IntSwapper();
...
swapper.Swap(var1, var2);
// now var1 should be 14 and var2 12
```

Program 6.3 shows a possible declaration of class `IntSwapper` and Program 6.4 a program the uses it. The execution of the program is shown in Figure 6.5. As you can see our first attempt at writing class `IntSwapper` clearly didn't work! Why not? Simply because the parameters are passed by value, there is no way for the `Swap` method of class `IntSwapper` to change the values of its actual parameters, `var1` and `var2`. Hence, `var1` and `var2` have exactly the same value after the invocation of `Swap` is complete as they had before!

```
/* A class that provides a method to */
/*   swap the values of its parameters */
class IntSwapper
{
   public void Swap(int num1, int num2)
   {
      int tmp;

      tmp = num1;
      num1 = num2;
      num2 = tmp;
   }
}
```

Program 6.3   Class `IntSwapper`.

```
/* A program that tries to use a method to swap */
/* the values of two variables */

using tcdIO;

class SwapProgram
{
   public static void Main()
   {
      Terminal terminal;
      int var1, var2;
      IntSwapper swapper;

      /* create an object to represent the terminal */
      terminal = new Terminal();

      /* create the IntSwapper */
      swapper = new IntSwapper();

      /* Read in some numbers */
      var1 = terminal.ReadInt("Enter value of var1: ");
      var2 = terminal.ReadInt("Enter value of var2: ");

      /* swap them */
      swapper.Swap(var1, var2);
```

```
      /* Write out the numbers */
      terminal.WriteLine("Value of var1 is now: " + var1 + ".");
      terminal.WriteLine("Value of var2 is now: " + var2 + ".");
   }
}
```

Program 6.4   A program to swap the values of two `int` variables.

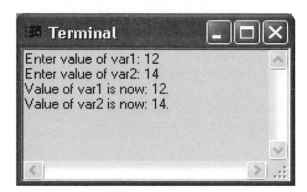

Figure 6.5   The execution of Program 6.4.

On the other hand, if the values that we wanted to swap were contained in objects, we would be able to swap them. For example, let's say we had a class called `IntBox` whose instances each contain a single value of type `int` as shown in Program 6.5.

We can now write a method to swap the values stored in two instances of class `IntBox` as shown in Program 6.6. Notice that we use the methods provided by class `IntBox` to retrieve the values stored in each of the objects passed as parameters to the `Swap` method and to store new values into each object.

```
/* A class whose instances contain a single int */
class IntBox
{
   private int value;

   /* initialize a new IntBox */
   public IntBox(int v)
   {
      this.value = v;
   }

   /* change the value contained in the current IntBox */
   public void SetValue(int v)
   {
      this.value = v;
   }

   /* return the value contained in the current IntBox */
   public int GetValue()
   {
      return this.value;
   }
}
```

Program 6.5   Class `IntBox`.

```
/* A class that provides a method to */
/* swap the values of its parameters */
class IntSwapper
{
   public void Swap(IntBox num1, IntBox num2)
   {
      int tmp;

      /* first save the value contained in num1 */
      tmp = num1.GetValue();
      /* now change the value contained in num1 */
      /* to be the same as that contained in num2 */
      num1.SetValue(num2.GetValue());
      /* finally, change the value contained in num2 */
      /* to be the original value from num1 */
      num2.SetValue(tmp);
   }
}
```

Program 6.6   Class `IntSwapper` (revised).

```
/* A program to swap the contents of two objects */

using tcdIO;

class SwapProgram
{
   public static void Main ()
   {
      Terminal terminal;
      IntBox box1, box2;
      IntSwapper swapper;

      /* create an object to represent the terminal */
      terminal = new Terminal();

      /* create the IntSwapper */
      swapper = new IntSwapper();

      /* Read in some numbers */
      box1 = new IntBox(terminal.ReadInt("Enter value of box1: "));
      box2 = new IntBox(terminal.ReadInt("Enter value of box2: "));

      /* swap them */
      swapper.Swap(box1, box2);

      /* Write out the numbers */
      terminal.WriteLine("Value of box1 is now: " + box1.GetValue() + ".");
      terminal.WriteLine("Value of box2 is now: " + box2.GetValue() + ".");
   }
}
```

Program 6.7   A program to swap the contents of two objects.

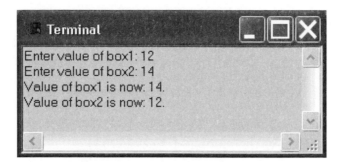

Figure 6.6   The execution of Program 6.7.

A program that uses the `IntBox` and `IntSwapper` classes is shown in Program 6.7 and its output in Figure 6.6. Notice that the values contained in `box1` and `box2` have been modified as a result of the invocation of the `Swap` method just as we intended!

Class Variables and Methods

So far, we've taken the view that a class is solely a description of a set of objects that represent the same kind of entity. As such, a class declaration includes a list of the instance variables contained in each instance of the class together with a list of the methods to which the instances of the class can respond. In fact, there is slightly more to a C# class than just that! In particular, it is possible for a class to have attributes and methods that belong to the class itself rather than to its individual instances.

An attribute that belongs to the class itself is known as a *class variable* (as opposed to an *instance variable*). While every instance of a class has its own individual copy of each instance variable declared by the class, only a single copy of each class variable exists and that copy is *shared* between all the instances of the class. Consequently, any instance of the class can read or modify the value of a class variable.

A method that applies to the class itself is known as a *class method*. Class methods are invoked on the class itself rather than on a specific instance of the class. We have already seen, and indeed used, some class methods! A good example is the method `Math.Sqrt` that we used in writing the `Overlaps` method in class `Circle`. Did you notice that when we used `Math.Sqrt` we never created an object on which to invoke the method? We didn't need to because `Sqrt` is actually a class method provided by class `Math`. Thus, `Sqrt` is invoked on the class rather than on a specific instance of the class. To invoke a class method we use the `.` (dot) operator as usual and can pass parameters to the method in the normal way. However, rather than specifying a particular object on which to invoke the method, we always specify the name of the class.

Declaring Class Variables and Methods

A class variable or method is declared by labeling it with the keyword `static` in the class definition. Thus, `Sqrt` is declared as follows in class `Math`:

```
public static double Sqrt(double d);
```

Notice that the keyword `static` comes after the keyword `public` and before the type of value returned by the method. Having declared `Sqrt` to be `static`, we can now invoke it on the class `Math` as in:

```
double result = Math.Sqrt(2.47783);
```

but we can't invoke it on an instance of class `Math`. For example, we can't write:

```
Math mathObject = new Math();
double result = mathObject.Sqrt(2.47783);
```

Why not? Simply because `Sqrt` is a class method and not an instance method!

As an example of the use of class variables and methods, let's write a class, call it `ObjectCounter`, that keeps count of the number of instances of the class that have been created. Clearly `ObjectCounter` will need to provide an attribute, let's call it `numInstances`, to be used to store the number of instances of the class that have been created so far. `numInstances` will need to be incremented every time that an instance of the class is created (i.e., by the constructor). Our class will also need to provide a method to allow the current value of `numInstances` to be retrieved when necessary – let's call it `GetNumInstances`. A first attempt at writing class `ObjectCounter` is shown in Program 6.8.

Now let's write a program that illustrates the use of the class. Our program will simply use a loop that creates a new object on each iteration. Just for fun, the program will keep references to the last three objects created while older objects will be discarded. In addition, after each

```
/* A class that is capable of keeping */
/* count of its instances */
class ObjectCounter
{
    private int numInstances = 0;    // number of instances of class
    private string name;             // each instance has a name

    /* initialize a new instance with given name */
    public ObjectCounter(string name)
    {
        /* initialize name */
        this.name = name;
        /* count new instance */
        this.numInstances = this.numInstances + 1;
    }

    /* return number of existing instances */
    public int GetNumInstances()
    {
        return this.numInstances;
    }

    /* return name associated with current object */
    public string GetName()
    {
        return this.name;
    }
}
```

Program 6.8   Class `ObjectCounter`.

object is created and initialized, the number of objects created so far will be printed. The full program is shown in Program 6.9 and its output in Figure 6.7.

Clearly, we've done something wrong, but what? The problem is that, as we declared it in Program 6.8, numInstances is an instance variable. Thus, every instance of the class has its own distinct copy of this variable. Moreover, our constructor causes the copy of this variable

```
/* A program to illustrate the need for */
/* class variables and methods */

using tcdIO;

class CounterProgram
{

   public static void Main()
   {
      Terminal terminal;
      ObjectCounter last, secondLast, thirdLast;
         // keep three instances
      int count, number;

      /* create an object to represent the terminal */
      terminal = new Terminal();

      /* get number to create - at least 3 */
      number = terminal.ReadInt("Enter number of instances to create: ");
      while (number < 3)
      {
         number = terminal.ReadInt("Enter number of instances to create: ");
      }

      /* create first three */
      count = 3;
      thirdLast = new ObjectCounter("Some name");
      terminal.WriteLine("Class currently has: "
                         + thirdLast.GetNumInstances() + " instances.");
      secondLast = new ObjectCounter("Some name");
      terminal.WriteLine("Class currently has: "
                         + secondLast.GetNumInstances() + " instances.");
      last = new ObjectCounter("Some name");
      terminal.WriteLine("Class currently has: "
                         + last.GetNumInstances() + " instances.");

      /* create the rest */
      while (count < number)
      {
         thirdLast = secondLast;
         secondLast = last;
         last = new ObjectCounter("Some name");
         terminal.WriteLine("Class currently has: "
                            + last.GetNumInstances() + " instances.");
         count = count + 1;
      }
   }
}
```

Program 6.9   A program to illustrate the need for class variables.

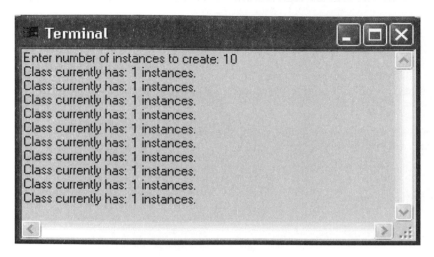

Figure 6.7   The execution of Program 6.9.

in each instance of the class to have the value 1. As you can see in Figure 6.7 every call to GetNumInstances in our program returns this value – the value of the numInstances variable in the object on which it is invoked. We can visualize the situation as in Figure 6.8.

To solve the problem, we need to make numInstances a class variable so that there is only one copy of this variable that is shared by all instances. In addition, we can make GetNumInstances a class method that we invoke on the class itself rather than on any one of its instances as shown is Program 6.10. Clearly, it makes sense to ask the class how many instances it has rather than to ask any particular instance of the class.

Program 6.11 shows our revised program and Figure 6.9 its output. Notice that GetNumInstances is now invoked on the class rather than an object. Figure 6.10 shows the variables and objects used by the program. Notice that there is now only a single copy of the variable numInstances.

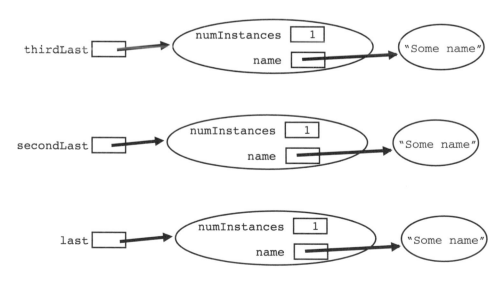

Figure 6.8   The variables and objects of Program 6.9.

```
/* A class that is capable of keeping */
/* count of its instances (revised) */
class ObjectCounter
{
   private static int numInstances = 0;   // class keeps count of instances
   private string name;                    // each instance has a name

   /* initialize a new instance with given name */
   public ObjectCounter(string name)
   {
      /* initialize name */
      this.name = name;
      /* count new instance */
      numInstances = numInstances + 1;
   }

   /* return number of existing instances */
   public static int GetNumInstances()
   {
      return numInstances;
   }

   /* return name associated with current object */
   public string GetName()
   {
      return this.name;
   }
}
```

Program 6.10   Class ObjectCounter (revised).

```
/* A program to illustrate the use of */
/* class variables and methods */

using tcdIO;

class CounterProgram
{

   public static void Main()
   {
      Terminal terminal;
      ObjectCounter last, secondLast, thirdLast; // keep three instances
      int count, number;

      /* create an object to represent the terminal */
      terminal = new Terminal();

      /* get number to create - at least 3 */
      number = terminal.ReadInt("Enter number of instances to create: ");
      while (number < 3)
      {
         number = terminal.ReadInt("Enter number of instances to create: ");
      }
```

```
    /* create first three */
    count = 3;
    thirdLast = new ObjectCounter("Some name");
    terminal.WriteLine("Class currently has: "
                    + ObjectCounter.GetNumInstances() + " instances.");
    secondLast = new ObjectCounter("Some name");
    terminal.WriteLine("Class currently has: "
                    + ObjectCounter.GetNumInstances() + " instances.");
    last = new ObjectCounter("Some name");
    terminal.WriteLine("Class currently has: "
                    + ObjectCounter.GetNumInstances() + " instances.");

    /* create the rest */
    while (count < number)
    {
        thirdLast = secondLast;
        secondLast = last;
        last = new ObjectCounter("Some name");
        terminal.WriteLine("Class currently has: "
                    + ObjectCounter.GetNumInstances() + " instances.");
        count = count + 1;
    }
  }
}
```

Program 6.11   A program to illustrate the use of class variables and methods.

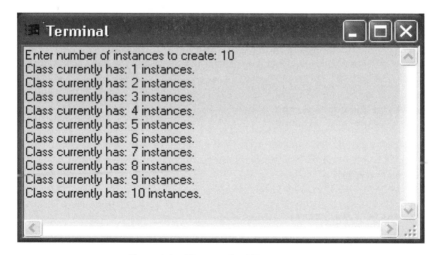

Figure 6.9   The execution of Program 6.11.

As you can see in Program 6.10, the instance methods of a class can access any class variables provided by the class. For example, the constructor of class `ObjectCounter` uses the `numInstances` class variable. Likewise, the class methods can use any class variables provided by the class. For example, in Program 6.10, `GetNumInstances` also uses `numInstances`. However, class methods *cannot* access the instance variables of the class. Instance variables are associated with the individual instances of a class. Class methods aren't invoked on a particular instance of the class and hence have no corresponding instance variables. In fact, a class method can be invoked on a class even if that class has no instances!

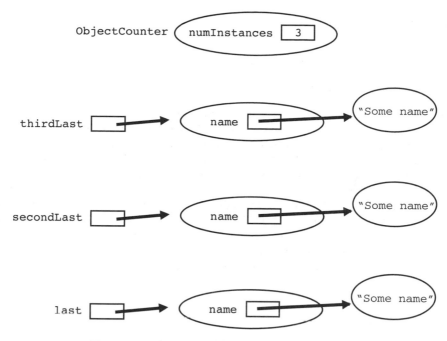

Figure 6.10   The variables and objects used by Program 6.11.

For the same reason, class methods cannot use `this`. When a class method is executing there is no current object and hence `this` has no value. Of course, if a class method creates an object or is given a reference to an object as a parameter, it can use that object as normal.

Using Class Methods

Class methods should be used sparingly. Nevertheless, they are often useful. They are often used to implement commands that don't properly apply to any particular instance of a class but are somehow associated with the entities represented by the instances of the class – our `GetNumInstances` method is a good example.

Class methods are also often used to implement generally useful commands that don't apply to any particular type of object. The `Sqrt` method of class `Math` is a good example. Obviously its useful to have a method that is capable of calculating square roots so that we don't have to do it ourselves every time that we need to take a square root. However, it's not so obvious what object, or indeed what class of object, such a method should be applied to! The solution is to make it a class method. In fact, there are numerous classes whose only purpose is to provide collections of such generally useful methods. Class `Math` is one example. Not only does it provide a class method to calculate square roots, but also class methods to perform a variety of other mathematical functions including calculating sines and cosines, and taking the absolute value of a number. All of these functions are provided as class methods. In fact, all the methods provided by class `Math` are class methods!

Classes like `Math` that exist only to provide collections of useful methods are usually referred to as utility classes. They usually have the common characteristic that they only provide `static` methods and hence, there is never any reason to create an instance of one of these classes.

Main is static

One other place where `static` methods always appear is in the program class of a C# program! Remember that the `Main` method is always declared:

```
public static void Main();
```

Yep, `Main` is always a `static` method. If you think about it, this makes good sense. `Main` is invoked by the CLR to start a program executing. At that point, no objects have been created. If there are no objects, it's not possible to invoke a method on an object. Hence, `Main` is declared to be class method so that it can be invoked by the CLR to get the program running.

As you can now appreciate there really is nothing very special about a program class other than the fact that is has a method called `Main` that can be called by the CLR! In fact, the program class can declare any instance variables and methods, as well as any class variables and methods, that we feel appropriate. As a general rule, you shouldn't provide instance variables and methods or class variables in your program classes. It is sometimes useful to provide additional class methods that can be called by `Main` to perform a task that may need to be carried out several times in the course of the program and which doesn't apply to any particular object.

Using Class Variables

In general, the use of class variables is best avoided. There are really very few places where such variables are ever needed.

On the other hand, all constants are implicitly declared to be `static`. This means that the constant value is associated with the class rather than with every individual instance of the class. Clearly, since the value of the constant can't be changed, it makes sense not to copy it in every individual instance of the class, but rather to store it only once in the class. For example, the constant `PI` in class `Circle` was declared

```
private const double PI = 3.1416;
```

and is considered `static` even though the keyword `static` doesn't, and indeed can't, appear in its declaration.

The Scope Rules of C#

Have you noticed that we often declare entities with the same identifier in different parts of a program? For example, we often declare the same identifier in different classes and, indeed, often even declare the same identifier several times within the same class. We might, for example, use the identifier `radius` for the name of an instance variable in class `Circle` and the name of a local variable in the `Main` method of a program that manipulates circles. Moreover, the `Overlaps` and `Centre` methods of class `Circle` both use the identifier `other` as the name of their formal parameter.

Clearly, being able to reuse identifiers in this way is a good idea. Apart from anything else, it saves us having to continually think up new identifiers! More importantly, it allows different parts of a program to be developed independently and without detailed knowledge of the other parts of the program. If identifiers could not be reused in different parts of a program, then every programmer would have to be aware of all the other identifiers that were being used everywhere else in the program! In a large project, which involved hundreds of programmers, this would almost certainly be impossible!

Nevertheless, if the same identifier can be used to mean different things at different points in a program, or even within a single class, there is a risk of ambiguity arising. If we are not careful, it might not be possible to say exactly what the meaning of a particular identifier at a particular point in the program is. Clearly, we need some rules to allow us to uniquely establish what any identifier refers to at any point in a program. Such rules are called the *scope rules* of a programming language. This section provides an overview of the scope rules of C#. As it happens, the detailed scope rules of C# are quite complex, so we'll limit ourselves to introducing the most important rules here and introduce some of the others later as the need arises.

Class Scope

The *scope* of a declaration is the region of the program within which the entity declared can be referred to using its identifier. For example, as Figure 6.11 shows, the scope of the

```
class Circle
{
    private const double PI = 3.1416;
    private double x, y;
    private double radius;

    public Circle(double x, double y, double radius)
    {
        ...
    }

    public double GetX()
    {
        ...
    }

    public double GetY()
    {
        ...
    }

    public double GetRadius()
    {
        ...
    }

    public double CalculateArea()
    {
        ...
    }

    public double CalculateCircumference()
    {
        ...
    }

    public bool Overlaps(Circle other)
    {
        ...
    }
    ...
}
```

The scope of `radius`

Figure 6.11   The scope of the `radius` instance variable.

```
class Circle
{

    public Circle(double x, double y, double radius)
    {
        ...
    }

    public double GetX()
    {
        ...
    }

    public double GetY()
    {
        ...
    }

    public double GetRadius()
    {
        ...
    }

    public double CalculateArea()
    {
        ...
    }

    public double CalculateCircumference()
    {
        ...
    }

    public bool Overlaps(Circle other)
    {
        ...
    }


    private const double PI = 3.1416;
    private double x, y;
    private double radius;
}
```

The scope of `radius`

Figure 6.12   The scope is unaffected by the order of declaration.

instance variable `radius` is the entire class. In other words, we can use the identifier `radius` anywhere within class `Circle` to refer to the instance variable with that name declared in the class.

In general, the scope of an instance variable or method declaration is the entire class in which it is declared. An instance variable or method declaration is said to have *class scope*. Class scope extends from the opening "{" of the class declaration to the closing "}".

Although we don't recommend it, the scope rules allow an instance variable to be declared at the end of the class declaration (or indeed between the declarations of any two methods) and not just at its beginning. Nevertheless, its scope is still the entire class as shown in Figure 6.12.

Block Scope

The scope of a local variable declaration is the *block* in which it appears. What's a block? A block is simply that part of a program between an opening brace and the matching closing brace. In

```
public bool Overlaps(Circle other)
{
    double distance, x, y;

    x = other.GetX() - this.x;
    y = other.GetY() - this.y;
    distance = Math.Sqrt((x * x) + (y * y));
    return distance <= (other.GetRadius() + this.radius);
}
```

(a)

```
public bool Overlaps(Circle other)
{
    double x = other.GetX() - this.x;
    double y = other.GetY() - this.y;
    double distance = Math.Sqrt((x * x) + (y * y));
    return distance <= (other.GetRadius() + this.radius);
}
```

(b)

Scope of
distance

```
public bool Overlaps(Circle other)
{
    double x = other.GetX() - this.x;
    double y = other.GetY() - this.y;
    distance = Math.Sqrt((x * x) + (y * y));
    double distance;
    return distance <= (other.GetRadius() + this.radius);
}
```

(c)

Figure 6.13   Block scope.

the Overlaps method shown in Figure 6.13(a), the scope of the local variable distance is the block forming the body of the method. Again, although we don't recommend it, the scope rules allow a local variable to be declared anywhere within a block – not just at its beginning. Thus, we could rewrite Overlaps as shown in Figure 6.13(b) so that distance is not declared until it is actually needed. As before, its scope remains the entire block forming the body of the method. Note however, that unlike an instance variable, the use of a local variable cannot precede its declaration so Figure 6.13(c) is not allowable even though the assignment to distance is within its scope.

Nested Blocks

Blocks can be nested. In other words, one block can contain a number of other blocks as illustrated in Figure 6.14, which shows a version of the Fibonacci program that we wrote in Chapter 5. In this case, both the if and else branches of the if statement and the body of the while loop constitute nested blocks. The block corresponding to the body of the while loop is nested within the block constituting the if branch of the if statement. Likewise, both the if and else branches of the if statement are nested within the block constituting the Main method.

```
               class Factorial
               {
                 public static void Main ()
                 {
                   Terminal terminal;
                   int factorialN = 1;
Block 1            int n;

                   terminal = new Terminal();
                   n = terminal.ReadInt("Enter n: ");
                   if (n > 1)
Block 2            {
                     while (n > 1)
Block 3              {
                       factorialN = factorialN * n;
                       n = n - 1;
                     }
                     terminal.WriteLine("n! is: " + factorialN + ".");
                   }
                   else
Block 4            {
                     terminal.WriteLine("Unable to calculate " + n + "!");
                   }
                 }
               }
```

Figure 6.14   Nested blocks.

Scope of
`factorialN`

```
class Factorial
{
  public static void Main ()
  {
    Terminal terminal;
    int factorialN = 1;
    int n;

    terminal = new Terminal();
    n = terminal.ReadInt("Enter n: ");
    if (n > 1)
    {
      while (n > 1)
      {
        factorialN = factorialN * n;
        n = n - 1;
      }
      terminal.WriteLine("n! is: " + factorialN + ".");
    }
    else
    {
      terminal.WriteLine("Unable to calculate " + n + "!");
    }
  }
}
```

Figure 6.15   Block scope in the presence of nested blocks.

```
class Factorial
{
  public static void Main ()
  {
    Terminal terminal;
    int n;

    terminal = new Terminal();
    n = terminal.ReadInt("Enter n: ");
    if (n > 1)
    {
      int factorialN = 1;
      while (n > 1)
      {
        factorialN = factorialN * n;
        n = n - 1;
      }
      terminal.WriteLine("n! is: " + factorialN + ".");
    }
    else
    {
      terminal.WriteLine("Unable to calculate " + n + "!");
    }
  }
}
```

Scope of
factorialN

Figure 6.16   Local variables can be declared in nested blocks.

The scope of a local variable declaration includes not only the block in which the declaration occurs but also, as Figure 6.15 shows, any nested blocks. In Figure 6.15, the scope of the local variable factorialN extends over the if and while statements too.

C# allows a local variable to be declared within any block and not just the outermost block of a method. For example, as Figure 6.16 shows, the local variable factorialN could have been declared in the block corresponding to the if part of the if statement. As before, the scope of the variable is the block in which it appears, in this case limited to the if part of the if statement. In other words, factorialN can't be used elsewhere in the method such as in the else part of the if statement.

As you might expect, once a local variable has been declared in some block, no other local variable with the same identifier can be declared in a nested block. On the other hand, it is possible for a method to declare a local variable with the same name as an instance variable of its class. The two can be distinguished because the instance variable can be referred to using this.

Formal Parameter Scope

The scope of a formal parameter is the body of the method to which it is a parameter. Thus, as Figure 6.17 shows, the scope of the formal parameter other is the body of the Overlaps method.

Scope of
other

```
public bool Overlaps(Circle other)
{
  double distance, x, y;

  x = other.GetX() - this.x;
  y = other.GetY() - this.y;
  distance = Math.Sqrt((x * x) + (y * y));
  return distance <= (other.GetRadius() + this.radius);
}
```

Figure 6.17   The scope of a formal parameter.

Like a local variable, a formal parameter can have the same identifier as an instance variable – we've seen lots of examples of this already. An instance variable can be distinguished from a formal parameter using `this`.

More surprisingly, a formal parameter can have the same identifier as a local variable of the same method. In this case, the use of the identifier in the scope of the local variable declaration always denotes the corresponding local variable and *not* the formal parameter of the same name. In some sense, the declaration of the local variable supersedes the declaration of the formal parameter. In C#'s terminology local variables are said to *hide* formal parameters with the same identifier.

Overloading Methods

In C#, as well as in a number of other object-oriented programming languages, a class can declare several methods with the *same* identifier as long as each has a different set of formal parameters. Methods with the same name but different formal parameters are said to be *overloaded*. For example, Program 6.12 shows yet another revised version of class `Circle` in which both the `Circle` constructor and the `Overlaps` method are overloaded. In other words two different versions of the constructor are provided as well as two different versions of the `Overlaps` method. Either constructor can be used to initialize a new instance of the class. Likewise, either version of `Overlaps` can be invoked on any instance of class `Circle`. Because the formal parameters of the different versions of an overloaded method are different, C# can determine from the actual parameters supplied when the method is invoked which version of the method is intended to be executed. Method overloading is useful where a class has a set of methods that perform similar functions using different inputs.

Two methods with the same identifier must differ in either:

- the number of formal parameters that they take,
- the types of the formal parameters that they take, or
- the order in which formal parameters of the same type occur.

For example, given a class that declares the method:

```
public void Print(float number, int pos)
{
  // print number at position pos on the current line
}
```

```
/* A class whose instances represent circles (revised) */

using System;

class Circle
{
   private const double PI = 3.1416;
   private double x, y; // position
   private double radius;

   /* initialize a new circle located at position (0.0,0.0) */
   public Circle(double radius)
   {
      this.x = 0.0;
      this.y = 0.0;
      this.radius = radius;
   }

   /* initialize a new circle located at position (x, y) */
   public Circle(double x, double y, double radius)
   {
      this.x = x;
      this.y = y;
      this.radius = radius;
   }

   /* return x coordinate of circle */
   public double GetX()
   {
      return this.x;
   }

   /* return y coordinate of circle */
   public double GetY()
   {
      return this.y;
   }

   /* return radius of circle */
   public double GetRadius()
   {
      return this.radius;
   }

   /* calculate area of circle */
   public double CalculateArea()
   {
      return PI * this.radius * this.radius;
   }

   /* calculate circumference of circle */
   public double CalculateCircumference()
   {
      return 2.0 * PI * this.radius;
   }
```

```
/* move circle to specified location */
public void MoveTo(double x, double y)
{
    this.x = x;
    this.y = y;
}

/* move specified circle to the same location */
/* as the current circle */
public void CentreAt(Circle other)
{
    if ((object)this != (object)other)
    {
        /* no need to move current circle */
        other.MoveTo(this.x, this.y);
    }
}

/* check if circle is at specified location */
/* and put it there if not */
public bool IsAt(double x, double y)
{
    if ((this.x == x) && (this.y == y))
    {
        /* circle is already at the specified position */
        return true;
    }
    else
    {
        /* circle is not at the specified *
        /* position so move it */
        this.x = x;
        this.y = y;
        return false;
    }
}

/* check if specified circle overlaps with current circle */
public bool Overlaps(Circle other)
{
    double distance, x, y;

    if ((object)this == (object)other)
    {
        /* other refers to the current circle and a circle */
        /* always overlaps with itself so return true */
        return true;
    }
    else
    {
        /* other refers to a different circle *
        /* get distance between centres of circles */
        x = other.GetX() - this.x;
        y = other.GetY() - this.y;
```

```
         distance = Math.Sqrt((x * x) + (y * y));
         /* determine if circles overlap */
         return distance <= (other.GetRadius() + this.radius);
      }
   }

   /* check if specified circle overlaps with current circle */
   public bool Overlaps(double x, double y, double radius)
   {
      /* first get distance between centres of circles */
      x = x - this.x;
      y = y - this.y;
      double distance = Math.Sqrt((x * x) + (y * y));
      /* determine if circles overlap */
      return distance <= (radius + this.radius);
   }
}
```

Program 6.12   Class `Circle` (revised).

we could also declare:

```
public void Print(float number, int x, int y)
{
   // print number at position (x, y) on the screen
}
```

in the same class since this version of `Print` takes a different number of parameters. Likewise, we could declare:

```
public void Print(int number, int pos)
{
   // print number at position pos on the current line
}
```

since this version of `Print` takes parameters of different types. Finally, we might also include:

```
public void print(int pos, float number)
{
   // print number on line pos of the screen
}
```

since, although this version of `Print` takes the same types of parameters as our original version, the parameters of different types occur in a different order. Note, however, that we can't include:

```
public void Print(int pos, int number)
{
   // print number on line pos of the screen
}
```

because we already have a version of `Print` that takes two `int`s as its parameters even though the identifiers of the corresponding parameters (and presumably their meaning) are different.

It's worth pointing out that the types returned by the different versions of an overloaded method may be different although this is not significant in distinguishing between the different versions. For example, given:

```
public void Print(float number, int pos)
{
   // print number at position pos on the current line
}
```

we can also have

```
public int Print(float number, int x, int y)
{
   // print number at position (x, y) on screen
}
```

but only because the number of parameters is different! We could not have

```
public int Print(float number, int pos)
{
   // print number at position pos on the current line
}
```

because, although the return type is different, the number, types and order of the parameters is the same.

Overloaded methods are very common. As in our `Circle` class, overloaded constructors are particularly common – we often want to be able to initialize new instances of a class in different ways specified by means of different sets of parameters. For example, we will often have a constructor that takes no parameters and initializes a new object to some default state. We may provide a constructor that takes an object of the same class as a parameter and initializes the new object to the same state as the specified object. We will usually also provide one or more further constructors that take parameters corresponding to different subsets of the instance variables of the object.

Object Deletion and Destructors

As we know, new objects are created by using the new operator and are usually initialized by means of constructors provided by their class. Once created, an object *exists* for as long as it remains accessible from the program that created it, i.e., while some variable or some other accessible object contains a reference to it. As we saw, when an object is no longer accessible, it is garbage and will eventually be deleted by C#.

Just before it deletes an instance of a class, C# invokes a special method, called a *destructor*, on that object (if it has one). While constructors are use to initialize newly created objects, destructors are invoked on existing objects just before they are about to be deleted. Since objects are deleted by C#, destructors are always invoked by C# rather than by programs or other objects.

Destructors give objects an opportunity to tidy up their state just before being deleted! For example, say we had an object that opened a network connection to another computer in order to transfer data to or form that computer as part of its normal operation. The object may eventually become garbage because no other object retains a reference to it. However, before the object is deleted it should be given an opportunity to close its network connection. As this point, the object is only known to C#. Hence, the way this is accomplished is by providing a special method that can be invoked by C# just before deleting the object. The code for this method is provided as part of the class declaration and can be written to do any appropriate tidying up that might be necessary. For example, it might close any open network connections still maintained by the object.

Declaring a Destructor

Essentially, a destructor is a method takes no parameters and returns no result. Its identifier is the same as the name of its class but preceded by a ˜ (tilde). Thus, the destructor for class `Circle` would be called `˜Circle`. Moreover, a destructor can't be overloaded – a class can provide only a single destructor. Other than that, a destructor is a normal instance method and can, of course, access all the instance variables of the object on which it is invoked.

A destructor is optional. A class need not provide a destructor if there is no need for its instances to perform any tidying up before being deleted. In fact, the normal situation is that classes do not provide a destructor. If a destructor is provided by a class, C# guarantees to invoke the method on the every instance of the class exactly once before the object is deleted. Since it's unpredictable when a garbage object will be deleted, it's equally unpredictable when exactly its destructor will be invoked. C# makes no guarantees about this nor about the order in which the destructors of different objects will be invoked with respect to the order in which the objects become garbage!

Keeping Track of the Number of Instances of a Class

As an example of the use of a destructor, let's modify our `ObjectCounter` class so that it keeps count of the number of instances of the class that *exist* at any time. Notice that our previous version of `ObjectCounter`, shown in Program 6.11, only keeps track of the number of instances that have been *created*. In particular, it does not take account of the fact that some of those instances may have been deleted (by C#) because they became garbage. Thus, when an instance of the class is about to be deleted we want to decrement the `numInstances` class variable maintained by the `ObjectCounter` class. So, we need a way of knowing exactly when an instance of the class is (about to be) deleted. Happily, a destructor will provide us with just this! We simply need to add a destructor to class `ObjectCounter` that decrements `numInstances` whenever it is invoked (since the destructor being invoked corresponds to an instance of the class being deleted).

Program 6.13 shows the resulting class declaration and Program 6.14 a program that uses it. If fact, we added another class variable to `ObjectCounter` to keep count of the number of

```
/* A class that is capable of keeping */
/* count of its instances (revised) */
class ObjectCounter
{
    private static int numInstances = 0;  // number of existing instances
    private static int numDeleted = 0;    // number of instances deleted
    private string name;                  // each instance has a name

    /* initialize a new instance with given name */
    public ObjectCounter(string name)
    {
        /* initialize name */
        this.name = name;
        /* count new instance */
        numInstances = numInstances + 1;
    }
```

```
    /* return number of existing instances */
    public static int getNumInstances()
    {
        return numInstances;
    }

    /* return number of deleted instances */
    public static int getNumDeleted()
    {
        return numDeleted;
    }

    /* return name associated with current object */
    public string getName()
    {
        return this.name;
    }

    /* decrement instance count when object deleted */
    ~ObjectCounter()
    {
        numInstances = numInstances - 1;
        numDeleted = numDeleted + 1;
    }
}
```

Program 6.13 Class ObjectCounter (revised).

```
/* A program to illustrate the use of destructors */

using tcdIO;

class CounterProgram
{
    public static void Main()
    {
        Terminal terminal;
        ObjectCounter last, secondLast, thirdLast;
        // keep three instances
        int createCount, deleteCount = 0, number;

        /* create an object to represent the terminal */
        terminal = new Terminal();

        /* get number to create - at least 3 */
        number = terminal.ReadInt("Enter number of instances to create: ");
        while (number < 3)
        {
            number = terminal.ReadInt("Enter number of instances to create: ");
        }

        /* create first three */
        createCount = 3;
        thirdLast = new ObjectCounter("Some name");
        secondLast = new ObjectCounter("Some name");
        last = new ObjectCounter("Some name");
```

```
      /* create the rest */
      while (createCount < number)
      {
         thirdLast = secondLast;
         secondLast = last;
         last = new ObjectCounter("Some name");
         createCount = createCount + 1;
         /* Write message if more objects have been deleted */
         if (ObjectCounter.getNumDeleted() > deleteCount)
         {
            /* some more objects have been deleted */
            deleteCount = ObjectCounter.getNumDeleted();
            terminal.WriteLine("Class now has: "
                        + ObjectCounter.getNumInstances()  + " instances ("
                        + ObjectCounter.getNumDeleted() + " deleted).");
         }
      }
      /* all done! */
      terminal.WriteLine("Finished!");
   }
}
```

Program 6.14   A program to illustrate the use of destructors.

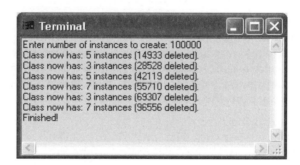

Figure 6.18   The execution of Program 6.14.

instances of the class that have been deleted, together with another class method to return the value of this counter when requested. This allows Program 6.14 to determine when another object has been deleted and print out a corresponding message!

Notice that Program 6.14 only keeps references to the last three objects created at any time. Thus, most of the objects created by the program become garbage as soon as three further objects have been created. C# eventually deletes these garbage objects. Just before deleting each object, C# invokes its destructor on the object. Figure 6.18 shows what happens if we ask the program to create a sufficiently large number of objects. Notice that a lot of objects have been created (and made garbage) before we begin to see objects being deleted!

Case Study: Complex Numbers

To conclude this chapter, we will look as writing a class whose instances represent complex numbers, together with a program that allows arithmetic to be performed on a complex number.

To begin with, let's have a quick recap on complex numbers. A complex number is composed of two parts: a *real part* and an *imaginary part*. The real part is a real number while the imaginary part represents a coefficient of iota (iota is the square root of -1). Thus, examples of complex numbers include:

$$5.0 + 24.9i \quad -34.67 + 0.9i \quad 104.56 - 67.8i \quad -45.23i$$

where i represents iota. Given two complex numbers $C_1 = x_1 + y_1 i$ and $C_2 = x_2 + y_2 i$, then:

$$C_1 + C_2 = (x_1 + x_2) + (y_1 + y_2)i$$

$$C_1 - C_2 = (x_1 - x_2) + (y_1 - y_2)i$$

$$C_1 * C_2 = (x_1 x_2 - y_1 y_2) + (x_1 y_2 + x_2 y_1)i$$

$$C_1/C_2 = (x_1 x_2 + y_1 y_2)/(x_2^2 + y_2^2) + (x_2 y_1 + x_1 y_2)/(x_2^2 + y_2^2)i \quad \text{iff } (x_2^2 + y_2^2) \text{ is not 0.}$$

Additionally, if $C_1 = x_1 + y_1 i$ then the *conjugate* of C_1 is $= x_1 - y_1 i$.

As usual, we begin writing our class, `ComplexNumber`, by considering what attributes the class should provide. In this case, it seems to be quite clear that every instance of `ComplexNumber` should have two attributes representing the real and imaginary parts of the corresponding complex number, i.e., we should provide two instance variables,

```
private double re; private double im;
```

Next we need to consider how a new instance of `ComplexNumber` should be initialized. As we noted previously, it is quite common for a class to provide a number of overloaded constructors to initialize different instances of the class in different ways. In the case of a complex number, we could imagine initializing the number to be zero, to have some specified values for its real and imaginary parts, or to be the same as some other specified complex number. This would mean providing three constructors as follows:

```
public ComplexNumber();
public ComplexNumber(double re, double im);
public ComplexNumber(ComplexNumber other);
```

Each of the constructors initializes the `re` and `im` attributes of the new object with the appropriate values. In the case of the third constructor, this means that we need some way of extracting the values of its attributes from an existing instance of the class. Thus, we will provide the methods:

```
public double GetRe();
```

and

```
public double GetIm();
```

to do just that.

What other methods should `ComplexNumber` provide? Obviously we will want methods to implement each of the arithmetic operations on a complex number, perhaps a method to return the conjugate of a complex number, and a method to obtain a `string` representing the value of the complex number – `ToString`.

The arithmetic operations are all similar. They all take a parameter of type `ComplexNumber` giving the number to add to, subtract from, multiply or divide the current number respectively. Importantly, performing an arithmetic operation changes the current number but does not require that we return any value except in one case. The method that performs division of complex numbers must be prepared for the possibility that the requested division is not possible and hence returns a `bool` result to indicate whether or not the division was actually carried out. Thus the headings of the corresponding methods are:

```
public void Add(ComplexNumber other);
public void Subtract(ComplexNumber other);
public void Multiply(ComplexNumber other);
public bool Divide(ComplexNumber other);
```

The methods that perform arithmetic mostly just update the `re` and `im` attributes of the object on which they are invoked according to the rules above. `Divide` uses an `if` statement to ensure that the division is possible before attempting to update `re` and `im` and returns the appropriate result in each part of the `if` statement. Both `Multiply` and `Divide` have to be careful not to overwrite the original value of `re` in the current object before it is used to calculate the new value of `im`. To do so, the original value of `re` is saved in the local variable `x` in both cases.

To return the conjugate of a complex number we simply create and return a new instance of `ComplexNumber` initialized from the attributes of the current number.

```
public ComplexNumber Conjugate();
```

`ToString` is also straightforward and simply constructs a `string` from the real and imaginary parts of the current complex number. The only complication is making sure that the sign between the real and imaginary parts is correct: a '+' when the imaginary part is positive and a '−' when it is negative. An `if` statement is used to work out what sign to use and the `static` method `Abs` from class `Math` to take the absolute value of `im` so as to make sure that any '−' is not printed twice.

The full class declaration is shown in Program 6.15 and a program that uses it in Program 6.16. This program follows the standard format for any program that reads and processes a sequence of commands from the user. It uses a `while` loop to repeatedly read commands until the `EXIT` command is entered and a nested `if` statement to determine what the current command is.

```
/* A class whose instances represent complex numbers */
using System;
class ComplexNumber
{
   private double re;
   private double im;

   /* initialize a new complex number to zero */
   public ComplexNumber()
   {
      this.re = 0.0;
      this.im = 0.0;
   }

   /* initialize new complex number to be equal */
   /* to specified complex number */
   public ComplexNumber(ComplexNumber other)
   {
      this.re = other.GetRe();
      this.im = other.GetIm();
   }
```

```csharp
/* initialize new complex number with specified values */
public ComplexNumber(double re, double im)
{
    this.re = re;
    this.im = im;
}

/* return real part of current complex number */
public double GetRe()
{
    return this.re;
}

/* return imaginary part of current complex number */
public double GetIm()
{
    return this.im;
}

/* add specified complex number to current complex number */
public void Add(ComplexNumber other)
{
    this.re = this.re + other.GetRe();
    this.im = this.im + other.GetIm();
}

/* subtract specified complex number from current complex number */
public void Subtract(ComplexNumber other)
{
    this.re = this.re - other.GetRe();
    this.im = this.im - other.GetIm();
}

/* multiply current complex number by specified complex number */
public void Multiply(ComplexNumber other)
{
    double x = this.re;
    // save real part of original complex number

    this.re = (this.re * other.GetRe()) - (this.im * other.GetIm());
    this.im = (x * other.GetIm()) + (this.im * other.GetRe());
}

/* divide current complex number by specified complex */
/* number if possible Return true if sucessful, false otherwise */
public bool Divide(ComplexNumber other)
{
    double x = this.re;
    // save real part of original complex number
    double divisor = (other.GetRe() * other.GetRe())
                            + (other.GetIm() * other.GetIm());

    /* check if division is possible */
    if (divisor != 0.0)
    {
        this.re = ((this.re * other.GetRe())
                        + (this.im * other.GetIm())) / divisor;
```

```
            this.im = ((this.im * other.GetRe())
                                    - (x * other.GetIm())) / divisor;
            return true;
         }
         else
         {
            return false;
         }
      }

      /* return conjugate of current complex number */
      public ComplexNumber Conjugate()
      {
         return new ComplexNumber(this.re, -this.im);
      }

      /* return a string representing
       * the current complex number */
      public string Tostring()
      {
         string sign = "+";

         if (im < 0)
         {
            sign = "-";
         }
         return this.re + sign + Math.Abs(this.im) + "i";
      }
}
```

Program 6.15   Class ComplexNumber.

```
/* A program to perform arithmetic on complex numbers */

using tcdIO;

class ComplexProgram
{
   private const string EXIT = "e";

   public static ComplexNumber ReadComplex(Terminal t, string p)
   {
      t.WriteLine(p);
      double r = t.ReadDouble("Re: ");
      double i = t.ReadDouble("Im: ");
      return new ComplexNumber(r, i);
   }

   public static void Main()
   {
      Terminal terminal;
      ComplexNumber number1, number2;
      string op;

      /* create an object to represent the terminal */
      terminal = new Terminal();
```

```
    /* Read the first complex number */
    number1 = ReadComplex(terminal, "Enter first complex number");
    op = terminal.ReadString("Enter operation (+, -, *, /, e<xit>): ");
    while (!op.Equals(EXIT))
    {
        if (op.Equals("+"))
        {
            number2 = ReadComplex(terminal, "Enter number");
            number1.Add(number2);
            terminal.WriteLine(number1.Tostring());
        }
        else if (op.Equals("-"))
        {
            number2 = ReadComplex(terminal, "Enter number");
            number1.Subtract(number2);
            terminal.WriteLine(number1.Tostring());
        }
        else if (op.Equals("*"))
        {
            number2 = ReadComplex(terminal, "Enter number");
            number1.Multiply(number2);
            terminal.WriteLine(number1.Tostring());
        }
        else if (op.Equals("/"))
        {
            number2 = ReadComplex(terminal, "Enter number");
            if (number1.Divide(number2))
            {
                terminal.WriteLine(number1.ToString());
            }
            else
            {
                terminal.WriteLine("Unable to divide "
                                + number1 + " by " + number2 + ".");
            }
        }
        op = terminal.ReadString("Enter operation: ");
    }
    terminal.WriteLine("Finished!");
    }
}
```

Program 6.16   A program to perform arithmetic on complex numbers.

Since this program frequently needs to read complex numbers from the user, the program class actually provides a class method, `ReadComplex`, to read in the real and imaginary parts of a complex number and create a corresponding instance of class `ComplexNumber`. Since, `ReadComplex` isn't a method of class `Terminal`, it actually takes a parameter of type `Terminal` to identify the terminal from which to read, as well as a `string` with which to prompt the user.

```
public static ComplexNumber ReadComplex(Terminal t, string p);
```

This is the first time that we have seen a program class that provides a method other than `Main`. The program class of a C# program is a completely normal class except that no instances of the class are usually created. As a result, any methods provided by this class should be `static` and are, in any case, usually intended to be used only by `Main` (or another method of the same class) to perform operations that occur frequently in the program.

You might wonder why we didn't make `ReadComplex` a method on class `ComplexNumber`. The reason is that we want `ComplexNumber` to be reusable in lots of different programs that provide different forms of user interface. How input/output should be implemented depends heavily on the style of user interface provided by the program and may differ radically from one program to another. If we put the code to read complex numbers in class `ComplexNumber`, the style in which it is done might not be appropriate for all programs and would then need to be rewritten in different programs. Hence, as a rule, it makes more sense for any code that deals with input/output to be left to the program and its user interface to implement in whatever way is appropriate for that particular program.

Summary

- every instance method executes *in the context of* some object – *the current object* for the program
- during the execution of an instance method, `this` always refers to the current object
- `void` is used in place of the return type of a method to specify that the method does not return a result
- the *actual parameters* to a method invocation are used to initialize the corresponding *formal parameters* of the method
- actual parameters are usually *passed by value*
- the formal parameters of a method can be used as if they were local variables declared within that method
- when using call-by-value it is *not* possible for a method to modify its actual parameters
- a method *can* modify an object to which it is passed a reference as a parameter
- a class can have its own attributes and methods
- class attributes and methods are labeled with the keyword `static`
- the *scope* of a declaration is the region of the program within which the entity declared can be referred to using its identifier
- multiple *overloaded* versions of a method can be provided in the same class as long as they take different parameters
- a class can provide a *destructor* to allow an object to tidy itself up before being deleted

Exercises

(1) Consider the following C# class declaration:

```
class xxx {
  public void yyy(int num1, int num2)
  {
    int tmp;
    tmp = num1;
    num1 = num2;
    num2 = tmp;
  }
}
```

Write fragments of code to call the yyy method of class xxx where:

- the actual parameters are literals;
- the actual parameters are variables;
- the actual parameters are expressions involving one or more operators.

What does the yyy method actually do (in particular, what effect does it have on its actual parameters)?

(2) Design a class Rectangle whose instances represent rectangles with position as well as length and breadth. Include any constructors and methods that you think appropriate, including the method Overlaps to report whether or not two rectangles overlap with each other.

(3) If you didn't include it already, add an overloaded version of Overlaps to class Rectangle to report whether or not the current rectangle overlaps with a specified circle.

(4) Rewrite the Traveling Salesperson program so that it uses a class method to create and initialize new instances of City with required.

(5) Design a class whose instances represent individual playing cards. Include methods to report whether or not the current card is of the same suit (hearts, spades, clubs, or diamonds) as a specified card and whether or not the current card has the same rank (Ace, King, Queen, Jack, two–ten) as a specified card.

(6) Write a class that represents a poker hand (i.e., a collection of five different playing cards). Include methods to report whether or not the hand:

- is a flush (i.e., five cards of the same suit),
- is a straight (i.e., five consecutively ranked cards of any suit),
- is a straight flush (i.e., five consecutively ranked cards of the same suit),
- is a royal flush (i.e., ace, king, queen, jack and ten of the same suit),
- is a poker (i.e., four cards of the same rank),
- contains three of a kind (i.e., three cards of the same rank),
- is a full house (i.e., three cards of the same rank with a pair of cards of another rank),
- contains two pairs (i.e., of cards of the same rank),
- contains one pair.

Abstraction and Encapsulation 7

This chapter:

- introduces the idea of an *abstraction* as a description of the essential properties of an entity
- describes how classes represent abstractions of the entities of interest to a program
- introduces *encapsulation* as the means of hiding the implementation of an abstraction from its users
- describes the use of the keywords `public` and `private` in more detail
- describes how C#'s *properties* are used to encapsulate instance variables
- describes how a class can define operators that apply to instances of the class

As discussed in Chapter 1, the essential idea behind the object-oriented approach to computer programming is that dividing a program into meaningful chunks, which can be written separately, offers lots of advantages. In the object-oriented approach to writing a program, chunks are chosen to represent the entities with which the program deals. The interesting behaviour of each type of entity is then defined by a corresponding class. When we come to write a new program, we first try to identify the types of entity with which the program deals. This allows us to decide what classes we will need to write. Subsequently, we have to decide exactly what behaviour each class should provide. In other words, we have to describe the essential properties of the entities that we are trying to represent and that are relevant to our program. Such a description is usually referred to an *abstraction*. This process of designing meaningful abstractions of the entities of interest to a program is clearly at the heart of object-oriented programming.

Abstractions focus on the behaviour that the entities of interest exhibit rather than on how that behaviour is implemented. Clearly, writing a class whose instances actually exhibit the desired behaviour involves another level of complexity. Another essential feature of the object-oriented approach is that the users of a class shouldn't have to be aware of that complexity but only of the behaviour defined by the abstraction that the class represents. The process of hiding this complexity is referred to as *encapsulation*.

Together abstraction and encapsulation allow us to divide up programs into chunks that are not only meaningful to the program at hand but are also largely independent of each other. As such, they are at the very heart of the object-oriented approach to computer programming, as we will discuss in the remainder of this chapter.

Abstraction

Let's begin our discussion of abstraction by saying exactly what we mean by the term "abstraction". Simply put, *an abstraction is a description of the essential properties of an entity that are of interest.* We often talk about "abstraction" or "building an abstraction of an entity" as the process of describing those essential properties of some entity.

A key part of building an abstraction of some entity is obviously identifying what the essential properties of interest are. Clearly, this depends on the type of entity that we are considering. However, it also depends on the context is which we are using the abstraction. Notice that our definition talks about the *essential* properties *of interest*. The phrase "of interest" implies that only a subset of the properties of an entity may need to be taken into account. The phrase "essential" implies that we have to be careful not to miss any properties of interest. In some sense, we must try to identify the smallest complete subset of the entity's properties that are relevant to us. Why? Mainly, because we want to minimize complexity. By focusing on fewer properties we can hopefully simplify the abstraction and hence increase the ease with which it can be understood and, eventually, implemented.

As an example, let's consider building an abstraction of a city. What are the essential properties of a city? Clearly, it depends on what our interest in the city is. From the perspective of a city planner, essential properties might include the population of the city, its demographic make up, the types and places of employment available, the availability of public utilities, such as water and power, and infrastructure, such as roads and public transportation. On the other hand, from the perspective of a visitor or potential visitor to the city, essential properties might include what places of interest there are to visit, what kinds of accommodation are available, what restaurants are available, and what kind of public transportation is available

As you can see, building an abstraction is a very *subjective* process. There is no *right* abstraction of a particular entity, although there will certainly be abstractions that are more appropriate than others in different circumstances.

In general, an abstraction focuses on the *behaviour* of the entity in question rather than its implementation. In other words, an abstraction tells us what the entity does rather than how it does it. Put another way, it tells us how we might make use of the entity in question rather than how we might construct such as entity. For example, a meaningful abstraction of a car, from a driver's perspective, would tell us how to drive the car, i.e., what controls are available, what the effect of each control is, and what we have to do to operate each control. It wouldn't describe how the controls work or what components are necessary to make them work. We don't need to know anything about how an engine is constructed in order to drive a car and, indeed, many drivers don't! These details aren't essential to the abstraction. It's enough to know that to make the car go faster, we push the accelerator, while to make it go slower we push the brake pedal.

Abstraction in Object-oriented Programming

A key part of object-oriented programming is identifying the essential properties of the entities with which the program deals that are of interest. These essential properties are captured in the definition of a class whose instances represent those entities. As such, *classes represent abstractions of the entities of interest to some program.*

Since, building an abstraction is a subjective process, different classes might be required to represent the same type of entity in different circumstances. Thus, there is unlikely to be a single class that is appropriate for representing a given type of entity in every program although the same class might be reused in several programs that have similar views of the type of entity concerned.

The behaviour of entities of some type is usually captured in the set of methods provided by the corresponding class. When designing a class we must provide a set of methods that accurately captures the behaviour of entities of that type. Initially, we focus on what methods are required and what role each method plays (rather than on how it works). This allows us to decide on the name, formal parameters, and return type of each method – what we have previously called the method's heading and what is usually called its *signature*. The result of this process is a complete list of the methods to be provided by the class. Such a list is known as the *interface* or *protocol* of the class. The interface of the class defines the abstraction supported by the class.

For example, Program 7.1 shows the interface of the ComplexNumber class from Chapter 6. Notice that the interface only describes the methods to be provided by the class. In particular, it doesn't describe the state provided by instances of the class nor how the methods are actually implemented. Program 7.1 defines an abstraction of a complex number as something that can be created, added, subtracted, multiplied, and divided without saying how this behaviour is implemented.

Importantly, the interface of a class should provide all the information that is required in order to be able to use the class. The interface of a class serves as the interface between the users of the class and the implementers of the class. Once the signatures of all the methods provided by a class are known, other classes and programs that use the class can be written. Notice that users don't need to know how the methods are implemented in order to be able to use them – they only need to know their signatures. Once the interface of the class has been defined, and assuming that it doesn't change, the users and implementers of the class can work independently of each other. In some sense the interface represents an agreement between the users and the implementers as to their division of responsibilities. In particular, the implementers are agreeing to implement a certain abstraction with certain behaviour.

Unfortunately, while the signatures of the methods tell us exactly how to invoke each method individually, they don't tell us anything about the order in which different methods of a class should be invoked. It is very often the case that the methods of a class can only be invoked in a certain sequence. For example, Program 7.2 shows the interface of a class whose instances represent library books. Implicitly, certain methods can only meaningfully be invoked if other methods have already been invoked. For example, it is only meaningful to invoke RenewLoan on a library book that has already been borrowed by invoking BorrowBook and not yet returned with ReturnBook. Describing the allowable sequences in which the methods of a class can meaningfully be invoked is an important part of defining its interface. Unfortunately, C# provides no means of formally specifying such sequences (although notations for describing them do exist in other languages). Thus, it becomes the responsibility of the designer of the class to document these allowable sequences by means of comments associated with the signature of each method as we have done in Program 7.2. Although informal, this approach ensures that the interface of each class includes all the information that users of the class might need in order to use the class correctly.

Encapsulation

Only the interface of a class should need to be known to its users. How that interface is implemented should always remain hidden. There are many good reasons for this. One of the

```
/* The interface of a class whose instances */
/* represent complex numbers */
class ComplexNumber
{
    /* initialize a new complex number to zero */
    public ComplexNumber();

    /* initialize new complex number to be equal */
    /* to specified complex number */
    public ComplexNumber(ComplexNumber other);

    /* initialize new complex number with specified values */
    public ComplexNumber(double re, double im);

    /* return real part of current complex number */
    public double GetRe();

    /* return imaginary part of current complex number */
    public double GetIm();

    /* Add specified complex number to current complex number */
    public void Add(ComplexNumber other);

    /* subtract specified complex number from current complex number */
    public void Subtract(ComplexNumber other);

    /* multiply current complex number by specified complex number */
    public void Multiply(ComplexNumber other);

    /* divide current complex number by specified complex */
    /* number if possible Return true if sucessful, false otherwise */
    public bool Divide(ComplexNumber other);

    /* return conjugate of current complex number */
    public ComplexNumber Conjugate();

    /* report whether or not specified complex number */
    /* is equal to current complex number */
    public bool Equals(ComplexNumber other);

    /* return a string representing the current complex number */
    public override string ToString();
}
```

Program 7.1   The ComplexNumber interface.

most important is that it makes the job of the users so much easier if they don't have to worry about how the classes that they use are implemented. For example, we've used the Terminal class in many of the programs that we've written without ever having to think about how that class was implemented.

From the perspective of the implementers of a class, hiding implementation details also makes life easier. It gives the implementers of a new class the freedom to implement the abstraction in any way that they think fit. Moreover, it also allows them to *change* their implementation without affecting the users of the class as long as the agreed interface remains unchanged.

```
/* The interface of a class whose instances */
/* represent library books */
class LibraryBook
{
    /* initialize a new instance representing a book with the */
    /* specified author, title, publisher, year of publication, */
    /* and shelf mark */
    public LibraryBook(string author, string title,
                            string publisher,int year, string shelfMark);

    /* return the author of the book */
    public string GetAuthor();

    /* return the title of the book */
    public string GetTitle();

    /* return the publisher of the book */
    public string GetPublisher();

    /* return the year of publication of the book */
    public int GetYear();

    /* return the shelf mark of the book */
    public string GetShelfMark();

    /* record the fact that the book has been borrowed by the specfied */
    /* user This operation is only possible if the book is not already */
    /* on loan and has not been reserved by another user */
    /* Return true if successful, false otherwise */
    public bool BorrowBook(LibraryUser borrower);

    /* return date on which the book is due to be returned */
    /* This operation is only possible if the book is on loan */
    /* Return null if the book is not currently on loan */
    public Date DueBack();

    /* report whether or not the book is currently on loan */
    /* Return true if so, false otherwise */
    public bool IsOnLoan();

    /* renew a loan on a book This operation if only possible */
    /* if the book is on loan to the specifed user, this loan has not */
    /* previously been renewed, and the book is not reserved by another */
    /* user Return true if successful, false otherwise */
    public bool RenewLoan(LibraryUser borrower);

    /* reserve a book on behalf of a specified user This operation is */
    /* only possible if the book is on loan to a different user */
    /* and has not already been reserved by the specified user */
    /* Return true if successful, false otherwise */
    public bool ReserveBook(LibraryUser reserver);

    /* record the fact that the book is being returned by the specified */
    /* user This operation is only possible if the book is on loan to */
    /* the specified user Return true if successful, false otherwise */
    public bool ReturnBook(LibraryUser borrower);
```

```
/* report whether or not the return of the book is currently overdue */
/* Return true if so, false otherwise */
public bool IsOverdue();
}
```

Program 7.2 The `LibraryBook` interface.

The process of hiding all the details of an entity that do not contribute to its essential characteristics is called *encapsulation*. Encapsulation hides the implementation of an abstraction from its users. For this reason encapsulation is often referred to as *information hiding*.

In terms of object-oriented programming, encapsulation allows us to hide both how the state of an object is represented as well as the details of how the object's methods work. How the state of an object is represented often dictates how its methods work. Thus, hiding the way in which the state of an object is represented allows us to change that representation later and ensures that we also have the freedom to change the way in which the methods work if necessary.

For example, consider the interface to the `Date` class shown in Program 7.3. When implementing the class `Date` we might decide to store the current date using three instance variables as follows:

```
private int day;    // 1...31
private int month;  // 1...12
private int year;   // 1900-2100
```

However, this in not the only way in which a date can be recorded. The month might equally well be recorded as a string such as "`May`" or "`July`". More radically, we might record the current date as a count of the number of seconds that have elapsed since some arbitrary date such as the 1st of January 1900:

```
private int numSeconds; // since 1/1/1900
```

This isn't as crazy as it sounds – some computer systems do in fact use this approach to recording dates and times! Thus, both approaches are valid and have different advantages and disadvantages in different circumstances. The important thing to realize is that users of the `Date` class should not need to be aware of which approach we are using in order to successfully use the class. Moreover, if we decide to change our approach later, users of the class will not be affected and can continue to use the class without even being aware of the change.

As Figure 7.1 shows, methods are often seen as providing a buffer between the users of an abstraction and its state. In other words, methods encapsulate the state of an object. In this view, the only way of accessing the state of an object is via the methods defined by the interface of its class.

Access Modifiers

Following our philosophy that the implementation of a class, including the way in which the state of its instances is represented, should be hidden, we have so far described a style of programming in which all objects are *fully encapsulated*. The only interactions between objects have been by means of invocations of their respective methods. In all of the programs

```
/* The interface of a class whose */
/* instances represent dates */
class Date
{
    /* initialize date to specified values */
    /* year - a year between 1900 and 2100 */
    /* month - a month between 1-12 */
    /* day - day of the month between 1-31 */
    /* Leave date uninitialized if parameters are invalid */
    public Date (int year, int month, int day);

    /* Initialize a date from a string of the form "dd/mm/yyyy" */
    /* Leave date uninitialized if str is null or represents */
    /* a badly formatted string */
    public Date (string str);

    /* return the year */
    public int GetYear();

    /* return the month */
    public int GetMonth();

    /* return the day of the month */
    public int GetDay();

    /* check whether this date comes before the specified date */
    /* Returns true if the current date comes before the specified */
    /* date; false otherwise */
    public bool Before(Date when);

    /* check whether this date comes after the specified date */
    /* Returns true if the current date comes after the specified */
    /* date; false otherwise */
    public bool After(Date when);

    /* compare current date with the specified date */
    /* Return true if the dates are the same; false otherwise */
    public bool Equals(Date when);

    /* returns true if the current year is a leap year */
    public bool IsLeapYear();

    /* return the number of days between the current date and the */
    /* specified date (> 0 if current date comes after specified date) */
    public int DaysBetween(Date when);

    /* convert a date to a string of the form "dd/mm/yyyy" */
    public override string ToString();

    /* returns true if the specified year is a leap year */
    public static bool IsLeapYear(int year);
}
```

Program 7.3   The Date interface.

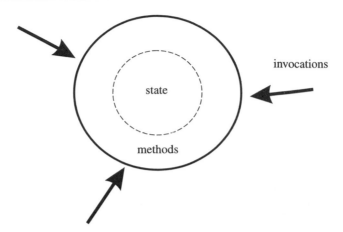

Figure 7.1 Methods encapsulate the state of an object.

that we have written so far, objects, even instances of the same class, never access the instance variables of other objects directly. As we will see, C# actually allows an object to access the instance variables of *another* object directly in certain circumstances. While this is possible, you should note that it results in the implementation details of a class being exposed to its users (who are now necessarily aware of what instance variables the class provides). Thus, allowing the instance variables of an object to be accessed directly represents a weakening of encapsulation and is not normally to be recommended.

public **and** private

C# allows us to distinguish instance variables and methods of a class that are intended to be visible to its users from those that intended to be hidden using the keywords public and private. So far, all of our classes have provided public (visible) methods and private (hidden) instance variables. However, it is possible for a class to provide both public instance variables and private methods! public and private are called *access modifiers* because they are used to modify the type of access to an object's instance variables and methods that is allowed.

The keyword public is used to designate those properties provided by a class that constitute the interface to the class. Thus, a property that is labeled as being public is part of the interface of the class, will be known to users of the class, and, importantly, cannot have its declaration changed in any way without affecting users of the class. Normally, only methods should be made public. Implementation details such as what instance variables are used to implement those methods should be kept hidden by labeling them as private.

The keyword private is used to designate those aspects of a class declaration that constitute implementation details. Users of a class cannot use its private instance variables or methods. As such the private instance variables and methods of a class are completely encapsulated. In general, all instance variables should be private allowing us to change the implementation of a class without exposing the change to its users.

Using `private` Instance Variables

Instance variables that are labeled `private` can only be used within the class in which they are declared. However, all the instances of a class have direct access to the `private` instance variables of all the other instances of the same class.

For example, in Chapter 6 we wrote a class `ComplexNumber` that declared two `private` instance variables to store the real and imaginary parts of each complex number. In order to carry out the methods to add, subtract, multiply, and divide complex numbers, the current instance of `ComplexNumber` needed to be able to retrieve the real and imaginary parts of another complex number. This was achieved by having it invoke the `GetRe` and `GetIm` methods on the other object. However, one instance of `ComplexNumber` can always access the instance variables of another instance of the class directly even if those instance variables are `private`. For example, within the Add method of class `ComplexNumber` we can replace the line

```
this.re = this.re + other.GetRe();
```

with

```
this.re = this.re + other.re;
```

to have the current object obtain the value of the `re` instance variable of the complex number referred to by `other`. Hence, we can rewrite class `ComplexNumber` as shown in Program 7.4.

```
/* A class whose instances represent */
/* complex numbers (revised) */
using System;
class ComplexNumber
{
    private double re;
    private double im;

    /* initialize a new complex number to zero */
    public ComplexNumber()
    {
        this.re = 0.0;
        this.im = 0.0;
    }

    /* initialize new complex number to be equal */
    /* to specified complex number */
    public ComplexNumber(ComplexNumber other)
    {
        this.re = other.re;
        this.im = other.im;
    }

    /* initialize new complex number with specified values */
    public ComplexNumber(double re, double im)
    {
        this.re = re;
        this.im = im;
    }
```

```
/* return real part of current complex number */
public double GetRe()
{
   return this.re;
}

/* return imaginary part of current complex number */
public double GetIm()
{
   return this.im;
}

/* add specified complex number to current complex number */
public void Add(ComplexNumber other)
{
   this.re = this.re + other.re;
   this.im = this.im + other.im;
}

/* subtract specified complex number from current complex number */
public void Subtract(ComplexNumber other)
{
   this.re = this.re - other.re;
   this.im = this.im - other.im;
}

/* multiply current complex number by specified complex number */
public void Multiply(ComplexNumber other)
{
   double x = this.re;
   // save real part of original complex number

   this.re = (this.re * other.re) - (this.im * other.im);
   this.im = (x * other.im) + (this.im * other.re);
}

/* divide current complex number by specified complex */
/* number if possible Return true if sucessful, false otherwise */
public bool Divide(ComplexNumber other)
{
   double x = this.re;
   // save real part of original complex number
   double divisor = (other.re * other.re) + (other.im * other.im);

   /* check if division is possible */
   if (divisor != 0.0)
   {
      this.re = ((this.re * other.re) +
                            (this.im * other.im)) / divisor;
      this.im = ((this.im * other.re) - (x * other.im)) / divisor;
      return true;
   }
   else
   {
      return false;
   }
}
```

```
/* return conjugate of current complex number */
public ComplexNumber Conjugate()
{
   return new ComplexNumber(this.re, -this.im);
}

/* report whether or not specified complex number */
/* is equal to current complex number */
public bool Equals(ComplexNumber other)
{
   if ((object)this == (object)other)
   {
      return true;
   }
   else
   {
      return (this.re == other.re) && (this.im == other.im);
   }
}

/* return a string representing the current complex number */
public override string ToString()
{
   string sign = "+";

   if (this.im < 0)
   {
      sign = "-";
   }
   return this.re + sign + Math.Abs(this.im) + "i";
}
}
```

Program 7.4   Class ComplexNumber.

Note that we still provide the methods GetRe and GetIm to return the values of the real and imaginary parts of the complex number. However, these methods are intended for use by other classes that use class ComplexNumber rather than for use within class ComplexNumber itself. Thus, from the point of view of users of the class, its implementation details remain hidden and its instance variables are still fully encapsulated.

Using public Instance Variables

There may be times when it is allowable to provide public rather than private instance variables in a class, i.e., where we really are prepared to expose the implementation of the class to its users. Class ComplexNumber might be an example. If we are sure that we will never want to store the value of a complex number other than by using instance variables of type double to represent its real and imaginary parts, then we might make re and im public as in Program 7.5.

Given this version of the class, re and im can now be accessed directly by instances of *any* other class. For example, instead of writing,

```
realPart = number.GetRe();
```

```csharp
/* A class whose instances represent */
/* complex numbers (revised) */
using System;
class ComplexNumber
{
   public double re;
   public double im;

   /* initialize a new complex number to zero */
   public ComplexNumber()
   {
      this.re = 0.0;
      this.im = 0.0;
   }

   /* initialize new complex number to be equal */
   /* to specified complex number */
   public ComplexNumber(ComplexNumber other)
   {
      this.re = other.re;
      this.im = other.im;
   }

   /* initialize new complex number with specified values */
   public ComplexNumber(double re, double im)
   {
      this.re = re;
      this.im = im;
   }

   /* add specified complex number to current complex number */
   public void Add(ComplexNumber other)
   {
      this.re = this.re + other.re;
      this.im = this.im + other.im;
   }

   /* subtract specified complex number from current complex number */
   public void Subtract(ComplexNumber other)
   {
      this.re = this.re - other.re;
      this.im = this.im - other.im;
   }

   /* multiply current complex number by specified complex number */
   public void Multiply(ComplexNumber other)
   {
      double x = this.re;
      // save real part of original complex number

      this.re = (this.re * other.re) - (this.im * other.im);
      this.im = (x * other.im) + (this.im * other.re);
   }
```

```
/* divide current complex number by specified complex */
/* number if possible Return true if sucessful, false otherwise */
public bool Divide(ComplexNumber other)
{
   double x = this.re;
   // save real part of original complex number
   double divisor = (other.re * other.re) + (other.im * other.im);

   /* check if division is possible */
   if (divisor != 0.0)
   {
      this.re = ((this.re * other.re) + (this.im * other.im)) / divisor;
      this.im = ((this.im * other.re) - (x * other.im)) / divisor;
      return true;
   }
   else
   {
      return false;
   }
}


/* return conjugate of current complex number */
public ComplexNumber Conjugate()
{
   return new ComplexNumber(this.re, -this.im);
}


/* report whether or not specified complex number */
/* is equal to current complex number */
public bool Equals(ComplexNumber other)
{
   if ((object)this == (object)other)
   {
      return true;
   }
   else
   {
      return (this.re == other.re) && (this.im == other.im);
   }
}


/* return a string representing the current complex number */
public override string ToString()
{
   string sign = "+";

   if (this.im < 0)
   {
      sign = "-";
   }
   return this.re + sign + Math.Abs(this.im) + "i";
}
}
```

Program 7.5 Class ComplexNumber (revised).

to retrieve the real part of a complex number, `number`, we might write

```
realPart = number.re;
```

As a result, there is no longer any need to provide the methods `GetRe` and `GetIm`. In this new scenario, instances of any class can access the `re` and `im` instance variables of any instance of `ComplexNumber` and treat it as a variable of type `double`. Of course, this means that they can also change the value of `re` or `im`. For example, we might write

```
number.re = 3.456;
```

or

```
number.im = number.im * 8 2;
```

Notice that this has significantly changed our definition of what the essential properties of a complex number are. In particular, we are now allowing the parts of a complex number to be *independently* and *arbitrarily* changed whereas they could previously only be changed as the result of performing one of the arithmetic operations that we defined for `ComplexNumber`! Thus, this class provides a different interface and hence represents a different abstraction of a complex number. We should think very carefully as to whether we want to allow this or not when defining the interface to our class: it may be an appropriate choice or it may be an inappropriate choice depending on our intended use of the class.

The Dangers of `public` Instance Variables

We have already noted that providing `public` instance data in a class may make it more difficult to change the implementation of that class subsequently. Anything that is labeled as `public` constitutes part of the interface of the class and, hence, cannot be changed without affecting other users of the class.

Moreover, the use of `public` instance data may have other implications affecting the *validity* of the abstractions that we define. We already encountered the issue of whether or not it was valid to allow the real and imaginary parts of a complex number to be modified independently and arbitrarily. As another example, we might provide a version of class `Circle` in which the `radius` instance variable is `public`. However, doing so significantly changes the definition of what a circle is. Under our previous definition, a circle was something that, once it had been created, could not change its size. Under this definition it can!

Moreover, since `radius` is of type `double`, it is now possible for a program to make the `radius` of a circle negative! While it is arguable whether the real and imaginary parts of a complex number can be changed independently or even whether the radius of a circle can be changed, it should be absolutely clear that a circle cannot have a negative radius. Hence, our new `Circle` interface does not represent a valid abstraction of a circle. This definition of the `Circle` interface permits its instances to behave in ways that are not consistent with the entity to be represented.

As another example, consider what would happen if we defined the interface to class `Date` as in Program 7.7. Notice that the `day`, `month`, and `year` instance variables are now `public` and consequently part of the interface. Unfortunately, having made this change, we now open up the possibility of having an instance of `Date` containing a value such as 31/2/1997 or 56/13/1894 or even −34/45/0 none of which should be allowable!

```
/* A class whose instances represent circles */
/* with a public instance variable */
class Circle
{
    public const double PI = 3.1416;
    public double radius;

    /* initialize new circle object */
    public Circle(double radius)
    {
        this.radius = radius;
    }

    /* calculate area of circle */
    public double CalculateArea()
    {
        return this.radius * this.radius * PI;
    }

    /* calculate circumference of circle */
    public double CalculateCircumference()
    {
        return 2.0 * PI * this.radius;
    }
}
```

Program 7.6   Class `Circle`.

Thus, the golden rule is that *encapsulation protects the validity of the abstractions that we are defining*. Defining an abstraction as a collection of methods that are executed in response to invocations ensures that objects always have the opportunity to make sure that their state is valid and that only allowable modifications can be carried out at any time.

Accessors and Modifiers

As an alternative to providing public instance variables, we can always provide methods to allow the instance variables to be examined or modified in allowable ways whenever necessary. For example, while our original version of class `ComplexNumber` has methods to retrieve the real and imaginary parts of a `ComplexNumber`, we could equally well include methods to modify the real and imaginary parts.

```
public void SetRe(double re)
{
    this.re = re;
}
public void SetIm(double im)
{
    this.im = im;
}
```

Our `ComplexNumber` class would then include a set of methods to allow us to query the value of its instances variables (`GetRe` and `GetIm`) and another set to allow us to change the values of its instance variables (`SetRe` and `SetIm`). As we noted before, it is quite common for a class to provide such methods. The former are often referred to as *accessor*

```
/* The interface of a class whose */
/* instances represent dates (revised) */
class Date
{
   public int year;
   public int month;
   public int day;

   /* initialize date to specified values */
   /* year - a year between 1900 and 2100 */
   /* month - a month between 1-12 */
   /* day - day of the month between 1-31 */
   /* Leave date uninitialized if parameters are invalid */
   public Date (int year, int month, int day);

   /* Initialize a date from a string of the form "dd/mm/yyyy" */
   /* Leave date uninitialized if str is null or represents */
   /* a badly formatted string */
   public Date (string str);

   /* check whether this date comes before the specified date */
   /* Returns true if the current date comes before the specified */
   /* date; false otherwise */
   public bool Before(Date when);

   /* check whether this date comes after the specified date */
   /* Returns true if the current date comes after the specified */
   /* date; false otherwise */
   public bool After(Date when);

   /* compare current date with the specified date */
   /* Return true if the dates are the same; false otherwise */
   public bool Equals(Date when);

   /* returns true if the current year is a leap year */
   public bool IsLeapYear();

   /* return the number of days between the current date and the */
   /* specified date (> 0 if current date comes after specified date) */
   public int DaysBetween(Date when);

   /* convert a date to a string of the form "dd/mm/yyyy" */
   public override string ToString();

   /* returns true if the specified year is a leap year */
   public static bool IsLeapYear(int year);
}
```

Program 7.7 The Date interface (revised).

methods and the latter as *modifier* methods. The significant difference between this approach and the use of public instance variables is that we can now change the way in which the state of a complex number is stored without changing its interface. We could for example, store the complex number using polar coordinates. This would require us to change the implementation of all of the methods but would not require us to change the signatures of the existing methods.

If we use this approach with the `radius` instance variable of class `Circle`, we could ensure that the radius was never given a negative value by including an appropriate `if` statement in the modifier method.

```
public void SetRadius(double radius)
{
   if(radius > 0.0)
      this.radius = radius;
}
```

Notice that this method only changes the instance variable when the parameter is positive and non-zero, thereby protecting our circle abstraction.

Properties

As we noted in the previous section, it is often the case that classes provide accessor and modifier methods to allow users to access the instance variables of its instances in a controlled way. So much so, in fact, that C# provides a special way of defining accessors and modifiers while providing users of a class with the illusion that they are accessing an instance variable directly.

Program 7.8 is a revised version of class `Circle` that provides a *property* called `radius` that can be used as if it were an instance variable. The radius property is defined by the `get` and `set` methods while the actual radius is stored in the private instance variable `radiusValue`. Thus, although there is no public instance variable called `radius` in class `Circle`, given an instance of `Circle`, referred to by a variable `disc`, we can still write:

```
double r = disc.radius;  // get value of radius property
disc.radius = 50.7;      // set value of radius property
disc.radius = -75.0;     // radius property is still 50.7
```

The first assignment causes the property's `get` method to be invoked returning the value of the radius. The second assignment causes the property's `set` method to be invoked to give a new value to the property, which is actually stored as the value of `radiusValue`. Note that the final assignment also causes the `set` method to be invoked but doesn't cause the value of `radiusValue` to be changed.

Defining a Property

Rather like an instance variable, a property is defined by specifying its type and its name. Unlike an instance variable, a property is not a container for a value but is defined by a pair of methods, `get` and `set`, that are called implicitly whenever the value of the property is required or an attempt to assign a value to the property is made. These methods are introduced by the keywords `get` and `set` respectively in the definition of the property.

The `get` method is invoked whenever an attempt to retrieve the value of the property is made. Thus, the `get` method is implemented as a function that returns a value of the same type at the property. The signature of the `get` method is implicit and only the statements making up its body have to be specified as in Program 7.8.

The set method is invoked in response to an attempt to assign a value to the property. While get implicitly returns a value of the same type as the property, set implicitly has a single formal parameter of the same type as the property (referred to by the identifier value) and returns no result, i.e., it is a procedure. The value that is to be assigned to the property is passed as the actual parameter to set and can be used in any appropriate way within the method. For example, in Program 7.8, the value to be assigned to the radius property becomes the value of the formal parameter value within the set method where it is used in the if statement and in the assignment to radiusValue.

As another example, Program 7.9 is a class whose instances represent temperatures. Class Temperature provides a single public instance variable, degreesCelsius, to store a temperature in degrees Celsius but also allows the temperature to be accessed in Fahrenheit using the property degreesFahrenheit. The get and set methods of the degreesFahrenheit property perform the necessary conversions between Celsius and

```
/* A class whose instances represent circles with a radius property */
class Circle
{
   public const double PI = 3.1416;
   private double radiusValue;

   /* initialize new circle object */
   public Circle(double radiusValue)
   {
      this.radiusValue = radiusValue;
   }

   /* allow radius to be retrieved or changed */
   /* to a new positive value */
   public double radius
   {
      get
      {
         return this.radiusValue;
      }
      set
      {
         if (value > 0.0)
            this.radiusValue = value;
      }
   }

   /* calculate area of circle */
   public double CalculateArea()
   {
      return this.radiusValue * this.radiusValue * PI;
   }

   /* calculate circumference of circle */
   public double CalculateCircumference()
   {
      return 2.0 * PI * this.radiusValue;
   }
}
```

Program 7.8   Class Circle (revised).

```
/* A class whose instances represent temperatures */
/* expressed in Celsius or Fahrenheit */
class Temperature
{
   /* store temperature in Celsius */
   public double degreesCelsius;

   /* initialize new temperature with Celsius value */
   public Temperature(double degreesCelsius)
   {
      this.degreesCelsius = degreesCelsius;
   }

   /* allow temperature to be stored and retrieved in Fahrenheit */
   public double degreesFahrenheit
   {
      get
      {
         return ((this.degreesCelsius * 9.0) / 5.0) + 32.0;
      }
      set
      {
         this.degreesCelsius = ((value - 32.0) / 9.0) * 5.0;
      }
   }
}
```

Program 7.9 Class Temperature.

Fahrenheit values. Users of the class can choose to work in either Celsius or Fahrenheit as follows

```
...
temperature.degreesCelsius = 15.6; // cool day
fahrenheitTemperature =
   temperature.degreesFahrenheit; // 60.08
temperature.degreesFahrenheit = 32.0; // update property
celsiusTemperature = temperature.degreesCelsius; // 0
```

Although implemented differently, the property degreesFahrenheit is used in the same way as the public instance variable degreesCelsius.

Note that both the radius property in class Circle and the degreesFahrenheit property in class Temperature make use of other instance variables to store their values. Of course, the value of a property can be calculated and recorded in any way, for example, based on the values of several instance variables as for any other method.

Finally, it is worth noting that a property may have no get or no set method associated with it. A property with no get method, a so-called *write-only property*, is somewhat unusual. Providing a *read-only property*, one that has no set method, would be similar to providing an accessor for a private instance variable without providing a corresponding modifier as, in fact, we have done in many of the classes that we have written. Making an attempt to retrieve the value of a write-only property or to change the value of a read-only property is obviously not allowed!

Defining Operators for Objects

Our `ComplexNumber` class defines a set of methods to perform arithmetic with complex numbers including `add`, `subtract`, `divide`, and `multiply`. For example, to add two complex numbers we invoke `Add` on one of the numbers passing the other number as a parameter to the method.

```
ComplexNumber c1, c2;
...
c1.Add(c2);
...
```

In contrast, to add integers we can use the + operator. You might ask why we can't use the + operator with complex numbers too. It's a good question. It would seem very natural to be able to write

```
ComplexNumber c1, c2;
...
c1 = c1 + c2;
...
```

to add two complex numbers. In fact C# will allow us to do just that provided that we define just how the + operator should work for complex numbers in the corresponding class. We can likewise provide complex number specific definitions of other operators including the other arithmetic operators and the relational operators.

Given that we already have a definition of the + operator that applies to integers (and some other types) providing a definition of + for complex numbers is equivalent to *overloading* the + operator. Remember that an overloaded method is one for which different versions, which apply to different types of parameters, exist. C# also allows *operator overloading* by allowing a class to provide its own definitions for operators.

Defining an Overloaded Operator

In C#, an overloaded operator is implemented as a `static` method. Defining an overloaded operator is therefore essentially the same as defining any other `static` method except that rather than giving the method an arbitrary name, its identifier is replaced with the operator to be overloaded preceded by the keyword `operator`. For example, to overload the + operator to perform addition of complex numbers, we write:

```
public static ComplexNumber operator +(ComplexNumber c1,
   ComplexNumber c2)
```

Notice that since `operator +` is a `static` method, which will not be invoked on a particular instance of the class, it requires two `ComplexNumber` parameters to specify the numbers to be added. As defined it also returns a result of type `ComplexNumber`.

Rational Numbers

As a more complete example of the use of operator overloading, let's write a class whose instances represent rational numbers, i.e., numbers of the form N/D, where N (the numerator) and D (the denominator) are integers, and that provides methods to perform arithmetic on rational numbers. Given two rational numbers $R_1 = n_1/d_1$ and $R_2 = n_2/d_2$, then:

$$R_1 + R_2 = (n_1 d_2 + n_2 d_1)/d_1 d_2$$

$$R_1 - R_2 = (n_1 d_2 - n_2 d_1)/d_1 d_2$$

$$R_1 * R_2 = n_1 n_2/d_1 d_2$$

$$R_1/R_2 = n_1 d_2/d_1 n_2.$$

In our class we will represent the numerator and denominator explicitly as the instance variables of each rational number.

```
private int n, d; // numerator and denominator
```

Of course, we can implement the arithmetic operations as methods in the usual way. For example, addition may be implemented as:

```
public RationalNumber Add(RationalNumber other)
{
    return new RationalNumber
            (this.n*other.d + other.n*this.d, this.d*other.d);
}
```

Notice that the result is returned as a new instance of `RationalNumber` rather than by updating one or other of the original numbers. Given this definition it is straightforward to overload the + operator to perform rational addition.

```
public static RationalNumber operator +(RationalNumber r1,
                                        RationalNumber r2)
{
    return r1.Add(r2);
}
```

Given two rational numbers, let's call them `first` and `second`

```
RationalNumber first, second, result;
```

We can now say

```
result = first.Add(second);
```

by invoking the Add method directly or, perhaps more naturally,

```
result = first + second;
```

using the overloaded + operator. Program 7.10 shows the full class definition.

```csharp
/* A class whose instances represent rational numbers */
using tcdIO;
public class RationalNumber
{
   private int n, d;   // numerator and denominator

   /* Constructor to initialize new rational number */
   /* Assumes d > 0 - i.e., not negative or zero */
   public RationalNumber(int n, int d)
   {
      this.n = n;
      this.d = d;
   }

   /* return numerator */
   public int GetN()
   {
      return this.n;
   }

   /* return numerator */
   public int GetD()
   {
      return this.d;
   }

   /* return value of number as a double */
   public double GetValue()
   {
      double n, d;
      n = this.n;
      d = this.d;
      return n / d;
   }

   /* add another rational number to the current rational number */
   /* to give another rational number */
   public RationalNumber Add(RationalNumber other)
   {
      return new RationalNumber
                     (this.n*other.d + other.n*this.d, this.d*other.d);
   }


   /* subtract another rational number from the current rational number */
   /* to give another rational number */
   public RationalNumber Subtract(RationalNumber other)
   {
      return new RationalNumber
                     (this.n*other.d - other.n*this.d, this.d*other.d);
   }


   /* multiply the current rational number by another rational number */
   /* to give another rational number */
   public RationalNumber Multiply(RationalNumber other)
   {
      return new RationalNumber(this.n*other.d, this.d*other.d);
   }
```

```
/* divide the current rational number by another rational number */
/* to give another rational number */
public RationalNumber Divide(RationalNumber other)
{
    return this.Multiply(new RationalNumber(other.d, other.n));
}

/* addition operator */
public static RationalNumber operator +(RationalNumber r1,
                                        RationalNumber r2)
{
    return r1.Add(r2);
}

/* subtraction operator */
public static RationalNumber operator -(RationalNumber r1,
                                        RationalNumber r2)
{
    return r1.Subtract(r2);
}

/* multiplication operator */
public static RationalNumber operator *(RationalNumber r1,
                                        RationalNumber r2)
{
    return r1.Multiply(r2);
}

/* division operator */
public static RationalNumber operator /(RationalNumber r1,
                                        RationalNumber r2)
{
    return r1.Divide(r2);
}

/* return rational number as a string for printing */
public override string ToString()
{
    return this.n + "/" + this.d;
}
}
```

Program 7.10   Class `RationalNumber`.

Overloading the Equality Operators

We saw in Chapter 4, that the == and != operators are used to compare objects to see if
they have the same value. By default, objects are considered equal if the values of all of their
instances variables are the same. While this is a good basis for deciding on the equality of
instances of most classes, it is not necessarily correct for all classes. For example, consider the
following example involving our `RationalNumber` class:

```
RationalNumber oneHalf = new RationalNumber(1, 2);
RationalNumber twoQuarters = new RationalNumber(2, 4);
...
if (oneHalf == twoQuarters)
```

```
{
  // equal
} else {
  //not equal
}
```

Unfortunately, this comparison will always be `false` even though the two rational numbers are equal. The problem arises because the same rational number can be represented in different ways by our class. Thus, although the instances variables of the two instances of `RationalNumber` have different values, the instances are equal. To solve the problem we need to define our own version of the == operator that takes account of the fact that there may be different representations of the same number using the rule that given two rational numbers $R_1 = n_1/d_1$ and $R_2 = n_2/d_2$, then

$R_1 == R_2$ if and only if $n_1 d_2 = n_2 d_1$

```
public static bool operator ==(RationalNumber r1,
                               RationalNumber r2)
{
  return r1.n * r2.d == r2.n * r1.d;
}
```

Notice that the overloaded == operator returns a result of type `bool` as it always must. Now that we have overloaded the == operator for class `RationalNumber`, C# requires that we also overload the != operator too. In fact, C# also requires that if we overload < for a class we must also overload > and, likewise, if we overload <=, we must overload >=, which makes good sense because these operators are intended to complement each other. The definition of != for `RationalNumber` might be as follows:

```
public static bool operator !=(RationalNumber r1,
                               RationalNumber r2)
{
  return r1.n * r2.d != r2.n * r1.d;
}
```

Case Study: Complex Numbers Revisited

To complete this chapter, we will revisit our complex number class one last (well, maybe not!) time. Program 7.11 shows a complete definition of class `ComplexNumber`, while Program 7.12 uses the class to performs arithmetic on complex numbers.

The class shown in Program 7.11 represents a small modification to our previous `ComplexNumber` class, which mainly differs in the fact that we have added overloaded operators to perform complex arithmetic and comparison. Notice that we have also changed the way in which the arithmetic instance methods work so that rather than updating the current number with the result of the operation, they return the result as a new instance of the class or, in the case of division, `null` if the operation cannot be carried out. This is a better design than the previous one in the presence of overloaded operators, since it means that the operands to the operators are not changed as a side effect of the operation.

```
/* A class whose instances represent */
/* complex numbers with arithmetic operators */
using System;
class ComplexNumber
{
   public double re;
   public double im;

   /* initialize a new complex number to zero */
   public ComplexNumber()
   {
      this.re = 0.0;
      this.im = 0.0;
   }

   /* initialize new complex number to be equal */
   /* to specified complex number */
   public ComplexNumber(ComplexNumber other)
   {
      this.re = other.re;
      this.im = other.im;
   }

   /* initialize new complex number with specified values */
   public ComplexNumber(double re, double im)
   {
      this.re = re;
      this.im = im;
   }

   /* add specified complex number to current complex number */
   public ComplexNumber Add(ComplexNumber other)
   {
      return new ComplexNumber(this.re + other.re, this.im + other.im);
   }

   /* subtract specified complex number from current complex number */
   public ComplexNumber Subtract(ComplexNumber other)
   {
      return new ComplexNumber(this.re - other.re, this.im - other.im);
   }

   /* multiply current complex number by specified complex number */
   public ComplexNumber Multiply(ComplexNumber other)
   {
      return new ComplexNumber((this.re * other.re) - (this.im * other.im),
                     (this.re * other.im) + (this.im * other.re));
   }

   /* divide current complex number by specified complex */
   /* number if possible Return answer if sucessful, null otherwise */
   public ComplexNumber Divide(ComplexNumber other)
   {
      double divisor = (other.re * other.re) + (other.im * other.im);

      /* check if division is possible */
      if (divisor != 0.0)
```

```
    {
        return new ComplexNumber(((this.re * other.re) +
            (this.im * other.im)) / divisor,
                ((this.im * other.re) - (this.re* other.im)) / divisor);
    }
    else
    {
        return null;
    }
}

/* return conjugate of current complex number */
public ComplexNumber Conjugate()
{
    return new ComplexNumber(this.re, -this.im);
}

/* report whether or not specified complex number */
/* is equal to current complex number */
public override bool Equals(object o)
{
    return this == (ComplexNumber)o;
}

public override int GetHashCode()
{
    return 0;
}

/* addition operator */
public static ComplexNumber operator +(ComplexNumber c1,
                                        ComplexNumber c2)
{
    return c1.Add(c2);
}

/* subtraction operator */
public static ComplexNumber operator -(ComplexNumber c1,
                                        ComplexNumber c2)
{
    return c1.Subtract(c2);
}

/* multiplication operator */
public static ComplexNumber operator *(ComplexNumber c1,
                                        ComplexNumber c2)
{
    return c1.Multiply(c2);
}

/* division operator */
public static ComplexNumber operator /(ComplexNumber c1,
                                        ComplexNumber c2)
{
    return c1.Divide(c2);
}

/* equality operator */
```

```
        public static bool operator ==(ComplexNumber c1,
                                       ComplexNumber c2)
        {
            /* We can't compare non existent objects, so */
            /* if either reference is null, we'll return false. */
            if ( null == (object)c1 || null == (object)c2)
                return false;
            else
                return (c1.re == c2.re) && (c1.im == c2.im);


        }

        /* inequality operator */
        public static bool operator !=(ComplexNumber c1,
                                       ComplexNumber c2)
        {
            /* We can't compare non existent objects, so */
            /* if either reference is null, we'll return false. */
            if ( null == (object)c1 || null == (object)c2)
                return false;
            else
                return (c1.re != c2.re) || (c1.im != c2.im);
        }

        /* return a string representing the current complex number */
        public override string ToString()
        {
            string sign = "+";

            if (this.im < 0)
            {
                sign = "-";
            }
            return this.re + sign + Math.Abs(this.im) + "i";
        }
    }
```

Program 7.11   Class `ComplexNumber` (revised).

```
/* A program to perform arithmetic on complex numbers */

using tcdIO;

class ComplexProgram
{
    private const string EXIT = "e";

    public static ComplexNumber ReadComplex(Terminal t, string p)
    {
        t.WriteLine(p);
        double r = t.ReadDouble("Re: ");
        double i = t.ReadDouble("Im: ");
        return new ComplexNumber(r, i);
    }

    public static void Main()
    {
        Terminal terminal;
```

```
ComplexNumber number1, number2, result;
string op;

/* create an object to represent the terminal */
terminal = new Terminal();

op = terminal.ReadString("Enter operation (+, -, *, /, e<xit>): ");
while (!op.Equals(EXIT))
{
    if (op.Equals("+"))
    {
        number1 = ReadComplex(terminal, "Enter first number");
        number2 = ReadComplex(terminal, "Enter second number");
        result = number1 + number2;
        terminal.WriteLine(result.ToString());
    }
    else if (op.Equals("-"))
    {
        number1 = ReadComplex(terminal, "Enter first number");
        number2 = ReadComplex(terminal, "Enter second number");
        result = number1 - number2;
        terminal.WriteLine(result.ToString());
    }
    else if (op.Equals("*"))
    {
        number1 = ReadComplex(terminal, "Enter first number");
        number2 = ReadComplex(terminal, "Enter second number");
        result = number1 * number2;
        terminal.WriteLine(result.ToString());
    }

    else if (op.Equals("/"))
    {
        number1 = ReadComplex(terminal, "Enter first number");
        number2 = ReadComplex(terminal, "Enter second number");

        // Do the di
        if ((object)(result = number1/number2) != null)
        {
            terminal.WriteLine(result.ToString());
        }
        else
        {
            terminal.WriteLine("Unable to divide "
                + number1 + " by "
                + number2 + ".");
        }
    }
    op = terminal.ReadString("Enter operation: ");
}
terminal.WriteLine("Finished!");
}
}
```

Program 7.12 A program to perform arithmetic on complex numbers.

Summary

- an *abstraction* is a description of the essential properties of an entity that are of interest
- classes represent abstractions of the entities of interest to some program
- the *signature* of a method describes its name, formal parameters and return type
- the *interface* or *protocol* of a class lists the complete set of public instance variables and methods provided by the class
- the interface of a class defines the abstraction supported by the class
- *encapsulation* hides all the details of an entity that do not contribute to its essential characteristics
- encapsulation hides the implementation of an abstraction from its users
- the `public` keyword is used to designate those properties of a class that constitute the interface of the class
- the `private` keyword is used to designate those properties of a class that constitute implementation details
- encapsulation protects the *validity* of the abstractions that we define
- make all instance variables `private` except in exceptional circumstances
- *accessor* and *modifier* methods allow users of a class to access the instance variables of its instances in a controlled way
- C# provides *properties* as a way of encapsulating instance variables
- *operator overloading* allows a class to provide its own definitions for commonly used operators

Exercises

(1) Complete the declaration of class `LibraryBook` making sure that your implementation of each of the methods detects when a method is invoked on a library book out of context.

(2) Implement the `Date` interface using separate instance variables to store the day, month, and year.

   Hint: watch out for leap years!

(3) Repeat Exercise 2 using an instance variable of type `int` containing the number of days since January 1st 1900 to record the date.

(4) A queue is a list of items arranged in the order in which the items were originally added to the list, i.e., the least recently added item is always at the head of the queue while the most recently added item is always at the back of the queue. Furthermore, only the item at the head of the queue can be removed at any time although further items can always be added to the end of the queue. Design the interface of a class whose instances represent queues of people. Make sure to describe the allowable sequences in which the methods of the class can be invoked.

(5) Design the interface of a class whose instances represent appointment diaries.

More About Types and Values 8

This chapter:

- distinguishes between accessing data by value and by reference
- introduces *value types* – types whose values are accessed by value rather than by reference
- describes how `structs` are used to introduce new value types
- introduces an alternative way to pass parameters to methods

In Chapter 3 we introduced the idea of a *type* as a set of values. We saw that C# provides 13 *simple types*, whose values represent fundamental entities such as numbers and single characters, and also allows us to introduce new types as classes. We saw that each class introduces a corresponding type whose values are the instances of the class. Moreover, we saw that because variables of such class types do not contain instances of the class but rather references to instances, these class types are called *reference types* in C#. In this chapter, we will look at how to define types whose values are stored directly in variables, rather like the values of the simple types. Such types are called *value types* and, in fact, all C#'s simple types are defined as value types. C# allows us to introduce our own values types in much the same way as we can use classes to introduce our own reference types. In this chapter, we will look in detail at the differences between reference types and value types.

Value Types vs. Reference Types

Consider Figure 8.1, which shows the contents of two variables, my`Salary` of type `int` and my`Boss` of type `Person`. What should be immediately apparent is the while my age is stored directly in the my`Age` variable, the my`Boss` variable only contains a reference to the object representing my boss and not the value of the corresponding object, which is stored elsewhere. As we saw previously, an important consequence of this is that several variables of type `Person` might refer to this object value and be used to access it. For example, if my boss had a salary of $58 000 (lucky guy!), we might say:

```
Person manager = myBoss; // now refers to same object as myBoss
manager.IncreaseSalary(10000);    // increase salary
int salary = myBoss.GetSalary();  // returns 68,000
```

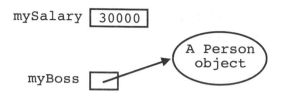

Figure 8.1   Values versus references.

We get this result because both method invocations, although performed using different variables, are directed to the same object. This object is always accessed indirectly via its references. We say that accesses to the object's value take place *by reference*.

In contrast, consider what happens when we assign the value of mySalary to another variable and then change it. Let's say mySalary is initially $30 000.

```
int yourSalary = mySalary;           // copy value to yourSalary
yourSalary = yourSalary + 10000;  // you get an increase
                                     // but I don't
```

In this case, when we change the value stored in yourSalary, it has no effect on the value stored in mySalary. Although the value of yourSalary came from mySalary, because the values are stored in the variables themselves rather than elsewhere, the values of the two variables are independent. Changes to one, don't affect the other. In this case, we say that the variables are accessed *by value*. Figure 8.2 shows the results.

Notice that for reference types, assignment between variables copies a reference from one variable to another but leaves the value to which the source variable referred unaffected. With

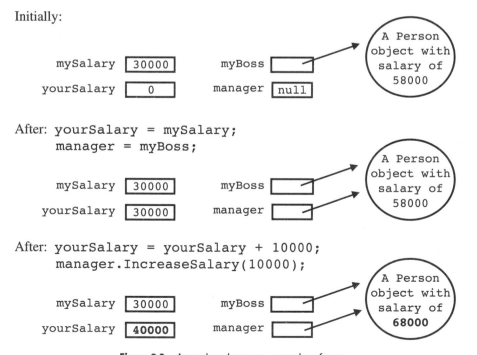

Figure 8.2   Access by value versus access by reference.

simple types, assignment makes a new independent copy of the value, which can be changed separately later.

Simple Types as Value Types

In fact, C#'s simple types are a subset of a more general category of types whose values are stored directly in variables and are copied by assignment. These types are collectively called *value types*. Value types come in two guises: pre-defined value types (the simple types) and user-defined value types, which can be introduced by programmers as we will see later in the chapter.

User-defined Value Types

For now, let's imagine that we have already defined our own value type whose values represent complex numbers rather like instances of the ComplexNumber class from Chapters 6 and 7. Each value of this type will consist of a pair of doubles for the real and imaginary parts of the complex number. Let's call our type ComplexNumberValue. Figure 8.3 shows what a variable of type ComplexNumberValue might look like compared with a variable of type ComplexNumber. Notice that while the ComplexNumber variable contains a reference to a ComplexNumber object, the ComplexNumberValue variable contains the pair of doubles itself.

Figure 8.4 shows the effect of introducing two further variables of types ComplexNumber-Value and ComplexNumber and assigning the values of our original variables to them. Both ComplexNumber variables new refer to the same ComplexNumber value (i.e., object) while the two ComplexNumberValue variables contain independent copies of the same value.

As our example illustrates, we now have two options for any type that we can define. We can define it as a reference type, by means of a class, or we can define it as a value type, as we will describe below. Since, we are doing object-oriented programming, most of the entities with which our programs will deal, will be objects defined by classes and accessed by reference. In particular, this ensures that we can easily keep a one-to-one correspondence between objects and the entities that they represent, which is usually desirable. For example, performing assignments between variables of reference types will result in the references being copied and not the objects concerned being duplicated. Sometimes we will want to use value types, usually in much the same way that the simple types are used, to represent simple values. ComplexNumberValue above is a good example.

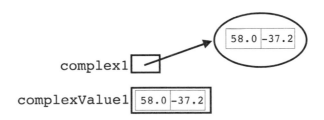

Figure 8.3 ComplexNumber versus ComplexNumberValue.

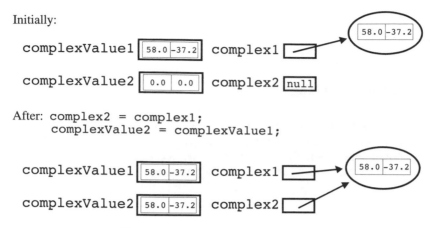

Figure 8.4   Assignment of complex numbers.

Defining Value Types – `structs`

Just as a reference type is introduced by a class definition, a new value type can be introduced by a *struct definition*. In fact, a struct definition is very similar to a class definition except that it is introduced by the keyword `struct` rather than the keyword `class`. The term `struct` is short for "structure" and is used for historical reasons. We often use the term "struct" to refer to a value of a type defined by a struct definition too!

As Figure 8.5 shows, a struct can have both attributes and methods just like a class. Indeed, with a few exceptions that we will discuss below, a struct can have pretty much all the same features as a class, including overloaded constructors and methods, fields (we use the term field to refer to the attributes of a struct), and properties as well as `static` methods and fields. For example, Program 8.1 shows the definition of `struct ComplexNumberValue`. This definition is almost identical to class `ComplexNumber` as shown in Chapter 7. In particular, it provides all the same methods for performing arithmetic on complex numbers. The major difference between values of type `ComplexNumber` and `ComplexNumberValue` is the way in which they are stored and accessed, by reference in the case of `ComplexNumber` and by value in the case of `ComplexNumberValue` as we saw in Figures 8.3 and 8.4.

```
struct <struct name>
{

    <list of fields>

    <list of methods>

}
```

Figure 8.5   The syntax of a `struct` declaration.

```csharp
/* A struct whose values represent */
/* complex numbers with arithmetic operators */
using System;
struct ComplexNumberValue
{
   public double re;
   public double im;

   /* initialize new complex number to be equal */
   /* to specified complex number */
   public ComplexNumberValue(ComplexNumberValue other)
   {
      this.re = other.re;
      this.im = other.im;
   }

   /* initialize new complex number with specified values */
   public ComplexNumberValue(double re, double im)
   {
      this.re = re;
      this.im = im;
   }

   /* add specified complex number to current complex number */
   public ComplexNumberValue Add(ComplexNumberValue other)
   {
      return new ComplexNumberValue(this.re + other.re,
         this.im + other.im);
   }

   /* subtract specified complex number from current complex number */
   public ComplexNumberValue Subtract(ComplexNumberValue other)
   {
      return new ComplexNumberValue(this.re - other.re, this.im -
         other.im);
   }

   /* multiply current complex number by specified complex number */
   public ComplexNumberValue Multiply(ComplexNumberValue other)
   {
      return new ComplexNumberValue((this.re * other.re) -
         (this.im * other.im),
                  (this.re * other.im) + (this.im * other.re));
   }

   /* Divide current complex number by specified complex number.
    *
    * In the event of a divide by zero, the result will be infinity.
    * This can happen to either or both of the real and imaginary part.
    *
    * To test for infinity call double.IsInfinity().  */
   public ComplexNumberValue Divide(ComplexNumberValue other)
   {
      double divisor = (other.re * other.re) + (other.im * other.im);
      return new ComplexNumberValue(((this.re * other.re)
         + (this.im * other.im)) / divisor,
            ((this.im * other.re) - (this.re* other.im)) / divisor);
   }
```

```csharp
/* return conjugate of current complex number */
public ComplexNumberValue Conjugate()
{
   return new ComplexNumberValue(this.re, -this.im);
}

/* report whether or not specified complex number */
/* is equal to current complex number */

public override bool Equals(object o)
{
   return this == (ComplexNumberValue)o;
}

public override int GetHashCode()
{
   return 0;
}

// addition operator
public static ComplexNumberValue operator +(ComplexNumberValue c1,
                 ComplexNumberValue c2)
{
   return c1.Add(c2);
}

// subtraction operator
public static ComplexNumberValue operator -(ComplexNumberValue c1,
                 ComplexNumberValue c2)
{
   return c1.Subtract(c2);
}

// multiplication operator
public static ComplexNumberValue operator *(ComplexNumberValue c1,
                 ComplexNumberValue c2)
{
   return c1.Multiply(c2);
}

// division operator
public static ComplexNumberValue operator /(ComplexNumberValue c1,
                 ComplexNumberValue c2)
{
   return c1.Divide(c2);

}

// equality operator
public static bool operator ==(ComplexNumberValue c1,
           ComplexNumberValue c2)
{
   return c1.Equals(c2);
}
```

```
// inequality operator
public static bool operator !=(ComplexNumberValue c1,
           ComplexNumberValue c2)
{
   return !c1.Equals(c2);
}

/* return a string representing the current complex number */
public override string ToString()
{
   string sign = "+";

   if (this.im < 0)
   {
      sign = "-";
   }
   return this.re + sign + Math.Abs(this.im) + "i";
}
}
```

Program 8.1   Struct ComplexNumberValue.

Creating Structs

There are, of course, a few differences between classes and structs. Firstly, as Program 8.1 illustrates, a struct cannot provide a constructor that takes no formal parameters although one is provided for each struct by default. This default parameterless constructor initializes all the fields of the struct with default values. Hence, we can create a new value of type ComplexNumberValue as:

```
ComplexNumberValue c1, c2;
c1 = new ComplexNumberValue();       // use default constructor
c2 = new ComplexNumberValue(4.5, 7.4); // use our constructor
```

even though we didn't include a constructor that takes no parameters in the declaration of our struct. It is however required that our constructors give values to all the fields of the struct before finishing, which is sensible even if it wasn't the case for a class definition.

If a struct provides only public fields, then we can actually create a new struct without using the new operator at all. Since structs are stored directly in variables, there is no need to create the struct separately from the variable. However, we still have to give values to all the fields of the struct before we can use it. If all the fields are public, we can do this using simple assignment. For example, if our re and im attributes were public we could write:

```
ComplexNumberValue c1; // introduce variable to hold struct
c1.re = 4.5;           // give value to field re
c2.im = 7.4;           // give value to field im
```

This works because the values of the fields are stored in the variable c1 created as a result of the variable declaration and only need to be given values before the struct is used.

Using Structs

Syntactically, structs are accessed in exactly the same ways that objects are. For example, Program 8.2 shows a program that performs arithmetic on complex numbers using values

```
/* A program to perform arithmetic on complex numbers */

using tcdIO;

class ComplexValueProgram
{
   private const string EXIT = "e";

   public static ComplexNumberValue ReadComplex(Terminal t, string p)
   {
      t.WriteLine(p);
      double r = t.ReadDouble("Re: ");
      double i = t.ReadDouble("Im: ");
      return new ComplexNumberValue(r, i);
   }

   public static void Main()
   {
      Terminal terminal;
      ComplexNumberValue number1, number2, result;
      string op;

      /* create an object to represent the terminal */
      terminal = new Terminal();

      op = terminal.ReadString(
         "Enter operation (+, -, *, /, e<xit>): ");
      while (!op.Equals(EXIT))
      {
         if (op.Equals("+"))
         {
            number1 = ReadComplex(terminal, "Enter first number");
            number2 = ReadComplex(terminal, "Enter second number");
            result = number1 + number2;
            terminal.WriteLine(result.ToString());
         }
         else if (op.Equals("-"))
         {
            number1 = ReadComplex(terminal, "Enter first number");
            number2 = ReadComplex(terminal, "Enter second number");
            result = number1 - number2;
            terminal.WriteLine(result.ToString());
         }
         else if (op.Equals("*"))
         {
            number1 = ReadComplex(terminal, "Enter first number");
            number2 = ReadComplex(terminal, "Enter second number");
            result = number1 * number2;
            terminal.WriteLine(result.ToString());
         }
         else if (op.Equals("/"))
         {
            number1 = ReadComplex(terminal, "Enter first number");
            number2 = ReadComplex(terminal, "Enter second number");
            if ((object)(result = number1/number2) != null)
            {
               terminal.WriteLine(result.ToString());
            }
```

```
        else
        {
            terminal.WriteLine("Unable to divide "
                + number1 + " by "
                + number2 + ".");
        }
    }
    op = terminal.ReadString("Enter operation: ");
    }
    terminal.WriteLine("Finished!");
    }
}
```

Program 8.2   A program to perform arithmetic on complex number values.

of type ComplexNumberValue to represent the complex numbers. Compare the program with the version in Chapter 7 that does the same thing using objects of type ComplexNumber to represent complex numbers. The programs are almost identical apart from the names of the types being used.

It is of course important to realize that while the assignments to variables of type ComplexNumber in the program in Chapter 7 are copying object references, those to variables of type ComplexNumberValue in Program 8.2 are copying struct values. Importantly, the same applies to the values passed as parameters to the various methods or returned as their results.

For example, in class ComplexNumber, method Add receives a reference to another instance of ComplexNumber as a parameter, eventually creates a new instance of ComplexNumber and returns a reference to it as its result. In contrast, in struct ComplexNumberValue, method Add receives a ComplexNumberValue as a parameter, eventually creates a new value of type ComplexNumberValue and returns a copy of it as its result. In particular, because parameters are passed by value, the Add method, receives a copy of its actual parameter. Thus, any changes made to the value have no effect on the actual parameter in exactly the way as if the parameter had been of a simple type.

Differences Between Classes and Structs

Apart from the way in which structs are created and initialized, the differences between class and structs are relatively minor in terms of the features of classes that we have seen already. The other important difference is that structs are not garbage collected. They exist for as long as the variable that contains them is in scope and are deleted when the variable goes out of scope, just like values of simple types. Essentially, structs are expected to be created and deleted very dynamically. Consequently, a struct may not include a destructor.

Simple Types as Structs

We've seen that both the simple types and structs are examples of value types. In fact, in C#, the simple types are actually represented as structs that define the methods, and implicitly the operators, available to manipulate values of simple types. Figure 8.6 summarizes the different categories of types that we have met in C#.

Type int is actually represented by a struct called Int32. As Figure 8.7 shows, the other simple types are similarly represented by corresponding structs. Because, values of type int are actually considered structs, we can invoke methods on them just as we can on other

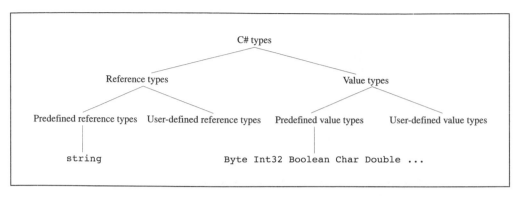

Figure 8.6 Types in C#.

structs. For example, Int32 provides a ToString method for integers so that given a variable result of type int we can say:

```
terminal.println("Result is:" + result.ToString());
```

or even

```
terminal.println("Result is:" + 15.ToString());
```

Similarly, Int32 provides a static method called parse to convert a string into an int. To read an integer from the terminal we might say:

```
int input = int.Parse(terminal.readString("Enter input:"));
```

where Parse, being static, is invoked on int rather than a specific value of type int.

Passing Parameters by Reference

In Chapter 7, we tried to write a method to swap the values of two integer variables. We soon discovered that with C#'s usual way of passing parameters by value this wasn't possible. Our

Type	C# struct
sbyte	SByte
short	Int16
int	Int32
long	Int64
byte	Byte
ushort	UInt16
uint	UInt32
ulong	UInt64
float	Single
double	Double
decimal	Decimal
char	Char
bool	Boolean

Figure 8.7 C#'s predefined value types.

method was intended to be called with two variables as actual parameters and to change the contents of those variables as a result of its execution:

```
int var1 = 12, var2 = 14;
swapper = new IntSwapper();
...
swapper.Swap(var1, var2);
// now var1 should be 14 and var2 12
```

However, because the parameters were passed by value, the method only received a copy of the value of each variable and wasn't able to manipulate the variables directly. Put another way, the effect of passing parameters by value is only to initialize the values of the formal parameters with the values of the actual parameters. As we saw, changes made to the formal parameters during the course of a method have no effect on the corresponding actual parameters.

To write our Swap method as we had intended, we would need to be able to *link* the formal parameters of the method to its actual parameters for the duration of the method, so that any changes to the formal parameters were immediately reflected in the actual parameters. Rather than being copies of the same value, both the actual and the formal parameters would then refer to the same value in much the same way that two variables of a reference type can refer to the same object. As it turns out, C# allows us to do just that!

```
/* A class that provides a method to
   swap the values of its parameters */
class IntSwapper
{
    public void Swap(ref int num1, ref int num2)
    {
        int tmp;

        tmp = num1;
        num1 = num2;
        num2 = tmp;
    }
}
```

Program 8.3 Class IntSwapper (revised).

Program 8.3, is a modified version of the IntSwapper class providing a version of the Swap method that allows the values of the actual parameters to be swapped. Notice that the formal parameters to Swap are labeled with the keyword ref. When a method with a ref parameter is invoked, the corresponding actual parameter must be a variable and the formal and actual parameters are linked together for the duration of the method. Changes to the formal parameter are reflected immediately in the corresponding actual parameter. Program 8.4 is a program that uses an IntSwapper to swap the values of two variables. The execution of the program is shown in Figure 8.8. As you can see, the program works as expected! Notice that in Program 8.4 the actual parameters var1 and var2 are also labeled with the keyword ref in the method invocation. While this may seen like unnecessary duplication of effort, C# requires it! At least, it should make it clear to anyone reading the program that the values of those variables are likely to be changed as a side-effect of the method invocation.

Figure 8.9 illustrates exactly what happens as the method executes. Initially, var1 and var2 are given the values 12 and 37. When the method is invoked, the formal parameter num1 is *linked* to var1 and num2 to var2. In particular, the values of var1 and var2 are *not*

```
/* A program that swaps the values of two integer */
/* variables using a method */
using tcdIO;
class SwapProgram
{
   public static void Main()
   {
      Terminal terminal;
      int var1, var2;
      IntSwapper swapper;

      /* create an object to represent the terminal */
      terminal = new Terminal();

      /* create the IntSwapper */
      swapper = new IntSwapper();

      /* Read in some numbers */
      var1 = terminal.ReadInt("Enter value of var1: ");
      var2 = terminal.ReadInt("Enter value of var2: ");

      /* swap them */
      swapper.Swap(ref var1, ref var2);

      /* Write out the numbers */
      terminal.WriteLine("Value of var1 is now: " + var1 + ".");
      terminal.WriteLine("Value of var2 is now: " + var2 + ".");
   }
}
```

Program 8.4   A program to swap the value of two int variables (revised).

copied to num1 and num2 – there is only one copy of the values maintained by the program. The assignment to num1 causes the value of the var1 to change. Likewise, the assignment to num2 causes the value of var2 to change. In some sense, num1 and num2 are acting as if they were references to the values held in var1 and var2. For this reason, this mode of passing parameters is referred to as *pass by reference* in contrast to the usual method of *pass by value*.

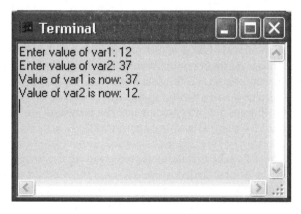

Figure 8.8   The execution of Program 8.4.

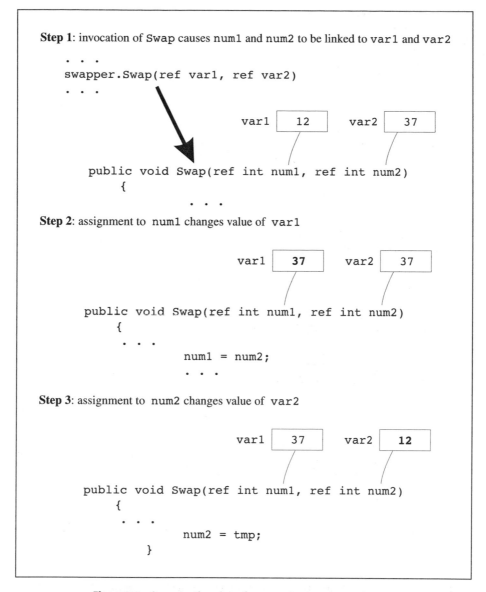

Figure 8.9   Swapping the values of two actual parameters step by step.

Passing User-defined Structs by Reference

Just like values of simple types, values of structs are also normally passed by value. For example, in struct ComplexNumberValue, the value of the actual parameter to the Add method is copied to the corresponding formal parameter. However, any struct can be passed by reference in the same way that a value of a simple type can.

For example, we could write a simple method to swap the values of two variables of type ComplexNumberValue following the same pattern as our Swap method from class IntSwapper.

```
/* A program that swaps the values of two complex */
/* number variables using a method */
using System;
using tcdIO;
class SwapComplexProgram
{
   public static ComplexNumberValue ReadComplex(Terminal t, string p)
   {
      t.WriteLine(p);
      double r = t.ReadDouble("Re: ");
      double i = t.ReadDouble("Im: ");
      return new ComplexNumberValue(r, i);
   }

   public static void Main()
   {
      Terminal terminal;
      ComplexNumberValue complex1, complex2;
      ComplexSwapper swapper;

      /* create an object to represent the terminal */
      terminal = new Terminal();

      /* create the ComplexSwapper */
      swapper = new ComplexSwapper();

      /* Read in some numbers */
      complex1 = ReadComplex(terminal, "Enter value of complex1: ");
      complex2 = ReadComplex(terminal, "Enter value of complex2: ");

      /* swap them */
      swapper.Swap(ref complex1, ref complex2);

      /* Write out the numbers */
      terminal.WriteLine("Value of complex1 is now: " + complex1 + ".");
      terminal.WriteLine("Value of complex2 is now: " + complex2 + ".");
   }
}
```

Program 8.5 A program to swap the value of two ComplexNumberValue variables.

```
public void SwapComplexValues(ref ComplexNumberValue c1,
   ref ComplexNumberValue c2) {
   ComplexNumberValue tmp;
   tmp = c1;
   c1 = c2;
   c2 = tmp;
}
```

Since the formal parameters are labeled as ref parameters, the actual parameters must be variables to which c1 and c2 will be linked for the duration of each invocation of SwapComplexValues. Program 8.5 shows a program that uses this method to swap the values of two variables of type ComplexNumberValue and Figure 8.10 the results of running it.

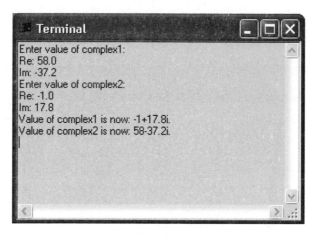

Figure 8.10   The execution of Program 8.5.

Perhaps not surprisingly, we can also pass object references by reference. This allows a method to change the contents of an actual parameter of a reference type in addition to being able to access (and possibly change) the object referred to by the actual parameter.

As an example, here's yet another a method that swaps the values of its actual parameters which are this time of type `ComplexNumber`.

```
public void SwapComplex(ref ComplexNumber c1,
    ref ComplexNumber c2) {
    ComplexNumber tmp;
    tmp = c1;
    c1 = c2;
    c2 = tmp;
}
```

Figure 8.11 shows the effect of using this method to swap the values of two variables of type `ComplexNumber`. Notice that it is the contents of the two variables that are changed by the method and not the contents of the two objects to which they refer.

By way of contrast here's a method that swaps the contents of two instances of `ComplexNumber`.

```
public void SwapComplex (ComplexNumber c1,
    ComplexNumber c2) {
    ComplexNumber tmp = new ComplexNumber();
    tmp.re = c1.re; tmp.im = c1.im;
    c1.re = c2.re; c1.im = c2.im;
    c2.re = tmp.im; c2.re = tmp.im;
}
```

Figure 8.12 shows the effect of using this method. Obviously, the difference between swapping object references and swapping the contents of an object is significant, especially

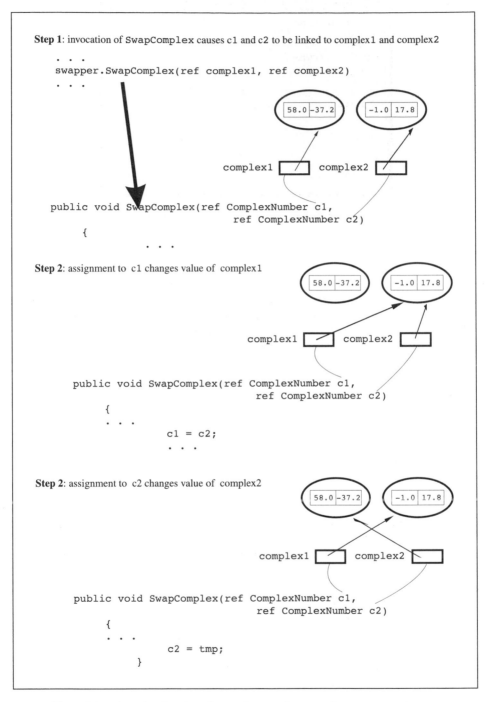

Figure 8.11   Swapping the values of `ComplexNumber` actual parameters step by step.

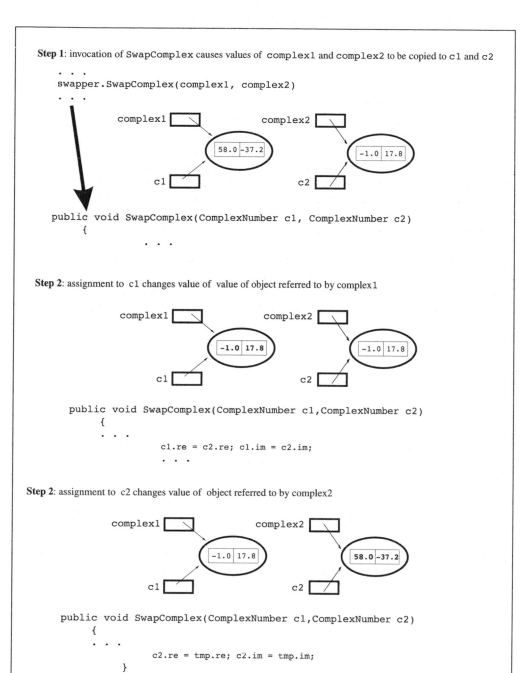

Figure 8.12   Swapping the values of two `ComplexNumber` objects step by step.

when we consider that there may be several variables referring to the same object and changes to the object's contents are visible through all of those variables.

`ref` **and** `out`

As we have seen, when the formal parameter to a method is a `ref` parameter, the corresponding actual parameter must be a variable and must have been labeled with `ref` in the method invocation. Moreover, C# requires that the actual parameter has already been given a value. Implicitly, the actual parameter is being used both to pass information to the method (i.e., the value that it had before the method was invoked) and to receive results from the method (i.e., the changed value that it will have received once the method has been completed). Sometimes, a parameter is *only* intended to receive a result from a method and not to provide information to the method. In this case, the parameter may be labeled with the keyword `out` instead of `ref`.

When the formal parameter to a method is an `out` parameter, the call by reference mechanism is still used and the corresponding actual parameter must still be a variable. However, in this case the actual parameter must be labeled with the keyword `out` in the method invocation and need not have already been given a value before the invocation takes place.

Case Study: Intersecting Line Segments

To illustrate the various features that we have introduced in this chapter, we will consider writing a program to determine whether segments of two straight lines intersect. Each line segment will be defined by a start point and an end point where each point is a point in two-dimensional space. Of course, we will have to watch out for the fact that the lines may be parallel to each other and therefore do not intersect or, if they are not parallel, that their point of intersection does not lie within the segments of interest.

There are various strategies that we could use to determine whether two line segments intersect. For example, when we know the algebraic equations of the corresponding lines, we can use the method of simultaneous equations to find their point of intersection. Given the equations of two lines in the form

$$\text{Line1} : a_1\,x + b_1\,y = c_1$$
$$\text{Line2} : a_2\,x + b_2\,y = c_2$$

solving these equations for x and y gives us the point of intersection of the lines (if a solution is possible). To use this strategy with our line segments, we need to be able to find the equations of the corresponding lines given the start and end points of the line segments. Moreover, we need to be aware that the solution to the equations (i.e., the point of intersection) need not lie on the part of the line that is within the segment in which we are interested.

Given two points on a line (x_1, y_1) and (x_2, y_2), we can calculate the slope (m) of the line as $(y_2 - y_1)/(x_2 - x_1)$ as long as $(x_2 - x_1)$ is not zero. Given m, we can calculate the coefficients $(a, b$ and $c)$ of the equation of the line as:

$$a = -m \quad b = 1 \quad c = (-m \cdot x_1) + y_1.$$

Finally, given the equations of two lines as above, their point of intersection can be found by:

$$x = (b_1 c_2 - c_1 b_2)/(b_1 a_2 - a_1 b_2)$$
$$y = (a_1 c_2 - c_1 a_2)/(a_1 b_2 - b_1 a_2)$$

as long as $a_1 b_2$ is not equal to $a_2 b_1$, which indicates that the lines are parallel.

Identifying the Classes

As usual our first task is to identify the classes to be written. Apart from the program class, let's call that LineProgram, classes to represent line segments (LineSegment) and points (Point) seem like obvious candidates. Notice, however, that an instance of Point is simply a pair of real numbers. Moreover, each LineSegment will need to contain two points to define its start and end. These points should be fully encapsulated, in particular, to prevent changes to the Point objects causing the line to move! Given these observations, it makes sense to define Point as a struct rather than a class, so that each instance of LineSegment will embed the values of its points internally.

Apart from its start and end points, every LineSegment has an equation defined by three real numbers. We might consider introducing a class to represent such equations, but again it makes sense to represent an equation as a struct since it is really only a set of numbers that should be treated together. For this reason we introduce struct Equation.

Identifying the Methods

Class LineSegment will obviously need to provide a constructor that takes a pair of points as inputs. It will also provide methods to allow its start and end point to be queried as well as a method to allow its equation to be obtained. LineSegment can also provide methods to allow features of the line such as its slope, midpoint, and length to be calculated. Finally, it will provide the method to determine if two line segments intersect. By now, writing the headings of these methods should provide no difficulty. However, the CalculateSlope and GetEquation methods are worth a little further consideration.

Our approach to calculating a slope only works if the x coordinates of the two points of the line segment are not the same. Hence, GetSlope should indicate when the slope can't be determined. To achieve this we have it return a bool value to indicate success or failure and return the actual slope as the value of an out parameter that will be given a value by the method if the slope can be calculated.

```
/* calculate slope of line if not infinite */
public bool CalculateSlope(out double slope)
```

```
/* A struct whose values represent points */
using System;
struct Point {
   public double x;   // used to store x coordinate of the point
   public double y;   // used to store y coordinate of the point

   /* declare a constructor to initialize new points */
   public Point(double x, double y)
   {
         this.x = x;
         this.y = y;
   }

   /* a method to calculate the distance between two points */
   public double CalculateDistance(Point other) {
      double tmpX = other.x - this.x; // (x2 - x1)
         double tmpY = other.y - this.y; // (y2 - y1)
         return Math.Sqrt((x*x) + (y*y));
   }
}
```

Program 8.6   Struct `Point`.

GetEquation is similar in that our approach to determining the equation of the line depends on being able to calculate the slope of the line. Success or failure will be indicated by a result of type bool and the equation returned as the value of an out parameter.

```
/* get coefficients of equation of line if possible */
public bool GetEquation(out Equation equation)
```

Notice that in this case the out parameter is of the user-defined type Equation.
    The resulting struct and class definitions are shown in Programs 8.6–8.9.

```
/* A struct whose values represent equations of the form ax + by = c*/
struct Equation {
   public double a, b, c;   // coefficients of the equation

   /* declare a constructor to initialize new equation*/
   public Equation(double a, double b, double c)
   {
      this.a = a;
      this.b = b;
      this.c = c;
   }
}
```

Program 8.7   Struct `Equation`.

```
/* A class whose instances represent line segments */
using tcdIO;
class LineSegment {
   private Point left, right;

   /* initialize new instances of class Line */
   public LineSegment(Point left, Point right)
   {
      this.left = left; // copy parameters
      this.right = right;
   }

   /* return a copy of the left coordinate of the current line */
   public Point GetLeft()
   {
      return this.left;
   }

   /* return a copy of the right coordinate of the current point */
   public Point GetRight()
   {
      return this.right;
   }

   /* calculate length of line */
   public double CalculateLength()
   {
      return left.CalculateDistance(right);
   }

   /* calculate midpoint of line */
   public Point CalculateMidpoint()
   {
      return new Point((left.x + right.x)/2, (left.y + right.y)/2);
   }

   /* calculate slope of line if not infinite */
   public bool CalculateSlope(out double slope)
   {
      if ((right.x - left.x) != 0.0)
      {
         slope = (right.y - left.y)/(right.x - left.x);
         return true;
      }
      else
      {
         slope = 0;
         return false;
      }
   }

/* get coefficients of equation of line if possible */
   public bool GetEquation(out Equation equation)
   {
      double m; // slope of line
      if (this.CalculateSlope(out m))
      {
         equation.a = -m;
```

```
         equation.b = 1;
         equation.c = left.y - (m * left.x);
         return true;
      }
      else
      {
         equation.a = -m;
         equation.b = 1;
         equation.c = left.y - (m * left.x);
         return false;
      }
   }

   /* report whether given a point of the same line is on the line segment */
   public bool IsOn(Point point)
   {
      return ((left.x <= point.x) && (point.x <= right.x))
         || ((right.x <= point.x) && (point.x <= left.x));
   }

   /* report whether line segment intersects with another */
   public bool Intersects(LineSegment other)
   {
      /* first try to solve simultaneous equations for */
      /* point of intersection of corresponding lines */
      Equation e1, e2;
      Point intersect;

      if(this.GetEquation(out e1)
         && other.GetEquation(out e2))
      {
         if ((e1.b * e2.a) != (e1.a * e2.b))
         {
            /* there is an intersection */
            intersect.x = (((e1.b * e2.c) - (e1.c * e2.b))
               / ((e1.b * e2.a) - (e1.a * e2.b)));
            intersect.y = (((e1.a * e2.c) - (e1.c * e2.a))
               / ((e1.a * e2.b) - (e1.b * e2.a)));
            /* now see if the point of intersection is on */
            /* both line segments */
            return this.IsOn(intersect) && other.IsOn(intersect);
         }
         else
         {
            /* parallel lines */
            return false;
         }
      }
      else
      {
         /* infinite slope */
         return false;
      }
   }
}
```

Program 8.8 Class LineSegment.

```
/* A program to determine if two line segments intersect */

using tcdIO;

class LineProgram
{

    public static LineSegment ReadLineSegment(Terminal t, string p)
    {
        t.WriteLine(p);
        return new LineSegment(
            new Point(t.ReadDouble("x1: "), t.ReadDouble("y1: ")),
            new Point(t.ReadDouble("x2: "), t.ReadDouble("y2: ")));
    }

    public static void Main()
    {
        Terminal terminal;
        LineSegment line1, line2;


        /* create an object to represent the terminal */
        terminal = new Terminal();

        /* read line segments */
        line1 = ReadLineSegment(terminal, "Enter first line");
        line2 = ReadLineSegment(terminal, "Enter second line");

        /* check for intersection */
        if (line1.Intersects(line2))
        {
            terminal.WriteLine("Line segments intersect.");
        }
        else
        {
            terminal.WriteLine("Line segments do not intersect.");
        }
    }
}
```

Program 8.9   A program to determine if line segments intersect.

Summary

- variables whose type is a value type contain values that are copied by assignment
- variables of reference types contain references to values that are not copied by assignment
- the simple types are examples of predefined value types
- user-defined values types can be defined as structs
- structs are defined and used in much the same way as classes
- the simple types are represented as structs
- parameters can be passed by reference as well as by value
- a method can change an actual parameter that is passed by reference
- an actual parameter to be passed by reference must therefore be a variable
- parameters to be passed by reference are labeled with ref or out

- ref parameters are used to provide information to a method and to receive a result from that method
- out parameters are used only to receive a result from a method

Exercises

(1) Consider the following C# class declaration:

```
class xxx {
  void yyy(ref int num1, int num2) {
    int tmp;
    tmp = num1;
    num1 = num2;
    num2 = tmp;
  }
}
```

Write fragments of code to call the yyy method of class xxx where:

- some of the actual parameters are literals;
- some of the actual parameters are variables;
- some of the actual parameters are expressions involving one or more operators.

What does the yyy method actually do (in particular, what effect does it have on its actual parameters)?

(2) Write a program to perform arithmetic on rational numbers, where rational numbers are represented by structs. Make sure to introduce appropriate operators.

(3) Consider the class whose instance represented people that you wrote in Chapter 3. Would it be appropriate to use structs rather than objects to represent people? Draw some diagrams to illustrate the implications of doing so?

(4) Type long can represent a very large range of integer numbers (-2^{63} to $2^{63} - 1$). Define a new type, doubleLong, that represents integers in the range -2^{127} to $2^{127} - 1$.

Characters, Strings and Things　9

This chapter:

- motivates the need for programs to be able to process textual data including individual characters and strings
- describes type `char` – the simple type provided by C# to represent single characters
- describes class `string` – the C# class whose instances represent immutable strings of characters
- describes class `StringBuilder` – the C# class whose instances represent mutable strings of characters

Many of the programs that we have seen in previous chapters have dealt with strings of characters in one form or another. We saw in Chapter 3 that C# provides a class especially to represent such strings of characters – the class `string`. We have used strings to print messages on the screen and to store messages entered by the users of our programs. Moreover, we have already seen how to use string concatenation to make a new string by joining two existing strings.

Apart from joining different strings together, none of our programs performed any other kinds of modifications on the strings with which they dealt. You can probably imagine circumstances where a program might need to change some of the characters that make up a string, or add some additional characters into the middle of a string, or perhaps even delete characters from a string. The ability to perform this kind of string manipulation is an important requirement for many different kinds of program that deal with text. The word processor that I am using to write this book is a good example. If we imagine that this word processor is written in C# and that every line of text is represented by a string of characters, then clearly there will be times when I will need to modify these strings as I edit the text. For example, I may need to correct misspelled words, capitalize words, add punctuation, or delete poorly chosen words.

Happily, C# provides a whole range of facilities to allow programs to perform this kind of string manipulation and we will look at many of them later in this chapter. However, before we can look any further at strings and string manipulation, we need to look at how C# handles the building blocks from which strings are composed – individual characters.

Working with Characters – Type `char`

As we saw briefly in Chapter 3, C# provides a simple type to represent individual characters. This type is called `char`. The possible values of type `char` are individual characters such as

275

"A", ";" or "x". In fact, the set of possible values of type char includes pretty much every *printable character* that you can think of! It includes not only the characters that we are familiar with from English but also a variety of different characters found in other languages such as Greek and Russian that use completely different character sets. The ability to write programs that can deal with such characters is obviously important if we want our programs to be usable throughout the world, and especially, when we come to write programs that will be globally accessible over the Internet. As well as these printable characters, type char includes various *non-printable characters*. These invisible characters include characters such as the "line feed" character, which is used to designate the end of a line of text, and the "carriage return" character, which, when printed, causes the cursor to move back to the beginning of the current line.

Writing Character Literals

In a program we can usually write values (literals) of type char by enclosing the character concerned in single quotes. The use of the single quotes is necessary in order to distinguish the character value to which we want to refer from the characters making up the text of the program! Thus, the following are all examples of character literals:

```
'='   'A'   'a'   '"'  (double quote)   'x'   '_'   '9'
```

Notice that without the single quotes = would be the assignment operator, A would be a single-letter identifier, and 9 a literal of type int.

The Unicode Character Encoding System

Every value of type char is represented by a 16-bit code number. Thus, when a character value is to be stored in a computer's memory, what is actually stored is the code number representing that character. Since every code number is 16 bits long, C# can represent up to 65536 different characters. For example, here are the code numbers used to represent each of characters in the list above:

```
'='(61)     'A'(65)    'a'(97)     '"'(34)
'x'(120)    '_'(95)    '9'(57)
```

Of course, these codes weren't chosen randomly (even if it appears from the examples that this might have been the case!). The assignment of code numbers to different characters is the subject of an internationally accepted standard known as the Unicode Standard. Because this code is internationally accepted it means that text produced by any program will be recognized as the same text by every other program that uses the Unicode Standard (whether or not that program happens to be written in C# or any other language shouldn't matter!). Moreover since the Unicode Standard assigns different codes to all the different characters found in the different languages covered by the standard, there is never any ambiguity about exactly which character is intended as there could be if different standards were used to assign codes to different languages.

The fact that characters are represented as numbers gives us another way to write a character literal in a program. Every character can also be written by giving its code number preceded by the symbol \u (a backslash followed immediately by a lowercase u). The character still has to be written in single quotes and the code number has to be written as a hexadecimal number. For example, the characters in the list above could be written:

```
'\u003D'('=')     '\u0041'('A')     '\u0061'('a')
'\u0022'('"')
'\u0078'('x')     '\u005F'('_')     '\u0039'('9')
```

Given a choice between using `'A'` and `'\u41'`, the former is clearly preferable. However, the latter scheme allows us to write any possible character including the non-printable characters. For example, some of the commonly used non-printable characters that we might want to include in a program can be represented as follows:

```
'\u000a' (line feed)        '\u000d' (carriage return)

'\u0008' (backspace)        '\u0009' (tab)
```

This scheme also solves another problem that you may have noticed – it gives us a way of representing the single quote:

```
'\u0027' (single quote)
```

Escape Sequences

Although this scheme is very flexible, it is a bit ugly. Realizing this, the designers of C# provided some special shorthand symbols to represent commonly used character values. These special symbols are called *escape sequences*. The most commonly used escape sequences are shown in Figure 9.1. Notice that they are all introduced by a single backslash. For this reason the backslash character is known as the *escape character*. Moreover, because backslash is used to introduce an escape sequence, we usually have to use the escape sequence for backslash itself whenever we want to write the literal representing backslash in a C# program.

`'\n'`	linefeed	`'\u000a'`
`'\r'`	carriage return	`'\u000d'`
`'\b'`	backspace	`'\u0008'`
`'\t'`	tab	`'\u0009'`
`\''`	double quote	`'\u0022'`
`\'`	single quote	`'\u0027'`
`\\`	backslash	`'\u005c'`

Figure 9.1   Escape sequences for commonly used character values.

The ASCII Character Encoding System and Control Characters

The first 128 character codes defined by the Unicode Standard (i.e., the characters `'\u0000'` to `'\u007f'`) correspond to the character codes used by the older ASCII character encoding

	0	1	2	3	4	5	6	7	8	9	A	B	C	D	E	F
0	NUL ^@	STX ^A	SOT ^B	ETX ^C	EOT ^D	ENQ ^E	ACK ^F	BEL ^G	BS ^H	HT ^I	LF ^J	VT ^K	FF ^L	CR ^M	SO ^N	SI ^O
10	DLE ^P	DC1 ^Q	DC2 ^R	DC3 ^S	DC4 ^T	NAK ^U	SYN ^V	ETB ^W	CAN ^X	EM ^Y	SUB ^Z	ESC ^[	FS ^\	GS ^]	RS ^^	US ^_
20	Space	!	"	#	$	%	&	'	(	)	*	+	,	-	.	/
30	0	1	2	3	4	5	6	7	8	9	:	;	<	=	>	?
40	@	A	B	C	D	E	F	G	H	I	J	K	L	M	N	O
50	P	Q	R	S	T	U	V	W	X	Y	Z	[	\	]	^	_
60	`	a	b	c	d	e	f	g	h	i	j	k	l	m	n	o
80	p	q	r	s	t	u	v	w	x	y	z	{	|	}	~	DEL

Figure 9.2   Characters `'\u0000'` to `'\u007f'`.

standard. ASCII stands for the "American Standard Code for Information Interchange" and is, like Unicode, essentially a standard for assigning code numbers to characters. We mention it here because it is still widely used in other programming languages. However, ASCII is a 7-bit code and only defines 128 characters. These characters happen to be those that are used most commonly used in English including the upper and lowercase English alphabet, the decimal digits, and many common punctuation marks.

Characters `'\u0000'` to `'\u001f'` are the so-called *control characters*. These are characters that have special meaning when displayed on a terminal or printer, or when transmitted between computers. For example, the line feed character (`'\u000a'` or `'\n'`) is an example of a control character. Control characters are often referred to by the key combination used to generate the character on the keyboard. For example, line feed can be referred to as "control-j" (usually written as ^J) because it can be generated by simultaneously pressing the <CONTROL> and <j> keys on the keyboard. Figure 9.2 lists the first 128 characters, their codes and, in the case of the control characters, the corresponding key combinations used to type them.

char **Variables and Assignment**

We can declare and initialize variables of type `char` (whether instance variables in a class declaration or local variables in a method) in the usual way. For example,

```
char myInitial = 'V';
```

declares a single variable called `myInitial` that is capable of storing a single `char` value and gives it an initial value of `'V'`.

```
char firstInitial = 'V', middleInitial ='J';
```

declares two separate `char` variables called `firstInitial` and `middleInitial` respectively and gives them appropriate initial values.

As ever, we can use assignment to change the value stored in a `char` variable.

```
myInitial = 'D';
```

stores the value `'D'` into the variable `myInitial` overwriting its previous value. The statement

```
char firstLetter = myInitial;
```

stores the current value of the variable `myInitial` into the variable `firstLetter`.

We can also declare constants of type `char`, and indeed generally use type `char` in any of the ways that we previously used other simple types such as `int` and `double`. Thus, we can also have:

- expressions that give values of type `char`,
- methods that take parameters of type `char`, and
- methods that return values of type `char`.

Reading and Writing Characters

Perhaps the most important operations that we can perform on characters are those to read characters from the user and print characters on the screen.

As for the other simple types, a value of type `char` can be printed out using the `WriteLine` method from class `Terminal`. However, note that a single character is not a string! Thus, if we have a variable called `firstInitial` of type `char`, we can't say:

```
terminal.WriteLine(firstInitial);
```

since the parameter passed to `WriteLine` must be of type `string` rather than type `char`. However, we could write

```
terminal.WriteLine("Hello " +firstInitial+ ". " +name+"!");
```

In this case, the value of `firstInitial` is converted to type `string` and concatenated with the string `"Hello "` before being printed.

Sometimes we will want to be able to print out a single character on its own. For these cases we can use the method `WriteChar`, which is also provided by class `Terminal`. `WriteChar` takes a single `char` as its only parameter and prints the corresponding character at the next position on the screen. Thus, we could say:

```
terminal.WriteChar('A');
```

or

```
terminal.WriteChar(firstInitial);
```

Class `Terminal` also provides a method for reading a single character from the user. Not surprisingly this method is called `ReadChar`. `ReadChar` is a little different from its counterparts for reading integers and floating-point numbers. Firstly, it doesn't take any parameter. Secondly, it doesn't wait for the user to press the <ENTER> key before returning the next character entered. Finally, it doesn't print the character that was entered on the screen.

Using ReadChar and WriteChar

As an example of reading and writing characters form the user, let's write a program that reads a list of characters entered by the user and counts how many characters are in the list. Since users usually like to see what they're typing, we will want our program to echo, i.e., print out, each character on the screen as it reads it in.

Since the program has to read a list of characters from the terminal and since we don't know in advance how many characters will be entered, we will use a loop to repeatedly read in a single character at a time using `ReadChar`. The character will need to be stored in a variable so that we can subsequently print it out using `WriteChar`. Moreover, we will need to keep a count of how many characters the program has read and increment the count for each new character.

Knowing what the body of the loop has to do, we now need to think about the terminating condition. How will the program know when to stop reading characters? We need to have some way for the user to indicate the end of the list of characters. The simplest solution is to use a designated character as the sentinel marking the end of the list. By convention, the end of a stream of characters is usually marked by the so-called *end-of-file* character. Which character actually represents the end-of-file character depends on the operating system running on the computer. For example, on computers that run the Unix operating system, it's the ^D character. On PCs running Windows operating systems it's ^Z. Let's assume that our program is to run on a PC and so use ^Z as the end-of-file character. Thus, we can ask the user to enter ^Z to designate the end of the list of characters and test for the presence of this character in the terminating condition of the loop. Program 9.1 shows the resulting program.

There are a few points worth noting about the program. Firstly, notice that we have used a `char` constant to define the end-of-file character using the `\u` notation to specify the actual value of the character. This allows us to easily change the program to use a different character to mark the end of the list should we need to. Secondly, notice the way in which we combined reading in the character, storing it in a variable, *and* testing if it was the end-of-file character into the terminating condition of the loop! The value of the expression

```
ch = terminal.ReadChar()
```

is the character that has just been read, which is then compared with the `char` value EOF. As this example illustrates, we can compare `char` values for equality and inequality. Figure 9.3 shows the result of running the program. Note that each character appears on the screen only once and that this is the result of the call to `WriteChar` in the body of our loop.

Using '\n'

Program 9.2 is a variation of Program 9.1 in which each character is written on a separate line. To start a new line after each character we simply print out a single new line character ('\n') using `WriteChar`. Figure 9.4 shows the result.

Converting Between Characters and Their Unicode Codes

Given a character it is often useful to be able to determine the Unicode code number associated with that character. Likewise, given a number in the range covered by the Unicode code, it may sometimes be necessary to convert that number into the corresponding character.

```
/* A program to illustrate Reading and writing */
/* characters Reads a list of characters entered by the user, */
/* counts them, and Writes out each on the terminal screen */

using tcdIO;

class EchoCharacter
{
    /* use ^Z as the end of file character */
    private const char EOF = '\u001A';

    public static void Main()
    {
        Terminal terminal;
        char ch;         // the character
        int count = 0; // the number of characters so far

        /* create an object to represent the terminal */
        terminal = new Terminal();

        terminal.WriteLine("Enter a list of characters
            (^Z to finish).");

        while ((ch=terminal.ReadChar()) != EOF)
        {
            count = count + 1;         // count character
            terminal.WriteChar(ch);    // echo character
        }
        terminal.WriteLine("The list had " + count + " characters.");
    }
}
```

Program 9.1   A program to illustrate reading and writing characters.

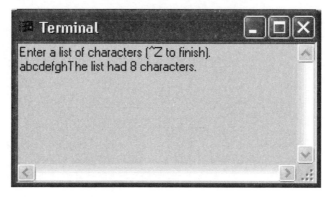

Figure 9.3   The execution of Program 9.1.

```
/* A program to illustrate the use of '\n' */
/* Reads a list of characters entered by the user, counts them, */
/* and Writes out each on a separate line of the screen */

using tcdIO;

class EchoCharacterPerLine
{
    /* use ^Z as the end of file character */
    private const char EOF = '\u001A';

    public static void Main()
    {
        Terminal terminal;
        char ch;        // the character
        int count = 0;

        /* create an object to represent the terminal */
        terminal = new Terminal();

        terminal.WriteLine("Enter a list of characters
            (^Z to finish).");
        while ((ch=terminal.ReadChar()) != EOF)
        {
            count = count + 1;        // count character
            terminal.WriteChar(ch);   // echo character
            terminal.WriteChar('\n'); // start a new line
        }
        terminal.WriteLine("The list had " + count + " characters.");
    }
}
```

Program 9.2   A program to illustrate the use of ' \n '.

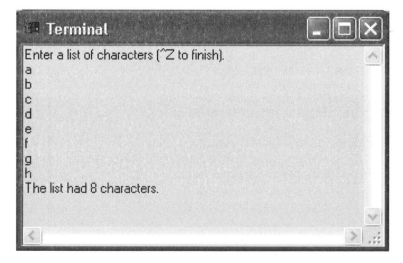

Figure 9.4   The execution of Program 9.2.

Determining the Unicode for a Character

Program 9.3 is yet another variation of Program 9.1. This time, as well as printing out each character that is entered, we print out the Unicode code number for the character.

As Program 9.3 illustrates, determining the Unicode value of a character is very easy. We simply assign the char value to a variable of type int! You may be surprised that C# allows this, since a character is clearly not an integer number. In fact, C# interprets type char as being another integer type and hence allows values of type char to be assigned to variables of type int and long and their unsigned counterparts. The value stored into the integer variable is, of course, the code number used to represent the character value.

By the way, notice the output from our program shown in Figure 9.5. The last two characters entered were control characters – ^G and ^X, in fact. Although they can't be displayed on the screen, their codes are displayed correctly.

Determining the Character Corresponding to a Unicode Code

Program 9.4 illustrates the reverse process: converting a Unicode code number into the corresponding character value. The idea is the same – simply assign the code number to

```
/* A program to illustrate conversion between characters and */
/* Unicode codes Reads a list of characters entered by the user, */
/* counts them, and Writes out the code number of each */

using tcdIO;

class EchoUnicode
{
    /* use ^Z as the end of file character */
    private const char EOF = '\u001A';

    public static void Main()
    {
        Terminal terminal;
        char ch;        // the character
        int unicode;    // its code number
        int count = 0;

        /* create an object to represent the terminal */
        terminal = new Terminal();

        terminal.WriteLine("Enter a list of characters
           (^Z to finish).");
        while ((ch=terminal.ReadChar()) != EOF)
        {
            count = count + 1;          // count character
            terminal.WriteChar(ch);     // echo character
            unicode = ch;               // calculate its code number
            terminal.WriteLine(": " + unicode);// Write out the code number
        }
        terminal.WriteLine("The list had " + count + " characters.");
    }
}
```

Program 9.3   A program to illustrate conversion between characters and Unicode codes.

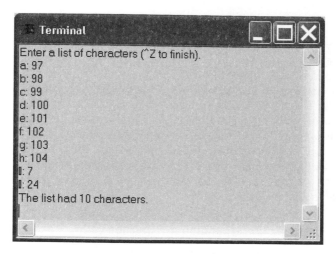

Figure 9.5 The execution of Program 9.3.

```
/* A program to illustrate conversion between Unicode */
/* codes and characters Reads a list of codes entered by the user, */
/* counts them, and Writes out the corresponding characters */

using tcdIO;

class Unicode2Char
{
    public static void Main()
    {
        Terminal terminal;
        int unicode;    // a code number
        char ch;        // the corresponding character
        int count = 0;

        /* create an object to represent the terminal */
        terminal = new Terminal();

        terminal.WriteLine("Enter a list of codes (-1 to finish).");
        while ((unicode=terminal.ReadInt("Enter code: ")) >= 0)
        {
            /* first make sure that we have a 16-bit value */
            if (unicode <= 0xffff)
            {
                count = count + 1;
                ch = (char)unicode;         // determine character
                terminal.WriteChar(ch);     // echo character
                terminal.WriteChar('\n');   // start a new line
            }
        }
        terminal.WriteLine("The list had " + count + " characters.");
    }
}
```

Program 9.4 A program to illustrate conversion between Unicode codes and characters.

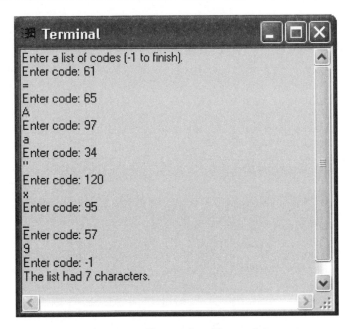

Figure 9.6 The execution of Program 9.4.

a variable of type char. However, since this isn't a safe operation (because the value of an arbitrary integer may be too large to store into a variable of type char), C# requires that we use a type cast to indicate that we really want to perform this operation. Note the use of an if statement to ensure that the number entered by the user is in the allowable range before we try to convert it into the corresponding character. The result of running the program is shown in Figure 9.6.

Comparison of Character Values

Because characters are represented as numbers we can use all the numeric relational operators to compare characters. In fact, we've already seen the use of the != operator to compare two char values for inequality in Program 9.1. However, we can also use the ==, !=, >, <, >=, and <= operators to compare char values. For the purposes of comparison, characters are ordered according to their Unicode code numbers. Thus, characters with lower code numbers are *less than* characters with higher code numbers. For example, '!' (33) is less than '5' (53), which is itself less than 'A' (65). If you study Figure 9.2, you'll notice a few interesting patterns:

- the characters representing the digits occur in the order of the values they represent,
- the characters representing the uppercase letters occur in alphabetic order,
- the characters representing the lowercase letters also occur in alphabetic order,
- the uppercase letters have consecutive code numbers,
- likewise, the lowercase letters have consecutive code numbers.

Unfortunately, this means that all uppercase letters have lower code numbers than any lowercase letter. For example, this means that while 'A' <= 'B' is true and 'a' <= 'b' is true, 'a' <= 'B' is surprisingly false!

```
/* A program to illustrate comparison of characters */
/* Reads a list of characters entered by the user, */
/* counts them, and Writes out any uppercase letters entered */

using tcdIO;

class EchoCapital
{
    /* use ^Z as the end of file character */
    private const char EOF = '\u001A';

    public static void Main()
    {
        Terminal terminal;
        char ch;
        int countChars = 0, countCaps = 0;

        /* create an object to represent the terminal */
        terminal = new Terminal();

        terminal.WriteLine("Enter a list of characters
            (^Z to finish).");
        while ((ch=terminal.ReadChar()) != EOF)
        {
            countChars = countChars + 1;    // count all characters
            if ((ch >= 'A') && (ch <= 'Z'))
            {
                countCaps = countCaps + 1;    // count uppercase letters
                terminal.WriteChar(ch);       // echo uppercase letters
            }
        }
        terminal.WriteLine("\nThe list had " + countChars + " characters");
        terminal.WriteLine("of which " + countCaps + " were uppercase
            letters.");
    }
}
```

Program 9.5   A program to illustrate comparison of characters.

Using Character Comparison

To illustrate the use of character comparison, Program 9.5 is yet another variation of Program 9.1. This version of the program reads a list of characters as before, but only prints out those that represent uppercase letters (see Figure 9.7). Thus, the body of the loop now uses an if statement to test whether or not the current character is an uppercase letter. To do so, it has to check that the character comes after 'A' and before 'Z'. The corresponding condition is:

```
((ch >= 'A') && (ch <= 'Z')
```

as shown in the program.

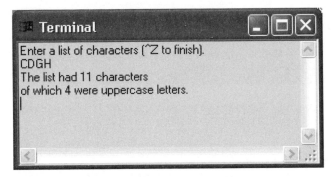

Figure 9.7   The execution of Program 9.5.

Struct `Char`

As for the other simple types, the type `char` is actually defined as a C# struct type called `Char`. As ever, we can usually ignore this detail. However, it is worth noting that struct `Char` provides a set of useful, mostly `static`, methods for processing characters. A subset of the most useful methods provided by struct `Char` is shown in Program 9.6. These methods fall into three main categories:

- methods to determine what category a particular character falls into: `IsLower`, `IsUpper`, `IsDigit`, `IsLetter`, `IsLetterOrDigit`, `IsControl`, `IsWhiteSpace`
- methods to convert between upper and lowercase letters: `ToLower` and `ToUpper`
- methods to convert between digits and their numeric values: `GetNumericValue`.

```
/* Some of the methods provided by struct Char - a struct whose */
/* values represent individual characters (extract) */
struct Char
{
    /* return true if the specified char is a lowercase letter */
    public static bool IsLower(char ch);

    /* returns true if the character at the specified index */
    /* of the specified string is a lowercase character */
    public static bool IsLower(string str, int index);

    /* return true if the specified char is an uppercase letter */
    public static bool IsUpper(char ch);

    /* returns true if the character at the specified index of the */
    /* specified string is an uppercase character */
    public static bool IsUpper(string str, int index);

    /* return true if the specified char is a digit */
    public static bool IsDigit(char ch);

    /* returns true if the character at the specified index of the */
    /* specified string is a digit */
    public static bool IsDigit(string str, int index);
```

```
/* return true if the specified char is a letter */
public static bool IsLetter(char ch);

/* return true if the character at the specified index of the */
/* specified string is a letter */
public static bool IsLetter(string str, int index);

/* return true if the specified character is a letter or digit */
public static bool IsLetterOrDigit(char ch);

/* returns true if the character at the specified index of the */
/* specified string is a letter or a digit */
public static bool IsLetterOrDigit(string str, int index);

/* return the lowercase equivalent of the specified char or, if */
/* the char has no lowercase equivalent, return the char itself */
public static char ToLower(char ch);

/* return the uppercase equivalent of the specified char, */
/* if any, or otherwise return the char itself */
public static char ToUpper(char ch);

/* return true if the specified char is a control character */
public static bool IsControl(char ch);

/* return true if the character at the specified index of the */
/* specified string is a control character */
public static bool IsControl(string str, int index);

/* return true if the specified char is a white space */
public static bool IsWhiteSpace(char ch);

/* return true if the character at the specified index of the */
/* specified string is a white space */
public static bool IsWhiteSpace(string str, int index);

/*return the numeric value of the specified char */
public static short GetNumericValue(char ch);

/*return the numeric value of the character at the specified */
/* index of the specified string */
public static short GetNumericValue(string str, int index);
}
```

Program 9.6   Class Character (extract).

To illustrate the use of the methods in struct Char, let's write a program to read hexadecimal numbers from the user and print out their decimal equivalents. Our program will need to read the number character by character, starting with the leftmost (or most significant) digit since that's the order in which the digits are normally entered. As we read each character, the value of that character as a hexadecimal digit must be obtained and added to a running total for the value of the number entered so far. However, we must remember that each new digit entered means that all the previous digits now represent higher powers of 16. To take account of this fact we need to multiply the value of the running total by 16 before adding on the value of the most recent (or least significant) digit read.

```
/* A program to illustrate the use of struct Char */
/* Reads a hexadecimal integer from the keyboard */

using tcdIO;
using System;

class ReadHex
{
    private const int HEX = 16;

    public static void Main()
    {
        Terminal terminal;
        char ch;
        int number = 0, value;

        /* create an object to represent the terminal */
        terminal = new Terminal();

        /* ask the user to enter the number */
        terminal.Write("Please enter hexademical number: ");

        /* Read first character */
        ch = Char.ToUpper(terminal.ReadChar());
        /* while character represents a hex. digit, process it */
        while(Char.IsDigit(ch) || (('A' <= ch) && (ch <= 'F')) )
        {
            /* echo character */
            terminal.WriteChar(ch);
            if (Char.IsDigit(ch))
                value = (int)Char.GetNumericValue(ch);
            else
                value = (int)ch - (int)'A' + 10;
            /* update running total */
            number = number * HEX + value;
            /* Read next character */
            ch = Char.ToUpper(terminal.ReadChar());
        }
        /* Write the result on a new line */
        terminal.WriteLine("\nDecimal equivalent is: " + number + ".");
    }
}
```

Program 9.7   A program to illustrate the use of struct Char.

One question remains, when should the program stop reading characters? A simple solution is to stop once a character that doesn't represent a hexadecimal digit has been entered.

Notice the use of ToUpper to convert each character to uppercase as its read; this avoids us having to worry about the distinction between upper and lowercase letters in the rest of the program. We use IsDigit to determine whether or not a character entered is a decimal digit and GetNumericValue to get its decimal value if so. To get the value corresponding to the hexadecimal digits 'A' to 'F', we get the Unicode value of each and subtract the Unicode value of 'A', to get a value in the range 0 to 5, and then add 10 to get the corresponding value in the range 10 to 15. The full program is shown in Program 9.7 and its output in Figure 9.8.

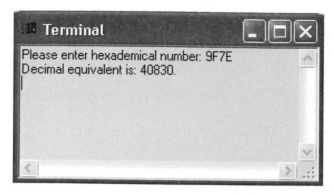

Figure 9.8 The execution of Program 9.7.

All About Strings

As we've already seen a *string* represents a sequence of characters. In C# strings are usually represented by objects that are instances of the C# class `string`. C# allows string literals to be written as sequences of characters enclosed in double quotes and uses an object to represent such a literal. Now that we know a little more about characters, it's worth pointing out that a string can contain any character that we want to include. Thus, the following are all valid ways to introduce a new string.

```
"This is a string"
"Here\'s a string that includes a single quote!"
"Here\'s another that includes a double quote (\")!"
"This string extends\n over two lines"
"Using Unicode is \u004F.\004B. too!"
```

Representation of Strings

Internally, C# represents a string as an *indexed* sequence of characters as shown in Figure 9.9. Thus, every character in a string is labeled with a unique index number that can be used to refer to that character within the string. Consecutive index numbers are allocated to characters starting at 0 for the leftmost character in the string. The value of the highest index number for a given string depends on the number of characters in the string.

We can use index numbers to access the individual characters in a string. To do so, we specify both the name of a variable that refers to the string and the index of the required character in the string enclosed within [ ] (i.e., a pair of square brackets). Of course, we have to be sure that the index is valid for the instance of `string` that we are accessing. To allow us to check that the index number is indeed within the allowable range we can use the read-only property `Length` provided by class `string`.

```
public int Length;
```

`Length` returns the number of characters contained in the string on which it is invoked. The valid index numbers for a string `str` are the numbers between 0 and `str.Length-1` inclusive. For example, given:

```
string message = "Today is Friday!";
```

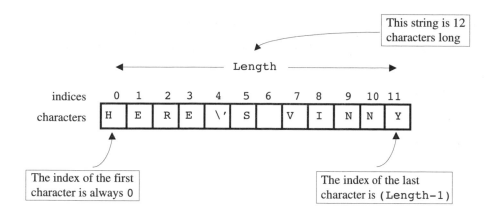

Figure 9.9   A string is an indexed sequence of characters.

then

```
message.Length  // 17
message[0]   // is 'T'
message[2]   // is '-'
message[16]  // is '!'
```

and

```
message[17] // causes an exception!
```

Accessing the Individual Characters of a String

As an example of accessing the individual characters in a string, let's write a program that counts the number of uppercase letters contained in a string entered by the user. As usual we can read in the string using ReadString. We will then need to use a loop to move through each of the characters in the string and for each character check, using an if statement, whether or not that character is an uppercase letter. We will use an int variable, let's call it index, to hold the index number of the current character. We can initialize index to 0 and keep executing the loop while index is less than or equal to the length of the string less 1. At the end of each iteration of the loop we need to increment index in order to move to the next character in the string. The full program is shown in Program 9.8 and its output in Figure 9.10.

It's perhaps worth taking a look at the execution of Program 9.8 in more detail. Figure 9.11 traces trough the execution of the program when the user enters the string "VinnY". Notice that, since the length of the string is 5, the body of the loop is executed once for each value of index from 0 to 4. On each iteration of the loop, index has a different value and refers to a different character from the string.

Reading Hexadecimal Numbers Revisited

As another example, Program 9.9 is a modified version of Program 9.7 to read a hexadecimal integer from the keyboard and print out its decimal equivalent. Rather than reading a single character at a time, this version of the program reads the entire string of characters representing the number at once using ReadString. It then uses a loop to move through

```
/* A program to illustrate the use of [] to access */
/* the individual characters of a string Counts the number of */
/* uppercase characters contained in a string entered by the user */

using tcdIO;
using System;

class CountCapitals
{
   public static void Main()
   {
      Terminal terminal;
      string sentence;
      int index = 0, count = 0;

      /* create an object to represent the terminal */
      terminal = new Terminal();

      /* Read the string from the user */
      sentence = terminal.ReadString("Please enter your string.");
      terminal.WriteLine("The string has " + sentence.Length
         + " characters");
      /* move through the string character by character */
      while (index <= sentence.Length-1)
      {
         /* check if the character is an uppercase letter */
         if (Char.IsUpper(sentence[index]))
         {
            /* if yes, increment count */
            count = count + 1;
         }
         /* move to next character */
         index = index + 1;
      }
      terminal.WriteLine("of which " + count + " are uppercase letters.");
   }
}
```

Program 9.8   A program to illustrate the use of string indexing.

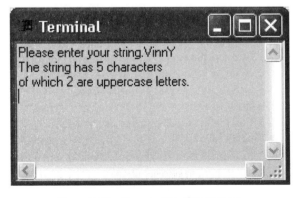

Figure 9.10   The execution of Program 9.8.

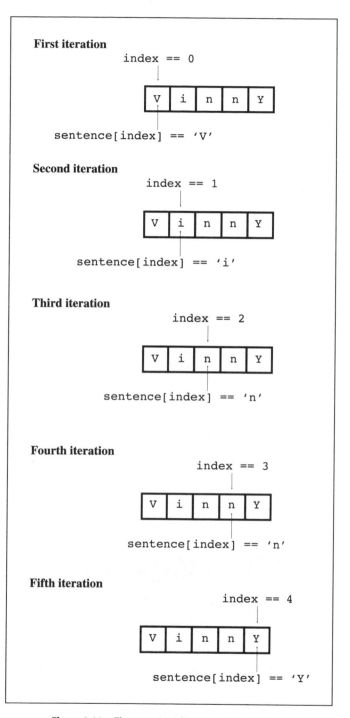

Figure 9.11   The execution of Program 9.8 in detail.

```
/* A program to illustrate the use of [] */
/* Reads a hexidecimal integer from the keyboard */

using tcdIO;
using System;

class ReadHex
{
   private const int HEX = 16;
   private const int ALLOWABLEDIGITS = 8;

   public static void Main()
   {
      Terminal terminal;
      string input;
      int index = 0, number = 0, value;

      /* create an object to represent the terminal */
      terminal = new Terminal();

      /* Read the hexadecimal number from the user */
      input = terminal.ReadString("Please enter hexademical number: ");

      /* check that the number can be represented as an int */
      if (input.Length <= ALLOWABLEDIGITS)
      {
         /* while there are more valid hex. digits, process then */
         while ((index <= input.Length - 1)
            && (Char.IsDigit(input[index])
               || (('A' <= input[index]) && (input[index]<= 'F'))))
         {
            if (Char.IsDigit(input[index]))
               value = (int)Char.GetNumericValue(input[index]);
            else
               value = (int)input[index] - (int)'A' + 10;
            /* update running total */
            number = number * HEX + value;
            /* move to next character */
            index = index + 1;
         }
         /* now find out why the loop terminated */
         if (index == input.Length)
            terminal.WriteLine("Decimal equivalent is: " + number + ".");
         else
            terminal.WriteLine("The only characters allowed are 0-9
               and A-F.");
      }
      else
      {
         terminal.WriteLine("This number is too big to be
            converted to int.");
      }
   }
}
```

Program 9.9 A program to illustrate the use of string indexing.

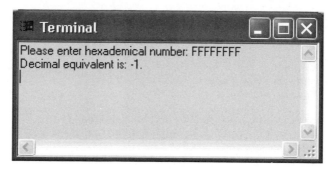

Figure 9.12   The execution of Program 9.9.

the string character by character as before and converts each hexadecimal digit to the corresponding integer value.

In Program 9.9, all the characters entered by the user are read in together. This gives rise to two potential problems. First, the number may be too large to represent as an `int`. In particular, if the user enters more than eight hexadecimal digits, the number will not be representable as an `int`. Of course, we can easily check for this possibility by looking at the length of the string entered by the user (using an `if` statement) before trying to perform the conversion.

Another potential problem is that some of the characters entered by the user may not be valid hexadecimal digits. In our previous program we stopped reading characters once a non-hexadecimal digit was entered. In this program all the characters entered are part of the string. As the program visits each character it therefore has to be prepared for the possibility that the character is invalid. We have to decide what to do if such a character is found in the string. The best solution is to stop the program and report the error to the user. Hence, the terminating condition of our loop should cause the loop to stop both when the end of the string is reached and when an invalid character is found in the string. Since there are now two ways of terminating the loop, we need to test what happened after the execution of the loop is complete. If we made it to the end of the string then the index should be equal to the length of the string, otherwise it won't! The execution of the program is shown in Figure 9.12.

Further `string` Methods

Class `string` provides a range of useful methods for doing different types of string processing – far too many, in fact, for us to cover here! Program 9.10 describes a subset of the most useful methods provided by this class.

In general, these methods fall into one of three main categories, as follows:

- methods to compare complete strings and sub-strings of a string with each other: `Equals`, `StartsWith`, `EndsWith`,
- methods to search a string for occurrences of a specified character or string: `IndexOf`, `LastIndexOf`,
- methods to produce new strings from the contents of an existing string either by extracting a sub-string of the string, joining the string to another string, or replacing characters of the string with other characters (such as their uppercase or lowercase equivalents): `Substring`, `Insert`, `Remove`, `Replace`, `ToLower`, `ToUpper`.

We'll take a brief look at these methods in action in the following sections.

```
/* A class whose instances represent strings (extract) */
class String
{
    /* compares the current string to the specified string. Returns */
    /* true if str is not null and represents the same sequence */
    /* of characters as the current string.  */
    public bool Equals(string str);

    /* compares string str1 to string str2. Returns */
    /* true if str1 is not null and represents the same sequence */
    /* of characters as string  str2 */
    public static bool Equals(string str1, string str2);

    /* returns the index within the current string of the first */
    /* occurrence of the specified character or */
    /* -1 if the character does not occur */
    public int IndexOf(char ch);

    /* returns the index within the current string of the first */
    /* occurrence of the specified character, starting the search */
    /* at the specified index. Returns -1 if the character doesn't occur */
    public int IndexOf(char ch, int beginIndex);

    /* returns the index within the current string of the first */
    /* occurrence of the specified substring or -1 if the substring */
    /* does not occur */
    public int IndexOf(string str);

    /* returns the index within the current string of the first */
    /* occurrence of the specified substring, starting at the specified */
    /* index or -1 if the substring does not occur */
    public int IndexOf(string str, int beginIndex);

    /* returns the index within the current string of the first */
    /* occurence of the specified character, starting the search */
    /* at the specified index and searching the specified number */
    /* of elements */
    public int IndexOf(char ch, int beginIndex, int count);

    /* returns the index within the current string of the first */
    /* occurence of the specified string, starting the search  */
    /* at the specified index and searching the specified number */
    /* of elements */
    public int IndexOf(string str, int beginIndex, int count);

    /* returns the index within the current string of the last */
    /* occurence of the specified character or -1 if the character */
    /* does not occur The string is searched backwards */
    public int LastIndexOf(char ch);

    /* returns the index within the current string of the last */
    /* occurence of the specified character, searching backward */
    /* starting at the specified index */
    /* Retunrs -1 if the character does not occur before that index */
    public int LastIndexOf(char ch, int beginIndex);

    /* returns the index within the current string of the rightmost */
    /* occurrence of the specified substring or -1 if it does not occur */
    public int LastIndexOf(string str);
```

```
/* returns the index within the current string of the last */
/* occurrence of the specified substring searching backward starting */
/* at the specified index */
/* Returns -1 if it does not occur before that index */
public int LastIndexOf(string str, int beginIndex);

/* returns the index within the current string of the last */
/* occurence of the specified character, starting the search */
/* at the specified index and searching the specified number */
/* of elements */
public int IndexOf(char ch, int beginIndex, int count);

/* returns the index within the current string of the last */
/* occurence of the specified string, starting the search  */
/* at the specified index and searching the specified number */
/* of elements */
public int IndexOf(string str, int beginIndex, int count);

/* returns a new string that is a substring of the current string */
/* beginning at the specified index and extending to the end of */
/* this string. Throws an exception if  beginIndex is out of range */
public string Substring(int beginIndex);

/* returns a new string that is a substring of the current string */
/* beginning at the specified index and extending to the character */
/* at index endIndex - 1 */
/* Throws an exception if beginIndex or endIndex is out of range */
public string Substring(int beginIndex, int endIndex);

/* returns a new string resulting from replacing all occurrences */
/* of ch1 in the current string with ch2 */
public string Replace(char ch1, char ch2);

/* returns a new string resulting from replacing all occurrences */
/* of str1 in the current string with str2 */
public string Replace(string str1, string str2);

/* returns a new string resulting from converting all of the  */
/* characters in the current string to lowercase */
public string ToLower();

/* returns a new string resulting from converting all of the */
/* characters in the current string to uppercase */
public string ToUpper();

/* returns true if the current string starts with */
/* the specified string */
public bool StartsWith(string str);

/*returns true if the current string ends with */
/* the specified string */
public bool EndsWith(string str);

/* returns a new string resulting from inserting */
/* the specified string */
/* at the specified index */
public string Insert(int beginIndex, string str);
```

```
/* returns a new string resulting from removing the specified number */
/* of characters from the specified index */
public string Remove(int beginIndex, int count);
}
```

Program 9.10   Class string (extract).

Comparing Strings

We've already seen that we can compare two strings to see if they contain the same sequence of characters using the == operator. Sometimes, for example, where we want to compare a known string with a string of text entered by the user of a program, we would like the comparison to ignore the case of any letters in the string. For example, if we ask the user a question and want to know if the answer is the string "yes", we could write

```
if (answer == "yes") {
    // the answer was "yes"
    ...
```

Unfortunately, this condition will be false if the user entered "YES", or "Yes", or even "yeS", although any of these combinations should probably be interpreted as being a positive response!

For these cases we can use the ToLower method to make a string containing the lowercase equivalent of the user's answer before doing the comparison:

```
if (answer.ToLower() == "yes") {
    // the answer was "yes" or "YES" or "Yes" or "yeS" or
    ...
```

Comparing Sub-strings

Apart from allowing us to compare a complete string with another string, class string allows the sub-string at the beginning or end of a string to be compared with another string using the methods StartsWith and EndsWith.

For example, to check if the user's response begins with the string "Do it" we could write:

```
if (answer.ToLower().StartsWith("Do it"))...
```

or to check if the user's response ends with the string "now!", we could write:

```
if (answer.ToLower().EndsWith("now!"))...
```

Searching a String for a Character or Sub-string

One important operation that we often need to perform is searching a string for occurrences of a specified character or sequence of characters. Fortunately, class string also provides the overloaded methods IndexOf and LastIndexOf to do just that! IndexOf can be used to find the first or subsequent occurrences of a specified character or sub-string in a string. IndexOf searches the string from left to right. LastIndexOf is similar but searches the string from right to left. Both IndexOf and LastIndexOf return the index at which the character or sub-string was found or –1 (an impossible index value) when they can't find any further occurrences of the required character or sub-string.

As an example of the use of IndexOf and LastIndexOf, Program 9.11 searches a string entered by the user for all occurrences of the character 'y' and the sub-string "Vinny", first from left to right and then from right to left. In each case we use a loop to move through the string by repeatedly calling IndexOf or LastIndexOf to find the next occurrence. The terminating condition causes the loop to stop when there are no further occurrences of 'V' or "Vinny" in the string.

```
/* A program to illustrate searching a string */
/* Searches a string entered by the user for all occurrences */
/* of the character 'V' and the sub-string "Vinny" */
/* first from left to right and then from right to left */

using tcdIO;

class SearchString
{
   private const char SEARCHCHAR = 'y';
   private const string SEARCHSTRING = "Vinny";

   public static void Main()
   {
      Terminal terminal;
      string input;
      int index = 0;

      /* create an object to represent the terminal */
      terminal = new Terminal();

      /* Read the string to be searched form the user */
      input = terminal.ReadString("Please enter the string
         to be searched.\n>");

      /* search for required character starting at position 0 */
      terminal.WriteLine("Searching left to right for "
         + SEARCHCHAR + " ...");
      while (index < input.Length
            && (index = input.IndexOf(SEARCHCHAR, index)) != -1)
      {
         /* Write out position */
         terminal.WriteLine("\'" + SEARCHCHAR + "\' found at index "
            + index);
         /* restart search at following character */
         index = index + 1;
      }

      /* search for required string starting at position 0 */
      index = 0; // be careful to reset index
      terminal.WriteLine("Searching left to right for "
         + SEARCHSTRING + " ...");
      while (index < input.Length
            && (index = input.IndexOf(SEARCHSTRING, index)) != -1)
      {
         /* Write out position */
         terminal.WriteLine("\"" + SEARCHSTRING + "\" found at index "
            + index);
```

```
        /* restart search at following character */
        index = index + 1;
    }

    /* search for required character starting at end of string */
    index = input.Length - 1;
    terminal.WriteLine("Searching right to left for "
        + SEARCHCHAR + " ...");
    while (index >= 0
           && (index = input.LastIndexOf(SEARCHCHAR, index)) != -1)
    {
        /* Write out position */
        terminal.WriteLine("\'" + SEARCHCHAR + "\' found at index "
            + index);
        /* restart search at previous character */
        index = index - 1;
    }

    /* search for required string starting at end of string */
    index = input.Length - 1; // be careful to reset index
    terminal.WriteLine("Searching right to left for "
        + SEARCHSTRING + " ...");
    while (index >= 0 &&
           (index = input.LastIndexOf(SEARCHSTRING, index)) != -1)
    {
        /* Write out position */
        terminal.WriteLine("\"" + SEARCHSTRING + "\" found at index "
            + index);
        /* restart search at previous character */
        index = index - 1;
    }
    terminal.WriteLine("Searching complete.");
    }
}
```

Program 9.11   A program to illustrate searching a string.

Notice that in Program 9.11 the return values from IndexOf and LastIndexOf are used subsequently to determine the position from which to start searching for the next occurrence of the character or sub-string during the next iteration of the loop! The execution of the program is shown in Figure 9.13.

Creating New Strings from an Existing String

Class string also provides a variety of ways to create a new string out of the characters contained in an existing string. The most important thing to know about these methods is that they *don't* modify the original string in any way. They simply create new strings based on the contents of the existing string.

For example, we've already seen the string concatenation operator (+) being used to make a new string by joining two existing strings. For example, given:

```
string name, christianName = "Vinny", surName = "Cahill";
```

we could write:

```
name = christianName + surName; // name is now "VinnyCahill"
```

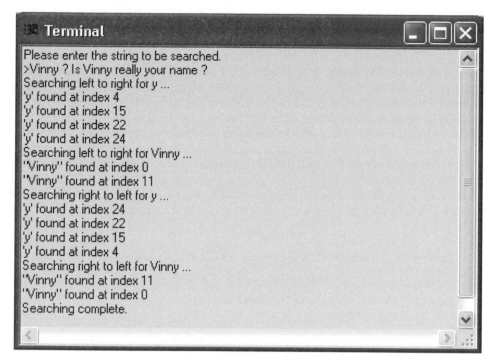

Figure 9.13   The execution of Program 9.11.

Another useful method in this category is the overloaded method `Substring`. `Substring` can be used to create a string that contains a contiguous subset of the characters from the string on which it is invoked. For example, given:

```
name = "Vinny Cahill";
```

then

```
name.Substring(6);
```

returns the new string `"Cahill"`, i.e., the portion of `name` extending from position 6 to the end of the string.

```
name.Substring(0, 5);
```

returns the new string `"Vinny"`. Notice that in this case the required sub-string is specified by giving the index of the first character from the existing string to be included in the new string and the number of characters to be included.

Class `string` also provides methods to create new strings by inserting, removing, or replacing characters in an existing string. For example, given `name` as before

```
name.Insert(6, "J. ");
```

returns the new string `"Vinny J. Cahill"`, i.e., with the string `"J. "` inserted starting at position 6.

```
name.Remove(3, 2).Insert(3, "cent");
```

returns the new string `"Vincent Cahill"` by first removing the two characters `"ny"` starting at position 3 and then inserting the string `"cent"` at position 4 in the resulting string.

Class `StringBuilder`

Apart from the fact that a C# string contains a sequence of characters, perhaps its most important characteristic is that it is *immutable*. Once a string has been created there is absolutely no way to modify it. We can't extend it; we can't shorten it; and we certainly can't replace any of the characters contained in the string with different characters. We can use a string as a basis for creating a new string that is a sub-string of the original or the result of concatenating the original with some other string. We can even create a new string in which some of the characters of the original have been replaced by different characters. However, we can never modify the original string. That said, we sometimes need the flexibility to be able to make arbitrary modifications to the contents of a string, especially without having to go to the expense of creating a whole new object for each modification! The C# class `StringBuilder` provides just this flexibility! An extract of this class is shown in Program 9.12.

```
/* A class whose instances represent string builders (extract) */
class StringBuilder
{
    /* initialize an empty string builder */
    public StringBuilder();

    /* initialize a string builder to contain the same sequence of */
    /* characters as the specified string */
    public StringBuilder(string str);

    /* gets or sets the length of this instance */
    public int Length {get; set;}

    /* gets or sets the maximum number of characters that */
    /* can be contained in this instance */
    public int Capacity {get; set;}

    /* append a copy of the specified string to the con-
tents of the string builder */
    public StringBuilder Append(string str);

    /* append the string representation of the parameter to the */
    /* contents of the string builder */
    public StringBuilder Append(char c);
    public StringBuilder Append(int i);
    public StringBuilder Append(long l);
    public StringBuilder Append(float f);
    public StringBuilder Append(double d);
    public StringBuilder Append(bool b);

    /* insert the specified string into the string builder */
    /* at the specified index */
    public StringBuilder Insert(int index, string str);

    /* insert the string representation of the parameter into the */
    /* contents of the string builder at the specified index */
    public StringBuilder Insert(int index, char c);
    public StringBuilder Insert(int index, int i);
```

```
public StringBuilder Insert(int index, long l);
public StringBuilder Insert(int index, float f);
public StringBuilder Insert(int index, double d);
public StringBuilder Insert(int index, bool b);

/* return a new string representing the contents */
/* of the string builder */
public string ToString();
}
```

Program 9.12   Class StringBuilder (extract).

Like an instance of class string, an instance of class StringBuilder contains a sequence of characters. However, while the contents of a string instance cannot be modified, the contents of a StringBuilder can. The characters contained within a StringBuilder can be replaced individually with different characters, new characters can be added to a StringBuilder, and existing characters can be removed.

Representation of StringBuilder

As Figure 9.14 shows a StringBuilder object, like a string, is an indexed collection of characters. Unlike a string, a StringBuilder has both a *current length* and a *current capacity*. The length of a StringBuilder describes how many characters are currently contained in the StringBuilder. Its capacity describes how many characters may (currently) be stored in the StringBuilder. In fact, we usually don't have to worry about the capacity of a StringBuilder since C# will usually increase the capacity to allow more characters to be added to the StringBuilder when necessary.

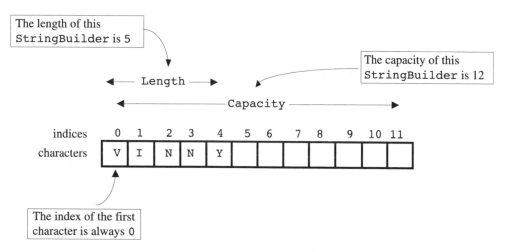

Figure 9.14   A StringBuilder is an indexed sequence of characters.

Class `StringBuilder` provides two read/write properties to allow the length and capacity of a `StringBuilder` object to be determined or modified as necessary:

```
public int Length;
```

and

```
public int Capacity;
```

Remember that, in the case of a `StringBuilder`, both the length and the capacity can change as characters are added and removed! If the value assigned to `Length` is less than the current length of the `StringBuilder`, it is truncated. If the length is set to a value greater than the current capacity, the capacity is adjusted to be the same as the specified length. Assigning a value that is less than the current capacity to `Capacity` causes an exception.

We can access the individual characters contained in a `StringBuilder` by specifying both the name of a variable that refers to the `StringBuilder` object and the index of the required character enclosed within [ ] as for strings. The index must be less than `Length`. Given

```
StringBuilder name;
char letter;
```

we can retrieve the character at position 5 in the object using

```
letter = name[5];
```

Moreover, we can actually replace a character in the object using the method

```
name[5] = letter;
```

In either case, we have to be careful that the index value we supply is in the range 0 to `name.Length-1`. In other words, we can only use these methods to access characters that are already contained in the buffer. Notice that while `name` denotes a `StringBuffer`, `name[5]` effectively denotes a `char` variable in which we can store and retrieve individual characters.

Accessing the Individual Characters in a `StringBuilder` Object

Let's write a program that does more or less the same thing that the `Replace` method of class `string` does: replaces all occurrences of some specified character in a string with a different character.

We will want to read the string, the character to be replaced, and the new character from the user. Having read the string, the program can create a `StringBuilder` containing the same characters using the `StringBuilder` constructor that takes a string as its parameter. Then we will need to use a loop to move through each of the positions in the buffer one-by-one. We can check whether the character at the current position in the buffer is the character to be replaced and, if so, store the new character at that position in the buffer.

The terminating condition for the loop ensures that the loop stops once every position in the object has been checked. To write out the new string, we need to convert the contents of the object back into a string. The easiest way to achieve this is to invoke the `ToString` method on the `StringBuilder` to create a new string containing the same characters as the `StringBuilder`. Program 9.13 shows the full program and Figure 9.15 its output.

```
/* A program to illustrate the use of [] */
/* Reads a string and two characters and replaces all */
/* occurances of the first character with the second character */

using tcdIO;
using System.Text;

class ReplaceCharacter
{
    public static void Main()
    {
        Terminal terminal;
        int index = 0;
        string targetString;
        StringBuilder buffer;
        char oldChar, newChar;

        /* create an object to represent the terminal */
        terminal = new Terminal();

        /* Read the string to be modified from the user */
        targetString = terminal.ReadString("Please enter
            your string \n>");
        /*put the string into a new buffer */
        buffer = new StringBuilder(targetString);

        /* Read the characters */
        terminal.Write("Enter character to be replaced \n>");
        oldChar = terminal.ReadChar();
        terminal.WriteChar(oldChar);
        terminal.Write("\nEnter new character \n>");
        newChar = terminal.ReadChar();
        terminal.WriteChar(newChar);

        /* now replace all occurances of old character with */
        /* new character */
        while (index <= buffer.Length-1)
        {
            if (buffer[index] == oldChar)
            {
                buffer[index] =  newChar; // replace character
            }
            index = index + 1; // move to next character
        }

        /* retrieve the string from the buffer */
        targetString = buffer.ToString();
        terminal.WriteLine("\nThe modified string is:\n\""
            + targetString + "\".");
    }
}
```

Program 9.13 A program to illustrate changing a `StringBuilder` object.

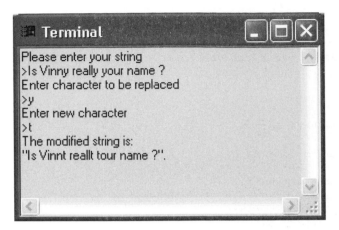

Figure 9.15   The execution of Program 9.13.

Appending Data to a `StringBuilder`

Apart from individually accessing and replacing the characters contained in a `String-Builder`, we can also add characters to the end of the object, i.e., after the characters that are already contained in the buffer, using one of the many overloaded versions of the `Append` method. For example, there are versions of `Append` that can be used to append a single character or a string of characters to a buffer. In each case, the length of the buffer is increased to reflect the addition of more characters. The capacity of the buffer may also be increased if the buffer wasn't already big enough to accommodate the additional characters.

For example, suppose we have a `StringBuilder` called `clock` with a capacity of 16 and containing the 11-character string `"The time is"`. Figure 9.16 shows the effect of executing the statement

```
clock.Append(" four o\'clock");
```

Notice that the new characters have been added directly after the existing characters and that the buffer has grown to accommodate them!

It's worth re-emphasizing that `Append` is overloaded to take values of various different types including all the simple types as its parameter. In each case, the given value is first converted to a `string` and then the corresponding characters are added to the `StringBuilder`.

Inserting Data into a `StringBuilder`

As well as appending data to the end of a `StringBuilder` we can also insert characters into the middle of the characters that are already present in the object using one of the overloaded versions of the `Insert` method. As for `Append`, there are versions of `Insert` that can be used to insert a single character or a string of characters. In each case, `Insert` takes two parameters: the index at which the characters are to be inserted and the description of the characters to be inserted. As before, the length of the buffer is increased to reflect the addition of more characters and its capacity may be increased as necessary.

Before:

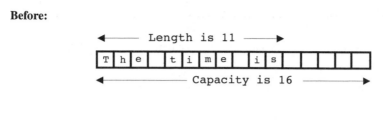

```
clock.Append(" four o\'clock");
```

After:

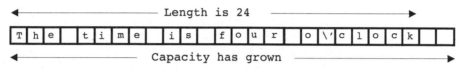

Figure 9.16   The effect of appending characters to a `StringBuilder`.

For example, given a `StringBuilder` called name with a capacity of 16 and containing the 11-character string "`Donal LaffertY`". Figure 9.17 shows the effect of executing the statement

```
name.Insert(5, " C.");
```

Before:

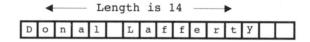

```
name.Insert(5, " C");
```

After:

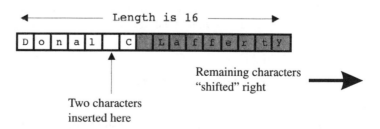

Figure 9.17   The effect of inserting characters into a `StringBuilder`.

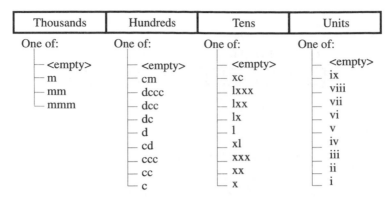

Figure 9.18 The format of a Roman numeral.

Notice that the new characters have been inserted starting at position 5 and that the object has grown to accommodate them! Moreover, notice that `Insert` is not destructive. The existing characters are not overwritten, they are simply *shifted* right by a number of spaces.

`Insert` is also overloaded to take values of various different types, including all the simple types as its second parameter. In each case, the given value is first converted to a `string` and then the corresponding characters are inserted into the `StringBuilder` at the position specified by the first parameter.

Case Study: Roman Numerals

In order to see `string` and `StringBuilder` in action, let's write a program to perform arithmetic on Roman numerals. Our program should at least be able to accept Roman numerals entered by the user, add or subtract them, and print out the result as a Roman numeral.

Hopefully, you've encountered Roman numerals before. If not, don't worry! A Roman numeral is simply a way of writing a positive decimal integer using various sequences of letters to represent the decimal digits. For example, the Roman numeral "mcmxcvii" represents the number 1997.

While you may not think it, the rules for translating between a decimal number and its Roman numeral equivalent are surprisingly straightforward. First off, note that the characters used in the Roman numeral system and their decimal values are as follows:

i = 1, v = 5, x = 10, l = 50, c = 100, d = 500, m = 1000.

Actually, these characters are only sufficient to represent the numbers from 0 to 3999 – higher numbers can be represented but need further characters. We'll limit ourselves to this range for now!

As Figure 9.18 shows, a Roman numeral is written in base 10 using appropriate combinations of these characters to represent the individual digits. For example, the digits 1 to 9 are written as follows:

i, ii, iii, iv, v, vi, vii, viii, and ix

while the decades (10 to 90) follow a similar pattern:

x, xx, xxx, xl, l, lx, lxx, lxxx, and xc

and likewise the hundreds. Thousands are written using one to three "m"s and there is no character to represent zero.

Thus, our previous example 1997, is one thousand ("m") followed by nine hundreds ("cm"), nine tens ("xc") and seven units ("vii") or, putting it all together, "mcmxcviii".

Class `RomanNumeral`

Hopefully, it's clear to you that our program should use a class to represent Roman numerals. Every instance of class `RomanNumeral` will represent one number. Class `RomanNumeral` will also provide the methods to add and subtract Roman numerals.

Defining the Attributes of `RomanNumeral`

Now let's look in detail at what attributes and methods should be provided by the class. The first question is what attributes do Roman numerals have? Clearly, we need to store the value of the Roman numeral. We might consider storing the value (e.g., "mcmxcvii") as an instance of `string`. However, if we take this approach performing addition and subtraction will be very difficult! You should realize that we can represent the value of a Roman numeral just as well as a single `int` (e.g., 1997) and, in doing so, make performing addition and subtraction very easy. Thus, the value of the Roman numeral will be contained in a single attribute of type `int`:

```
private int value;
```

The methods of the class will encapsulate this value and ensure that it is always in the allowable range 0–3999. For this reason, i.e., to prevent arbitrary integers being stored in `value`, this instance variable is `private`. So, internally, the state of a Roman numeral is held as a single `int`. Only when the Roman numeral is being read in or printed out will this value be converted from or to the corresponding string of characters.

We don't need any further instance variables, but it will be useful to define some constants for use in the program. For example, we will introduce constants to represent the maximum value of one of our Roman numerals and to represent the characters that are allowed in a Roman numeral. These constants will be used in the class itself and may also be useful to other classes and programs that deal with Roman numerals and, hence, are declared to be `public`.

Defining the Constructors of `RomanNumeral`

Having decided on what attributes are to be provided, we now need to decide on the methods. First off, let's think about constructors: how might we want to initialize a Roman numeral? Clearly, we need to be able to initialize a Roman numeral from the string representing its value. Hence, we will provide one constructor that takes a single parameter of type `string`. We might also want to initialize a Roman numeral from an `int` value or from the value of another Roman numeral. Finally, we might want to be able to initialize a Roman numeral to zero. Hence, we will provide four constructors as follows:

```
/* initialize a RomanNumeral to zero */
public RomanNumeral()
/* initialize a RomanNumeral with the value given by str */
public RomanNumeral(string str)
/* initialize a RomanNumeral to the specified value */
public RomanNumeral(int number)
/* initialize a RomanNumeral with the value of numeral */
public RomanNumeral(RomanNumeral numeral)
```

One point to note is that the constructors that take a string or an integer as their parameter have to be prepared to deal with the possibility that the parameter doesn't represent a valid Roman numeral. For example, the integer parameter might be negative or too large. The string parameter might be null or badly formed in some other way (although an empty string should be acceptable). In these cases the constructor should initialize the value of the Roman numeral to zero.

Defining the Methods of `RomanNumeral`

What other methods should we provide? Clearly, we will need the methods to actually add and subtract Roman numerals:

```
/* add value of numeral to the current RomanNumeral */
public int AddRoman(RomanNumeral numeral)
/* subtract value of numeral from the current RomanNumeral */
public int SubtractRoman(RomanNumeral numeral)
```

Both of these methods have to be prepared for the possibility that the result is outside the range that can be represented as a Roman numeral. For example, the result may be too large in the case of addition or negative in the case of subtraction. In these cases we will leave the value of the current Roman numeral unchanged and report the error to the caller of the method by returning −1 as its result.

Apart from these methods we should provide an `Equals` method to compare Roman numerals and `ToString` to return the string representation of a Roman numeral.

So far, we have identified two methods concerned with the conversion between the integer value of a Roman numeral and its string representation. Our constructor needs to be able to take a string and determine the corresponding integer value, while `ToString` needs to be able to determine the corresponding string from the value stored in an instance of `RomanNumeral`. In fact, methods to perform the conversion from a Roman string to an integer and vice versa might be generally useful methods to make available to any program that deals with Roman numerals. Hence, it seems like a good idea to implement this functionality in two separate methods that can also be used by the constructor and `ToString` as necessary.

The methods `ConvertRomanStringToInt` and `ConvertIntToRomanString` don't really apply to any particular instance of `RomanNumeral`. Instead, they are really utility methods that perform conversions between strings and integers. As such, they should probably be declared as `static` methods:

```
/* convert a string representing a roman numeral to an int */
public static int ConvertRomanStringToInt(string str)
/* return the Roman numeral string for the given value */
public static string ConvertIntToRomanString(int number)
```

When writing these methods we have, of course, to be prepared for the possibility that the parameter may not be valid. For example, in the case of `ConvertRomanStringToInt`, the given string may be null or not represent a valid Roman numeral. In the case of `ConvertIntToRomanString`, the int may be negative or too large.

Converting an `int` to a Roman Numeral and Vice Versa

Most of the methods provided by class `RomanNumeral` are quite straightforward (they are, after all, mostly concerned with integer addition and subtraction). However, the methods to perform the conversions are a little trickier. We'll look at each of them in turn.

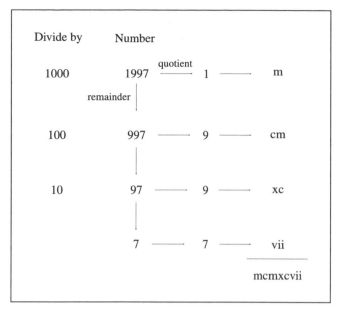

Figure 9.19   Converting an integer to a Roman numeral.

To convert an integer to a Roman numeral, we need to break down the integer into its thousands, hundreds, tens and units components and work out the corresponding characters to use to represent each digit. To extract the number of thousands in the integer we divide it by 1000 and take the quotient. The remainder from the division leaves the rest of the number to be converted. For example, Figure 9.19 shows how 1997 is converted to a Roman numeral.

`ConvertIntToRomanString` uses a `StringBuilder` to store the characters of the `RomanNumeral`. As characters are generated (from left to right) they are appended to the end of the buffer. When the conversion is complete, the contents of the buffer are converted to a `string`. Note that `ConvertIntToRomanString` uses a private method, `UpdateBuffer`, to append the appropriate sequence of characters to the buffer depending on the current digit and whether it represents hundreds (represented by a combination of "m", "d", and "c"), tens ("c", "l", and "x") or units ("x", "v", and "i").

To convert a Roman string to an integer, we need to scan the string from left to right and check which allowable combinations of characters are present, determine their corresponding values, and add the values to a running total. In this case, we first look for characters representing thousands followed by any of the character combinations representing hundreds (as shown in Figure 9.18) and likewise for tens and units. Notice that the character combinations representing the hundreds are mutually exclusive, resulting in a nested `if` statement being used to check for each case. The same is true of the character combinations representing the tens and units. If, having checked for all the legal combinations of characters, we find that there are still characters in the string that have not been accounted for, it means that the string did not represent a valid Roman numeral.

The full code for class `RomanNumeral` is shown in Program 9.14 and a simple program that uses the class in Program 9.15.

```
/* A class whose instances represent Roman numerals */

using System.Text;
using System;

class RomanNumeral
{
    /* declare constants to represent the */
    /* characters allowed in a Roman numeral */
    /* and the maximum value of a Roman numeral */
    public const char I = 'i';
    public const char V = 'v';
    public const char X = 'x';
    public const char L = 'l';
    public const char C = 'c';
    public const char D = 'd';
    public const char M = 'm';
    public const int MAXNUMERAL = 3999;
    /* declare the attributes of a Roman nnumeral */
    private int value;     // just an integer value
    /* declare constructors */
    /* initialize a new RomanNumeral to zero */
    public RomanNumeral()
    {
        value = 0;
    }

    /* initialize a new RomanNumeral with the value specified by */
    /* the given string if the string represents a valid */
    /* Roman numeral or zero otherwise */
    public RomanNumeral(string str)
    {
        if ((str == null) || ((this.value = ConvertRomanStringToInt(str))
            == -1))
        {
            /* an invalid roman numeral */
            this.value = 0;
        }
    }

    /* initialize a new RomanNumeral with the specified value if this */
    /* value can be represented by a Roman numeral or zero otherwise */
    public RomanNumeral(int number)
    {
        if ((number >= 0) && (number <= MAXNUMERAL))
            this.value = number;
        else
            this.value = 0;
    }

    /* initialize a new RomanNumeral with the same value as */
    /* the specified RomanNumeral */
    public RomanNumeral(RomanNumeral numeral)
    {
        this.value = numeral.value;
    }
```

```
/* declare instance methods */
/* add the value of the specified RomanNumeral to the current */
/* RomanNumeral if the resulting value is not too large */
/* to be represented as a Roman numeral */
public int AddRoman(RomanNumeral numeral)
{
   /* first check that result will be in range */
   if (value + numeral.value <= MAXNUMERAL)
      return this.value = this.value + numeral.value;
   else
      return -1;
}

/* subtract the value of a specified RomanNumeral from the */
/* current RomanNumeral if the resulting value will be positive */
public int SubtractRoman(RomanNumeral numeral)
{
   if (value >= numeral.value)
      return this.value = this.value - numeral.value;
   else
      return -1;
}

/* check if two RomanNumerals have the same value */
public bool Equals(RomanNumeral numeral)
{
   return this.value == numeral.value;
}

/* return the string representing the current RomanNumeral */
public override string ToString()
{
   return ConvertIntToRomanString(this.value);
}

/* return the value of the current RomanNumeral */
public int GetValue()
{
   return this.value;
}

/* declare static methods */
/* check if the specified character is allowed in a roman numeral */
public static bool IsRomanDigit(char digit)
{
   /* convert character to upper case to make life easy */
   digit = Char.ToUpper(digit);
   /* check if the character is one of the allowable set */
   return (digit == I) || (digit == V) || (digit == X) ||
      (digit == L) || (digit == C)|| (digit == D) ||(digit == M);
}

/* convert a roman numeral to an integer Return 0 if str empty and -1
/* if string is null or  does not represent a valid roman numeral */
public static int ConvertRomanStringToInt(string str)
{
   int number = 0; // the value of the roman numeral
   int index = 0;  // current position in string
```

```csharp
if (str == null)
   return -1;
else if (str.Equals(""))
   return 0;
else
{
   /* try to convert the string */
   str = str.ToLower();
   /* check for the presence of 0-3 Ms */
   /* be careful not to run off the end of the string */
   int mCount = 0;
   while ((index <= str.Length-1)
      && (str[index] == M)
      && (mCount < 3))
   {
      number = number + 1000;
      mCount = mCount + 1;
      index = index + 1;
   }

   /* now check for presence of hundreds */
   /* always be careful not to run off the end of the string */
   if ((index <= str.Length-2)
      && (str[index] == C)
      && (str[index+1] == M))
   {
      /* CM */
      number = number + 900;
      index = index + 2;
   }
   else if ((index <= str.Length-1)
      && (str[index] == D))
   {
      /* D */
      number = number + 500;
      index = index + 1;
      /* might be followed by 0-3 Cs */
      int cCount = 0;
      while ((index <= str.Length-1)
         && (str[index] == C)
         && (cCount < 3))
      {
         number = number + 100;
         cCount = cCount + 1;
         index = index + 1;
      }
   }
   else if ((index <= str.Length-2)
      && (str[index] == C)
      && (str[index+1] == D))
   {
      /* CD */
      number = number + 400;
      index = index + 2;
   }
   else
   {
      /* look for 0-3 Cs */
```

```
      int cCount = 0;
      while ((index <= str.Length-1)
          && (str[index] == C)
          && (cCount < 3))
      {
          number = number + 100;
          cCount = cCount + 1;
          index = index + 1;
      }
  }

  /* now check for presence of tens */
  if ((index <= str.Length-2)
      && (str[index] == X)
      && (str[index+1] == C))
  {
      /* XC */
      number = number + 90;
      index = index + 2;
  }
  else if ((index <= str.Length-1)
      && (str[index] == L))
  {
      /* L */
      number = number + 50;
      index = index + 1;
      /* might be followed by 0-3 Xs */
      int xCount = 0;
      while ((index <= str.Length-1)
          && (str[index] == X)
          && (xCount < 3))
      {
          number = number + 10;
          xCount = xCount + 1;
          index = index + 1;
      }
  }
  else if ((index <= str.Length-2)
      && (str[index] == X)
      && (str[index+1] == L))
  {
      /* XL */
      number = number + 40;
      index = index + 2;
  }
  else
  {
      /* look for 0-3 Xs */
      int xCount = 0;
      while ((index <= str.Length-1)
          && (str[index] == X)
          && (xCount < 3))
      {
          number = number + 10;
          xCount = xCount + 1;
          index = index + 1;
      }
  }
```

```
    /* now check for presence of units */
    if ((index <= str.Length-2)
       && (str[index] == I)
       && (str[index+1] == X))
    {
       /* IX */
       number = number + 9;
       index = index + 2;
    }
    else if ((index <= str.Length-1)
       && (str[index] == V))
    {
       /* V */
       number = number + 5;
       index = index + 1;
       /* might be followed by 0-3 Is */
       int iCount = 0;
       while ((index <= str.Length-1)
          && (str[index] == I)
          && (iCount < 3))
       {
          number = number + 1;
          iCount = iCount + 1;
          index = index + 1;
       }
    }
    else if ((index <= str.Length-2)
       && (str[index] == I)
       && (str[index+1] == V))
    {
       /* IV */
       number = number + 4;
       index = index + 2;
    }
    else
    {
       /* look for 0-3 Is */
       int iCount = 0;
       while ((index <= str.Length-1)
          && (str[index] == I)
          && (iCount < 3))
       {
          number = number + 1;
          iCount = iCount + 1;
          index = index + 1;
       }
    }

    /* checked all legal possibilites so we should be */
    /* at the end of the sting */
    if (index == str.Length)
       return number;
    else
       return -1;
  }
}
```

```
/* return a string representing the roman numeral whose value */
/* is number or null if number cannot be represented as a */
/* roman numeral (note: 0 is represented as an empty string) */
public static string ConvertIntToRomanString(int number)
{
    /* first check that number can be represented as a Roman numeral */
    if ((number >= 0) && (number <= MAXNUMERAL))
    {
        /* if so convert the number to a roman numeral */
        /* make a StringBuilder to hold the digits */
        StringBuilder buffer = new StringBuilder();

        /* extract thousands from number */
        int Ms = number / 1000;
        number = number % 1000;
        /* add appropriate number of "M"s to buffer */
        while (Ms > 0)
        {
            buffer.Append("m");
            Ms = Ms - 1;
        }

        /* extract hundreds from number */
        int Cs = number / 100;
        number = number % 100;
        /* add appropriate hundreds characters to buffer */
        UpdateBuffer(buffer, Cs, "c", "d", "m");

        /* extract tens from number */
        int Xs = number / 10;
        number = number % 10;
        /* add appropriate tens characters to buffer */
        UpdateBuffer(buffer, Xs, "x", "l",  "c");

        /* add appropriate units characters to buffer */
        UpdateBuffer(buffer, number, "i", "v",  "x");

        /* now return the string in lower case */
        return buffer.ToString();
    }
    else
    {
        return null;
    }
}

/* private method used to update buffer with digits of numeral */
private static void UpdateBuffer(StringBuilder buffer, int n,
    string one, string five, string ten)
{
    switch (n)
    {
        case 1:
            buffer.Append(one);
            break;
```

```
               case 2:
                  buffer.Append(one + one);
                  break;
               case 3:
                  buffer.Append(one + one + one);
                  break;
               case 4:
                  buffer.Append(one + five);
                  break;
               case 5:
                  buffer.Append(five);
                  break;
               case 6:
                  buffer.Append(five + one);
                  break;
               case 7:
                  buffer.Append(five + one + one);
                  break;
               case 8:
                  buffer.Append(five + one + one + one);
                  break;
               case 9:
                  buffer.Append(one + ten);
                  break;
               case 10:
                  buffer.Append(ten);
                  break;
         }
      }
}
```

Program 9.14   Class RomanNumeral.

```
/* A program to perform addition */
/* and subtraction of Roman numerals */

using tcdIO;

class RomanProgram
{
   private const string EXIT = "e";
   private const string ADD = "a";
   private const string SUB = "s";

   public static void Main()
   {
      Terminal terminal;
      RomanNumeral num1, num2;
      string command, numeral;

      /* create an object to represent the terminal */
      terminal = new Terminal("Roman Numberals program");

      command = terminal.ReadString("Enter add, subtract, exit.\n");
      command = command.ToLower();
      while (!command.StartsWith(EXIT))
      {
         /* make sure the command is valid */
```

```
        if (command.StartsWith(ADD) || command.StartsWith(SUB))
        {
            /* Read in the numbers */
            numeral = terminal.ReadString("Enter first number> ");
            num1 = new RomanNumeral(numeral);
            terminal.WriteLine("Num1 is: " + num1.GetValue() + ".");
            numeral = terminal.ReadString("Enter second number> ");
            num2 = new RomanNumeral(numeral);
            terminal.WriteLine("Num2 is: " + num2.GetValue() + ".");
            /* carry out the command */
            if (command.StartsWith(ADD))
            {
                if (num1.AddRoman(num2) != -1)
                    terminal.WriteLine("Result is: " + num1.ToString()
                        + " (" + num1.GetValue() + ").");
                else
                    terminal.WriteLine("Sorry, the result is too large!");
            }
            else if (command.StartsWith(SUB))
            {
                if (num1.SubtractRoman(num2) != -1)
                    terminal.WriteLine("Result is: " + num1.ToString()
                        + " (" + num1.GetValue() + ").");
                else
                    terminal.WriteLine("Sorry the result is negative.");
            }
        }
        /* get the next command */
        command = terminal.ReadString("Enter add, subtract, exit.\n");
        command = command.ToLower();
    }
    terminal.WriteLine("Done.");
    }
}
```

Program 9.15 A program to perform addition and subtraction of Roman numerals.

Summary

- type char represents *single* characters
- every value of type char is represented by a 16-bit code number
- C# uses the Unicode character coding scheme
- a string represents a *sequence* of characters
- all strings are represented by instances of class string
- strings are *immutable*
- internally a string is implemented as an *indexed* sequence of characters
- the individual characters contained in a string can be accessed using their index numbers
- class string provides lots of useful methods for comparing, searching, and creating (new) strings
- class StringBuilder provides the ability to modify strings
- the characters contained in a StringBuilder can be accessed or replaced individually
- further characters can be inserted into or appended on to a StringBuilder

Exercises

(1) Say which of the following are valid string literals:

```
"This is a simple string"
"This isn't such a simple string"
'a'
"John said "I don\'t know" and he didn\'t!"
"\"\\n\" is very useful!"
```

(2) Write a method that takes a `string` as a parameter and reports either the number of uppercase letters, the number of lowercase letters, or the number of digits contained in the `string` as requested by the caller of the method. Write a program that uses your method.

(3) Write a method that takes a `string` as a parameter and returns a new `string` containing the characters of the original `string` in reverse order.

(4) If you look at an Irish social security number, you'll see that it consists of a sequence of digits followed by a letter. The letter is determined from the values of the digits and is used to ensure that you don't make a mistake when quoting the number.
Write a C# program that, when given a ten-digit number as input, calculates a unique "check" character corresponding to the given number according to the following rules:

- add the five pairs of digits contained in the number
- take the remainder of dividing the result by 26
- select the letter in that position of the alphabet assuming the 'A' is in position 0, 'B' in position 1, etc.

For example, if the input is 1122334455, your program should calculate

(11 + 22 + 33 + 44 + 55) % 26 giving 9

and so give 'J' as the "check" character.

(5) A palindrome is a word that is spelt the same backwards and forwards (e.g., "level" or "deed"). Write a method that takes a `string` as a parameter and reports whether or not the contents of the `string` represents a palindrome.

(6) Write a method that reports whether or not the contents of a `string` passed as a parameter to the method represents a valid C# comment (i.e., begins with "/*" and ends with "*/" or begins with "//").

(7) Consider an exam consisting of ten true or false type questions. A solution to the exam can be represented as a string of ten characters where each character is either 'T', if the answer to the corresponding question is true or 'F', if the answer to the corresponding question is false. For example, the string "TFFTTFFFTT" indicates that the answers to questions 1, 4, 5, 9, and 10 are true, while the answers to questions 2, 3, 6, 7, and 8 are false. Write a program to mark such an exam. The program should read and store the string representing the correct solution, and should then read the identification number and the string representing the solution for each candidate who took the exam and print out the mark obtained by that candidate.

Hint: use appropriate classes.

(8) An employee's time card can be represented as a string of characters with the following layout:

Position in string:	Data:
0–19	Employee name
20	Contains 'C' if employee works in city
21	Contains 'U' if employee is a member of a union
22–25	Employee identification number
26	Blank
27–28	Number of regular hours worked
29	Blank
30–33	Hourly rate (pounds and pence)
34	Blank
35–36	Number of dependants
37	Blank
38–39	Number of overtime hours worked

Write a program that reads such strings from its user and for each one prints the following information:

- the employee's gross pay (= regular hours * hourly rate + overtime hours * hourly rate * 1.5),
- the employee's income tax (= 0.14 * (gross pay – 13 * number of dependants)),
- the employee's city tax (= 4% of gross pay if the employee works in the city),
- the employee's union dues (= 6% of net pay (i.e., after income and city tax have been deducted) if the employee is a member of the union.

Managing Collections of Data – Arrays in C# 10

This chapter:

- motivates the need for programs to be able to manage collections of data that are organized as lists or tables
- introduces *arrays* as one means of implementing such collections in C#
- describes the `for` and `foreach` loops, iteration statements that are often used when working with arrays
- describes the *autoincrement* and *autodecrement* operators – a convenient way to increment or decrement the value of a variable
- describes the use of *indexers*, methods that allow the contents of an object to be accessed based on the value of an index
- describes how *command line arguments* are used to provide information to a program each time that it is executed

Suppose that we wanted to write a program to be used to maintain the student records for a school. Our program would need to maintain some information about each of the students including their personal details, information about the courses that they were taking, and their grades. By now, I'm sure that you'll instantly recognize that we would need to introduce a class `Student` whose instances could be used to represent the individual students. One instance of the class would presumably be used to represent each student in the school. However, the really interesting thing to notice is that, at any time, our program might have to keep track of hundreds of instances of class `Student` even for a relatively small school! Given what we have learned already, the program might need to use hundreds of different variables to hold (references to) these objects while the program was running. Even if we knew at the time that we were writing the program how many students were in the school (and how could we?), using so many variables would certainly make for a long and confusing program. Moreover, remembering which variables contained the objects corresponding to particular students would be a nightmare! Clearly, this approach just isn't feasible. What we need is a way of representing a collection of entities (such as a collection of students) that doesn't require us to know in advance how many entities will be in the collection, doesn't require us to declare a separate variable for each entity, and provides a convenient way for us to access the individual entities when necessary. One way of managing such a collection in C# is known as an *array*. We'll look at arrays in detail in the remainder of this chapter.

Arrays – The Basics

We saw in Chapter 10 that an instance of string or StringBuilder can be thought of as an *indexed collection* of characters. In a similar way, an array is an *indexed collection of values*. In C#, arrays can contain values of *any* type (not just characters as was the case with string and StringBuilder). For example, we can have an array containing integers, an array containing floating-point numbers, an array containing students (i.e., objects that represent students), an array containing cars, or even an array containing strings! In fact, we can have arrays that contain values of any type that we can declare in C#. Any given array can usually only contain values of one type. Thus, we might have an array containing integers and another array containing students, but not an array containing both integers and students!

Figure 10.1 shows some examples of arrays: an array of integers, an array of characters, and an array of strings. The individual sub-components of an array are called its *elements* and their type is called the *element type* of the array. As for the characters of a string or StringBuilder, the elements of an array are indexed starting at 0 for the first element. Arrays that contain values of value types, including simple types such as int or float, store those values in the individual elements of the array. Arrays that contain values of reference types, such as Student or string, store references to the corresponding objects. Thus, the individual elements of the array act as if they were variables of the corresponding types. You might even think of an array as a collection of variables of the same type joined together! As Figure 10.1 shows, different arrays can contain different numbers of elements.

An array of int

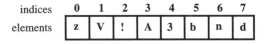

An array of char

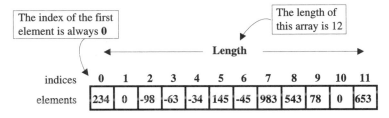

An array of string

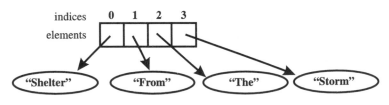

Figure 10.1   Some arrays.

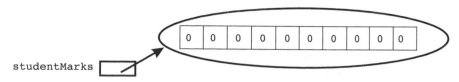

Figure 10.2   The `studentMarks` array.

Declaring an Array

C# provides the means to introduce new types whose values are arrays of some existing type. These new types are called *array types*. All array types are also reference types. Put another way, individual arrays are objects of the corresponding array type.

For example, to declare a variable capable of holding (a reference to) an array of `int`, we write:

```
int[] studentMarks;
```

using the `[ ]` (two square brackets with no space between them) notation to indicate that the variable `studentMarks` will hold (a reference to) an array of `int` rather than a single `int`. The type of the variable `studentMarks` is "array of `int`" and is a reference type.

This declaration gives us a variable of type "array of `int`", but it doesn't give us a new array. Since arrays are objects, a new array is created using the new operator as usual. For example, we might say:

```
studentMarks = new int[10];
```

to create a new array capable of containing ten integers and store a reference to it in the variable `studentMarks` as shown in Figure 10.2. Notice that the number of elements to be contained in the array is specified when we create the array by using the `[ ]` notation again. Once we have created an array, we can't change its size later. Thanks to its declaration as having type "array of `int`", `studentMarks` can contain (a reference to) *any* array of integers. So, we might later do:

```
studentMarks = new int[50];
```

or even

```
studentMarks = new int[(noOfExams+noOfProjects)*noOfTerms];
```

Notice that the number of elements to be contained in the new array can be given by an `int` expression.

Creating Arrays of Objects

To create an array capable of storing a list of students, we might write:

```
Student[] classMembers = new Student[10];
```

This declares a new variable, `classMembers`, whose type is "array of `Student`" and immediately creates an array capable of containing ten instances of `Student`. Similarly,

```
string[] sentence = new string[NUMWORDS];
```

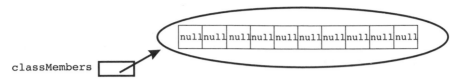

Figure 10.3 The `classMembers` array.

declares a variable, `sentence`, whose type is "array of `string`" and creates an array capable of holding NUMWORDS strings.

In all of these examples, the arrays that we have created are initially empty. Thus, the `studentMarks` array is capable of holding a number of `int`s but we haven't yet stored any values into the individual elements of the array. As Figure 10.2 shows, all the elements are initialized to zero. Likewise, the `classMembers` array is capable of holding a number of `Students` but we haven't yet stored any objects in the array. All the elements are therefore initialized to `null` as shown in Figure 10.3.

Accessing the Individual Elements of an Array

Each individual element of an array can be treated as if it were a *variable* of the array's element type. To refer to a particular element of an array, we specify both the name of a variable that refers to the array and the index of the required element using the [ ] notation again. For example,

- to refer to the first element of the array referred to by `studentMarks` we write `studentMarks [0]` (remember that the index of the first element of an array is always 0);
- to refer to the fifth element of the array referred to by `classMembers`, we write `classMembers[4]`;
- to refer to the last element of the array referred to by `sentence`, we write `sentence[NUMWORDS-1]` (since there are NUMWORDS elements in the array);
- we can use any expression of type `int` that returns a valid index for the array within [ ]. A valid index is any value between 0 and one less than the length of the array. To allow us to find out its length, every array has a `public` read-only property called `Length` that gives the number of elements in the array. For example, to refer to the last element of `sentence`, we could write:

```
sentence[sentence.Length-1]
```

Using Arrays

As a very simple example of the use of arrays, Program 10.1 creates a three-element array of `int`, reads in three numbers from the user, stores them in separate elements of the array, and then prints out their sum on the screen. In this example, the elements of the array are being used as if they were variables of type `int`. Thus, we use `ReadInt` to read the value into each element and integer addition to add the values of the three elements.

Clearly, we could just as easily have written Program 10.1 using three integer variables. However, arrays really come into their own when we need to deal with larger collections of values or when we don't know in advance how many values we will have to deal with. For example, Program 10.2 is similar to Program 10.1 except that the user of the program specifies

```
/* a program to illustrate accessing the */
/* elements of an array */

using tcdIO;

class AccessArray
{
    public static void Main()
    {
        Terminal terminal;
        int[] numberArray; // declare a variable to hold the array
        int sum;

        /* create an object to represent the terminal */
        terminal = new Terminal();

        /* create a three element array of integers */
        numberArray = new int[3];

        /* now Read values into each of the elements of the array */
        numberArray[0] = terminal.ReadInt("Enter value of first element: ");
        numberArray[1] = terminal.ReadInt("Enter value of second element: ");
        numberArray[2] = terminal.ReadInt("Enter value of third element: ");

        /* sum the contents of the array */
        sum = numberArray[0] + numberArray[1] + numberArray[2];

        /* finally, Write out the result */
        terminal.WriteLine("The sum of the elements is " + sum + ".");
    }
}
```

Program 10.1   A program to illustrate accessing the elements of an array.

the size of the array to be created. This means that we don't know in advance how big our array is going to be and, in fact, different size arrays may be created each time that the program is run.

In Program 10.2 we read in the size of the array from the user, making sure that the specified size is positive and non-zero. Obviously, it makes no sense to create an array with a negative number of elements! The required size is stored in a variable and the value of this variable is then used to specify the size of the array to be created by new. Because we don't know how many elements are in the array until the program is actually running, we need to use loops both to read in the elements of the array from the user and to sum the elements. Both loops use a variable, index, to hold the index of the current element of the array. index is initialized to 0, the index of the first element, before each loop and incremented at the end of each iteration. Thus, the value of index is used to access a different element of the array on each iteration of the loop using the [ ] notation. The terminating condition for both loops uses the Length property of numberArray to ensure that the loop terminates once the last element of the array has been processed. Notice that both loops visit every element of the array exactly once no matter how big the array actually is. Figure 10.4 shows the result of running the program for a ten-element array.

```csharp
/* a program to illustrate accessing the */
/* elements of an array using a loop */

using tcdIO;

class AccessArray
{
   public static void Main()
   {
      Terminal terminal;
      int[] numberArray; // declare a variable to hold the array
      int size;          // declare a variable to hold size of array
      int index;         // declare a variable to index the array
      int sum = 0;

      /* create an object to represent the terminal */
      terminal = new Terminal();

      /* ask the user for the size of the array */
      /* and make sure its positive */
      size = terminal.ReadInt("Enter size of array required: ");
      while (size <= 0)
      {
         size = terminal.ReadInt("Enter size of array required: ");
      }

      /* create an array of the appropriate size */
      numberArray = new int[size];

      /* now Read values into each of the elements of the array */
      index = 0;  // start at element zero
      while (index <= numberArray.Length-1)
      {
         numberArray[index] = terminal.ReadInt("Element " + index + ": ");
         /* move to next element */
         index = index + 1;
      }

      /* sum the contents of the array */
      index = 0;  // start at element zero
      while (index <= numberArray.Length-1)
      {
         sum = sum + numberArray[index];
         /* move to next element */
         index = index + 1;
      }

      /* finally, Write out the result */
      terminal.WriteLine("The sum of the elements is " + sum + ".");
   }
}
```

Program 10.2 A program to illustrate accessing the elements of an array using a loop.

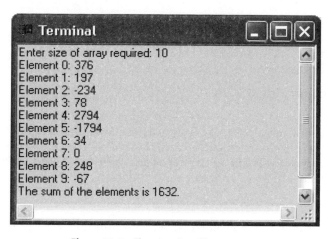

Figure 10.4   The execution of Program 10.2.

Vector Addition

As a further example, let's think about writing a program to perform addition on vectors. A vector represents the coordinates of a point in N-dimensional space. For example, a vector representing a point in three-dimensional space consists of three real numbers giving the x, y, and z coordinates of the point in question, e.g., (234.6, 567.89, 34.67). Likewise, a vector with four dimensions consists of a collection of four real numbers, and, in general, a vector of N dimensions, a collection of N real numbers.

To write our program we will introduce a class, Vector, whose instances represent individual vectors. Class Vector should provide at least the ability to initialize a new vector of the required size, to retrieve the contents of a vector (so that they can, for example, be printed out), and to add one vector to another.

Before looking in detail at its methods, we need to consider what attributes class Vector should provide. As we noted, a vector is essentially a list of real numbers. Clearly, using an array to store this list of numbers is a good choice. All the more so because we don't know in advance what the dimension of the vector, and hence the number of coordinates to be stored, is going to be. Class Vector will therefore provide an attribute of type "array of double" declared as follows:

```
private double[] vectorData;
```

Notice that this declaration only indicates that every instance of Vector includes a list of doubles. It doesn't say how many numbers will be contained in this list, and, in fact, the number of elements in the array can vary from one instance of Vector to another, as we will see. Also note that the vectorData attribute is private since we don't want the coordinates to be accessible other than through the methods of class Vector.

Should Vector provide any other attributes? Since instances of Vector can represent vectors of different sizes, we might include an attribute giving the size of the current vector. However, such an attribute would be redundant because we can always use the Length property of the vectorData array to find out the size. Thus, the class need provide only a single attribute.

Next, we need to think about how to initialize a new Vector. As is often the case, there is more than one way in which a new vector could be initialized. For example, we might initialize a new vector so that the values of all of its coordinates are zero. We might initialize a new vector with some specified set of values. Or, we might initialize a new vector to be the same as another vector. This suggests providing a set of overloaded constructors for class `Vector`. Our first constructor will take the size of vector to be represented as a parameter and initialize all the coordinates of the vector to zero, i.e.

```
public Vector(int N)
```

One point to note here is that the value of `N` should always be positive. As shown in Program 10.3, this constructor creates an array of the required size, assigns it to `vectorData` and uses a loop to set each individual element of the array to `0.0`.

Our second constructor will take an array of `doubles` as a parameter and use the contents of the array to initialize the new vector, i.e.,

```
public Vector(double[] other)
```

As can be seen in Program 10.3, this constructor uses the `Length` property of the array `other` to determine how big the new vector is to be and then creates an array of the appropriate size to hold the data. Each element of the new array is then initialized from the corresponding element of `other` by means of a loop that, much like the two loops in Program 10.2, visits each element of the array exactly once.

There are a couple of really important points illustrated by this version of the constructor. First, it shows that an array can be a parameter to a constructor or, indeed, any other method. Notice how an array type is specified in a parameter list – by giving its element type followed by `[ ]`. Second, you may wonder why we bothered to create a new array in the `Vector` constructor at all since the constructor is actually passed a perfectly good array as its parameter. However, the array passed to the constructor may be accessed outside of class `Vector` by any part of the program that has a reference to it. A vector's data should be completely encapsulated within an instance of `Vector`. Hence, each instance of `Vector` creates its own array to store its data and keeps the only reference to that array privately. Thus, access to the contents of the array is only possible by means of the methods provided by class `Vector`.

Our third constructor will take another instance of vector as its parameter and initialize the new vector to be the same at the vector specified by the parameter, i.e.,

```
public Vector(Vector other)
```

This constructor is very similar to the previous constructor. It uses the `Length` property of the `vectorData` array belonging to the vector `other` to determine how big the new vector is to be and then creates an array of the appropriate size to hold the data. Each element of the new array is then initialized from the corresponding element of the `vectorData` array in `other` using a loop. Notice that this constructor accesses the `vectorData` array in the object passed as its parameter even though `vectorData` is declared to be `private`. Remember that the methods of a class can always access the `private` instance variables of all instances of that class and not just those of the instance on which they are invoked.

To allow the contents of a vector to be retrieved, we provide the method `GetVectorData` as follows:

```
public double[] GetVectorData()
```

Notice that the data of the vector is returned as an array of `doubles`. As you can see, an array can also be the return value of a method. In this case, the return type of the method is specified by giving the element type of the array followed by `[ ]`. The most important thing to say about this method is that it does not simply return the array referred to by `vectorData` as its result. Remember that we want to encapsulate this array within the current instance

```
/* a class whose instances represent N-dimensional vectors */
class Vector
{
   private double[] vectorData; // the vector

   /* create vector of specified size and initialize all elements to 0.0 */
   /* assumes that N is greater than 0 */
   public Vector(int N)
   {
      int i = 0;

      /* create an array of size N */
      this.vectorData = new double[N];
      /* initialize each element to 0.0 */
      while (i <= this.vectorData.Length-1)
      {
         this.vectorData[i] = 0.0;
         i = i + 1;
      }
   }

   /* create vector initialized from the specified array of doubles */
   public Vector(double[] other)
   {
      int i = 0;

      /* create an array whose size is the same as the array other */
      this.vectorData = new double[other.Length];
      /* initialize each element from corresponding element of other */
      while (i <= vectorData.Length-1)
      {
         this.vectorData[i] = other[i];
         i = i + 1;
      }
   }

   /* create vector initialized from the specified vector */
   public Vector(Vector other)
   {
      int i = 0;

      /* create an array whose size is the same as the Vector other */
      this.vectorData = new double[other.vectorData.Length];
      /* initialize each element from corresponding element of other */
      while (i <= this.vectorData.Length-1)
      {
         this.vectorData[i] = other.vectorData[i];
         i = i + 1;
      }
   }

   /* return vector data */
   public double[] getVectorData()
   {
      double[] data;
      int i = 0;
```

```
    /* first make a new array to hold the data */
    data = new double[this.vectorData.Length];
    /* copy each element of vectorData to new array */
    while (i <= this.vectorData.Length-1)
    {
        data[i] = this.vectorData[i];
        i = i + 1;
    }
    /* return the data */
    return data;
}


/* add specified vector to current vector if both */
/* vectors are the same length Return true if */
/* addition is possible, false otherwise */
public bool addVector(Vector other)
{
    int i = 0;

    /* check that vectors are the same length */
    if (this.vectorData.Length == other.vectorData.Length)
    {
        /* add corresponding elements of each vector */
        while (i <= this.vectorData.Length-1)
        {
            this.vectorData[i] = this.vectorData[i] + other.vectorData[i];
            i = i + 1;
        }
        return true;
    }
    else
    {
        return false;
    }
}
}
```

Program 10.3 Class Vector.

of Vector. If we were to return (a reference to) this array, then other parts of the program could access its elements directly using this reference. Instead, we create a new array of the same size, copy the elements of the vectorData array to the new array and return the new array as our result.

Finally, the AddVector method adds another vector, which is passed as the parameter, to the current vector:

```
public bool AddVector(Vector other)
```

AddVector has to be prepared for the possibility that the two vectors are of different sizes, in which case they can't be added. Hence, AddVector returns a bool value to indicate whether or not the addition was actually performed. We use an if statement to compare the sizes of the two vectors before trying to perform the addition. To actually do the addition, AddVector simply uses a loop to move though the arrays contained in each of the vectors adding the corresponding elements. Again, the same variable is used to index both arrays so that each iteration of the loop accesses the same position in each array.

```
/* a program to illustrate the use of arrays */

using tcdIO;

class VectorProgram
{
    public static void Main()
    {
        Terminal terminal;
        Vector firstVector, secondVector;
        double[] data;
        int i, size;

        /* create an object to represent the terminal */
        terminal = new Terminal();

        /* ask the user for the size of the vectors */
        size = terminal.ReadInt("Enter size of vectors: ");
        /* make sure that the size is positive */
        while (size < 1)
        {
            size = terminal.ReadInt("Enter size of vectors: ");
        }

        /* create an array to hold vector data */
        data = new double[size];

        /* Read in the data of the first vector and */
        /* use it to initialize the vector */
        terminal.WriteLine("Reading " + size + " element vector.");
        /* Read a value into each element of the data array */
        /* from 0 to data.Length-1 */
        i = 0;
        while (i <= data.Length-1)
        {
            data[i] = terminal.ReadDouble("Enter element " + (i+1) + ": ");
            i = i + 1;
        }
        /* create first vector */
        firstVector = new Vector(data);

        /* Read in the data of the second vector and */
        /* use it to initialize the vector */
        terminal.WriteLine("Reading " + size + " element vector.");
        /* Read a value into each element of the data array */
        /* from 0 to data.Length-1 */
        i = 0;
        while (i <= data.Length-1)
        {
            data[i] = terminal.ReadDouble("Enter element " + (i+1) + ": ");
            i = i + 1;
        }
        /* create second vector */
        secondVector = new Vector(data);

        /* since we can be sure that the vectors are the */
        /* same size go ahead and add the vectors */
        firstVector.addVector(secondVector);
```

```
    /* Write out the answer */
    data = firstVector.getVectorData();
    terminal.WriteLine(data.Length + " element vector is:");
    /* Write out the value of each element of the data array */
    /* from 0 to data.Length-1 */
    i = 0;
    while (i <= data.Length-1)
    {
        terminal.WriteDouble(data[i]); terminal.WriteLine("");
        i = i + 1;
    }

    /* Write a message to say that the program is finished */
    terminal.WriteLine("Finished!");
  }
}
```

Program 10.4   A program to illustrate the use of arrays.

Program 10.4 shows a simple program that uses class Vector to add two vectors of the same size. To initialize each vector, the program first reads in an array of doubles from the user and uses the appropriate Vector constructor to initialize a new instance of Vector with the contents of the array. It then uses the AddVector method to add the vectors and the GetVectorData method to retrieve the results before printing them out.

Array Initializers

C# provides a convenient shorthand for creating and initializing an array as part of the declaration of an array variable. For example, to create and initialize a five-element array of int referred to by the variable numberList, we can simply write:

```
int[] numberList = {345, -34, 98763, 0, 45};
```

i.e., we give a list containing the initial value to be stored in each element of the array separated by commas and enclosed in braces. When such a declaration is used, the size of the array to be created is determined from the number of values provided in the list. In the example above, there are five values in the list, so a five-element array is created. The values are taken from left to right to initialize elements of the array. Given, the declaration above we get:

numberList[0] is 345, numberList[2] is 98763, and numberList[4] is 45.

In fact, we can use any expression of the correct type to provide the value for each element of the array. For example, to create a five-element array of ints, we could write:

```
int[] numberList = {val1, val1+val2, val1*2, 0, val2*val2};
```

where val1 and val2 are variables of type int. To create a five-element array of strings we might write:

```
string[] names = {"Vinny", "Cahill", "Donal", "Lafferty",
null};
```

In this case, the first four elements of the array are initialized with the specified `strings` while the fifth is set to `null`. We might even create a three-element array of `Vectors` in the same way:

```
Vector[] vecs = {new Vector(5), new Vector(7), new
Vector(9)};
```

In this case, each of three elements is initialized with a newly created instance of `Vector`.

The `for` Loop

We have already seen that C# provides a number of iteration statements, including the `while` and `do` statements, designed to allow us to have some sequence of statements executed a variable number of times. The `for` statement or `for` loop, is another such iteration statement provided by C#. `for` loops are usually used when the number of times that a loop is to be executed is controlled by a counter. However, the `for` loop is really just a shorthand form of the `while` loop and can be used wherever a `while` loop can be used.

The Syntax of the `for` Loop

Figure 10.5 shows the syntax of the `for` loop. As you can see, it's a little complicated. A `for` loop is introduced by the keyword `for`. Following the keyword, and enclosed in brackets, is an *initialization statement*, a *condition*, and an *update statement* all separated by semicolons. The body of the loop follows and is usually enclosed in braces. The initialization statement is, as the name suggests, intended to allow any initialization required to be carried out before the loop is executed. For example, if the execution of the loop is controlled by a counter, then the initialization statement would normally be used to give the counter its initial value. The condition is the terminating condition for the loop. As in a `while` loop, the body of the `for` loop will be executed repeatedly for as long as this condition remains `true`. Again, if the `for` loop is controlled by a counter, then this condition would be used to check if the counter has reached its final value. The update statement is used to perform any update required after each iteration of the loop. If the execution of the loop is controlled by a counter, the update statement could be used to increment or decrement its value after each iteration.

```
for (<initialisation statement>;
     <condition>;
     <update statement>) {

   <statement sequence>

}
```

Figure 10.5   The syntax of the C# `for` loop.

Flow of Control Through a `for` Loop

Figure 10.6 shows the flow of control through a `for` loop. Notice that when a `for` loop is executed the initialization statement is always executed first. After that, execution of the loop

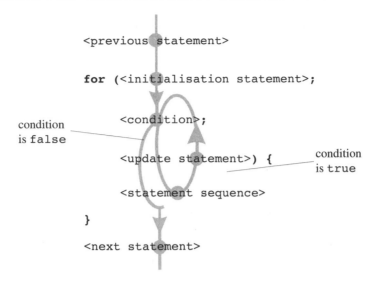

Figure 10.6   The flow of control through a `for` loop.

proceeds in much the same way as for a `while` loop: the terminating condition is tested. If the condition is `true`, the body of the loop is executed and control returns to the terminating condition. If the terminating condition becomes `false`, the execution of the `for` statement ends. The only major difference is that when the execution of the body of the loop is finished and before the terminating condition is re-evaluated, the update statement is re-executed. Note that while the initialization statement is only executed once, the update statement is executed after each iteration of the loop.

Replacing a `while` Loop with a `for` Loop

Program 10.5 is a typical example of a program that uses a counter to control the execution of a `while` loop. The program prints out the numbers from one up to some value entered by the user. The variable `currentNumber` is used as the counter to keep track of how many iterations of the loop have been carried out. Notice that:

- `currentNumber` is initialized to 1 before the execution of the loop begins
- the terminating condition for the loop tests whether or not `currentNumber` has reached its final value, and
- after each iteration of the loop `currentNumber` is updated by adding one to its value.

The `while` loop in Program 10.5 is an ideal candidate to be replaced by a `for` loop. Program 10.6 shows the resulting program. Notice that the initialization of `currentNumber`, the terminating condition that tests the value of `currentNumber`, and the updating of `currentNumber` have all been placed in the heading of the `for` loop. In fact, `currentNumber` has even been declared in the initialization part of the `for` loop! A variable that is declared in the initialization part of a `for` loop can only be used in the `for` loop. In other words, its scope is limited to the `for` loop.

```
/* a program to illustrate */
/* the use of a counter to control a loop */

using tcdIO;

class UserChoice
{
   public static void Main()
   {
      Terminal terminal;
      int usersChoice;
      int currentNumber = 1; // start at 1

      /* create an object to represent the terminal */
      terminal = new Terminal();

      /* get the user's number */
      usersChoice = terminal.ReadInt("Enter the highest
         number to write: ");

      /* now Write out the list */
      terminal.WriteLine("The list is:");
      while (currentNumber <= usersChoice)
      {
         /* Write out the value of currentNumber */
         terminal.WriteInt(currentNumber);
         /* increment currentNumber */
         currentNumber = currentNumber + 1;
      }

      /* Write a message to say that the program is finished */
      terminal.WriteLine("Finished!");
   }
}
```

Program 10.5   A program to illustrate the use of a counter to control a loop.

```
/* a program to illustrate the use of the for loop */

using tcdIO;

class UserChoice
{
   public static void Main()
   {
      Terminal terminal;
      int usersChoice;

      /* create an object to represent the terminal */
      terminal = new Terminal();

      /* get the user's number */
      usersChoice = terminal.ReadInt("Enter the highest
         number to write: ");

      /* now Write out the list */
      terminal.WriteLine("The list is:");
```

```
    for (int currentNumber = 1;
       currentNumber <= usersChoice;
       currentNumber = currentNumber + 1)
    {
       /* Write out the value of currentNumber */
       terminal.WriteInt(currentNumber);
    }

    /* Write a message to say that the program is finished */
    terminal.WriteLine("Finished!");
  }
}
```

Program 10.6   A program to illustrate the use of the for loop.

Using a for loop in this way separates the code concerned with controlling the execution of the loop neatly from the code that is intended to be executed repeatedly.

Using a for Loop to Visit All the Elements of an Array

Loops whose executions are controlled by the value of a counter are actually very common. The most common use of such loops is actually when dealing with indexed collections such as strings, StringBuilders, and arrays. A very typical use of a for loop is when writing a loop that accesses all of the elements of an array. For example, we can rewrite class Vector to make use of for loops as shown in Program 10.7.

```
/* a class whose instances represent */
/* N-dimensional vectors (revised) */
class Vector
{
    private double[] vectorData; // the vector

    /* create vector of specified size and initialize all elements to 0.0 */
    /* assumes that N is greater than 0 */
    public Vector(int N)
    {

        /* create an array of size N */
        this.vectorData = new double[N];
        /* initialize each element to 0.0 */
        for (int i = 0; i <= vectorData.Length-1; i = i + 1)
        {
            this.vectorData[i] = 0.0;
        }
    }

    /* create vector initialized from the specified array of doubles */
    public Vector(double[] other)
    {

        /* create an array whose size is the same as the array other */
        this.vectorData = new double[other.Length];
        /* initialize each element from corresponding element of other */
        for (int i = 0; i <= this.vectorData.Length-1; i = i + 1)
```

```
        {
            this.vectorData[i] = other[i];
        }
    }


    /* create vector initialized from the specified vector */
    public Vector(Vector other)
    {

        /* create an array whose size is the same as the Vector other */
        this.vectorData = new double[other.vectorData.Length];
        /* initialize each element from corresponding element of other */
        for (int i = 0; i <= this.vectorData.Length-1; i = i + 1)
        {
            this.vectorData[i] = other.vectorData[i];
        }
    }


    /* return vector data */
    public double[] getVectorData()
    {
        double[] data;

        /* first make a new array to hold the data */
        data = new double[this.vectorData.Length];
        /* copy each element of vectorData to new array */
        for (int i = 0; i <= this.vectorData.Length-1; i = i + 1)
        {
            data[i] = this.vectorData[i];
        }
        /* return the data */
        return data;
    }


    /* add specified vector to current vector if both */
    /* vectors are the same length Return true if */
    /* addition is possible, false otherwise */
    public bool addVector(Vector other)
    {

        /* check that vectors are the same length */
        if (vectorData.Length == other.vectorData.Length)
        {
            /* add corresponding elements of each vector */
            for (int i = 0; i <= vectorData.Length-1; i = i + 1)
            {
                this.vectorData[i] = this.vectorData[i] + other.vectorData[i];
            }
            return true;
        }
        else
        {
            return false;
        }
    }
}
```

Program 10.7   Class Vector (revised).

```
for (int i = 0;
     i <= array.Length-1;
     i++) {

   <process element array[i]>

}
```

Figure 10.7 A template for accessing all the elements of an array in turn.

Notice that the variable used to hold the index of the current element of the array, in this case i, is declared and initialized to 0 in the initialization part of the for loop. The value of the index variable is compared with one less than the length of the array in the condition. Finally, i is incremented in the update part of the for loop. As Figure 10.7 shows, this is the standard way of writing any loop that needs to access every element of an array in turn.

The Autoincrement and Autodecrement Operators

You may have noticed that we often need to increment, or indeed decrement, the value of a variable containing a number. To do so, we usually write something like:

```
i = i + 1; // increment i
```

As you know by now, the effect of this statement is to add 1 to the current value of i. Moreover, since = is an operator, this statement is also an expression whose value is the new value of i. For example, if i is 9, the effect of the statement

```
terminal.WriteInt(i=i+1);
```

is to change the value of i to 10 and then to write out the value 10.

Since incrementing and decrementing a variable are so common, C# provides a shorthand notation for performing this operation in the form of the so-called *autoincrement* (++) and *autodecrement* (--) operators. ++ and -- are unary operators, i.e., they are applied to a single operand, the variable whose value is to be incremented or decremented. Both can be used in either prefix or postfix forms, i.e., written before or after their operand respectively. For example, if i is 9, then using the postfix form of ++ as in

```
i++
```

increments i to 10. However, the value of this expression is 9, i.e., the value of i *before* it was incremented. The fact that i is written before ++ is intended to indicate that the value before the increment is used. On the other hand, using the prefix form of ++ as in

```
++i
```

also increments i to 10 but has 10 as its value, i.e., the value of i *after* it is incremented.
    Similarly, using the postfix form of -- as in

```
i--
```

decrements the value of i. If the value of i is 10 then the effect of this statement is to set i to 9. The value of the expression is 10, the value of i before the assignment. Finally, using the prefix form

```
--i
```

also decrements i but has 9 as its value.

The autoincrement and autodecrement operators are commonly used to update a variable that is being used to index an array. For example, notice that we used the autoincrement operator in our template for accessing the elements of an array in Figure 10.7.

Array Overflow

Let's say we have an array of doubles as follows:

```
double[] numberArray = {34.5, -739.52, 78.32, 23567.09,
                        0.02};
```

i.e., an array of five elements whose indices range from 0 to 4. What do think happens if we try to access numberArray [-1] or numberArray [10] as in

```
numberArray[-1] = 4.5;
```

or

```
myDouble = numberArray[10];
```

Clearly, there is no element of numberArray with index –1 or index 10. Thus, any attempt to access such an element causes an exception (actually the IndexOutOfRangeException exception). Accessing, or rather trying to access, a non-existent element of an array is usually referred to as *array overflow* and is a very common mistake, particularly when using a loop to process the elements of an array. We will cover exceptions in more detail in a future chapter.

Searching an Array – A First Attempt

Consider writing code to search an array of doubles for the value -1.0. The basic strategy is to use a loop to check each element of the array in turn to see if it is equal to -1.0, stopping once an element with that value is found. Notice that unlike our previous examples, this loop does not necessarily access every element of the array. The required value might be contained in the first element of the array, or the second element, or the third element. Thus, the loop might only need to visit one or two or three elements of the array. On the other hand, the required value might be contained in the last element of the array, in which case our loop would have to visit every element. Moreover, there is also a possibility that the required value may not be contained in the array at all!

In any case, we have to be careful when writing the terminating condition that the loop does not cause array overflow. In general, we need to make sure that before using a variable to index an array, the variable lies within the index range of the array. One possible solution is shown in Program 10.8.

Notice that we start off with the index variable being zero. In the terminating condition for the loop we check whether the current element of the array contains the required value or not, and also check that the loop has not reached the end of the array, before moving to the

```
/* a program to illustrate searching an array */

using tcdIO;

class SearchArray
{
    public static void Main()
    {
        Terminal terminal;
        double[] numberArray;
        int i;

        /* create an object to represent the terminal */
        terminal = new Terminal();

        /* create a ten element array */
        numberArray = new double[10];

        /*  Read values into all the elements of the array */
        for (i = 0; i <= numberArray.Length-1; i++)
        {
            numberArray[i] = terminal.ReadInt("Enter element " + i + ": ");
        }

        /* search the array for -1.0 */
        i = 0; // start at position 0
        while ((numberArray[i] != -1.0) && (i <= numberArray.Length-1))
        {
            /* move to the next element of the array */
            i++;
        }

        /* check if the required value was found */
        if (numberArray[i] ==  -1.0)
            terminal.WriteLine("-1 found at position " + i + ".");
        else
            terminal.WriteLine("-1 not found in array.");
    }
}
```

Program 10.8   A program to illustrate searching an array.

next element. Figure 10.8 shows the operation of the program when the array contains –1.0 at position 5.

As expected the program correctly reports the position at which –1.0 is located. Figure 10.9 shows what happens when the array does not contain –1.0.

As you can see, even though we took precautions against array overflow, we still managed to run off the end of the array. Why? Well, when index is 9, the terminating condition is,

```
(numberArray[9] != -1.0) && (index <= 9)
```

which is true, so we execute the body of the loop and increment index again. Now we evaluate the terminating condition with index being equal to 10

```
(numberArray [10] != -1.0) && (index <= 9)
```

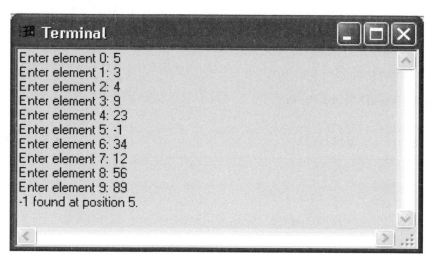

Figure 10.8   The execution of Program 10.8 when the array contains −1 . 0.

i.e. we try to access `numberArray[10]` even though the condition

```
index <= 9
```

is `false`.

Searching an Array – Second Attempt

The solution is simply to change the order of the two conditions so that we check that `index` is in the required range before we try to use it to access an element of the array as shown in Program 10.9. Notice that our new terminating condition relies on the short-circuit evaluation of `&&`. When the condition

```
index <= numberArray.Length-1
```

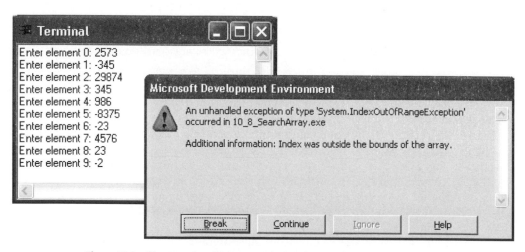

Figure 10.9   The execution of Program 10.8 when the array does not contain −1 . 0.

```
/* a program to illustrate searching an array (revised) */

using tcdIO;

class SearchArray
{
    public static void Main()
    {
        Terminal terminal;
        double[] numberArray;
        int i;

        /* create an object to represent the terminal */
        terminal = new Terminal();

        /* create a ten element array */
        numberArray = new double[10];

        /*  Read values into all the elements of the array */
        for (i = 0; i <= numberArray.Length-1; i++)
        {
            numberArray[i] = terminal.ReadInt("Enter element " + i + ": ");
        }

        /* search the array for -1.0 */
        i = 0; // start at position 0
        while ((i <= numberArray.Length-1) && (numberArray[i] != -1.0))
        {
            /* move to the next element of the array */
            i++;
        }

        /* check if the required value was found */
        if ((i <= numberArray.Length-1) && (numberArray[i] ==  -1.0))
            terminal.WriteLine("-1 found at position " + i + ".");
        else
            terminal.WriteLine("-1 not found in array.");
    }
}
```

Program 10.9 A program to illustrate searching an array (revised).

is false, the second part of the condition, which accesses numberArray[index], will not be evaluated. Notice too that, once the loop terminates, index may be greater than numberArray.Length-1 if -1.0 was not found in the array. Hence, we also had to modify the condition in the if statement following the loop. Again, the general strategy is to *make sure that the index variable is in range before trying to use it to access the array.* Figure 10.10 shows what happens when our revised program is used to search an array that does not contain -1.0.

This program again serves as a template for any program that needs to search the elements of an array for some value as shown in Figure 10.11.

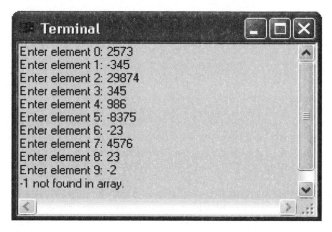

Figure 10.10   The execution of Program 10.9 when the array does not contain −1.0.

The foreach Loop

When dealing with collections such as arrays and strings, we often need to process all the elements in the collection individually in some way without actually changing the contents of the collection. For example, imagine calculating the average value of the numbers stored in an array. To accomplish this we would need to visit each element, read its value, and add it to some running total. Clearly we can do this using a simple for loop. For example, given

```
double averageSalary;
double[] salaries; // employee salaries
...
```

```
int i = 0;

while ((i <= array.Length-1)
        && (array[i] != <value>)) {

   i++;

}

if ((i <= array.Length-1)
    && (array[i] ==  <value>)){

   // value found at position i

} else {

   // value not contained in array

}
```

Figure 10.11   A template for searching an array for a value.

we might write:

```
for(int i = 0; i <= salaries.Length-1; i++) {
   averageSalary = averageSalary + salaries[i];
}
averageSalary = averageSalary / salaries.Length;
```

Here, every iteration of the loop uses the value of a different element of the array, without changing that value. In this case the individual elements are identified by their indices. Since cases like this are so common, C# provides a shorthand for writing these kind of loops by means of the foreach loop.

The Syntax of the foreach Loop

Figure 10.12 shows the syntax of the foreach loop. Happily, it's very simple! A foreach loop is introduced by the keyword foreach. Following the keyword, and enclosed in brackets, is a variable declaration, consisting of a type name and identifier, and an expression denoting a collection. The variable declaration and expression are separated by the keyword in. The body of the loop follows and is usually enclosed in braces. The variable is referred to as the *iteration variable* and its type should be the same as the element type of the collection. Its scope is the body of the foreach loop.

```
foreach (<type> <identifier> in
         <collection expression>) {

    <statement sequence>

}
```

Figure 10.12   The syntax for the foreach statement.

Flow of Control Through a foreach Loop

The body of a foreach loop is executed once for each element of the specified collection. On each iteration of the loop the value of the next element of the collection is made available as the value of the iteration variable, i.e, the next element of the collection is effectively assigned to the iteration variable for the duration of this iteration and can be used within the body of the loop. For example, the for loop in our previous example can be replaced by:

```
foreach(double salary in salaries) {
   averageSalary = averageSalary + salary;
}
averageSalary = averageSalary / salaries.Length;
```

In this case, the iteration variable is salary and is of type double, i.e., the element type of the salaries array. On each iteration of the loop, one element of salaries is implicitly assigned to salary and used in calculating the running total within the body of the loop. The loop continues until every element of salaries has been processed.

The nice feature of the foreach loop is that C# looks after managing the index used to access the collection and retrieving the values of the elements, leaving us to concentrate on what we want to do with the value of each element. However, the iteration variable is always read-only, i.e., we can never assign a value to this variable ourselves – only C# has that privilege! Also note that unlike the for loop we don't have an index variable that we can use to keep track of our current position in the collection or to modify the contents of one of its elements. Thus, the foreach loop is intended strictly for situations where we want to use the values of all the elements of a collection without modifying the contents of the collection. It provides a convenient shorthand for these cases but is not nearly as flexible as using a for (or indeed a while) loop.

Managing Tables – Two-dimensional Arrays

In C#, the elements of an array can be of *any* other type. For example, the type of the elements might be a value type, such as int, double, or char or a reference type, such as string, Vector, or Person. In particular, this means that the type of the elements can be another array type! Thus, the individual elements of one array can actually contain other arrays. As we will see, this allows us to use arrays to implement tables of data as well as lists.

For example, consider declaring a variable to store the marks obtained by each of the students in a class for each of their weekly exercises:

- the class consists of many students: we can use an "array of students" to represent the class,
- each student has one mark for each exercise: we can use an "array of marks" to represent each student,
- we can use an integer to represent each individual mark.

Thus, the full set of marks can be stored as an array of arrays of integers!

To declare a variable to hold such as array, we write

```
int[][] courseMarks; // an array of arrays of int
```

Notice the use of [ ][ ] to indicate that we want an array of arrays! To create the array, we write:

```
courseMarks = new int[NUMSTUDENTS][];
for (int s = 0; s <= courseMarks.Length-1; s++) {
  courseMarks[s] = new int[NUMEXERCISES];
}
```

where NUMSTUDENTS specifies how many student arrays we need and NUMEXERCISES how many marks are to be recorded for each student. Notice that we first create the containing array and subsequently each of its sub-arrays. Figure 10.13 shows what the resulting array might look like if NUMSTUDENTS were 4 and NUMEXERCISES were 10. Each row of the table corresponds to the array of marks for one student. Each element of this array is a single mark.

An array that contains other arrays, such as our courseMarks array, is usually referred to as being a *two-dimensional array*. In C# terminology the number of dimensions in an array is also called its *rank*.

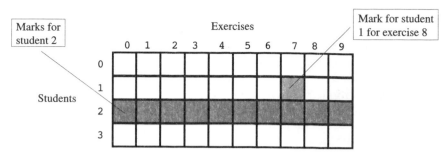

Figure 10.13   The `courseMarks` array.

To record the fact that student 1 got a mark of 9 in exercise 8, we write

```
courseMarks[1][8] = 9;
```

where:

- `courseMarks[1]` is the entry for student 1 in the class array and is itself an array,
- `courseMarks[1][8]` is the entry for exercise 8 in the array for student 1 and is a single integer.

As another example, consider declaring an array to represent a lecture timetable. Let's assume that individual lectures are represented by instances of class `Lecture` and that lectures can occur on the hour at any time between 09:00 hrs and 16:00 hrs, Monday through Friday. We can use a two-dimensional array indexed by day and hour as follows:

```
Lecture[][] timetable = new Lecture[NUMDAYS][];
for (int d = 0; d <= timetable.Length-1; d++) {
  timetable[d] = new Lecture[NUMLECTURES];
}
```

Figure 10.14 shows the structure of the resulting array.

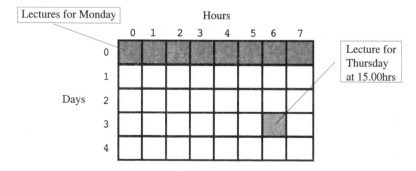

Figure 10.14   The `timetable` array.

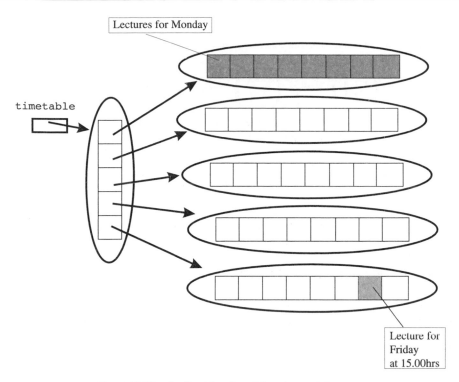

Figure 10.15   An alternative view of the `timetable` array.

To schedule a lecture on Monday at 12:00 hrs we might write:

```
timetable[0][3] = new Lecture("Programming", "Room 5");
```

where:

- `timetable[0]` is the entry for Monday in the timetable array and is itself an array,
- `timetable[0][3]` is the entry for 12.00 hrs in Monday's array and contains an instance of `Lecture`.

Note that the expression `timetable[0]` denotes an array of lectures, i.e., its type is "array of `Lecture`" – not surprising given that we said `timetable` is an array of arrays! Strictly speaking, `timetable[0]` stores a reference to an array object as shown in Figure 10.15 since each of the rows is a separate object.

Because of the way that two-dimensional arrays are implemented as arrays of arrays, there is no way to refer to a single column of such an array as a single unit. We can refer to the whole two-dimensional array (e.g., `timetable`), one row of the array (e.g., `timetable[2]`, which is itself an array), or one element of a row (e.g. `timetable[2][0]`, a single `Lecture`).

On the other hand, this approach allows us some additional flexibility. For example, each of the arrays contained in another array can be a different size:

```
int[][] grid = {{23, 45, 56, 67},
                {35, 46, 57, 98, 34, 45},
                {23, 45}}
```

In this example, `grid` is a two-dimensional array of `int`. `grid` contains 3 elements, each of which is itself an array of `int`. `grid[0]` is a four-element array, `grid[1]` a six-element

combine row 1 of first matrix with column 2 of second matrix to form element [1][2] of result

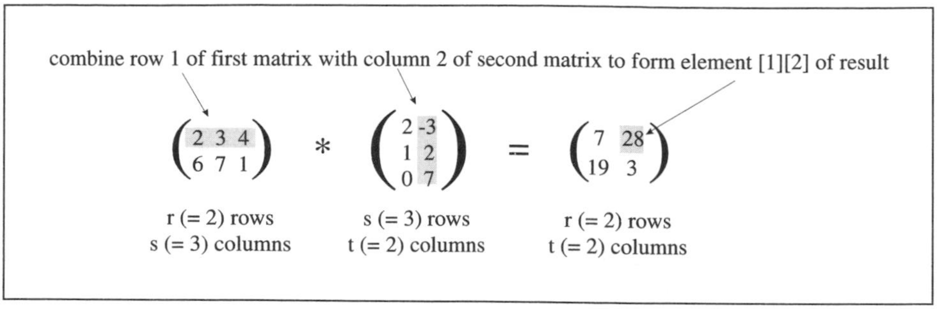

$$\begin{pmatrix} 2 & 3 & 4 \\ 6 & 7 & 1 \end{pmatrix} \quad * \quad \begin{pmatrix} 2 & -3 \\ 1 & 2 \\ 0 & 7 \end{pmatrix} \quad = \quad \begin{pmatrix} 7 & 28 \\ 19 & 3 \end{pmatrix}$$

r (= 2) rows   s (= 3) rows   r (= 2) rows
s (= 3) columns   t (= 2) columns   t (= 2) columns

Figure 10.16 An example of matrix multiplication.

array and `grid[2]` a two-element array. Notice that we can, as usual, use an initializer to create and initialize a two-dimensional array.

Working with Two-dimensional Arrays

As an example of the use of two-dimensional arrays, let's write a program to implement matrix multiplication. A matrix is essentially a two-dimensional grid of numbers (integers in our case). We can multiply two matrices only if the number of columns in the first matrix is the same as the number of rows in the second one. For example, given an r by s matrix M_1 (i.e., one with r rows and s columns) and an s by t matrix M_2, we can multiply M_1 by M_2 to give an r by t matrix as the result. Figure 10.16 shows how the multiplication is carried out.

To write our program we will of course introduce a class `Matrix` whose instances represent individual matrices. `Matrix` will provide a set of overloaded constructors to initialize new matrices, a method to allow the contents of the current matrix to be retrieved, and, finally, a method to multiply the current matrix by another matrix to yield a new matrix.

The data of each matrix can be stored as a two-dimensional array of `int`. Thus, class `Matrix` provides a single attribute:

```
private int[][] mData;
```

Note that this declaration does not specify how big the matrix will be. Thus, instances of `Matrix` can represent matrices of different sizes.

Our first `Matrix` constructor will take the dimensions of the new matrix as its parameters and initialize the matrix to contain zero in every element (assuming, of course, that the dimensions supplied are positive):

```
public Matrix (int rows, int cols);
```

This constructor will need to create a two-dimensional array of the required size and fill every element with 0. Thus, it will need to visit every element of every row of the array and set the value of that element. To do so it uses two `for` loops. One loop iterates through all the rows of the matrix in turn. For each row, the other loop iterates through all the column positions in that row.

Given an array referred to by `mData`, `mData.Length` tells us how many rows are in the array. Thus, to write a `for` loop that visits each row we write:

```
for (int r = 0; r <= mData.Length-1; r++) {
  /* visit row r */
}
```

```
for (int r = 0; r <= array.Length-1; r++) {

    for (int c = 0; c <= array[r].Length-1; c++) {

        <process element array[r][c]>

    }
}
```

Figure 10.17   A template for accessing all the elements of a two-dimensional array in turn.

Each row of mData is itself an array. Thus, mData[r].Length gives the number of elements in the array corresponding to row r. To visit every element of row r, we need another loop:

```
for (int c = 0; c <= mData[r].Length-1; c++) {
    /* visit element c of row r */
}
```

Putting all of this together, to visit every element of the array the Matrix constructor combines these two loops as follows:

```
for (int r = 0; r <= mData.Length-1; r++) {
    for (int c = 0; c <= mData[r].Length-1; c++) {
        mData[r][c] = 0;
    }
}
```

This construct is referred to as a *nested* for *loop*. Just as a single for loop is normally used to visit all the elements of a one-dimensional array, nested for loops are usually used to visit all the elements of a two-dimensional array as shown in Figure 10.17. Notice that this approach works even when the number of elements in each row of the array is different since the inner for loop uses the Length property of the *current* row to determine how many elements it has to visit.

Our second constructor initializes a new instance of Matrix from the contents of a two-dimensional array of ints supplied as its single parameter:

```
public Matrix(int[][] other);
```

Of course, it's quite allowable to have a two-dimensional array as a parameter to a constructor or other method. This version of the constructor creates a new two-dimensional array to hold the data and then uses nested for loops again to copy the parameter array, element by element, to the new array. Notice that the dimensions of the array are given by other.Length for the number of rows and other[0].Length for the number of columns (which is fine assuming that all the other rows have the same number of elements as row 0!).

The final constructor initializes a new instance of Matrix to be the same as another instance of Matrix supplied as its single parameter:

```
public Matrix(Matrix other);
```

As before, this constructor creates a new two-dimensional array of the appropriate size and copies data into it, element by element, from the mData array in other using nested for loops.

To allow the contents of a matrix to be retrieved, `Matrix` provides the method `GetMatrixData` as follows:

```
public int[][] GetMatrixData();
```

Notice that the data of the matrix is returned as a two-dimensional array of `int`s. As you can see, a two-dimensional array can also be the return value of a method. `GetMatrixData` creates a new array of the same size as `mData` and again uses nested `for` loops to copy the elements of the `mData` array to the new array before returning the new array as its result.

The `MultiplyMatrix` method multiples the current matrix by the matrix specified as its parameter if possible, i.e., if the number of columns in the current matrix (as given by `matrixData[0].Length`) is equal to the number of rows in the specified matrix (as given by `other.matrixData.Length`). `MultiplyMatrix` returns a `bool` result to indicate whether or not multiplication was possible:

```
public bool MultiplyMatrix(Matrix other);
```

To carry out the multiplication we need to combine all rows of the current matrix with each column of the other matrix in turn. Thus, we need a loop to iterate over all the rows in the current matrix, i.e.,

```
for (int r = 0; r <= mData.Length-1; r++){
    /* combine row r of current matrix */
    /* with all columns of other matrix */
}
```

So, we need a nested loop to iterate over each column of the *other* matrix in turn:

```
for (int r = 0; r <= mData.Length-1; r++){
    for (int c = 0; c <= other.mData[0].Length-1; c++) {
        /* combine row r of current matrix */
        /* with column c of other matrix */
    }
}
```

To combine row r of the current matrix with column c of the other matrix we need to sum the partial results obtained by multiplying the corresponding elements of the row and the column. This requires yet another nested loop!

```
int sum = 0;
for (int e = 0; e <= mData[r].Length-1; e++){
    sum = sum + (mData[r][e] * other.mData[e][c]);
}
```

The full implementation of the method is shown in Program 10.10.

A program that uses class `Matrix` to perform matrix multiplication is shown in Program 10.11. The program reads the dimensions (`r`, `s`, and `t`) of the two matrices to be multiplied and then reads in the data of each matrix in turn. Note that nested `for` loops are used yet again to read in the data for each matrix into a two-dimensional array that becomes the parameter to the `Matrix` constructor. `MultiplyMatrix` is then used to perform the multiplication and `GetMatrixData` to retrieve the data from the result matrix for printing out to the screen.

```
/* a class whose instances represent matrices */
/* Uses Jagged Arrays */

using tcdIO;

class Matrix {
  private int[][] mData; // the matrix

  /* initialize matrix of specified dimensions to zero everywhere */
  /* assumes that both dimensions are positive */
  public Matrix(int rows, int cols) {
     mData = new int[2][];
     mData[0] = new int[rows];
     mData[1] = new int[cols];
     for(int r = 0; r <= mData.GetLength(0)-1; r++)
        for(int c = 0; c <= mData[1].GetLength(0)-1; c++)
           mData[r][c] = 0;
  }

  /* create matrix initialized from the specified 2-d array of ints */
  /* assumes that all rows of the specified array are the same size */
  public Matrix(int[][] other) {
     mData = new int[2][];
     mData[0] = new int[other.GetLength(0)];
     mData[1] = new int[other.GetLength(0)];
     for(int r = 0; r <= mData.GetLength(0)-1; r++)
        for(int c =0; c<= mData[1].GetLength(0)-1; c++)
           mData[r][c] = other[r][c];
  }

  /* create matrix initialized from the specified matrix */
  public Matrix(Matrix other) {
     mData[0] = new int[other.mData.GetLength(0)];
     mData[1] = new int[other.mData.GetLength(0)];
     for(int r = 0; r <= mData.GetLength(0)-1; r++)
        for(int c =0; c<= mData[1].GetLength(0)-1; c++)
           mData[r][c] = other.mData[r][c];

  }

  /* return matrix data */
  public int[][] GetMatrixData() {
     int[][] data;

     /* first make a new array to hold the data */
     data = new int[2][];
       data[0] = new int[mData.GetLength(0)];
       data[1] = new int[mData.GetLength(0)];

     /* copy each element of mData to new array */
     for(int r = 0; r <= mData.GetLength(0)-1; r++)
     {
        for(int c = 0; c <= mData[1].GetLength(0)-1; c++)
        {
           data[r][c] = mData[r][c];
        }
     }
```

```
      /* return the data */
      return data;
   }

   /* multiply current matrix by specified matrix */
   /* if the number of columns in current matrix equals */
   /* number of rows in specified matrix */
   /* Return new matrix if multiplication possible or */
   /* null if multiplication is not possible */
   public Matrix MultiplyMatrix(Matrix other) {

      /* first check that the matrices can be multiplied */
      /* by comparing number of colums in current matrix with */
      /* number of rows in other matrix */
      if (mData[0].GetLength(0) == other.mData[1].GetLength(0)) {
         /* multiplication is possible */
         /* create a new matrix to hold the result */
         Matrix result = new Matrix(mData.GetLength(0),
            other.mData[0].GetLength(0));

         /* for all rows of current matrix */
         for (int r = 0; r <= mData.GetLength(0)-1; r++) {
           /* for all columns of other matrix */
           for (int c = 0; c <= other.mData[0].GetLength(0)-1; c++) {
              /* combine current row of current matrix */
              /* with current column of other matrix */
              int sum = 0;
              for (int e = 0; e <= mData[r].GetLength(0)-1; e++) {
                 sum = sum + mData[r][e] * other.mData[e][c];
              }
              /* store the result in the result matrix */
              result.mData[r][c] = sum;
           }
         }
         return result;
      } else {
         /* multiplication is not possible */
         /* return null */
         return null;
      }
   }
}
```

Program 10.10   Class Matrix.

```
/* a program to illustrate the use of 2-dimensional arrays */
/* Uses Jagged Arrays */

using tcdIO;

class MatrixProgram
{
   public static void Main()
   {
      Terminal terminal;
      Matrix firstMatrix, secondMatrix, resultMatrix;
```

```
int r, s, t = 0;
int[][] data;

/* create an object to represent the terminal */
terminal = new Terminal();

/* ask the user for the dimensions of the matrices */
r = terminal.ReadInt("Enter number of rows in first matrix: ");
s = terminal.ReadInt("Enter number of colums in first matrix: ");
t = terminal.ReadInt("Enter number of colums in second matrix: ");
/* make sure that all the dimensions are valid */
while ((r < 2) || (s < 2) || (t < 2))
{
    r = terminal.ReadInt("Enter number of rows in first matrix: ");
    s = terminal.ReadInt("Enter number of columns in first matrix: ");
    t = terminal.ReadInt("Enter number of columns in
        second matrix: ");
}

/* create and initialize first matrix */
data = new int[2][];
data[0] = new int[r];
data[1] = new int[s];

terminal.WriteLine("Reading " + r + " by " + s + " matrix.");
/* go through all rows of data */
for (int i = 0; i <= data.GetLength(0)-1; i++)
{
    /* for each row Read a value into every element of that row */
    for (int j = 0; j <= data[1].GetLength(0)-1; j++)
    {
        data[i][j] =
            terminal.ReadInt("Enter element [" + i + "," + j + "]: ");
    }
}
terminal.WriteLine("Instantiating first Matrix\n");
firstMatrix = new Matrix(data);

/* create and initialize second matrix */
data = new int[2][];
data[0] = new int[s];
data[1] = new int[t];

terminal.WriteLine("Reading " + s + " by " + t + " matrix.");
/* go through all rows of data */
for (int i = 0; i <= data.GetLength(0)-1; i++)
{
    /* for each row Read a value into every element of that row */
    for (int j = 0; j <= data[1].GetLength(0)-1; j++)
    {
        data[i][j] =
            terminal.ReadInt("Enter element [" + i + "," + j + "]: ");
    }
}
terminal.WriteLine("Instantiating second matrix \n");
secondMatrix = new Matrix(data);

/* multiply matrices */
```

```
    resultMatrix = firstMatrix.MultiplyMatrix(secondMatrix);
    terminal.WriteLine("Multiplied matrices \n");

    /* Write out the result */
    data = resultMatrix.GetMatrixData();
    terminal.WriteLine(data.GetLength(0) + " by "
        + data[1].GetLength(0) + " matrix is: ");
    /* go through all rows of data */
    for (int i = 0; i <= data.GetLength(0)-1; i++)
    {
        /* for each row Write out value of every element of that row */
        for (int j = 0; j <= data[1].GetLength(0)-1; j++)
        {
            terminal.Write(data[i][j] + " ");
        }
        /* start a new line after each row */
        terminal.WriteLine("");
    }

    /* Write a message to say that the program is finished */
    terminal.WriteLine("Finished!");
    }
}
```

Program 10.11   A program to illustrate the use of two-dimensional arrays.

Rectangular Arrays

As we have seen C# allows us to define two-dimensional arrays as arrays containing other arrays. For example, as Figure 10.15 shows, our two-dimensional timetable array is actually represented as six array objects – one object for the timetable that refers to five other array objects corresponding to each day of the working week. As we saw, this approach leaves open the possibility of having so-called *jagged arrays*, in which each of the rows of the array is a different size. For example, given a two-dimensional array of int such as:

```
    int[][] jaggedArray = new int[5][];
```

we could assign arrays of different lengths to each of the five elements since each can contain any array of int. Figure 10.18, shows the result of the following set of assignments:

```
    jaggedArray[0] = new int[5];   // a row with 5 elements
    jaggedArray[1] = new int[3];   // a row with 3 elements
    jaggedArray[2] = new int[4];   // a row with 4 elements
    jaggedArray[3] = new int[5];   // a row with 5 elements
    jaggedArray[4] = null;         // an empty row
```

As an alternative, C# also allows a two-dimensional array to be represented as a single object that can be indexed in two dimensions. This approach is somewhat less flexible in that it requires all the rows of the array to be the same length. Thus, arrays that are represented in this way are known as *rectangular arrays*.

Using Rectangular Arrays

To declare a variable to hold a rectangular array, we write

```
    int[,] courseMarks; // a rectangular array of int
```

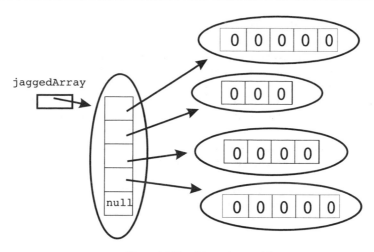

Figure 10.18   A jagged array of `int`.

Instead of using `[ ][ ]` to indicate that we want an array of arrays, we write `[ , ]` to indicate that we want one array with two dimensions. We can create the array with new by specifying the size of each dimension. Thus,

```
courseMarks = new int[5, 8];
```

results in the creation of a rectangular array object with five rows, where every row has eight elements of type `int` as shown in Figure 10.19. Notice that the entire array, being a single object, is created at the same time.

To record the fact that student 1 got a mark of 9 in exercise 4, we write

```
courseMarks[1,4] = 9;
```

where the indices for each dimension are written within a single pair of `[ ]` brackets but separated by a comma. To retrieve the mark awarded to student 2 for exercise 4 we write:

```
studentMark = courseMarks[2,4];
```

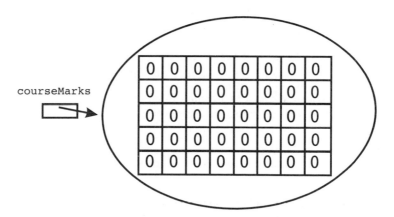

Figure 10.19   A rectangular array of `int`.

Because the array is a single object, it now makes no sense to index the array in one dimension only, e.g., courseMarks[2] is not defined.

In the case of a rectangular array, the Length attribute gives the number of elements in the array as before, although it should be noted that this is the total number of elements in all dimensions. Thus, the length of our courseMarks array is 40 (i.e., 5 × 8). When iterating over the contents of an array we will often want to be able to determine the number of rows and the number of columns in the array, i.e., the length of each individual dimension. For this purpose a rectangular array provides a method, GetLength, that returns the length of a given dimension of the array. For example, to write a nested for loop to initialize every element of the courseMarks array to 0, we can write:

```
for (int r = 0; r <= courseMarks.GetLength(0); r++){
  for (int c = 0; c <= courseMarks.GetLength(1); c++){
    courseMarks[r,c] = 0;
  }
}
```

where the dimensions are numbered from 0 so that courseMarks.GetLength(0) returns the length of the first dimension, i.e., the number of rows and course-Marks.GetLength(1) returns the length of the second dimension, i.e., the number of columns. Of course this nested for loop will work with any size of array.

As a more complete example of the use of rectangular arrays, Program 10.12, is a modified version of the matrix multiplication program that uses rectangular arrays, which makes sense given that matrices should always be rectangular!

```
/* A class whose instances represent matrices */

using tcdIO;

class Matrix
{
   private int[,] mData; // the matrix

   /* initialize matrix of specified dimensions to zero everywhere */
   /* assumes that both dimensions are positive */
   public Matrix(int rows, int cols)
   {
      this.mData = new int[rows,cols];
      for (int r = 0; r <= this.mData.GetLength(0)-1; r++)
      {
         for (int c = 0; c <= this.mData.GetLength(1)-1; c ++)
         {
            this.mData[r,c] = 0;
         }
      }
   }

   /* create matrix initialized from the specified 2-d array of ints */
   /* assumes that all rows of the specified array are the same size */
   public Matrix(int[,] other)
   {
      this.mData = new int[other.GetLength(0), other.GetLength(1)];
      for (int r = 0; r <= this.mData.GetLength(0)-1; r++)
```

```
      {
         for (int c = 0; c <= this.mData.GetLength(1)-1; c ++)
         {
            this.mData[r,c] = other[r,c];
         }
      }
   }

   /* create matrix initialized from the specified matrix */
   public Matrix(Matrix other)
   {
      this.mData = new int[other.mData.GetLength(0),
         other.mData.GetLength(1)];
      for (int r = 0; r <= this.mData.GetLength(0)-1; r++)
      {
         for (int c = 0; c <= this.mData.GetLength(1); c ++)
         {
            this.mData[r,c] = other.mData[r,c];
         }
      }
   }

   /* return matrix data */
   public int[,] getMatrixData()
   {
      int[,] data;

      /* first make a new array to hold the data */
      data = new int[this.mData.GetLength(0),this.mData.GetLength(1)];
      /* copy each element of mData to new array */
      for (int r = 0; r <= this.mData.GetLength(0)-1; r++)
      {
         for (int c = 0; c <= this.mData.GetLength(1)-1; c ++)
         {
            data[r,c] = this.mData[r,c];
         }
      }
      /* return the data */
      return data;
   }

   /* multiply current matrix by specified matrix */
   /* if the number of columns in current matrix equals */
   /* number of rows in specified matrix */
   /* Return new matrix if multiplication possible or */
   /* null if multiplication is not possible */
   public Matrix multiplyMatrix(Matrix other)
   {

      /* first check that the matrices can be multiplied */
      /* by comparing number of colums in current matrix with */
      /* number of rows in other matrix */
      if (this.mData.GetLength(1) == other.mData.GetLength(0))
      {
         /* multiplication is possible */
         /* create a new matrix to hold the result */
         Matrix result = new Matrix(this.mData.GetLength(0),
            other.mData.GetLength(1));
```

```
            /* for all rows of current matrix */
            for (int r = 0; r <= this.mData.GetLength(0)-1; r++)
            {
                /* for all columns of other matrix */
                for (int c = 0; c <= other.mData.GetLength(1)-1; c++)
                {
                    /* combine current row of current matrix */
                    /* with current column of other matrix */
                    int sum = 0;
                    for (int e = 0; e <= this.mData.GetLength(1)-1; e++)
                    {
                        sum = sum + this.mData[r,e] * other.mData[e,c];
                    }
                    /* store the result in the result matrix */
                    result.mData[r,c] = sum;
                }
            }
            return result;
        }
        else
        {
            /* multiplication is not possible */
            /* return null */
            return null;
        }
    }
}
```

Program 10.12   Modification of class `Matrix` to use rectangular arrays.

Indexers – Accessing Arbitrary Objects by Index

We've seen that many different types of objects encapsulate collections of values, often as one- or two-dimensional arrays but also potentially as instances of `string` or `StringBuilder`. For example, both class `Vector` and class `Matrix` encapsulate collections of integers. In the case study in the final section of this chapter we will introduce a class `TimeTable` that keeps a collection of `Lecture` objects. Very often we will want to write accessor and modifier methods that allow elements of these collections to be retrieved or modified in a controlled way, i.e., without requiring us to make the collection `public`. Such methods will often take the index value identifying the element to be accessed as a parameter. For example, we could add an accessor to the `Vector` class to retrieve the value of a specified element of its `vectorData` array:

```
    public int GetElement(int index) {
        if ((0 <= index) && (index <= vectorData.Length-1)) {
            return vectorData[index];
        }
    }
```

Given this definition (and a `Vector` object) we can then write:

```
    myElement = myVector.GetElement(myIndex);
```

Given that providing such methods is quite common, C# allows a class to provide properties that are parametrized by an index value in order to identify one element in a collection that is maintained by the class. Such a property is called an *indexer*. An equivalent indexer for class `Vector` would be:

```
public int this[int index] {
  get {
    if ((0 <= index) && (index <=
    this.vectorData.Length-1)) {
      return this.vectorData[index];
    }
  }
}
```

The indexer is called `this` and takes as a parameter the index value to be used. Note that, unusually, the formal parameter is enclosed in square brackets. Given this definition we can then write:

```
myElement = myVector[myIndex];
```

i.e., we can use the familiar [ ] notation to index the vector object (even through it is not itself an array!). We could also allow the contents of our vector to be changed by extending the indexer:

```
public int this[int index] {
  get {
    if ((0 <= index) && (index <=
    this.vectorData.Length-1)) {
      return this.vectorData[index];
    }
  }
  set {
    if ((0 <= index) && (index <=
    this.vectorData.Length-1)) {
      this.vectorData[index] = value;
    }
  }
}
```

Note the use of the implicit parameter, `value`, in the `set` part of the indexer. Given this definition we can then write:

```
myVector[myIndex] = myElement;
```

to modify the contents of one element of the vector's array. In this case the value of `myElement` becomes the value of the implicit `value` parameter to `set` when the indexer is executed.

Overloading Indexers

While the value used to index an array or string is always an integer, the formal parameter of an indexer can be of any type that we want to use to identify a value in our collection. Moreover, just as we can overload other methods, C# allows us to overload indexers so that we can access the same collection of values using indices of different types.

As an example, let's consider writing a class whose instances represent the kind of phone book that you might have built-in to your mobile phone. At least on my mobile, the built-in phone book allows me to store a small collection of entries in which each entry contains a single name and a phone number. The phone book allows me to add and remove entries and to lookup a number by entering the corresponding name. Moreover, when I receive a call the phone looks up the number from which the call came and displays the name of the caller if the number corresponds to an entry in my phone book. In effect, the phone book can be accessed by name (as is commonly the case) or by phone number.

Our C# class, let's call it `MobilePhoneBook`, will clearly need to maintain a collection of phone book entries. We can implement entries as instances of a class `MobilePhoneBookEntry` with each containing as attributes a name, of type `string`, and a phone number, of type `int`. The collection of entries maintained by an instance of `MobilePhoneBook` is then naturally implemented as an array of `MobilePhoneBookEntry`. `MobilePhoneBook` will also need to keep track of the number of entries currently contained in the array. Thus, the attributes of `MobilePhoneBook` might be:

```
MobilePhoneBookEntry[] entries;
int numEntries;
```

Of course, `MobilePhoneBook` will need to provide a constructor to initialize a new empty phone book of the required size and methods to add and remove entries, which might fail if there is no space in the phone book or the entry is not present respectively:

```
public MobilePhoneBook(int size);
public bool AddEntry(string name, int phoneNumber);
public bool RemoveEntry(string name);
```

Now let's think about looking up our phone book for an entry corresponding to a name or a number. Clearly, we could provide methods to implement this. However, since we are really accessing a collection it is convenient to implement this by providing two (overloaded) read-only indexers, one of which takes a string as its index parameter and the other an integer. The former will return the phone number as its result while the latter will return a name.

```
// return -1 when no matching entry found
public int this[string name];
// return null when no matching entry found
public string this[int number];
```

Both have to be prepared for the possibility that the index value specified is invalid in some way (e.g., the string may be `null` or the integer negative) and that no appropriate entry is found in the phone book. Programs 10.13 and 10.14 show the resulting class definitions. Now, given

```
MobilePhoneBook myPhoneBook;
string friendsName; int friendsNumber;
```

a program can now look up a phone book by:

```
friendsName = myPhoneBook[friendsNumber];
```

or

```
friendsNumber = myPhoneBook[friendsName];
```

provided that it is careful to check that the result doesn't indicate an error!

```
/* A struct whose values represent entries in a phone book */
struct MobilePhoneBookEntry
{
    private string name;
    private int phoneNumber;

    /* declare a constructor to initialize a new entry */
    /* Assumes name is not null and phoneNumber > 0 */
    public MobilePhoneBookEntry(string name, int phoneNumber)
    {
        this.name = name;
        this.phoneNumber = phoneNumber;
    }

    /* provide read-only properties to get name and number */
    public string entryName
    {
        get
        {
            return this.name;
        }
    }

    public int entryNumber
    {
        get
        {
            return this.phoneNumber;
        }
    }
}
```

Program 10.13   Class MobilePhoneBookEntry

```
/* A struct whose instances represent simple phone books */
struct MobilePhoneBook
{
    private const int NUMSLOTS = 10;
    private MobilePhoneBookEntry[] entries; // the phone book
    private int numEntries;

    /* constructor */
    public MobilePhoneBook(int size) {
        if (size > 0)
            entries = new MobilePhoneBookEntry[size];
        else
            entries = new MobilePhoneBookEntry[NUMSLOTS];
        numEntries = 0;
    }

    /* assumes name is not null and phoneNumber > 0 */
    public bool AddEntry(string name, int phoneNumber) {
        if (numEntries < entries.Length)
        {
            entries[numEntries++] = new MobilePhoneBookEn-
try(name, phoneNumber);
```

```
         return true;
   }
   else
      return false;
}

/* assumes name is not null */
public bool RemoveEntry(string name) {
   /* first look for the required entry */
   int i = 0; // start at position 0
   while ((i <= entries.Length-1) && (entries[i].entryName != name))
   {
      i++;
   }
   if ((i <= entries.Length-1) && (entries[i].entryName ==  name))
   {
      /* found at position i - remove it by */
      /* shifting remaining elements left */
      for (int r = i; r < entries.Length-1; r++)
      {
         entries[r] = entries[r+1];
      }
      numEntries--;
      return true;
   }
   else
      return false;
}

/* return -1 when no matching entry found */
/* assumes name is not null */
public int this[string name] {
   get {
      /* first look for the required entry */
      int i = 0; // start at position 0
      while ((i <= entries.Length-1) && (entries[i].entryName != name))
      {
         i++;
      }
      if ((i <= entries.Length-1) && (entries[i].entryName ==  name))
         /* found at position i - */
         return entries[i].entryNumber;
      else
         return -1;
   }
}


/* return null when no matching entry found */
public string this[int number] {
   get {
      /* first look for the required entry */
      int i = 0; // start at position 0
      while ((i <= entries.Length-1) &&
         (entries[i].entryNumber != number))
      {
         i++;
      }
```

```
          if ((i <= entries.Length-1) &&
              (entries[i].entryNumber ==  number))
              /* found at position i - */
              return entries[i].entryName;
          else
              return null;
      }
    }
}
```

Program 10.14   Class MobilePhoneBook.

Notice that, in this case, the indices being used to look up the collection correspond to the name and phone number contained in the entries and not the indices of the array used to store our phone book.

Indexing in Two or More Dimensions

Just as we can have arrays that are indexed in two or more dimensions, C# allows us to write indexers that take two or more parameters to be used to index an arbitrary collection. For example, we might add an indexer to our Matrix class that takes two parameters and uses them to index the matrixData array.

```
public int this[int x, int y] {
  get {
    if ((0 <= x) && (index <= this.matrixData.Length-1) &&
        (0 <= y) && (index <=
          this.matrixData[0].Length-1)) {
      return this.matrixData[x][y];
    }
  }
  set {
    if ((0 <= x) && (index <= this.matrixData.Length-1) &&
        (0 <= y) && (index <=
          this.matrixData[0].Length-1)) {
      this.matrixData[x][y] = value;
    }
  }
}
```

Given an instance of Matrix, we can now write:

```
myElement = myMatrix[x, y];
```

or

```
myMatrix[x,y] = myElement;
```

Essentially, instances of Matrix can now be treated as if they were rectangular arrays (even though the array contained in each element is jagged)!

Command Line Arguments

Many programs allow their users to supply some parameters to the program when it is executed. Like the parameters that are passed to a method when it is invoked, the parameters supplied to a program are used to provide information that the program needs in order to do its job. For example, if you use the Windows command prompt, you may have used the copy program to make a copy of a file. Obviously, copy needs to be told the name of the file to copy and the name of the file to which it is to be copied. For example, to copy the file sourceFile.txt to targetFile.txt, the appropriate command is:

```
copy sourceFile.txt targetFile.txt
```

In this case, copy is the name of a program and sourceFile.txt and targetFile.txt are its parameters. Properly speaking, such parameters are called *program parameters* or *command line arguments* since their values are written on the command line for the program.

C# provides the means for command line arguments to be supplied to C# programs in a similar manner. For example, if we were using a version of copy that was written in C#, we could supply command line arguments to the program as follows:

```
copy.exe sourceFile.txt targetFile.txt
```

i.e., by writing the values of the command line arguments after the name of the program to be executed.

All very well, but how does a C# program actually get hold of the command line arguments that were provided when it was executed? Well, the first thing to notice is that command line arguments are always strings. For example, our copy program takes two command line arguments, the strings "sourceFile.txt" and "targetFile.txt". When a C# program is executed with commands line arguments, C# gathers up all the strings representing command line arguments provided by the user into an array of string and passes this array as a parameter to the Main method of the program.

Any program that is expecting command line arguments should overload the Main method to take this array of string as a parameter:

```
static void Main(string[] args);
```

Here, args will be a list of the command line arguments that were passed to the program when it was executed with each argument being contained in a separate element of the array. In the case of our copy program, args would be an array of two elements with args[0] containing the string "sourceFile.txt" and args[1] the string "targetFile.txt".

In general, the number of arguments that were supplied is given by args.Length. C# usually interprets spaces on the command line as separating different arguments. Otherwise, a command line argument can be any string and can be used in any way that the program wants.

Conventions for Passing Command Line Arguments

While a command line argument can be any string, certain conventions have evolved concerning the format in which arguments are usually written on the command line. You should make sure that your programs also adhere to these conventions.

In general, there are three different types of command line arguments that may be provided:

- *options* – arguments that consist of a single word (the option name),
- *options with values* – arguments that consists of a single word (the option name) followed by one or more words that specify values related to that option (option values),
- *flags* – arguments that consist of only a single character.

By convention, option names and flags are always immediately preceded with a single minus sign (-).

For example, let's say we want to write a simple program, `Greet`, that prints a greeting to its user on the screen. This program might accept up to three options as follows:

- `-name <string>`, the value of the `name` option should be a string giving the name of the user to be greeted,
- `-times <number>`, the value of the `times` option should be the number of times that the greeting is to be printed,
- `-upper`, an option, which if present, indicates that the greeting should be printed in upper case.

Note that the first two options require a value to be specified along with the option name, while the third option is used to control how the greeting is printed. The program might also accept some flags:

- `-p` if present, indicates that the program should pause after each greeting,
- `-s` if present, indicates that the program should skip a line after each greeting.

So, to print a greeting to Vinny five times in uppercase, skipping a line and pausing after each greeting we could write:

```
> greet.exe -name vinny -times 5 -upper -s -p
```

By convention, options and flags should be accepted in any order except where an option requires one or more values. In that case the values should be entered directly after the option name. Convention also dictates that it should be allowable to combine a sequence of flags into a single word. Thus, the following should also be acceptable:

```
> greet.exe -times 5 -ps -upper -name vinny
```

Finally, it's good practice to have your programs print a *usage message* that describes the allowable arguments whenever the user enters incorrect arguments. For example, entering

```
> greet.exe -times -pk -upper -name vinny
```

should cause a message of the form:

```
Usage: greet [-name string] [-times number] [-upper] [-ps]
```

to be printed where square brackets ([ ]) are used to denote optional command line arguments.

Writing a Program that Accepts Command Line Arguments

Given that we now know all about arrays and `strings`, writing a program that accepts command line arguments isn't too difficult. For example, Program 10.15 shows the `greet` program whose command line arguments are described above.

```
/* a program to illustrate the use of command line */
/* arguments  writes a greeting on the screen and takes up to five */
/* arguments as follows: */
/*  -name <string>: the name of the user to be greeted */
/*  -times <number>: the number of times to Write the greeting */
/*  -upper: whether or not to write the greeting in upper case */
/*  -p: whether or not to pause after each greeting */
/*  -s: whether or not to skip a line after each greeting */

using tcdIO;

class Greet
{
    private const string USAGE =
    "Usage: CmdLineProgram [-name string] [-times number] [-upper] [-ps]";

    public static void Main(string[] args)
    {
        Terminal terminal;
        string argument;
        char flag;
        int i = 0;
        bool error = false;
        string greeting;
        /* give all the arguments default values */
        string name = "";
        int times = 1;
        bool upper = false, pause = false, skip = false;

        /* create an object to represent the terminal */
        terminal = new Terminal();

        /* now parse the command line */
        while (!error && i <= args.Length-1 && args[i].StartsWith("-"))
        {
            /* get the next argument and increment i */
            argument = args[i++];

            /* check for each possibility in turn */
            if (argument.Equals("-name"))
            {
                /* look for name being careful not to cause overflow */
                if (i <= args.Length-1)
                {
                    name = args[i++];  // the next string is as-
sumed to be the name
                }
                else
                {
                    error = true;      // no name supplied
                }
            }
            else if (argument.Equals("-times"))
            {
                /* look for number of times being careful not to cause
                   overflow */
                if (i <= args.Length-1)
                {
```

```
            times = int.Parse(args[i++]); // convert string to number
         }
         else
         {
            error = true;                        // no value supplied
         }
      }
      else if (argument.Equals("-upper"))
      {
         upper = true;
      }
      else
      {
         /* check for flags ignoring leading '-' */
         for (int j = 1; j <= argument.Length-1; j++)
         {
            flag = argument[j];
            switch (flag)
            {
               case 'p':
                  pause = true;
                  break;
               case 's':
                  skip = true;
                  break;
               default:
                  error = true;
                  break;
            }
         }
      }
   }
   /* now execute the program */
   if (error || i < args.Length)
   {
      terminal.WriteLine(USAGE);
   }
   else
   {
      greeting = "Hello " + name + "!";      // use name
      if (upper)                             // use upper
         greeting = greeting.ToUpper();
      for (int j = 1; j <= times; j++)
      {      // use times
         terminal.WriteLine(greeting);
         if (skip)                                // use skip
            terminal.WriteLine("");
         if (pause)
         {                              // use pause
            terminal.WriteLine("Hit any key to continue...");
            terminal.ReadChar();
         }
      }
      terminal.WriteLine("Finished.");
   }
  }
 }
}
```

Program 10.15   A program to illustrate the use of command line arguments.

The first thing to realize in understanding this program is that given a command line such as:

```
> greet.exe -name vinny -times 5 -upper -p -s
```

the args array passed to Main will contain seven elements corresponding to the seven strings on the command line ("-name", "Vinny", "-times", "5", "-upper", "-p", and "-s"). The individual strings might represent option names, option values, flags, or sequences of flags combined.

We can use a loop to work our way through the args array, with each iteration of the loop processing one, or possibly more, strings. The terminating condition for the loop should cause the loop to stop when we discover any error, when we run out of strings, or when we discover that the next string to be processed doesn't represent a command line argument (i.e., doesn't begin with a '–'). Hence, an outline of the loop is:

```
bool error = false;
int i = 0; // index
while (!error && i <= args.Length-1 && args[i].StartsWith("-
")){
    /* get the next argument and increment i */
    argument = args[i++];
    /* process argument */
    ...
}
```

On each iteration, we process the string contained in argument using a nested if statement to determine what, if any, argument it represents.

When looking for an option that requires no parameters, we simply compare the current string with the expected option name, for example:

```
if (argument == "-upper") {
    upper = true;
} else {
    /* check a different possibility */
}
```

When looking for an option that requires a value, we again compare the current string with the expected option name. However, having identified the presence of such an option, we then need to retrieve its value(s) being careful that the option name wasn't the last string on the command line:

```
if (argument == "-name") {
    if (i <= args.Length-1) {
        name = args[i++]; // the next string should be the name
    } else {
        error = true; // no name supplied
    }
} else {
    /* check a different possibility */
}
```

If the value of the option is a number, then we need to convert the string representing the value to the corresponding number. For example, in the case of an integer, we might use the parse method from struct int to do the job:

```
if (argument == "-times") {
  if (i <= args.Length-1) {
    times = int.parse(args[i++]);
  } else {
    error = true; // no value supplied
  }
} else {
  /* check a different possibility */
}
```

Finally, when examining a string that may represent one or more flags, we can use a `for` loop combined with a `switch` statement to examine each character of the string in turn beginning after the leading '–' (i.e., at position 1 in the string):

```
for (int j = 1; j <= argument.Length-1; j++) {
  flag = argument[j];
  switch (flag) {
    case 'p':
      pause = true;
      break;
    case 's':
      skip = true;
      break;
    default:
      error = true;
      break;
  }
}
```

Program 10.15 pulls all of these pieces together and actually serves as a good basis for writing any C# program that needs to process command line arguments.

Case Study: Managing a Lecture Timetable

As usual, we finish this chapter with a case study that employs most of what we have covered up to now. This time, we'll look at writing a C# program to be used by the students of some school to manage their weekly timetable, or in other words to keep track of the times and locations of their various lectures. Our program should allow students to add or remove lectures from their timetables as well as look up the timetable for a particular hour or day. We'll assume that lectures only occur on the hour at any time between 09:00 hrs and 16:00 hrs, Monday through Friday.

To begin with, we need to identify what classes will be required. The timetable for a student is clearly a candidate to be represented as an object. Such an object could potentially store descriptions of all the lectures that have been scheduled during the week. Individual lectures might also be represented as objects. In that case, the timetable would contain (references to) the objects representing the individual lectures. In addition to the classes representing the timetable and its constituent lectures, we will also need a class to implement the interface to the user of the timetable program. So, we will have three classes: `Lecture`, `Timetable`, and the program class `TimetableProgram`. We'll look at each of these in turn.

An instance of class `Lecture` should describe one scheduled lecture. As such, it should include attributes such as the subject of the lecture, the name of the lecturer, its venue, and, of course, the day and hour at which the lecture is scheduled. The subject, lecturer, and venue are conveniently represented as `string`s, while the day and hour can be represented as `int`s. For example, we can use 1 to represent Monday, 2 Tuesday, and so forth. Of course, we will need to ensure that the values of the day and hour attributes are always within the allowed ranges. Hence, we will make these attributes `private` to class `Lecture`.

Obviously class `Lecture` will need to provide a constructor to initialize new instances of `Lecture` as follows:

```
public Lecture(string s, string i, string v, int d, int h);
```

Once created, each instance of `Lecture` should be immutable – a rescheduled lecture can be represented by a new instance of the class. Hence, the only methods that need to be provided are methods to retrieve the attributes of a `Lecture` when required. We will also provide an implementation of `ToString` to return a `string` describing the lecture. We can conveniently use this method elsewhere in the program whenever we need to print out the details of a lecture. Creating a `string` from the attributes of a `Lecture` is straightforward as can be seen in Program 10.16. The only complication arises because the day is stored as an `int` rather than a `string`. We can use a `switch` statement to translate this `int` to the corresponding `string` and concatenate it with the `string` to be returned by `ToString`.

```
/* a struct whose instances represent lectures */

struct Lecture
{
   private string subject;
   private string instructor;
   private string venue;
   private int day;  // 1-5 for Monday-Friday
   private int hour; // 9-16 for 09.00hrs-16.00hrs

   /* initialsie a new instance of Lecture */
   /* Assumes that 1 <= d <= 5 and 9 <= h <= 16 */
   public Lecture(string s, string i, string v, int d, int h)
   {
      subject = s;
      instructor = i;
      venue = v;
      day = d;
      hour = h;
   }

   /*  Initialize Blank entry */
   public bool Initialize()
   {
      subject = null;
      instructor = null;
      venue = null;
      day = 0;
      hour = 0;
      return true;
   }
```

```
/* Test for empty lecture slot */
public bool IsEmpty()
{
   if(this.subject == null && this.instructor == null &&
      this.venue == null
      && this.day == 0 && this.hour == 0)
      return true;
   else
      return false;
}

/* return subject */
public string GetSubject()
{
   return subject;
}

/* return instructor */
public string GetInstructor()
{
   return instructor;
}

/* return venue */
public string GetVenue()
{
   return venue;
}

/* return a string describing the lecture */
public override string ToString()
{
   string message =  subject + " lecture by " + instructor
      + "\n in " + venue + " at " + hour + ".00hrs on ";
   switch (day)
   {
      case 1:
         message = message + "Monday.";
         break;
      case 2:
         message = message + "Tuesday.";
         break;
      case 3:
         message = message + "Wednesday.";
         break;
      case 4:
         message = message + "Thursday.";
         break;
      case 5:
         message = message + "Friday.";
         break;
   }
   return message;
}

}
```

Program 10.16   Class Lecture.

Now for class `Timetable`! A timetable is intended to keep track of the scheduling of a set of lectures. As such, it should provide methods to record the scheduling of a new lecture at a specified day and time, to obtain details of the lecture scheduled at a particular time or on a particular day, and to delete a lecture from the timetable. We've already seen that most of the information describing a scheduled lecture will be stored in a corresponding object. That being the case, an instance of class `Timetable` is really a container for instances of class `Lecture`. The main responsibility of the `Timetable` class is to provide access to these objects. Thus, class `Timetable` needs to provide a convenient data structure for storing a set of `Lecture`s that can be looked up by day or by day and time. One way of achieving this is to use a two-dimensional array of `Lecture` indexed by day and time:

```
private Lecture[][] timetable;
timetable = new Lecture[5][]; // 5 days
for (int d = 0; d <= timetable.Length-1; d++) {
   timetable[d] = new Lecture[8]; //8 hours per day
}
```

Here, each element of the array is capable of storing a reference to the object representing the corresponding lecture. If there is no lecture scheduled at the corresponding time, the value of the element will be `null`.

Given this data structure, we can use the first index to retrieve all the lectures scheduled on a particular day and both indices to retrieve the lecture scheduled at a particular hour on a particular day. For example,

- `timetable[day]` has type "array of `Lecture`" (`Lecture[]`) that corresponds to the array of lectures for day `day`. Some of the elements of this array may be `null`.
- `timetable[day][hour]` gives the instance of `Lecture` representing the lecture on the specified day at the specified hour or `null` if there is no such lecture.

The methods of class `Timetable` can easily be written to insert elements into or retrieve elements from the `timetable` array. As Program 10.17 shows, their main responsibility becomes ensuring that the day and hour specified fall within the allowable ranges so that array overflow does not occur. In fact, this is a very good example of using methods to encapsulate

```
/* a class whose instances represent timetables */

class Timetable
{
   public const int NUMDAYS = 5;      // Monday-Friday only
   public const int STARTHOUR = 9;    // 09.00hrs
   public const int FINISHHOUR = 16;  // 16.00hrs
   public const int NUMHOURS = FINISHHOUR - STARTHOUR + 1;

   private Lecture[,] timetable; // the timetable

   /* create and initialize two-dimensional array */
   /* to hold timetable data */
   public Timetable()
   {
      this.timetable = new Lecture[NUMDAYS,NUMHOURS];
      for (int d = 0; d <= this.timetable.GetLength(0)-1; d++)
      {
         for (int h = 0; h <= this.timetable.GetLength(1)-1; h++)
```

```
        {
            this.timetable[d,h].Initialize();
        }
    }
}

/* schedule a lecture for the specified day and time */
/* Day should be 1-5 and hour 9-16 */
/* Return true if sucessful and false if day or hour are invalid */
public bool schedule(int day, int hour, Lecture lecture)
{

    /* check that the day and hour are valid */
    if ((day >= 1) && (day <= NUMDAYS)
        && (hour >= STARTHOUR) && (hour <= FINISHHOUR))
    {
        /* add lecture to timetable */
        this.timetable[day-1,hour-STARTHOUR] = lecture;
        return true;
    }
    else
    {
        return false;
    }
}

/* delete the lecture occuring on the specified day and time */
/* Day should be 1-5 and hour 9-16 */
/* Return true if sucessful and false if day or hour are invalid */
public bool delete(int day, int hour)
{

    /* check that the day and hour are valid */
    if ((day >= 1) && (day <= NUMDAYS)
        && (hour >= STARTHOUR) && (hour <= FINISHHOUR))
    {
        /* return scheduled lecture */
        this.timetable[day-1, hour-STARTHOUR].Initialize();
        return true;
    }
    else
    {
        return false;
    }
}

/* lookup the lecture occuring on the specified day and time */
/* Day should be 1-5 and hour 9-16 */
/* Return false if day or hour are invalid */
public bool lookup(int day, int hour, out Lecture result)
{
    result = this.timetable[day-1,hour-STARTHOUR];

    /* check that the day and hour are valid */
    if ((day >= 1) && (day <= NUMDAYS)
        && (hour >= STARTHOUR) && (hour <= FINISHHOUR))
        return true;
```

```
        else
            return false;
    }

    /* lookup the lectures occuring on the specified day */
    /* Return null if day is not between 1 and 5 */
    public bool lookup(int day, out Lecture[] result)
    {
        /* return scheduled lectures */
        result = new Lecture[this.timetable.GetLength(1)];
        for(int i=0;i<this.timetable.GetLength(1);i++)
        {
            result[i] = this.timetable[day-1,i];
        }

        /* check that the day is valid */
        if ((day >= 1) && (day <= NUMDAYS))
            return true;
        else
            return false;
    }
}
```

Program 10.17 Class Timetables.

and protect a private data structure! Most of the methods of class Timetable simply use an if statement to ensure that the indices are valid and then access the timetable array as appropriate. By the way, you may also notice that the methods of class Timetable accept and return (references to) instances of class Lecture. Thus, the instances of Lecture referred to by an instance of Timetable may also be referred to by other parts of the program independently of the timetable. This is acceptable only because instances of Lecture are immutable once they have been created. Therefore, it's not possible for another part of the program to modify the contents of a slot in a timetable without using the correct method of class Timetable. If instances of Lecture could be modified, it would be more appropriate for the methods of class Timetable to make a copy of each Lecture object to which they are passed a reference so that the contents of the timetable are completely encapsulated. For example, classes Vector and Matrix in previous examples use this strategy.

Finally, class TimetableProgram provides the user interface to the timetable. Essentially, it accepts commands and associated data from the user and translates that input into a call to the appropriate method on an instance of Timetable as shown in Program 10.18.

```
/* a program to manage a student's weekly lecture timetable */

using tcdIO;

class TimetableProgram
{
    /* define the commands understood by the program */
    public const int SCHEDULE = 1;
    public const int DELETE = 2;
    public const int HOUR = 3;
    public const int DAY = 4;
    public const int LEAVE = 5;
    public const string WARNING =
    "Lectures are scheduled 9.00hrs-16.00hrs, Monday-Friday";
```

```csharp
public static void Main()
{
    Terminal terminal;
    Timetable timetable;
    int command, day, hour;
    string subject, instructor, venue;
    Lecture lecture;
    Lecture[] lectures;

    /* create an object to represent the terminal */
    terminal = new Terminal();

    /* create an object to represent the timetable */
    timetable = new Timetable();

    do
    {
        /* repeatedly ask the user for commands */
        terminal.WriteLine("Enter command as follows:");
        terminal.WriteLine(" 1 to add a lecture to the timetable");
        terminal.WriteLine(" 2 to delete a lecture from the timetable");
        terminal.WriteLine(" 3 to lookup the lecture at a
            particular time");
        terminal.WriteLine(" 4 to list the lectures on a
            particular day");
        terminal.WriteLine(" 5 to leave the program");
        command = terminal.ReadInt("Enter your command> ");
        switch (command)
        {
            case SCHEDULE:
                /* add a lecture to the timetable */
                /* first create an object to represent the lecture */
                subject = terminal.ReadString("Enter subject> ");
                instructor = terminal.ReadString("Enter
                    instructor's name> ");
                venue = terminal.ReadString("Enter venue> ");
                /* get the day and time at which the lecture
                    is to be scheduled */
                day = terminal.ReadInt("Enter day (1-5)> ");
                hour = terminal.ReadInt("Enter time (9-16)> ");
                lecture = new Lecture (subject, instructor, venue,
                    day, hour);
                /* add the lecture */
                if (timetable.schedule(day, hour, lecture))
                {
                    terminal.WriteLine(lecture.ToString());
                }
                else
                {
                    terminal.WriteLine(WARNING);
                }
                break;
            case DELETE:
                /* delete a lecture from the timetable */
                /* get the day and time at which the lecture
                    is to be deleted */
```

```
            day = terminal.ReadInt("Enter day (1-5)> ");
            hour = terminal.ReadInt("Enter time (9-16)> ");
            /* delete the lecture */
            if (timetable.delete(day, hour))
            {
                terminal.WriteLine("Lecture deleted.");
            }
            else
            {
                terminal.WriteLine(WARNING);
            }
            break;
        case HOUR:
            /* lookup the lecture at a partular time */
            /* get the day and time at which the lecture is
               scheduled */
            day = terminal.ReadInt("Enter day (1-5)> ");
            hour = terminal.ReadInt("Enter time (9-16)> ");
            /* lookup the lecture */
            if(timetable.lookup(day, hour, out lecture))
            {
                terminal.WriteLine(lecture.ToString());
            }
            else
            {
                terminal.WriteLine(WARNING);
            }
            break;
        case DAY:
            /* list the lectures on a particular day */
            /* get the day */
            day = terminal.ReadInt("Enter day (1-5)> ");
            /* lookup the lecture */
            if(timetable.lookup(day, out lectures))
            {
                for (int i = 0; i <= lectures.Length-1; i++)
                {
                    if(!lectures[i].IsEmpty())
                    terminal.WriteLine(lectures[i].ToString());
                }
            }
            else
            {
                terminal.WriteLine("Lectures are only scheduled
                    Monday-Friday");
            }
            break;
        }
    } while (command != LEAVE);
    terminal.WriteLine("Finished!");

    }
}
```

Program 10.18 A program to manage a student's weekly lecture timetable.

Notice that most of the error checking is left to the `Timetable` class and the program uses `if` statements to check whether or not an invocation of a method on the `Timetable` succeeded. The branch of the `switch` statement that deals with listing the lectures that occur on a given day uses a `for` loop to iterate through every element of the array of `Lectures` returned by the `Lookup` method from class `Timetable`. It then uses an `if` statement to check whether or not each element actually contains a scheduled lecture before trying to print out its details.

Summary

- *arrays* allow programs to manage collections of data that are organized as lists or tables
- an array is an indexed collection of values
- arrays are *objects*
- arrays can contain values of *any* type
- any given array can only contain values of *one* type, the *element type* of the array
- the elements of an array are indexed starting at 0 for the first element
- to refer to a particular element of an array, we specify the index of the required element using the [ ] notation
- *array initializers* provide a convenient way of creating and initializing an array as part of the declaration of an array variable
- the `for` and `foreach` statements are iteration statements
- the `for` statement is a shorthand form of the `while` statement
- `for` loops are usually used when the number of times that a loop is to be executed is controlled by a counter
- a single `for` loop is normally used to visit all the elements of a one-dimensional array in turn
- a `foreach` loop can also be used to process each element of a collection in turn
- the *autoincrement* and *autodecrement* operators can be used to increment or decrement the value of a variable
- an array whose elements contain other arrays is known as a *two-dimensional array*
- *nested `for` loops* are usually used to visit all the elements of a two-dimensional array
- *command line arguments* are used to pass information to a program when it is executed

Exercises

(1) A theatre has 20 spotlights mounted over its stage. Each spotlight can be on, off or dimmed. Write a class whose instances represent individual lights and use your class in a program that allows its user to control the lights (e.g., to turn a particular light on or off or to dim a light that is on).

(2) Consider an English sentence composed of a sequence of characters (i.e., uppercase or lowercase letters, digits, punctuation marks and spaces). Write a `static` method that, given a sentence, returns the number of times that each letter of the alphabet occurs in the sentence. Use your method in a program that reads some sentences from its user and prints out a description of how many times each letter occurs in each sentence.

Hint: what is the return type of the method?

(3) Write a class whose instances represent polynomials with integer coefficients and which provides methods to add and to multiply polynomials. For example, if

$$P(x) = x^3 + 3x^2 + 1 \quad \text{and} \quad Q(x) = x^2 + 5x$$

then

$$P(x) + Q(x) = x^3 + 4x^2 + 5x + 1$$

$$P(x) * Q(x) = x^5 + 8x^4 + 15x^3 + x^2 + 5x.$$

(4) Using only the methods provided by class Terminal, write a static method that, given an array of student examination marks (where each mark is between 1 and 10 with one student's mark per array element), outputs the information contained in the array as a histogram with marks on the horizontal axis and the number of students who obtained that mark on the vertical axis.

(5) The Josephus Ring Sequence is obtained by removing the nth number remaining in a ring of numbers 1...m. For, example if n is 3 and m is 8, then the ring is:

$$
\begin{array}{ccc}
8 & & 1 \\
7 & & 2 \\
6 & & 3 \\
5 & & 4 \\
\end{array}
$$

and the sequence is 1, 4, 7, 3, 8, 6, 2, 5.
Write a C# program that reads the values of n and m from its user and prints out the Josephus ring sequence for the given values.

(6) Write your own version of class StringBuilder using an array of char to hold the current contents of the buffer.

(7) Add the following methods to class Matrix:

- a method to return the index of the largest element in a specified row of the current matrix,
- a method to determine whether or not the current matrix has a *saddle point*. A saddle point is an element that is both the largest in its row and the smallest in its column.

(8) A *magic square* is an N by N array of positive integers, such that the sums of the values in each row, column, and diagonal are equal. Making use of a class MagicSquare, write a C# program that reads the size of a magic square and its contents, and then verifies that the square is indeed magic.
For example, given the input

$$
\begin{array}{cccc}
\multicolumn{4}{c}{4} \\
16 & 9 & 2 & 7 \\
6 & 3 & 12 & 13 \\
11 & 14 & 5 & 4 \\
1 & 8 & 15 & 10 \\
\end{array}
$$

your program should report that this is indeed a 4 by 4 magic square (since all the rows, columns, and diagonals sum to 34).

This chapter:

- presents the *has-a* and the *is-a* relationships and demonstrates them in the context of a non-trivial programming problem
- motivates the need for inheritance and presents its syntax
- introduces the concepts of a *base class* and a *derived class*
- distinguishes how public, private, and protected modify access to the members of a class
- discusses the implications of *inheritance* on type, including interchangeability of derived class objects and base class objects
- introduces the concept of *compile-time* and *run-time type*, and the associated operators as and is
- introduces the concept of *overloading* and *overriding* of base class methods
- introduces the concept of *interfaces* as a specification of type without an accompanying implementation

So far we have only scratched the surface of the capabilities available in an object-oriented programming language. To fully appreciate the power of an object-oriented language such as C#, we need to understand the concept of inheritance. As we will see in this chapter, inheritance allows us to vastly improve the reusability and maintainability of our code.

In this chapter we motivate the need for inheritance by first exploring the relationships that exist between objects and that exist between classes. We then look at how we would implement these relationships. As we will see, the language mechanisms introduced thus far are inadequate for implementing is-a relationships. To solve this problem, we introduce the concept of inheritance and the C# mechanisms that support its use. At the same time, we present other associated language mechanisms that are used in conjunction with inheritance to make code easier to write and easier to maintain over the long term.

Two Key Relationships: Has-A and Is-A

If you view the world in terms of objects, then you will notice that objects often relate to each other in one of two ways. Either an object may be contained within another or the class of an object maybe a subcategory of the class of another object. These scenarios correspond to the *has-a* and *is-a* relationships that we will discuss in this section.

Has-A

In object-oriented programming, the *has-a* relationship describes situations in which one object is a constituent element of another. For example, a vehicle is, roughly speaking, composed of a body, engine, and some wheels. In this case, the vehicle maintains a has-a relationship with respect to its engine. The same relationship exists between the vehicle and the body, and the vehicle and each of its wheels.

We can represent a has-a relationship by making the constituent object a field of the containing object. To represent the vehicle has-a engine relationship, a class describing a vehicle object would contain a field corresponding to the engine. Likewise, we would add fields corresponding to the body and each of the wheels. A crude version of the resulting `Vehicle` class is shown in Program 11.1.

Is-A

An *is-a* relationship occurs when one category of object has all the data and behaviour of another, plus some extras that make it more specific than the other. This situation arises when objects of one class are a more specialized version of objects of another. For example, in real life a lorry is-a vehicle. Both have a body, wheels, and an engine. However, the lorry is more specialized. It has a container either attached or on a trailer that allows the lorry to transport large quantities of materials. Also, the lorry is limited in the number of people it can transport. That said, the similarities between an object to represent a lorry and one to represent a vehicle

```
// Support classes for Vehicle
class Engine {}
class Body {}
class Wheel {}

// Quick example of a vehicle to get across the point of
// the has-a relationship.
class Vehicle {
  private Engine vehicleEngine;
  private Body   vehicleBody;
  private Wheel  frontLeft;
  private Wheel  frontRight;
  private Wheel  rearLeft;
  private Wheel  rearRight;

  public Vehicle( Engine engine, Body body,
                      Wheel fl, Wheel fr,
                      Wheel rl, Wheel rr )
  {
    this.frontLeft = fl;
    this.frontRight = fr;
    this.rearLeft = rl;
    this.rearRight = rr;
    this.vehicleEngine = engine;
    this.vehicleBody = body;
  }
}
```

Program 11.1   `Vehicle` class demonstrating how to code a has-a relationship.

```
// Support classes for Vehicle and Lorry
class Container {}

// Quick example of a lorry to get across the point of
// the is-a relationship
class Lorry {
  // Members specific to a lorry
  public Lorry( Container load, Engine engine, Body body,
                                 Wheel fl, Wheel fr,
                                 Wheel rl, Wheel rr )
  {
    this.load = load;
    this.frontLeft = fl;
    this.frontRight = fr;
    this.rearLeft = rl;
    this.rearRight = rr;
    this.vehicleEngine = engine;
    this.vehicleBody = body;
  }
  private Container load;

  // Members the same as in a Vehicle
  private Engine vehicleEngine;
  private Body   vehicleBody;
  private Wheel  frontLeft;
  private Wheel  frontRight;
  private Wheel  rearLeft;
  private Wheel  rearRight;
}
```

Program 11.2   Lorry class demonstrating how to code an is-a relationship.

are so strong that we could base the design of a class Lorry on the class Vehicle. The only significant difference would be the addition of an extra field to represent the container, and a change in constructor to ensure the field is properly initialized. Such an implementation of the Lorry class is shown in Program 11.2.

Keep in mind that is-a relationships occur between a more specialized class and its more general cousin, but not between objects with overlapping functionality. An is-a relationship implies that objects of one class contain the same functionality and data of objects of another. Fundamentally, the more specialized version could be used in place of the other. However, objects with overlapping functionality do not have this fundamental relationship. For instance, a passenger van and a lorry do not have an is-a relationship. A passenger van could not be used in place of a lorry truck because it lacks the container to allow it to transport items such as a cow. Likewise, a truck cannot be used in place of a passenger van. It lacks the seating capacity to move people safely and comfortably.

Demonstrating Is-A and Has-A

We will exercise our understanding of is-a and has-a relations during the design of a class that models insurance customers for an insurance company. So far we have seen the is-a and has-a relationships implemented in relatively simple classes. While simplicity avoids introducing distractions that obscure our point, it does not further our understanding of these relations or demonstrate programming issues that arise when these relations exist between objects and classes in the program. In this section, we introduce the distraction of class design issues. As the design progresses, we examine the classes produced to see what is-a and has-a relations exist, and what implications these relations have for the implementation of our design.

Take a car insurance company that tracks clients to make it easier to determine their premium and to bill them for their insurance. The car insurance company calculates a premium based on the client's age and gender. In this case, being under the age of 25 causes the premiums to double. Since the company has found males to have a much worse accident record, being male doubles the premium in addition to any increase due to age. For the purposes of mailing bills to clients, the company needs to know the client's name and home address. The client's address will change from time to time, but changes of address will not affect the client's premium or policy.

Tracking the client's age is more problematic than it seems. Based on the insurance company's requirements, an object describing a client should record the client's age for use in calculating their insurance premium. Simply storing their age is not a great solution, since it will have to be updated as time moves on. An alternative is to record the client's birthday and then recalculate their age based on the current date. As we have seen in previous chapters, determining whether a person meets an age criteria when their birthday is known is more complex than doing so when their actual age is known. With a birthday, three times more data is involved. Managing these data as independent fields makes construction error prone. Either a method is added to set the birthday or the constructor parameter list is made longer, and it becomes easy to mistakenly switch fields in the birthday such as day and month. In either case, an additional method will have to be added to handle the comparison of the current date and the birthday. Certainly, these requirements can implemented, but they obfuscate the point of the class, which is to represent a person.

To isolate the complexity of representing and manipulating the client's birthday, we introduce a `Date` class, shown in Program 11.3. This class encapsulates the year, month, and day data corresponding to a date, and provides the `YearsDifference` method for determining the difference in years between two dates. Using a `Date` class instance to represent a client's birthday allows us to clearly distinguish birthday data from other data in the person class. It also ensures that the `YearsDifference` method does not clutter the insurance client class. Finally, it allows a date to be passed as a single parameter.

To simplify tracking gender it makes sense to use a numeric value, but a constant should be supplied to guarantee the correct interpretation of this stored value. Aside from age, the client's gender is required to calculate a client's premium. The insurance company has noted that male drivers are more at risk of having an accident, so they must be identified so that their premium can be scaled to include this added risk. Thus, the gender must be stored so that a client can be quickly identified as being male. Using a string is not a good idea, because it leaves too much freedom to set the gender to an unrecognized value. Although we might expect a user to use "M" or "male", they might choose to use "boy" or "guy". A better strategy is to supply constants that represent the gender. The constant values could be strings, but numeric values will work just as well. For instance, the client class might supply the following constants:

```
// These constants are used in conjunction with gender.
public const int MALE = 1;
public const int FEMALE = 2;
```

```
class Date {
  /* declare the instance variables */
  private int day;    // should be in the range 1..31 depending on month
  private int month;  // should be in the range 1..12
  private int year;   // should be positive, four digit number

  /* class Date Assumes that y, m, and d represent a valid date */
  public Date(int y, int m, int d) {
    day = d;
    month = m;
    year = y;
  }

  // Method to determine difference, in years, between the stored
  // date and another date.
  public int YearsDifference ( Date other ) {
    int difference;

    difference = other.year - this.year;

    // Correct for month and day
    if ( this.month > other.month ) {
      difference--;
    }
    else if ( (other.month == this.month) && (this.day > other.day) ) {
      difference--;
    }

    return difference;
  }
}
```

Program 11.3 Date class.

The client object must also store the mailing address in a well encapsulated form. Very important to an insurance company is the ability to bill their clients. In our case this is done by mail, and a mailing address consists of the client's name and their home address. The only version of the client's name we are interested in is the one that appears on their mail. A single string can be used to store this. The home address consists of several pieces of information: the street address, city, country, and postal code. These could be stored in separate fields. However, placing them directly in the client's class introduces the same complexity issues that we tried to avoid when storing the birth date field. It would be better to encapsulate street address details in a separate object such as those defined by the Address class, shown in Program 11.4. Aside from a constructor, this class need only supply a method to return a string representing the mailing address, as it would appear on an envelope.

The resulting InsuranceClient class is shown in Program 11.5. The class contains the fields that we discussed along with methods to access, and in one case modify, these fields. The CurrentAge method determines the age of the person given the current date. BillingAddress simply returns the street address of the client, while Relocate allows the street address to be updated. The most complex method is InsuranceRate, which supplies a quote for the monthly cost of insurance based on the current date. This quote takes into account the gender and age of the person. Note, the base premium value is chosen arbitrarily and is not meant to reflect current rates!

```
class Address {
  private string street;
  private string town;
  private string country;
  private string postalCode;

  /* initialize a new instance of Address */
  public Address(string s, string t, string c, string p) {
    street = s;
    town = t;
    country = c;
    postalCode = p;
  }

  /* return the address, as it should appear on an envelope */
  public override string ToString() {
    return (street + "\n" + town + "\n" + country
                   + "\n" + postalCode + "\n");
  }
}
```

Program 11.4   Address class.


```
class InsuranceClient
{
  private string  name;
  public const int  MALE = 1, FEMALE = 2; // Constants for gender
  private    int      gender;
  private    Date     birthDay;
  private    Address home;

  public  InsuranceClient(string name, int gender,
                          Date birthDay, Address home){
    this.name      = name;
    this.gender    = gender;
    this.birthDay  = birthDay;
    this.home      = home;
  }

  public int CurrentAge(Date today) {
    return birthDay.YearsDifference(today);
  }
  public void Relocate(Address newHome) { this.home = newHome; }

  public Address BillingAddress() { return home; }

  public string Name() {return name;}

  public double InsuranceRate(Date today){
    double multiplier = 1, basePremium = 100;

    if ( InsuranceClient.MALE == gender )
      multiplier *= 2;
    if ( this.CurrentAge(today) < 25 )
      multiplier *= 2;

    return (multiplier * basePremium);
  }
}
```

Program 11.5   InsuranceClient class for car insurance company.

You have probably noticed that all the data members that we have added to the `InsuranceClient` each have an obvious has-a relationship with an `InsuranceClient` object. Take, for example, the client's birthday. In real-life, a person's birthday forms part of their identity: it dictates when they may drive and remembering someone's birthday is an important way to recognize a friendship. Thus, making a birthday object part of a client object is obvious. The same is true for the street address and the name string.

In the spirit of keeping our software system realistic, we should expand the insurance client scenario to include more types of clients. In this day and age it is not unreasonable for an insurance company to package insurance with other services. Let us revisit our car insurance company example, and add requirements for a second line of business that packages car insurance with financial services. In this case, our insurance company will offer to handle the payroll system at a very competitive rate for those companies that can convince their employees to enroll in the insurance company's car insurance. Thus, the insurance company will generate monthly pay slips and distribute them along with a salary cheque to each worker in the company. In this new scenario, the insurance company will have to track not only purchasers of their insurance, but also the details of salaried employees.

While the payslip is straightforward, employee salaries in our example are dependent on a base amount scaled according to technical expertise and worker seniority. The payslip need only include the employee's name, home address, and salary. On the other hand, an employee's salary is calculated by adding any bonus payments to a common base salary. The base salary is chosen arbitrarily to be 10 000. Having some sort of technical training represents a bonus of 100% of base salary. Seniority is also highly regarded, and after the first year of work an employee automatically receives an increase of 50% of base salary. Finally, the salary and the price paid for car insurance have no effect on each other.

Now that the additional requirements of an insured employee have been established, we must come up with a class to model these employees. Clearly, the `InsuranceClient` class will not suffice. It does not have the payroll and salary functionality that are the hallmark of the insured employee. However, the insured employee and the insurance client do maintain an is-a relation. The insured employee contains all the functionality required of the original `InsuranceClient` objects, which thus forms a basis for the design of an insured employee class. That is, the insured employee class can exploit the existing methods and fields of the `InsuranceClient` class. Using the language constructs learned so far, we have modeled is-a relationships by including the source code of one class in the class of the other. This approach is taken in Program 11.6 where the bottom half of the `InsuredEmployee` class is an exact copy of the `InsuranceClient`'s fields and methods.

```
class InsuredEmployee {
  Date startDate;
  int training;
  public const int Technical = 1, Other = 2;   // Training levels

  public InsuredEmployee(string name, int gender, Date birthDay,
                    Address home, Date startDate, int training ) {
    this.startDate = startDate;
    this.training = training;
    this.name     = name;
    this.gender   = gender;
    this.birthDay = birthDay;
    this.home     = home;
  }
```

```
public string Payslip(Date today) {
  return (this.Name()+ "\n"+this.BillingAddress()+ "\n"
                      + this.Salary(today).ToString() +"\n");
}

public double Salary(Date today) {
  double bonus = 1, baseSalary = 10000;

  if ( startDate.YearsDifference(today) > 1 )
    bonus *= 1.5;

  if ( training == InsuredEmployee.Technical )
    bonus *= 2.0;

    return baseSalary * bonus;
}


// These data members and methods are identical
// to those in InsuranceClient!
private string  name;
public const int  MALE = 1, FEMALE = 2; // Constants for gender
private    int      gender;
private    Date     birthDay;
private    Address home;

public int CurrentAge(Date today) {
  return birthDay.YearsDifference(today);
}
public void Relocate(Address newHome) { this.home = newHome; }

public Address BillingAddress() { return home; }

public string Name() {return name;}

public double InsuranceRate(Date today){
  double multiplier = 1, basePremium = 100;
  if ( InsuranceClient.MALE == gender )
    multiplier *= 2;
  if ( this.CurrentAge(today) < 25)
    multiplier *= 2;

  return (multiplier * basePremium);
}
}
```

Program 11.6   InsuredEmployee class for car insurance company.

The first half of Program 11.6 is of note because it is not implemented by code obtained from the InsuranceClient. In InsuredEmployee we have added the Salary method. The method calculates an employee's salary, taking into account the employee's level of training and seniority. The training level is recorded in a data member with the aid of two constants, Technical and Other, which describe the different categories of training. To determine seniority, InsuredEmployee records the date at which employment began in the startDate and calculates the length of service using this and the current date, which is passed to the `Salary` method as a parameter. Finally, the method `Payslip` has been added. It determines the salary using the `Salary` method and generates the text of the payslip using the salary, name, and address that are already present in the `InsuranceClient` details.

Problems with Implementing Is-A Relationships

Our *copy-and-paste strategy* for modeling the is-a relationship has tangible drawbacks. The strategy forces us to maintain multiple copies of the same code: one copy in the more general class and a copy in every specialization of the general class. Secondly, we have type compatibility issues that prevent the reuse of code client code. If the client code creates methods that use the more general object, it would be helpful if this code were able to manipulate the more specialized object without having to be rewritten. However, method calls need to specifically state the type of their parameter, and type rules prevent the use of objects in method calls whose type is incompatible with the method's parameter types.

The code maintenance issue is exposed when the `InsuranceClient` class and `InsuredEmployee` class must undergo the same revisions. Given a few years of operation the insurance company may decide to recognize its better customers. One way to distinguish the better customers is to calculate which customers have spent the most on insurance. This is simplistic because it does not take into account the amount a customer has cost the insurance company in claims in determining who is a better customer. Since all customers will be examined when determining who better customers are, both customers modeled by `InsuranceClient` and `InsuredEmployee` objects should both be examined. Consequently, the revisions to determine better customers will have to be applied to both classes.

A revision of `InsuranceClient` that meets this requirement is shown in Program 11.7. This version contains new functionality to track the total amount of premiums a client has paid. A new field, called `totalPremiums`, accumulates the amount spent on insurance. This field is set to zero when an `InsuranceClient` object is created. Whenever `InsuranceRate`

```
class InsuranceClient {
  private string  name;
  public const int  MALE = 1, FEMALE = 2; // Constants for gender
  private    int      gender;
  private    Date     birthDay;
  private    Address home;
  private    double   totalPremiums = 0;

  public  InsuranceClient(string name, int gender, Date birthDay,
        Address home) {
    this.name      = name;
    this.gender    = gender;
    this.birthDay = birthDay;
    this.home      = home;
  }

  public int CurrentAge(Date today) { return
        birthDay.YearsDifference(today); }
  public void Relocate(Address newHome) { this.home = newHome; }
  public Address BillingAddress() { return home; }
```

```
public string Name() {return name;}
public double TotalPremiums() { return totalPremiums; }

public double InsuranceRate(Date today) {
  double multiplier = 1, basePremium = 100;

  if ( InsuranceClient.MALE == gender )  multiplier *= 2;
  if ( this.CurrentAge(today) < 25)  multiplier *= 2;

  this.totalPremiums += (multiplier * basePremium);
  return (multiplier * basePremium);
  }
}
```

Program 11.7 InsuranceClient updated to track total premiums paid.

is called, the calculated premium is added to totalPremiums before the method returns to the caller. The method TotalPremiums provides access to the value accumulated.

While our copy-and-paste strategy can quickly update the InsuredEmployee class, the strategy becomes more tedious and error prone as common features of InsuredEmployee and InsuranceClient evolve. The requirement to track the total amount of premiums exists in the InsuredEmployee class as well. Since we are maintaining an is-a relationship, it is okay to manually copy code to calculate the total premium from InsuranceClient to the InsuredEmployee class. That is, if we remember to. It cannot be taken for granted that the InsuredEmployee class will be updated, because there is no indication in its source code that it has an is-a relationship with the InsuranceClient class! This is not the only problem. The insurance company may decide to add new types of clients. Rather than applying the copy-and-paste strategy between two classes, it may have to be applied to a multitude of classes. This generates considerable work! Hence the copy-and-paste strategy quickly becomes unmanageable.

The problem with copy-and-paste from the client code's perspective is that the duplicate versions of the client code must be created for each class involved in the is-a relationship. Take for example a method used to generate an insurance invoice. The CreateInsuranceInvoice method in Program 11.8 is an implementation of one such method. It extracts the billing address and insurance premium from an InsuranceClient class object. While CreateInsuranceInvoice makes use of methods that are present in both the InsuranceClient and InsuredEmployee classes, CreateInsuranceInvoice only works for InsuranceClient class objects. The compiler will not let an InsuredEmployee object be referred to by a variable of type InsuranceClient. Thus, in Program 11.8 this method call

```
DemoReuseProgram.CreateInsuranceInvoice(benny, today );
```

compiles fine, but the following method call generates a compiler error.

```
DemoReuseProgram.CreateInsuranceInvoice(betty, today );
```

The type incompatibility problem in Program 11.8 can be solved with *parameter overloading*. Essentially, two versions of the same method are written. Each has a different type specification for the purchaser parameter: one specifies purchaser as an InsuranceClient class object and the other specifies purchaser as an InsuredEmployee object. This approach is shown in Program 11.9.

While overloading makes calls to client code elegant, it comes with some horrendous maintenance issues. The elegance of overloading is that the compiler finds an appropriate

```
class DemoReuseProgram    {
  public static void Main() {
    Date bennyBorn = new Date(1975, 01, 01);
    Address bennyHome = new Address("Pearse Street", "Dublin",
                                    "Ireland", "Dublin 2");
    InsuranceClient benny = new InsuranceClient( "Benny",
                    InsuranceClient.MALE,bennyBorn, bennyHome );
    Date bettyBorn = new Date(1975, 01, 01);

    Address bettyHome = new Address("Townsend Street", "Dublin",
                                    "Ireland", "Dublin 2");
    Date bettyHired = new Date(2000, 01, 01);

    InsuredEmployee betty = new InsuredEmployee( "Betty",
                      InsuredEmployee.FEMALE , bettyBorn, bettyHome,
                      bettyHired, InsuredEmployee.Technical );
    Date today = new Date(2001, 10, 01);

    DemoReuseProgram.CreateInsuranceInvoice(benny, today );   // OK
    DemoReuseProgram.CreateInsuranceInvoice(betty, today );   // No good!
  }

  static string CreateInsuranceInvoice(InsuranceClient purchaser,
                                       Date today)
  {

    string postalAddress = purchaser.BillingAddress().ToString();
    string coverageCost = purchaser.InsuranceRate(today).ToString() ;

    return (postalAddress + coverageCost);
  }
}
```

Program 11.8   Method available for `InsuranceClient`, but not for `InsuredEmployee`.

```
class DemoReuse {
  public static void Main() {
    Date bennyBorn = new Date(1975, 01, 01);
    Address bennyHome = new Address("Pearse Street", "Dublin",
                                    "Ireland", "Dublin 2");
    InsuranceClient benny = new InsuranceClient( "Benny",
                    InsuranceClient.MALE, bennyBorn, bennyHome );
    Date bettyBorn = new Date(1975, 01, 01);

    Address bettyHome = new Address("Townsend Street","Dublin",
                                    "Ireland", "Dublin 2");
    Date bettyHired = new Date(2000, 01, 01);
    InsuredEmployee betty = new InsuredEmployee( "Betty",
                    InsuredEmployee.FEMALE , bettyBorn,
                    bettyHome, bettyHired, InsuredEmployee.Technical );

    Date today = new Date(2001, 10, 01);
    DemoReuse.CreateInsuranceInvoice(benny, today );  // OK
    DemoReuse.CreateInsuranceInvoice(betty, today );  // Uses overloaded
                                                      // version.
  }
```

```
static string CreateInsuranceInvoice(InsuranceClient purchaser,
                                     Date today)
{
  string postalAddress = purchaser.BillingAddress().ToString();

  string coverageCost = purchaser.InsuranceRate(today).ToString() ;

  return (postalAddress + coverageCost);
}

static string CreateInsuranceInvoice(InsuredEmployee purchaser,
                                     Date today)
{
  string postalAddress = purchaser.BillingAddress().ToString();

  string coverageCost = purchaser.InsuranceRate(today).ToString() ;

  return (postalAddress + coverageCost);
}
}
```

Program 11.9 Method overloading provides a version of `CreateInsuranceInvoice` for `Insurance-Client` and `InsuredEmployee`.

method regardless of the actual type of the variable being used. However, there is a drawback when the overloaded versions of a method are identical. Testing is overly time-consuming. In Program 11.9, two tests are required to verify the correct operation of what is essentially the same code. Maintenance of the overloaded method is also a pain as changes for the same code must be written twice, once for each method. Imagine if the overloaded method had to support 20 types of insurance client! It would be much more elegant if we could somehow get one version of the code to work for both types of objects.

Introducing Inheritance

The inheritance operation is an alternative to the copy-and-paste implementation of an is-a relationship. *Inheritance* is a language construct that is applied during the implementation of a class. It establishes an is-a relationship between a new class being implemented and an existing one. The effect of inheritance is that the compiler includes all the members of the existing class in the new class. As a result, the class being implemented is a *specialization* of the existing class.

The syntax for inheritance is applied to the name of a class. To select a class for inheritance, the declaration of the name of the class being written is followed with a colon and the name of the existing class from which we intend to inherit members. For example, we can revise the `Truck` example implemented in Program 11.2 using inheritance. The result is shown in Program 11.10. Notice that the constructor makes use of the `base` keyword. We will explain the meaning of this keyword later in this section.

To help in the discussion of inheritance, it is useful to introduce terminology for the classes involved. The existing class from which members are being inherited is called the *base class*. The new class that is being implemented is the *derived class*, since it derives some of its members from the base class. In C#, a derived class can only inherit from one base class. In general this is referred as *single-root inheritance*.

```
// Support class for Lorry
class Container {}

class Lorry : Vehicle {
  public Lorry( Container load, Engine engine, Body body,
                    Wheel fl, Wheel fr, Wheel rl, Wheel rr )
                  : base( engine,  body, fl,  fr, rl,  rr )
  {
    this.load = load;
  }

  private Container load;
}
```

Program 11.10   Implementation of class Lorry using inheritance.

The term *inherited members* refers to the fields, properties, and methods available in the base class that get added to the derived class. These members can be inherited directly or indirectly. Directly inherited members are those declared in the base class, while indirectly inherited members are those that were added to the base class if it made use of inheritance. Classes from which a derived class inherits directly and indirectly form the derived class' *inheritance chain*.

There is one important exception to the inheritance rule. The constructor methods of a base class are not included in the derived class. However, they can be accessed using the base keyword. Also, a special syntax is available for calling a base class constructor before the derived class constructor runs. This is done by following the derived class' constructor with a colon, and then using the base keyword as if it were the name of the constructor. This use of the base keyword is demonstrated in Program 11.10.

The ability of inheritance to include members of an existing class allows us to avoid the maintenance problems of the copy-and-paste strategy of implementing is-a relationships. First, we can reuse the functionality of the base class with very few lines of code. A re-implementation of the InsuredEmployee class in Program 11.11 demonstrates the use of inheritance to elegantly include InsuranceClient functionality. Not only has our implementation of InsuredEmployee shrunk from that of Program 11.6, but also inheritance establishes a continuing link between the InsuranceClient and InsuredEmployee classes that simplifies class maintenance. Recall from the discussion in the previous section that, using copy-and-paste, we had to manually update the InsuredEmployee class every time the InsuranceClient class changed. Instead, inheritance automatically updates InsuredEmployee with any modifications to the InsuranceClient class as soon as the former is recompiled.

```
class InsuredEmployee : InsuranceClient {
  Date startDate;
  int training;
  public const int Technical = 1, Other = 2;  // Training levels

  public InsuredEmployee(string name, int gender, Date birthDay,
                  Address home, Date startDate, int training )
                : base( name, gender, birthDay, home) {
    this.startDate = startDate;
    this.training = training;
  }
```

```
public string Payslip(Date today) {
  return (this.Name()+ "\n"+this.BillingAddress()+ "\n"
                      + this.Salary(today).ToString() +"\n");
}

public double Salary(Date today) {
  double bonus = 1, baseSalary = 10000;

  if ( startDate.YearsDifference(today) > 1 )
    bonus *= 1.5;

  if ( training == InsuredEmployee.Technical )
    bonus *= 2.0;

    return baseSalary * bonus;
  }
}
```

Program 11.11   Implementation of `InsuredEmployee` using inheritance.

Effects of Access Modifiers on Inheritance

The accessibility of a class' members dictates what code can access the member. Previously, we were introduced to the `public` and `private` accessibility modifiers. In this section we will see that these have slightly more meaning in the context of inheritance. Also, a new modifier called `protected`, is introduced and we will see how it works in conjunction with inheritance.

Review of Public and Private

Recall our discussion of `public` and `private` keywords in Chapter 7. At that point we described `public` and `private` keywords as *access modifiers* because they controlled which methods had access to an object's members. Specifically, the `private` keyword prevents access to a member of an object to all code outside the scope of the object's class declaration. That is, to all code not written inside a class' declaration. The purpose of this mechanism is to mark details of an object as being implementation dependent. In contrast, the `public` keyword allows any code to access a member regardless of scope. That is, regardless to where the code is declared. The purpose of the `public` keyword is to specify members that are part of an objects public interface.

A simple example in Program 11.12 demonstrates the use of `public` and `private` on a class' members. Let us start by examining how the access modifiers affect the class' methods. `AccessDemo` has two methods, one private and the other public. Both `PublicMethod` and `PrivateMethod` can be called by code declared inside the scope of the `AccessDemo` class. However, in the `AccessProgram` class, calls cannot be made to `PrivateMethod`, because code in the `AccessProgram` class is outside the scope of `AccessDemo`. Thus, the line

```
myObject.PrivateMethod(); // Error!
```

generates a compile-time error stating that `PrivateMethod` is inaccessible. By not allowing access to `PrivateMethod` to users of `AccessDemo` objects, we have freed the hands of the `AccessDemo` class' programmer to remove or change the parameters to the method at will.

The example also examines the effects on the data members `valueA` and `valueB`. Both fields are accessible from within the scope of the `AccessDemo` class. So the following call

```
using tcdIO;

class AccessDemo {
  public  int valueA = 1;
  private int valueB = 2;

  private void PrivateMethod(Terminal terminal) {
    // Accessing member methods from AccessDemo
    this.PublicMethod(terminal);              // OK
    terminal.WriteLine("Method called!");

    // Accessing data members from AccessDemo
    this.valueA = this.valueB + 1;            // OK
  }

  public void PublicMethod(Terminal terminal) {
    // Accessing member methods from AccessDemo
    this.PrivateMethod(terminal);             // OK

    // Accessing data members from AccessDemo
    this.valueA = this.valueB + 1;            // OK
  }
}

class AccessProgram {
  static public void Main() {
    Terminal terminal = new Terminal();
    AccessDemo accessObject = new AccessDemo();

    // Accessing member methods from AccessProgram
    accessObject.PublicMethod(terminal);  // OK
    accessObject.PrivateMethod(terminal); // Error!

    // Accessing data members from AccessProgram
    accessObject.valueA = accessObject.valueB + 1; // Error!
    accessObject.valueA =  1;                       // OK
  }
}
```

Program 11.12   Demonstration of `private` and `public` access modifiers.

```
    this.valueA = this.valueB + 1;
```

can be made from within `PublicMethod` and `PrivateMethod`. However, only public data members can be accessed from outside the class. Thus, making a similar call from within `AccessProgram` causes a compilation error.

Affect of `public` and `private` in the Context of Inheritance

Although a derived class will include all the members declared in its base class, the members are not necessarily accessible. That is, inheritance does not bypass the rules imposed by accessibility modifiers. A member labeled `public` will always be accessible outside the class in which it was declared, so a derived class will have full access to members declared public. The members labeled `private`, but included by inheritance will not be accessible from the derived class. We must stress that they will be present in objects of the derived class. Thus, inherited methods that make use of inherited private data members will still operate correctly. However, the derived class will not be able to manipulate these data members directly. The same is true for inherited private methods.

To clarify the accessibility semantics for inherited members, Program 11.13 demonstrates what access is available and not available when a derived class is written and when it is used. In the program, class `AccessInheritance` inherits directly from the `AccessDemo` class originally shown in Program 11.12. `AccessInheritance` will be able to use the public members of `AccessDemo`, and in this case we see that it is able to perform the following operations without error:

```
this.valueA = 1;              // OK
this.PublicMethod(terminal);  // OK
```

However, `AccessInheritance` cannot make accesses to the `valueB` data member and `PrivateMethod` method. Thus, the following code results in compiler errors:

```
this.valueB = 1;              // Error!
this.PrivateMethod(terminal); // Error!
```

Likewise, the accessibility errors occur when `AccessProgram` accesses private members of an `AccessInheritance` object.

```
using tcdIO;

class AccessInheritance : AccessDemo {
  public void TestAccess(Terminal terminal) {

    // Private members off limits!
    this.valueB = 1;                 // Error! Data inaccessible due
                                     // to its protection level
    this.PrivateMethod(terminal);    // Error! Method inaccessible due
                                     // to its protection level

    // Public members available!
    this.valueA = 1;                 // OK
    this.PublicMethod(terminal);     // OK
  }
}

class AccessProgram {
  static public void Main() {
    Terminal terminal = new Terminal();
    AccessDemo accessObject = new AccessDemo();

    // Accessing member methods from AccessProgram
    accessObject.PublicMethod(terminal);   // OK
    accessObject.PrivateMethod(terminal);  // Error!

    // Accessing data members from AccessProgram
    accessObject.valueA = accessObject.valueB + 1; // Error!
    accessObject.valueA = 1;                       // OK
  }
}
```

Program 11.13   Using `public` and `private` inherited members.

```
using tcdIO;

class AccessInheritance : AccessDemo {
  public void TestAccess(Terminal terminal) {

    // Private members off limits!
    base.valueB = 1;                    // Error! Data inaccessible due
                                        // to its protection level
    base.PrivateMethod(terminal);  // Error! Method inaccessible due
                                        // to its protection level

    // Public members available!
    base.valueA = 1;              // OK
    base.PublicMethod(terminal);  // OK
  }
}
```

Program 11.14   Accessing inherited members through base.

While it is clear that public members are being added to AccessInheritance via inheritance, it is not as obvious that the private members are included. Via inheritance public methods declared in AccessDemo are accessible in instances of AccessInheritance. We can call these methods directly as we did for PublicMethod in Program 11.13. The private members are included as well, but we cannot access them directly. Instead, we can deduce the presence of these members in the class from calls to the inherited PublicMethod method, which is dependent on private methods and fields. We can rely on the compiler to complain if PublicMethod made use of non-existent or inaccessible fields and methods. That these errors do not occur in Program 11.13 indicates that these calls are still accessible from AccessInheritance and AccessProgram.

Note that inherited members can be accessed using the base keyword as well as the this keyword. The Program 11.14 version of AccessInheritance has identical behaviour to the Program 11.13 version. Although base refers to the inherited class, it does not circumvent the access modifiers.

Introducing a New Access Modifier: protected

Another type of access semantics, called protected access, can be applied to members of a class. To specify protected access, use the protected keyword in place of the public or private keyword when declaring a member. For example, in Program 11.15 we have revised the implementation of AccessDemo to make the valueB field and the PrivateMethod method protected. As you might have guessed, protected access has similar semantics to the private access. As with private members, protected members cannot be accessed by unrelated classes. So the following code in Program 11.15 results in errors:

```
accessObject.PrivateMethod(terminal);               // Error!
accessObject.valueA = accessObject.valueB + 1; // Error!
```

The protected access modifier was not introduced until now because it is only of interest in the context of inheritance. Members that have protected accessibility can only be accessed from inside the scope of the class being defined, called the *containing class* or classes that have that class in their inheritance chain. Thus, any derived class that inherits a protected member

```
using tcdIO;

class AccessDemo {
  public    int valueA = 1;
  protected int valueB = 2;                               // changed access

  protected void PrivateMethod(Terminal terminal) { // changed access
    // Accessing member methods from AccessDemo
    this.PublicMethod(terminal);                    // OK
    terminal.WriteLine("Method called!");

    // Accessing data members from AccessDemo
    this.valueA = this.valueB + 1;                  // OK
  }

  public void PublicMethod(Terminal terminal) {
    // Accessing member methods from AccessDemo
    this.PrivateMethod(terminal);                   // OK

    // Accessing data members from AccessDemo
    this.valueA = this.valueB + 1;                  // OK
  }
}

class AccessProgram {
  static public void Main() {
    Terminal terminal = new Terminal();
    AccessDemo accessObject = new AccessDemo();

    // Accessing member methods from AccessProgram
    accessObject.PublicMethod(terminal);  // OK
    accessObject.PrivateMethod(terminal); // Error!

    // Accessing data members from AccessProgram
    accessObject.valueA = accessObject.valueB + 1; // Error!
    accessObject.valueA =  1;                       // OK
  }
}
```

Program 11.15   Program 11.12 revised to use the `protected` access modifier instead of `private`.

directly or indirectly can access that member. Classes that do not have the containing class in their inheritance chain cannot access the member at all.

To demonstrate protected access, let us turn to Program 11.16. Here we have created a class that takes advantage of the new implementation of `AccessDemo` from Program 11.15. The new class, `AccessInheritance`, inherits all the members of `AccessDemo`, which is consistent with our understanding of inheritance. Unlike previous versions of `AccessInheritance`, `valueB`, and `PrivateMethod` are accessible. Thus, calls such as

```
this.valueB = 1;
this.PrivateMethod(terminal);
```

```
using tcdIO;

class AccessInheritance : AccessDemo
{
  public void TestAccess(Terminal terminal) {
    // Protected members available!
    this.valueB = 1;               // OK
    this.PrivateMethod(terminal);  // OK

    // Public members available!
    this.valueA = 1;               // OK
    this.PublicMethod(terminal);   // OK
  }
}

class AccessProgram {
  static public void Main() {
    Terminal terminal = new Terminal();
    AccessDemo accessObject = new AccessDemo();

    // Accessing member methods from AccessProgram
    accessObject.PublicMethod(terminal);   // OK
    accessObject.PrivateMethod(terminal);  // Error!

    // Accessing data members from AccessProgram
    accessObject.valueA = accessObject.valueB + 1; // Error!
    accessObject.valueA =  1;                       // OK
  }
}
```

Program 11.16   Program 11.13 revised to use the `protected` access modifier instead of `private`.

no longer generate compile-time errors. There is still no way to bypass the accessibility instructions made when `valueB` and `PrivateMethod` were declared. Despite being directly accessible from `AccessInheritance`, the `AccessProgram` cannot access `valueB` or call `PrivateMethod` even if it is using an `AccessInheritance` object instead of an `AccessDemo` object.

Giving the derived class implementation details of its base class seems to violate encapsulation rules of object-oriented programming, but this knowledge is required to allow correct implementation of many is-a relationships. We said that fully encapsulated objects did not let any implementation details be accessed from outside the class. Fields that methods rely on were made private to prevent users of a class' objects from writing code that was dependent on their availability. By restricting access to these fields, we are free to revise the innards of an object without needing to revise the users of the object. Exposing details using the `protected` keyword would seem to violate our encapsulation. However, derived classes represent a special case. The assumption that a derived class is completely independent from the base class is inconsistent with the use of inheritance to simplify programming the derived class. For instance, the is-a relationship between the `InsuredEmployee` and `InsuranceClient` classes can be exploited with inheritance to simplify the coding of `InsuredEmployee`. However, the inheritance approach requires that `InsuredEmployee` access to the home and name fields of `InsuranceClient` to correctly generate a payslip.

```
class  InsuranceClient {

  protected string  name;    // [NEW:  access level is protected]
  protected Address home;    // [NEW:  access level is protected]

  ...

}

class  InsuredEmployee : InsuranceClient
{

  ...

  // [NEW:  name, home can be accessed directly!]
  public string Payslip(Date today) {
    return (this.name + "\n" + this.home + "\n"
          + this.Salary(today).ToString() + "\n")
  }

  ...

}
```

Figure 11.1 Simplification of Program 11.6 by revising access modifiers used in `InsuranceClient`.

Given our comments in the previous paragraph, we should look at re-implementing `InsuranceClient` and `InsuredEmployee` to exploit the `protected` access modifier. When we originally implemented `InsuredEmployee` in Program 11.6, we were lucky because public methods were available to access name and home. If the `BillingAddress` had added the name to the address, and if a method to get the name did not exist, then the `Payslip` method of the `InsuredEmployee` class might not have been so easy to create. Figure 11.1 shows a portion of the `InsuranceClient`, which is revised to expose commonly used members to derived classes. In the same figure, you will note that we have revised the implementation of the `Payslip` method in `InsuredEmployee` to take advantage of these revisions.

When inheritance does maintain full encapsulation, the resulting base and derived classes may not share an is-a relationship. Focusing on maintaining full encapsulation of the base class will lead to the use of inheritance for combining rather than extending behaviour. By *extending*, we mean that a clear is-a relationship exists between the base class and the derived class. Thus, the `InsuredEmployee` extends the `InsuranceClient`. Full encapsulation rules would frown on the code in Figure 11.11, where `InsuredEmployee` uses implementation details of `InsuranceClient`. In contrast, *combining* refers to the use of inheritance in situations where a clear is-a relationship does not exist. For instance, we could use inheritance to add web-browsing capabilities to the `InsuranceClient` class by deriving from a class that implements a web browser. Clearly, the `InsuranceClient` does not need to know any implementation details of the web browser, and full encapsulation is easy to maintain. However, their composition would not make much sense as `InsuranceClient` does not have an is-a relationship with a web browser!

Implications of Inheritance on Type

Inheritance is more than a quick way to simplify maintenance of class definitions. Inheritance has real implications for type. For instance, inheritance allows a class to implement another type. This section will look closely at the implications of this statement.

Substituting Derived Class Objects for Base Class Instances

The *type* assigned to a reference type variable describes the operations an object assigned to the variable must support. Any implementation of the reference type is fine so long as it supports these operations. As well as defining a type, a class defines an implementation for that type. So naturally an instance of the class that defines a type also implements the type defined by that class. Thus, it can be assigned to variables of that type. For example, instances of our `InsuranceClient` class can be assigned to a variable of type `InsuranceClient`, as we see in the code below:

```
InsuranceClient benny = new InsuranceClient( "Benny",
            InsuranceClient.MALE, bennyBorn, bennyHome );
```

The same holds for derived classes. They define a new type for which they provide an implementation, and instances of the derived class can be assigned to variables of the derived class' type. For instance, `InsuredEmployee` is a derived class, which we can instantiate and assign to a variable of that type:

```
InsuredEmployee betty = new InsuredEmployee( "Betty",
            InsuredEmployee.FEMALE, bettyBorn,
            bettyHome, bettyHired,
            InsuredEmployee.Technical );
```

What is less obvious is that a derived type also implements its base class type. Ergo, an instance of derived class can be assigned to a variable of its base class' type! Thus, it is perfectly legal to assign an instance of `InsuredEmployee` to a variable of type `InsuranceClient`, as we see here:

```
InsuranceClient someInsuranceClient =
    (InsuranceClient) betty;
```

The `InsuranceClient` type only guarantees that a fixed set of public, protected and private operations can be executed on the referenced object. It does not mean that the object referenced cannot support other operations. The assignment of an `InsuredEmployee` object to an `InsuranceClient` variable is legal because the inheritance mechanism has included all the members of the base class in the derived class. At the very least, all the operations available for an `InsuranceClient` object are available in an `InsuredEmployee` object. In fact, instances of a class can be used in place of instances of every class in its inheritance chain, since a class implements every type that it inherits from.

We can exploit the substitution properties of derived class objects to avoid the need to create methods with duplicate functionality as we did in Program 11.9. Recall that we initially implemented the is-a between `InsuranceClient` and `InsuredEmployee` by manually copying source from the `InsuranceClient` class to the `InsuredEmployee`. This copy-and-paste strategy generated unrelated classes. As a result, we had to create duplicate versions of `CreateInsuranceInvoice` for each class in the is-a relationship, as we did in Program 11.9. In contrast, inheritance creates new classes related to the class from

```
class DemoReuseProgram    {
  public static void Main() {
    Date bennyBorn = new Date(1975, 01, 01);
    Address bennyHome = new Address("Pearse Street", "Dublin",
                                    "Ireland", "Dublin 2");
    InsuranceClient benny = new InsuranceClient( "Benny",
                    InsuranceClient.MALE,bennyBorn, bennyHome );
    Date bettyBorn = new Date(1975, 01, 01);

    Address bettyHome = new Address("Townsend Street", "Dublin",
                                    "Ireland", "Dublin 2");
    Date bettyHired = new Date(2000, 01, 01);

    InsuredEmployee betty = new InsuredEmployee( "Betty",
                        InsuredEmployee.FEMALE, bettyBorn, bettyHome,
                        bettyHired, InsuredEmployee.Technical );
    Date today = new Date(2001, 10, 01);

    DemoReuseProgram.CreateInsuranceInvoice(benny, today );   // OK
    DemoReuseProgram.CreateInsuranceInvoice(betty, today );   // OK
  }

  static string CreateInsuranceInvoice(InsuranceClient purchaser,
                                       Date today)
  {
    string postalAddress = purchaser.BillingAddress().ToString();
    string coverageCost = purchaser.InsuranceRate(today).ToString() ;

    return (postalAddress + coverageCost);
  }
}
```

Program 11.17   Exploiting inheritance for code reuse.

which they derive. Not only can objects of these derived classes be assigned to variables of their base class type, but the derived class object can also be used in place of base class objects in method calls. Thus, the version of `CreateInsuranceInvoice` written for variables of type `InsuredEmployee` is unnecessary and can be removed. Calls to the method made with an `InsuredEmployee` object as a parameter will be executed by the version that takes an `InsuranceClient`. We can revise the code shown in Program 11.9 with a new version shown in Program 11.17.

Compile-time and Run-time Type

To describe the two classes involved in defining a variable's type and that of the object it references, we introduce the concepts of compile-time type and run-time type. It is confusing that a variable has a type that corresponds to a class, but that a different class can define the object that the variable refers to. Consequently, the terms compile-time type and run-time type exist to distinguish between the two types. The *compile-time type* of a variable does not change. It is fixed at compilation in the declaration of the variable. For example, we can declare a variable with a compile-time type of `InsuranceClient` in the following statement:

```
InsuranceClient jenny;
```

```
class TypeProgram
{
  static public void Main()
  {
    Date jennyBorn = new Date(1970, 01, 01);
    Address jennyHome = new Address("Nassau Street", "Dublin",
                                    "Ireland", "Dublin 2");
    Date jennyHired = new Date(1999, 01, 01);

    InsuranceClient jenny = new InsuredEmployee( "Jenny",
                                  InsuredEmployee.FEMALE , jennyBorn,
                                  jennyHome, jennyHired,
                                  InsuredEmployee.Technical );

    Date bennyBorn = new Date(1975, 01, 01);
    Address bennyHome = new Address("Pearse Street", "Dublin",
                                    "Ireland", "Dublin 2");
    InsuranceClient benny = new InsuranceClient( "Benny",
                                  InsuranceClient.MALE, bennyBorn,
                                  bennyHome );
  }
}
```

Program 11.18 Compile-time type versus run-time type.

In contrast, the *run-time type* is the class that implements the object to which a variable refers. Since a variable can be assigned a different object at any point, the run-time type can vary as the code executes. In Program 11.18, the compile-time type of benny and jenny is InsuranceClient, which is the type used in their declaration. However, benny and jenny have different run-time types. benny is assigned an instance of InsuranceClient, which becomes its run-time type. On the other hand, jenny is assigned an instance of InsuredEmployee, which becomes its run-time type.

The run-time type is of significance when we want to pass an object reference between variables of different type, because it tells us what compile-time types the referenced object supports. An object can support multiple compile-time types. For instance, objects of class InsuredEmployee implement both the InsuredEmployee and InsuranceClient types, while objects of class InsuranceClient only implement the InsuranceClient type. Objects that implement multiple types can be referred to by variables of any of the supported types. An object of type InsuredEmployee can be assigned to a variable of compile-time type InsuranceClient:

```
InsuranceClient jenny = new InsuredEmployee( "Jenny",
    InsuredEmployee.FEMALE, jennyBorn, jennyHome,
    jennyHired, InsuredEmployee.Technical );
```

or to a variable of compile-time type InsuredEmployee:

```
InsuredEmployee jenny = new InsuredEmployee( "Jenny",
    InsuredEmployee.FEMALE, jennyBorn, jennyHome,
    jennyHired, InsuredEmployee.Technical );
```

Knowing that objects can support multiple compile-time types, we need a way to overcome C# rules that prevent assignment between variables of different types. Normally, assigning one variable to another requires that they match in type. In Program 11.19, the assignment of an

```
class TypeProgram
{
  static public void Main()
  {
    Date jennyBorn = new Date(1970, 01, 01);
    Address jennyHome = new Address("Nassau Street", "Dublin",
                                    "Ireland", "Dublin 2");
    Date jennyHired = new Date(1999, 01, 01);

    InsuranceClient jenny = new InsuredEmployee( "Jenny",
                                  InsuredEmployee.FEMALE , jennyBorn,
                                  jennyHome, jennyHired,
                                  InsuredEmployee.Technical );

    InsuredEmployee employeeAA = jenny;     // Error!
  }
}
```

Program 11.19 Problems assigning between variables with different compile-time types.

`InsuranceClient` variable to an `InsuredEmployee` variable causes an error because the two variables differ in type, and C# is unable to implicitly convert the `InsuranceClient` variable `jenny` into the `InsuredEmployee` variable `employeeA`. However, we can use a conversion to temporarily convert the `jenny` `InsuranceClient` variable into an `InsuredEmployee` reference. The syntax of a conversion is to prefix the variable being converted with the desired type enclosed in round brackets. For instance, to convert the `jenny` variable to an `InsuredEmployee` reference we would write:

```
(InsuredEmployee) jenny
```

To assign this reference to the `employeeA` variable of type `InsuranceClient`, we would write:

```
InsuredEmployee employeeA = (InsuredEmployee) jenny;
```

When inheritance is used, C# automatically generates two conversions for the derived class. An implicit conversion is created to convert references to derived objects to references to base class objects. An *implicit conversion* does not require that the user write the conversion themselves. Instead, C# handles calling the conversion. As we said before, a derived class will always implement its base class type. If the source variable has the derived class as its compile-time type, then the object that is referenced will at least implement all the types supported by the derived class. A conversion to the base class type will always work, because the object will always support the base class type. Recognizing this fact, C# sees no need to be explicit about such conversions. For instance, in Program 11.20, the assignment of an `InsuredEmployee` variable to an `InsuranceClient` variable does not make use of the conversion operation. In particular, the assignment of `employeeA` to `jenny` does not cause any problems.

The second conversion generated by inheritance is used to change a base class object reference to a derived class object reference. The conversion has to be called explicitly, because it may fail. Specifically, there is no guarantee that the object being referenced actually implements the derived class' type. If the run-time type of the source variable is that of the derived class' type, the conversion will succeed. In Program 11.21, this situation occurs when the `jenny` variable is assigned to the `employeeA` variable.

```
class TypeProgram
{
  static public void Main()
    {
    Date jennyBorn = new Date(1970, 01, 01);
    Address jennyHome = new Address("Nassau Street", "Dublin",
                                    "Ireland", "Dublin 2");
    Date jennyHired = new Date(1999, 01, 01);

    InsuredEmployee employeeA = new InsuredEmployee( "Jenny",
                                   InsuredEmployee.FEMALE , jennyBorn,
                                   jennyHome, jennyHired,
                                   InsuredEmployee.Technical );

    InsuranceClient jenny = employeeA;      // OK
  }
}
```

Program 11.20   Implicit conversion handles assignment of derived type variable to variable of one of its inherited types.

Because jenny has a compile-time type of InsuranceClient and employeeA has a compile-time type of a derived class called InsuredEmployee, an *explicit conversion* must be used. jenny references an InsuredEmployee object so jenny's run-time type is InsuredEmployee. The InsuredEmployee class supports both the InsuredEmployee and the InsuranceClient type. So this object can be assigned to variables with the compile-time type InsuredEmployee, such as jenny or the compile-time type InsuredEmployee, such as employeeA. Accordingly, there is not a problem with the explicit conversion.

However, the same conversion fails if the run-time type of the source variable does not support the derived class' type. This is the case in Program 11.22 when we attempt to assign benny to employeeB. benny refers to an InsuranceClient object, so that is its run-time type. The InsuranceClient class does not implement the InsuredEmployee type, as it does not derive directly or indirectly from that class. The conversion operation deals with this problem by generating a run-time error that if not handled will terminate the program!

```
class TypeProgram {
  static public void Main()
    {
    Date jennyBorn = new Date(1970, 01, 01);
    Address jennyHome = new Address("Nassau Street", "Dublin",
                                    "Ireland", "Dublin 2");
    Date jennyHired = new Date(1999, 01, 01);

    InsuranceClient jenny = new InsuredEmployee( "Jenny",
                               InsuredEmployee.FEMALE , jennyBorn,
                               jennyHome, jennyHired,
                               InsuredEmployee.Technical );

    InsuredEmployee employeeA = (InsuredEmployee)jenny;
  }
}
```

Program 11.21   Successful conversion between different compile-time types.

```
class TypeProgram
{
   static public void Main()
   {
      Date bennyBorn = new Date(1975, 01, 01);
      Address bennyHome = new Address("Pearse Street", "Dublin",
         "Ireland", "Dublin 2");

      InsuranceClient benny = new InsuranceClient( "Benny",
         InsuranceClient.MALE,
         bennyBorn, bennyHome );

      // The following compiles, but generates a runtime error!
      InsuredEmployee employeeB = (InsuredEmployee)benny;
   }
}
```

Program 11.22   Failed conversion between different compile-time types.

To know what compile-time types a variable can be converted to, the variable's run-time type must be determined. One approach is to use user-defined methods. For instance, we might use an ad hoc scheme whereby the run-time type of an object is recorded in a protected string field that is added to the base class. In the case of the InsuranceClient, a protected clientType string along with a read-only public property called ClientType would suffice:

```
protected string clientType;
public string ClientType { get { return clientType; } }
```

Only the constructor knows the type of the object being instantiated, so we have to update the constructors for InsuranceClient and InsuredEmployee to set the clientType to a value that corresponds to the class that defines the object. The updated versions are shown in Figure 11.2. Although clientType is set to InsuranceClient when

```
public  InsuranceClient(string name, int gender, Date birthDay, Address home)
{
    this.clientType = "InsuranceClient";
    This.name      = name;
    this.gender    = gender;
    this.birthDay  = birthDay;
    this.home      = home;
}


public InsuredEmployee(string name, int gender, Date birthDay,
                       Address home, Date startDate, int training )
                  : base( name, gender, birthDay, home)
{
    this.clientType = "InsuredEmployee";
    this.startDate = startDate;
    this.training = training;
}
```

Figure 11.2   Contructors for InsuranceClient and InsuredEmployee updated to record run-time type.

InsuredEmployee calls base, the variable is changed to "InsuredEmployee" in the body of the InsuredEmployee constructor.

With the property and updated constructors in place, inspecting the type of an object is a matter of checking the value of the ClientType property. In Program 11.23, we use the property to determine if benny and jenny can be assigned to an InsuredEmployee variable. This will avoid any run-time errors. The output is shown in Figure 11.3

C# offers the built-in operators is and as to determine if a conversion is possible. The is operator examines the run-time type of a variable to see if it supports a specific type. If the type is supported, true is returned, otherwise false is returned. The syntax for the

```csharp
using tcdIO;

class TypeTestingProgram
{
    static public void Main()
    {
        Terminal terminal = new Terminal();

        Date jennyBorn = new Date(1970, 01, 01);
        Address jennyHome = new Address("Nassau Street","Dublin",
                                        "Ireland", "Dublin 2");
        Date jennyHired = new Date(1999, 01, 01);

        InsuranceClient jenny = new InsuredEmployee( "Jenny",
                                        InsuredEmployee.FEMALE, jennyBorn,
                                        jennyHome, jennyHired,
                                        InsuredEmployee.Technical );

        Date bennyBorn = new Date(1975, 01, 01);
        Address bennyHome = new Address("Pearse Street", "Dublin",
                                        "Ireland", "Dublin 2");

        InsuranceClient benny = new InsuranceClient( "Benny",
                                        InsuranceClient.MALE,
                                        bennyBorn, bennyHome );

        InsuredEmployee employee;
        if (jenny.ClientType == "InsuredEmployee")
        {
            employee = (InsuredEmployee) jenny;
            terminal.WriteLine("jenny's run-time type can be assigned " +
                        "to an InsuredEmployee variable");
        }
        else
        {
            terminal.WriteLine("jenny's run-time type does not support " +
                        "the InsuredEmployee type");
        }

        if (benny.ClientType == "InsuredEmployee")
        {
            employee = (InsuredEmployee) benny;
            terminal.WriteLine("benny's run-time type can be assigned " +
                        "to an InsuredEmployee variable.");
```

```
      }
      else
      {
         terminal.WriteLine("benny's run-time type does not " +
                            "support the InsuredEmployee type");
      }
   }
}
```

Program 11.23 Using the ad hoc scheme for determining run-time type.

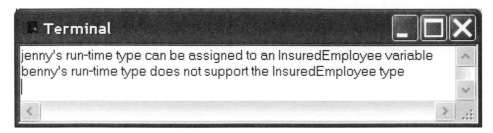

Figure 11.3 Output from Program 11.23.

operation is:

```
<variable name> is <type>
```

For example, we could ask the benny variable of Program 11.23 if it supports the InsuredEmployee type with the code in Figure 11.4.

As an alternative to inspecting a variable's run-time type, the as operator allows a conversion to be made that is guaranteed not to generate an error. Should the run-time type of a variable not support the conversion, a null reference will be assigned to the target variable. The syntax for the operator is:

```
<variable name> as <desired type>
```

Rather than writing (InsuredEmployee) jenny as we did in Figure 11.5, we could instead write "jenny as InsuredEmployee", with no change in functionality. There is a difference if we write "benny as InsuredEmployee" rather than "(Insured-Employee) benny". Normally, the conversion would fail and generate a run-time error. However, as will return a null rather than generate a run-time error.

```
InsuredEmployee employee;
if (benny is InsuredEmployee)
{
      employee = (InsuredEmployee) benny;
      terminal.WriteLine("benny's run-time type can be assigned to an"  +
                         " InsuredEmployee variable.");
}
else
{
      terminal.WriteLine("benny's run-time type does not support the" +
                         " InsuredEmployee type.");
}
```

Figure 11.4 Using the is operator for determining run-time type.

```
InsuredEmployee employee;
employee = benny as InsuredEmployee;
if (benny != null)
{
     terminal.WriteLine("benny's run-time type can be assigned to an"  +
                     " InsuredEmployee variable.");
}
else
{
     terminal.WriteLine("benny's run-time type does not support the" +
                     " InsuredEmployee type.");
}
```

Figure 11.5   Using the `as` operator for determining run-time type.

The behaviour of `is` and `as` is so similar that a conversion implemented using `as` can always be implemented with a conversion implemented with `is`. For example, we could revise the `is` operator example in Figure 11.4 with the version in Figure 11.5

Changing Existing Methods in a Derived Class

A powerful tool in object-oriented programming is the ability to vary how a method behaves given the context in which it is called. One example of this is overloading a method name. That is, in the same class we define methods with the same name, but different parameters. When the method is called, the version to execute is selected by examining the types and number of parameters supplied.

Inheritance in C# gives us two powerful tools for changing the behaviour of methods: overloading and overriding. *Overloading* allows us to re-declare an existing method in a derived class. Implementations of the existing and new declarations are available in derived class objects, but the one used in a method call depends on the referencing variable. Effectively, the behaviour of the method changes depending on the compile-time type of the referencing variable.

In contrast, *overriding* allows us to create new implementations of existing methods without re-declaring the method. A method is overridden when the implementation of an inherited method is revised. Unlike overloading, we are modifying the implementation of an existing method, rather than introducing a new one. With overriding, the method's implementation has changed for all the types that the derived class implements. This includes the type declared by the derived class and all the types in the derived class' inheritance chain. So, for objects of this derived class, the same implementation will be used in calls to that method regardless of the compile-time type of a variable that references the object. For this reason, we say that the method's implementation is decided by the variable's run-time type.

In the next couple of sections, we will go over the concepts of overloading and overriding in more detail. The semantics and syntax will be explained with the help of some examples, and we will use each feature when we make revisions to the classes that model our insurance clients.

Overloading

In general, overloading implies that the same method name is being used to define different methods. We have seen overloading before. In Program 11.8, we generated insurance premium invoices using `CreateInsuranceInvoice`. However, we found that another version of `CreateInsuranceInvoice` was required to generate invoices for instances of the `InsuredEmployee` class. In Program 11.9, we ended up with two methods with identical names, distinguished by a slight variation in calling parameters. The two methods were side by side in the same class, but knowing their differences in calling parameters allowed one method or the other to be used.

Previously, it was impossible to define two methods in the same class with the same *signature*. The *signature* of a method includes all the details required to call the method. Beyond the method name, the signature includes the number and type of parameters and the return type of the method. It does not include the accessibility modifiers. Thus, our two versions of `CreateInsuranceInvoice`, now pictured in Figure 11.6, shared the same name, but differed in signature, as their parameter lists had different types.

Inheritance allows us to take overloading a step further as it allows the definition of multiple methods with identical signatures. Restrictions on reusing a signature do not apply when a new method is declared with the same signature as an inherited method. The fact that a new method is being declared is reflected in the syntax used to declare an overloading method. To overload a method inherited from an existing class, the keyword new must be used. new is placed between the accessibility modifier and the method's return type specification. For example, if the `InsuredEmployee` class overloaded the `CurrentAge` method, the declaration would look like this:

```
public new int CurrentAge(Date today)
```

In fact, we can imagine that the `InsuredEmployee` might actually want to do this in

```
class DemoReuse {

    ...

  static string CreateInsuranceInvoice(InsuranceClient purchaser, Date today)
  {
    string postalAddress = purchaser.BillingAddress().ToString();

    string coverageCost = purchaser.InsuranceRate(today).ToString() ;

    return (postalAddress + coverageCost);
  }

  static string CreateInsuranceInvoice(InsuredEmployee purchaser, Date today)
  {
    string postalAddress = purchaser.BillingAddress().ToString();

    string coverageCost = purchaser.InsuranceRate(today).ToString() ;

    return (postalAddress + coverageCost);
  }
```

Figure 11.6   Overloaded versions of `CreateInsuranceInvoice`.

```
      public new int CurrentAge(Date today)
      {
            return startDate.YearsDifference(today);
      }
```

Figure 11.7 Overloaded version of CurrentAge to return employee seniority.

order to implement a method that returned the employee's seniority. An updated version of
InsuredEmployee would include the method in Figure 11.7.

Overloading methods in a derived class, such as InsuredEmployee, does not change
the implementation of the types inherited from the base class. Consequently, the new method
declaration only applies in cases when the new type is being used. Thus, a call to the method
using a variable whose compile-time type is that of the base class results in the execution of the
inherited method declaration. To access the new declaration, the new type must be accessed. To
do so, a variable must be used whose compile-time type is that of the derived class. Assuming
the method in Figure 11.7 is added to the InsuredEmployee class, we can expect the results
of calling CurrentAge on an InsuredEmployee object to vary depending on whether
we reference it with an InsuranceClient variable or an InsuredEmployee variable.

```
using tcdIO;

class InsuredEmployee : InsuranceClient
{
   private Date startDate;
   private int training;
   public const int Technical = 1, Other = 2;  // Training levels

   public InsuredEmployee(string name, int gender, Date birthDay,
      Address home, Date startDate, int training )
      : base( name, gender, birthDay, home)
   {
      this.startDate = startDate;
      this.training = training;
   }

   public string Payslip(Date today)
   {
      return (this.Name()+ "\n"+this.BillingAddress()+ "\n"
         + this.Salary(today).ToString() +"\n");
   }

   public double Salary(Date today)
   {
      double bonus = 1, baseSalary = 10000;

      if ( startDate.YearsDifference(today) > 1 )
         bonus *= 1.5;

      if ( training == InsuredEmployee.Technical )
         bonus *= 2.0;

      return baseSalary * bonus;
   }
```

```
    public new int CurrentAge(Date today)
    {
        return startDate.YearsDifference(today);
    }
}

class OverloadingTestProgram
{
    static void Main()
    {
        Terminal terminal = new Terminal();

        // Insurance purchaser profile
        Date jennyBorn = new Date(1970, 01, 01);
        Address jennyHome = new Address("Nassau Street","Dublin",
                "Ireland", "Dublin 2");
        Date jennyHired = new Date(1999, 01, 01);
        InsuranceClient client = new InsuredEmployee( "Jenny",
                                    InsuredEmployee.FEMALE , jennyBorn,
                                    jennyHome, jennyHired,
                                    InsuredEmployee.Technical );
        InsuredEmployee employee = (InsuredEmployee)client;

        // Age as an InsuranceClient
        Date today = new Date(2001, 10, 01);
        terminal.WriteLine("Jenny as a client is "
                        + client.CurrentAge(today)
                                    + " years old.");
        // Age as an InsuredEmployee
        terminal.WriteLine("Jenny as an employee is "
                                    + employee.CurrentAge(today)
                                    + " years old.");
    }
}
```

Program 11.24   Accessing overloaded versions of `CurrentAge` in an `InsuredEmployee` object.

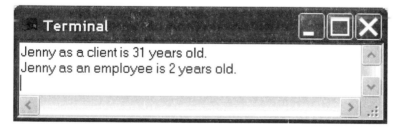

Figure 11.8   Output of Program 11.24.

Program 11.24 demonstrates overloading by using `CurrentAge` with both types of variable. The result is shown in Figure 11.8.

It is important to note that both methods are included in objects of the derived class, but only one is unhidden at any time. Without including both methods, the same object would find it impossible to vary the method being accessed according to the referencing variable's compile-time type. Even though two methods have the same signature, only one

```
using tcdIO;

class A {
  public string DefiningClass() { return "declared in class A"; }
}

class B:A { }

class C:B {
  public new string DefiningClass() { return "declared in class C"; }
}

class D:C { }

class OverloadingTest {
  public static void Main()
    {
       Terminal terminal = new Terminal();

    D d = new D();
    A a = d;
    B b = d;
    C c = d;

    terminal.WriteLine("Variable a uses DefiningClass: "
                               + a.DefiningClass());
    terminal.WriteLine("Variable b uses DefiningClass: "
                               + b.DefiningClass());
    terminal.WriteLine("Variable c uses DefiningClass: "
                               + c.DefiningClass());
    terminal.WriteLine("Variable d uses DefiningClass: "
                               + d.DefiningClass());
  }
}
```

Program 11.25   Simple demonstration of declaring and using overloaded methods.

version of these methods will be available to a given compile-time type. Thus, we say that the inaccessible methods are *hidden*. With a series of inheritance operations, a class may even have several methods that share the same signature. Again, all but one will be hidden for a given compile-time type.

The rules for *hiding* are that overloaded methods hide the inherited methods only for the new derived type and all its descendants. The new method is hidden when the derived object is referenced by a variable of the base class type or any of the other classes in the inheritance chain. Program 11.25 provides an excellent example of the hiding that goes on when methods are overloaded and inherited. In this example, we focus on an object of class D, which has the classes A, B, and C in its *inheritance chain*. Instances of class D inherit two declarations of DefiningClass, one from class A and another from class C. However, only one will be unhidden at any given time. As a newly declared method will hide previous declarations for the derived type and the descendants of the derived type, the DefiningClass method declared in class C will be used when an instance of class D is referenced by a variable of compile-time type C or D. In the case of compile-time types A and B, the existing declaration in class A will be accessed. The execution of the program confirms our expectations, and

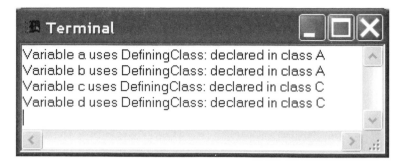

Figure 11.9   Output from executing Program 11.25.

Figure 11.9 displays the program's results.

Overriding

Overloading does not modify existing methods. Although inherited methods may be hidden, depending on the compile-time type of the referencing variable, their behaviour is left unchanged. Code written to exploit base class methods is not affected by overloading, which is a major advantage. An example of such code is the InsuranceRate method declared in the InsuranceClient class of Program 11.7 and pictured in Figure 11.10. The method makes use of CurrentAge to calculate the cost of insurance, and it expects CurrentAge to return the age of the client. If the method is executed on an InsuredEmployee object there will be two versions of CurrentAge available. One will calculate the worker's seniority and another will calculate the number of years the worker has been alive. However, InsuranceRate is declared in the InsuranceClient class, where the compile-time type of the this variable is InsuranceClient. Thus, calls to CurrentAge made in the InsuranceClient class will always access the method declared in the InsuranceClient class. Thus, the additive property of overloading guarantees that the new version of CurrentAge declared in InsuredEmployee will not interfere with InsuranceRate.

Overloading cannot solve all problems where a method needs to behave differently for a new class. Some problems require the same method to have different behaviour depending on the object being referenced, rather than on the compile-time type of the referencing variable. Imagine that the customer's contact phone number has to be added to the insurance invoice we generated with CreateInsuranceInvoice in Program 11.9. In this case, we would add functionality to the InsuranceClient to return the client's phone number. The method

```
public double InsuranceRate(Date today)
{
      double multiplier = 1, basePremium = 100;

      if ( InsuranceClient.MALE == gender )  multiplier *= 2;
      if ( this.CurrentAge(today) < 25)  multiplier *= 2;

      this.totalPremiums += (multiplier * basePremium);
      return (multiplier * basePremium);
}
```

Figure 11.10   InsuranceRate method revisited.

```
static string CreateInsuranceInvoice(InsuranceClient purchaser, Date today)
{
    string postalAddress = purchaser.BillingAddress().ToString();
    string coverageCost = purchaser.InsuranceRate(today).ToString() ;
    string contactNumber = purchaser.DaytimePhoneNumber().ToString() ;

    return (postalAddress + coverageCost);
}
```

Figure 11.11 Supplying more contact details in CreateInsuranceInvoice.

might be written as follows:

```
public string DaytimePhoneNumber() { return this.homeNumber; }
```

Presumably the field homeNumber would be added to the InsuranceClient, and its value set in the InsuranceClient constructor. CreateInsuranceInvoice would be updated to make use of this information as shown in Figure 11.11. Because InsuredEmployee inherits from InsuranceClient, it would inherit the same DaytimePhoneNumber method. However, an InsuredEmployee is more likely to be at work during the day than at home. In this case, DaytimePhoneNumber should be written as follows:

```
public string DaytimePhoneNumber() { return this.workNumber; }
```

Unlike homeNumber, workNumber would be a field declared in the Insured-Employee class and not in InsuranceClient. After overloading, this method gives the InsuredEmployee class two versions of DaytimePhoneNumber. One created by the InsuranceClient class and the other created by the InsuredEmployee class itself. However, the new version defined in InsuredEmployee is hidden when instances of InsuredEmployee are referred to by variables of type InsuranceClient. Thus, CreateInsuranceInvoice supplies the incorrect DaytimePhoneNumber for InsuredEmployee objects, because it references them with a variable of type InsuranceClient.

Overriding offers an alternative to overloading that allows us to properly implement DaytimePhoneNumber. The override mechanism revises the implementation of an inherited method for objects of the derived class. By overriding a method rather than overloading it, the method's implementation is tied to the class of the object rather than the type of the variable referencing the object. Based on our definition of run-time and compile-time types, overriding ties the method's implementation to the run-time type, whereas overloading ties the implementation to the compile-time type of the referencing variable. So, regardless of the type of the variable referencing instances of the derived class, the new implementation of the method will be accessed. Of course, this approach is not without difficulties. Because a variable's run-time type is likely to change during the execution of a program, it is hard to know the exact behaviour of a method if it can be overridden. To make the programmer aware of possible changes in behaviour, base class methods must explicitly permit overriding when they are declared. This is achieved by declaring the method with the virtual keyword after the access modifier, but before the return type. To allow our initial definition of DaytimePhoneNumber to be overridden, we would have to declare it in the InsuranceClient class it as follows:

```
public virtual string DaytimePhoneNumber() {
    return
    this.homeNumber; }
```

Once a method is declared as `virtual` it can be overridden in derived classes using the override keyword. To revise the implementation of DaytimePhoneNumber in the InsuredEmployee class, we would use the following declaration:

```
public override string DaytimePhoneNumber() {
   return
   this.workNumber; }
```

Program 11.26 uses updated versions of InsuredEmployee and InsuranceClient to demonstrate that when implemented with overriding, the DaytimePhoneNumber method

```
using tcdIO;

class InsuranceClient
{
   private string  name;
   public      const int  MALE = 1, FEMALE = 2; // Constants for gender
   private     int     gender;
   private     Date    birthDay;
   private     Address home;
   private     double  totalPremiums = 0;
   protected string homeNumber;

   public  InsuranceClient(string name, int gender, Date birthDay,
                                    Address home, string homeNumber)
   {
      this.name    = name;
      this.gender  = gender;
      this.birthDay = birthDay;
      this.home    = home;
      this.homeNumber = homeNumber;
   }

   public int CurrentAge(Date today) { return
            birthDay.YearsDifference(today); }
   public void Relocate(Address newHome) { this.home = newHome; }
   public Address BillingAddress() { return home; }
   public string Name() {return name;}
   public double TotalPremiums() { return totalPremiums; }

   public double InsuranceRate(Date today)
   {
      double multiplier = 1, basePremium = 100;


      if ( InsuranceClient.MALE == gender )  multiplier *= 2;
      if ( this.CurrentAge(today) < 25)  multiplier *= 2;

      this.totalPremiums += (multiplier * basePremium);
      return (multiplier * basePremium);
   }

   public virtual string DaytimePhoneNumber()
   {
      return this.homeNumber;
   }
}
```

```
class InsuredEmployee : InsuranceClient
{
    private Date startDate;
    private int training;
    private string workNumber;

    public const int Technical = 1, Other = 2;   // Training levels

    public InsuredEmployee(string name, int gender, Date birthDay,
                           Address home, Date startDate, int training,
                           string homeNumber, string workNumber)
                  : base( name, gender, birthDay, home, homeNumber)
    {
        this.startDate = startDate;
        this.training = training;
        this.workNumber = workNumber;
    }

    public string Payslip(Date today)
    {
        return (this.Name()+ "\n"+this.BillingAddress()+ "\n"
            + this.Salary(today).ToString() +"\n");
    }

    public double Salary(Date today)
    {
        double bonus = 1, baseSalary = 10000;

        if ( startDate.YearsDifference(today) > 1 )
            bonus *= 1.5;

        if ( training == InsuredEmployee.Technical )
            bonus *= 2.0;

        return baseSalary * bonus;
    }

    public new int CurrentAge(Date today)
    {
        return startDate.YearsDifference(today);
    }

  public override string DaytimePhoneNumber()
    {
        return this.workNumber;
    }
}

class Test {
  static void Main() {
      Terminal terminal = new Terminal();
    Date jennyBorn = new Date(1970, 01, 01);
    Address jennyHome = new Address("Nassau Street","Dublin",
                "Ireland", "Dublin 2");
    Date jennyHired = new Date(1999, 01, 01);
    string jennyPhone = "555-4321";
    string jennyWork  = "555-1113";
```

```
        InsuranceClient client = new InsuredEmployee( "Jenny",
                                    InsuredEmployee.FEMALE ,
                                    jennyBorn, jennyHome, jennyHired,
                                    InsuredEmployee.Technical,
                                jennyPhone, jennyWork );
        InsuredEmployee employee = (InsuredEmployee)client;

        // Contact number as an InsuranceClient
        Date today = new Date(2001, 10, 01);
        terminal.WriteLine("Jenny as a client can be reached at "
                            + client.DaytimePhoneNumber() );

        // Contact number as an InsuredEmployee
        terminal.WriteLine("Jenny as an employee can be reached at "
                            + employee.DaytimePhoneNumber() );
    }
}
```

Program 11.26   Demonstrating the result of overriding `DaytimePhoneNumber`.

will always report the correct value for an `InsuredEmployee` object regardless of the compile-time type of the variable used to reference it. The output from the program is shown in Figure 11.12.

Figure 11.12   Execution of Program 11.26.

Although we used override on `DaytimePhoneNumber` once, it is possible to override a method multiple times. In Program 11.27 the method `DefiningClass` is overridden multiple times. This program demonstrates the result of calling `DefiningClass` when an object of each of the classes is referenced by a variable of compile-time type A. The output of the program is shown in Figure 11.13.

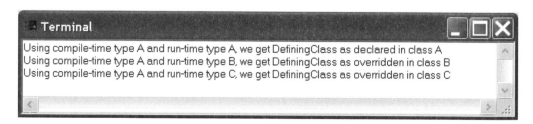

Figure 11.13   Execution of Program 11.27.

```
using tcdIO;

class A
{
    public virtual string DefiningClass() {
        return "DefiningClass as declared in class A"; }
}
class B:A
{
    public override string DefiningClass() {
        return "DefiningClass as overridden in class B"; }
}
class C:B
{
    public override string DefiningClass() {
        return "DefiningClass as overridden in class C"; }
}

class OverloadingTest
{
    public static void Main()
    {
        Terminal terminal = new Terminal();
        A a1 = new A();
        A a2 = new B();
        A a3 = new C();

        terminal.WriteLine("Using compile-time type A "
                            + "and run-time type A, we get "
                            + a1.DefiningClass());
        terminal.WriteLine("Using compile-time type A "
                            + "and run-time type B, we get "
                            + a2.DefiningClass());
        terminal.WriteLine("Using compile-time type A "
                            + "and run-time type C, we get "
                            + a3.DefiningClass());
    }
}
```

Program 11.27   Overriding a method multiple times.

Interfaces

Using classes to define types has drawbacks when the time comes to completely re-implement the type. As well as specifying the type, a class will define an implementation for the type. As we have seen, redefining the implementation of a class-defined type involves inheriting from the class that defined the type, and then overriding the type's methods. Note that overloading is not sufficient because it does not change the implementation of the inherited class' methods. Using inheritance and overriding has a few drawbacks. The type's methods have to be written with the virtual keyword so that they can be overloaded. Assuming the derived class is going to completely re-implement the inherited type, the members that it inherits from the base class become junk because they go unused. Finally, a derived class implements every type in its inheritance chain. Thus, implementing multiple types in the same class requires several inheritance operations to get all the desired types in the inheritance chain. If a type

```
interface PotentialDriver
{
   bool LegalTo-
Drive (Date today);
   bool HasLicense { get; set; }
}
```

Program 11.28 `PotentialDriver` interface.

is going to be completely re-implemented, the existing implementation only hinders the new implementation.

Interfaces offer a way to define a type without specifying its implementation. An *interface* only specifies a type's public operations. Thus, private and protected members are not allowed. To guarantee that no implementation details are included in the type, fields are excluded from interfaces. As an alternative, properties can be included in interfaces. Methods can be added, because their signature does not give away any implementation details. With these points in mind, let's look at an example interface specified in Program 11.28. This interface defines a type called `PotentialDriver`, with a method `LegalToDrive` to determine if the implementing object is allowed to drive. The interface also has a property `HasLicense` that indicates whether the implementing object has a driver's license. Incidentally, the motivation for defining the type as an interface is that the criteria for driving eligibility varies widely from country to country so that any default implementation has a high probability of being incorrect.

Although there seems to be similarity between the syntax used to define a class and that used to define an interface, the two are quite different. Interfaces use the keyword `interface` in place of `class`. By default, all the members of an interface are public. In fact, it is an error to apply an access modifier to the members of an interface. In order to declare methods without an implementation, a semicolon is placed after the method declaration rather than curly brackets. The same approach is used for the `get` and `set` methods of any properties included in the interface. As with properties defined in a class, interface properties need not include both a `set` and a `get`.

The syntax to implement an interface is similar to that used to create a derived class. A class selects an interface for implementation using the same syntax used to select a base class. The interface name is placed beside the class name with a separating comma in between. For the `InsuranceClient` class to implement the `PotentialDriver` interface we would write:

```
class InsuranceClient: PotentialDriver {
   /* body of class here */
}
```

With inheritance only one base class can be selected. However, a class can implement multiple interfaces. Additional interfaces are named after the first in a comma-separated list. Selection of interfaces does not prevent the class from using inheritance. However, the base class must appear first in the list of types that the class implements. If `InsuredEmployee` implemented the `PotentialDriver` type, the class would be defined as follows:

```
class InsuredEmployee: InsuranceClient, PotentialDriver {
   /* body of class here */
}
```

Remember that the members of an interface have to be implemented as public members. Otherwise they will not match the requirements of the interface. A complete version of the class

InsuredEmployee that implements PotentialDriver is pictured in Program 11.29. For this version of InsuredEmployee, the birthday field of InsuranceClient has to be changed from private to protected to allow InsuredEmployee to calculate the age properly.

```
class InsuredEmployee : InsuranceClient, PotentialDriver
{
    private Date startDate;
    private int training;
    private string workNumber;

    public const int Technical = 1, Other = 2;  // Training levels

    public InsuredEmployee(string name, int gender, Date birthDay,
        Address home, Date startDate, int training,
        string homeNumber, string workNumber)
        : base( name, gender, birthDay, home, homeNumber)
    {
        this.startDate = startDate;
        this.training = training;
        this.workNumber = workNumber;
    }

    public string Payslip(Date today)
    {
        return (this.Name()+ "\n"+this.BillingAddress()+ "\n"
            + this.Salary(today).ToString() +"\n");
    }

    public double Salary(Date today)
    {
        double bonus = 1, baseSalary = 10000;

        if ( startDate.YearsDifference(today) > 1 )
            bonus *= 1.5;

        if ( training == InsuredEmployee.Technical )
            bonus *= 2.0;

        return baseSalary * bonus;
    }

public new int CurrentAge(Date today)
    {
        return startDate.YearsDifference(today);
    }

    public override string DaytimePhoneNumber()
    {
        return this.workNumber;
    }

    // Potential Driver implementation
```

```
    public bool LegalToDrive(Date today)
    {
        if (birthDay.YearsDifference(today) > 18 && this.HasLicense)
        {
            return true;
        }
        return false;
    }

    bool hasLicense = true;
    public bool HasLicense
    {
        get { return hasLicense; }
        set { hasLicense = value; }
    }
}
```

Program 11.29   Version of `InsuredEmployee` that implements the `PotentialDriver` type.

```
using tcdIO;

class InterfaceImplementationProgram
{
    static void Main()
    {
        Terminal terminal = new Terminal();

        // Insurance purchaser profile
        Date jennyBorn = new Date(1970, 01, 01);
        Address jennyHome = new Address("Nassau Street", "Dublin",
                                                "Ireland", "Dublin 2");
        string jennyPhone = "555-4321";
        string jennyWork  = "555-1113";
        Date jennyHired = new Date(1999, 01, 01);
        InsuredEmployee employee = new InsuredEmployee("Jenny",
                                    InsuredEmployee.FEMALE, jennyBorn,
                                    jennyHome, jennyHired,
                                    InsuredEmployee.Technical,
                                        jennyPhone, jennyWork );
        // Current date
        Date today = new Date(2001, 10, 01);

        // InsuredEmployee implements the PotentialDriver type
        PotentialDriver person = (PotentialDriver)employee;
        person.HasLicense = true;
        terminal.WriteLine("With a license, can Jenny drive? "
                                    + person.LegalToDrive(today) );
    }
}
```

Program 11.30   Using a variable with the compile-time type `PotentialDriver`.

Figure 11.14   Execution of Program 11.30.

Types defined by an interface are like any other type. Thus, we can create variables whose compile-time type is that of the interface. However, we cannot instantiate instances of an interface. Interfaces do not have implementations. Thus, they do not have the constructor necessary for instantiation. As an alternative, interface-type variables can reference objects that implement the type defined by the interface. In Program 11.30, the `person` variable with a compile-time type of `PotentialDriver` is assigned a reference to an `InsuredEmployee` object. The result of the program is shown in Figure 11.14.

Note that the methods defined to support `PotentialDriver` are also part of the `InsuredEmployee` type. So, we can call them with a variable of compile-time type `InsuredEmployee`. In Program 11.31, we revise Program 11.30 to demonstrate this concept. As a result, we get the information output in Figure 11.15.

Structs, Inheritance and Boxing

C# does not allow the use of inheritance with structs, however structs can implement interfaces. The syntax used to implement interfaces in structs is the same as that used with class. However, the compiler will block any attempt to derive a class with a struct. To demonstrate the implementation of an interface, the `DriversLicense` struct in Program 11.32 implements the `PotentialDriver` interface of Program 11.28.

Recall that C# models value type and reference type variables quite differently. Reference type variables hold references to objects, while value type variables hold data. This is best understood by looking at what is done when one variable is assigned to another. With reference type variables, assignment copies the object reference contained in the right-hand side variable to the left-hand side variable. In the following assignment, the reference to a string is copied from the `myName` to the `myFullName` variable. After the code is executed, both variables refer to the same string object:

```
String myName = "John Doe";
String myFullName = my Name;
```

With value type variables, assignment copies the value stored in the right-hand side variable to the left-hand side variable. For example, in the following assignment an approximation for `PI` is copied from one `double` to another. After the code executes, there will be two copies of the value, with one stored in `PI` and the other stored in `PI_Again`

```
Double PI = 3.1415;
Double PI_Again = PI;
```

A problem could occur in this model when value type variables are assigned to reference type variables or vice versa. Our `DriversLicense` struct defines a value type, so a

```
using tcdIO;

class InterfaceImplementationProgram
{
    static void Main()
    {
        Terminal terminal = new Terminal();

        // Insurance purchaser profile
        Date jennyBorn = new Date(1970, 01, 01);
        Address jennyHome = new Address("Nassau Street", "Dublin",
            "Ireland", "Dublin 2");
        string jennyPhone = "555-4321";
        string jennyWork  = "555-1113";
        Date jennyHired = new Date(1999, 01, 01);
        InsuredEmployee employee = new InsuredEmployee("Jenny",
            InsuredEmployee.FEMALE, jennyBorn,
            jennyHome, jennyHired,
            InsuredEmployee.Technical,
            jennyPhone, jennyWork );
        // Current date
        Date today = new Date(2001, 10, 01);

        // InsuredEmployee implements the PotentialDriver type
        PotentialDriver person = (PotentialDriver)employee;
        person.HasLicense = true;
        terminal.WriteLine("With a license, can Jenny drive? "
            + person.LegalToDrive(today) );

        // Interface members are part of the InsuredEmployee type
        employee.HasLicense = false;
        terminal.WriteLine("Without a license, can Jenny drive? "
            + employee.LegalToDrive(today));

    }
}
```

Program 11.31   Using interface methods and properties with an `InsuredEmployee` reference.

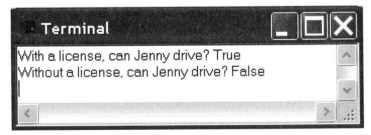

Figure 11.15   Execution of Program 11.31.

```
struct DriversLicense : PotentialDriver
{
    string name;
    Date birthday;

    public DriversLicense(string name, Date birthday)
    {
        this.name = name;
        this.birthday = birthday;
    }

    public string Name
    {
        get { return name; }
    }

    // Potential driver
    public bool LegalToDrive (Date today)
    {
        return true;
    }

    public bool HasLicense
    {
        // If they have a license, they will allows be
        // a potential driver!
        get { return true; }
        set   {}
    }
}
```

Program 11.32   Implementing the `PotentialDriver` interface with a struct.

`DriversLicense` variable contains the fields defined in the struct rather than referring to an object that contains the fields. However, `DriversLicense` also defines an implementation of `PotentialDriver`. The difficulty is that interface variables are reference type variables. This allows the interface variable to avoid knowing any details about the implementation of the interface. As a reference type, an interface variable can refer to any kind of object. In contrast, implementing an interface type variable as a value type requires assumptions be made about the interface's implementation. Specifically, the value type variable must reserve enough space to accommodate the implementation's fields. The problem is that value type variables, such as structs that implement interfaces, should be able to be assigned to reference type variables. Otherwise, it would not be possible for structs to properly implement interfaces.

The difficulty is solved with *boxing* and *unboxing*. Boxing refers to the creation of an object corresponding to a value type variable. Boxing is exploited to allow a struct type variable to be assigned to an interface type variable. Boxing occurs in the code below:

```
DriversLicense femaleDriver;
string name = "Kate";
Date birthday = new Date(1974, 4, 4);

femaleDriver = new DriversLicense(name, birthday);
PotentialDriver insuranceCandidate = femaleDriver;
```

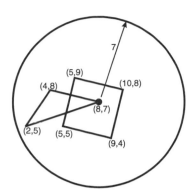

Figure 11.16   Overlapping shape scenario (only the triangle and square overlap).

When the `DriversLicense` struct is assigned a `PotentialDriver` type variable, an object with the same fields and methods as a `DriversLicense` struct is created and initialized with the fields of the struct being assigned. A reference to this object is then assigned to the `PotentialDriver` variable. In the example above, this occurs when `femaleDriver` is assigned to `insuranceCandidate`. Structs can always be boxed, so a conversion is not required to trigger the boxing. Since boxing generates an object and all value types can be boxed, C# can guarantee that regardless of type, any variable can be assigned to a variable of type `object`. Unboxing occurs when an interface variable is assigned to a struct type variable. As we mentioned, interface variables reference objects. In some cases, these objects are boxed structs, and can be converted back to value type variables using a conversion. Since it is not known whether the object referenced by an interface type variable is a boxed version of the struct type until run time, an explicit conversion is required to initiate unboxing. C# exploits unboxing, and the ability of any boxed value type to be unboxed, to allow a value type referenced by a variable of type `object` to be assigned to a variable of that value type.

Case Study

The subject of our case study is a program to determine if any number of two-dimensional shapes overlaps. To simplify the programming requirements, the set of shapes to handle is limited. Included in this set are circles, squares, and rectangles, which we modeled in previous chapters. For variety, pentagons and triangles must also be handled by the program. Shapes are considered to overlap only if their perimeters share one or more points. Thus in Figure 11.16, the triangle and square overlap each other, but they do not overlap the circle in which they are contained.

To assist in modeling shapes and finding shared points, a `Point` and a `Segment` class are provided with considerable functionality. The public methods and properties provided in each class are shown in Programs 11.33 and 11.34 respectively. Note that the implementation of each class is not given.

It is tempting to immediately implement classes corresponding to triangle, square, rectangle, and pentagon shapes. The first shape, a triangle, is defined by a set of three points. We can model this has-a relationship by making these points both the parameters of the constructor and fields of the class. The only complication is that instances of the `Point` class can be modified or more formally they are mutable. Simply referencing the `Point` objects

```
class Point
{
    public Point(double x, double y) {}
    public Point(Point pt) {}
    public double X { get; }
    public double Y { get; }
    public double Distance(Point other);
}
```

Program 11.33 Methods available in the Point class.

```
class Segment
{
    public Segment(Point p1, Point p2) {}
    public bool DoesItIntersect ( Segment other);
    public double Slope { get; }
    public double YIntercept {get; }
    public bool Parallel(Segment other);
    public bool OnSegment(Point p);
    public Segment PerpendicularSegment(Point pt1);
    public double MinDistance(Point pt);
    public double MaxDistance(Point pt);
}
```

Program 11.34 Methods available in the Segment class.

passed to the constructor opens the door to possible modification of a Triangle object's private data. To avoid this scenario, a copy of each Point parameter should be made and a reference to this copy stored in the Triangle class. Copying is simplified by the presence of a *copy constructor* in the Point class. That is, one of the constructors in the Point class takes in a reference to an existing Point and returns a copy of this object. A partial design for a triangle class is shown in Program 11.35.

By varying the number of Point objects in the constructor and fields, it is easy to create definitions for the pentagon and rectangle shapes. Sample definitions for rectangles and pentagons are shown in Programs 11.36 and 11.37. Note that squares can be modeled so easily by rectangles that it makes little sense to make a separate class to represent squares.

A more thorough examination of these shapes reveals that they can be represented with considerably less code by creating a more general polygon class. With the introduction of

```
public class Triangle
{
    //  Data fields
    private Point pt1, pt2, pt3;

    public Triangle(Point pt1, Point pt2, Point pt3)
    {
        this.pt1 = new Point(pt1);
        this.pt2 = new Point(pt2);
        this.pt3 = new Point(pt3);
    }
}
```

Program 11.35 Partial design of a class to model triangles.

```
public class Rectangle
{
   //  Data fields
   private Point pt1, pt2, pt3, pt4;

   public Rectangle (Point pt1, Point pt2, Point pt3, Point pt4)
   {
      this.pt1 = new Point(pt1);
      this.pt2 = new Point(pt2);
      this.pt3 = new Point(pt3);
      this.pt4 = new Point(pt4);
   }
}
```

Program 11.36   Partial design of a class to model rectangles.

arrays, the parameters of the `Triangle`, `Rectangle`, and `Pentagon` could be made identical. Likewise, the private `Point` fields could be stored in a single array object, which should make each class' fields identical. Finally, the creation of copies of the constructor parameters could be done in a loop that varied the number of `Point` objects created according to the number of elements in an array passed to the constructor. These changes give rise to a single `Polygon` class, shown in Program 11.38, which is capable of replacing the `Triangle`, `Rectangle`, and `Pentagon` classes. This new class reduces the code required to represent polygon shapes by approximately one-third.

In contrast to triangles, rectangles, and pentagons, circles cannot be easily represented by a polygon class. A circle consists of a single point, defining its centre and a radius describing the location of its circumference. The class in Program 11.39 models a circle.

Which methods to supply with our classes depends on the algorithm used to determine if two shapes overlap. This algorithm varies depending on the kind of shapes that are being examined for overlap. The program may be examining two circles, a circle and a polygon, or two polygons. In the first scenario, two circles overlap if their circumferences share a point. In this situation the distance between the centres of the two circles is no greater than the sum of their radii and no less than the difference of their radii. Another way of stating this condition is that the nearest point on the second circle is within the circumference of the first, and the

```
public class Pentagon
{
   //  Data fields
   private Point pt1, pt2, pt3, pt4, pt5;

   public Pentagon (Point pt1, Point pt2, Point pt3, Point pt4, Point pt5)
   {
      this.pt1 = new Point(pt1);
      this.pt2 = new Point(pt2);
      this.pt3 = new Point(pt3);
      this.pt4 = new Point(pt4);
      this.pt5 = new Point(pt5);
   }
}
```

Program 11.37   Partial design of a class to model pentagons.

```
public class Polygon
{
    //  Data fields
    private Point[] pts;

    public Polygon(Point[] pts)
    {
        this.pts = new Point[pts.Length];

        for ( int i = 0; i< this.pts.Length; i++)
        {
            this.pts[i] = new Point(pts[i]);
        }
    }
}
```

Program 11.38 Partial design of a class to model any polygon.

furthest point on the second is outside the circumference of the first. Of course, if either of these points is on the circumference, the circles overlap. In the second scenario, a circle and a polygon overlap if one of the polygon's segments intersects the circle's circumference. A simple way to determine this condition is to first determine the points on the polygon that are closest to and furthest from the centre of the circle. If the closest point is within the circle, and the furthest outside the circle, then at some point the polygon must intersect the arc of the circle. Again, if the distance from either point is equal to the radius, then the point is on the circumference, and the polygon still overlaps. The final scenario involves two polygons. Here, two polygons overlap if any of their segments intersect. This can be determined using linear algebra and the equation of a line. Fortunately, the segment class provides a method to determine if two segments intersect. With these algorithms in mind, we can choose methods for each class.

In the Circle class, the method to detect overlap must be overloaded. A single method will determine whether or not a circle overlaps with another shape. The name of this method, Overlaps, is chosen arbitrarily. Since the program is not required to report the location of overlap, it will suffice for Overlaps to return a Boolean value. However, two versions of Overlaps are required. One will handle Circle objects, while the other will handle Polygon objects. Declarations for each are shown in Program 11.40. Notice that the bodies of both Overlaps methods are identical. They rely on the ability to determine the closest and furthest points from the centre of this circle. To do so they call the methods

```
public class Circle
{
    Point centre;
    double radius;

    public Circle(Point centre, double radius)
    {
        this.centre = new Point(centre);
        this.radius = radius;
    }
}
```

Program 11.39 Partial design of a class to model a circle.

```csharp
using System;

public class Circle
{
    Point centre;
    double radius;

    public Circle(Point centre, double radius)
    {
        this.centre = new Point(centre);
        this.radius = radius;
    }

    public bool Overlaps(Polygon other)
    {
        double minDist = other.MinDistanceToPoint(this.centre);
        double maxDist = other.MaxDistanceToPoint(this.centre);

        if (this.OnCircumference(minDist) || this.OnCircumference(maxDist))
            return true;
        else if (this.WithinRadius(minDist) && this.OutsideRadius(maxDist))
            return true;
        else
            return false;
    }

    public bool Overlaps(Circle other)
    {
        double minDist = other.MinDistanceToPoint(this.centre);
        double maxDist = other.MaxDistanceToPoint(this.centre);

        if (this.OnCircumference(minDist) || this.OnCircumference(maxDist))
            return true;
        else if (this.WithinRadius(minDist) && this.OutsideRadius(maxDist))
            return true;
        else
            return false;
    }

    public double MinDistanceToPoint(Point pt)
    {
        double distance = this.centre.Distance(pt) - this.radius;
        return Math.Abs(distance);
    }

    public double MaxDistanceToPoint(Point pt)
    {
        double distance = this.centre.Distance(pt) + this.radius;
        return Math.Abs(distance);
    }

    private bool WithinRadius(double distance)
    {
        if ( (float)distance <= (float)this.radius)
            return true;
        else
```

```
            return false;
    }

    private bool OnCircumference(double distance)
    {
        if ( Math.Abs((float)distance-(float)this.radius) <= float.Epsilon)
            return true;
        else
            return false;
    }

    private bool OutsideRadius(double distance)
    {
        if ( (float)distance >= (float)this.radius)
            return true;
        else
            return false;
    }

    public bool Intersects(Segment sg)
    {
        double minDist = sg.MinDistance(centre);
        double maxDist = sg.MaxDistance(centre);

        if (this.OnCircumference(minDist) || this.OnCircumference(maxDist))
            return true;
        else if (this.WithinRadius(minDist) && this.OutsideRadius(maxDist))
            return true;
        else
            return false;
    }
}
```

Program 11.40   Complete implementation of the `Circle` class without inheritance.

`MinDistanceToPoint` and `MaxDistanceToPoint`, which have been added to the `Circle` class and the `Polygon` class (shown in Program 11.41).

In the `Polygon` class, the implementation of `Overlaps` relies on different methods than it does in the `Circle` class. Once again, two versions of `Overlaps` are used. One will detect overlap with a `Circle`, and another detects overlap with a `Polygon` object. As with the `Circle` class, both implementations of `Overlaps` have identical bodies. For each side in the polygon, a `Segment` object is created. The method then determines if the segment shares a point with the other shape by calling the `Intersects` method on that shape. For the `Polygon` class in Program 11.41 this method creates a `Segment` object for each side and uses the `DoesItIntersect` method of the `Segment` class to see if the parameter shares a point with any of the shape's sides. The `Intersects` method included in the `Circle` class, Program 11.40, uses the same principle as the `Circle` class' `Overlaps` method.

Using the polymorphism available in C#, we can remove the duplicate code in the `Overlaps` method. In C#, *polymorphism* refers to the ability of a derived class to re-implement the methods of its base class. This allows the programmer to access methods re-implemented in the derived class using a variable that is declared to reference the base class. In the case of the `Polygon` class, polymorphism allows us to write a single version

```
public class Polygon
{
   Point[] pts;

   public Polygon(Point[] pts)
   {
      this.pts = new Point[pts.Length];

      for ( int i = 0; i< this.pts.Length; i++)
      {
         this.pts[i] = new Point(pts[i]);
      }
   }

   public bool Overlaps(Polygon other)
   {
      for ( int i = 0; i<this.pts.Length; ++i)
      {
         Segment sgPoly = new Segment(this.pts[i],
                              this.pts[(i+1)%this.pts.Length]);
         if ( other.Intersects(sgPoly) )
            return true;
      }
      return false;
   }

   public bool Overlaps(Circle other)
   {
      for ( int i = 0; i<this.pts.Length; ++i)
      {
         Segment sgPoly = new Segment(this.pts[i],
                              this.pts[(i+1)%this.pts.Length]);
         if ( other.Intersects(sgPoly) )
            return true;
      }
      return false;
   }

   public double MinDistanceToPoint(Point pt)
   {
      Segment sg1 = new Segment(this.pts[0], this.pts[1]);
      double minDist = sg1.MinDistance(pt);

      for ( int i = 0; i<this.pts.Length; ++i)
      {
         Segment sg = new Segment(this.pts[i],
                              this.pts[(i+1)%this.pts.Length]);
         double currDist = sg.MinDistance(pt);

         if (currDist < minDist)
         {
            minDist = currDist;
         }
      }
      return minDist;
   }
```

```
public double MaxDistanceToPoint(Point pt)
{
    Segment sg1 = new Segment(this.pts[0], this.pts[1]);
    double maxDist = sg1.MaxDistance(pt);

    for ( int i = 0; i<this.pts.Length; ++i)
    {
        Segment sg = new Segment(this.pts[i],
                                    this.pts[(i+1)%this.pts.Length]);
        double currDist = sg.MaxDistance(pt);
        if (currDist > maxDist)
        {
            maxDist = currDist;
        }
    }
    return maxDist;
}

public bool Intersects(Segment sg)
{
    for ( int i = 0; i<this.pts.Length; ++i)
    {
        Segment sgPoly = new Segment(this.pts[i],
                                    this.pts[(i+1)%this.pts.Length]);
        if ( sgPoly.DoesItIntersect(sg) )
            return true;
    }
    return false;
}
}
```

Program 11.41 Complete implementation of the `Polygon` class without inheritance.

```
public class Shape
{
  protected Shape() {}

  public virtual double MinDistanceToPoint(Point pt) {return 0;}
  public virtual double MaxDistanceToPoint(Point pt) {return 0;}
  public virtual bool Intersects(Segment sg) {return false;}
  public virtual bool Overlaps(Shape other) {return false;}
}
```

Program 11.42 Shape base class.

of the Overlaps method to which we can pass either Polygon or Circle references. The restriction on polymorphism is that only classes with a common type can be used interchangeably. Fortunately, both circles and polygons are types of shapes. These is-a relationships make it natural to create a Shape class from which both the Circle and Polygon class derive. As we have seen in our discussion of inheritance, only methods in the base class can be called with a reference to the base class. Thus, the methods on which Overlaps relies must also be in the base class. The resulting base class, Shape, is shown in Program 11.42. Since we never want to use instances of the Shape class, we have made it impossible to instantiate the class by omitting any constructors other than the default, which we declare as protected. The methods that Shape implements are declared as virtual to allow their implementation to be revised in derived classes. The implementation of these methods in the Shape class is not important as it will not be used. The return calls are added to allow the class to compile properly.

By revising the Circle and Polygon class, we combine the two Overlaps methods into one. New versions of the Circle and Polygon are shown in Programs 11.43 and 11.44.

```csharp
using System;

public class Circle : Shape {
  Point centre;
  double radius;

  public Circle(Point centre, double radius) {
    this.centre = new Point(centre);
    this.radius = radius;
  }

  public override bool Overlaps(Shape other) {
    double minDist = other.MinDistanceToPoint(this.centre);
    double maxDist = other.MaxDistanceToPoint(this.centre);

    if (this.OnCircumference(minDist) || this.OnCircumference(maxDist))
      return true;
    else if (this.WithinRadius(minDist) && this.OutsideRadius(maxDist))
      return true;
    else
      return false;
  }

  public override double MinDistanceToPoint(Point pt){
    double distance = this.centre.Distance(pt) - this.radius;
    return Math.Abs(distance);
  }

  public override double MaxDistanceToPoint(Point pt) {
    double distance = this.centre.Distance(pt) + this.radius;
    return Math.Abs(distance);
  }

  public override bool Intersects(Segment sg) {
    double minDist = sg.MinDistance(centre);
    double maxDist = sg.MaxDistance(centre);

    if (this.OnCircumference(minDist) || this.OnCircumference(maxDist))
      return true;
    else if (this.WithinRadius(minDist) && this.OutsideRadius(maxDist))
      return true;
    else
      return false;
  }
  private bool WithinRadius(double distance) {
    if ( (float)distance <= (float)this.radius)
      return true;
```

```
      else
        return false;
  }

  private bool OnCircumference(double distance) {
    if ( Math.Abs((float)distance-(float)this.radius) <= float.Epsilon)
      return true;
    else
      return false;
  }

  private bool OutsideRadius(double distance){
    if ( (float)distance >= (float)this.radius)
      return true;
    else
      return false;
  }
}
```

Program 11.43 Circle updated to inherit from Shape class.

```
public class Polygon : Shape {
  Point[] pts;

  public Polygon(Point[] pts) {
        this.pts = new Point[pts.Length];

    for ( int i = 0; i< this.pts.Length; i++){
      this.pts[i] = new Point(pts[i]);
    }
  }

  public override bool Overlaps(Shape other) {
    for ( int i = 0; i<this.pts.Length; ++i) {
      Segment sgPoly = new Segment(this.pts[i],
              this.pts[(i+1)%this.pts.Length]);
      if ( other.Intersects(sgPoly) )
        return true;
    }
    return false;
  }

  public override double MinDistanceToPoint(Point pt) {
    Segment sg1 = new Segment(this.pts[0], this.pts[1]);
    double minDist = sg1.MinDistance(pt);

    for ( int i = 0; i<this.pts.Length; ++i){
      Segment sg = new Segment(this.pts[i],
              this.pts[(i+1)%this.pts.Length]);
      double currDist = sg.MinDistance(pt);

      if (currDist < minDist) {
        minDist = currDist;
      }
    }
```

```
      return minDist;
  }

  public override double MaxDistanceToPoint(Point pt) {
    Segment sg1 = new Segment(this.pts[0], this.pts[1]);
    double maxDist = sg1.MaxDistance(pt);

    for ( int i = 0; i<this.pts.Length; ++i){
      Segment sg = new Segment(this.pts[i],
              this.pts[(i+1)%this.pts.Length]);
      double currDist = sg.MaxDistance(pt);
      if (currDist > maxDist) {
        maxDist = currDist;
      }
    }
    return maxDist;
  }

  public override bool Intersects(Segment sg) {
    for ( int i = 0; i<this.pts.Length; ++i) {
      Segment sgPoly = new Segment(this.pts[i],
              this.pts[(i+1)%this.pts.Length]);
      if ( sgPoly.DoesItIntersect(sg) )
        return true;
    }
    return false;
  }
}
```

Program 11.44 `Polygon` updated to inherit from `Shape` class.

These classes now derive from the Shape class. Using the override keyword, each class re-implements the Shape class methods shown in Program 11.42.

Finally, we can exploit the inheritance relationship between Circle and Polygon objects to simplify the main body of our overlapping shapes program. Rather than store the various shapes in arrays corresponding to their types, our OverlappingShapeDetector class pictured in Program 11.45 uses a single array. Using a nested for loop, the program is able to compare each of the shapes input by the user with each of the other shapes. Any overlaps are reported as they are detected. While this program is not perfect, it is sufficient to correctly detect the overlap conditions in Figure 11.16, as shown in a screen shot of the program's results in Figure 11.17.

```
using tcdIO;

class OverlappingShapeDetector {

  // Static terminal variable can be accessed without
  // needing to pass the terminal object as a parameter.
  static Terminal terminal;

  static void Main() {
    Shape[] shapes;
```

```
    terminal = new Terminal("Overlapping Shape Finder");

    // Request number of shapes.
    int numShapes = terminal.ReadInt("Please enter the number "
                                      + "of shapes to examine:");
    shapes = new Shape[numShapes];

    // Get details on each shape
    for ( int i = 0; i < shapes.Length ; i++) {
      char isCircle = terminal.ReadChar("Is this shape a circle?"
                                        + " (Y/N)");
      terminal.WriteString("");

      if (isCircle == 'y' || isCircle == 'Y')
        shapes[0] = GetCircleInput();
      else
        shapes[i] = GetPolygonInput();
    }

    // Determine which shapes overlap
    for (int i = 0; i < shapes.Length ; i++)
      for (int j = i+1; j < shapes.Length; j++)
        if ( shapes[i].Overlaps(shapes[j]) )
           terminal.WriteString("Shape " + i + "overlaps shape " + j);
  }

  static Shape GetCircleInput() {
    terminal.WriteString("Taking input for CIRCLE: ");
    double x = terminal.ReadDouble("Enter X coordinate: ");
    double y = terminal.ReadDouble("Enter Y coordinate: ");
    double r = terminal.ReadDouble("Enter radius: ");

    return (Shape)new Circle(new Point(x,y), r);
  }

  static Shape GetPolygonInput() {
    Point[] corners;
    terminal.WriteString("Taking input for POLYGON: ");
    int sides = terminal.ReadInt("Enter number of corners: ");
    corners = new Point[sides];

    for (int i = 0 ; i < sides; i++) {
      terminal.WriteString("Enter data for corner " + i);
      double x = terminal.ReadDouble("Enter X coordinate: ");
      double y = terminal.ReadDouble("Enter Y coordinate: ");
      corners[i] = new Point(x,y);
    }
    return (Shape)new Polygon(corners);
  }
}
```

Program 11.45 OverlappingShapeDetector class.

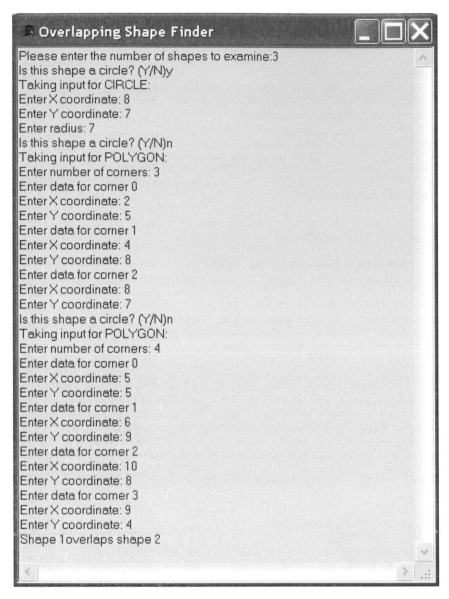

Figure 11.17 Execution of Overlapping Shape Detector.

Summary

- has-a relationships are represented with fields. Is-a relationships are best represented by inheritance
- the class being inherited from is the base class, and the class inheriting members from the base class is the derived class
- in a derived class, the base keyword can be used to refer to members inherited from the base class

- all members of the base class are included in the derived class, regardless of accessibility
- `protected` members are accessible in the class in which they were declared and any class that inherits them directly or indirectly
- the type specified when a variable is declared is its compile-time type; the class or struct of the object assigned to the variable is the run-time type
- objects of a particular class support the type defined by the class and every type defined by classes in its inheritance hierarchy
- the `is` keyword tests a variable to see if a variable's run-time type supports a particular compile-time type
- the `as` keyword performs a conversion from one compile-time type to another that returns `null` on a bad conversion rather than generating a run-time error
- the `new` keyword is used to declare a method that overloads an inherited method with the same signature
- the `virtual` keyword in the declaration of a method allows the method to be overridden in derived classes
- the `override` keyword overrides an inherited method by replacing its implementation with a newly defined one
- the `interface` keyword is used to define a new type without specifying its implementation
- structs cannot make use of inheritance, but they can implement interfaces

Exercises

(1) For each set of objects, identify the has-a and is-a relationships.
- Set 1: A banana, an orange, a fruit, a seed.
- Set 2: A pencil case, a pen, paper, pencil, eraser, rucksack.
- Set 3: Mobile phone, dialpad, Nokia, Motorola, battery, display screen.
- Set 4: Beverage, Coke, Soft drink, liquid, water.

(2) Create a class for the objects in Exercise 1. Use inheritance to model the is-a relationships and use fields to model the has-a relations.

(3) Observe the `Angle` class defined below; create two classes that derive from it. One derived class should store the angle in degrees, while the other should store the angle in radians.

```
class Angle {
    protected Angle() {}

    public virtual double InRadians(){return 0}
    public virtual double InDegrees(){return 0}
    public virtual double Tan(){return 0}
    public virtual double Cos(){return 0}
    public virtual double Sin(){return 0}
}
```

(4) Create a program that reports the perimeter of a triangle based on the length of any two sides and the angle between these sides. Allow the user to enter the angle in radians or degrees. Make use of both classes created in Exercise 3, but do not use any variables whose type is defined by either of these classes. Furthermore, ensure that the triangle is represented as an object.

(5) Use inheritance to create a new version of the triangle class in Exercise 4 that allows the user to determine the area of the triangle. Change the program written for Exercise 4 to report the area of the triangle along with its perimeter.

(6) Create two classes to represent a rectangle. One should describe the shape of the rectangle with points. The other should use the triangle class defined in Exercise 5. Use objects of these classes in a program to calculate the area and perimeter of the rectangles.

(7) Create a common base class for the rectangle representations that allows the program defined in Exercise 6 to operate without using variables of the two rectangle types. Make sure this base class contains the perimeter and area of the rectangle in data fields that are not public and that the base class cannot be instantiated.

Error Handling 12

This chapter:

- introduces the *stack* data structure, and identifies its most basic operations. An implementation of the stack will be the focus of our error-handling discussion
- discusses how to avoid run-time errors with simple error checking
- discusses the alternatives for dealing with errors
- explains how to organize error information to improve feedback with encapsulated error information
- introduces the concept of *exceptions* and *exception handling*
- introduces syntax for defining, *throwing* and *catching* exceptions
- identifies three categories of exceptions that C# automatically generates

We are going to look at error handling in the context of a *stack*. A stack is a commonly used data structure that stores variables. Since the concept of a stack may be new, the first section of this chapter will explain the theory of a stack, and present a class that implements the stack's operations. Fortunately, these operations are few and relatively simple. By their nature, it is easy to accidentally add or remove too many items from a stack. Thus, there is always a need to guard against errors even during normal operation. As we will see, stacks are useful in the discussion of several approaches to error handling.

During this chapter, we will progress from obvious approaches to error handling to more advanced strategies that rely on exception handling mechanisms. Initially, our error-handling strategy will be based on programming mechanisms we have already explored. However, their drawbacks will lead us to draw up new criteria for an error-handling system. As we will see, this "better" error-handling system will require the introduction of an exception programming mechanism. By the end of this chapter, we will demonstrate that using exceptions significantly improves a program's error-handling system.

Understanding Stacks

In programming terminology, a stack is a data structure that provides *LIFO access* to data. In general, the purpose of a data structure is to store data in an organized fashion so that it can be accessed later in a specific order. There are different kinds of data structures used in programming, but the stack is one of the most common by far. The term LIFO refers to the order in which data inserted into the stack is accessed. In the case of a stack, the last item in is the first item out. Shortening this ordering to *last in, first out* and taking the first letter of each word gives us the acronym LIFO. An excellent analogy for a stack is a pile of papers on a desk. As papers arrive, they are added to the top of the pile. As the pile grows, the last items added are always at the top, while the first items remain at the bottom, closest to the desk. When items are removed from the pile, they are always removed from the top. The first items removed are the last items to be added to the pile. Thus, the papers in the pile are accessed in LIFO order. Because of its LIFO properties and ability to store data, a pile of papers has all the properties of a stack.

To develop an intuitive feel for how stacks work, we will develop an implementation for a simple stack to contain integer values. Our first concern is how to store all the data that has been added. The obvious solution is to create variables to which we can assign integer values. Since the information stored has no particular meaning as far as the stack is concerned, an array is well suited to storing data added to the stack. The array allows us to allocate several variables in a single statement. As we will see, the array's ability to index data has several advantages when it comes to adding and removing data. A stack user will not access the array directly. Instead, two operations are made available for adding and removing data from the stack. For historical reasons, the operations are called *pop* and *push*. Pop is responsible for returning data, while push is responsible for inserting data into the stack. Since the stack user need not know the array exists, the array can be implemented as a private field as shown here:

```
private int[] stackData;
```

Of course, the writer of the stack class would have to decide what size to initialize this field to. Either user input or an arbitrary number can be chosen.

We need to develop a strategy for managing the array so that it not only records the incoming data, but is also able to tell us the relative order in which items were added. An array will have a number of elements capable of storing incoming data. Unfortunately, we cannot blindly pick elements to store the incoming data. The responsibility of a stack is to organize the data so that the last item inserted with a push command will be the first item returned if a pop command is completed. For this reason, we need to know the most recently added item. In fact, we need to know the exact order in which items were added.

A simple approach to obtaining LIFO behaviour is to emulate what we did with the pile of paper. Namely, to start filling the array, starting from the bottom. Since arrays do not have tops and bottoms per se, we will start filling from element zero, and continue filling the array by inserting incoming elements in the free element adjacent to the most recently filled element. Figure 12.1 visualizes this approach. To operate the array like a pile requires that we know the location of the last item added to the stack. We cannot determine this location by looking at the elements of the array. An array element will always look like an integer regardless of

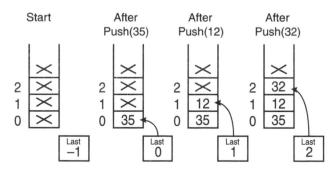

Figure 12.1   Visualizing stack semantics for an array.

whether or not it contains an inserted value. Instead, we will need an extra field to store the index of the last item. The following declaration will create the required field:

```
private int last;
```

In this case, the name last is arbitrary. We could choose any name, but "last" is a good brief explanation of the data stored in the variable.

After deciding where and how to store the stack's data, we have to design the methods to add and remove data. Recall, we called these operations push and pop. Push is responsible for adding data to the array, so the code in its body must find the next available space in the array. According to our design, we always add new data in the empty element beside the array element with the last item that was added. The array element with the last item added is always indexed by last. Since integers are added from the start of the array, all the elements between last and the array start will be occupied. So, the next unoccupied element is the one after that indexed by last. Thus, incrementing last by one will supply the index at which to store the incoming data. After storing the data, the push method should update last to reflect that data has been added to the array. The following implementation meets these criteria:

```
public void Push(int newValue) {
    int emptyLocation = last +1;
    this.stackData[emptyLocation] = newValue;
    last = last + 1;
}
```

or more concisely:

```
public void Push(int newValue) {
    this.stackData[++last] =
    newValue; }
```

Figure 12.2 takes the stack array pictured in Figure 12.1 and shows the effect on the stack's array after the method call Push(46) is made.

The pop operation is the antithesis of the push operation. Pop must remove the item most recently added to the stack. This item is quite easy to find, as it is indexed by last. After determining the most recently added item, we do not need to remove it from the array per se. It will suffice to record the item's element number, and then update last with the index of the new most recently added integer. Recall that we added items to the array from the start. Thus, the new most recently added item is the one beside the last. So last need only be decremented. The value at the recorded element number is then returned. The following code is a possible implementation of pop:

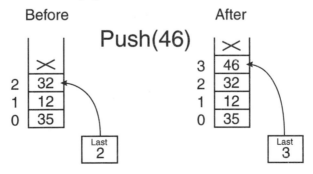

Figure 12.2 Changes to the stack in Figure 12.1 due to calling Push(46).

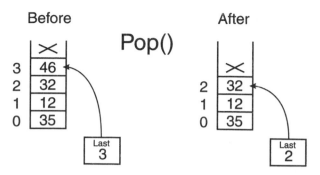

Figure 12.3 Changes to the stack in Figure 12.2 due to calling `Pop()`.

```
public int Pop() {
   int locationToReturn = last;

   /* update last */
   last = last - 1;
   return this.stackData[locationToReturn];
}
```

or more concisely:

```
public int Pop() { return (this.stackData[last--];) }
```

Figure 12.3 takes the stack array pictured in Figure 12.2 and shows the effects on the stack's array after a Pop method call is made. The value returned by this operation is 46.

A complete implementation of a stack is `IntegerStack`, illustrated in Program 12.1. Since the stack operations have to access all the stack's private data, the stack is best encapsulated

```
/* IntegerStack class implements a basic stack. */

public class IntegerStack {
  int[] stackData;
  int last = -1; /* Stacks always start out empty */

  public IntegerStack(int size) { this.stackData = new int[size]; }

  public void Push(int newValue) { this.stackData[++last] = newValue; }

  public int Pop() { return this.stackData[last--]; }

  public override string ToString() {
    string result = "";

    for ( int i = 0 ; i <= last ; i++)   {
      result = result + "item " + i.ToString() + ": "
                    + this.stackData[i].ToString() + " \n";
    }
    return result;
  }
}
```

Program 12.1 `IntegerStack` class implements a basic stack.

in a single object and its implementation requires only one class. `IntegerStack` solves the problem of what size of array to allocate by allowing the user to select the maximum number of items the array can contain. The constructor initializes `last` to –1 to accommodate the implementation of `Push`. `Push` increments `last` by one each time an item is added. The first item added to the array will be stored at index 0, so the first time `Push` increments `last` the result should also be 0. This will only be the case if `last` starts with the value –1. A new implementation of the `ToString` method has been created to print out all the contents of the stack. This method is not required for the stack to function properly, but it is handy for demonstrating the operation of the stack throughout this chapter.

Program 12.2 illustrates the use of an `IntegerStack` object. The program asks the user the maximum number of items the stack can contain, and then creates a stack with the corresponding size. Calls to `Push` are used to add multiples of two

```
/* StackDemo class demonstrates the operation of a stack*/
using tcdIO;

class StackDemo {
  static void Main() {
    /* Create Variables required by the method. */
    Terminal terminal;
    IntegerStack stack;
    int stackSize;

    /* Create a new terminal for communicating with the user. */
    terminal = new Terminal("Demonstration of a Stack");

    /* get details of parcel from user*/
    stackSize = terminal.ReadInt("Please enter the stack size: ");

    /* Create a stack according to the user specified size. */
    stack = new IntegerStack(stackSize);

    /* Fill the stack with arbitrary data */
    for ( int i = 0 ; i < stackSize ; i++ ) {
      terminal.WriteLine("Pushing " + (2*i).ToString()+ " into stack.");
      stack.Push(2*i);
    }

    /* Display contents of the stack */
    terminal.WriteLine("The stack contains the following items:");
    terminal.WriteLine(stack.ToString());

    /* Remove half the items in the stack. */
    for ( int i = 0 ; i < (stackSize / 2) ; i++ ) {
      terminal.WriteLine("Popping: " + stack.Pop().ToString()
                         + " removed from stack");
    }

    /* Display contents of the stack */
    terminal.WriteLine(stack.ToString());
  }
}
```

Program 12.2   `StackDemo` class demonstrates the operation of a stack.

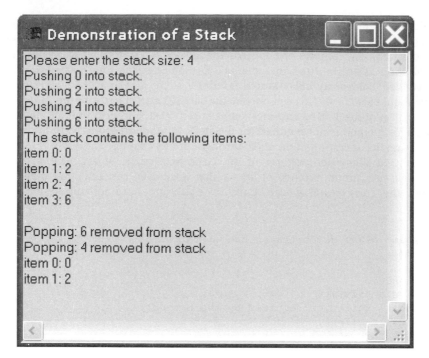

Figure 12.4 Sample operation of the `StackDemo` class.

to the stack. The value being pushed is reported prior to the push calls, so that the user can see the order in which values are entered in the stack. A call to `ToString` reveals the contents of the stack's array before half the items are removed using `Pop` method calls. The result of each `Pop` call is reported to the terminal. The user can verify the LIFO behaviour of the stack by comparing the order in which items were pushed with the order in which values are returned by pop. Finally, another `ToString` call is made to see the updated contents of the stack's array. Figure 12.4 illustrates the operation of the `StackDemo` program for a stack size of four elements.

Dealing with Errors

`IntegerStack` is not a very good stack implementation, because stacks should deal with misuse in an elegant fashion. Recall from Program 12.1 that `IntegerStack` does not provide details on the number of items it contains or the number of items it could contain. Thus, it is impossible to know when the stack is empty or full without knowing the total number of `Pop` and `Push` calls made on an `IntegerStack` object. Without the ability to verify whether the stack is full or empty, we can reasonably expect a stack user to accidentally remove items when the stack has none or to accidentally add too many items to the stack. Either of these mistakes causes the stack's methods to access the stack's storage array with an invalid array element index. For example, if the array is empty, the value of `last` will be −1. In this case,

```
/* StackErrorDemo tries to add too much to a stack. */
using tcdIO;

class StackErrorDemo {
  static void Main() {
    /* Create Variables required by the method. */
    Terminal terminal;
    IntegerStack stack;
    int stackSize;

    /* Create a new terminal for communicating with the user. */
    terminal = new Terminal("Demonstration of a Stack");

    /* Set the stack size to 4 */
    terminal.WriteLine("Demonstration of our IntegerStack class");
    stackSize = 4;

    /* Create a stack according to the user specified size. */
    stack = new IntegerStack(stackSize);

    /* Try to fill stack with more data than the stack can contain. */
    for ( int i = 0 ; i < stackSize+1 ; i++ ) { stack.Push(2*i); }
  }
}
```

Program 12.3   StackErrorDemo tries to add too much values to a stack.

a Pop call will try to return the value of array element -1, which is an element that does not exist!

```
/* If last is -1, this method tries to access
   this.stackData[-1] */
public int Pop() { return (this.stackData[last--];) }
```

In the code above, a run-time error occurs as soon as the attempt is made to access an invalid array element. By *run-time error*, we mean that C# will notice that a non-existent array element is being accessed and stop the program at the point the access was attempted. If the program was started from within Visual Studio, a dialog detailing the error encountered will appear on the screen. An example of the dialog shown appears in Figure 12.5. This dialog was generated during the execution of Program 12.3, where we attempted to put one too many items into an instance of IntegerStack. Thus, IntegerStack's current strategy for dealing with misuses is to immediately terminate!

In this section, we develop an approach to error handling that provides feedback using our existing knowledge of C# language mechanisms. We start by introducing simple error checking with minimal feedback. Pass by reference variables are used where methods need to return multiple pieces of information. In the subsequent subsection, we explore how the error feedback can be improved. Finally, we take advantage of objects to encapsulate error information.

Simple Error Checking

Preventing the misuse of IntegerStack from terminating our program is a matter of stopping Push and Pop from using an invalid index number to access an array element. In

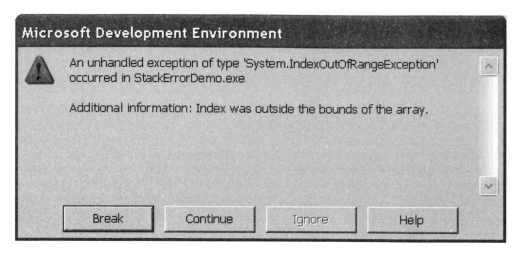

Figure 12.5   Program 12.3 fails when too many elements are added to the stack.

the case of Push, the danger is that too many items will be added to the stack. When the array is already full, Push will try to add a new value to a non-existent element after the end of the array. This scenario can be avoided if Push first verifies that the array is not already full before determining the index at which to store incoming data. For Pop, the danger is that the stack has no elements. As we pointed out previously, when the stack is empty Pop will try to return to the value of a non-existent array element before the start of the array. This scenario can be avoided by determining whether the stack is empty before ever attempting to remove data from the array.

A defensive programming strategy for IntegerStack should also provide callers of Push and Pop with feedback as to the success or failure of the operation. While it is undesirable to terminate the program when a Push or Pop operation cannot go ahead, it is important to give the caller some indication as to the success of the operation. For example, it would be annoying to add 500 values to a stack, only to have it discard 400 values because there is only room for 100 integers!

Most likely a Push or Pop will succeed, so feedback should not be onerous to interpret. For example, a Boolean or integer value can be quickly tested in a conditional statement. Returning an integer is useful if there is more than one cause of an error, because each value can be associated with a particular cause of failure. However, Push and Pop each have only one source of failure, thus a Boolean value should suffice for indicating whether these operations succeeded or not. From a coding point of view, feedback should be easily testable. Making the error code the return value of a method means the method call itself can be tested in a conditional statement. Finally, feedback should be consistent. We want to see both Push and Pop return feedback with the same mechanism, and the values returned should have the same meaning for both methods. Otherwise, a programmer may become confused about the meaning of a return code.

The new version of Push, shown in Program 12.4 meets our requirements for error checking and for providing feedback. Notice that the method's declaration has been changed. Previously, Push did not return a value, but now it returns a Boolean value to indicate the success of the operation. To catch errors, the method contains a new conditional statement

```
/* New version of IntegerStack with added error checks */

public class IntegerStack {
  int[] stackData;
  int last;

  public IntegerStack(int size) {
    this.stackData = new int[size];
    last = -1;
  }

  public bool Push(int newValue) {
    /* Return false if the array is already full. */
    if ( last+1 == this.stackData.Length) { return false; }
    this.stackData[++last] = newValue;
    return true;
  }

  public int Pop() { return (this.stackData[last--]); }

  public override string ToString() {
    string result = "";
    for ( int i = 0 ; i <= last ; i++) {
      result = result + "item " + i.ToString() + ": "
                      + this.stackData[i].ToString() + " \n";
    }
    return result;
  }
}
```

Program 12.4 IntegerStack updated with error checking in the Push method.

that verifies that the array is not already full. This statement checks if the variable `last` indexes the last element of the `stackData` array, as shown below:

```
/* Return false if the array is already full */
if ( last+1 == this.stackData.Length ) { return false; }
```

If the error checking is satisfied and the new value is added to the stack's storage array, the method returns `true`. Figure 12.6 shows the use of the updated `IntegerStack`, implemented in Program 12.4, with the test program in Program 12.5. Rather than crashing, the program reports failures of `Push` calls when too many items are added to the stack.

To implement the `Pop` method to specification, we make use of reference parameters to return multiple values from the method. The strategy taken in the `Push` method was to use the return value to indicate whether the operation succeeded or failed. This worked well because the method was not already returning a value. However, the `Pop` method in Program 12.4 needs to return the value of the integer being popped:

```
public int Pop() { return (this.stackData[last--]); }
```

The dilemma we face is the need to return information about the success of the operation and the value that is the result of the operation. To return the Boolean error code instead, we can change `Pop` to return the value being popped with a pass by reference parameter. Recall we discussed pass by reference in Chapter 8. The new declaration for `Pop` is:

```
public bool Pop(ref int popValue) {
```

```
/* Exercises the error handling of the Push method */
using tcdIO;

class StackErrorDemo  {
  static void Main() {
    /* Create Variables required by the method. */
    Terminal terminal;
    IntegerStack stack;
    int stackSize;

    /* Create a new terminal for communicating with the user. */
    terminal = new Terminal("Demonstration of a Stack");
    terminal.WriteLine("Overfilling an IntegerStack object:");

    /* Create a stack to hold three integers. */
    stackSize = 3;
    stack = new IntegerStack(3);

    /* Fill the stack with data. */
    for ( int i = 0 ; i < stackSize+1 ; i++ ) {
      terminal.Write("Adding item " + i.ToString() + " result is ");
      terminal.WriteLine(stack.Push(2*i).ToString() );
    }
  }
}
```

Program 12.5   Demonstration of Push method error checking in Program 12.4.

Finally, error checking has to be added to prevent Pop for executing when the stack is already full. The following code checks for this condition, and returns the appropriate error code:

```
/* Return false if the array is already empty. */
if (last == -1) {return false; }
```

The resulting version of IntegerStack is shown in Program 12.6.

A new test program, Program 12.7, illustrates the error handling that has been added to the Pop method. In this update of StackErrorDemo, the class attempts to take out one too many items from the stack. Figure 12.7 illustrates the results of a sample program execution.

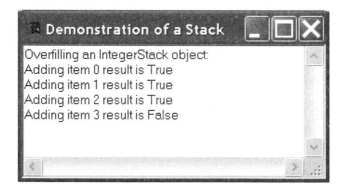

Figure 12.6   Execution of Program 12.5.

```
/* IntegerStack with error checking in the Pop method */

public class IntegerStack {
  int[] stackData;
  int last;
  public IntegerStack(int size) {
    this.stackData = new int[size];
    last = -1;
  }
  public bool Push(int newValue) {
    /* Return false if the array is already full. */
    if ( last+1 == this.stackData.Length) { return false; }
    this.stackData[++last] = newValue;    return true;
  }

  public bool Pop(ref int popValue) {
    /* Return false if the array is already empty. */
    if (last == -1) { return false; }
    popValue = this.stackData[last--];
    return true;
  }

  public override string ToString() {
    string result = "";
    for ( int i = 0 ; i <= last ; i++) {
      result = result + "item " + i.ToString() + ": "
                      + this.stackData[i].ToString() + " \n";
    }
    return result;
  }
}
```

Program 12.6   IntegerStack with error checking in the Pop method.

Better Error Messages

While there are tangible benefits to returning an error code, error codes have drawbacks when it comes to determining their meaning. Up until now our error codes have been rather uninformative. Replying with a Boolean value can indicate that an error has occurred, but it does not indicate much more information than that. We have to infer the meaning of the error code returned by a method from the comments in the method's declaration or by inspecting the method's implementation. It would be much handier if our error codes explained the exact nature of the problem in language the programmer could understand. At the same time, it would be nice to retain the advantages of a numeric error code that can be quickly tested to determine if the method completed without error.

Pass by reference can be exploited to return a text-based error code with a plain English description of the problem, which complements the numeric error code. One option for providing more detailed information about an error is to return a string with an English-language explanation of the problem that occurred. For instance, if Push found that the array was already full, it might indicate so with the following string:

```
errorInfo = "Push failed, stack is already full!";
```

This string can be quickly analyzed by a programmer, because it states the nature of the problem rather than referencing a list of error codes documented elsewhere. However, the

```
/* Exercises the error handling of the Pop method */
using tcdIO;

class StackErrorDemo {
  static void Main() {
    /* Create Variables required by the method. */
    Terminal terminal;
    IntegerStack stack;
    int stackSize;

    /* Create a new terminal for communicating with the user. */
    terminal = new Terminal("Demonstration of a Stack");
    terminal.WriteLine("Over emptying an IntegerStack object:");

    /* Create a stack to hold three integers. */
    stackSize = 3;
    stack = new IntegerStack(3);

    /* Fill the stack with data. */
    for ( int i = 0 ; i < stackSize ; i++ ) {
      terminal.Write("Adding item " + i.ToString() + " result is ");
      terminal.WriteLine(stack.Push(2*i).ToString() );
    }

    /* Remove more data than the stack can contains. */
    int popValue =0;
    for ( int i = 0; i <= stackSize; i++ ) {
      terminal.Write("Removing item " + i.ToString() + " result is ");
      terminal.WriteLine(stack.Pop(ref popValue).ToString() );
    }
  }
}
```

Program 12.7   Exercises the error handling of the Pop method.

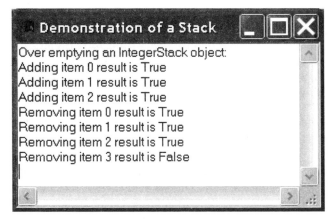

Figure 12.7   Sample execution of Program 12.7.

```
/* An IntegerStack with more informative error messages.*/
public class IntegerStack {
  int[] stackData;
  int last;

  public IntegerStack(int size) {
    this.stackData = new int[size];
    last = -1;
  }

  public bool Push(int pushValue, ref string errorInfo) {
    if ( last+1 == this.stackData.Length)
    {
      errorInfo = "Push failed, stack is already full!";
      return false;
    }
    this.stackData[++last] = pushValue;
    return true;
  }

  public bool Pop(ref int popValue, ref string errorInfo) {
    if (last == -1) {
      errorInfo = "Pop failed, stack is already empty!";
      return false;
    }
    popValue = this.stackData[last--];
    return true;
  }

  public override string ToString() {
    string result = "";
    for ( int i = 0 ; i <= last ; i++) {
      result = result + "item " + i.ToString() + ": "
                      + this.stackData[i].ToString() + " \n";
    }
    return result;
  }
}
```

Program 12.8   An `IntegerStack` with more informative error messages.

text string does not replace the need for a numeric return code that initially indicates the occurrence of an error. Testing a numeric code is much more elegant than comparing text. Numeric literals occupy less space, which makes the test code more concise and less complex. Not only does a test for a string occupy more space, but the test is error prone. Spelling and case sensitivity of strings make mistakes more likely. Also, strings are apt to change subtly, for instance when the programmer notices that the error message has been misspelled. To allow both pieces of error information to be returned, we can add more reference parameters to Push and Pop. An updated version of Push would be declared as follows:

```
public bool Push(int pushValue, ref string errorInfo) {
```

We see a complete implementation of text-based error information in Program 12.8, where error string parameters have been added to the Push and Pop methods.

Program 12.9 takes advantage of the text error information that has been added to IntegerStack in Program 12.8. This version of StackErrorDemo tries to add too many

```
/* Program to demonstrate IntegerStack's more informative error mes-
sages.*/
using tcdIO;

class StackErrorDemo {
  static void Main() {
    /* Create Variables required by the method. */
    Terminal terminal;
    IntegerStack stack;
    int stackSize;

    /* Create a new terminal for communicating with the user. */
    terminal = new Terminal("Demonstration of a Stack");

    /* Get stack size from user*/
    terminal.WriteLine("Demonstration of our IntegerStack class");
    stackSize = terminal.ReadInt("Please enter the stack size: ");

    /* Create a stack according to the user specified size. */
    stack = new IntegerStack(stackSize);

    /* Fill the stack with one to many pieces of data. */
    for ( int i = 0 ; i < stackSize+1 ; i++ ) {
      string failureMessage ="";
      bool pushResult;
      terminal.Write("Adding item " + i.ToString() + " result is ");
      pushResult = stack.Push(2*i,ref failureMessage);
      terminal.WriteLine(pushResult.ToString());
      if (!pushResult) {
        terminal.WriteLine("Error message: " + failureMessage);
      }
    }

    /* Remove more data than the stack can contains. */
    for ( int i = 0; i <= stackSize; i++ ) {
      string failureMessage ="";
      bool popResult;
      int   popValue = 0;
      terminal.Write("Removing item " + i.ToString() + " result is ");
      popResult = stack.Pop(ref popValue, ref failureMessage);
      terminal.WriteLine( popResult.ToString() );

      if (!popResult) {
        terminal.Write( "Error message: " + failureMessage );
      }
    }
  }
}
```

Program 12.9 Program to demonstrate `IntegerStack`'s more informative error messages.

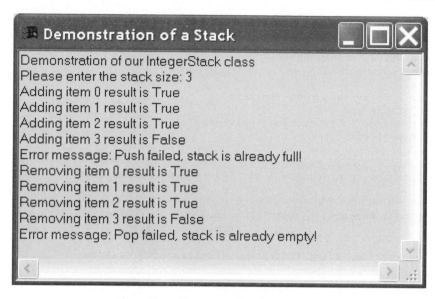

Figure 12.8   Sample execution of Program 12.9.

items to the stack, and then tries to remove an item from an empty stack. Whenever a method fails, that is, when it returns `false`, the text version of the error message is printed. The output from the program is pictured in Figure 12.8

Grouping Error Information

Using multiple parameters to pass error codes is unruly, makes a method call more complex and is hard to maintain. Depending on the amount of information associated with each error, several parameters may be required to hold the error information. Recall the declaration of the Pop method defined in Program 12.8:

```
public bool Pop(ref int popValue, ref string errorInfo) {
```

To call `Pop`, we had to declare a string variable to pass as the `errorInfo` parameter. Assuming the method usually succeeds, this parameter will be rarely used, resulting in a lot of wasted time declaring and passing an unnecessary variable. Another problem is that error reporting misses out on the benefits of proper encapsulation. When the number of parameters passed to a method increases, it becomes more and more difficult to ascertain which are related to error reporting, and which are used for normal operation. Also, we cannot easily maintain the error information. Should the error reporting change subtly in future versions of our stack, we not only have to modify the method's parameters, but we have to update existing users so that they include the correct number of parameters. While using multiple parameters solves the immediate problem of allowing multiple forms of error information, the approach is not suitable for serious programming.

An alternative to using multiple parameters is to define a class that describes all error information. For example, the Boolean and string error information returned by `Push` and `Pop` have become fields of an object defined by class `StackError` defined in Program 12.10. Now, `Push` and `Pop` need only return an instance of `StackError` with the error codes set correctly. As a bonus, the `StackError` constructor, shown below, sets the numeric and

```
/* StackError combines all error information into one object.*/

public class StackError {
  private string errorMessage;
  private bool success;

  /* Take a positive outlook on life */
  public StackError() {
    errorMessage = "Everything's alright.";
    success = true;
  }

  public string ErrorMessage { get  {  return errorMessage;  }
                               set  {  errorMessage = value; } }

  public bool Success  {  get  {  return success;  }
                          set  {  success = value; } }

  public override string ToString() { return errorMessage; }
}
```

Program 12.10   `StackError` combines all error information into one object.

text error codes to values that avoid further work on the part of Pop and Push when either operation succeeds:

```
// Take a positive outlook on life
public StackError() {
    errorMessage = "Everything's alright.";
    success = true;
}
```

The reason for exposing numeric and text data as properties rather than methods is to give StackError objects a similar feel to the data parameters that they replace. For instance, the code Push used to set the text error code would change from:

```
ErrorInfo = "Push failed, stack is already full!";
```

to

```
errorInfo.ErrorMessage =
    "Push failed, stack is already full!";
```

Regardless, the StackError object does provide the same functionality of the multiple parameters we were using.

The advantage of defining an object to store all the error information is that it solves the problems with using multiple parameters. Returning an object of this class avoids the need to contaminate the method parameters with variables unrelated to the normal operation of the method. Based on the updated implementation of IntegerStack in Program 12.11, the declaration of Push changes from:

```
public bool Push(int pushValue, ref string errorInfo)
```

to

```
public StackError Push(int pushValue)
```

```
/* A stack that returns an error object. */

public class IntegerStack {
  int[] stackData;
  int last;

  public IntegerStack(int size) {
    this.stackData = new int[size];
    last = -1;
  }

  public StackError Push(int pushValue) {
    StackError errorInfo = new StackError();
    if ( last+1 == this.stackData.Length) {
      errorInfo.ErrorMessage = "Push failed, stack is already full!";
      errorInfo.Success = false;
    } else {
      this.stackData[++last] = pushValue;
    }
    return errorInfo;
  }

  public StackError Pop(ref int popValue) {
    StackError errorInfo = new StackError();
    if (last == -1) {
      errorInfo.ErrorMessage = "Pop failed, stack is already empty!";
      errorInfo.Success = false;
    } else {
      popValue = this.stackData[last--];
    }
    return errorInfo;
  }

  public override string ToString() {
    string result = "";
    for ( int i = 0 ; i <= last ; i++) {
      result = result + "item " + i.ToString() + ": "
                      + this.stackData[i].ToString() + " \n";
    }
    return result;
  }
}
```

Program 12.11   A stack that returns an error object.

Notice that by using `StackError` objects we can focus all the error-handling information into the return value, rather than requiring the declaration of variables to pass as parameters. Of further benefit is the ability to change the error information without the need to update the method's parameters or the objects that call these methods. We need simply to update the definition of `StackError` with new fields and methods. So using encapsulating error information in an object is worth the effort.

Throwing Exceptions

The last section culminated with an error-handling strategy that provided excellent feedback to method callers and was flexible to changes in error codes. In this strategy, method callers are notified of errors by means of an object passed back in the return code of the called method. This object contains different descriptions of the error ranging from a Boolean flag that indicates whether something went wrong, to a text description of the probable cause of the error. From a programming perspective, the method parameter list is *clean* in that it is free of error-related parameters. Also, the method that produces error information is flexible to change, because the data in the error object is free to change without affecting the way in which the method is called. Indeed, the strategy was an excellent solution for dealing with errors that commonly occur during stack usage.

Our strategy does not implement nicely when a method's return value cannot be commandeered for error handling or when an error message object has to be returned several times before a method caller is found to handle the error. Take the case of constructors. They return instances of a class, and this is non-negotiable! We can turn to pass by reference parameters to transport the error-handling object to a constructor caller. However, we are trying to avoid putting error-handling information in the parameters, because using the parameters introduces an inconsistency with other methods that do use the return code for error information. Secondly, the method that can handle an error may not be directly calling the method that generates the error. Take the example of a program that handles errors in its `Main` method, but uses another method to add sets of numbers to a stack. Such a program is pictured in Program 12.12. This program makes use of an instance of the `IntegerStack` class defined in Program 12.11. The stack is filled with arbitrary data in a method called `PushData`. `PushData` examines the `StackError` object returned each time `Push` is called to see if the operation completed successfully. If a problem is encountered, then `PushData` immediately returns the `StackError` object to its caller. In the case of Program 12.12, a problem is always encountered, because more items are pushed than the stack can accommodate. The propagation of the `StackError` object is pictured in Figure 12.9

In Program 12.12, not much code is required to propagate the `StackError` object. However, the propagation becomes more code intensive when the number of method invocations between the error object creator and handler increases. Figure 12.10 pictures a more complex scenario. In this case, we have to add extra functionality to the intermediate methods to immediately return the `StackError` object to `Main`. Not only is this time consuming for the programmer, but the repetitiveness of the work makes it prone to errors.

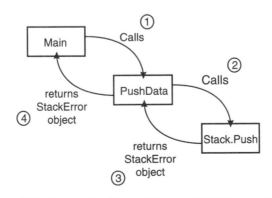

Figure 12.9 Propagation of `StackError` object in Program 12.12.

```
/* Generating error objects that need to be returned multiple times be-
fore they are properly handled */
using tcdIO;

class StackErrorDemo {
  /* Static terminal need not be passed as a parameter. */
  static Terminal terminal;

  public static void Main() {
    /* Create Variables required by the method. */
    IntegerStack stack;
    int items2Push;

    /* Create a new terminal for communicating with the user. */
    terminal = new Terminal("Demonstration of a Stack");
    terminal.WriteLine("Demonstration of error object propagation");

    /* We have arbitrarily decided to push 4 values. */
    items2Push = 4;

    /* Deliberately make the stack to small for items to push */
    stack = new IntegerStack(items2Push-1);

    /* Ask PushData to place arbitrary data on the stack. */
    StackError error  = PushData(stack, items2Push);

    if (error.Success != true ) {
      terminal.WriteLine("Stack method generated an error!");
      terminal.WriteLine("Custom error message: " + error.ToString());
    }
  }

  public static StackError PushData(IntegerStack stack, int numPushes){

    /* Start with an error code that indicates success */
    StackError errorCode = new StackError();

    for ( int i = 0; i < numPushes; i++  ) {

      /* State what we are doing */
      terminal.WriteLine("Pushing " + i.ToString() + " onto stack.");

      /* Add an item to the stack. */
      errorCode = stack.Push(2*i);

      /* Stop immediately if there is a problem! */
      if ( errorCode.Success != true ) break;
    }
    return errorCode;
  }
}
```

Program 12.12   Generating error objects that need to be returned multiple times before they are properly handled.

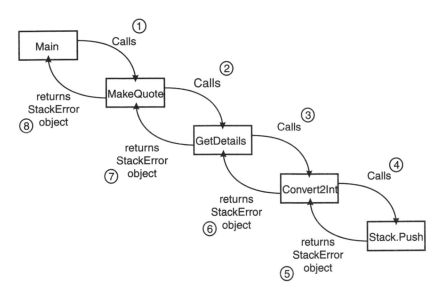

Figure 12.10   Propagation steps for a `StackError` object in a more complex program.

C# solves problems with our current error-handling strategy with a mechanism that avoids reliance on return values for moving error code objects and that guarantees uniformity in these objects. The major drawback with our error-handling strategy was its dependence on method return values for shifting control from the point at which an error was spotted to the point at which the program deals with the error. As we observed in the preceding paragraph, this approach is not always feasible, and becomes annoyingly code intensive as the distance between error detection and error-handling code grows. A completely new approach to shifting control is to *throw exceptions*. By *exception*, we mean an object that contains all the error code information associated with a problem the program has spotted. By *throwing*, we mean jumping from the line of code at which an error was detected to lines of code that deal with the error. Throwing can shift control without the use of reference parameters or return values. Unlike other means of flow control, such as `break` and `return`, throwing allows control to shift to code in a method that may not have directly called the current method. As for guaranteeing uniformity in error code objects, all exception objects must inherit from a common base class called `Exception`. This class gives all exceptions useful methods and fields. For instance, the base class defines a field that contains a text description of the error that has occurred. Thus, exceptions provide more powerful error-handling mechanisms that allow us to express our error-handling strategy more concisely and consistently.

The following three subsections introduce exceptions and present a new version of `IntegerStack` that makes use of exception mechanisms. Error handling with exceptions or *exception-handling* as it is often referred to as, is written in three parts. First, the exception object is defined. Next, `throw` statements are embedded in error checks. Finally, `try/catch` blocks are defined by code that calls methods that throw exceptions. These new mechanisms are applied to upgrade the error handling for the `IntegerStack` so that it deals with `Push` and `Pull` errors with exceptions. In addition, we tackle error scenarios not well supported by the definition of `IntegerStack` in Program 12.11. Be sure to keep a careful eye on the examples as each exception mechanism is introduced.

```
/* StackError revised to inherit from System.Exception */
using System;

public class StackError : Exception {
  private string errorMessage;
  private bool success;

  // Take a positive outlook on life
  public StackError() {
    errorMessage = "Everything's alright.";
    success = true;
  }

  public string ErrorMessage {    get  {  return errorMessage;  }
                                  set  {  errorMessage = value; }  }

  public bool Success {    get  {  return success;  }
                           set  {  success = value; }  }

  public override string ToString() { return errorMessage; }
}
```

Program 12.13   StackError revised to inherit from Exception.

Defining an Exception Class

A programmer is free to put whatever details they want in an exception, so long as it derives from class Exception. An exception is an object that contains the error information that we want to transmit to other parts of the program. Exception objects can be custom-made by the programmer, but as mentioned they must have Exception in their inheritance hierarchy. Thus, they must directly or indirectly inherit from Exception class. The Exception class contains methods that the C# exception handling mechanism relies on. If an object not derived from Exception is used as an exception, the compiler will generate the following error:

```
"The type caught or thrown must be derived from
System.Exception"
```

Thus, we can change StackError to define an exception by having it inherit from Exception, as we have done in Program 12.13.

Throwing an Exception

Exceptions are only thrown at specific points in the code where we have used the throw keyword. We have to explicitly define points at which exception objects are thrown. Exceptions are usually thrown from within conditional statements that look for errors. For instance, an if statement might test program variables to determine if a method is being used incorrectly or examine the results of an operation to see if the values generated fall within a range of valid values. If an error condition has occurred, the program will execute the body of the conditional statement. In the body, an exception object is created to describe the problem that was detected, and the exception is thrown. Throws are initiated using the keyword throw in conjunction with an exception object, as shown in Figure 12.11, thus exceptions are only used when an error has been detected.

```
throw <some_exception_object>;
```

Figure 12.11 Syntax for throwing an exception.

In Program 12.14, we have revised the constructor to thrown an exception if an unreasonable size is used when an `IntegerStack` is constructed. The size of a stack corresponds to the number of elements that the stack can contain. Having a zero or negative sized stack would be unreasonable, as a stack that cannot contain any elements is useless. If this condition occurred, we would want an exception to be thrown that indicated an error had occurred and that the cause was an unreasonable value for the stack size. In Program 12.14, the constructor has been revised to detect invalid stack sizes using the following conditional:

```
if (size <= 1 )
```

If this condition happens to be `true`, the body of the `if` statement creates an exception, stores an explanation of its cause, and uses a `throw` statement to pass the exception to another piece of code that can handle the problem. The body of the conditional is shown below:

```
{
    /* Create the exception */
    StackError errorInfo = new StackError();
    /* Store details on the error */
    errorInfo.ErrorMessage = "Push() failed, stack is"
        +"already full!";
    errorInfo.Success = false;
    /* Throw the exception */
    throw errorInfo;
}
```

As well as adding new error-handling capabilities to the stack constructor, exception-based error handling has been introduced to the `Push` and `Pop` methods in Program 12.14.

The confusing part of a `throw` statement is understanding what statement is executed after `throw`. Code must be written explicitly to expect and handle an exception in a process called *catching*. This code is defined separately from the code that generates the exceptions, and is covered in the next section.

Catching Exceptions

A programmer must anticipate the generation of an exception by putting code that may generate an exception in a `try/catch` block. The effect of a `throw` statement is to have the program look back at the source code that it has executed. This begins with the code executed just before the `throw` statement and continues until the beginning of a `try` block is encountered. As the program rolls back to the start of the `try` block, any objects that were created are destroyed. This is handled automatically by C#'s garbage collector facility. A `try` block can be easily recognized, as it starts with the keyword `try`, followed by some statements enclosed in curled brackets. Following the `try` block, a `catch` block is added to deal with the exceptions that are generated by the `try` block code. A `catch` block starts with the keyword `catch` and a declaration, in round brackets, that identifies the type of exception that the

```
/* IntegerStack with exception based error handling */
using System;

public class IntegerStack {
  int[] stackData;
  int last;

  public IntegerStack(int size) {
    // Throw an exception if the stack size is invalid
    if (size <= 1 ) {
      /* Create the exception */
      StackError errorInfo = new StackError();

      /* Store details on the error */
      errorInfo.ErrorMessage = "IntegerStack constructor failed," +
                                        " stack too small!";
      errorInfo.Success = false;

      /* Throw the exception */
      throw errorInfo;
    }
    this.stackData = new int[size];
    last = -1;
  }

  public void Push(int pushValue) {

     /* If the stack is full, throw an exception */
    if ( last+1 == this.stackData.Length) {
      StackError errorInfo = new StackError();
      errorInfo.ErrorMessage = "Push() failed, stack is already full!";
      errorInfo.Success = false;
      throw errorInfo;
    }
    this.stackData[++last] = pushValue;
    return;
  }

  public void Pop(ref int popValue) {
    /* If the stack is empty, throw an exception */
    if (last == -1) {
      // Create exception object
      StackError errorInfo = new StackError();
      errorInfo.ErrorMessage = "Pop() failed, stack is already empty!";
      errorInfo.Success = false;
      throw errorInfo;
    }
    popValue = this.stackData[last--];
    return;
  }

  public override string ToString() {
    string result = "";
    for ( int i = 0 ; i <= last ; i++) {
      result = result + "item " + i.ToString() + ": "
        + this.stackData[i].ToString() + " \n";
    }
    return result;
  }
}
```

Program 12.14   IntegerStack with exception-based error handling.

```
try {
       // any code that may throw an exception that we want
       // to take care of.
}
catch (Exception theExeception) {
       // Code executed when an exception of type Exception is
       // thrown.  This code can access information in the
       // exception object using the reference variable theException.
}
```

Figure 12.12   Syntax of a try/catch block.

catch block can take care of and the variable name used to refer to the exception object in the catch block. The syntax for a try/catch block is shown outlined in Figure 12.12.

Note that multiple catch blocks can be defined for the same try. The first catch block, whose parameter type is supported by the exception object thrown, contains the code executed in response to a throw. If none of these catch blocks are supported by the exception object's run-time type, the program will continue rolling back to search for another try block, whose catch block it will examine. Note that a try/catch block can appear in a different method than the throw statement. Thus, there is no knowledge at the point that an exception is thrown as to where the exception is going to be caught. It is the responsibility of the programmer to organize a try/catch block to intercept any exceptions that are thrown.

As a concrete example, we have created a revision of StackErrorDemo in Program 12.15 that uses a try/catch block to intercept exceptions thrown by the IntegerStack of Program 12.14. From IntegerStack's definition in Program 12.14, we know the constructor, Push and Pop methods can generate exceptions. Thus, the constructor call is contained in the try block. While there is no direct call to Push, the method PushData makes calls to Push. Should a call to Push throw an exception, the program will return from PushData looking for a try/catch block that can handle a StackError exception. PushData no longer needs to return a StackError object; however, it should be called from inside the try code of a try/catch block that can deal with StackError exceptions. The catch block executed in response to an exception throw accesses details stored in the exception object using the reference variable error defined in round brackets along side the catch keyword. While Program 12.15 has only one catch block, it is possible for multiple catch blocks to follow a try block.

Using Program 12.15, we can see how throwing exceptions allows constructors to return error codes and avoids the need for code to propagate the error object. By selecting an unreasonable stack size, the user can generate a StackError exception in the IntegerStack constructor. This is the case in Figure 12.13, where using a stack size of zero demonstrates exception handling with a constructor. It is important to mention that control passes to a catch block as soon as an exception is encountered. This means that the code in the try block beyond the point that an exception is encountered will not be executed. Thus, "How many times to Push?" does not appear in Figure 12.13 and none of the PushData calls are made. If a valid stack size is specified and more items are selected for pushing than the stack can accommodate, we can trigger an exception in Push that will force both the Push and the PushData methods to return. This situation is pictured in Figure 12.14. Notice that there is no explicit code in PushData of Program 12.15 to pass the StackError object from the Push method to the Main method. With this example we can see how throwing exceptions has solved the problems with our previous error-handling implementation.

```
/* Catch exceptions thrown by the StackInteger class. */
using tcdIO;

class StackErrorDemo {
  /* Static terminal need not be passed as a parameter. */
  static Terminal terminal;

  static void Main() {
    /* Create Variables required by the method. */
    IntegerStack stack;
    int stackSize, pushCalls;

    /* Create a new terminal for communicating with the user. */
    terminal = new Terminal("Demonstration of a Stack");
    terminal.WriteLine("Demonstration of exceptions in IntegerStack");

    /* Get a stack size from the user.  */
    stackSize = terminal.ReadInt("Please enter the stack size: ");

    try {
      stack = new IntegerStack(stackSize);

      /* Get the number of items to add from the user. */
      pushCalls = terminal.ReadInt("How many times to Push?");
      PushData(stack, pushCalls);
    }  catch (StackError error) {
      terminal.WriteLine("Stack method generated an error!");
      terminal.WriteLine("Exception type:      " + error.Message);
      terminal.WriteLine("Custom error message: " + error.ToString());
    }
  }

  public static void PushData(IntegerStack stack, int numPushes){
    for ( int i = 0; i < numPushes ; i++ ) {

      /* State what we are doing */
      terminal.WriteLine("Pushing " + i.ToString() + " onto stack.");

      /* Add an item to the stack. */
      stack.Push(2*i);
    }
  }
}
```

Program 12.15   Catch exceptions thrown by the Program 12.14 StackInteger class.

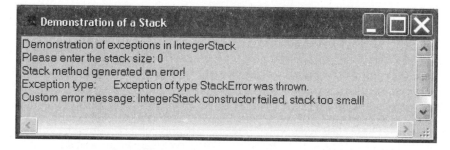

Figure 12.13   Generating an exception in the IntegerStack constructor.

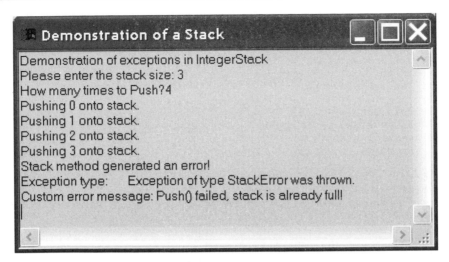

Figure 12.14   Generating an exception that is thrown across several methods.

C# Defined Exceptions

As well as allowing the user to create and throw exceptions, C# has built-in exceptions to protect and notify the program when language constructs are misused. Up until now, we saw the use of `try/catch` blocks to catch exceptions generated by methods we called. These methods contained explicit `throw` statements triggered when an error in the method's operation was detected. However, there are errors that occur purely from the misuse of C# language constructs. Exceptions are thrown when variable data is incorrectly accessed, when invalid conversions are made or when integer arithmetic operations fail. Rather than terminate the program when these errors occur, C# throws exceptions with the expectation that the program will catch them. If the exceptions are not caught, then the program is forced to terminate. Fortunately, we can catch exceptions generated by C# language constructs in the same way we catch user defined exceptions.

Program 12.16, `ArrayAccess`, demonstrates an *invalid data access* when more elements are added to an array than it can handle. In this program, the user is requested to select the array size and the number of elements stored in the array. However, the program assumes that the array is large enough to accommodate all the number of values added. When the number of elements to add is greater than the number of elements in the array, the program accesses a non-existent array element. Rather than let the program crash, `ArrayAccess` anticipates incorrect access by putting the array accesses in a `try` block. After printing the details of the error, the program continues execution after the `catch` block. Figure 12.15 pictures the program's output when the user triggers a run-time error.

Program 12.17 demonstrates the consequences of an *invalid conversion*. Here, two classes are defined, one a derived class of the other. As we discussed in Chapter 11, an explicit conversion is defined in a derived class that allows variables of the base class type to be converted to variables of the derived class' type. The reason the conversion is explicit is that it may fail. Specifically, a base object cannot be referenced by a variable of a derived class' type. Thus a variable of base class type, which refers a base class object, cannot be converted to a variable of derived class type. Should this occur, C# throws an exception as it does for an invalid data access. If a `try/catch` block can be found that handles an `InvalidCastException`,

```
/* Demonstrates catching an invalid data access on an array. */
using System;
using tcdIO;

class ArrayAccess {
  static void Main() {
    /* Create Variables required by the method. */
    Terminal terminal;
    int[] intArray;
    int arraySize, index;

    /* Create a new terminal for communicating with the user. */
    terminal = new Terminal("Demonstration of array element access");

    /* Get the array size from the user. */
    arraySize=terminal.ReadInt("How many elements are in the array? ");

    /* Get array element to access. */
    index=terminal.ReadInt("Which element should a value be stored in? ");

    try {
      /* Create the array */
      intArray = new int[index];

      /* Store an item in the array */
      intArray[index] = 1;

    } catch (Exception error) {
      terminal.WriteLine("Caught an exception!");
      terminal.WriteLine(error.Message);
      terminal.WriteLine(error.ToString());
    }
  }
}
```

Program 12.16   Demonstrates catching an invalid data access on an array.

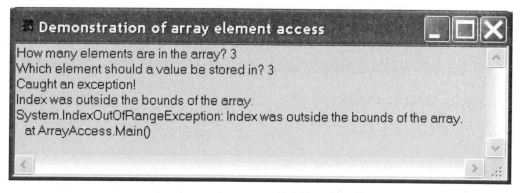

Figure 12.15   Sample execution of Program 12.16.

```
/* Example of an invalid conversion.*/
using System;
using tcdIO;

class A { /* Contents are not important */ }

class B : A { /* Contents are not important */ }

class BadConversion
{
  static void Main() {
    /* Create Variables required by the method. */
    Terminal terminal;
    A superClassObject;
    B subClassObject;

    /* Create a new terminal for communicating with the user. */
    terminal = new Terminal("Demonstration a bad conversion");

    superClassObject = new A();

    try {
      /* Sometime B's can be A's, so we'll use an explicit
       * conversion to see if that is the case today
       */
      subClassObject = (B)superClassObject;

      /* Print the result */
      terminal.WriteLine("Success!" );
    } catch (Exception error) {
      terminal.WriteLine("Caught an exception!");
      terminal.WriteLine(error.Message);
      terminal.WriteLine(error.ToString());
    }
  }
}
```

Program 12.17   Example of an invalid conversion.

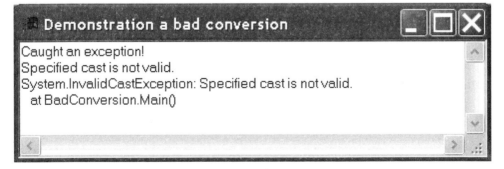

Figure 12.16   Sample execution of Program 12.17.

```
/* Allows a divide by zero arithmetic error. */
using System;
using tcdIO;

class DivideByZero {
  static void Main() {
    /* Create Variables required by the method. */
    Terminal terminal;
    int dividend, divisor, quotient;

    /* Create a new terminal for communicating with the user. */
    terminal = new Terminal("Demonstration of division of integers");

    /* Get the array size from the user. */
    dividend = terminal.ReadInt("Dividend? ");

    /* Get array element to access. */
    divisor = terminal.ReadInt("Divisor? ");

    try {
      /* Do the division and write the result. */
      quotient = dividend/divisor;
      terminal.WriteLine("The result is " + quotient.ToString() );
    } catch (Exception error) {
      terminal.WriteLine("Caught an exception!");
      terminal.WriteLine(error.Message);
      terminal.WriteLine(error.ToString());
    }
  }
}
```

Program 12.18   Allows a divide by zero arithmetic error.

the catch will be executed and execution will resume after the catch block. In the case of Program 12.17, the program catches the exception and prints out details of the error. The run-time operation of the program is pictured in Figure 12.16.

Finally, Program 12.18 demonstrates the results of attempting an invalid arithmetic operation on an integer numeric type. For this example we have chosen the divide by zero error. This error should be familiar, as it is as apt to happen on a handheld calculator as it is to happen in a C# program. When the error is detected, C# throws a DivideByZeroException object. Figure 12.17 demonstrates the output of Program 12.18 as it prints out the details of the divide by zero error.

Case Study

Anyone who examines the case study in Chapter 11 closely will notice two important problems with the classes used to solve the overlapping shapes problem. First, the Polygon class allows us to create a shape with less than three points. For instance, we could create a Polygon with no sides. In this case, the Overlaps() method, shown in Figure 12.18, will cause an exception when it tries to create a Segment object with only one point. This exception will crash the program. Secondly, the OverlappingShapeDetector class has a bug that crashes the

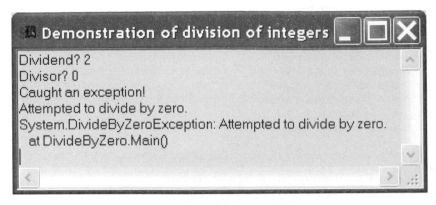

Figure 12.17   Sample execution of Program 12.18.

program. If a circle is selected for anything other than the first shape, the program crashes. The problem lies with our user input loop, shown in Figure 12.19. Here, the index of circle shape is always '0', when it should be 'i' so that it can vary according to which shape is being input. The program should put a reference to a Circle object in the shapes array element corresponding to the shape being input. However, the element may instead contain a null reference. When a null reference is used as a parameter to an Overlaps call, the program fails.

The long-term solution to these problems is to add exceptions to the Shape class implementations. One solution to the problems of our program is to carefully screen input to prevent the creation of unreasonable shapes or the use of Shape methods with unreasonable

```
public override bool Overlaps(Shape other) {
  for ( int i = 0; i<this.pts.Length; ++i) {
    Segment sgPoly = new Segment(this.pts[i],
                                  this.pts[(i+1)%this.pts.Length]);
    if ( other.Intersects(sgPoly) )
      return true;
  }
  return false;
}
```

Figure 12.18   Overlaps method in class Polygon.

```
// Get details on each shape
for ( int i = 0; i < shapes.Length ; i++) {
    char isCircle = terminal.readChar("Is this shape a circle? (Y/N)");
    terminal.WriteString("");

    if (isCircle == 'y' || isCircle == 'Y')
        shapes[0] = GetCircleInput();
    else
        shapes[i] = GetPolygonInput();
}
```

Figure 12.19   Portion of OverlappingShapeDetector that causes problems when any shape is a circle other than the first shape input.

```
using System;

public class ShapeException : System.Exception  {
  // Some premade error codes to simplify seeding exceptions.
  public const string NoOther = "You called Overlaps() with "
                                          + "a null reference!";
  public const string TooFewSides = "A polygon has at least 3 sides!";
  public const string General = "An exception occurred in a Shape "
                                          + "class implementation";

  // We reuse the base constructor
  public ShapeException(string msg):base(msg) {}

  // Default construction contains a relevant message.
  public ShapeException() : this(General) {}
}
```

Program 12.19   Class `ShapeException` describes exceptions thrown by implementations of the `Shape` class.

parameters. In this case, the program would prevent a user from inputting a polygon with fewer than three sides. Likewise, the `Overlaps` calls could be modified so they returned `false` should their `Shape` parameter be `null`. Unfortunately, screening the input to the program does not prevent other users of the `Polygon` class from making the same mistake. Also, there is no way for the `Overlaps` method to indicate that an error has occurred as there is no room in the return value for additional information explaining the reason why two `Shape` objects do not overlap. Without this information, the error in Figure 12.19 could not be detected. A better approach to stopping the creation of invalid `Polygon` objects is to throw an exception in the constructor. Also, exceptions can be used to return error information from the `Overlaps` method without changing its return type. So, exceptions offer a way to indicate the presence of errors that does not modify the existing methods and which is easily reusable in other programs.

The error detection code in classes that derive from class `Shape` should throw exception objects defined by a unique class. The exception object does not have to contain many details on the cause of the error. A string with a text explanation describing the problem will suffice, and such a string is already available in `Exception` class objects. However, creating a unique exception object class makes it more convenient to detect `Shape`-class exceptions. C# allows the definition of `catch` blocks that are executed for a specific type of exception object. Having an exception class unique to shapes allows the definition of `catch` blocks to respond to problems specific to `Shape` objects. Thus, we define the `ShapeException` class, which is pictured in Program 12.19. C# requires that this class inherit from the `Exception` class, so we exploit the string defined in `Exception` rather than create a string field in `ShapeException`. Notice that `ShapeException` defines string constants to correspond to common error conditions. This is intended to make the error messages returned by implementations of the `Shape` type more consistent. The position of these constants guarantees that users of the `ShapeException` class will be able to access the strings.

With the definition of the `ShapeException` class, we can report the detection of errors in the `Polygon` and `Circle` classes. The `Polygon` class needs to stop the creation of polygons with fewer than three points. In Program 12.20, the `Polygon` constructor has been updated to throw a `ShapeException` object when not enough points are used. The error message is a constant defined in the `ShapeException` class. The `Polygon` class also needs to ensure that the parameter to the `Overlaps` method is valid. If the parameter is `null`,

```csharp
using System;

public class Polygon : Shape {
  Point[] pts;

  public Polygon(Point[] pts) {
    this.pts = new Point[pts.Length];

    // Check validity of constructor parameters.
    if (this.pts.Length < 3)
      throw new ShapeException(ShapeException.TooFewSides);

    for ( int i = 0; i< this.pts.Length; i++){
      this.pts[i] = new Point(pts[i]);
    }
  }

  public override bool Overlaps(Shape other) {

    // Verify that the other parameter references an object!
    if (other == null)
      throw new ShapeException(ShapeException.NoOther);

    for ( int i = 0; i<this.pts.Length; ++i) {
      Segment sgPoly = new Segment(this.pts[i],
         this.pts[(i+1)%this.pts.Length]);
      if ( other.Intersects(sgPoly) )
        return true;
    }
    return false;
  }

  public override double MinDistanceToPoint(Point pt) {
    Segment sg1 = new Segment(this.pts[0], this.pts[1]);
    double minDist = sg1.MinDistance(pt);

    for ( int i = 0; i<this.pts.Length; ++i){
      Segment sg = new Segment(this.pts[i],
         this.pts[(i+1)%this.pts.Length]);
      double currDist = sg.MinDistance(pt);

      if (currDist < minDist) {
        minDist = currDist;
      }
    }
    return minDist;
  }

  public override double MaxDistanceToPoint(Point pt) {
    Segment sg1 = new Segment(this.pts[0], this.pts[1]);
    double maxDist = sg1.MaxDistance(pt);

    for ( int i = 0; i<this.pts.Length; ++i){
      Segment sg = new Segment(this.pts[i],
         this.pts[(i+1)%this.pts.Length]);
      double currDist = sg.MaxDistance(pt);

      if (currDist > maxDist) {
        maxDist = currDist;
```

```
    }
  }
  return maxDist;
}

public override bool Intersects(Segment sg) {
  for ( int i = 0; i<this.pts.Length; ++i) {
    Segment sgPoly = new Segment(this.pts[i],
        this.pts[(i+1)%this.pts.Length]);
    if ( sgPoly.DoesItIntersect(sg) )
      return true;
  }
  return false;
}
}
```

Program 12.20   Update of `Polygon` class to catch invalid arguments to the constructor and the `Overlaps` method.

a `ShapeException` object is thrown. Once again, the error message is defined by a string constant. The `Circle` class need only update its `Overlaps` method to validate the method parameter. The updated portion of class `Circle` is shown in Program 12.21.

```
using System;

public class Circle : Shape {
  Point centre;
  double radius;

  public Circle(Point centre, double radius) {
    this.centre = new Point(centre);
    this.radius = radius;
  }

  public override bool Overlaps(Shape other) {
    // Verify that the other parameter references an object!
    if (other == null)
      throw new ShapeException(ShapeException.NoOther);

    double minDist = other.MinDistanceToPoint(this.centre);
    double maxDist = other.MaxDistanceToPoint(this.centre);

    if (this.OnCircumference(minDist) || this.OnCircumference(maxDist))
      return true;
    else if (this.WithinRadius(minDist) && this.OutsideRadius(maxDist))
      return true;
    else
      return false;
  }

  public override double MinDistanceToPoint(Point pt){
    double distance = this.centre.Distance(pt) - this.radius;
    return Math.Abs(distance);
  }
```

```
public override double MaxDistanceToPoint(Point pt) {
  double distance = this.centre.Distance(pt) + this.radius;
  return Math.Abs(distance);
}

public override bool Intersects(Segment sg) {
  double minDist = sg.MinDistance(centre);
  double maxDist = sg.MaxDistance(centre);

  if (this.OnCircumference(minDist) || this.OnCircumference(maxDist))
    return true;
  else if (this.WithinRadius(minDist) && this.OutsideRadius(maxDist))
    return true;
  else
    return false;
}
private bool WithinRadius(double distance) {
  if ( (float)distance <= (float)this.radius)
    return true;
  else
    return false;
}

private bool OnCircumference(double distance) {
  if ( Math.Abs((float)distance-(float)this.radius) <= float.Epsilon)
    return true;
  else
    return false;
}

private bool OutsideRadius(double distance){
  if ( (float)distance >= (float)this.radius)
    return true;
  else
    return false;
}
}
```

Program 12.21   Update of `Circle` class to catch invalid arguments to the `Overlaps` method.

With these changes in place, the `OverlapDetectorProgram` will correctly automatically report invalid input, but `try/catch` blocks are required to make use of this information. By default, any uncaught exceptions in C# will cause the program to terminate. If the program is running from inside a development environment, a dialog will be displayed indicating the error message stored in the exception that was thrown. An example of this dialog is shown in Figure 12.21, and was generated by the program input in Figure 12.20.

While the dialog reports that "A polygon has at least 3 sides!", the user is not given the opportunity to revise their input. To do so, the `OverlappingDetectorProgram` would have to catch the exception and prompt the user for new input. In Program 12.22, the `Main` method has been revised to catch exceptions generated when `Circles` or `Polygons` are created. The exception's error message is reported, and the user has a chance to correct the information that they supplied for the shape. A demonstration of the improved error handling is provided in Figure 12.22, where the user attempts to create an invalid polygon. The program rebuffs the users input when an exception is caught by the input loop. The problem is reported

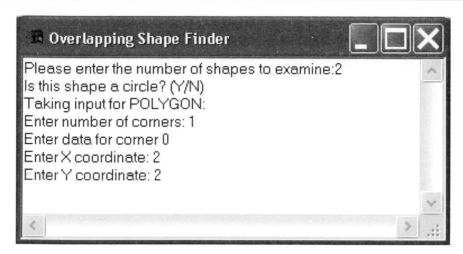

Figure 12.20   Input to create an invalid `Polygon` object.

to the user, and they are asked to input the shape data again. In addition, the program catches any exceptions that are generated when `Overlaps` is called. While the user may not be able to correct these problems, at least they are aware that the program's results may not be correct. Another demonstration is provided in Figure 12.23, where the `Circle` input bug is triggered. Here the program correctly reports that `Overlaps` is called with an invalid parameter. The programmer will have to fix the problem, but at least they now know the cause.

Our updated classes generate exceptions only for very specific errors. It is still possible that the `Shape` class and its derivatives throw exceptions not defined by the `ShapeException`. These will not be problems that we have anticipated in our error checking code, and it's reasonable to expect that they are uncommon or that they indicate problems that cannot be reasonably handled by the `catch` blocks that we have defined.

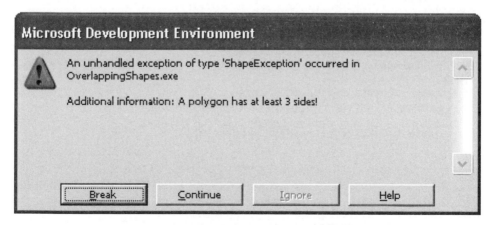

Figure 12.21   Consequences of input used in Figure 12.20.

```csharp
using System;
using tcdIO;

class OverlappingShapeDetector {

  // Static terminal variable can be accessed without
  // needing to pass the terminal object as a parameter.
  static Terminal terminal;

  static void Main() {
    Shape[] shapes;

    terminal = new Terminal("Overlapping Shape Finder");

    // Request number of shapes.
    int numShapes = terminal.ReadInt("Please enter the number" +
                                     " of shapes to examine:");
    shapes = new Shape[numShapes];

    // Get details on each shape
    for ( int i = 0; i < shapes.Length ; i++) {
      char isCircle = terminal.ReadChar("Is this shape a circle? (Y/N)");
      terminal.WriteString("");

      try {
        if (isCircle == 'y' || isCircle == 'Y')
          shapes[0] = GetCircleInput();
        else
          shapes[i] = GetPolygonInput();
      }
      catch (ShapeException problem){
        terminal.WriteString(problem.Message);
        terminal.WriteString("Please try entering that one again!");

        // Decrement loop counter
        --i;
      }
    }

    // Determine which shapes overlap
    for (int i = 0; i < shapes.Length ; i++){
      for (int j = i+1; j < shapes.Length; j++){
        try {
          if ( shapes[i].Overlaps(shapes[j]) )
            terminal.WriteString("Shape " + i + "overlaps shape " + j);
        }
        catch (ShapeException problem){
          terminal.WriteString("Problem matching Shape "
                               + i + " to "+ j + ":");
          terminal.WriteString(problem.Message);
        }
      }
    }
  }

  static Shape GetCircleInput() {
    terminal.WriteString("Taking input for CIRCLE: ");
```

```
        double x = terminal.ReadDouble("Enter X coordinate: ");
        double y = terminal.ReadDouble("Enter Y coordinate: ");
        double r = terminal.ReadDouble("Enter radius: ");

        return (Shape)new Circle(new Point(x,y), r);
    }

    static Shape GetPolygonInput() {
        Point[] corners;
        terminal.WriteString("Taking input for POLYGON: ");
        int sides = terminal.ReadInt("Enter number of corners: ");
        corners = new Point[sides];

        for (int i = 0 ; i < sides; i++) {
            terminal.WriteString("Enter data for corner " + i);
            double x = terminal.ReadDouble("Enter X coordinate: ");
            double y = terminal.ReadDouble("Enter Y coordinate: ");
            corners[i] = new Point(x,y);
        }
        return (Shape)new Polygon(corners);
    }
}
```

Program 12.22 Update of Main method in OverlappingShapeDetector class to catch invalid arguments to the constructor and the Overlaps method.

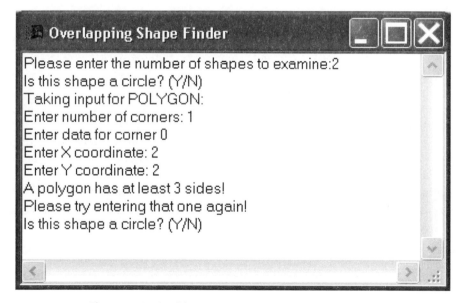

Figure 12.22 Invalid Polygon error is caught by Program 12.22.

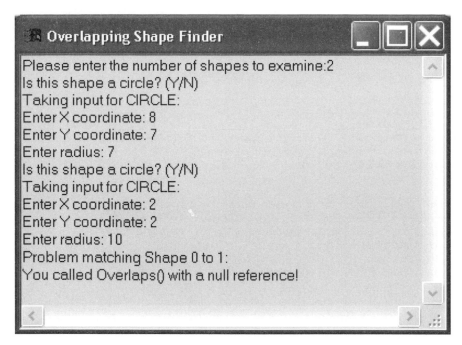

Figure 12.23 Results when `Circle` input bug of Program 12.22 is triggered.

Summary

- a stack data structure stores information that is retrieved in a LIFO order; two methods, `Push` and `Pop`, are provided to add and remove data from the stack
- good error checking should be consistent in the values used to indicate an error and in the way error information is returned to the caller
- error information should be informative; we saw that combining several pieces of information in one object simplified error reporting
- error reporting should not make calling methods of an object cumbersome; using exceptions to pass error information avoids cluttering a method's parameter list with parameters unrelated to normal execution
- exception objects are defined by classes that inherit from the `Exception` class
- a `try`/`catch` block specifies a set of `catch` blocks that handle specific types of exceptions generated by the code enclosed by the `try` block
- the `throw` keyword passes an exception object to the first type-compatible `catch` block of an enclosing `try` block

Exercises

(1) Use the stack program of Program 12.4 to store the letters of the alphabet and print them in reverse order. Use as few lines of code as possible.

(2) Create a class that implements a queue. A *queue* is similar to a stack, except that items are removed in FIFO (first in, first out) order. Instead of the method names `Push` and `Pop`, a queue uses the method names `Enqueue` and `Dequeue` for methods to insert and remove items from the queue object. Unlike a stack, the queue's next free element and next element to remove cannot be tracked with the same variable. Instead, they have to be recorded independently.

Create an application to store the alphabet in your queue and then to read out the data.

(3) A naive implementation of queue will only be able to store a value once in each element of the storage array field. This is because the calculation of the next available element does not take into account the elements that become free at the start of the Queue object's storage array. The elements are freed whenever `Dequeue` is called. Take, for example, a queue that uses a ten-element array for storage. If the last item inserted is in element 9 and the next item to remove is in element 6, then elements 0 through 5 could be used. To take advantage of this space, the `Enqueue` method must realize that the next element after number 9 is number 0.

Create a version of class Queue that is able to take advantage of storage array elements freed by calls to `Dequeue`. Write a program that adds all the letters of the alphabet and removes them in the order they were added. However, be sure to use a queue that uses a ten-element array to store inserted items.

(4) The queue we wrote for Exercise 3 needs to stop the user from inserting too many items into the queue. Add throws to the constructor, `Enqueue` and `Dequeue` methods as we did to the `IntegerStack` in Program 12.14, and create a new class to describe the exception objects that are thrown.

Create a program that uses this new implementation of Queue. It should have an interface that allows the user to select the queue size, to add items to the queue and remove items from the queue. In this case, the items added should describe people.

(5) The integer type provides the `Parse` method which converts strings to integer values. However, if the string contains invalid characters the `Parse` method throws an exception. For instance, `int.Parse("z12")` will cause an exception to be thrown.

With this in mind, create a calculator program that allows the user to add, multiply, subtract, and divide numbers. In the user interface you must read in all data as strings and convert to integer values using the `Parse` method. Incorrect input should be reported to the user, and another opportunity must be given to input the correct data. Be sure to catch any exceptions that are generated by divide by zero problems!

(6) So far we have used one class to define all of the exception objects thrown in a program. However, a method can potentially throw exception objects of different classes.

Re-implement the `LibraryBook` class created for Chapter 7, Exercise 1 with revisions to the error-handling system. Instead of returning `false` when a call to `BorrowBook`, `RenewLoan`, `ReserveBook`, or `ReturnBook` cannot execute properly, generate an exception. Use separate classes to define exception objects for each cause of failure for each method. To demonstrate that the revised error-handling system works according to specification, create a program that triggers every possible exception. This program need not take input from the user, but it must terminate normally. Specifically, it must catch and report any exceptions that are thrown.

GUI Development 13

This chapter:

- introduces the concept of a *form* and that of a *control*
- demonstrates the usefulness of Visual Studio's Designer for editing the layout and setting the properties of forms and their controls
- introduces the concept of an *event*, and gives an overview of the *publisher–subscriber* event model used by C#
- explains what a *delegate type* is and how it is defined
- explains how an event field is defined and what purpose the event field serves
- demonstrates the use of elementary controls such as buttons and labels
- introduces mouse events to which controls can respond
- introduces the concept of a modal dialog box

As with other C# applications, classes form the backbone of a *graphical user interface* (or *GUI* for short). GUI development hinges on the use of pre-made classes that implement windows and controls that are placed in these windows. These ready-made classes considerably reduce the coding effort required to display windows and interact with the user. As an added benefit, they make our windows look and feel like those used by other applications on our computer. Broadly speaking, a *control* is any item that is able to display itself and respond to user interaction. An example of a control placed in a window would be the "Cancel" button found on many dialog boxes. Each control corresponds to a different class, but their basic functionality is specified in a common base class. Since the concepts learned working with basic controls apply to any control, we will introduce a limited number of GUI pre-made classes.

GUI development is simplified by using tools to write the code for us. In previous chapters, we wrote our classes from beginning to end, and possibly inherited behaviour from other classes. In GUI development, the task of constructing windows and the placement of controls on them can be automated significantly. Indeed, Visual Studio provides a Designer tool that can generate a considerable amount of code automatically. The Designer is useful for organizing the layout of a window as well as configuring the properties of the window and controls on that window. Features of the Designer will be presented throughout this chapter.

A more significant problem in GUI development is the erratic nature of user input. Previously terminal programs were able to predict what the user would type next because information was requested in a fixed order. With GUIs, any control on a window can be manipulated at any time. To model this kind of interaction we introduce the concept of an *event* that corresponds to some kind of action by the user. By creating methods to respond to every possible event, we can allow the user to pick the order in which input is added to a window. Programming in terms of events requires two new constructs: the delegate and the

481

event field. Event constructs and the event model are discussed in the second section of this chapter.

GUI Design

In this section we introduce the concepts required to develop GUIs for our programs. We start by introducing the form. A *form* is a class that defines a piece of real estate on our screen. A form is of little interest until additional controls are placed on it. As we will see, controls are able to respond to user actions. Forms have a has-a relationship with controls. Without the necessary feedback to see what it is that we have created, we could spend a lot of time getting the form's layout correct. Fortunately, Visual Studio provides a very powerful editor that allows us to design our form and place controls graphically. The editor or Designer as Visual Studio calls it, actually writes code for us that it places in the form class. Using the Designer we can quickly assemble dialog boxes and main windows for our applications.

Introducing Forms

An application that contains forms requires an entirely different project from one that uses the console. When projects are created in Visual Studio, the option is given to select a template corresponding to the type of application being created. This dictates the initial set of classes added to the application and makes sure that the build instructions for the project are suited

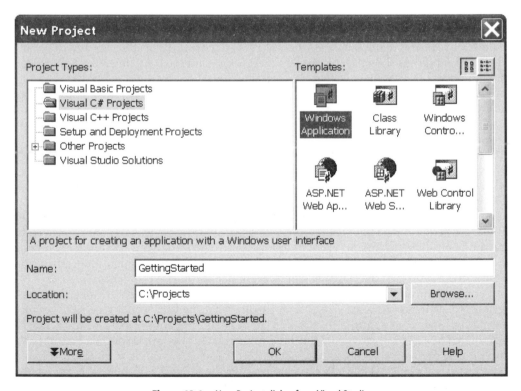

Figure 13.1   New Project dialog from Visual Studio.

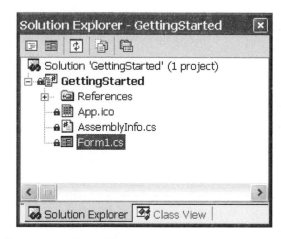

Figure 13.2   Files initially added to a Windows Application project.

to what is being compiled. GUI projects are best served by the Windows Application template. Indeed, when we select the Windows Applications template, as is done in Figure 13.1, the help message states "A project for creating an application with a Windows user interface".

Classes derived from the Form class are the focal point of GUI development. The initial project created by the Windows Application template, and pictured in Figure 13.2, contains a

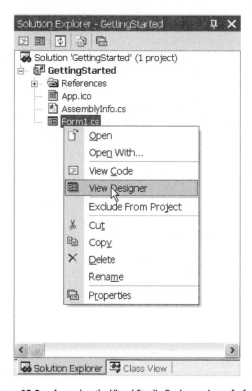

Figure 13.3   Accessing the Visual Studio Designer view of a form.

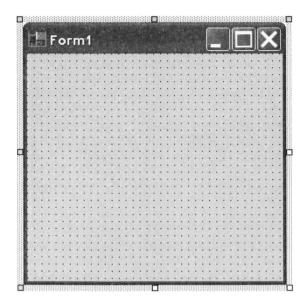

Figure 13.4   Rendering by Visual Studio of a window generated by objects of the Form1 class.

few files of which one is called `Form1`. This file contains the declaration of a class called `Form1` that inherits from the `Form` class in the `System.Windows.Forms` namespace. Simply put, the `Form` class defines the windows that are used by graphical interfaces. More precisely, the objects instantiated from classes derived from `class Form` correspond to the windows that are displayed by an application. To simplify the terminology, we will refer to these classes in general as *forms*. To get an immediate look at the window specified by `Form1`, we can display it in Visual Studio's Designer. The Designer is activated using the right click menu of

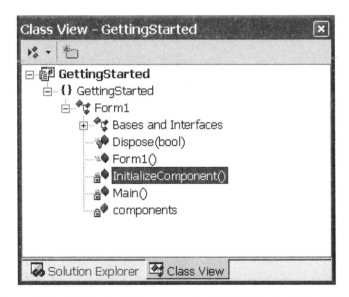

Figure 13.5   Methods, data fields and properties initially defined in the Form1 class.

the Solution Explorer, as shown in Figure 13.3. The window displayed by the Designer should look very similar to that in Figure 13.4. We will discuss more advanced uses for Designer later in this section. While the `Form` class provides the basic design and functionality of a window, it will have to be customized to suit our needs. For instance, our `Form1` class has already customized the title of the window to say "Form1". More complex applications are likely to have many windows; each corresponding to an object defined by a form. Hence the importance of making changes to classes derived from `Form` rather than the `Form` class itself!

The appearance of a form is largely controlled by properties inherited from the `Form` base class. As we can see from the class view pictured in Figure 13.5, the `Form1` class has very few methods, one data field called `components`, and no properties. However, the `Form` base class implements numerous properties with a variety of purposes. Some properties allow values to be used to control the appearance of the windows. The `Width` and `Height` properties set the dimensions of the form's window, while the `Text` property sets the title of the window. In contrast, some properties are Booleans that indicate the presences of a standard control. `MinimizeBox` and `MaxmizeBox` control the availability of minimize and maximize buttons on the right-hand side of the window's title bar. By revising a form class' code, we can specify these values programmatically. First, the class' code must be opened for editing. This is done in a fashion similar to that used in Figure 13.3 to open the form in the Designer, except that the "View Code" option is selected as pictured in Figure 13.6.

Figure 13.6 Accessing the code view of a form.

```csharp
using System;
using System.Drawing;
using System.Collections;
using System.ComponentModel;
using System.Windows.Forms;
using System.Data;

namespace GettingStarted
{
    /// <summary>
    /// Summary description for Form1.
    /// </summary>
    public class Form1 : System.Windows.Forms.Form
    {
        /// <summary>
        /// Required designer variable.
        /// </summary>
        private System.ComponentModel.Container components = null;

        public Form1()
        {
            //
            // Required for Windows Form Designer support
            //
            InitializeComponent();

            //
            // TODO: Add any constructor code after InitializeComponent call
            //
            this.Text = "This is our very first GUI window!";
            this.Width = 500;
            this.MaximizeBox = false;
            this.MinimizeBox = false;
        }

        /// <summary>
        /// Clean up any resources being used.
        /// </summary>
        protected override void Dispose( bool disposing )
        {
            if( disposing )
            {
                if (components != null)
                {
                    components.Dispose();
                }
            }
            base.Dispose( disposing );
        }

        #region Windows Form Designer generated code
        /// <summary>
        /// Required method for Designer support - do not modify
        /// the contents of this method with the code editor.
        /// </summary>
        private void InitializeComponent()
        {
```

```
        //
        // Form1
        //
        this.AutoScaleBaseSize = new System.Drawing.Size(6, 15);
        this.ClientSize = new System.Drawing.Size(292, 260);
        this.Name = "Form1";
        this.Text = "Form1";
    }
    #endregion

    /// <summary>
    /// The main entry point for the application.
    /// </summary>
    [STAThread]
    static void Main()
    {
        Application.Run(new Form1());
    }
}
}
```

Program 13.1   Initial Form1 class with several properties modified in the constructor.

In the code view, we can make changes to the properties we have just mentioned. To demonstrate, Program 13.1 has been changed significantly from the initial Form1 class. The maximize and minimize boxes have been removed, the title has changed, and the window starts out much wider than the previous version. We can verify the effect of changing these properties by compiling the application and looking at the window that is displayed, which is shown in Figure 13.7.

Forms do not become interesting until we start adding controls. A form is rather bare, as it does not contain any useful input devices such as buttons. Nor does it have any output items

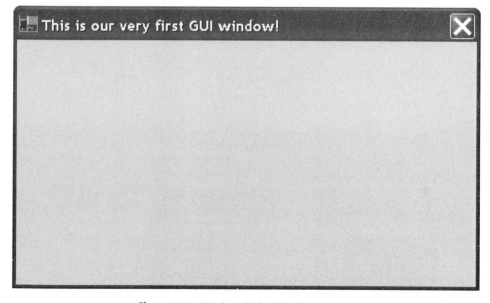

Figure 13.7   Windows displayed by Program 13.1.

such as textboxes. The functionality of these items is implemented in objects defined by other classes. In the next section we will discuss controls and then apply them in order to make our forms useful vehicles for input and output.

Introducing Controls

A *control* is an object that responds to user input and is able to display images on the screen. All controls are defined by classes that inherit from the Control class. This base class provides very general capabilities for handling user input, be it from a mouse or the keyboard. As well, controls can handle input from other sources. For instance, when the operating system's colour scheme changes, the operating system will send out messages alerting controls to the change. The Control class also provides functionality for displaying and updating the control's image on the computer monitor. Indeed, the Control class is a base class of all classes used to interact graphically with the user.

The capability of a control is much more general than that of a form. Forms are more narrowly defined than controls. Forms stake out real estate on the computer screen, but the user input that they respond to is limited. The user can do little more than move a window around the screen. They can also resize the form when the mouse is positioned over the borders or when the minimize or maximize buttons are used. The Control class has none of these capabilities built-in. Rather it provides methods to support displaying images and capturing the actions of a user. Control developers must inherit from the Control class and customize the capabilities of a control, just as form developers do with the Form class. Indeed, the Form class itself inherits from the Control class which makes it a type of control. This relationship is pictured in the inheritance hierarchy presented in Figure 13.8.

A form acts as a container for other controls. At first it may seem odd that a form class, a type of control, is able to contain other controls. However, this is not the chicken and the egg problem it seems. Containment simply means that objects of the form class maintain a

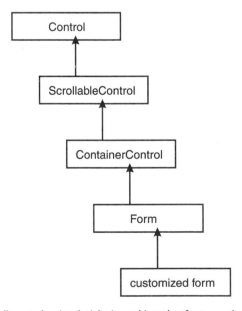

Figure 13.8   Inheritance diagram showing the inheritance hierarchy of a Form class back to class Control.

has-a relationship with several control objects. These control objects become data members of the form's class. Being controls, items such as a button or a textbox might be able to display themselves on the screen by themselves. However, this makes little sense, as several controls such as a button and a textbox cannot interact with the user coherently if they are displayed independently. Imagine having to switch windows from the textbox in which you entered some text to press the OK button that causes the data to be processed! By being able to collect several controls in one window, we can organize the controls for a specific purpose. A form class gains the capability to act as a container by inheriting from the `ContainerControl` class, pictured in the `Form` class' inheritance hierarchy in Figure 13.8.

To exploit the container capabilities of a form, we have to guarantee access to the control objects to be contained and properly register them with the form. Typically, a form maintains references to control objects with fields. While a reference to a control can be passed to the object, it is more common that the form instantiates the control objects. Having access to the objects does not guarantee that they will be displayed by the form, as demonstrated by Program 13.2. This program is an update of Program 13.1. The program looks different as we have removed some of the unused blocks of comments included when Visual Studio created the class `Form1`. More importantly, we have updated the fields to include references to two buttons and a label control. The label control is used to display read-only information to the user. While the constructor properly initializes the controls, they will not yet be displayed by a `Form1` object. Figure 13.9 shows the form displayed when the program is compiled and executed.

```
using System;
using System.Drawing;
using System.Collections;
using System.ComponentModel;
using System.Windows.Forms;
using System.Data;

namespace GettingStarted
{
    public class Form1 : System.Windows.Forms.Form
    {
        private System.ComponentModel.Container components = null;

        // These field store references to our controls
        private Button leftButton, rightButton;
        private System.Windows.Forms.Label feedbackLabel;

        public Form1()
        {
            //
            // Required for Windows Form Designer support
            //
            InitializeComponent();

            // Setup the overall form.
            this.Text = "Simple use of controls";
            this.Size = new System.Drawing.Size(304, 232);
            this.MaximizeBox = false;
            this.MinimizeBox = false;

            // Initialize control objects.
```

```csharp
        // create the label
        this.feedbackLabel = new Label();
        this.feedbackLabel.Location = new System.Drawing.Point(76, 48);
        this.feedbackLabel.Size = new System.Drawing.Size(154, 24);
        this.feedbackLabel.Text = "No button pressed, yet!";
        // create right button
        this.rightButton = new Button();
        this.rightButton.Location = new System.Drawing.Point(168, 112);
        this.rightButton.Size = new System.Drawing.Size(88, 40);
        this.rightButton.Text = "Right";

        // create left button
        this.leftButton = new Button();
        this.leftButton.Location = new System.Drawing.Point(24, 112);
        this.leftButton.Size = new System.Drawing.Size(88, 40);
        this.leftButton.Text = "Left";
    }

    protected override void Dispose( bool disposing )
    {
        if( disposing )
        {
            if (components != null)
            {
                components.Dispose();
            }
        }
        base.Dispose( disposing );
    }

    #region Windows Form Designer generated code
    /// <summary>
    /// Required method for Designer support - do not modify
    /// the contents of this method with the code editor.
    /// </summary>
    private void InitializeComponent()
    {
        //
        // Form1
        //
        this.AutoScaleBaseSize = new System.Drawing.Size(6, 15);
        this.Name = "Form1";
        this.Text = "Form1";
    }
    #endregion

    /// <summary>
    /// The main entry point for the application.
    /// </summary>
    [STAThread]
    static void Main()
    {
        Application.Run(new Form1());
    }
}
}
```

Program 13.2   Program 13.1 modified to include controls and a different title.

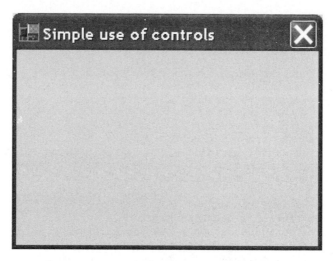

Figure 13.9   Form displayed when Program 13.2 executes.

To make controls viewable and responsive, they have to be registered with a form's
`ControlCollection` object. Each form uses its own instance of a `ControlCollection`
object to manage its collection of controls. The object is accessed from the `Controls`
property that is present in all classes that inherit from `ContainerControl`. The
`ContainerControl` supplies methods to add and remove objects from its collection.

```
using System;
using System.Drawing;
using System.Collections;
using System.ComponentModel;
using System.Windows.Forms;
using System.Data;

namespace GettingStarted
{
    public class Form1 : System.Windows.Forms.Form
    {
        private System.ComponentModel.Container components = null;

        // These field store references to our controls
        private Button leftButton, rightButton;
        private System.Windows.Forms.Label feedbackLabel;

        public Form1()
        {
            //
            // Required for Windows Form Designer support
            //
            InitializeComponent();

            // Setup the overall form.
            this.Size = new System.Drawing.Size(304, 232);
            this.MaximizeBox = false;
            this.MinimizeBox = false;
```

```
        // Initialize control objects.

        // create the label
        this.feedbackLabel = new Label();
        this.feedbackLabel.Location = new System.Drawing.Point(76, 48);
        this.feedbackLabel.Size = new System.Drawing.Size(154, 24);
        this.feedbackLabel.Text = "No button pressed, yet!";

        // create right button
        this.rightButton = new Button();
        this.rightButton.Location = new System.Drawing.Point(168, 112);
        this.rightButton.Size = new System.Drawing.Size(88, 40);
        this.rightButton.Text = "Right";

        // create left button
        this.leftButton = new Button();
        this.leftButton.Location = new System.Drawing.Point(24, 112);
        this.leftButton.Size = new System.Drawing.Size(88, 40);
        this.leftButton.Text = "Left";

        // Register the objects with the form
        this.Controls.Add(this.feedbackLabel);
        this.Controls.Add(this.rightButton);
        this.Controls.Add(this.leftButton);
    }

    /// <summary>
    /// Clean up any resources being used.
    /// </summary>
    protected override void Dispose( bool disposing )
    {
        if( disposing )
        {
            if (components != null)
            {
                components.Dispose();
            }
        }
        base.Dispose( disposing );
    }

    #region Windows Form Designer generated code
    /// <summary>
    /// Required method for Designer support - do not modify
    /// the contents of this method with the code editor.
    /// </summary>
    private void InitializeComponent()
    {
        //
        // Form1
        //
        this.AutoScaleBaseSize = new System.Drawing.Size(6, 15);
        this.ClientSize = new System.Drawing.Size(296, 192);
        this.Name = "Form1";
        this.Text = "Simple use of controls";
    }
    #endregion
```

```
/// <summary>
/// The main entry point for the application.
/// </summary>
[STAThread]
static void Main()
{
    Application.Run(new Form1());
}
    }
}
```

Program 13.3   Program 13.2 updated to properly display controls.

Program 13.3 uses the Add method of the ContainerControl object to register the buttons and label for display. As a result, they are now displayed on Form1 objects when we execute the program as shown in Figure 13.10.

Our approach to adding controls to a form can be improved significantly, as can the functionality of those controls. For instance, the buttons in Figure 13.10 would be far more interesting if they did something! Currently, we can click them as much as we want, but no code has been written to respond to the clicks. This code will be written after we have had a chance to introduce the concept of events, and show how C# models events. In the meantime, it would greatly simplify our work as programmers if we could take advantage of a graphical tool to help us position controls on a form. Indeed, Visual Studio's Designer is a very powerful tool for that specific purpose. Before moving on to discuss events, we will look at how Visual Studio's Designer helps us write code.

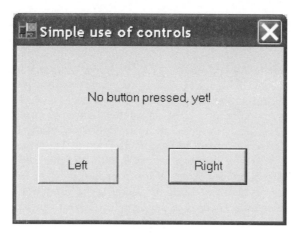

Figure 13.10   Form displayed when Program 13.3 executes.

Using the Visual Studio Designer

Visual Studio's Designer provides drag and drop placement and positioning of a wide variety of controls. We described how to use a form in the Designer at the beginning of this section, and demonstrated the process in Figure 13.3. However, we did not discuss how to access the plethora of controls that can be placed on the form. A selection of controls is available in the Designer's Toolbox. By default this window remains hidden on the left-hand side of the

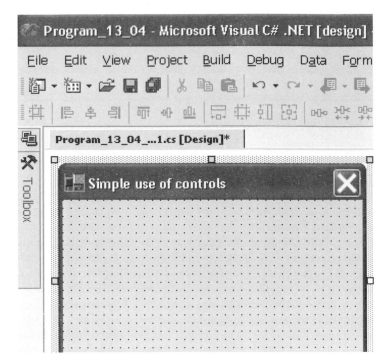

Figure 13.11   Toolbox menu when it is hidden.

Visual Studio window, and only slides into view when the pointer is placed over the Toolbox label or its hammer and wrench icon. This icon and the Toolbox label can be seen to the left in Figure 13.11.

When the Toolbox menu appears, pushing the "Windows Forms" button causes a menu of controls to appear, as shown in Figure 13.12. An alternative way to access the Toolbox window is to use the Toolbox option in the View menu.

Controls can be placed on the form by selecting them from the Toolbox and drawing their outline on the form. The Designer gives an up to date view of the controls on the form. Moreover, it allows a selected control to be quickly resized. The series of dots on the form represent intersection points in an imaginary grid. The Designer simplifies placement and resizing of controls by limiting the corners of controls placed on the form to grid points. The Designer also allows the form to be resized by dragging the sides and corner of the form. In Figure 13.13, we have used the Toolbox to duplicate the layout generated by the code added to the constructor in Program 13.3.

The Designer's graphical editing capabilities cannot be relied upon to completely describe the appearance of a form. In Figure 13.13, some items such as the form's title are still not correct. To allow their correction, Visual Studio supplies a comprehensive Properties dialog. The dialog for a form is immediately displayed by right clicking on the form's backdrop and selecting the Properties option in the dialog that appears. This menu is pictured in Figure 13.14.

The Properties dialog that appears allows the value of each of the form's properties to be edited. Where possible, the choices for a property are limited to the set of values in the dropdown list, as is the case for `MinimizeBox` in Figure 13.15. The final result of using the Designer and the Properties dialog to describe the Program 13.3 form is shown in Figure 13.16. Note that the grid lines are superimposed by the designer and do not appear when the program runs.

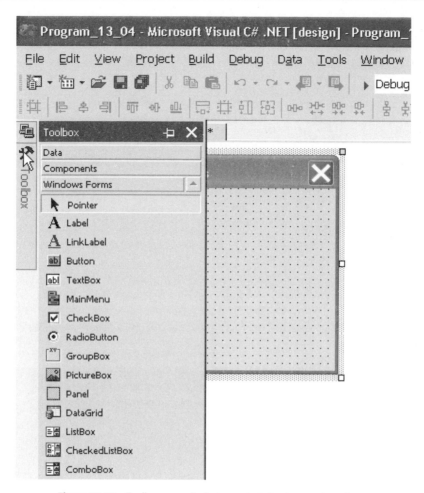

Figure 13.12 Toolbox menu displaying controls for placement on a form.

The Designer works by generating code and placing it in the target form's class. In Program 13.3, the form's constructor was modified to instantiate controls and add them to the `ControlCollection` object. In addition, the properties controlling the form's size, title, and title bar buttons were set. Rather than modifying the constructor, Visual Studio's Designer modifies a method by the name of `InitializeComponent`. In this method, the Designer writes code that would have had to be created manually. The method is activated when the form is instantiated. This is done by a call to the method that is added to the form's constructor when the form class was added to the project. Usually the Designer-generated code is hidden by the code editor, and in its place is the message "`Windows Form Designer generated code`" as shown in Figure 13.17. However, it can be viewed by clicking on the "+" symbol to the left of the message. We can see the generated code in the `InitializeComponent` method of Program 13.4. Note that the generated code corresponds quite closely to the code added to the constructor in Program 13.3.

To add behaviour to our forms will require an understanding of how events work in the C# environment. In this section we saw that using Visual Studio's Designer can speed the coding of layout and property settings of a form containing some buttons and a label. Moreover,

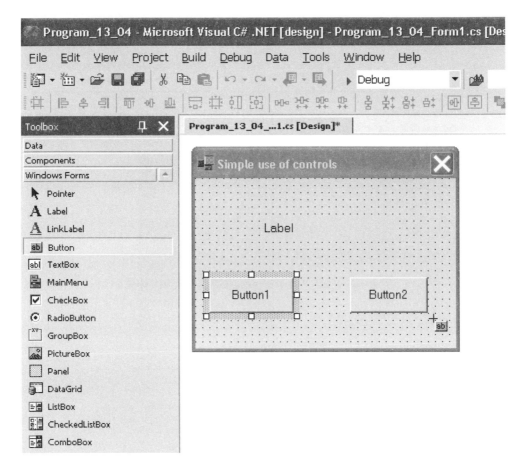

Figure 13.13   View of form in designer after work on constructor code in Program 13.3 has been duplicated.

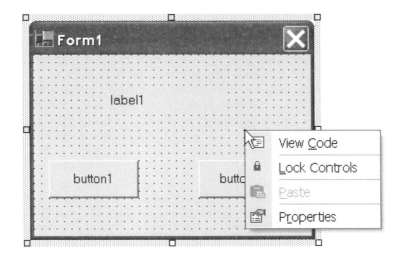

Figure 13.14   Opening a form's properties dialog.

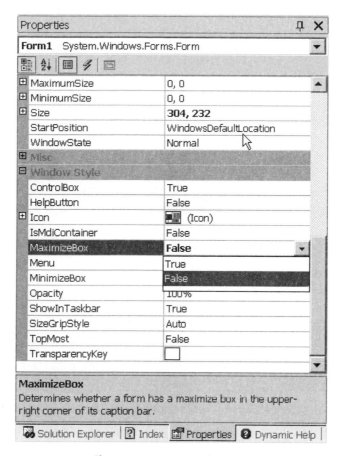

Figure 13.15   Properties for a form.

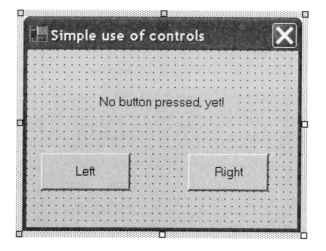

Figure 13.16   Form built using Visual Studio's Designer and Properties dialog.

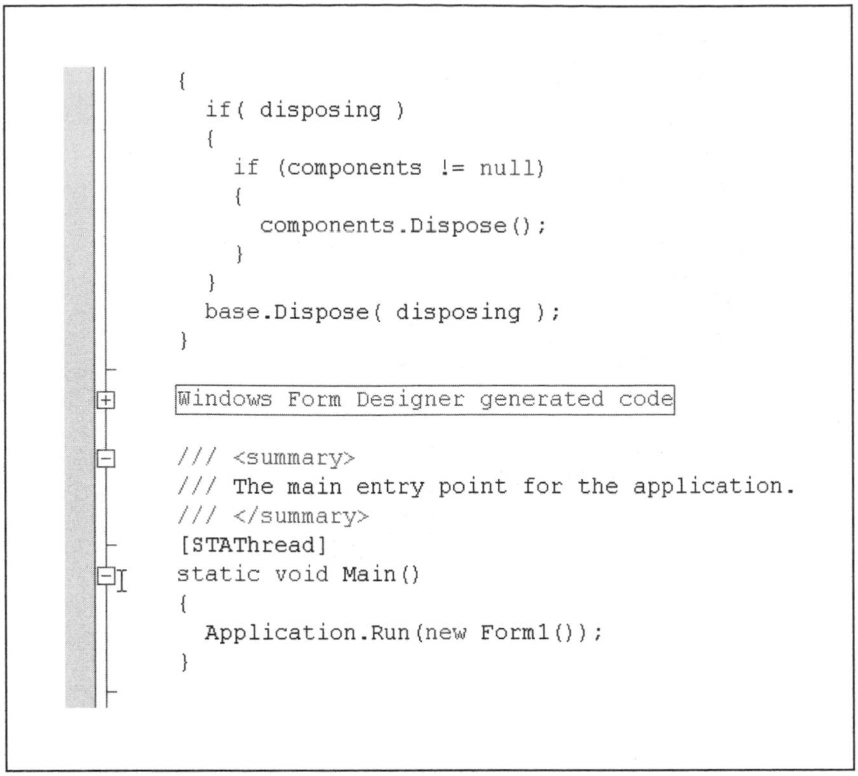

```
            {
              if( disposing )
              {
                if (components != null)
                {
                  components.Dispose();
                }
              }
              base.Dispose( disposing );
            }

    Windows Form Designer generated code

            /// <summary>
            /// The main entry point for the application.
            /// </summary>
            [STAThread]
            static void Main()
            {
              Application.Run(new Form1());
            }
```

Figure 13.17   View of Program 13.4 when Visual Studio hides the Designer-generated code.

```csharp
using System;
using System.Drawing;
using System.Collections;
using System.ComponentModel;
using System.Windows.Forms;
using System.Data;

namespace GettingStarted
{
    public class Form1 : System.Windows.Forms.Form
    {
        private System.ComponentModel.Container components = null;

        // These field store references to our controls
        private System.Windows.Forms.Label label1;
        private System.Windows.Forms.Button button1;
        private System.Windows.Forms.Button button2;

        public Form1()
        {
            //
            // Required for Windows Form Designer support
            //
            InitializeComponent();
```

```
   // Setup the overall form.
   this.Text = "Simple use of controls";
   this.ClientSize = new System.Drawing.Size(296, 192);
   this.MaximizeBox = false;
   this.MinimizeBox = false;

}


/// <summary>
/// Clean up any resources being used.
/// </summary>

protected override void Dispose( bool disposing )
{
   if( disposing )
   {
      if (components != null)
      {
         components.Dispose();
      }
   }
   base.Dispose( disposing );
}

#region Windows Form Designer generated code
/// <summary>
/// Required method for Designer support - do not modify
/// the contents of this method with the code editor.
/// </summary>
private void InitializeComponent()
{
   this.label1 = new System.Windows.Forms.Label();
   this.button1 = new System.Windows.Forms.Button();
   this.button2 = new System.Windows.Forms.Button();
   this.SuspendLayout();
   //
   // label1
   //
   this.label1.Location = new System.Drawing.Point(76, 48);
   this.label1.Name = "label1";
   this.label1.Size = new System.Drawing.Size(154, 24);
   this.label1.TabIndex = 0;
   this.label1.Text = "No button pressed, yet!";
   //
   // button1
   //
   this.button1.Location = new System.Drawing.Point(16, 112);
   this.button1.Name = "button1";
   this.button1.Size = new System.Drawing.Size(96, 40);
   this.button1.TabIndex = 1;
   this.button1.Text = "Left";
   //
   // button2
   //
   this.button2.Location = new System.Drawing.Point(176, 112);
   this.button2.Name = "button2";
```

```
        this.button2.Size = new System.Drawing.Size(88, 40);
        this.button2.TabIndex = 2;
        this.button2.Text = "Right";
        //
        // Form1
        //
        this.AutoScaleBaseSize = new System.Drawing.Size(6, 15);
        this.ClientSize = new System.Drawing.Size(296, 192);
        this.Controls.AddRange(new System.Windows.Forms.Control[] {
                                            this.button2,
                                            this.button1,
                                            this.label1});
        this.MaximizeBox = false;
        this.MinimizeBox = false;
        this.Name = "Form1";
        this.Text = "Simple use of controls";
        this.ResumeLayout(false);

    }
    #endregion

    /// <summary>
    /// The main entry point for the application.
    /// </summary>
    [STAThread]
    static void Main()
    {
        Application.Run(new Form1());
    }
  }
}
```

Program 13.4   Code generated by the Visual Studio Designer.

the Designer can be used to edit any control. However, using controls effectively for user interaction requires that we can respond to what the user is doing at run time. This code will require the use of events, which we will discuss in detail in the next section.

Understanding Events

Events can be thought of as "things" that cause a message to be passed from one object to another. In the context of GUIs, these things are actions by the application's user, and the messages contain information about what the user did. For example, a mouse event message might give details on a mouse click such as the coordinates of the pointer at the time of the click and the name of the button that was clicked. When the user interacts with the computer, these messages are generated by the operating system and passed to the form to which they correspond. This form is then responsible for distributing the message to the controls associated with the location of the click. Of course, a mouse click is just one kind of event.

We will describe the *Publisher–Subscriber idiom* used by C# to model events by way of an example. This rather intimidating sounding model, pictured in Figure 13.18 has only three key elements, and as such is fairly easy to grasp. The key elements are the Event Message, the Event Handler, and the Event Field. We will discuss each element in turn as we build an

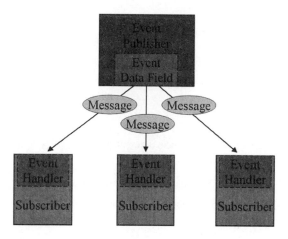

Figure 13.18   Overview of the Publisher–Subscriber event model used in C#.

event-based model of an imaginary fire alarm system. The fire alarm system models a fire alarm button and the fire alarm bell that is activated when the button is pushed. This system is visualized in Figure 13.19.

As we mentioned, *event messages* are objects that contain information describing the event that occurred. While these objects could be defined by any class, C# uses the convention that events have the `EventArgs` class in their inheritance hierarchy. This convention is strictly followed in the event messages defined for GUI actions. In the case of our fire alarm system, an event message will be passed from the push button to the alarm bell. The only information that might be of interest is the cause of the fire alarm. This information can be contained in a string field. For instance, the system might be being tested rather than there being an actual fire. In this case, the cause string in the event message might state "`Remain calm, this is just a test!`". A suitable definition of the push event message is shown in Program 13.5.

An *event handler* must be supplied by the subscriber in order to receive events from the publisher. A *subscriber* is an object that wishes to be notified of the occurrence of an event. When the event occurs, the subscriber will be passed the event's message object. This message is passed using a method call. The *event publisher* makes a call to the subscriber's event handler method and passes the event message as one of the method's parameters. The event handler's parameters and return type are rigidly defined. In fact, a special keyword is used in C# to allow this specification to be given a name. When the keyword `delegate` is applied to a method declaration that ends with a semicolon instead of a body, a method is not added to the class

Figure 13.19   Fire alarm system composed of a fire alarm button connected to a fire bell.

```
using System;

class PushEventArgs : EventArgs {
  private string cause;
  public string Cause { get{ return cause; } }

  public PushEventArgs(string cause) {
    this.cause = cause;
  }
}
```

Program 13.5   `PushEventArgs` class describes the event message passed when an alarm push event occurs.

```
delegate void PushEventHandler(object source, PushEventArgs e);
```

Program 13.6   `PushEventHandler` describes the parameters and return types of the event handler a subscriber must supply to receive an alarm push event.

in which the declaration appears. Instead, the method's name becomes associated with a type describing any method that takes the same parameters and uses the same return type. In C# terminology, method specifications created with the `delegate` keyword are referred to as *delegate types* or *delegates*. By convention, C# requires that all event handler delegates have two arguments. The first identifies the publisher of the event, while the second references the event message object. Since any type of publisher object can be referenced by a variable of type `object`, the first parameter is always of type `object`. The second will vary according to the class of the event message that is passed. For example, the fire alarm system will want to pass a reference to a `PushEventArgs` object. Finally, an event handler cannot return a value. In Program 13.6, an event handler named `PushEventHandler` is declared using the `delegate` keyword. Notice that we have to state explicitly that the return type of the event handler is specified as `void`. This declaration need not occur in a class, as the keyword `delegate` declares a type. A subscriber class that correctly implements the event handler is shown in Program 13.7. As expected, instances of this class will model the alarm bell in our fire alarm system.

The publisher object is able to specify an event as a field, which simplifies the distribution of event messages significantly and allows subscribers to register for events in a uniform manner. In C#, *event fields* are specified by combining the name of an event handler specification and the `event` keyword. For instance, an event field that requires subscribers to implement the `PushEventHandler` event handler would be declared as follows:

```
public event PushEventHandler PushEvent;
```

```
using tcdIO;

class AlarmBell {

  public void RingBell(object source, PushEventArgs e) {
    Terminal terminal = new Terminal("Fire alarm warning!");
    terminal.WriteString(e.Cause);
  }

}
```

Program 13.7   Subscriber class for the alarm push event.

```
class FireAlarmButton {

  public event PushEventHandler PushEvent;

  protected void OnPush(PushEventArgs e) {
    if (PushEvent != null)
      PushEvent(this, e);
  }
  public void TestFireAlarm() {
    OnPush(new PushEventArgs("Remain calm, this is just a test!") );
  }
}
```

Program 13.8   Publisher class for the alarm push event.

An event field has two purposes. From the point of view of subscriber objects, the event field acts as a container for all the event handlers that event subscribers have registered with publisher. To support the subscriber's view, two operations are available to manipulate the event. The += operator allows subscribers to register their event handler method with the publisher, while the –= operator allows subscribers to remove their event handler from the list of methods that will be called when an event occurs. For example, an instance of the AlarmBell class of Program 13.7 could register with the PushEvent event contained in an object called publisher with the following code:

```
AlarmBell subscriber = new AlarmBell();
publisher.PushEvent +=
    new PushEventHandler(subscriber.RingBell);
```

Note the syntax used in the statement above. To the left of += is a reference to the event field. Obtaining a reference to an event field is as straightforward as accessing a public field of an object. In the statement above, the referenced field is the PushEvent event field of an instance of the FireAlarmButton class of Program 13.8. To the right of +=, the code new PushEventHandler(subscriber.RingBell) creates a new object to correspond to an invocation of the RingBell method. Creating an object to correspond to the event handler raises the question "what is the class of this object?" In the case of event handlers, the class name is the delegate type used to specify the event handler's parameters and return type. Finally, the += operator registers this new object with the event field. From the point of view of a publisher, the event field simplifies the distribution of the event message objects to the set of subscribers. The publisher can invoke an event field as if it were the name of an event handler itself. The event field will then use the parameters it is passed to call each of the event handler methods registered with the event field. Using this mechanism, the OnPush method in Program 13.8 is able to transmit the event message object to all subscribers of the PushEvent event field.

The best way to understand how the publisher and subscriber classes fit together is to use them in a program where an event is raised. In Program 13.9 a subscriber object registers with the event of a publisher object. You will recognize the subscriber object's class from Program 13.7 and the publisher variable's class from Program 13.8. An event is raised when some condition causes the publisher to create an event message object and distribute it to registered subscribers of the event. This occurs in Program 13.9 when the TestFireAlarm method of the publisher is invoked. After TestFireAlarm creates an event message, it uses PushEvent to handle the distribution of the message object to all the subscribers of the event. When the subscriber object receives this message, it creates a Terminal class object

```
class EventDemoProgram {

  static void Main(string[] args) {

    // Create an event publisher object
    FireAlarmButton publisher = new FireAlarmButton();

    // Create an event subscriber object
    AlarmBell subscriber = new AlarmBell();

    // Register the event listener with the event source.
    publisher.PushEvent += new PushEventHandler(subscriber.RingBell);

    // Kick off event.
    publisher.TestFireAlarm();
  }
}
```

Program 13.9   Alarm push event demonstration program.

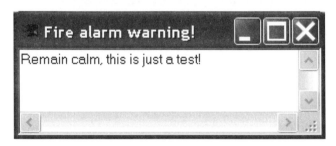

Figure 13.20   Results of Program 13.9.

that displays the contents of the message. This window, shown in Figure 13.20, announces that there is no need to get excited as the alarm is only a test.

Understanding how to operate a GUI with C# requires only a shallow understanding of events. Specifically, events are raised any time the user interacts with controls on the form. By registering with the appropriate event handlers, our forms can exhibit the kind of behaviour typical of a user interface. Fortunately, getting started with GUI development does not require that we know how to define event messages or event fields, as these will already be defined by the controls in use on a form. Thus, developing fairly interesting GUIs requires only that we be comfortable with creating event handlers and registering them with an event field.

Operating the GUI

Armed with an understanding of events, we should decide on what behaviour to add to the useless form developed in the first section of this chapter, an image of which appears in Figure 13.21. Since we are just starting to learn GUI programming, the requirements should start out rather simple. For a start, we can aim to program the form to respond to button clicks. There needs to be some visible and satisfying feedback to indicate that code is in place to detect the button clicks. For this it should suffice to update the text in the label to indicate which button was clicked. For instance, if the left button is clicked, the label's text should

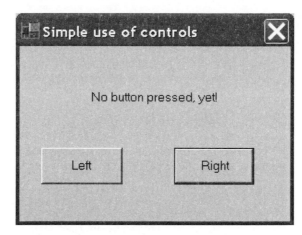

Figure 13.21   Form displayed when Program 13.3 executes.

change to something like "`Left button was clicked`". The resulting dialog is shown in Figure 13.22. Likewise, clicking on the right button should change the label to display "`Right button was clicked`".

With a firm purpose in mind, we can investigate what mouse events can be detected by the button. Recall that we said GUI programming involves creating a response to events that correspond to interesting user input. All controls publish a set of events defined by the `Control` base class. Among these events are a series of conditions caused by the user manipulating the mouse. Understandably, these events all start with the prefix `Mouse`. A list and summary of each is available in the Visual Studio manuals. This list appears in Figure 13.23. The Visual Studio Help is kind enough to distinguish events from methods and properties with an icon, which explains the cartoon lightning bolt to the left of each event's name.

From the list of summaries, it appears that the `MouseDown` event will correspond to the clicking of a button, so we will be interested in attaching behaviour to this event. Of secondary interest are some of the terms used in the descriptions of mouse related events. *Focus*, used

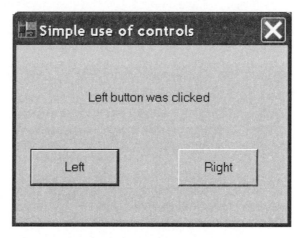

Figure 13.22   Updates to form when the Left button is clicked.

.NET Framework Class Library

Control Members

MouseDown	Occurs when the mouse pointer is over the control and a mouse button is pressed.
MouseEnter	Occurs when the mouse pointer enters the control.
MouseHover	Occurs when the mouse pointer hovers over the control.
MouseLeave	Occurs when the mouse pointer leaves the control.
MouseMove	Occurs when the mouse pointer is moved over the control.
MouseUp	Occurs when the mouse pointer is over the control and a mouse button is released.
MouseWheel	Occurs when the mouse wheel moves while the control has focus.

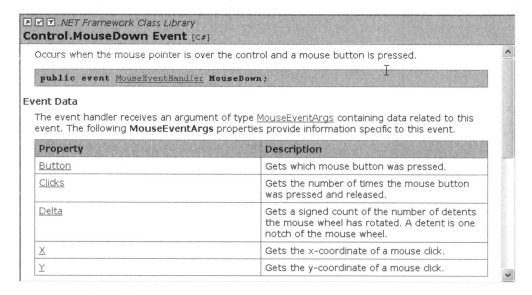

Figure 13.23 Summary of Mouse event fields defined in `Control` class.

in the `MouseWheel` description, refers to input focus. When a control has input focus, it receives keyboard events that occur when the user types on the keyboard. Usually a control signals that it has focus by appearing subtly highlighted. In Figure 13.21 the Right button has focus. Notice that it differs slightly from the Left button, which does not have focus. This situation is reversed in Figure 13.22, where the Left button has focus. The term *enter* used in the description of `MouseEnter` refers to the point in time at which the mouse position changes from being not above any part of the control to being above any part of the control. Likewise, the term *leave* used in the description of `MouseLeave` refers to when the mouse pointer moves from on top of a control to some point not on that control. Based on our survey of events, we will have to respond to `MouseDown` events that are received by our buttons.

.NET Framework Class Library

Control.MouseDown Event [C#]

Occurs when the mouse pointer is over the control and a mouse button is pressed.

```
public event MouseEventHandler MouseDown;
```

Event Data

The event handler receives an argument of type MouseEventArgs containing data related to this event. The following **MouseEventArgs** properties provide information specific to this event.

Property	Description
Button	Gets which mouse button was pressed.
Clicks	Gets the number of times the mouse button was pressed and released.
Delta	Gets a signed count of the number of detents the mouse wheel has rotated. A detent is one notch of the mouse wheel.
X	Gets the x-coordinate of a mouse click.
Y	Gets the y-coordinate of a mouse click.

Figure 13.24 Detailed description of the `MouseDown` field in the `Control` class.

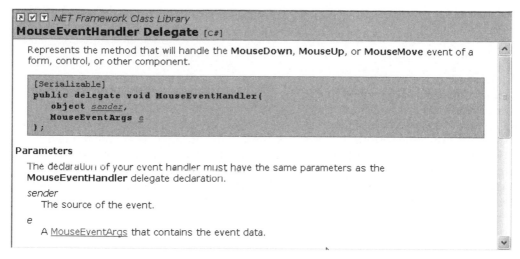

Figure 13.25 MouseEventHandler delegate type's specification for an event handler method.

To respond to MouseDown events of a button, an event handler method must be created and registered with the button's MouseDown event field. The event handler we write must conform to the specification provided by the MouseDown event field. Looking at the help topic describing the MouseDown field in Figure 13.24, we see that the event handler is specified by the MouseEventHandler delegate type.

The MouseDown help contains a link to a description of the MouseEventHandler delegate. This description is pictured in Figure 13.25 and supplies details on the parameters and return type specified by the delegate. Since the delegate describes an event handler, it should come as no surprise that the return type is void and that the first parameter is an object reference.

Based on the description of the MouseEventHandler delegate, the following method would be a suitable event handler for the MouseDown event of the button marked "Left":

```
public void leftButton_MouseDown(object sender,
    MouseEventArgs e) {}
```

The choice of leftButton_MouseDown for the method's name will help us distinguish this method from the event handler for the button marked "Right". We have decided that pressing the button marked "Left" will modify the text in the label control of the form. In fact, Text is a property of the label control, and changing its value at run-time will update the text displayed by the label. An update of leftButton_MouseDown that changes the text displayed by the label control is shown below:

```
public void leftButton_MouseDown(object sender,
    MouseEventArgs e) {
        this.feedbackLabel.Text = "Left button was clicked";
}
```

In order to access the label control, we will want to place our event handler in the form's class where the label is a data field. Using the += operator introduced in the previous section, the code to register the event handler should look like the following:

```
// Register event handlers for the buttons on the form
this.leftButton.MouseDown +=
    new MouseEventHandler(this.leftButton_MouseDown);
```

With an understanding of the code required to implement and register the MouseDown event handlers, we can update Program 13.3.

In Program 13.10, we have added event handlers to allow the form's buttons to report that they have been clicked. The event handlers leftButton_MouseDown and rightButton_MouseDown use code described in the previous paragraph to modify the form's label to state which button was just pressed. In order for these event handlers to be triggered, they are registered with the MouseDown event field of their respective button. This occurs in the constructor sometime after the button objects are instantiated. The result of pressing the button marked "Right" is shown in Figure 13.26.

```
using System;
using System.Drawing;
using System.Collections;
using System.ComponentModel;
using System.Windows.Forms;
using System.Data;

namespace GettingStarted
{
    public class Form1 : System.Windows.Forms.Form
    {
        private System.ComponentModel.Container components = null;

        // These field store references to our controls
        private Button leftButton, rightButton;
        private System.Windows.Forms.Label feedbackLabel;

        public Form1()
        {
            //
            // Required for Windows Form Designer support
            //
            InitializeComponent();

            // Setup the overall form.
            this.Size = new System.Drawing.Size(304, 232);
            this.MaximizeBox = false;
            this.MinimizeBox = false;

            // Initialize control objects.

            // create the label
            this.feedbackLabel = new Label();
            this.feedbackLabel.Location = new System.Drawing.Point(76, 48);
            this.feedbackLabel.Size = new System.Drawing.Size(154, 24);
            this.feedbackLabel.Text = "No button pressed, yet!";

            // create right button
            this.rightButton = new Button();
            this.rightButton.Location = new System.Drawing.Point(168, 112);
            this.rightButton.Size = new System.Drawing.Size(88, 40);
            this.rightButton.Text = "Right";
```

```csharp
        // create left button
        this.leftButton = new Button();
        this.leftButton.Location = new System.Drawing.Point(24, 112);
        this.leftButton.Size = new System.Drawing.Size(88, 40);
        this.leftButton.Text = "Left";

        // Register the objects with the form
        this.Controls.Add(this.feedbackLabel);
        this.Controls.Add(this.rightButton);
        this.Controls.Add(this.leftButton);

        // Register event handlers for the buttons on the form
        this.leftButton.MouseDown +=
                new MouseEventHandler(this.leftButton_MouseDown);

        this.rightButton.MouseDown +=
                new MouseEventHandler(this.rightButton_MouseDown);
    }

    // Event handlers for dealing with mouse clicks.
    public void leftButton_MouseDown(object sender, MouseEventArgs e) {
     this.feedbackLabel.Text = "Left button was clicked";
    }

    public void rightButton_MouseDown(object sender, MouseEventArgs e) {
     this.feedbackLabel.Text = "Right button was clicked";
    }

    /// <summary>
    /// Clean up any resources being used.
    /// </summary>
    protected override void Dispose( bool disposing )
    {
        if( disposing )
        {
            if (components != null)
            {
                components.Dispose();
            }
        }
        base.Dispose( disposing );
    }

    #region Windows Form Designer generated code
    /// <summary>
    /// Required method for Designer support - do not modify
    /// the contents of this method with the code editor.
    /// </summary>
    private void InitializeComponent()
    {
        //
        // Form1
        //
        this.AutoScaleBaseSize = new System.Drawing.Size(6, 15);
        this.ClientSize = new System.Drawing.Size(296, 192);
    }
    #endregion
```

```
/// <summary>
/// The main entry point for the application.
/// </summary>
[STAThread]
static void Main()
{
    Application.Run(new Form1());
}
    }
}
```

Program 13.10   Update of Program 13.3 that responds to button clicks.

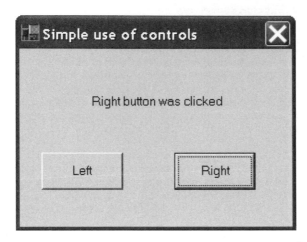

Figure 13.26   Result of pressing the button marked "Right" during the execution of Program 13.10.

Since mouse clicks are such a common occurrence in GUI programming, Visual Studio Designer provides a much simpler approach to creating an event handler to respond to clicks. Double clicking on a control viewed in the Designer will cause the Designer to automatically generate an event handler corresponding to the Click event, and register it with the control. Take, for example, the form in Figure 13.16 generated by the Designer. If we double click on the Left button, the Designer updates the InitializeComponent method shown in Program 13.4 to include the following specification for button1:

```
//
// button1
//
this.button1.Location = new System.Drawing.Point(16, 112);
this.button1.Name = "button1";
this.button1.Size = new System.Drawing.Size(96, 40);
this.button1.TabIndex = 1;
this.button1.Text = "Left";
this.button1.Click +=
    new System.EventHandler(this.button1_Click);
```

The last line of this specification is new. It registers an event handler for the button's Click event. This event handler, button1_Click, is new as well, and has been generated automatically by Visual Studio. Since Visual Studio cannot guess what functionality we have

Figure 13.27   Code editor open and ready to edit automatically generated event handler.

in mind for the event, the code editor is opened with the cursor positioned in the body of the new event handler, as shown in Figure 13.27.

The model for responding to events and manipulating controls introduced in this section is consistent for every control placed on a form. Whether we want to add buttons, drop down menus or textboxes, each of these controls will provide events to which we can attach behaviour. Of equal importance to the concept of events is the concept of properties. Using properties, controls such as textboxes, drop down lists and radio buttons can be inspected to see what input or selections a user has made. Building on an understanding of these basic concepts, a programmer should be able to build any form.

Case Study

To demonstrate the GUI programming principles learnt in this chapter, we will extend the Overlapping Shapes Detector Case Study introduced in Chapter 12. In this case, we want to create an amateurish GUI for the program. By amateurish, we mean simple. An advanced GUI might provide a grid and allow the user to draw shapes. However, it should suffice to move the original mechanism for specifying shapes from the Terminal class to a series of forms. Doing so will exercise our understanding of the use of properties to manipulate controls and the use of events to respond to user actions. Critical to GUI development is that the user interface is well defined before any coding begins. To guarantee that the interface is consistent and answers our needs, it is important that we have a firm specification for all the forms that the user will be using and for how the user will move from one form

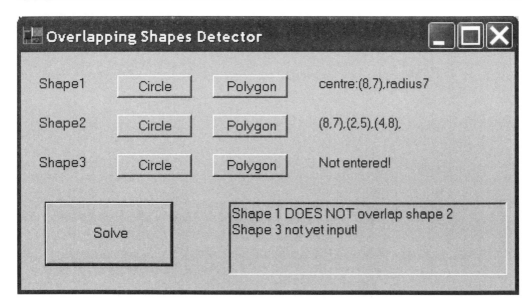

Figure 13.28 Main form used by Overlapping Shapes Detector.

to another. For this reason, the case study starts with a thorough discussion of the forms used in the Overlapping Shapes GUI before addressing the programming issues involved in implementing these forms.

The interface will centre on a single form that allows users to configure three shapes, provides details on the current configuration of each shape and reports overlapping conditions at the user's request. A sample of the form presented to application users is shown in Figure 13.28. Notice that the number of shapes will be limited to three. This limitation is in place to simplify the project. Along side each shape's label are buttons that correspond to the two types of wizards. The term *wizard* nicely describes a series of similar looking forms that guide the user through a configuration process. In this case, the user is configuring a shape to be used in the Overlapping Shapes Detector. By clicking on one of the buttons, the shape's type is set and a wizard is activated that allows the user to enter its input parameters. The shapes will display their parameters in a label to the right of the buttons after the shape is properly set up. Reporting which shapes overlap will be delayed until the user specifically requests the list of overlapping shapes. This is done by the pressing the label marked "Solve". The textbox control to the right of the Solve button will state the shapes that overlap. When the user is done with the program, it can be closed using the form's close button in the top right-hand corner.

Gathering data on the shapes will be done via a series of modal dialog boxes. As in previous versions of this program, the user will input the coordinates of the corners of a polygon or in the case of circles they will provide a centre point and radius. However, their input will be guided by a wizard specific to the shape being specified. This wizard will present the user with a series of modal dialog boxes, each of which will represent a separate step in specifying the dimensions of a shape. The term *modal dialog box* refers to the relatively simple concept of a form that cannot be ignored. Any form can be displayed as a modal dialog box. When a modal dialog box is being displayed by the application, the user is unable to switch to any of the other forms that the program is displaying on the screen. As we will see, programming

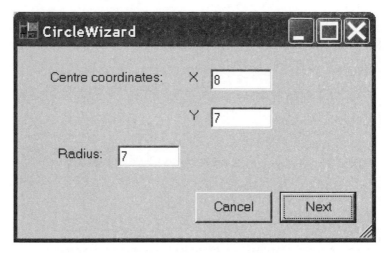

Figure 13.29 `CircleWizard` form used by the circle wizard.

a form to appear as a modal dialog is quite simple. Before we can begin programming, the design of the dialogs used by the wizard must be specified.

The circle wizard will use a form to gather details on the centre point and the radius of the circle. The form, shown in Figure 13.29 will allow the user to input details on the circle via three textboxes. If the user presses the Next button, the main form will update the shape's details with those provided by the form. However, if the Cancel button or the "X" button of the title bar is used, then the main form will ignore the user's input. Finally, the wizard will try to help the user by initializing the input fields to the values last entered by the user. These will be the values used last time the form was displayed.

The polygon wizard will first determine the number of sides in the polygon and then ask for the coordinates of each corner in the polygon. In our design, the polygon wizard uses multiple dialogs to obtain the number of corners in the polygon and the coordinates of each corner.

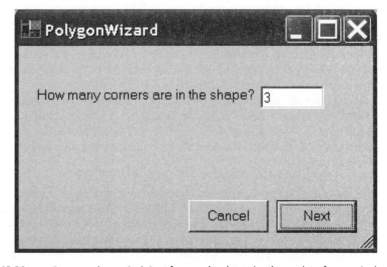

Figure 13.30 `PolygonWizardSides` form used to determine the number of corners in the polygon.

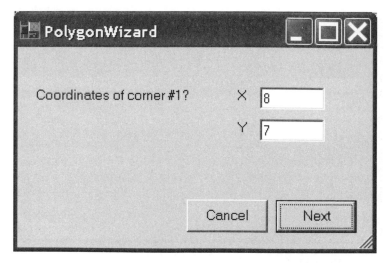

Figure 13.31   `PolygonWizardCorner` form used to determine the coordinates of a corner.

The wizard starts by asking for the number of sides in the polygon using the form pictured in Figure 13.30. We will refer to this form as the `PolygonWizardSides` form.

Once the number of corners is known, the wizard requests the coordinates for each corner using another form. This form, shown in Figure 13.31, has its label updated to correspond to the corner whose coordinates are being input. For instance, in Figure 13.31, the label requests the "Coordinates of corner #1". We will refer to this dialog as the `PolygonWizardCorner` form.

Any form can display itself as a modal dialog by calling its `ShowModal` method. The difficulty lies in determining why the dialog closed. Typically, dialogs close because the user has pressed some sort of OK button or some sort of Cancel button. However, there are several other reasons why a modal dialog might close. Thus, the `ShowModal` call returns an enumerated value corresponding to the condition that caused the dialog to close. The enumeration from which the value is selected is called `DialogResult`, and contains the values shown in Figure 13.32.

By selecting a value for the `DialogResult` property, we can cause clicks of a button to close the dialog and return an appropriate value. For instance, in the `CircleWizard` form of Figure 13.29, we can associate the Next button with the `DialogResult.OK` value by assigning that value to the button's `DialogResult` property. Setting the property is done most easily by selecting the button in the Designer and opening its properties using the right click menu, shown in Figure 13.33. The properties window supplies a limited set of values to associate with the `DialogResult` property, as shown in Figure 13.34. With an understanding of how to operate a modal dialog, we can move on to design methods to operate each of our wizards.

The application's interface will be implemented by a single class that will maintain the shape data, associate methods to operate wizards, and check for overlapping with interface buttons. The main form will be defined by a single class. Intuitively, we name this class `MainForm`. `MainForm` needs to avoid using code specific to the internals of the wizard forms. Take, for example, the creation of a `Circle` from input to the `CircleWizard` form. Should the `MainForm` create the `Circle` itself, it must learn which variables correspond to the textboxes that contain centre point coordinates and the radius. An additional problem is that

.NET Framework Class Library
DialogResult Enumeration [C#]

Members

Member name	Description
Abort	The dialog box return value is Abort (usually sent from a button labeled Abort).
Cancel	The dialog box return value is Cancel (usually sent from a button labeled Cancel).
Ignore	The dialog box return value is Ignore (usually sent from a button labeled Ignore).
No	The dialog box return value is No (usually sent from a button labeled No).
None	Nothing is returned from the dialog box. This means that the modal dialog continues running.
OK	The dialog box return value is OK (usually sent from a button labeled OK).
Retry	The dialog box return value is Retry (usually sent from a button labeled Retry).
Yes	The dialog box return value is Yes (usually sent from a button labeled Yes).

Figure 13.32   Values defined for the DialogResult Enumeration.

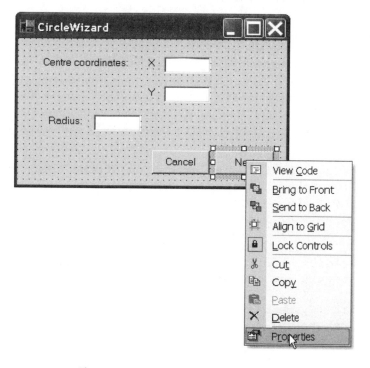

Figure 13.33   Viewing the properties of a button.

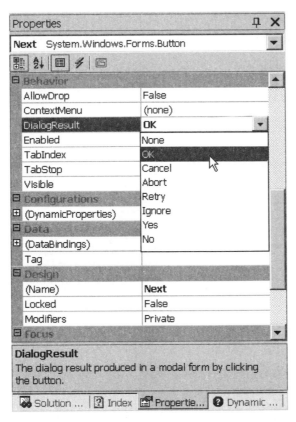

Figure 13.34   Setting up a button to close the form and return DialogResult when clicked.

by default the Designer labels these variables `private`. Should the variables be revised with the Designer, there is a strong chance that the `MainForm` code will break. The solution is to provide methods in each wizard form that return the user's input at as high a level as possible. Consequently, the `CircleWizard` form will provide the `GetCircle` method shown below:

```
public Circle GetCircle() {
    // Parsing will throw an exception if the text is not a
    // valid number. If it does, we return null;
    try {
        double x, y, radius;
        x = double.Parse(this.xCoord.Text);
        y = double.Parse(this.yCoord.Text);
        radius = double.Parse(this.radius.Text);
        return new Circle( new Point(x, y), radius);
    }
    catch (System.Exception e) {
        return null;
    }
}
```

Likewise, the `PolygonWizardSides` form will supply the `GetPolygonSides` method:

```
// Method that returns the number of sides in the polygon
public int GetPolygonSides() {
    // Parsing will throw an exception if the text is not a
    // valid number. If it does, we return null;
    try {
        return int.Parse(this.numSides.Text);
    }
    catch (System.Exception e) {
        return 0;
    }
}
```

Finally, the `PolygonWizardCorner` form will supply the `GetPolygonCorner` method shown here:

```
// Method that returns a Point object corresponding to
// a corner of the polygon
public Point GetPolygonCorner() {
    // Parsing will throw an exception if the text is not a
    // valid number. If it does, we return null;
    try {
        double x, y, radius;
        x = double.Parse(this.xCoord.Text);
        y = double.Parse(this.yCoord.Text);
        return new Point(x, y);
    }
    catch (System.Exception e) {
        return null;
    }
}
```

Note that each method determines what values the user input by *parsing*, or converting to numbers, the string from textboxes. The names of the textboxes were set in the Designer using the Name property of each control. `MainForm` will require a method to operate the `CircleWizard` form that first determines whether the Next button was used to close the form or if the Cancel button or Close title bar button was used. Only if the user presses the Next button should the shape be updated. To achieve this behaviour, we need only test the return value from a `ShowDialog` call on a `CircleWizard` object. A method meeting these requirements is shown below:

```
// Operates the CircleWizard form and stores results in
// the "this.shapes" field.
//
// BTW, CircleWizard form will contain the last set of info
// entered by the user, regardless of which shape that was.
//
private void circleWizard(int shapeNum) {
    // Determine the dimensions, but return without
    // changing shapes if user does not press OK.
    if ( circleDialog.ShowDialog() != DialogResult.OK)
        return;
```

```
   // Ask the CircleWizard for its input.
   Circle result = circleDialog.GetCircle();
   if (result != null) {
      this.shapes[shapeNum] = result;
   }
   return;
}
```

MainForm will also need a method to operate the polygon wizard. This method needs to first use the PolygonWizardSides form to determine the number of sides that the polygon will have. Naturally, an invalid count for the sides or closing the form by not pressing "Next" will cause the method to stop without updating the shape. Otherwise, the coordinates of each side will be determined using the PolygonWizardCorner form. The shape is only updated if the Next button is used to close the form and the form is able to convert the user's input into a Point object. The method polygonWizard, shown below, meets these requirements:

```
// Operates the PolygonWizard forms and stores results in
// the "this.shapes" field.
//
// BTW, PolygonWizard forms will contain the last set of info
// entered by the user, regardless of which shape that was.
//
private void polygonWizard(int shapeNum) {

   // Determine the number of sides, but return without
   // changing shapes if user does not press OK.
   if (this.polygonSidesDialog.ShowDialog() != DialogResult.OK)
      return;

   // If the number of sides is invalid, return without
   // changing shapes.
   int sides = this.polygonSidesDialog.GetPolygonSides();
   if (sides < 3)
      return;

   Point[] newPts = new Point[sides];

   for ( int i = 0; i < sides; i++) {
      // Determine the coordinates of this corner, but
      // return without changing shapes if user does not
      // press OK.
      if (this.polygonCornerDialog.ShowDialog()
            != DialogResult.OK)
         return;

      newPts[i] = this.polygonCornerDialog.GetPolygonCorner();
   }
   this.shapes[shapeNum] = new Polygon(newPts);
}
```

A separate method is required to determine whether the shapes overlap. Unlike the original interface to the Overlapping Shapes Detector, there is a chance that the array of shapes contains some null references. solveOverlaps, shown below, accounts for this problem by testing each shape reference used to see if it is null. As the method progresses, it continually updates a string variable which contains the results of the comparison. Notice the addition of the "\r\n" string to the end of each string stored in result. The textbox control interprets this string as a new line when it displays the result string.

```
// Method that updates the overlapInfo text box beside the
// "Solve" button with details on which shapes overlap.
private void solveOverlaps() {
    string result = "";

    // Cycle through every shape.
    for (int i = 0; i<this.shapes.Length; i++) {

        // Report if it is invalid
        if (shapes[i] == null) {
            result = result + "Shape " +i+" not yet input!"
                + "\r\n";
        }
        // Otherwise report whether it overlaps or not.
        else {
            for (int j = i+1; j< this.shapes.Length; j++) {

                // Don't do comparisons with null references
                if (this.shapes[j] == null)
                    continue;
                if (this.shapes[i].Overlaps(this.shapes[j])) {
                    result = result+ "Shape "+ i+
                        " overlaps shape " + j+ "\r\n";
                } else {
                    result = result+ "Shape "+ i+
                        " DOES NOT overlap shape "}
                        + j+ "\r\n";
                }
            }
        }
    }

    // Update the results
    this.overlapInfo.Text = result;
}
```

To get the MainForm to respond to button clicks, Click event handlers have to be added to all the buttons. Double clicking on every button in the Designer will generate and register a Click event handler. Each event handler has then to be modified to call the appropriate wizard except for the Solve button, which must be associated with the solveOverlaps method. The completed event handlers are shown below. Notice how after a wizard is called, the event handler will update the text message to its left. The names for each control used in MainForm were assigned using the Name property of the button, textbox or label.

```csharp
// Event handlers for shape buttons
private void circle1_Click(object sender, System.EventArgs e) {
   this.circleWizard(0);
   if (this.shapes[0] == null) {
      this.shape1Info.Text = "Not entered!";
   } else {
      this.shape1Info.Text = this.shapes[0].ToString();
   }
}
private void polygon1_Click(object sender,
      System.EventArgs e) {
   this.polygonWizard(0);
   if (this.shapes[0] == null) {
      this.shape1Info.Text = "Not entered!";
   } else {
      this.shape1Info.Text = this.shapes[0].ToString();
   }
}
private void circle2_Click(object sender,
   System.EventArgs e) {
      this.circleWizard(1);
   if (this.shapes[1] == null) {
      this.shape2Info.Text = "Not entered!";
   } else {
      this.shape2Info.Text = this.shapes[1].ToString();
   }
}
private void polygon2_Click(object sender, Sys-
tem.EventArgs e) {
   this.polygonWizard(1);

   if (this.shapes[1] == null) {
      this.shape2Info.Text = "Not entered!";
   } else {
      this.shape2Info.Text = this.shapes[1].ToString();
   }
}
private void circle3_Click(object sender, System.EventArgs e) {
   this.circleWizard(2);

   if (this.shapes[2] == null) {
      this.shape3Info.Text = "Not entered!";
   } else {
      this.shape3Info.Text = this.shapes[2].ToString();
   }
}
private void polygon3_Click(object sender,
      System.EventArgs e) {
   this.polygonWizard(2);

   if (this.shapes[2] == null) {
      this.shape3Info.Text = "Not entered!";
```

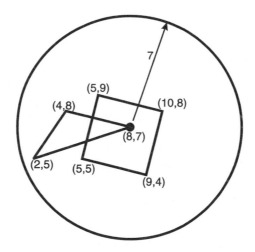

Figure 13.35   Test data for Overlapping Shapes Detector.

```
    } else {
        this.shape3Info.Text = this.shapes[2].ToString();
    }
}
// Event handler for "Solve" button
private void solve_Click(object sender, System.EventArgs e) {
    solveOverlaps();
}
```

As a test, we can apply test data in Figure 13.35 to the final implementation of MainForm. The expected results are shown in Figure 13.36.

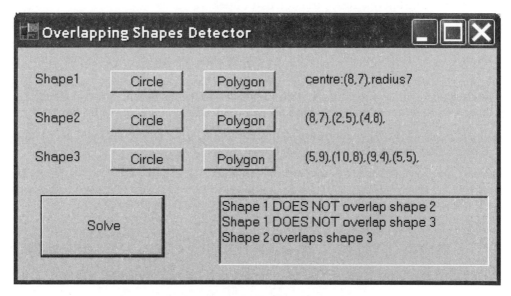

Figure 13.36   Event handler methods from the MainForm form.

Summary

In this chapter we learned that:

- all windows are defined by forms, which are classes derived from `class Form`
- Visual Studio's Designer facilitates coding the layout and properties of all controls
- the Toolbox supplies a variety of controls that can be placed on a form
- event handlers are used to code the behaviour of controls
- the `delegate` keyword is used to define a delegate type with the syntax shown below. (Note that the method declaration ends with a semicolon (i.e. "`;`") rather than a body with curly braces (i.e. "`{}`".)

    ```
    delegate <method declaration>;
    ```

- an event field is declared with the syntax:

    ```
    event <delegate type> <field name>;
    ```

- the += operator is used to register an event handler with an event field. When this is done, the event handler will be called when the event is triggered.

Exercises

(1) Create the `CircleWizard` form used in the Case Study. You are free to implement the `Circle` class however you wish.

(2) Create the `PolygonWizard` dialogs used in the Case Study. You are free to implement the `Polygon` class.

(3) Create the `MainForm` used in the Case Study. Ensure that it properly detects overlaps; i.e., include a Solve button that works! This may require that you review your solution to the intersecting lines exercise earlier on in the book.

(4) Provide publisher and subscriber classes to correspond to the scenario of a door bell being pressed. Two subscriber classes should respond to the event: a door chime and a warning light. Each subscriber should write a message to a `Terminal` object indicating the message that was received.

(5) Revise the previous application to take input from one form and send it to two others; i.e., there should be a form to correspond with each subscriber and each publisher.

(6) Write a party line application in which three input forms are available. When data is written to one of the windows, it is duplicated on the others.

(7) Create an interface for the dating agency program. You are welcome to choose any six criteria for matching clients of the agency. Be sure to design your forms in advance of implementing their behaviour!

This chapter:

- considers some of the issues that arise in the design of a large object-oriented program
- introduces the use of diagrams to represent the relationships between the classes in a program
- describes the design of a large object-oriented program that implements a simple library database management system

The previous chapters in this book introduced various aspects of object-oriented programming and C# in some detail. By now you should be reasonably comfortable writing small C# classes and the applications that use them. In this chapter, we will take a look at what's involved in writing a substantially larger program than those that we have considered until now.

As you know, at the heart of object-oriented programming is the idea that a large program can be tackled by dividing it up into a number of co-operating classes, which can then be written separately. The complexity of any single class needn't be much greater than that of any of the classes that we have written so far. The challenge in designing a large program is to identify the appropriate classes and the ways in which they co-operate. While our previous programs typically consisted of one or two classes, we can expect that any large program will consist of tens of classes that interact in complex ways. While our main concern previously was with writing each individual class, our main concern now must be with decomposing the program into an appropriate set of classes and assigning responsibilities to each class. Having done that, we can hopefully call on the material that we have covered in the previous chapters of the book to actually write each class in turn.

A Library Database Management System

The problem that we are going to consider is the design of a library database management system for a small library. The idea is to design a program that can be used by a librarian to keep track of the status of the books in the library, including whether or not they are currently on loan and, if so, to whom. To make the problem tractable, we will make a number of simplifying assumptions about the way in which our library system is to be used.

We assume that there is only a single librarian on duty at any time, i.e., there is only ever a single user of our system at a time. We assume that there are only a small number of potential users of the library and a reasonably small number of books. The system is only intended to keep track of the status of the books in the library as they are borrowed and, hopefully, returned. It is not intended to provide facilities to allow borrowers to search for particular books in the library catalogue, for example, by their subject matter or author. Thus, the system might more appropriately be used by an individual to keep track of their own personal book collection rather than by a large public library. For example, I have a hundred or so books on my shelves that are constantly being borrowed, and occasionally returned, by my students!

We will make one more assumption, which, unlike the others, is a little unreasonable. We will assume that the program does not need to store the information that it maintains *persistently*, i.e., on disk. Thus, we assume that the program runs continuously. If the program is ever shut down then all the information maintained by the program will be lost and will need to be entered again!

The Rules of the Library

Every library has rules about who can borrow what and when. Our library is no exception. Here are the rules that our program must enforce:

- any user may, subject to the rules below, borrow any book,
- a user may have at most three books on loan at any time,
- borrowed books must be returned within a fixed period of time and a fine is charged for each day that a book is overdue,
- a user may not borrow a book while holding any book that is overdue,
- a user may renew a loan for an additional period of time but only one consecutive renewal is allowed,
- a user may reserve a book that is already on loan provided that the book is not on loan to that user,
- a user may reserve as many books as required,
- reservations are handled on a "first come first served" basis, i.e., the first user to reserve the book will be the first to receive the book when it next becomes available,
- a loan may not be renewed if the book is already reserved.

Clearly, we could have imposed additional rules. For example, we could have different categories of user with different borrowing rights for different categories of books and so on. For now at least we'll keep it relatively simple!

The Functions of the Library Management System

Given the rules above, we are now in a position to identify what functions the library management system should support. In fact, most of its functions correspond to the types of requests that users of the library can make. Clearly, the system must

- allow a particular user to borrow a particular book,
- allow a user to return a book,
- allow a user to renew a loan on a book,
- allow a user to reserve a book,
- allow a user to cancel a reservation.

all subject to the rules above. In addition, the system will need to provide the ability to

- add and remove users of the library,

- add and remove books.

These seven operations describe the core of the functionality that the system is intended to provide. Again, you can probably imagine other functions that such a system might provide. For example, we might provide the ability to list which books are currently on loan or on loan to a particular user, the ability to find out which books are frequently borrowed by which users, which users have poor records of returning books on time and so on. Again, in order to make the problem tractable, we won't consider providing this sort of functionality now, although it is always wise to keep an eye towards how we might need to modify or extend a program in the future.

Identifying the Classes

As usual, our first step is to identify what classes are required to implement our program. As ever, we expect classes to represent the entities with which the program deals. In this case there seem to be two key types of entity: books and users. Entities of both types seem to be good candidates to be represented by objects. In addition, we will obviously need an application class that provides the user interface to the library system. Let's consider the possible responsibilities of each of these classes in turn.

The library book class (`LibraryBook`) should be responsible for storing the details of each book in the library, including keeping track of its current lending status. This class should allow a book to be borrowed, renewed, returned and reserved. Thus, `LibraryBook` is likely to be the class that is primarily responsible for enforcing the rules of the library. The methods provided by this class should therefore implement each of these operations. Among its fields are likely to be details of the current loan and any reservations for the book (when it is on loan).

The library user class (`LibraryUser`) should be responsible for recording all the information concerning one user of the library. Methods on the class should allow details of a user's loans and reservations to be recorded. Thus, the fields of `LibraryUser` are likely to include details of loans and reservations made by the user. Notice that there appears to be some possible duplication between the fields of `LibraryBook` and `LibraryUser`. An instance of `LibraryBook` will include details of any loan and any reservations for the book while an instance of `LibraryUser` will include details of any loans or reservations made by the user. Rather then replicating this information in two places, it seems more sensible to introduce two further classes to represent individual loans and reservations respectively (`LibraryLoan` and `LibraryReservation`).

`LibraryLoan` will be responsible for maintaining all the information concerning one loan while `LibraryReservation` will be responsible for maintaining information about one reservation request. Thus, each instance of `LibraryBook` will refer to the instance of `LibraryLoan` corresponding to the current loan while each instance of `LibraryUser` will keep a list of instances of `LibraryLoan` representing the loans made by the user. Thus, exactly one instance of `LibraryBook` and one instance of `LibraryUser` will refer to any single instance of `LibraryLoan`.

Each instance of `LibraryBook` will also have a list of instances of `LibraryReservation`, representing reservation requests for the book, and an instance of `LibraryUser` a list of instances of `LibraryReservation`, representing the reservations made by the user. Again, each instance of `LibraryReservation` will be referred to by exactly one instance of `LibraryBook` and one instance of `LibraryUser`.

The form (`MainLibraryInterfaceForm`) will implement the user interface to the library system and is responsible for all input/output performed by the program. It must accept requests from the librarian and translate these requests into invocations on the appropriate object(s).

At the user interface, books will normally be known by their shelf marks – an identifier that serves to uniquely identify every book in the library and its place in the library. Likewise, users will be known by library user identifiers. Nearly every operation in the system will require the selection of a book, user identifier, or both, so we will need a strategy for picking these. One approach is to select books by entering the book number and subject and then creating a shelf mark. Likewise, a library user can be selected by entering the user's identification number. Given the relatively small number of books and users intended for this software, it would be less error prone to pick a shelf marker from a list of all shelf markers, and to select the user from a list that supplied the user's name along with their details. In either case, the GUI should order the list according to shelf maker or user identifier. For this system to work, the GUI must maintain a mapping from a shelf mark to the corresponding instance of `LibraryBook` as well as a mapping from a user identifier to the corresponding instance of `LibraryUser`. To implement this mapping we will introduce two new classes `LibraryCatalogue` and `LibraryUserDatabase`. A single instance of `LibraryCatalogue` maintains a list of all the books in the library and allows the corresponding instance of `LibraryBook` to be retrieved given a shelf mark. Likewise, an instance of `LibraryUserDatabase` maintains a list of all the users of the library and allows the appropriate instance of `LibraryUser` to be retrieved given a user identifier. Furthermore, indexers should be available to allow the book and user objects to be accessed with a loop. This will facilitate the GUI to fill a list with selections.

Figure 14.1 is a class diagram summarizing the classes that we have identified, their responsibilities, and the most important relationships between them. Class diagrams are commonly used in the various methodologies that exist for the object-oriented analysis and design. Of course, different methodologies use different notations for drawing such diagrams. Figure 14.1 uses a notation based on *Unified Modeling Language (UML)*, a well-known object-oriented analysis and design methodology.

In UML each class is represented by a rectangle divided into three sections. The first section contains the name of the class, the second the names of its most important fields, and the third the names of its most important methods. Properties appear in the methods rectangle with the set and get capabilities listed. It's not necessary to include an exhaustive list of all the fields and methods of each class. The most important function of a class diagram is to give a sense of what classes are required and the role of each class.

In UML, lines drawn between the rectangles represent relationships between the corresponding classes. Different types of relationships between classes are possible. For the purposes of our example, we are interested in identifying has-a relationships between classes, i.e., identifying which classes have fields that refer to instances of the other classes. Thus, the line drawn between the `LibraryBook` and `LibraryLoan` classes indicates that each instance of `LibraryBook` has a field that refers to a single instance of `LibraryLoan` and that each instance of `LibraryLoan` has a field that refers to a single instance of `LibraryBook`. Similarly, the annotated line drawn between `LibraryUser` and `LibraryLoan` indicates that each instance of `LibraryUser` has a field that refers to between zero and three instances of `LibraryLoan`, while each instance of `LibraryLoan` refers to a single instance of `LibraryUser`.

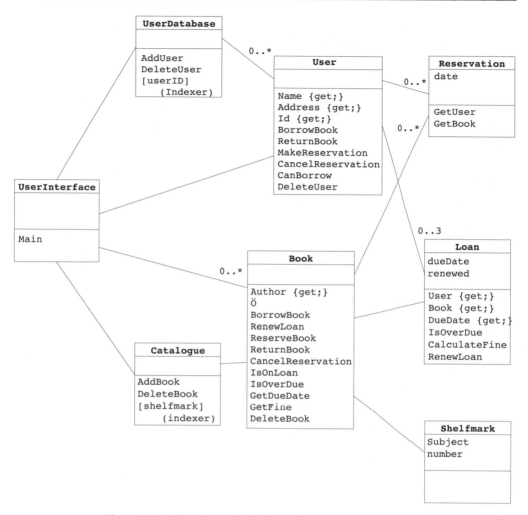

Figure 14.1   A class diagram for the library database management system.

The Classes in Detail

Having identified the main classes involved in the program we will now look at each class in turn. This section looks at the classes that run the backend of the software. The GUI forms that run the front end, otherwise known as the interface, will be discussed later in this chapter. Rather than trying to describe the implementation of each class in detail, we concentrate on describing the interface of each class and the most important fields provided by the class. We will also point out any implementation details that we feel are particularly interesting. Otherwise, the full code for the case study is provided in Appendix B.

Class LibraryBook

The heart of the library management system is the LibraryBook class whose instances record the details of each book in the library's collection and its status.

The methods of class `LibraryBook` are mostly fairly obvious. We will need to provide a constructor to initialize new instances of the class with information describing the book such as its title, author, publisher, year of publication and subject:

```
public LibraryBook(string title, string author,
    string publisher, int year, string subject)
```

We will also need to provide a set of properties to allow this information to be retrieved on request:

```
public string Author { get; }
public string Title { get; }
public string Publisher { get; }
public int Year { get; }
public string Subject { get; }
```

Notice that none of this information can be changed. Hence, there are no `set` methods defined for the properties. Notice too that the book's shelf mark is determined by the constructor based on the subject matter of the book. Hence, we should also provide a property to allow the shelf mark to be retrieved when necessary:

```
public LibraryShelfmark Shelfmark { get; }
```

Apart from these properties there is a set of methods to implement the main operations on library books that can be requested by users:

```
public int BorrowBook(LibraryUser borrower)
public int RenewLoan()
public int ReserveBook(LibraryUser reserver)
public int ReturnBook()
public bool CancelReservation(LibraryReservation reservation)
```

Both the `BorrowBook` and `ReserveBook` methods need to be passed the identity of the user who is attempting to borrow or reserve the book as a parameter. The most natural way to do this is to pass a reference to the appropriate instance of `LibraryUser` to each method. This reflects the fact that borrowing or reserving a book may result in the corresponding instance of `LibraryUser` being modified to record the new loan or reservation. `CancelReservation` likewise needs to be passed a parameter to identify the particular reservation to be canceled, however, neither `RenewLoan` nor `ReturnBook` need any parameters since there can only be one outstanding loan on a book at any time.

An important part of designing the interface to a class is to consider the possible return values from its methods – in other words, identifying the possible outcomes of the methods. In the case of class `LibraryBook`, it's important to realize that any given book can be in any one of four possible states during its lifetime. It can be:

- in the library and available for loan,
- in the library but held for some user who previously reserved the book,
- out on loan,
- out on loan but reserved by one or more users.

How each of the `LibraryBook` methods behaves depends on that state of the object when the method is invoked as well as on other factors such as the status of the user on whose behalf the request was made. Thus, in general, each of these methods should return a value to indicate what the effect of the invocation was. In general, there will be multiple possible outcomes so we can use an integer to represent each possibility. In the case of `BorrowBook` the possible outcomes are:

- the loan was granted,
- the loan was not granted because the book is currently out on loan,
- the loan was not granted because, although the book is in the library, it is being held for another user,
- the loan was not granted because the book is out and reserved by another user,
- the loan was not granted because the user is not allowed to borrow any further books.

For `RenewLoan` the possible outcomes are:

- the renewal was allowed,
- the renewal was not allowed because the book is not currently on loan,
- the renewal was not allowed because the book is being held for another user,
- the renewal was not allowed because the book is reserved by another user,
- the renewal was not allowed because the loan was already renewed or the return of the book is overdue.

For `ReserveBook` the possible outcomes are:

- the reservation was allowed,
- the reservation was not allowed because book is not currently on loan,
- the reservation was not allowed because the book is already on loan to the specified user,
- the reservation was not allowed because the book is being held but has already been reserved by the specified user.

For `ReturnBook` the possible outcomes are:

- the book was returned successfully,
- the book was returned successfully and is now being held for another user,
- the book was not returned because it was not on loan,
- the book was not returned because it was not on loan but is being held for another user.

For `CancelReservation`, there are only two meaningful outcomes: either the reservation was canceled or, for whatever reason, it was not. Since there are only two possible outcomes, the return type of the method is `bool`.

As well as the methods that implement user requests, we should also provide some methods to return information about the current status of the book. Methods in this category might include:

```
public bool IsOnLoan()
public bool IsOverdue()
public DateTime GetDueDate()
```

and

```
public int GetFine()
```

Notice the use of the C# library class `DateTime`, whose instances represent dates, as the return type for `GetDueDate`.

We will also need a method to be used when deleting a book from the system: for example to cancel any outstanding loans or reservations on the book. Deleting a book while it is on loan might represent the situation where a user who borrowed the book lost it:

```
public void DeleteBook()
```

Finally, we should override the standard methods `Equals` and `ToString` as for other classes. In order to override `Equals`, `GetHashCode` must also be overridden. The purpose of `GetHashCode` is to provide an `int` that as uniquely as possible identifies the object on which the method is called. Since the shelf mark uniquely identifies our book, we will use this object's `GetHashCode` to generate a hash code for objects of class `LibraryBook`.

Deciding on the fields to be provided by class `LibraryBook` is not too difficult. Clearly, we will need fields to store details of each book such as its title and author. The most important field will hold the current status of the book (whether it is in the library, in but held, on loan or on loan but reserved), i.e.,

```
private int status = IN; // could also be OUT, HELD, RESERVED
```

In addition, each book will have a field referring to the current loan on the book, if any:

```
private LibraryLoan currentLoan = null;
```

Notice that there is a strong relationship between the value of `status` and the value of `currentLoan`. If `status` is IN or HELD, `currentLoan` must be `null`; if `status` is OUT or RESERVED, then `currentLoan` must refer to some instance of `LibraryLoan`.

It will be useful for the GUI to be able to obtain the book's current status in the form of a string. For this, a property will do. Thus, we introduce the following:

```
public string Status { get; }
```

Finally, a book should keep a list of reservation requests pertaining to that book. The most straightforward way of doing this is to maintain an array of `LibraryReservation`:

```
private LibraryReservation[] currentReservations = null;
```

Notice that there is again a relation between the value of `status` and the value of `currentReservations`. If `status` is IN or OUT, `currentReservations` must be `null`, representing the fact that the book is not reserved; if `status` is HELD or RESERVED, then `currentReservations` must refer to an array of `LibraryReservation` with at least one element. We must be prepared for the number of elements contained in `currentReservations` to change as reservations are made, granted, and canceled. When the last outstanding reservation is granted `currentReservations` becomes `null`. When a reservation is subsequently made we will need to create a new array to hold this and future reservations until they are all granted or canceled. As more reservations are made we may even need to create a larger array to hold all the reservations.

Having considered the protocol to be supported by class `LibraryBook` and looked at its fields, you should now spend some time studying the operation of the methods and the available methods. Taken individually they are no more complicated than most of the methods that we have written previously.

Class LibraryUser

Instances of `LibraryUser` record the details concerning a single user of the library, including the loans and reservation requests made by the user. We will need to provide a constructor to initialize new instances of the class with information describing the user's personal details such as name and address:

```
public LibraryUser(string name, string address)
```

as well a set of properties to allow these details to be retrieved on request:

```
public string Name { get; }
public string Address { get; }
```

Potentially, the values of these properties might be changed over time, e.g., if the user moves house. However, we don't currently provide this functionality at the user interface to the library management system, so we won't provide set access in class `LibraryUser`. Allocation of user identifiers to users will be the responsibility of the constructor, hence we need to provide a property to allow a user's identifier to be retrieved when necessary:

```
public int Id { get; }
```

For the purposes of a GUI, it is useful to know the identifier that will be used for the next user that is created. This allows the identifier to be provided when details for a new user are entered, but the corresponding object has not yet been created. In this case, it is best to use a static property as we see here:

```
public static int NextId { get; }
```

Most of the other methods to be provided by `LibraryUser` correspond to the operations that can be requested by users. In designing the interface to these methods we need to realize that they are intended to be called from the `LibraryBook` class once the decision to allow the loan, renewal, or reservation request has been made and the corresponding instance of `LibraryLoan` or `LibraryReservation` obtained. Nevertheless, there may be circumstances where these methods could fail if invoked erroneously on an instance of `LibraryUser`:

```
public bool BorrowBook(LibraryLoan loan)
public bool ReturnBook(LibraryLoan loan)
public bool MakeReservation(LibraryReservation reservation)
public bool CancelReservation(LibraryReservation reservation)
```

Notice that each method takes an instance of `LibraryLoan` or `LibraryReservation` as its input and returns a `bool` result to indicate whether or not the method succeeded.

As well as the methods that handle loans and reservations, we need to provide a method to determine if a user is allowed to borrow further books:

```
public bool CanBorrow()
```

We will also need a method to be used when deleting a user form the system. In general a user may not be deleted while they have any loans outstanding (we clearly don't want to lose track of our books). Hence, this method may fail in this circumstance:

```
public bool DeleteUser()
```

Finally, we should override the standard methods `Equals` and `ToString` as for other classes. Whenever Equals is overridden, so must `GetHashCode` be overridden. For `LibraryUser` objects, the userID uniquely identifies the object. Since it is an `int`, we will return it in the `GetHashCode` method.

Apart from fields that store details of each user such as their name and address, the most important fields will be lists of the current loans and current reservations made by the user:

```
private LibraryLoan[] currentLoans = null;
private LibraryReservation[] currentReservations = null;
```

While `currentLoans` can contain at most the number of loans corresponding to the maximum number of loans that a user may make, we must be prepared for the number of elements contained in `currentReservations` to change as reservations are made, granted and canceled. Thus, `currentReservations` will need to be managed in much the same way as the corresponding field of class `LibraryBook`.

Classes `LibraryCatalogue` and `LibraryUserDataBase`

Our application will use a single instance of `LibraryCatalogue` to maintain a list of all the books in the library. In particular, that instance of `LibraryCatalogue` will contain a reference to every instance of `LibraryBook` representing a book in the library and will allow that reference to be obtained given the shelf mark of the book.

`LibraryCatalogue` provides a constructor to initialize a new catalogue as being empty and methods to insert a book into the catalogue and remove a book from the catalogue:

```
public LibraryCatalogue()
public bool AddBook(LibraryBook book, LibraryShelfmark mark)
public bool DeleteBook(LibraryShelfmark mark)
```

To retrieve a reference to a book given its shelf mark an indexer is used:

```
public LibraryBook this [LibraryShelfmark mark] { get; }
```

`AddBook` takes an instance of `LibraryBook` and the object representing its shelf mark as its parameters and returns a `bool` result to indicate whether or not it succeeded. Likewise, `DeleteBook` takes a shelf mark as its parameter and also returns a `bool` result to indicate whether or not it succeeded. For example, `DeleteBook` might fail if the shelf mark provided as its parameter is incorrect. Finally, the indexer takes a shelf mark as its parameter and returns a reference to the object representing the corresponding book if it was found in the catalogue or the value `null` otherwise.

A catalogue has only two fields: an array used to store the list of books and an integer used to keep count of how many books are currently in the catalogue:

```
private int numBooks;
private LibraryBook[] catalogue;
```

The list of books is maintained in the first `numBooks` elements of the array. Adding a book to the catalogue might require that a new larger array be created if the existing array is already full. Removing a book from the catalogue will normally require that the contents of all the following elements in the array be shifted down a place to maintain the constraint that the list of books is stored at the beginning of the array. The GUI will need to access this list on a regular basis to fill selection lists with details on each book. Consequently, we add an indexer to allow a `LibraryCatalogue` object to be treated as an array that returns `LibraryBook` objects. Should an invalid element be requested a `null` reference will be returned:

```
public LibraryBook this [int index] { get; }
```

This indexer is most useful if there is a mechanism to determine the maximum index value that can be used with the indexer. To duplicate the capabilities of an array, we provide a `Length` property that indicates the number of valid index numbers:

```
public int Length { get; }
```

The `LibraryUserDatabase` class is remarkably similar to the `LibraryCatalogue` class except that each instance maintains a list of references to instances of `LibraryUser` rather than `LibraryBook`. Moreover, instances of `LibraryUser` are identified by means of integer library user identifiers rather than shelf marks. Thus, `LibraryUserDatabase` provides a constructor to initialize a new empty database, methods to insert a user into the database and remove a user from the database, and an indexer to retrieve a references to users:

```
public LibraryUserDatabase()
public bool AddUser(LibraryUser user, int id)
public bool DeleteUser(int id)
public LibraryUser this [int id] { get; }
```

`AddUser` takes an instance of `LibraryUser` and an integer representing the user's identifier as its parameters and returns a `bool` result to indicate whether or not it succeeded. Likewise, `DeleteUser` takes a user identifier as its parameter and also returns a `bool` result to indicate whether or not it succeeded. Finally, the indexer takes an index as its parameter and returns a reference to the object representing the corresponding user if it was found in the database or `null` otherwise.

Like a catalogue, a user database has only two fields: an array used to store the list of users and an integer used to keep count of how many users are in the database:

```
private int numUsers;
private LibraryUser[] database;
```

Again the list of users is maintained in the first `numUsers` elements of the `database` array. Adding a user might require that a new larger array be created if the existing array is already full. Removing a user will normally require that the contents of all the following elements in the array be shifted down a place to maintain the constraint that the list of users is stored at the beginning of the array. As with `LibraryCatalogue` objects, the GUI interface will need to access this list on a regular basis to fill selection lists with details on library users. We will make use of the indexer to allow a `LibraryUserDatabase` object to be treated as an array that returns `LibraryUser` objects. However, we will need to know the maximum number of indexes that should be examined for a valid `LibraryUser` object reference. To do so, we provide a Length property that indicates the number of valid index numbers:

```
public int Length { get; }
```

Classes `LibraryLoan` and `LibraryReservation`

Instances of class `LibraryLoan` represent individual loans and, as such, store information such as (references to) the book and user concerned, the date on which the book is due to be returned, and whether or not the loan has already been renewed.

The constructor initializes a new instance of `LibraryLoan` given the book being borrowed and the user making the loan:

```
public LibraryLoan(LibraryBook book, LibraryUser user)
```

Among the responsibilities of the constructor is working out the date on which the book is due to be returned.

`LibraryLoan` also provides a set of properties to query the details of the loan:

```
public LibraryUser User { get; }
public LibraryBook Book { get; }
public DateTime DueDate { get; }
```

as well as a set of methods to determine whether or not the loan is overdue and what fine is due as a result:

```
public bool IsOverdue()
public int CalculateFine()
```

`LibraryLoan` also provides a method to renew a loan if permissible:

```
public bool RenewLoan()
```

`RenewLoan` may fail if the loan is overdue or has already been renewed and hence returns a `bool` result.

As usual, both `ToString` and `Equals` are overridden. `ToString` allows details of a loan to be displayed by the GUI, while `Equals` allows loan objects to be compared with each other. As a consequence, `GetHashCode` must be provided. Since a loan corresponds to only one book, and a book can only be loaned once, the result of the `LibraryBook`'s `GetHashCode` identifies the `LibraryLoan` object uniquely.

The fields of `LibraryLoan` are simply used to record the information describing the loan:

```
private LibraryBook book;
private LibraryUser user;
private DateTime dueDate;
private bool renewed;
```

`LibraryReservation` is even simpler that `LibraryLoan`. Instances of `Library-Reservation` simply contain a description of one reservation request, including (references to) the book and user concerned and the date on which the request was made. The constructor:

```
public LibraryReservation(LibraryBook book, LibraryUser user)
```

initializes this information from its parameters while the properties

```
public LibraryUser User { get; }
public LibraryBook Book { get; }
public DateTime Date { get; }
```

allow this information to be retrieved when required.

Again, both `ToString` and `Equals` are overridden. As a consequence, `GetHashCode` must be provided. Reservations are uniquely defined by their associated user, book and reservation date. We cannot uniquely identify the reservation without using data from each, however, performing an "XOR" on the results of calling `GetHashCode` on each method should generate a sufficiently unique value.

Struct `LibraryShelfmark`

Shelf marks have no behaviour. Consequently, a struct named `LibraryShelfmark` is used to represent shelf marks. In our program the shelf mark for a book is composed of its subject concatenated with a unique identifier.

LibraryShelfmark provides two constructors: one to initialize a shelf mark for a new book and the second to initialize an instance of LibraryShelfmark representing the shelf mark of an existing book. The first constructor takes the subject of the book whose shelf mark is being initialized as its parameter, allocates a new unique identifier for the book, and initializes the new LibraryShelfmark instance accordingly. The second constructor takes both the subject and unique identifier as parameters and uses them to initialize the new LibraryShelfmark instance correctly:

```
public LibraryShelfmark(string subject)
public LibraryShelfmark(string subject, int number)
```

Apart from the constructors, the only methods provided by LibraryShelfmark are overrides of the standard methods ToString and Equals. This reflects the fact that since shelf marks are simply used to identify books uniquely, the most important operation on a shelf mark is that to compare one shelf mark with another! Of course, two shelf marks are equal when both the subject and unique identifier match.

The fields of a shelf mark are used to store the subject and unique identifier:

```
private string subject;
private int number;
```

This last field can be the source of the value returned by the GetHashCode override required to override the Equals method.

However, class LibraryShelfmark also uses a class variable to store the next unique identifier that is available to be allocated:

```
private static int nextNumber = 0;
```

nextNumber is incremented each time that a unique identifier is allocated to an individual instance of LibraryShelfmark.

User Interface: Designing Our GUI

The final class to be considered is the application class MainLibraryInterfaceForm. As we discussed previously, this class is responsible for all input/output performed by the program. It provides a form with event handlers as well as a series of class methods that implement each of the commands available to users of the program. These event handlers are then associated with the click events of buttons on the form.

MainLibraryInterfaceForm is responsible for creating the library's catalogue and the user database before repeatedly prompting the user for commands and processing the resulting input. When an event is received, the MainLibraryInterfaceForm method responsible for handling that command is called. Typically, this method will:

- display a form to request further input such as the shelf mark of the book required or the identifier of the user concerned,
- use the catalogue and/or user database to obtain references to the corresponding LibraryBook or LibraryUser objects,
- invoke the appropriate method on the book or user to carry out the command, and
- interpret the value returned by that method invocation and display an appropriate message to the user.

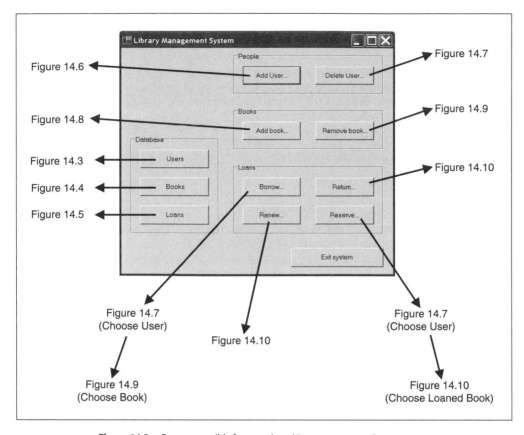

Figure 14.2   Forms accessible from `MainLibraryInterfaceForm`.

The design we have come up with relies on a series of forms to collect user data that are activated when buttons on a `MainLibraryInterfaceForm` object are pressed. Figure 14.2 pictures the main form and summarizes what windows are displayed when a button is pressed (Figures 14.3–14.10). The windows displayed are pictured in figures cited by the button that activates them. In some cases, multiple windows are required to gather user data. When a request can end in multiple outcomes, it is up to the `MainLibraryInterfaceForm` to display a dialog box indicating the operation's result. A full implementation of the system is available in Appendix B. For simplicity, this full program implements the GUI with class `MainForm` rather than class `MainLibraryInterfaceForm`.

ID	Name	Address	Loans	Fines
0	George Washington	Presidents Ave., Washington D.C.	0	
1	Napoleon Bonaparte	Emperors Way, Paris	0	
2	Winston Churchill	Ministers Alley, London	0	
3	Oscar Wilde	Westland Row, Dublin	0	

User Database

Figure 14.3   View User Database.

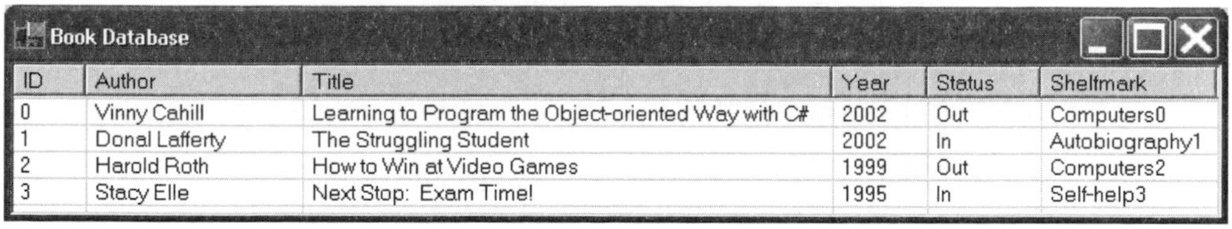

Book Database

ID	Author	Title	Year	Status	Shelfmark
0	Vinny Cahill	Learning to Program the Object-oriented Way with C#	2002	Out	Computers0
1	Donal Lafferty	The Struggling Student	2002	In	Autobiography1
2	Harold Roth	How to Win at Video Games	1999	Out	Computers2
3	Stacy Elle	Next Stop: Exam Time!	1995	In	Self-help3

Figure 14.4 View Book Database.

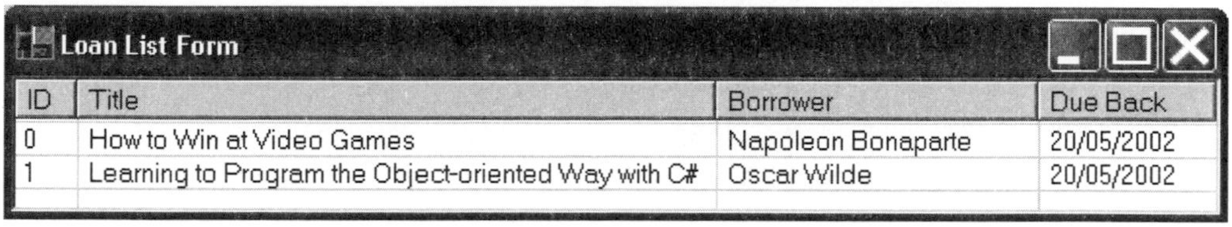

Loan List Form

ID	Title	Borrower	Due Back
0	How to Win at Video Games	Napoleon Bonaparte	20/05/2002
1	Learning to Program the Object-oriented Way with C#	Oscar Wilde	20/05/2002

Figure 14.5 View List of Loans.

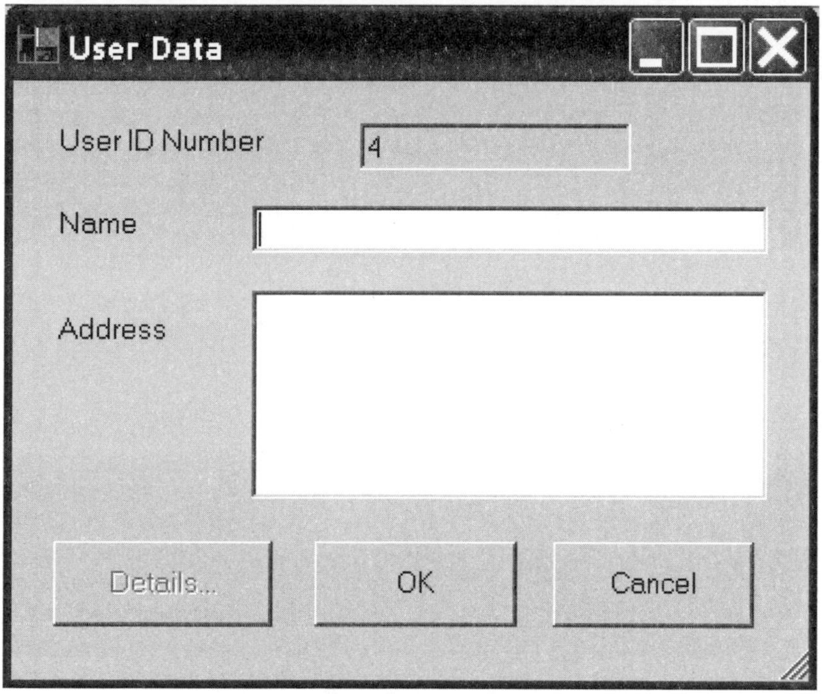

Figure 14.6 Gather User Data.

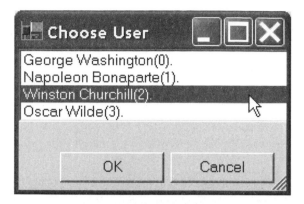

Figure 14.7   Choose User.

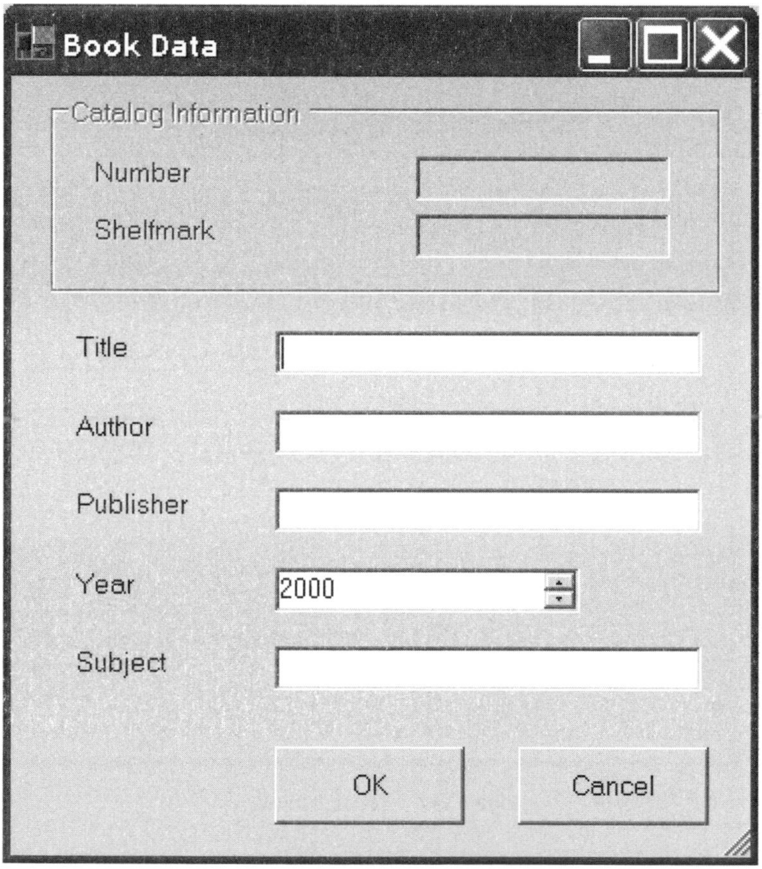

Figure 14.8   Gather Book Data.

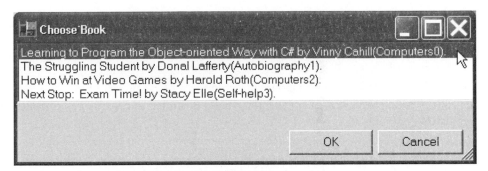

Figure 14.9   Choose Book.

Figure 14.10   Choosing a Loaned Book.

Summary

- a large program can be written by dividing it up into a number of co-operating classes that can be written separately
- the challenge in designing a large program is to identify the appropriate classes and the ways in which they co-operate
- class diagrams are commonly used to show the existence of classes and the relationships between them in a program
- when designing a class we concentrate on describing the interface of the class and the most important fields provided by the class
- an important part of designing the interface to a class is to consider the possible outcomes of its methods and hence to identify the possible return values from each method

Exercises

(1) Design and implement a simple stock control system for a warehouse. Your stock control system should maintain information about a number of different electrical components. Each component has a unique identification number. The system should maintain the level of stock of each component and produce warnings when stock levels fall below specified levels. It should be able to determine whether certain components are available, and, if so, in what quantity and also whether new supplies of those components are expected. It should also be able to determine the financial value of the stocks. In particular, the following commands should be supported with a GUI.

   (a) Enter a new component description.

The description should include the name of the component, its supplier, the current price of the component and the critical stock level below which a warning should be produced. The system should generate a unique identification number for the new component.

(b) Notify the system that new supplies of a component have now arrived.

The number of components delivered should be added to the number currently in stock.

(c) Remove a specified number of a particular component from the stocks.

If there are insufficient components in stock, an error should be produced. If, as a result of the withdrawal from the stocks, the level of that component falls below its critical level, then a warning should be produced.

(d) Notify the system that new supplies of a particular component have now been ordered.

(e) Inquire the level of stocks for a certain component.

The system should return the number of items currently in stock, whether this falls below the critical level, whether new supplies have been ordered and if so when they are expected to arrive, and, finally, the total financial value of the stocks of that component.

(f) List all the components and their descriptions, the financial value of the stock of each component, and the total value of all stock.

(g) List the description of a particular component.

(h) Change the price and/or critical level and/or description and/or supplier of a particular component.

(i) Remove all stocks of a particular component and delete all information pertaining to that component.

Note that this is different to (c) above in the case where after (c) above the stock level falls to zero, command (c) does not erase the description of the component from the system, whereas command (i) does.

(2) Design and implement a simple database system tailored towards the needs of a swimming club. A swimming club has many members of different ages and abilities who may swim at one or several training sessions per week (at most one a day). The club is also taking part in a league for which it is necessary to select one or more teams based on age and ability. The objective of your data base system is to automate the keeping of records for the club and the selection of teams. Thus, the database may contain information describing swimmers, training sessions and teams and should support the following commands with a GUI.

(a) Enter a new swimmer into the database.

The information maintained for each swimmer will include personal details such as name, address, and age, the swimmer's personal identification number, which training sessions are attended by the swimmer and details of the swimmers past performance in the various possible events (personal best, best training time, most recent competitive time).

(b) Update personal details for a given swimmer.

Note that this option may effect the swimmer's eligibility for a particular training session (see below).

(c) Remove a swimmer from the database.

(d) Update details of a swimmer's performance.

Enter a recent training or competitive time for a particular event and update the swimmer's record as appropriate. This option may entitle the swimmer to a place on a team (if any is in effect) or effect eligibility for a particular training session.

(e) Enter a new training session into the database.

Information describing the time, duration, and location of the session must be maintained as well as any qualification on those who are eligible to attend e.g. "only members of the 1st team may attend" or "only under-11 swimmers may attend".

(f) Add a swimmer to a session.

(g) Remove a training session from the database.

(h) Pick a league team.

Pick one or more teams according to the format given below. Teams should be chosen with the best possible swimmers in each place. Swimmers may not belong to more than one team. Once chosen a team remains in effect until new teams are next selected, subject to relevant changes as a result of commands (a), (b), or (d) above.

(i) List any of the following:

- all swimmers in the club (optionally giving personal details),
- all training sessions (optionally giving details),
- all swimmers who attend a particular training session, or
- all swimmers who are members of a particular team.

Note 1: swimming events.

Four competitive swimming strokes are recognized: Frontcrawl (F/C), Backcrawl (B/C), BreastStroke (B/S), and Butterfly (B/F). In addition, a swimmer may compete in the Individual Medley (I/M) event.

For each stroke races over a number of distances are run:

F/C (male):	50 m, 100 m, 200 m, 400 m, and 1500 m
F/C (female):	50 m, 100 m, 200 m, 400 m, and 800 m
B/C:	50 m, 100 m, and 200 m
Br/S:	50 m, 100 m, and 200 m
B/F:	50 m, 100 m, and 200 m
I/M:	200 m and 400 m

Note 2: composition of teams.

A league team consists of a male and a female team. Each (sub-)team consists of swimmers in four age groups: under-11, under-13, under-15, and senior where a swimmer is "under-11" if he/she was under 11 years of age on the 1st of January in the year in which the team was picked. A swimmer may swim in an older age group. A swimmer may swim in as many events as required. In each age group four events are held: 100 m F/C, 100 m B/C, 100 m Br/S, 100 m B/F. Finally, two swimmers from each club compete in each event.

Introducing the Internet and the World Wide Web

This chapter:

- introduces computer networks
- introduces the Internet as a world-wide computer network
- describes the World Wide Web as a means of accessing information that is stored on computers connected to the Internet
- introduces the Hyper-Text Mark-up Language (HTML) that is used to write documents to be published on the Web
- describes how to write a simple HTML document

In today's world computers rarely operate in isolation. Most computers are connected to one or more other computers so that their respective users can communicate with each other electronically, share information and collaborate in various other ways. A collection of two or more interconnected computers is usually referred to as *a computer network*. A computer network may be restricted to a single organization, such as company or school, or, as in the case of the Internet, span the entire world.

In this chapter we will take a brief look at the how the Internet is organized and describe one of the most important services supported by the Internet – the World Wide Web (WWW). We'll also look as how the information that is made available on the Web is usually structured using HTML – the Hypertext Mark-up Language.

The Internet

The Internet is a worldwide collection of interconnected computers. Users whose computers are connected to the Internet can use a variety of services supported by the Internet. For example, they can exchange electronic mail messages with other users. They can participate in electronic "chat rooms", usually referred to as *news groups* in Internet terminology, where they can discuss just about any topic you can imagine with other users who have similar interests. They can fetch files containing data and programs from other machines. They can run their programs on remote machines. Finally, and perhaps most importantly, they can browse hypertext documents that are published on the WWW.

Computers can be interconnected using a variety of different technologies. Most commonly, computers are connected by means of the telephone network by using a *modem*, a device that is capable of converting data from the format in which is it stored on a computer into electrical signals that can be transmitted over the telephone network and vice versa. In effect, a modem does for computer data what a telephone does for sounds.

Being able to physically interconnect computers is one thing, being able to provide useful services is quite another. Imagine a telephone conversation with a million people all tying to speak at once! Clearly, we need a set of rules that will allow different computers to engage in meaningful exchanges with each other. Such a set of rules is called a *communications protocol*. Communications protocols govern things like how computers are addressed, how their addresses are translated into, for example, phone numbers that can be used to contact them, and how and what kind of requests computers can make of each other. Of course, these protocols are implemented as (very complex) computer programs installed in all the machines that are participating in the network. What distinguishes the Internet is that all the computers that are connected to it use the same (set of) protocols, *the Internet Protocols*, to control their communication.

Perhaps surprisingly, there is really no central control of the Internet. Any computer can join as long as it can be physically connected to the other computers that form the Internet and abides by the rules of the Internet Protocols when communicating with other computers. Thus, the Internet is very much a co-operative. Computers join and leave the network frequently. Computers that are part of the network can retrieve information that has been made available by other computers by using the appropriate protocol to request that information when it is required. They can also make their own information available as long as they are prepared to abide by the rules of the protocol and return that information whenever it is requested by another computer.

Different protocols are used to provide different types of services. For example, there are protocols governing how electronic mail messages are exchanged (the Simple Mail Transfer Protocol or SMTP), how files are fetched from remote machines (the File Transfer Protocol – FTP), and how news group messages are distributed (the Network News Transfer Protocol – NNTP).

The World Wide Web

The Web is a service supported by the Internet that allows arbitrary information, made available by one machine, to be retrieved by any other machine on demand. Such information can include text, photographs, programs, animations, maps, audio tracks, videos, and pretty much any other type of information that you can think of. This information is structured as a collection of *web pages*. Most importantly, any web page can refer to any other web page by means of a *link* contained in the page. Notice, I said "any other web page". A page on one machine can refer to a completely independent page on a separate machine by means of a link. Once a page has been retrieved, the links contained in the page can be used to retrieve any, or all, of the corresponding pages. Thus, the Web can be viewed as an interconnected collection of pages containing arbitrary data that can be navigated by retrieving known pages and following the links that they contain to retrieve related pages. You can imagine the Web as a (huge) book containing lots and lots of pages. Unlike a traditional book whose pages are organized in a sequential order and are intended to be read in that order, web pages usually have no implied order. The expectation is that, having read one page, the reader will follow one of the possibly many links in that page to *some* other related page rather than the *next* page. A document organized in this manner, using links that can be followed to retrieve related information, is referred to as a *hypertext* document.

Uniform Resource Locators

Every page that is accessible via the Web has its own unique address, which can be used to retrieve that page as well as to link to it to other pages. Such an address is known as a *Uniform Resource Locator* or URL. For example, the URL for my personal web page or *home page*, is

```
http://www.dsg.cs.tcd.ie/~vjcahill
```

Since they can be used to refer to a variety of different types of data, URLs come is a variety of forms. The first part for the URL ("`http://`") specifies what type of URL this is and, especially, what protocol should be used to retrieve the associated page. This URL specifies that HTTP, the Hypertext Transfer Protocol, should be used. This is by far the most common form of URL. At least for now, we will ignore other forms. The second part of the URL ("`www.dsg.cs.tcd.ie`") is essentially the Internet address of the machine that is making the page available. The remainder of the URL ("`/~vjcahill`") is the local address of the page on that machine. Here are some further examples of URLs.

```
http://www.dsg.cs.tcd.ie/~laffertd
```

Notice that this URL refers to a different page but one being made available by the same machine.

```
http://www.tcd.ie/
```

This URL refers to another page exported by a different machine in Trinity College. Notice that this URL contains no local page address. Thus, this URL refers to the top level, or *index*, page made available by the machine `www.tcd.ie`.

Browsers, Clients, and Servers

A machine that makes pages available on the Web is usually referred to as a *web server*. Such a machine must run a special program, which understands the Hypertext Transfer Protocol, to accept requests for the pages that it has made available and return copies of the those pages on demand.

A machine that retrieves pages via the Web is usually called a *client*. A client must have the software necessary to make requests for pages on behalf of local users according to the rules of the protocol. Users, in turn, use a program called a *browser* to view web pages and request further pages to be retrieved. Popular web browsers such as Microsoft's Internet Explorer or Netscape's Communicator provide the means of requesting pages to be retrieved given their URLs and of displaying retrieved pages. Links within a page that has been retrieved are usually highlighted (typically by underlining) in the display. Clicking on such a link with the mouse usually causes the corresponding page to be retrieved and displayed providing a convenient way of fetching further pages without having to know their URLs in advance.

For example, Figure A.1 shows the result of running Microsoft's Internet Explorer. If we know the URL of a page that we want to view, we can type the URL in the text field labeled "Address" and press return to retrieve the page. For example, to retrieve my home page, we type its URL in the address field as shown in Figure A.2.

The page is then retrieved and displayed as shown in Figure A.3. Notice that the page includes a mix of text and graphics.

To retrieve further pages we now have two alternatives. If we want to retrieve another page whose URL we know, we can type the URL in the location field as before and the page will be retrieved and displayed in place of the current page. However, as with most web

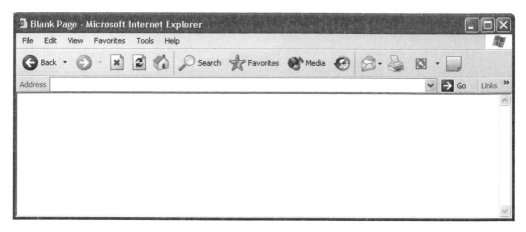

Figure A.1 Running a web browser.

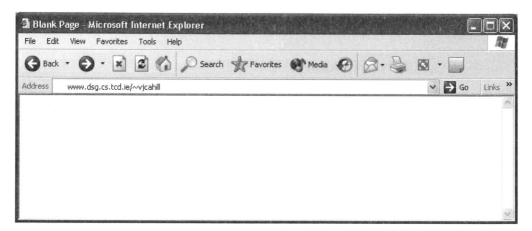

Figure A.2 Retrieving a web page whose URL we know.

pages, my page includes a number of links to other web pages. In fact, each of the underlined pieces of text on the page represents a link. If we click on any link with the mouse, the corresponding page will be retrieved. For example, Figure A.4 shows the result of clicking on the link "`Trinity College Dublin`". Notice that the URL for the new page is displayed in the address field. We can continue to browse the web by following any of the links on Trinity's page, typing in a known URL for a page that we want to visit or using the "Back" button on the browser to return to a previous page.

Writing Your Own Web Page

As we mentioned previously, all Web pages are written in a language known as the Hypertext Mark-up Language or HTML. Thus, most Web pages could more correctly be described as being *HTML documents*. Note however that HTML documents can refer to other sorts of documents, allowing them to also be retrieved via the Web. While it's not our intention to

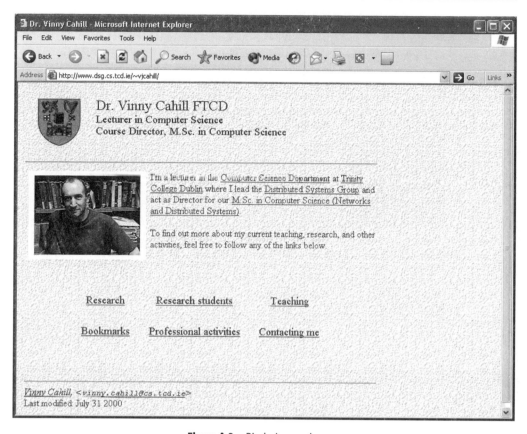

Figure A.3   Displaying a web page.

give a complete description of HTML, which would certainly take a whole book on its own, this section looks at the basics of HTML. Having read this section you will hopefully know enough about HTML to be able to write your own Web pages!

The first version of HTML was developed by Tim Berners-Lee at CERN, the European Laboratory for Particle Physics in Geneva. Subsequent versions of HTML have been standardized by the World Wide Web Consortium (W3C), the body that looks after most of the standards related to the operation of the Web. At the time of writing, the current version of HTML is version 4.0. To find out more about HTML and to keep up to date with developments in HTML look at the W3C's own HTML Web page at `http://www.w3.org/MarkUp/`.

The HTML Philosophy

For as long as computers have been used to process documents, there has been a need to define common document formats that allow documents, possibly generated by different word processing packages, to be exchanged between different types of computers. Over time hundreds of different formats for storing and exchanging documents have been proposed. Unlike previous proposals, HTML concentrates on document structure rather than formatting. As an example consider a user who is writing a report using a word processing package such as

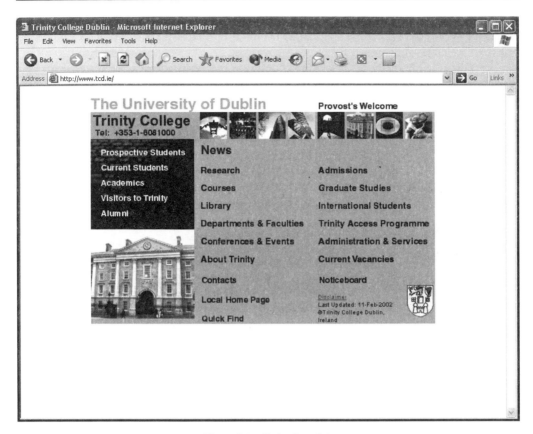

Figure A.4 Navigating a link.

Microsoft Word. Often the user will first type in the entire report and subsequently format it. For example, having typed in the report the user might change all the quotes to italics, make all the chapter headings bold and widen the margins a little. All of these format changes are stored with the document so that it is always displayed in the same way. Most document formats work similarly in that it's up to the user to format the document based on their knowledge of its structure.

In contrast, HTML allows the author of a document to explicitly indicate or *mark up*, the structure of the document. Thus, the author will enclose the title of the document with a set of *tags*, which simply indicate that the enclosed text represents the document's title. Similarly, when writing the abstract, the author encloses the abstract in a set of tags that indicate that the enclosed text constitutes the abstract. Thus, the author of an HTML document normally concentrates on indicating the structure of the document rather than its formatting. All the formatting is done automatically by the browser that is eventually used to view the document. Thus, the browser chooses a style for headings, quotations, and abstracts, and displays each part of a document using the appropriate formatting based on the way in which the document is marked up. This means that a document may look differently when viewed with different browsers but the way in which different documents are displayed by a particular browser will be consistent from document to document.

HTML Tags

As we mentioned earlier, an HTML document's structure is defined by sets of tags. A tag is simply a special symbol used to indicate the structure or format of the enclosed text. As a very simple first example let's look at the `title` tag used to indicate the title of an HTML document. To give an HTML document the title "Vinny's Home Page" we simply write

```
<title>Vinny's Home Page</title>
```

in our HTML document. As you can see, tags (almost) always appear in pairs. In general, all tags begin with `<tag_name>` and end with `</tag_name>`. Between the opening tag, in this case `<title>` and the closing tag, `</title>`, we have the content, in this case the title of the document. The title of an HTML document is usually displayed in the title bar of the browser window in which the corresponding HTML document is being displayed.

A Complete Web Page

Now that we know about the idea of tags, we can write a simple web page. Program A.1 is a complete HTML document describing a simplified version of my home page. Figure A.5 shows what the document looks like when displayed in a browser.

Let's take a closer look at the HTML document. The first line of the file is simply a comment, rather like a Java comment, which describes the web page. In particular, comments are not

```
<!-- Vinny's home page - version 1 -->
<html>
<head>
<title>Vinny's Home Page</title>
</head>

<body>
<h1>Vinny Cahill</h1>
<h3>Lecturer, Department of Computer Science, Trinity College Dublin</h3>

<p>
Hi!
</p>

<p>
Welcome to my home page. As you can see, I'm a lecturer in the
Computer
Science Department at
Trinity College, Dublin where I'm a member of the
Distributed Systems Group.
</p>

<p>
Some of the activities in which I am involved include teaching, research,
and, in my free time, swimming.
</p>

</body>
</html>
```

Program A.1   Vinny's Home Page – version 1.

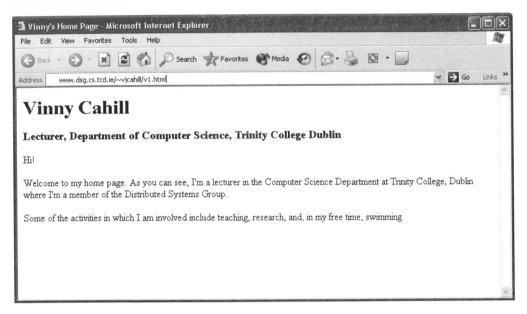

Figure A.5 Displaying Vinny's home page 1.

displayed by browsers as you can see in Figure A.5. In HTML, all comments appear, just as above, within a single comment tag

```
<!- comment -->
```

and can appear anywhere in a HTML document. Moreover, a comment can include several lines of text.

Every HTML document is enclosed within the `<html>` and `</html>` tags. These tags may appear redundant but they explicitly indicate that the enclosed document is an HTML document. Most HTML documents are composed of two distinct parts: a header and a body. The header is enclosed within the `<head>` and `</head>` tags and describes various properties of the document including, most commonly, its title. The title itself is introduced using the `<title>...</title>` tags as we've already seen. The real content of the document is given in its body, which is enclosed with the `<body>...</body>` tags.

In this case, the body of our document has a main heading, a sub-heading and three paragraphs of text. The main heading is enclosed within the `<h1>...</h1>` tags, which indicate that this heading is a level 1 heading. You can have up to six levels of headings. Usually, level 1 heading tags contain the main heading for the document. Level 2 might contain chapter headings, level 3 section headings, level 4 sub-section headings and so on. The browser chooses an appropriate font and size to display headings at different levels. In this case we've chosen level 3 for the sub-heading of the document. You can see the difference between the way in which the two headings are displayed in Figure A.5. Incidentally, this is a good example of specifying the document's structure rather than it formatting.

Finally, the text that appears between the paragraph tags `<p>...</p>` is formatted automatically by the browser to form a single paragraph irrespective of how the text is formatted in the HTML document. For example, the browser may remove multiple spaces and line breaks as necessary.

Tags and Attributes

As is obvious from Figure A.5, our web page isn't very eye-catching. Fortunately, HTML provides lots of ways for us to liven up web pages!

Let's begin by looking at our colour scheme. The background colour used when displaying our web page is normally chosen by the browser. In Microsoft's Internet Explorer this colour is white. However, in Netscape Communicator it happens to be a dull grey colour. We can use HTML to make the background colour consistent between browsers. For example, to specify that the page should always be displayed with a white background, we write:

```
<body bgcolor=white>
```

bgcolor (for "background colour") is an *attribute* of the <body> tag and white is the value that we have chosen for the colour. We could have chosen yellow, blue or red, or indeed any of a range of other colours that HTML supports.

Many HTML tags take attributes that affect the way in which they work. Most attributes are optional. For example, it's perfectly acceptable to use the <body> tag without an attribute just as we did in Program A.1. As we'll see later, some tags can take several attributes. In general, an attribute has a name, such as bgcolor, and is given a value by following the name with an = sign and the required value, such as white.

Including Images

A good way of livening up a web page is to include some pictures or *images*. Images are typically stored in separate files in one of a number of different image formats. Commonly used formats include those known as GIF, JPEG, PNG, and XBM. Different formats have different advantages and disadvantages. For example, the most commonly used formats are JPEG and GIF. JPEG images compress well and can therefore be stored in smaller files, which can be transmitted across the Internet more quickly. Unfortunately, we have to sacrifice some picture quality to compress the picture appropriately. On the other hand, GIF images tend to be larger but higher quality. It's worth bearing in mind that the number and size of images included in a web page will seriously affect the speed with which the page can be downloaded and displayed.

To include an image in a web page, we simply use the <img> tag. For example, we can add a picture of me to our web page as follows:

```
<img src="vinny_small.jpg">
```

In this case the value of the src attribute of the <img> tag is a URL for the file in which the picture is stored (enclosed in double quotes). Notice that we can use a *relative* URL as above (in which case the image is retrieved from the same directory as the HTML file) or we can specify the complete URL of the file as in:

```
<img src="http://www.cs.tcd.ie/~vjcahill/vinny_small.jpg">
```

Note that the latter allows a web page to include an image that is located *anywhere* on the web and not necessarily on the same machine as the HTML file. Notice also that this URL refers to a file that does not itself contain an HTML document. The browser can deduce from the file extension, ".jpg", that the URL refers to a JPEG image rather than a HTML document and hence can process and display it properly.

Obviously, the src attribute of the <img> tag is required. However, the <img> tag can also include a number of other optional attributes that allow us some control over how the

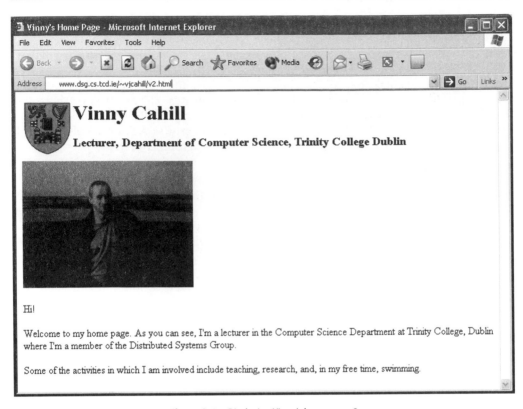

Figure A.6 Displaying Vinny's home page 2.

image is displayed on the page. For example, to display Trinity's crest on our page and have it aligned to the left margin of the page, we can write:

```
<img align=left src="tcdcrest.gif">
```

i.e., using the `align` attribute with the value `left`.

Program A.2 shows our modified web page and Figure A.6 how it is displayed by a browser. As expected, the background is now white and the page includes two images. Notice that since the crest is aligned to the left, the text that follows it is displayed to its right.

Links and Anchors

Hypertext links allow us to move freely to and from a block of text or an image to another relevant document by simply clicking on the link in the browser's window. In order to include such a link in an HTML document we use an HTML *anchor*. An anchor is essentially an HTML tag that specifies the URL of the related document and the text to be displayed at the point in the current document at which the link appears. The URL is specified as an attribute of the anchor, `<a>`, tag while the text is enclosed by the `<a>` tag and the corresponding `</a>` tag. For example to include a link to Trinity College's home page in our web page, we write:

```
<a href="http://www.tcd.ie/">Trinity College, Dublin</a>
```

The text between the `<a>...</a>` tags appears as a hypertext link in the document. The `href` attribute tells the browser where to locate the document to which the link refers.

```
<!-- Vinny's home page - version 2 -->
<html>
<head>
<title>Vinny's Home Page</title>
</head>

<body bgcolor=white>

<img align=left src="tcdcrest.gif">
<h1>Vinny Cahill</h1>
<h3>Lecturer, Department of Computer Science, Trinity College Dublin</h3>

<p>
<img src="vinny_small.jpeg">
</p>

<p>
Hi!
</p>

<p>
Welcome to my home page. As you can see, I'm a lecturer in the
Computer
Science Department at
Trinity College, Dublin where I'm a member of the
Distributed Systems Group.
</p>

<p>
Some of the activities in which I am involved include teaching, research,
and, in my free time, swimming.
</p>

</body>
</html>
```

Program A.2   Vinny's Home Page – version 2.

Instead of placing text within the <a> tag, we can include pretty much any HTML. For example, we could arrange that clicking on Trinity's crest also links us to Trinity's home page by using the <img> tag within the <a>...</a> tags as follows:

```
<a href="http://www.tcd.ie/"><img align=left src=
    "tcdcrest.gif"> </a>
```

The <img> tag is now nested within the <a> tag, in the same way that the whole of our HTML document is nested within the <body> tag.

Program A.3 shows a new revision of our web page that includes a number of links to other pages, while Figure A.7 shows how the page is displayed by the browser. Any text that represents a link to another document is underlined and displayed in a different colour (which usually depends on whether or not the link has already been followed). The crest is also outlined in the same colour as the other link text to indicate that it represents a link (unfortunately making the page rather ugly!).

```
<!-- Vinny's home page - version 3 -->
<html>
<head>
<title>Vinny's Home Page</title>
</head>

<body bgcolor=white>

<p>
<a href="http://www.tcd.ie/"><img align=left src="tcdcrest.gif"></a>
<h1>Vinny Cahill</h1>
<h3>Lecturer, Department of Computer Science, Trinity College Dublin</h3>
</p>

<p>
<img src="vinny_small.jpeg">
</p>

<p>
Hi!
</p>

<p>
Welcome to my home page. As you can see, I'm a lecturer in the
<a href="http://www.cs.tcd.ie/">Computer
Science Department</a> at <a href="http://www.tcd.ie/">
Trinity College, Dublin</a> where I'm a member of the
<a href="http://www.dsg.cs.tcd.ie/">Distributed Systems
Group</a>.
</p>

<p>
Some of the activities in which I am involved include teaching, research,
and, in my free time, swimming.
</p>

</body>
</html>
```

Program A.3 Vinny's Home Page – version 3.

Document Formatting with HTML

We noted already that HTML is designed primarily to allow document authors to indicate the structure of their documents rather than how they should be formatted. Formatting is expected to be left up to the browser. However, we also saw that HTML allows some formatting decisions to be specified by the document author. For example, we were able to specify the background colour for our document as well as how to align our images. In fact, there are many HTML tags concerned solely with formatting. These are referred to as *physical* tags as opposed to the *logical* tags used to indicate document structure (many of which also have attributes that describe formatting).

As a simple example of a physical tag, notice that we can specify that a particular piece of text is to be displayed in boldface by using the ... tag. For example, we might bold our greeting as follows:

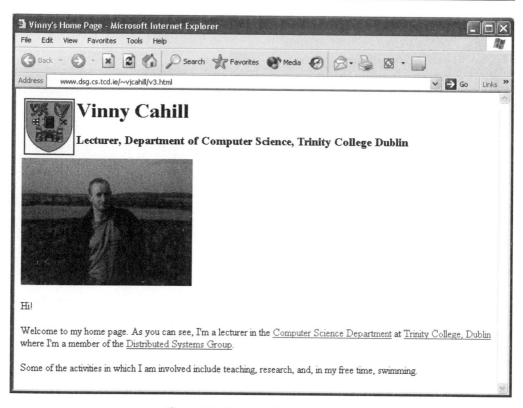

Figure A.7   Displaying Vinny's home page 3.

```
<b>Hi!</b>
```

We can also do other kinds of formatting such as including numbered or bulleted lists as well as tables of data. For example, an HTML unnumbered list is enclosed within the `<ul>...</ul>` tags with each individual item in the list being enclosed within the list item, `<li>...</li>`, tags. For example, we might include a list of my activities in our page as follows:

```
<ul>
<li> teaching,</li>
<li> research, and</li>
<li> in my free time, swimming.</li>
</ul>
```

Program A.4 shows the final version of our web page including these changes. Notice the use of the physical `<center>...</center>` tags to cause the list to be centred in the browser's window and the horizontal rule, `<hr>`, tag to draw a line across the display. As is good practice, the web page is signed with an email address at which I can be contacted by including an anchor with a special `mailto` URL that includes my email address. Figure A.8 shows how the final version of the page looks like when displayed.

Hopefully this section has given you a taste of what you can do using HTML. To find out about the many other tags and attributes supported by HTML look at any of the very many good books on HTML that are available. The World Wide Web Consortium's HTML page is

```
<!-- Vinny's home page - version 4 -->
<html>
<head>
<title>Vinny's Home Page</title>
</head>

<body bgcolor=white>

<img align=left src="tcdcrest.gif">
<h1>Vinny Cahill</h1>
<h3>Lecturer, Department of Computer Science, Trinity College Dublin</h3>

<hr>

<p>
<img src="vinny_small.jpeg">
</p>

<p>
<b>Hi!</b>
</p>

<p>
Welcome to my home page. As you can see, I'm a lecturer in the
<a href="http://www.cs.tcd.ie/">Computer
Science Department</a> at <a href="http://www.tcd.ie/">
Trinity College, Dublin</a> where I'm a member of the
<a href="http://www.dsg.cs.tcd.ie/">Distributed Systems
Group</a>.
</p>

<p>
Some of the activities in which I am involved include:
<center>
<ul>
<li> teaching,
<li> research, and
<li> in my free time, swimming.
</ul>
</center>
</p>

<hr>
<address><a href="mailto:vinny.cahill@cs.tcd.ie">vinny.cahill@cs.tcd.ie
</a></address>

</body>
</html>
```

Program A.4   Vinny's Home Page – version 4.

also a good place to look for information about HTML on-line. As well as including links to the complete (detailed) specification of HTML, it also includes many links to introductory and summary information on HTML.

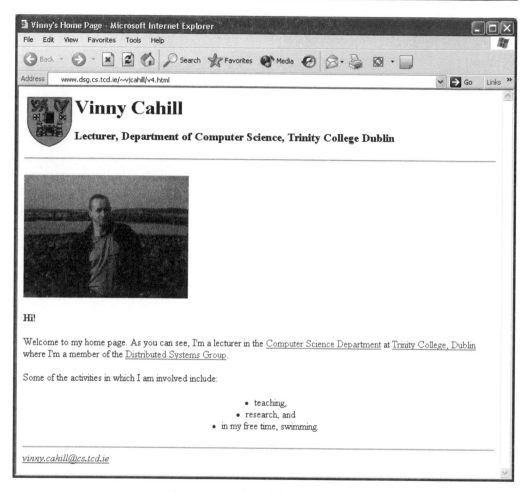

Figure A.8   Displaying Vinny's home page 4.

Summary

- a computer network is a collection of interconnected computers
- the Internet is a computer network that spans the entire world
- the Internet supports services such as electronic mail, file transfer, news groups, use of remote machines and the World Wide Web
- the Web provides access to pages of hypertext information made available by any of the computers connected to the Internet
- a Web browser is used to retrieve and display Web pages of interest
- a single Web page can include links to other Web pages located anywhere else on the Web
- HTML is used to write web pages
- HTML allows the structure of the information contained in a Web page to be marked up using tags and attributes

This chapter:

• provides source code for the Case Study mentioned in Chapter 14

```
using System.Globalization;
using System;

namespace LibraryDatabase
{
  public class LibraryBook
  {
    /* declare book status codes */
    public const int IN = 0;
    public const int OUT = 1;
    public const int HELD = 2;     // implies book is not on loan
    public const int RESERVED = 3; // implies book is on loan

    /* declare return values for methods */
    public const int BADBORROWER = 4;
    public const int BADRENEWAL = 5;

    /* declare attributes of book */
    private string author;
    private string title;
    private string publisher;
    private int year;
    private LibraryShelfmark shelfmark;
    private string subject;
    private int fine = 0;
    private int status = IN;
    /* when status is IN or HELD, currentLoan is null */
    /* when status is OUT or RESERVED, currentLoan is not null */
    private LibraryLoan currentLoan = null;
    /* when status is IN or OUT, numReservations is 0 */
    /* and currentReservations is null */
    /* when status is HELD or RESERVED, numReservations is > 0 */
    /* and currentReservations is not null */
    private int numReservations = 0;
    private LibraryReservation[] currentReservations = null;

    /* initialize a new instance representing a book with the */
    /* specified author, title, publisher, year of publication, */
    /* and subject */
    public LibraryBook(string title, string author, string publisher,
      int year, string subject)
    {
```

```csharp
    this.title = title;
    this.author = author;
    this.publisher = publisher;
    this.year = year;
    this.subject = subject;
    /* allocate new shelf mark to book */
    shelfmark = new LibraryShelfmark(subject);
}

/* return the author of the book */
public string Author { get { return author;} }

/* return the title of the book */
public string Title { get { return title; } }

/* return the publisher of the book */
public string Publisher { get { return publisher; } }

/* return the year of publication of the book */
public int Year { get { return year; } }

/* return the subject of the book */
public string Subject { get { return subject; } }

/* return the shelf mark of the book */
public LibraryShelfmark Shelfmark { get { return shelfmark; } }

/* delete the current book from the system */
public void DeleteBook()
{
    /* cancel any outstanding loan */
    if (currentLoan != null)
    {
        currentLoan.User.ReturnBook(currentLoan);
        currentLoan = null;
    }
    /* cancel any outstanding reservations */
    if (numReservations != 0)
    {
        for (int r = 0; r < numReservations; r++)
        {
            LibraryUser user = currentReservations[r].User;
            user.CancelReservation(currentReservations[r]);
            currentReservations[r] = null;
        }
        numReservations = 0;
        currentReservations = null;
    }
}

/* determine if book can be borrowed by the specfied user */
/* Records the loan if granted Returns: */
/*   IN: if the loan was granted */
/*   OUT: if the book is currently on loan */
/*   HELD: if the book is in and reserved by another user */
/*   RESERVED: if the book is out and reserved by another user */
/*   BADBORROWER: if loan was not granted becuase user is overquota */
public int BorrowBook(LibraryUser borrower)
{
    /* first check that the parameter is valid */
    if (borrower == null)
    {
```

```
      return BADBORROWER;
}
switch (status)
{
  case IN:
    if (borrower.CanBorrow())
    {
      status = OUT;
      currentLoan = new LibraryLoan(this, borrower);
      borrower.BorrowBook(currentLoan);
      return IN;
    }
    else
    {
      return BADBORROWER;
    }
  case HELD:
    if (borrower == currentReservations[0].User)
    {
      /* book is available to current borrower */
      /* delete the reservation */
      borrower.CancelReservation(currentReservations[0]);
      for (int r = 0; r < numReservations-1; r++ )
      {
        currentReservations[r] = currentReservations[r+1];
      }
      if (--numReservations == 0)
      {
        currentReservations = null;
      }
      /* now see if the book can be given to the borrower */
      if (borrower.CanBorrow())
      {
        if (numReservations == 0)
        {
          status = OUT;
        }
        else
        {
          status = RESERVED;
        }
        currentLoan = new LibraryLoan(this, borrower);
        borrower.BorrowBook(currentLoan);
        return IN;
      }
      else
      {
        if (numReservations == 0)
        {
          status = IN;
          return BADBORROWER;
        }
        else
        {
          status = HELD;
          return HELD;
        }
      }
    }
    else
    {
      /* book is not available to current borrower */
```

```
        return HELD;
      }
    default: // OUT, RESERVED
      return OUT;
  }
}


/* return date on which the book is due to be returned */
/* This operation is only possible if the book is on loan */
/* Return 0 if the book is not currently on loan */
public DateTime GetDueDate()
{
  if (currentLoan != null)
  {
    return currentLoan.DueDate;
  }
  else
  {
    return new DateTime(0);
  }
}

/* report whether or not the book is currently on loan */
/* Return true if so, false otherwise */
public bool IsOnLoan()
{
  return currentLoan != null;
}

/* determine if a loan can be renewed and record the renewal */
/* if allowed Returns */
/*  IN: if the book is not currently on loan */
/*  OUT: if the renewal is allowed */
/*  HELD: if the book is in and reserved by another user */
/*  RESERVED: if the book is out and reserved by another user */
/*  BADRENEWAL: if the renewal was not granted */
public int RenewLoan()
{
  switch (status)
  {
    case IN:
      return IN;
    case OUT:
      if (currentLoan.RenewLoan())
      {
        return OUT;
      }
      else
      {
        return BADRENEWAL;
      }
    case HELD:
      return HELD;
    default: // RESERVED
      return RESERVED;
  }
}

/* determine if a book can be reserved by the specified user */
/* and record the reservation if allowed Returns */
/*  IN: if the book is not currently on loan */
```

```
/*  OUT: if the book is already on loan to the specified user */
/*  HELD: if the book is in and reserved by the specified user */
/*  RESERVED: if the reservation is allowed */
/*  BADBORROWER: if parameter is null */
public int ReserveBook(LibraryUser reserver)
{
  int r = 0;
  bool alreadyReserved = false;

  /* first check that the parameter is valid */
  if (reserver == null)
  {
    return BADBORROWER;
  }
  switch (status)
  {
    case OUT:
      /* make sure that the book is not on loan to the user */
      if (!currentLoan.User.Equals(reserver))
      {
        status = RESERVED;
        numReservations = 1;
        currentReservations = new LibraryReservation[2];
        currentReservations[0] = new LibraryReservation(this, reserver);
        reserver.MakeReservation(currentReservations[0]);
        return RESERVED;
      }
      else
      {
        return OUT;
      }
    case RESERVED:
      /* find out if the user has already reserved the book */
      r = 0;
      alreadyReserved = false;
      while (!alreadyReserved && (r < numReservations))
      {
        alreadyReserved = currentReservations[r++].User.Equals(reserver);
      }
      /* allow reservation only if user hasn't already reserved */
      /* the book and has not already got the book on loan */
      if (!alreadyReserved && !currentLoan.User.Equals(reserver))
      {
        /* check that there is space in the reservations list */
        if (numReservations == currentReservations.Length)
        {
          /* make more space */
          LibraryReservation[] tmp
            = new LibraryReservation[currentReservations.Length+2];
          for (r = 0; r <= currentReservations.Length-1; r++)
          {
            tmp[r] = currentReservations[r];
          }
          currentReservations = tmp;
        }
        /* make the reservation */
        currentReservations[numReservations]
          = new LibraryReservation(this, reserver);
        reserver.MakeReservation(currentReservations[numReservations]);
        numReservations++;
        return RESERVED;
      }
```

```
      else if (alreadyReserved)
      {  // user has already reserved the book
        return RESERVED;
      }
      else
      {     // book is already on loan to the user
        return OUT;
      }
    case HELD:
      /* find out if the book is being held for the user */
      if (currentReservations[0].User.Equals(reserver))
      {
        return HELD;
      }
      else
      {
        /* find out if the user has already reserved the book */
        r = 0;
        alreadyReserved = false;
        while (!alreadyReserved && (r < numReservations))
        {
          alreadyReserved = currentReservations[r++].User.Equals(reserver);
        }
        /* allow reservation only if user hasn't already reserved */
        /* the book and has not already got the book on loan */
        if (!alreadyReserved && !currentLoan.User.Equals(reserver))
        {
          /* check that there is space in the reservations list */
          if (numReservations == currentReservations.Length)
          {
            LibraryReservation[] tmp
              = new LibraryReservation[currentReservations.Length+2];
            /* make more space */
            for (r = 0; r <= currentReservations.Length-1; r++)
            {
              tmp[r] = currentReservations[r];
            }
            currentReservations = tmp;
          }
          /* make the reservation */
          currentReservations[numReservations]
            = new LibraryReservation(this, reserver);
          reserver.MakeReservation(currentReservations[numReservations]);
          numReservations++;
          return RESERVED;
        }
        else if (alreadyReserved)
        { // user has already reserved the book
          return RESERVED;
        }
        else
        {     // book is already on loan to the user
          return OUT;
        }
      }
    default: // IN
      return IN;
  }
}

/* record the return of a book Returns */
/*  IN: if the book is not currently on loan */
```

```
/*  HELD: if the book is in and already reserved */
/*   OUT: if the book is successfully returned */
/*  RESERVED: if the book is successfully returned but */
/*            has already been reserved */
public int ReturnBook()
{
  switch (status)
  {
    case OUT:
      if (currentLoan.IsOverdue())
      {
        fine = currentLoan.CalculateFine();
      }
      currentLoan.User.ReturnBook(currentLoan);
      status = IN;
      currentLoan = null;
      return OUT;
    case RESERVED:
      if (currentLoan.IsOverdue())
      {
        fine = currentLoan.CalculateFine();
      }
      currentLoan.User.ReturnBook(currentLoan);
      status = HELD;
      currentLoan = null;
      return RESERVED;
    case IN:
      return IN;
    default:  // HELD:
      return HELD;
  }
}

/* report whether or not the return of the book is currently overdue */
/* Return true if so, false otherwise */
public bool IsOverdue()
{
  if (currentLoan != null)
  {
    return currentLoan.IsOverdue();
  }
  else
  {
    return false;
  }
}

/* clear any fine outstanding on the book */
/* Return the value of the fine */
public int GetFine()
{
  int f = fine;
  fine = 0;
  return f;
}

/* record the fact that the specified reservation has been cancelled */
/* Return true if successful, false otherwise */
public bool CancelReservation(LibraryReservation reservation)
{
  if ((reservation != null) && (numReservations != 0))
  {
```

```
    /* lookup the reservation in the book's list */
    int r = 0;
    while ((r <= currentReservations.Length-1)
       && !(currentReservations[r].Equals(reservation)))
    {
      r++;
    }
    /* check if the reservation was found in the list */
    if (currentReservations[r].Equals(reservation))
    {
      /* remove the reservation from the list */
      if (--numReservations == 0)
      {
        /* remove the only reservation and */
        /* change the status of the book */
        currentReservations = null;
        if (currentLoan == null)
        {
          status = IN;
        }
        else
        {
          status = OUT;
        }
      }
      else
      {
        for (int i = r; i <= currentReservations.Length-2; i++)
        {
          currentReservations[i] = currentReservations[i+1];
        }
      }
      return true;
    }
    else
    {
      /* reservation was not found in book's list */
      return false;
    }
  }
  else
  {
    /* parameter is null or book has no reservations */
    return false;
  }
}

public string GetStatus()
{
  switch(status)
  {
    case IN:
      return "In";
    case OUT:
    {
      if(this.IsOverdue())
        return "Overdue";
      else
        return "Out";
    }
    case HELD:
    {
```

```
        return "Held";
      }
      case RESERVED:
      {
        return "Reserved";
      }
    }
    return "Error";
  }

  /* indicate whether or not the current book */
  /* is equal to the specified book */
  public override bool Equals(object other)
  {
    LibraryBook otherBook = (LibraryBook)other;
    if (this == otherBook)
    {
      return true;
    }
    else
    {
      return shelfmark.Equals(otherBook.shelfmark);
    }
  }

  /* GetHashCode is required in order to override Equals
   * The function provides an int that as uniquely as possible
   * identifies this object instance. */
  public override int GetHashCode()
  {
    /* The shelfmark uniquely identifies our book, so
     * we use the shelfmark's HashCode! */
    return shelfmark.GetHashCode();
  }

  /* return a string representing the current book */
  public override string ToString()
  {
    return title + " by " + author +  "(" + shelfmark + ").";
  }
  }
}
```

Program B.1   class LibraryDatabase.

```csharp
namespace LibraryDatabase
{
  public class LibraryUser
  {
    /* declare max number of books that a user can borrow */
    private const int QUOTA = 3;

    /* declare next user id. number to allocate */
    private static int nextId = 0;

    // Shows next id number without actually creating an object
    public static int NextId { get {return nextId; } }

    /* declare attributes of user */
    private string name;
    private string address;
    private int userId;
    public int NumLoans
    {
      get
      { return numLoans;  }
    }
    public int NumReservations
    {
       get
       {  return numLoans;  }
    }
    public LibraryLoan[] Loans
    {
      get
      { return currentLoans;}
    }
    /* when numLoans is 0, currentLoans is null */
    private int numLoans = 0;
    private LibraryLoan[] currentLoans = null;
    /* when numReservations is 0, currentReservations is null */
    private int numReservations = 0;
    private LibraryReservation[] currentReservations = null;

    /* initialize a new instance representing a user with */
    /* the specified name and address */
    public LibraryUser(string name, string address)
    {
      this.name = name;
      this.address = address;
      userId = nextId++;
    }

    /* return name of current user */
    public string Name { get {return name;} }

    /* return address of current user */
    public string Address { get { return address; } }

    /* return id. number of current user */
    public int Id { get { return userId; } }

    /* delete the current user from the system */
    /* Users cannot be deleted while they have books on loan */
    /* Return true if successful, false otherwise */
    public bool DeleteUser()
    {
```

```
  if (numLoans == 0)
  {
    /* cancel any reservations by the current user */
    for (int r = 0; r < numReservations; r++)
    {
      LibraryBook book = currentReservations[r].Book;
      book.CancelReservation(currentReservations[r]);
      currentReservations[r] = null;
    }
    numReservations = 0;
    currentReservations = null;
    return true;
  }
  else
  {
    return false;
  }
}

/* determine if current user can borrow any more books */
/* A user can borrow books until they reach their quota */
/* provided that none of the books that they have on loan */
/* are overdue */
/* Return true if books can be borrowed, false otherwise */
public bool CanBorrow()
{
  bool allowed = numLoans < QUOTA;

  if (allowed && (numLoans > 0))
  {
    /* check that no existing loans are overdue */
    int l = 0;
    while (allowed && (l < numLoans))
    {
      allowed = !currentLoans[l++].IsOverdue();
    }
  }
  return allowed;
}

/* record the fact that the current user has made the specified loan */
/* Return true if successful, false otherwise */
public bool BorrowBook(LibraryLoan loan)
{
  if (loan != null)
  {
    if (numLoans == 0)
    {
      /* start new list */
      currentLoans = new LibraryLoan[QUOTA];
      /* and record loan */
      currentLoans[numLoans++] = loan;
      return true;
    }
    else if (numLoans < QUOTA)
    {
      /* just record loan */
      currentLoans[numLoans++] = loan;
      return true;
    }
    else
    {
```

```
        /* too many loans */
        return false;
      }
    }
    else
    {
      /* parameter is null */
      return false;
    }
}

/* record the fact that the current user has returned the specified loan */
/* Return true if successful, false otherwise */
public bool ReturnBook(LibraryLoan loan)
{
  if (loan != null && numLoans != 0)
  {
    /* lookup the loan in the user's list */
    int l = 0;
    while ((l <= currentLoans.Length-1) && !(currentLoans[l].Equals(loan)))
    {
      l++;
    }
    /* check if the loan was found in the list */
    if (currentLoans[l].Equals(loan))
    {
      /* remove the loan from the list */
      if (--numLoans == 0)
      {
        currentLoans = null;
      }
      else
      {
        for (int i = l; i <= currentLoans.Length-2; i++)
        {
          currentLoans[i] = currentLoans[i+1];
        }
      }
      return true;
    }
    else
    {
      /* loan was not found in user's list */
      return false;
    }
  }
  else
  {
    /* parameter is null or user has no loans */
    return false;
  }
}

/* record the fact that the current user has made the specified */
/* reservation Return true if successful, false otherwise */
public bool MakeReservation(LibraryReservation reservation)
{
  if (reservation != null)
  {
    if (numReservations == 0)
    {
      /* start new list */
```

```
        currentReservations = new LibraryReservation[10];
        /* and reservation */
        currentReservations[numReservations++] = reservation;
      }
      else if (numReservations == currentReservations.Length)
      {
        /* make more space in list */
        LibraryReservation[] tmp = new LibraryReservation[numReservations+10];
        for (int r = 0; r <= currentReservations.Length-1; r++)
        {
          tmp[r] = currentReservations[r];
        }
        currentReservations = tmp;
        /* and record reservation */
        currentReservations[numReservations++] = reservation;
      }
      else
      {
        /* just record reservation */
        currentReservations[numReservations++] = reservation;
      }
      return true;
    }
    else
    {
      return false;
    }
}

/* record the fact that the current user has cancelled a reservation */
/* Return true if successful, false otherwise */
public bool CancelReservation(LibraryReservation reservation)
{
    if ((reservation != null) && (numReservations != 0))
    {
      /* lookup the reservation in the user's list */
      int r = 0;
      while ((r <= currentReservations.Length-1)
         && !(currentReservations[r].Equals(reservation)))
      {
        r++;
      }
      /* check if the reservation was found in the list */
      if (currentReservations[r].Equals(reservation))
      {
        /* remove the reservation from the list */
        if (--numReservations == 0)
        {
          currentReservations = null;
        }
        else
        {
          for (int i = r; i <= currentReservations.Length-2; i++)
          {
            currentReservations[i] = currentReservations[i+1];
          }
        }
        return true;
      }
      else
      {
        /* reservation was not found in user's list */
```

```
        return false;
      }
    }
    else
    {
      /* parameter is null or user has no reservations */
      return false;
    }
  }

  /* indicate whether or not the current user */
  /* is equal to the specified user */
  public override bool Equals(object other)
  {
    LibraryUser otherUser = (LibraryUser) other;
    if (this == otherUser)
    {
      return true;
    }
    else
    {
      return userId == otherUser.userId;
    }
  }

  /* GetHashCode is required in order to override Equals
   * The function provides an int that as uniquely as possible
   * identifies this object instance. */
  public override int GetHashCode()
  {
    /* The userID uniquely identifies a LibraryUser, so
     * we use the userID instance variable */
    return this.userId;
  }

  /* return a string representing the current user */
  public override string ToString()
  {
    return name  +  "(" + userId + ").";
  }
}
}
```

Program B.2 class LibraryUser.

```csharp
using System.Globalization;
using System;

namespace LibraryDatabase
{
  public class LibraryLoan
  {
    private static int LOANPERIOD = 7; // days

    /* declare attributes of loan */
    private LibraryBook book;
    private LibraryUser user;
    private DateTime dueDate;
    private bool renewed - false;

    /* initialize a new object representing a loan of the */
    /* specified book to the specified user */
    public LibraryLoan(LibraryBook book, LibraryUser user)
    {
      this.book = book;
      this.user = user;
      /* set due date to be today's date plus seven days */
      dueDate = new DateTime();
      dueDate = DateTime.Today;
      dueDate = dueDate.AddDays(LOANPERIOD);
    }

    /* return object representing user who made the loan */
    public LibraryUser User { get { return user;} }

    /* return object representing book that was borrowed */
    public LibraryBook Book { get { return book;} }

    /* return date when book is due back */
    public DateTime DueDate { get { return dueDate; } }

    /* check if loan is overdue */
    /* Return true if so, false otherwise */
    public bool IsOverdue()
    {
      return (dueDate < DateTime.Today);
    }

    /* calculate fine due on book */
    public int CalculateFine()
    {
      /* first check if loan is overdue */
      if (dueDate < DateTime.Today)
      {
        /* if so work out how many days
        have elapsed between due date and today */
        TimeSpan numDays = (dueDate - DateTime.Today);
        return numDays.Days;
      }
      else
      {
        return 0;
      }
    }

    /* renew a loan A loan can only be renewed once */
    /* and only if it not overdue  Return true */
```

```
/* if successful, false otherwise */
public bool RenewLoan()
{
  if (!renewed && !IsOverdue())
  {
    dueDate = dueDate.AddDays(LOANPERIOD);
    renewed = true;
    return true;
  }
  else
  {
    return false;
  }
}


/* indicate whether or not the current loan */
/* is equal to the specified loan */
public override bool Equals(object other)
{
  LibraryLoan otherLoan = (LibraryLoan)other;

  if (this == otherLoan)
  {
    return true;
  }
  else
  {
    return book.Equals(otherLoan.book)
           && user.Equals(otherLoan.user);
  }
}

/* GetHashCode is required in order to override Equals
 * The function provides an int that as uniquely as possible
 * identifies this object instance. */
public override int GetHashCode()
{
  /* Only one book is allowed per loan, so the
   * Book's hash code uniquely identifies a
   * LibraryLoan */
  return this.book.GetHashCode();
}


/* return a string representing the current loan */
public override string ToString()
{
  return book + " on loan to " + user +  " until "
            + dueDate + ".";
}
  }
}
```

Program B.3 class LibraryLoan.

```csharp
using System.Globalization;
using System;

namespace LibraryDatabase
{
  public class LibraryReservation
  {
    private LibraryBook book;
    private LibraryUser user;
    private DateTime date= new DateTime();

    /* initialize a new object representing a reservation of the */
    /* specified book by the specified user */
    public LibraryReservation(LibraryBook book, LibraryUser user)
    {
      this.book = book;
      this.user = user;
    }

    /* return object representing user who made the reservation */
    public LibraryUser User { get { return user;} }

    /* return object representing book that was reserved */
    public LibraryBook Book { get { return book;} }

    /* return date when reservation was made */
    public DateTime Date { get { return date;} }

    /* indicate whether or not the current reservation */
    /* is equal to the specified reservation */
    public override bool Equals(object other)
    {
      LibraryReservation otherRsrv = (LibraryReservation)other;
      if (this == otherRsrv)
      {
        return true;
      }
      else
      {
        return book.Equals(otherRsrv.book)
                && user.Equals(otherRsrv.user);
      }
    }

    /* GetHashCode is required in order to override Equals
     * The function provides an int that as uniquely as possible
     * identifies this object instance. */
    public override int GetHashCode()
    {
      /* Reservations are uniquely defined by a User, Book and Date.
       * We cannot uniquely identified the reservation witout using
       * data from all three, so we XOR the HashCode from each. */
      return book.GetHashCode() ^ date.GetHashCode() ^ user.GetHashCode();
    }


    /* return a string representing the current reservation */
    public override string ToString()
```

```
    {
      return book + " reserved by " + user +  " on " + date + ".";
    }
  }

}
```

Program B.4 `class LibraryReservation`.

```
using System.Globalization;

namespace LibraryDatabase
{

  public class LibraryCatalogue
  {
    private const int SIZE = 3;
    private int numBooks;
    private LibraryBook[] catalogue;

    /* initialize an object representing an empty catalogue */
    public LibraryCatalogue()
    {
      numBooks = 0;
      catalogue = new LibraryBook[SIZE];
    }

    /* add the specifed book to the catalogue under the specifed shelf mark */
    public bool AddBook(LibraryBook book, LibraryShelfmark mark)
    {
      if ((book != null))
      {
        /* check if there is space available */
        if (numBooks < catalogue.Length)
        {
          /* if so, record book */
          catalogue[numBooks++] = book;
        }
        else
        {
          /* if not, make more space in list */
          LibraryBook[] tmp = new LibraryBook[catalogue.Length+SIZE];
          for (int b = 0; b <= catalogue.Length-1; b++)
          {
            tmp[b] = catalogue[b];
          }
          catalogue = tmp;
          /* and record reservation */
          catalogue[numBooks++] = book;
        }
        return true;
      }
      else
      {
        return false;
      }
    }

    /* delete the book with the specified shelfmark from the catalogue */
    public bool DeleteBook(LibraryShelfmark mark)
    {
      if (numBooks != 0)
      {
        /* look for the book in the catalogue */
        int b = 0;
        while ((b < catalogue.Length-1) && (catalogue[b] != null)
          && !(catalogue[b].Shelfmark.Equals(mark)))
        {
          b++;
        }
        /* check if the book was found in the catalogue */
```

```csharp
      if ((catalogue[b] != null) && (catalogue[b].Shelfmark.Equals(mark)))
      {
        /* remove the book from the list */
        for (int i = b; i <= catalogue.Length-2; i++)
        {
          catalogue[i] = catalogue[i+1];
        }
        catalogue[catalogue.Length-1]=null;
        numBooks--;
        return true;
      }
      else
      {
        /* book was not found in catalogue */
        return false;
      }
    }
    else
    {
      /* parameter is null or catalogue has no books */
      return false;
    }
  }

  public LibraryBook this [LibraryShelfmark mark]
  {
    get
    {
      if (numBooks != 0)
      {
        /* look for the book in the catalogue */
        int b = 0;
        while ((b < catalogue.Length-1) && (catalogue[b] != null)
          && !(catalogue[b].Shelfmark.Equals(mark)))
        {
          b++;
        }
        /* check if the book was found in the catalogue */
        if ((catalogue[b] != null) && (catalogue[b].Shelfmark.Equals(mark)))
        {
          return catalogue[b];
        }
        else
        {
          /* book was not found in catalogue */
          return null;
        }
      }
      else
      {
        /* parameter is null or catalogue has no books */
        return null;
      }
    }
  }

  public int Length {
    get {
      // Is the array initialized?
      if (catalogue == null)
        return 0;
      else
```

```
          return catalogue.Length;
      }
   }

   /* indexer to access LibraryBooks in catalogue */
   public LibraryBook this [int index]
   {
     get
     {
       // Is the array initialized?
       if (catalogue == null)
         return null;
       // Check the index limits
       else if (index < 0 || index >= catalogue.Length)
         return null;
       else
         return catalogue[index];
     }
   }
 }
}
```

Program B.5 class LibraryCatalogue.

```csharp
using System.Globalization;
namespace LibraryDatabase
{

  public class LibraryUserDatabase
  {
    private const int SIZE = 3;
    private int numUsers;
    private LibraryUser[] database;

    /* initialize an object representing an empty list of users */
    public LibraryUserDatabase()
    {
      numUsers = 0;
      database = new LibraryUser[SIZE];
    }

    /* add the specifed user to the database under the specifed user id. */
    public bool AddUser(LibraryUser user, int id)
    {
      if (user != null)
      {
        /* check if there is space available */
        if (numUsers < database.Length)
        {
          /* if so, record user */
          database[numUsers++] = user;
        }
        else
        {
          /* if not, make more space in list */
          LibraryUser[] tmp = new LibraryUser[database.Length+SIZE];
          for (int u = 0; u <= database.Length-1; u++)
          {
            tmp[u] = database[u];
          }
          database = tmp;
          /* and record reservation */
          database[numUsers++] = user;
        }
        return true;
      }
      else
      {
        return false;
      }
    }

    /* delete the user with the specified user id from the database */
    public bool DeleteUser(int id)
    {
      if (numUsers != 0)
      {
        /* look for the user in the database */
        int u = 0;
        while ((u < database.Length-1) && (database[u] != null)
            && (database[u].Id != id))
        {
          u++;
        }
```

```
      /* check if the user was found in the database */
      if ((database[u] != null) && (database[u].Id == id))
      {
        /* remove the user from the list */
        for (int i = u; i <= database.Length-2; i++)
        {
          database[i] = database[i+1];
        }
        numUsers--;
        return true;
      }
      else
      {
        /* user was not found in database */
        return false;
      }
    }
    else
    {
      /* database has no users */
      return false;
    }
  }

  /* indexer to access LibraryBooks in catalogue */
  public LibraryUser this [int id]
  {
    get
    {
      if (numUsers != 0)
      {
        /* look for the user in the database */
        int u = 0;
        while ((u < database.Length-1)
          && (database[u] != null) && (database[u].Id != id))
        {
          u++;
        }
        /* check if the user was found in the database */
        if ((database[u] != null) && (database[u].Id == id))
        {
          return database[u];
        }
        else
        {
          /* user was not found in database */
          return null;
        }
      }
      else
      {
        /* database has no users */
        return null;
      }
    }
  }

  public int Length {
    get {
      if (numUsers == 0)
```

```
        return 0;
      else
        return database.Length;
    }
  }
 }
}
```

Program B.6 `class LibraryUserDatabase.`

```
namespace LibraryDatabase
{

  public struct LibraryShelfmark
  {
    /* declare next shelf number to allocate */
    private static int nextNumber = 0;

    /* declare attributes of shelf mark */
    private string subject;
    private int number;

    /* initialize a new object representing the shelf */
    /* mark of a new book about the specified subject */
    public LibraryShelfmark(string subject)
    {
      this.subject = subject;
      number = nextNumber++;
    }


    /* initialize a new object representing the shelf */
    /* mark of an existing book */
    public LibraryShelfmark(string subject, int number)
    {
      this.subject = subject;
      this.number = number;
    }

    /* return a string representing the current shelf mark */
    public override string ToString()
    {
      return subject + number;
    }


    /* indicate whether or not the current shelf mark */
    /* is equal to the specified shelf mark */
    public override bool Equals(object other)
    {
      LibraryShelfmark otherMark = (LibraryShelfmark) other;
      if (this.subject.Equals(otherMark.subject)
            && this.number == otherMark.number)
        return true;
      else
        return false;
    }

    /* GetHashCode is required in order to override Equals
     * The function provides an int that as uniquely as possible
     * identifies this object instance. */
    public override int GetHashCode()
    {
      /* Shelfmarks are uniquely identified by the book number */
      return this.number;
    }
  }
}
```

Program B.7   struct LibraryShelfmark.

```csharp
using System;
using System.Drawing;
using System.Collections;
using System.ComponentModel;
using System.Windows.Forms;
using System.Data;

using LibraryDatabase;

namespace LibraryGUI
{
  /// <summary>
  /// Summary description for Form1.
  /// </summary>
  public class MainForm : System.Windows.Forms.Form
  {
    private LibraryCatalogue catalogue;
    private LibraryUserDatabase userDatabase;

    private System.Windows.Forms.GroupBox groupBox1;
    private System.Windows.Forms.GroupBox groupBox2;
    private System.Windows.Forms.GroupBox groupBox3;
    private System.Windows.Forms.Button btnAddUser;
    private System.Windows.Forms.Button btnDeleteUser;
    private System.Windows.Forms.Button btnAddBook;
    private System.Windows.Forms.Button btnRemoveBook;
    private System.Windows.Forms.Button btnBorrow;
    private System.Windows.Forms.Button btnRenew;
    private System.Windows.Forms.Button btnReserve;
    private System.Windows.Forms.GroupBox groupBox4;
    private System.Windows.Forms.Button btnUserList;
    private System.Windows.Forms.Button btnBookList;
    private System.Windows.Forms.Button btnLoanList;
    private System.Windows.Forms.PictureBox pictureBox1;
    private System.Windows.Forms.Button btnExit;
    private System.Windows.Forms.Button btnReturn;
    /// <summary>
    /// Required designer variable.
    /// </summary>
    private System.ComponentModel.Container components = null;

    public MainForm()
    {
      //
      // Required for Windows Form Designer support
      //
      InitializeComponent();

      //
      // TODO: Add any constructor code after InitializeComponent call
      //
      catalogue = new LibraryCatalogue();
      userDatabase = new LibraryUserDatabase();

      populateSample();
    }

    /// <summary>
    /// Clean up any resources being used.
    /// </summary>
    protected override void Dispose( bool disposing )
    {
```

```
      if( disposing )
      {
        if (components != null)
        {
          components.Dispose();
        }
      }
      base.Dispose( disposing );
  }

  #region Windows Form Designer generated code
  /// <summary>
  /// Required method for Designer support - do not modify
  /// the contents of this method with the code editor.
  /// </summary>
  private void InitializeComponent()
  {
    this.btnUserList = new System.Windows.Forms.Button();
    this.pictureBox1 = new System.Windows.Forms.PictureBox();
    this.btnBorrow = new System.Windows.Forms.Button();
    this.btnReserve = new System.Windows.Forms.Button();
    this.btnAddBook = new System.Windows.Forms.Button();
    this.btnRemoveBook = new System.Windows.Forms.Button();
    this.btnAddUser = new System.Windows.Forms.Button();
    this.btnLoanList = new System.Windows.Forms.Button();
    this.btnBookList = new System.Windows.Forms.Button();
    this.btnRenew = new System.Windows.Forms.Button();
    this.btnDeleteUser = new System.Windows.Forms.Button();
    this.btnReturn = new System.Windows.Forms.Button();
    this.btnExit = new System.Windows.Forms.Button();
    this.groupBox1 = new System.Windows.Forms.GroupBox();
    this.groupBox2 = new System.Windows.Forms.GroupBox();
    this.groupBox3 = new System.Windows.Forms.GroupBox();
    this.groupBox4 = new System.Windows.Forms.GroupBox();
    this.groupBox1.SuspendLayout();
    this.groupBox2.SuspendLayout();
    this.groupBox3.SuspendLayout();
    this.groupBox4.SuspendLayout();
    this.SuspendLayout();
    //
    // btnUserList
    //
    this.btnUserList.Location = new System.Drawing.Point(20, 30);
    this.btnUserList.Name = "btnUserList";
    this.btnUserList.Size = new System.Drawing.Size(144, 39);
    this.btnUserList.TabIndex = 0;
    this.btnUserList.Text = "Users";
    this.btnUserList.Click += new System.EventHandler(this.btnUserList_Click);
    //
    // pictureBox1
    //
    this.pictureBox1.Location = new System.Drawing.Point(51, 20);
    this.pictureBox1.Name = "pictureBox1";
    this.pictureBox1.Size = new System.Drawing.Size(133, 148);
    this.pictureBox1.TabIndex = 4;
    this.pictureBox1.TabStop = false;
    //
    // btnBorrow
    //
    this.btnBorrow.Location = new System.Drawing.Point(20, 30);
    this.btnBorrow.Name = "btnBorrow";
    this.btnBorrow.Size = new System.Drawing.Size(123, 39);
```

```
this.btnBorrow.TabIndex = 0;
this.btnBorrow.Text = "Borrow...";
this.btnBorrow.Click += new System.EventHandler(this.btnBorrow_Click);
//
// btnReserve
//
this.btnReserve.Location = new System.Drawing.Point(174, 89);
this.btnReserve.Name = "btnReserve";
this.btnReserve.Size = new System.Drawing.Size(123, 39);
this.btnReserve.TabIndex = 3;
this.btnReserve.Text = "Reserve...";
this.btnReserve.Click += new System.EventHandler(this.btnReserve_Click);
//
// btnAddBook
//
this.btnAddBook.Location = new System.Drawing.Point(20, 30);
this.btnAddBook.Name = "btnAddBook";
this.btnAddBook.Size = new System.Drawing.Size(123, 39);
this.btnAddBook.TabIndex = 0;
this.btnAddBook.Text = "Add book...";
this.btnAddBook.Click += new System.EventHandler(this.btnAddBook_Click);
//
// btnRemoveBook
//
this.btnRemoveBook.Location = new System.Drawing.Point(174, 30);
this.btnRemoveBook.Name = "btnRemoveBook";
this.btnRemoveBook.Size = new System.Drawing.Size(123, 39);
this.btnRemoveBook.TabIndex = 1;
this.btnRemoveBook.Text = "Remove book...";
this.btnRemoveBook.Click += new System.EventHandler(this.btnRemoveBook_Click);
//
// btnAddUser
//
this.btnAddUser.Location = new System.Drawing.Point(20, 30);
this.btnAddUser.Name = "btnAddUser";
this.btnAddUser.Size = new System.Drawing.Size(123, 39);
this.btnAddUser.TabIndex = 0;
this.btnAddUser.Text = "Add User...";
this.btnAddUser.Click += new System.EventHandler(this.btnAddUser_Click);
//
// btnLoanList
//
this.btnLoanList.Location = new System.Drawing.Point(20, 148);
this.btnLoanList.Name = "btnLoanList";
this.btnLoanList.Size = new System.Drawing.Size(144, 40);
this.btnLoanList.TabIndex = 2;
this.btnLoanList.Text = "Loans";
this.btnLoanList.Click += new System.EventHandler(this.btnLoanList_Click);
//
// btnBookList
//
this.btnBookList.Location = new System.Drawing.Point(20, 89);
this.btnBookList.Name = "btnBookList";
this.btnBookList.Size = new System.Drawing.Size(144, 39);
this.btnBookList.TabIndex = 1;
this.btnBookList.Text = "Books";
this.btnBookList.Click += new System.EventHandler(this.btnBookList_Click);
//
// btnRenew
//
this.btnRenew.Location = new System.Drawing.Point(20, 89);
this.btnRenew.Name = "btnRenew";
```

```
this.btnRenew.Size = new System.Drawing.Size(123, 39);
this.btnRenew.TabIndex = 2;
this.btnRenew.Text = "Renew...";
this.btnRenew.Click += new System.EventHandler(this.btnRenew_Click);
//
// btnDeleteUser
//
this.btnDeleteUser.Location = new System.Drawing.Point(174, 30);
this.btnDeleteUser.Name = "btnDeleteUser";
this.btnDeleteUser.Size = new System.Drawing.Size(123, 39);
this.btnDeleteUser.TabIndex = 1;
this.btnDeleteUser.Text = "Delete User...";
this.btnDeleteUser.Click += new System.EventHandler(this.btnDeleteUser_Click);
//
// btnReturn
//
this.btnReturn.Location = new System.Drawing.Point(174, 30);
this.btnReturn.Name = "btnReturn";
this.btnReturn.Size = new System.Drawing.Size(123, 39);
this.btnReturn.TabIndex = 1;
this.btnReturn.Text = "Return...";
this.btnReturn.Click += new System.EventHandler(this.btnRemove_Click);
//
// btnExit
//
this.btnExit.DialogResult = System.Windows.Forms.DialogResult.OK;
this.btnExit.Location = new System.Drawing.Point(358, 424);
this.btnExit.Name = "btnExit";
this.btnExit.Size = new System.Drawing.Size(195, 40);
this.btnExit.TabIndex = 5;
this.btnExit.Text = "Exit system";
this.btnExit.Click += new System.EventHandler(this.btnExit_Click);
//
// groupBox1
//
this.groupBox1.Controls.AddRange(new System.Windows.Forms.Control[] {
                                                this.btnDeleteUser,
                                                this.btnAddUser});
this.groupBox1.Location = new System.Drawing.Point(236, 10);
this.groupBox1.Name = "groupBox1";
this.groupBox1.Size = new System.Drawing.Size(317, 89);
this.groupBox1.TabIndex = 0;
this.groupBox1.TabStop = false;
this.groupBox1.Text = "People";
//
// groupBox2
//
this.groupBox2.Controls.AddRange(new System.Windows.Forms.Control[] {
                                                this.btnRemoveBook,
                                                this.btnAddBook});
this.groupBox2.Location = new System.Drawing.Point(236, 128);
this.groupBox2.Name = "groupBox2";
this.groupBox2.Size = new System.Drawing.Size(317, 89);
this.groupBox2.TabIndex = 1;
this.groupBox2.TabStop = false;
this.groupBox2.Text = "Books";
//
// groupBox3
//
this.groupBox3.Controls.AddRange(new System.Windows.Forms.Control[] {
                                                this.btnReserve,
                                                this.btnRenew,
```

```csharp
                                                       this.btnReturn,
                                                       this.btnBorrow});
    this.groupBox3.Location = new System.Drawing.Point(236, 247);
    this.groupBox3.Name = "groupBox3";
    this.groupBox3.Size = new System.Drawing.Size(317, 148);
    this.groupBox3.TabIndex = 2;
    this.groupBox3.TabStop = false;
    this.groupBox3.Text = "Loans";
    //
    // groupBox4
    //
    this.groupBox4.Controls.AddRange(new System.Windows.Forms.Control[] {
                                                       this.btnLoanList,
                                                       this.btnBookList,
                                                       this.btnUserList});
    this.groupBox4.Location = new System.Drawing.Point(20, 188);
    this.groupBox4.Name = "groupBox4";
    this.groupBox4.Size = new System.Drawing.Size(185, 207);
    this.groupBox4.TabIndex = 3;
    this.groupBox4.TabStop = false;
    this.groupBox4.Text = "Database";
    //
    // MainForm
    //
    this.AutoScaleBaseSize = new System.Drawing.Size(6, 15);
    this.ClientSize = new System.Drawing.Size(573, 479);
    this.Controls.AddRange(new System.Windows.Forms.Control[] {
                                              this.btnExit,
                                              this.pictureBox1,
                                              this.groupBox4,
                                              this.groupBox3,
                                              this.groupBox2,
                                              this.groupBox1});
    this.Name = "MainForm";
    this.Text = "Library Management System";
    this.groupBox1.ResumeLayout(false);
    this.groupBox2.ResumeLayout(false);
    this.groupBox3.ResumeLayout(false);
    this.groupBox4.ResumeLayout(false);
    this.ResumeLayout(false);

}
#endregion

/// <summary>
/// The main entry point for the application.
/// </summary>
[STAThread]
static void Main()
{
  Application.Run(new MainForm());
}

private void btnBookList_Click(object sender, System.EventArgs e)
{
  BookListForm booklist = new BookListForm();
  booklist.Catalogue = catalogue;
  booklist.ShowDialog(this);
}

private void btnAddUser_Click(object sender, System.EventArgs e)
{
```

```
    UserForm userform = new UserForm();

    userform.tbID.Text = LibraryUser.NextId.ToString();

    userform.ShowDialog(this);
    this.Visible = true;

    string name, address;
    int userId;
    LibraryUser user;

    name = userform.tbName.Text;
    address = userform.tbAddress.Text;

    if(name != "")
    {
      user = new LibraryUser(name, address);
      userId = user.Id;
      userDatabase.AddUser(user, userId);
    }
}

private void btnAddBook_Click(object sender, System.EventArgs e)
{
  BookForm bookform = new BookForm();
  bookform.ShowDialog(this);
  this.Visible = true;

  string title,author,publisher,subject;
  int year;

  title = bookform.tbTitle.Text;
  author = bookform.tbAuthor.Text;
  publisher = bookform.tbPublisher.Text;
  year = (int)bookform.updnYear.Value;
  subject = bookform.tbSubject.Text;

  LibraryBook book;
  LibraryShelfmark shelfmark;

  if(title != "")
  {
    book = new LibraryBook(title,author,publisher,year,subject);
    shelfmark = book.Shelfmark;
    catalogue.AddBook(book, shelfmark);
  }
}

private void btnUserList_Click(object sender, System.EventArgs e)
{
  UserListForm userlistform = new UserListForm();
  userlistform.UserDatabase = this.userDatabase;
  userlistform.ShowDialog(this);
}

private void btnLoanList_Click(object sender, System.EventArgs e)
{
  LoanListForm loanlistform = new LoanListForm();
  loanlistform.UserDatabase = this.userDatabase;
  loanlistform.ShowDialog(this);
}
```

```csharp
/// <summary>
/// Adds sample data for testing
/// </summary>
private void populateSample()
{
  LibraryUser tempUser = new LibraryUser("George Washington",
                                  "Presidents Ave., Washington D.C.");
  userDatabase.AddUser(tempUser,1);
  tempUser = new LibraryUser("Napoleon Bonaparte", "Emperors Way, Paris");
  userDatabase.AddUser(tempUser,1);
  tempUser = new LibraryUser("Winston Churchill", "Ministers Alley, London");
  userDatabase.AddUser(tempUser,1);
  tempUser = new LibraryUser("Oscar Wilde", "Westland Row, Dublin");
  userDatabase.AddUser(tempUser,1);

  LibraryBook tempBook = new LibraryBook(
    "Learning to Program the Object-oriented Way with C#",
    "Vinny Cahill",
    "Verlag Springer",
    2002,
    "Computers");

  LibraryShelfmark shelfmark;
  shelfmark = tempBook.Shelfmark;

  catalogue.AddBook(tempBook, shelfmark);

  tempBook = new LibraryBook(
    "The Struggling Student",
    "Donal Lafferty",
    "Confetti Press",
    2002,
    "Autobiography");

  shelfmark = tempBook.Shelfmark;
  catalogue.AddBook(tempBook, shelfmark);

  tempBook = new LibraryBook(
    "How to Win at Video Games",
    "Harold Roth",
    "Duck and Cover Press",
    1999,
    "Computers");

  shelfmark = tempBook.Shelfmark;
  catalogue.AddBook(tempBook,shelfmark);

  tempBook = new LibraryBook(
    "Next Stop:  Exam Time!",
    "Stacy Elle",
    "Guilty Feelings Press",
    1995,
    "Self-help");

  shelfmark = tempBook.Shelfmark;
  catalogue.AddBook(tempBook,shelfmark);

}

private void btnDeleteUser_Click(object sender, System.EventArgs e)
{
  LibraryUser user = pickUser();
```

```
    if(user != null)
      userDatabase.DeleteUser(user.Id);
  }

  private void btnRemoveBook_Click(object sender, System.EventArgs e)
  {
    LibraryBook book = pickBook();
    if(book!=null)
    {
      catalogue.DeleteBook(book.Shelfmark);
    }
  }

  private void btnBorrow_Click(object sender, System.EventArgs e)
  {
    borrowBook();
  }

  private LibraryUser pickUser()
  {
    UserPickerForm userpickerform = new UserPickerForm();
    userpickerform.UserDatabase = userDatabase;
    userpickerform.ShowDialog(this);
    return (LibraryUser)userpickerform.lbUsers.SelectedItem;
  }
  private LibraryBook pickBook()
  {
    BookPickerForm bookpickerform = new BookPickerForm();
    bookpickerform.Catalogue = catalogue;
    bookpickerform.ShowDialog(this);
    return (LibraryBook)bookpickerform.lbBooks.SelectedItem;
  }
  private LibraryLoan pickLoan()
  {
    LoanPickerForm loanpickerform = new LoanPickerForm();
    loanpickerform.UserDatabase = userDatabase;
    loanpickerform.ShowDialog(this);
    return (LibraryLoan)loanpickerform.lbLoans.SelectedItem;
  }
  private void borrowBook()
  {
    LibraryUser user = pickUser();
    LibraryBook book = pickBook();

    switch (book.BorrowBook(user))
    {
      case LibraryBook.IN:
        MessageBox.Show("Book due back on " +
          (book.GetDueDate()).ToString() + ".");
        break;
      case LibraryBook.OUT:
        MessageBox.Show("Book currently on loan to another user.");
        break;
      case LibraryBook.HELD:
      case LibraryBook.RESERVED:
        MessageBox.Show("Book already reserved for another user.");
        break;
      case LibraryBook.BADBORROWER:
        MessageBox.Show("User cannot borrow any further books.");
        break;
    }
```

```csharp
}

private void btnRemove_Click(object sender, System.EventArgs e)
{
  LibraryLoan loan = pickLoan();
  if(loan != null)
  {
    LibraryBook book = loan.Book;
    int fine;
    switch (book.ReturnBook())
    {
      case LibraryBook.IN:
      case LibraryBook.HELD:
        MessageBox.Show("Book not currently on loan.");
        break;
      case LibraryBook.OUT:
        MessageBox.Show("Book returned.");
        fine = book.GetFine();
        if (fine != 0)
        {
          MessageBox.Show("A fine of " + fine + "Euros is due.");
        }
        break;
      case LibraryBook.RESERVED:
        MessageBox.Show("Book returned but reserved for another user");
        fine = book.GetFine();
        if (fine != 0)
        {
          MessageBox.Show("A fine of " + fine + "Euros is due.");
        }
        break;
    }
  }
}

private void btnRenew_Click(object sender, System.EventArgs e)
{
  renewBook();
}

private void btnReserve_Click(object sender, System.EventArgs e)
{
  reserveBook();
}

private void reserveBook()
{
  LibraryUser user = pickUser();
  LibraryLoan loan = pickLoan();

  if(loan != null)
  {
    LibraryBook book = loan.Book;
    switch (book.ReserveBook(user))
    {
      case LibraryBook.IN:
        MessageBox.Show("Book not currently on loan.");
        break;
      case LibraryBook.OUT:
        MessageBox.Show("Book already on loan to this user.");
        break;
      case LibraryBook.HELD:
```

```
                MessageBox.Show("Book already reserved by this user.");
                break;
             case LibraryBook.RESERVED:
                MessageBox.Show("Book reserved.");
                break;
          }
       }
    }
    private void renewBook()
    {
       LibraryLoan loan = pickLoan();
       if(loan != null)
       {
          LibraryBook book = loan.Book;
          switch (book.RenewLoan())
          {
             case LibraryBook.IN:
                MessageBox.Show("Book not currently on loan.");
                break;
             case LibraryBook.OUT:
                MessageBox.Show("Book due back on " +
                   book.GetDueDate().ToString() + ".");
                break;
             case LibraryBook.HELD:
             case LibraryBook.RESERVED:
                MessageBox.Show("Book already reserved for another user.");
                break;
             case LibraryBook.BADRENEWAL:
                MessageBox.Show("Loan previously renewed.");
                break;
          }
       }
    }

    private void btnExit_Click(object sender, System.EventArgs e)
    {
       Close();
    }
  }
}
```

Program B.8   class MainForm based on Figure 14.2.

```csharp
using System;
using System.Drawing;
using System.Collections;
using System.ComponentModel;
using System.Windows.Forms;
using LibraryDatabase;
namespace LibraryGUI
{
  /// <summary>
  /// Summary description for BookForm.
  /// </summary>
  public class BookForm : System.Windows.Forms.Form
  {
    private System.Windows.Forms.Label label1;
    private System.Windows.Forms.Label label2;
    private System.Windows.Forms.Label label3;
    private System.Windows.Forms.Label label4;
    private System.Windows.Forms.Label label5;
    public System.Windows.Forms.TextBox tbTitle;
    public System.Windows.Forms.TextBox tbAuthor;
    public System.Windows.Forms.TextBox tbPublisher;
    public System.Windows.Forms.TextBox tbSubject;
    public System.Windows.Forms.NumericUpDown updnYear;
    private System.Windows.Forms.Button button1;
    private System.Windows.Forms.Button button2;
    private System.Windows.Forms.GroupBox groupBox1;
    public System.Windows.Forms.TextBox tbNumber;
    public System.Windows.Forms.TextBox tbShelfmark;
    private System.Windows.Forms.Label label7;
    private System.Windows.Forms.Label label6;
    /// <summary>
    /// Required designer variable.
    /// </summary>
    private System.ComponentModel.Container components = null;

    public BookForm()
    {
      //
      // Required for Windows Form Designer support
      //
      InitializeComponent();

      //
      // TODO: Add any constructor code after InitializeComponent call
      //
    }

    /// <summary>
    /// Clean up any resources being used.
    /// </summary>
    protected override void Dispose( bool disposing )
    {
      if( disposing )
      {
        if(components != null)
        {
          components.Dispose();
        }
      }
      base.Dispose( disposing );
    }
```

```
#region Windows Form Designer generated code
/// <summary>
/// Required method for Designer support - do not modify
/// the contents of this method with the code editor.
/// </summary>
private void InitializeComponent()
{
  this.label1 = new System.Windows.Forms.Label();
  this.label2 = new System.Windows.Forms.Label();
  this.label3 = new System.Windows.Forms.Label();
  this.tbAuthor = new System.Windows.Forms.TextBox();
  this.updnYear = new System.Windows.Forms.NumericUpDown();
  this.button1 = new System.Windows.Forms.Button();
  this.button2 = new System.Windows.Forms.Button();
  this.tbPublisher = new System.Windows.Forms.TextBox();
  this.tbSubject = new System.Windows.Forms.TextBox();
  this.tbTitle = new System.Windows.Forms.TextBox();
  this.label4 = new System.Windows.Forms.Label();
  this.tbShelfmark = new System.Windows.Forms.TextBox();
  this.tbNumber = new System.Windows.Forms.TextBox();
  this.groupBox1 = new System.Windows.Forms.GroupBox();
  this.label7 = new System.Windows.Forms.Label();
  this.label6 = new System.Windows.Forms.Label();
  this.label5 = new System.Windows.Forms.Label();
  ((System.ComponentModel.ISupportInitialize)(this.updnYear)).BeginInit();
  this.groupBox1.SuspendLayout();
  this.SuspendLayout();
  //
  // label1
  //
  this.label1.Location = new System.Drawing.Point(31, 128);
  this.label1.Name = "label1";
  this.label1.Size = new System.Drawing.Size(61, 29);
  this.label1.TabIndex = 0;
  this.label1.Text = "Title";
  //
  // label2
  //
  this.label2.Location = new System.Drawing.Point(31, 168);
  this.label2.Name = "label2";
  this.label2.Size = new System.Drawing.Size(61, 28);
  this.label2.TabIndex = 1;
  this.label2.Text = "Author";
  //
  // label3
  //
  this.label3.Location = new System.Drawing.Point(31, 207);
  this.label3.Name = "label3";
  this.label3.Size = new System.Drawing.Size(71, 29);
  this.label3.TabIndex = 2;
  this.label3.Text = "Publisher";
  //
  // tbAuthor
  //
  this.tbAuthor.Location = new System.Drawing.Point(133, 168);
  this.tbAuthor.Name = "tbAuthor";
  this.tbAuthor.Size = new System.Drawing.Size(215, 22);
  this.tbAuthor.TabIndex = 6;
  this.tbAuthor.Text = "";
  //
  // updnYear
  //
```

```
this.updnYear.Location = new System.Drawing.Point(133, 247);
this.updnYear.Maximum = new System.Decimal(new int[] {
                                                2100,
                                                0,
                                                0,
                                                0});
this.updnYear.Minimum = new System.Decimal(new int[] {
                                                1500,
                                                0,
                                                0,
                                                0});
this.updnYear.Name = "updnYear";
this.updnYear.Size = new System.Drawing.Size(154, 22);
this.updnYear.TabIndex = 11;
this.updnYear.Value = new System.Decimal(new int[] {
                                                2000,
                                                0,
                                                0,
                                                0});
//
// button1
//
this.button1.DialogResult = System.Windows.Forms.DialogResult.OK;
this.button1.Location = new System.Drawing.Point(133, 336);
this.button1.Name = "button1";
this.button1.Size = new System.Drawing.Size(96, 39);
this.button1.TabIndex = 12;
this.button1.Text = "OK";
//
// button2
//
this.button2.DialogResult = System.Windows.Forms.DialogResult.Cancel;
this.button2.Location = new System.Drawing.Point(256, 336);
this.button2.Name = "button2";
this.button2.Size = new System.Drawing.Size(96, 39);
this.button2.TabIndex = 13;
this.button2.Text = "Cancel";
this.button2.Click += new System.EventHandler(this.button2_Click);
//
// tbPublisher
//
this.tbPublisher.Location = new System.Drawing.Point(133, 207);
this.tbPublisher.Name = "tbPublisher";
this.tbPublisher.Size = new System.Drawing.Size(215, 22);
this.tbPublisher.TabIndex = 7;
this.tbPublisher.Text = "";
//
// tbSubject
//
this.tbSubject.Location = new System.Drawing.Point(133, 286);
this.tbSubject.Name = "tbSubject";
this.tbSubject.Size = new System.Drawing.Size(215, 22);
this.tbSubject.TabIndex = 9;
this.tbSubject.Text = "";
//
// tbTitle
//
this.tbTitle.Location = new System.Drawing.Point(133, 128);
this.tbTitle.Name = "tbTitle";
this.tbTitle.Size = new System.Drawing.Size(215, 22);
this.tbTitle.TabIndex = 5;
this.tbTitle.Text = "";
```

```
//
// label4
//
this.label4.Location = new System.Drawing.Point(31, 247);
this.label4.Name = "label4";
this.label4.Size = new System.Drawing.Size(51, 28);
this.label4.TabIndex = 3;
this.label4.Text = "Year";
//
// tbShelfmark
//
this.tbShelfmark.Location = new System.Drawing.Point(184, 59);
this.tbShelfmark.Name = "tbShelfmark";
this.tbShelfmark.ReadOnly = true;
this.tbShelfmark.Size = new System.Drawing.Size(128, 22);
this.tbShelfmark.TabIndex = 16;
this.tbShelfmark.Text = "";
//
// tbNumber
//
this.tbNumber.Location = new System.Drawing.Point(184, 30);
this.tbNumber.Name = "tbNumber";
this.tbNumber.ReadOnly = true;
this.tbNumber.Size = new System.Drawing.Size(128, 22);
this.tbNumber.TabIndex = 15;
this.tbNumber.Text = "";
//
// groupBox1
//
this.groupBox1.Controls.AddRange(new System.Windows.Forms.Control[] {
                                        this.tbNumber,
                                        this.tbShelfmark,
                                        this.label7,
                                        this.label6});
this.groupBox1.Enabled = false;
this.groupBox1.Location = new System.Drawing.Point(20, 10);
this.groupBox1.Name = "groupBox1";
this.groupBox1.Size = new System.Drawing.Size(338, 99);
this.groupBox1.TabIndex = 17;
this.groupBox1.TabStop = false;
this.groupBox1.Text = "Catalog Information";
//
// label7
//
this.label7.Location = new System.Drawing.Point(20, 59);
this.label7.Name = "label7";
this.label7.Size = new System.Drawing.Size(128, 29);
this.label7.TabIndex = 14;
this.label7.Text = "Shelfmark";
//
// label6
//
this.label6.Location = new System.Drawing.Point(20, 30);
this.label6.Name = "label6";
this.label6.Size = new System.Drawing.Size(128, 28);
this.label6.TabIndex = 10;
this.label6.Text = "Number";
//
// label5
//
this.label5.Location = new System.Drawing.Point(31, 286);
this.label5.Name = "label5";
```

```
      this.label5.Size = new System.Drawing.Size(61, 29);
      this.label5.TabIndex = 4;
      this.label5.Text = "Subject";
      //
      // BookForm
      //
      this.AutoScaleBaseSize = new System.Drawing.Size(6, 15);
      this.ClientSize = new System.Drawing.Size(373, 391);
      this.Controls.AddRange(new System.Windows.Forms.Control[] {
                                                  this.groupBox1,
                                                  this.button2,
                                                  this.button1,
                                                  this.updnYear,
                                                  this.tbSubject,
                                                  this.tbPublisher,
                                                  this.tbAuthor,
                                                  this.tbTitle,
                                                  this.label5,
                                                  this.label4,
                                                  this.label3,
                                                  this.label2,
                                                  this.label1});
      this.Name = "BookForm";
      this.Text = "Book Data";
      ((System.ComponentModel.ISupportInitialize)(this.updnYear)).EndInit();
      this.groupBox1.ResumeLayout(false);
      this.ResumeLayout(false);

    }
    #endregion

    private void button2_Click(object sender, System.EventArgs e)
    {
      this.tbAuthor.Text = this.tbNumber.Text = this.tbPublisher.Text =
          this.tbTitle.Text = this.tbSubject.Text = "";
    }
  }
}
```

Program B.9 class BookForm based on Figure 14.8.

```
using System;
using System.Drawing;
using System.Collections;
using System.ComponentModel;
using System.Windows.Forms;
using LibraryDatabase;
namespace LibraryGUI
{
  /// <summary>
  /// Summary description for BookListForm.
  /// </summary>
  public class BookListForm : System.Windows.Forms.Form
  {
    public System.Windows.Forms.ListView lvBooks;
    private System.Windows.Forms.ColumnHeader bookShelfmark;
    private System.Windows.Forms.ColumnHeader bookYear;
    private System.Windows.Forms.ColumnHeader bookStatus;
    private System.Windows.Forms.ColumnHeader bookID;
    private System.Windows.Forms.ColumnHeader bookAuthor;
    private System.Windows.Forms.ColumnHeader bookTitle;
    /// <summary>
    /// Required designer variable.
    /// </summary>
    private System.ComponentModel.Container components = null;

    public BookListForm()
    {
      //
      // Required for Windows Form Designer support
      //
      InitializeComponent();

      //
      // TODO: Add any constructor code after InitializeComponent call
      //
    }

    /// <summary>
    /// Clean up any resources being used.
    /// </summary>
    protected override void Dispose( bool disposing )
    {
      if( disposing )
      {
        if(components != null)
        {
          components.Dispose();
        }
      }
      base.Dispose( disposing );
    }

    #region Windows Form Designer generated code
    /// <summary>
    /// Required method for Designer support - do not modify
    /// the contents of this method with the code editor.
    /// </summary>
    private void InitializeComponent()
    {
      this.bookYear = new System.Windows.Forms.ColumnHeader();
      this.bookID = new System.Windows.Forms.ColumnHeader();
      this.bookAuthor = new System.Windows.Forms.ColumnHeader();
```

```
this.bookTitle = new System.Windows.Forms.ColumnHeader();
this.lvBooks = new System.Windows.Forms.ListView();
this.bookStatus = new System.Windows.Forms.ColumnHeader();
this.bookShelfmark = new System.Windows.Forms.ColumnHeader();
this.SuspendLayout();
//
// bookYear
//
this.bookYear.Text = "Year";
//
// bookID
//
this.bookID.Text = "ID";
this.bookID.Width = 46;
//
// bookAuthor
//
this.bookAuthor.Text = "Author";
this.bookAuthor.Width = 136;
//
// bookTitle
//
this.bookTitle.Text = "Title";
this.bookTitle.Width = 214;
//
// lvBooks
//
this.lvBooks.Columns.AddRange(new System.Windows.Forms.ColumnHeader[] {
                                            this.bookID,
                                            this.bookAuthor,
                                            this.bookTitle,
                                            this.bookYear,
                                            this.bookStatus,
                                            this.bookShelfmark});
this.lvBooks.Dock = System.Windows.Forms.DockStyle.Fill;
this.lvBooks.FullRowSelect = true;
this.lvBooks.GridLines = true;
this.lvBooks.MultiSelect = false;
this.lvBooks.Name = "lvBooks";
this.lvBooks.Size = new System.Drawing.Size(757, 376);
this.lvBooks.TabIndex = 0;
this.lvBooks.View = System.Windows.Forms.View.Details;
this.lvBooks.SelectedIndexChanged +=
    new System.EventHandler(this.lvBooks_SelectedIndexChanged);
//
// bookStatus
//
this.bookStatus.Text = "Status";
this.bookStatus.Width = 72;
//
// bookShelfmark
//
this.bookShelfmark.Text = "Shelfmark";
//
// BookListForm
//
this.AutoScaleBaseSize = new System.Drawing.Size(6, 15);
this.ClientSize = new System.Drawing.Size(757, 376);
this.Controls.AddRange(new System.Windows.Forms.Control[] {
                                            this.lvBooks});
this.Name = "BookListForm";
this.Text = "Book Database";
```

```
      this.ResumeLayout(false);

   }
   #endregion


   private LibraryCatalogue catalogue;
   public LibraryCatalogue Catalogue
   {
     get
     {
       return catalogue;
     }
     set
     {
       catalogue = value;
       populateListView();
     }
   }
   private void populateListView()
   {
     lvBooks.BeginUpdate();
     lvBooks.Items.Clear();

     string[] items;
     LibraryBook book;

     for(int i=0;i<catalogue.Length;i++)
     {
       book = catalogue[i];
       if(book != null)
       {
         items = new string[6];

         items[0] = i.ToString();
         items[1] = book.Author;
         items[2] = book.Title;
         items[3] = book.Year.ToString();
         items[4] = book.GetStatus();
         items[5] = book.Shelfmark.ToString();
         ListViewItem lvItem = new ListViewItem(items);
         lvBooks.Items.Add(lvItem);
       }
     }
     lvBooks.EndUpdate();
   }

   private void lvBooks_SelectedIndexChanged(object sender, System.EventArgs e)
   {

   }
 }
}
```

Program B.10 class BookListForm based on Figure 14.4.

```csharp
using System;
using System.Drawing;
using System.Collections;
using System.ComponentModel;
using System.Windows.Forms;
using LibraryDatabase;
namespace LibraryGUI
{
  /// <summary>
  /// Summary description for BookPickerForm.
  /// </summary>
  public class BookPickerForm : System.Windows.Forms.Form
  {
    public System.Windows.Forms.ListBox lbBooks;
    private System.Windows.Forms.Button btnOK;
    private System.Windows.Forms.Button btnCancel;
    /// <summary>
    /// Required designer variable.
    /// </summary>
    private System.ComponentModel.Container components = null;

    public BookPickerForm()
    {
      //
      // Required for Windows Form Designer support
      //
      InitializeComponent();

      //
      // TODO: Add any constructor code after InitializeComponent call
      //
    }

    /// <summary>
    /// Clean up any resources being used.
    /// </summary>
    protected override void Dispose( bool disposing )
    {
      if( disposing )
      {
        if(components != null)
        {
          components.Dispose();
        }
      }
      base.Dispose( disposing );
    }

    #region Windows Form Designer generated code
    /// <summary>
    /// Required method for Designer support - do not modify
    /// the contents of this method with the code editor.
    /// </summary>
    private void InitializeComponent()
    {
      this.lbBooks = new System.Windows.Forms.ListBox();
      this.btnOK = new System.Windows.Forms.Button();
      this.btnCancel = new System.Windows.Forms.Button();
      this.SuspendLayout();
      //
      // lbBooks
      //
```

```
    this.lbBooks.Anchor = (((System.Windows.Forms.AnchorStyles.Top |
        System.Windows.Forms.AnchorStyles.Bottom)
      | System.Windows.Forms.AnchorStyles.Left)
      | System.Windows.Forms.AnchorStyles.Right);
    this.lbBooks.ItemHeight = 16;
    this.lbBooks.Name = "lbBooks";
    this.lbBooks.Size = new System.Drawing.Size(379, 292);
    this.lbBooks.TabIndex = 0;
    //
    // btnOK
    //
    this.btnOK.Anchor = (System.Windows.Forms.AnchorStyles.Bottom |
        System.Windows.Forms.AnchorStyles.Right);
    this.btnOK.DialogResult = System.Windows.Forms.DialogResult.OK;
    this.btnOK.Location = new System.Drawing.Point(164, 316);
    this.btnOK.Name = "btnOK";
    this.btnOK.Size = new System.Drawing.Size(96, 28);
    this.btnOK.TabIndex = 1;
    this.btnOK.Text = "OK";
    this.btnOK.Click += new System.EventHandler(this.btnOK_Click);
    //
    // btnCancel
    //
    this.btnCancel.Anchor = (System.Windows.Forms.AnchorStyles.Bottom |
        System.Windows.Forms.AnchorStyles.Right);
    this.btnCancel.DialogResult = System.Windows.Forms.DialogResult.Cancel;
    this.btnCancel.Location = new System.Drawing.Point(266, 316);
    this.btnCancel.Name = "btnCancel";
    this.btnCancel.Size = new System.Drawing.Size(96, 28);
    this.btnCancel.TabIndex = 2;
    this.btnCancel.Text = "Cancel";
    this.btnCancel.Click += new System.EventHandler(this.btnCancel_Click);
    //
    // BookPickerForm
    //
    this.AutoScaleBaseSize = new System.Drawing.Size(6, 15);
    this.ClientSize = new System.Drawing.Size(373, 351);
    this.Controls.AddRange(new System.Windows.Forms.Control[] {
                                                this.btnCancel,
                                                this.btnOK,
                                                this.lbBooks});
    this.Name = "BookPickerForm";
    this.Text = "Choose Book";
    this.ResumeLayout(false);

}
#endregion

public LibraryCatalogue catalogue;

public LibraryCatalogue Catalogue
{
  get
  {
    return catalogue;
  }
  set
  {
    catalogue = value;
    populateListBox();
  }
}
```

```
    private void populateListBox()
    {
      for(int i=0;i<catalogue.Length;i++)
      {
        if(catalogue[i] != null)
        {
          this.lbBooks.Items.Add(catalogue[i]);
        }
      }
    }

    private void btnCancel_Click(object sender, System.EventArgs e)
    {
      this.lbBooks.ClearSelected();
    }

    private void btnOK_Click(object sender, System.EventArgs e)
    {

    }
  }
}
```

Program B.11 class BookPickerForm based on Figure 14.9.

```
using System;
using System.Drawing;
using System.Collections;
using System.ComponentModel;
using System.Windows.Forms;
using LibraryDatabase;
namespace LibraryGUI
{
  /// <summary>
  /// Summary description for LoanListForm.
  /// </summary>
  public class LoanListForm : System.Windows.Forms.Form
  {
    public System.Windows.Forms.ListView lvLoans;
    private System.Windows.Forms.ColumnHeader loanDueBack;
    private System.Windows.Forms.ColumnHeader loanID;
    private System.Windows.Forms.ColumnHeader loanTitle;
    private System.Windows.Forms.ColumnHeader loanBorrower;
    /// <summary>
    /// Required designer variable.
    /// </summary>
    private System.ComponentModel.Container components = null;

    public LoanListForm()
    {
      //
      // Required for Windows Form Designer support
      //
      InitializeComponent();

      //
      // TODO: Add any constructor code after InitializeComponent call
      //
    }

    /// <summary>
    /// Clean up any resources being used.
    /// </summary>
    protected override void Dispose( bool disposing )
    {
      if( disposing )
      {
        if(components != null)
        {
          components.Dispose();
        }
      }
      base.Dispose( disposing );
    }

    #region Windows Form Designer generated code
    /// <summary>
    /// Required method for Designer support - do not modify
    /// the contents of this method with the code editor.
    /// </summary>
    private void InitializeComponent()
    {
      this.lvLoans = new System.Windows.Forms.ListView();
      this.loanID = new System.Windows.Forms.ColumnHeader();
      this.loanTitle = new System.Windows.Forms.ColumnHeader();
      this.loanBorrower = new System.Windows.Forms.ColumnHeader();
      this.loanDueBack = new System.Windows.Forms.ColumnHeader();
```

```csharp
        this.SuspendLayout();
        //
        // lvLoans
        //
        this.lvLoans.Columns.AddRange(new System.Windows.Forms.ColumnHeader[] {
                                                    this.loanID,
                                                    this.loanTitle,
                                                    this.loanBorrower,
                                                    this.loanDueBack});
        this.lvLoans.Dock = System.Windows.Forms.DockStyle.Fill;
        this.lvLoans.GridLines = true;
        this.lvLoans.Name = "lvLoans";
        this.lvLoans.Size = new System.Drawing.Size(737, 336);
        this.lvLoans.TabIndex = 0;
        this.lvLoans.View = System.Windows.Forms.View.Details;
        //
        // loanID
        //
        this.loanID.Text = "ID";
        this.loanID.Width = 64;
        //
        // loanTitle
        //
        this.loanTitle.Text = "Title";
        this.loanTitle.Width = 188;
        //
        // loanBorrower
        //
        this.loanBorrower.Text = "Borrower";
        this.loanBorrower.Width = 218;
        //
        // loanDueBack
        //
        this.loanDueBack.Text = "Due Back";
        this.loanDueBack.Width = 90;
        //
        // LoanListForm
        //
        this.AutoScaleBaseSize = new System.Drawing.Size(6, 15);
        this.ClientSize = new System.Drawing.Size(737, 336);
        this.Controls.AddRange(new System.Windows.Forms.Control[] {
                                                    this.lvLoans});
        this.Name = "LoanListForm";
        this.Text = "Loan List Form";
        this.ResumeLayout(false);

    }
    #endregion

    LibraryUserDatabase userDatabase;
    public LibraryUserDatabase UserDatabase
    {
        get
        {
            return userDatabase;
        }
        set
        {
            userDatabase = value;
            populateListView();
        }
    }
```

```
private void populateListView()
{
  string[] items;
  LibraryUser user;

  int loancount=0;

  for(int i=0;i<userDatabase.Length;i++)
  {
    if(userDatabase[i] != null)
    {
      items = new string[4];
      user = userDatabase[i];
      for(int j=0;j<user.NumLoans;j++)
      {
        LibraryLoan loan = user.Loans[j];

        items[0] = loancount.ToString();
        items[1] = loan.Book.Title;
        items[2] = user.Name;
        items[3] = loan.DueDate.ToShortDateString();

        loancount++;

        ListViewItem lvItem = new ListViewItem(items);
        lvLoans.Items.Add(lvItem);
      }
    }
  }
}
}
```

Program B.12 class LoanListForm based on Figure 14.5.

```csharp
using System;
using System.Drawing;
using System.Collections;
using System.ComponentModel;
using System.Windows.Forms;
using LibraryDatabase;
namespace LibraryGUI
{
  /// <summary>
  /// Summary description for LoanPickerForm.
  /// </summary>
  public class LoanPickerForm : System.Windows.Forms.Form
  {
    public System.Windows.Forms.ListBox lbLoans;
    private System.Windows.Forms.Button btnOK;
    private System.Windows.Forms.Button btnCancel;
    /// <summary>
    /// Required designer variable.
    /// </summary>
    private System.ComponentModel.Container components = null;

    public LoanPickerForm()
    {
      //
      // Required for Windows Form Designer support
      //
      InitializeComponent();

      //
      // TODO: Add any constructor code after InitializeComponent call
      //
    }

    /// <summary>
    /// Clean up any resources being used.
    /// </summary>
    protected override void Dispose( bool disposing )
    {
      if( disposing )
      {
        if(components != null)
        {
          components.Dispose();
        }
      }
      base.Dispose( disposing );
    }

    #region Windows Form Designer generated code
    /// <summary>
    /// Required method for Designer support - do not modify
    /// the contents of this method with the code editor.
    /// </summary>
    private void InitializeComponent()
    {
      this.lbLoans = new System.Windows.Forms.ListBox();
      this.btnOK = new System.Windows.Forms.Button();
      this.btnCancel = new System.Windows.Forms.Button();
      this.SuspendLayout();
      //
      // lbLoans
      //
```

```csharp
    this.lbLoans.Anchor = (((System.Windows.Forms.AnchorStyles.Top |
        System.Windows.Forms.AnchorStyles.Bottom)
        | System.Windows.Forms.AnchorStyles.Left)
        | System.Windows.Forms.AnchorStyles.Right);
    this.lbLoans.ItemHeight = 16;
    this.lbLoans.Name = "lbLoans";
    this.lbLoans.Size = new System.Drawing.Size(379, 292);
    this.lbLoans.TabIndex = 0;
    //
    // btnOK
    //
    this.btnOK.Anchor = (System.Windows.Forms.AnchorStyles.Bottom |
        System.Windows.Forms.AnchorStyles.Right);
    this.btnOK.DialogResult = System.Windows.Forms.DialogResult.OK;
    this.btnOK.Location = new System.Drawing.Point(164, 316);
    this.btnOK.Name = "btnOK";
    this.btnOK.Size = new System.Drawing.Size(96, 28);
    this.btnOK.TabIndex = 1;
    this.btnOK.Text = "OK";
    //
    // btnCancel
    //
    this.btnCancel.Anchor = (System.Windows.Forms.AnchorStyles.Bottom |
        System.Windows.Forms.AnchorStyles.Right);
    this.btnCancel.DialogResult = System.Windows.Forms.DialogResult.Cancel;
    this.btnCancel.Location = new System.Drawing.Point(266, 316);
    this.btnCancel.Name = "btnCancel";
    this.btnCancel.Size = new System.Drawing.Size(96, 28);
    this.btnCancel.TabIndex = 2;
    this.btnCancel.Text = "Cancel";
    this.btnCancel.Click += new System.EventHandler(this.btnCancel_Click);
    //
    // LoanPickerForm
    //
    this.AutoScaleBaseSize = new System.Drawing.Size(6, 15);
    this.ClientSize = new System.Drawing.Size(373, 351);
    this.Controls.AddRange(new System.Windows.Forms.Control[] {
                                                this.btnCancel,
                                                this.btnOK,
                                                this.lbLoans});
  this.Name = "LoanPickerForm";
  this.Text = "Choose Loan";
  this.ResumeLayout(false);

}
#endregion

private LibraryUserDatabase userDatabase;
public LibraryUserDatabase UserDatabase
{
  get
  {
    return userDatabase;
  }
  set
  {
    userDatabase = value;
    populateListBox();
  }
}
private void populateListBox()
{
```

```
    LibraryUser user;

    for(int i=0;i<userDatabase.Length;i++)
    {
      if(userDatabase[i] != null)
      {
        user = userDatabase[i];
        for(int j=0;j<user.NumLoans;j++)
        {
          LibraryLoan loan = user.Loans[j];
          lbLoans.Items.Add(loan);
        }
      }
    }
  }

  private void btnCancel_Click(object sender, System.EventArgs e)
  {
    this.lbLoans.ClearSelected();
  }
 }
}
```

Program B.13   class `LoanPickerForm` based on Figure 14.10.

```csharp
using System;
using System.Drawing;
using System.Collections;
using System.ComponentModel;
using System.Windows.Forms;
using LibraryDatabase;
namespace LibraryGUI
{
  /// <summary>
  /// Summary description for UserForm.
  /// </summary>
  public class UserForm : System.Windows.Forms.Form
  {
    private System.Windows.Forms.Label label2;
    private System.Windows.Forms.Label label3;
    public System.Windows.Forms.TextBox tbName;
    public System.Windows.Forms.TextBox tbAddress;
    private System.Windows.Forms.Button btnOK;
    private System.Windows.Forms.Button btnCancel;
    private System.Windows.Forms.Label label1;
    public System.Windows.Forms.TextBox tbID;
    private System.Windows.Forms.Button btnDetails;
    /// <summary>
    /// Required designer variable.
    /// </summary>
    private System.ComponentModel.Container components = null;

    public UserForm()
    {
      //
      // Required for Windows Form Designer support
      //
      InitializeComponent();

      //
      // TODO: Add any constructor code after InitializeComponent call
      //
    }

    /// <summary>
    /// Clean up any resources being used.
    /// </summary>
    protected override void Dispose( bool disposing )
    {
      if( disposing )
      {
        if(components != null)
        {
          components.Dispose();
        }
      }
      base.Dispose( disposing );
    }

    #region Windows Form Designer generated code
    /// <summary>
    /// Required method for Designer support - do not modify
    /// the contents of this method with the code editor.
    /// </summary>
    private void InitializeComponent()
    {
      this.tbAddress = new System.Windows.Forms.TextBox();
```

```
this.btnOK = new System.Windows.Forms.Button();
this.tbID = new System.Windows.Forms.TextBox();
this.label1 = new System.Windows.Forms.Label();
this.btnDetails = new System.Windows.Forms.Button();
this.tbName = new System.Windows.Forms.TextBox();
this.btnCancel = new System.Windows.Forms.Button();
this.label2 = new System.Windows.Forms.Label();
this.label3 = new System.Windows.Forms.Label();
this.SuspendLayout();
//
// tbAddress
//
this.tbAddress.Location = new System.Drawing.Point(113, 99);
this.tbAddress.Multiline = true;
this.tbAddress.Name = "tbAddress";
this.tbAddress.Size = new System.Drawing.Size(245, 98);
this.tbAddress.TabIndex = 3;
this.tbAddress.Text = "";
//
// btnOK
//
this.btnOK.DialogResult = System.Windows.Forms.DialogResult.OK;
this.btnOK.Location = new System.Drawing.Point(143, 217);
this.btnOK.Name = "btnOK";
this.btnOK.Size = new System.Drawing.Size(96, 40);
this.btnOK.TabIndex = 6;
this.btnOK.Text = "OK";
//
// tbID
//
this.tbID.Location = new System.Drawing.Point(164, 20);
this.tbID.Name = "tbID";
this.tbID.ReadOnly = true;
this.tbID.Size = new System.Drawing.Size(128, 22);
this.tbID.TabIndex = 10;
this.tbID.Text = "";
//
// label1
//
this.label1.Location = new System.Drawing.Point(20, 20);
this.label1.Name = "label1";
this.label1.Size = new System.Drawing.Size(113, 28);
this.label1.TabIndex = 9;
this.label1.Text = "User ID Number";
//
// btnDetails
//
this.btnDetails.Enabled = false;
this.btnDetails.Location = new System.Drawing.Point(20, 217);
this.btnDetails.Name = "btnDetails";
this.btnDetails.Size = new System.Drawing.Size(103, 40);
this.btnDetails.TabIndex = 11;
this.btnDetails.Text = "Details...";
//
// tbName
//
this.tbName.Location = new System.Drawing.Point(113, 59);
this.tbName.Name = "tbName";
this.tbName.Size = new System.Drawing.Size(245, 22);
this.tbName.TabIndex = 2;
this.tbName.Text = "";
//
```

```
        // btnCancel
        //
        this.btnCancel.DialogResult = System.Windows.Forms.DialogResult.Abort;
        this.btnCancel.Location = new System.Drawing.Point(256, 217);
        this.btnCancel.Name = "btnCancel";
        this.btnCancel.Size = new System.Drawing.Size(96, 40);
        this.btnCancel.TabIndex = 8;
        this.btnCancel.Text = "Cancel";
        this.btnCancel.Click += new System.EventHandler(this.btnCancel_Click);
        //
        // label2
        //
        this.label2.Location = new System.Drawing.Point(20, 59);
        this.label2.Name = "label2";
        this.label2.Size = new System.Drawing.Size(62, 29);
        this.label2.TabIndex = 4;
        this.label2.Text = "Name";
        //
        // label3
        //
        this.label3.Location = new System.Drawing.Point(20, 109);
        this.label3.Name = "label3";
        this.label3.Size = new System.Drawing.Size(72, 19);
        this.label3.TabIndex = 5;
        this.label3.Text = "Address";
        //
        // UserForm
        //
        this.AutoScaleBaseSize = new System.Drawing.Size(6, 15);
        this.ClientSize = new System.Drawing.Size(378, 282);
        this.Controls.AddRange(new System.Windows.Forms.Control[] {
                                                    this.btnDetails,
                                                    this.tbID,
                                                    this.label1,
                                                    this.btnCancel,
                                                    this.btnOK,
                                                    this.label3,
                                                    this.label2,
                                                    this.tbAddress,
                                                    this.tbName});
        this.Name = "UserForm";
        this.Text = "User Data";
        this.ResumeLayout(false);

    }
    #endregion

    private void btnCancel_Click(object sender, System.EventArgs e)
    {
        this.tbAddress.Text = this.tbID.Text = this.tbName.Text = "";
    }
  }
}
```

Program B.14 class UserForm based on Figure 14.6.

```
using System;
using System.Drawing;
using System.Collections;
using System.ComponentModel;
using System.Windows.Forms;
using LibraryDatabase;
namespace LibraryGUI
{
  /// <summary>
  /// Summary description for UserListForm.
  /// </summary>
  public class UserListForm : System.Windows.Forms.Form
  {
    public System.Windows.Forms.ListView lvUsers;
    private System.Windows.Forms.ColumnHeader userAddress;
    private System.Windows.Forms.ColumnHeader userName;
    private System.Windows.Forms.ColumnHeader userID;
    private System.Windows.Forms.ColumnHeader userLoans;
    private System.Windows.Forms.ColumnHeader userFines;
    /// <summary>
    /// Required designer variable.
    /// </summary>
    private System.ComponentModel.Container components = null;

    public UserListForm()
    {
      //
      // Required for Windows Form Designer support
      //
      InitializeComponent();

      //
      // TODO: Add any constructor code after InitializeComponent call
      //
    }

    /// <summary>
    /// Clean up any resources being used.
    /// </summary>
    protected override void Dispose( bool disposing )
    {
      if( disposing )
      {
        if(components != null)
        {
          components.Dispose();
        }
      }
      base.Dispose( disposing );
    }

    #region Windows Form Designer generated code
    /// <summary>
    /// Required method for Designer support - do not modify
    /// the contents of this method with the code editor.
    /// </summary>
    private void InitializeComponent()
    {
      this.userAddress = new System.Windows.Forms.ColumnHeader();
      this.userID = new System.Windows.Forms.ColumnHeader();
      this.userFines = new System.Windows.Forms.ColumnHeader();
      this.userLoans = new System.Windows.Forms.ColumnHeader();
```

```
        this.userName = new System.Windows.Forms.ColumnHeader();
        this.lvUsers = new System.Windows.Forms.ListView();
        this.SuspendLayout();
        //
        // userAddress
        //
        this.userAddress.Text = "Address";
        this.userAddress.Width = 266;
        //
        // userID
        //
        this.userID.Text = "ID";
        //
        // userFines
        //
        this.userFines.Text = "Fines";
        //
        // userLoans
        //
        this.userLoans.Text = "Loans";
        //
        // userName
        //
        this.userName.Text = "Name";
        this.userName.Width = 124;
        //
        // lvUsers
        //
        this.lvUsers.Columns.AddRange(new System.Windows.Forms.ColumnHeader[] {
                                                    this.userID,
                                                    this.userName,
                                                    this.userAddress,
                                                    this.userLoans,
                                                    this.userFines});
        this.lvUsers.Dock = System.Windows.Forms.DockStyle.Fill;
        this.lvUsers.GridLines = true;
        this.lvUsers.Name = "lvUsers";
        this.lvUsers.Size = new System.Drawing.Size(737, 336);
        this.lvUsers.TabIndex = 0;
        this.lvUsers.View = System.Windows.Forms.View.Details;
        this.lvUsers.SelectedIndexChanged +=
            new System.EventHandler(this.lvUsers_SelectedIndexChanged);
        //
        // UserListForm
        //
        this.AutoScaleBaseSize = new System.Drawing.Size(6, 15);
        this.ClientSize = new System.Drawing.Size(737, 336);
        this.Controls.AddRange(new System.Windows.Forms.Control[] {
                                                        this.lvUsers});
        this.Name = "UserListForm";
        this.Text = "User Database";
        this.ResumeLayout(false);

    }
    #endregion

    private LibraryUserDatabase userDatabase;
    public LibraryUserDatabase UserDatabase
    {
        get
        {
            return userDatabase;
```

```
    }
    set
    {
      userDatabase = value;
      populateListView();
    }
  }
  private void populateListView()
  {
    string[] items;
    LibraryUser user;

    for(int i=0;i<userDatabase.Length;i++)
    {
      if(userDatabase[i] != null)
      {
        items = new string[5];
        user = userDatabase[i];
        items[0] = user.Id.ToString();
        items[1] = user.Name;
        items[2] = user.Address;
        items[3] = user.NumLoans.ToString();
        items[4] = "";

        ListViewItem lvItem = new ListViewItem(items);
        lvUsers.Items.Add(lvItem);
      }
    }
  }

  private void lvUsers_SelectedIndexChanged(object sender, System.EventArgs e)
  {

  }
 }
}
```

Program B.15 class UserListForm based on Figure 14.3.

```csharp
using System;
using System.Drawing;
using System.Collections;
using System.ComponentModel;
using System.Windows.Forms;
using LibraryDatabase;
namespace LibraryGUI
{
  /// <summary>
  /// Summary description for UserPickerForm.
  /// </summary>
  public class UserPickerForm : System.Windows.Forms.Form
  {
    public System.Windows.Forms.ListBox lbUsers;
    private System.Windows.Forms.Button btnOK;
    private System.Windows.Forms.Button btnCancel;
    /// <summary>
    /// Required designer variable.
    /// </summary>
    private System.ComponentModel.Container components = null;

    public UserPickerForm()
    {
      //
      // Required for Windows Form Designer support
      //
      InitializeComponent();

      //
      // TODO: Add any constructor code after InitializeComponent call
      //
    }

    /// <summary>
    /// Clean up any resources being used.
    /// </summary>
    protected override void Dispose( bool disposing )
    {
      if( disposing )
      {
        if(components != null)
        {
          components.Dispose();
        }
      }
      base.Dispose( disposing );
    }

    #region Windows Form Designer generated code
    /// <summary>
    /// Required method for Designer support - do not modify
    /// the contents of this method with the code editor.
    /// </summary>
    private void InitializeComponent()
    {
      this.lbUsers = new System.Windows.Forms.ListBox();
      this.btnOK = new System.Windows.Forms.Button();
      this.btnCancel = new System.Windows.Forms.Button();
      this.SuspendLayout();
      //
      // lbUsers
      //
```

```csharp
      this.lbUsers.Anchor = (((System.Windows.Forms.AnchorStyles.Top |
         System.Windows.Forms.AnchorStyles.Bottom)
        | System.Windows.Forms.AnchorStyles.Left)
        | System.Windows.Forms.AnchorStyles.Right);
      this.lbUsers.ItemHeight = 16;
      this.lbUsers.Name = "lbUsers";
      this.lbUsers.Size = new System.Drawing.Size(379, 292);
      this.lbUsers.TabIndex = 0;
      //
      // btnOK
      //
      this.btnOK.Anchor = (System.Windows.Forms.AnchorStyles.Bottom |
         System.Windows.Forms.AnchorStyles.Right);
      this.btnOK.DialogResult = System.Windows.Forms.DialogResult.OK;
      this.btnOK.Location = new System.Drawing.Point(164, 316);
      this.btnOK.Name = "btnOK";
      this.btnOK.Size = new System.Drawing.Size(96, 28);
      this.btnOK.TabIndex = 1;
      this.btnOK.Text = "OK";
      //
      // btnCancel
      //
      this.btnCancel.Anchor = (System.Windows.Forms.AnchorStyles.Bottom |
         System.Windows.Forms.AnchorStyles.Right);
      this.btnCancel.DialogResult = System.Windows.Forms.DialogResult.Cancel;
      this.btnCancel.Location = new System.Drawing.Point(266, 316);
      this.btnCancel.Name = "btnCancel";
      this.btnCancel.Size = new System.Drawing.Size(96, 28);
      this.btnCancel.TabIndex = 2;
      this.btnCancel.Text = "Cancel";
      this.btnCancel.Click += new System.EventHandler(this.btnCancel_Click);
      //
      // UserPickerForm
      //
      this.AutoScaleBaseSize = new System.Drawing.Size(6, 15);
      this.ClientSize = new System.Drawing.Size(373, 351);
      this.Controls.AddRange(new System.Windows.Forms.Control[] {
                                                    this.btnCancel,
                                                    this.btnOK,
                                                    this.lbUsers});
      this.Name = "UserPickerForm";
      this.Text = "Choose User";
      this.ResumeLayout(false);

}
#endregion

LibraryUserDatabase userDatabase;
public LibraryUserDatabase UserDatabase
{
  get
  {
    return userDatabase;
  }
  set
  {
    userDatabase = value;
    populateListBox();
  }
}
private void populateListBox()
{
```

```
        for(int i=0;i<userDatabase.Length;i++)
        {
          if(userDatabase[i] != null)
            lbUsers.Items.Add(userDatabase[i]);
        }
      }

    private void btnCancel_Click(object sender, System.EventArgs e)
    {
      this.lbUsers.ClearSelected();
    }
  }
}
```

Program B.16   class UserPickerForm based on Figure 14.7.

Index

!, *see* not operator
!=, *see* not equals operator
\n, *see* new line
\u, *see* unicode
*, *see* multiplication operator
*/, *see* comment
=, *see* assignment operator
+, *see* string concatenation operator,
    see concatentation
++, *see* autoincrement
+= operator, 503
--, *see* autodecrement
-= operator, 503
., *see* member access operator
/*, *see* comment
//, *see* comment
<, *see* less than operator
<=, *see* less than or equals operator
==, *see* equals operator
>, *see* greater than operator
>=, *see* greater than or equals operator
[,], *see* rectangular arrays
[ ], *see* arrays
[ ], *see* indexers
[ ], *see* square brackets
[ ] [ ], *see* arrays, arrays of arrays
&&, *see* and operator
| |, *see* or operator

A

abstraction, 221, 222, 249
abstractions, 235
access by reference, 252
access by value, 252
access modifiers, 228, 394
   protected, 397
accessor, 183, 237, 249
accessor methods, 236
actual arguments, *see* actual parameters
actual parameters, 186–188, 219
addition operator, 58, 63, 67
address, 26
and operator, 99, 127, 143
arithmetic expressions, 59
array initializers, 334
array types, 325
arrays, 323
   [ ], 325, 326

accessing, 326
array of arrays, 347
array overflow, 341
declaring, 325
element type, 324
elements, 324
encapsulation, 330
index of the first, 326
initialization, 326
Length, 326
method parameter, 330
new, 325
reference type, 324
return value, 330
searching, 341
summary, 379
template for searching, 345
value types, 324
as, 408
as operator, 409
ASCII, 277
assembler, 30, 46
assembly, 19, 35
assembly language, 28, 29, 46
assignment, 63, 67, 71–73, 75, 76, 92
assignment compatibility, 80
assignment operator, 71
assignment statement, 16
attributes, 3, 12, 21, 47
autodecrement, 340
autoincrement, 340

B

base class, 392
base keyword, 393
behaviour, 8, 177, 221–223
binary digit, 26
binary operators, 58
bit, *see* binary digit
block, 202, 203, 205
block scope, 202
bool, 50, 51, 98, 143
boxing, 425
   conversion, 426
brackets, 59
break, 130
break statement, 130
browser, 545